Looking Ahead

Independent School

Issues & Answers

Looking Ahead

Independent School Issues & Answers

Second Edition

Edited by Patrick F. Bassett & Craig Thorn

Avocus Publishing, Inc.
Gilsum, NH

Looking Ahead:
Independent School Issues & Answers 2nd Edition
Edited by Patrick F. Bassett &
Craig Thorn

Published by:

Avocus Publishing, Inc.
4 White Brook Road
Gilsum, NH 03448
603-357-0236
FAX: 603-357-2073
Orders: 800-345-6665

Printed in the United States of America
ISBN: 1-890-765-10-4: $21.95 Trade Paperback
Publication Date: March 2004

To my family, my best teachers, all.

—P.F. BASSETT

This book is dedicated to my father,
Craig Thorn III,
who knows how to look ahead
no matter what.

—CRAIG THORN IV

Contents

Communication

Curriculum

Technology

Acknowledgments

Pat Bassett would like to thank and acknowledge the legions of fellow travelers who have inspired him on his independent school journey, especially with his very tolerant colleagues who have routinely endured his various schemes and unsettling pronouncements. Of course, his main companion and reality-check, is his wife, Barbara, long-suffering but stoical fellow traveler beyond compare.

Craig Thorn IV would like to thank his best friend, Drea, for teaching him to think like a lawyer without having to be one. He would like to acknowledge Ernest Peter for his wry wit and sound friendship all these years. He would also like to thank Phillips Academy for its long support.

Introduction

Looking Ahead: Independent School Issues & Answers, 2nd Edition offers over sixty essays on six broad topics—finance, faculty, communication, curriculum, culture & community, and technology—that leading educators in independent schools feel represent the vital areas of discussion and development in private education today. In effect, *Looking Ahead* is a colloquium of educators from a wide variety of independent school perspectives sharing ideas that invite colleagues throughout the independent school world to engage in their own discussions about school.

You will find in this collection surprising connections between areas of discussion and schools, observing your own trends that emerge in essays that are engaging and open-ended. The writers herein offer their ideas, experiences, and anecdotes in the spirit of a continuing dialogue. Because the range of subjects is great, the active reader will appreciate a renewed sense of how complex and rich the independent school experience is. The contributors write clearly, but deeply about their topics of interest. So, the reader will not only learn much about what colleagues in all aspects of independent school life are thinking, but also, in many cases, what innovative experiments they are conducting.

Looking Ahead offers much sound, practical advice, as well. The reader will learn about efficient marketing techniques, curriculum mapping, strategies for conducting successful meetings, and useful technology between offices. The reader will see how the latest trends in educational theory inform diverse approaches to diverse problems. Most important, the reader will see the way all aspects of school life influence one another in ways that sometimes elude us during the daily business of the school day.

The book is divided into six sections. The first section focuses on financing the independent school. In this section, *Looking Ahead* covers topics including managing endowment, defining productivity, maintaining financial equilibrium, utilizing debt, and underwriting a new school. Underlying the essays in this section is the understanding that increasing expenses put enormous pressure on the tuition stream and force schools to come up with innovative approaches to generating new sources of revenues or adopting new methods of cost containment.

The second section studies the challenges schools face to attract and retain qualified faculty in a more competitive, more complex job market. Authors consider creative ways to compensate faculty, define career tracks, create job-sharing models, establish endowed chairs and teaching fellowships, and develop loyalty through professional development. That novel approaches to attracting and retaining faculty are a sound financial investment is a recurring theme in this section.

Effective communication in settings on and off the school campus is the subject of the third section of *Looking Ahead.* Essays on marketing a school's programs, communicating a school's mission, clarifying school policies to protect the school legally, and developing strategies for productive meetings comprise this section. The reader will find that schools of all kinds work hard to communicate a clear sense of themselves even as they strive to invite as many voices as possible into the mix.

In the fourth section of the book, devoted to curriculum, *Looking Ahead* features a variety of pieces ranging from theoretical statements about the modern independent school's curricular vision to specific examples of curricular review and innovation. Among the recurring themes in this section is a prevailing sense that schools should develop programs that invite students to play an increasing role in their own learning.

The fifth section of the book introduces a number of approaches to the idea of culture and community in an independent school environment. Essays on new definitions of diversity, the role a school should play in moral education, and global awareness offer striking ideas about the ways in which education is as much a part of the campus as it is the classroom. Coming from markedly different perspectives, the authors in this section arrive at strikingly similar conclusions about what culture and community might mean in the 21st century.

The final section of the book offers the latest ideas about technology, but not by offering specific software and hardware suggestions that soon will be dated. Rather, in the spirit of the whole book, this section introduces authors who look at the broad issues about technology in independent schools: from textbook to accounting book, teacher's aide to pedagogical philosophy. In this section, the reader will find pieces about student-centered learning, budgeting techniques, professional development, curricular aides, and the relationship between information systems and new ideas about education in general.

We present this second edition of *Looking Ahead* in the spirit of the first edition. This book is an invitation to educators to collaborate on issues that continue to challenge and intrigue us. We hope that *Looking Ahead* raises more questions than it answers, and provokes our colleagues to contribute their own questions. Along the way, we hope that our colleagues realize that, as different as our schools and our roles in them can be, we have much to say one another and much to learn from what we hear.

Craig Thorn
Andover, Massachusetts

Patrick Bassett
Washington, D.C.

FINANCE

Considering the Financing Challenge of the 21st Century Independent School

By Mark J. Mitchell

In the book *The Small College Guide to Financial Health: Beating the Odds,* the author Michael Townsley, Ph.D., asks "Will a flat economy, the stock market crash, changes in student preferences, tuition that outpaces inflation, and new forms of competition plunge small independent colleges into a sea of chronic financial distress?" Given that a 2001 survey of NAIS heads revealed that the second most-compelling challenge facing independent schools today is financing the school of the 21st century, most in the independent school community might be asking this same question, only replacing the word *colleges* with *schools*. This research makes it clear that many schools share the same pressing issues relative to financing—issues such as increasing teacher salaries, funding the ever-present need for implementing newest technologies, maintaining excellence of curriculum, communicating to constituencies, improving diversity, and managing facilities. Clearly funding these endeavors are difficult enough. Funding them while seeking to maintain affordability and market viability through minimizing tuition dependency, keeping tuition increases as low as possible, and supporting financial aid programs make the problem particularly complex and difficult to balance.

Informed by discussions and presentations delivered at the National Association of Independent Schools/National Business Officers Association Independent Schools Financing Symposium, this chapter explores the array of independent school financing challenges facing school leaders today. The financing challenges reviewed fall into one or more of the following four categories:

- Financing Trends and Challenges
- Pricing
- Fundraising
- New Ventures

Financing Trends and Challenges

What are the key trends and indicators that influence the nature of the challenging questions that independent schools are facing? According to Pat Bassett, NAIS president, and Sarah Daignault, executive director of NBOA, several key insights and questions set the context for understanding the complex nature of the financing conundrum.

- *On tuition and demand:* In the last ten years, median tuition among independent schools has significantly outpaced inflation growth. Adjusted for inflation, median tuition at day schools is up 38% in the last ten years. By comparison, the average tuition and fees among both four-year private and public colleges and universities have increased by 38% between 1992–93 and 2002–03, according to the College Board's *Trends in College Pricing, 2002*. At the same time, however, inquiries, applications, and enrollments have increased but not the number of acceptances per enrollee—reflecting a greater selectivity and competitive environment. Can or should schools continue this path? At what point will this begin to affect demand?
- *On factors driving tuition trends:* Data suggest that tuitions are higher primarily because schools are hiring more and more staff, up nearly 32% since 1992. The largest growth in staffing is in instructional support personnel—tutors, psychologists, and learning specialists (up 53.5%). Student/teacher ratios overall (including the instructional support staff) are down to 9:1 versus 11:1 a few years ago. Adding a curricular or extracurricular program is rarely met by eliminating another. Market-driven competition impacts the drive for the best technology and the most impressive facilities, which in turn impacts increased public relations, communications, marketing, and "cultivation" costs to spread the word about this quality to families, donors, and others. Meanwhile, it is interesting to note that since 1992 the student attrition rate has dropped, suggesting that these factors have led to improved value and better matching between schools and students. Can schools operate more efficiently—for example, cutting costs, increasing student-teacher ratios—and retain or improve quality?
- *On diversity trends:* Ethnic/racial diversity is increasing without a dramatic increase in the percentage of students receiving financial aid. Adjusted for inflation, the average financial aid grant is 38.1% higher than it was a decade ago, but that is because higher average awards are being offered to cover the skyrocketing tuition. However, only 1.8% more students received financial aid in 2002 than did in 1992. While ethnic diversity has improved, socio-economic diversity does not seem to have expanded much in the past decade. How can socio-economic diversity goals be reached?
- *On teachers' salaries:* Faculty pay continues to lag behind that of public school teachers. Adjusted for inflation, the median teacher salary has grown by just 11% in the past ten years. Bassett contended that the trends and data suggest that many of the resources gained from 38% growth in tuition rates and increased giving are being geared toward hiring more staff, not toward increasing salaries for teachers. How can schools maximize the use of highly qualified teachers and pay them at levels concomitant to both their education and the increasing demand for skilled teachers in order to attract and retain the best?
- *On teacher attrition:* Teacher attrition in independent schools remains low (around 10%) relative to comparable measures. Corporations in general lose 11% of staff

annually while public schools lose 13%. Smaller private schools lose a lot more—25%—perhaps because their salaries are seriously under market. Many teachers who leave independent schools are leaving the teaching field entirely, often within the first five years, which seems to be lifestyle-related in terms of career and salary ambition. Factors such as the mission of the school, small classes, disciplined environments, motivated students, and more control over curriculum make teaching in independent schools worth the financial sacrifice for many. Will these "psychic" rewards of working in independent schools be as compelling for the next generation of teachers?

Before tackling the interconnectedness of these issues and questions, Sarah Daignault discussed the importance of thinking out of the box, particularly if it is a "box" which, in the current financial environment, is not doing a particularly good job of holding in all the school's financial needs. But first, a critical question in this regard is "What is the box we're in?" The traditional model for budgeting in independent schools is built on a series of assumptions and goals that reflect a concept of quality that has become a standard that most schools do not want to change.

The four sides of the box are:

- *Keeping classes small.* Schools rely on the competitive advantage that personal, individualized attention brings in nurturing a student's personal, social, and intellectual growth. Although there is no research suggesting that a 9:1 ratio of students to faculty results in a better education than 10:1 or 11:1, schools may be wary of increasing class size because of the perception of decreased advantage in the marketplace.
- *Extending financial aid.* Schools recognize that offering financial aid serves a dual purpose of expanding access to schools and for improving student quality (i.e., enrollment management). The full-pay students are not always the best students and the best students may often need financial assistance to be part of the school community. But schools may be wary of extending more assistance if they can fill seats with more full-paying students.
- *Keeping tuition affordable.* Few schools charge tuition at a rate that reflects the actual cost of educating a student. As such, all families at nearly all schools receive some level of subsidy. Schools rely on annual fund and/or other charitable giving so as not to charge true cost. Real annual giving is up 28% in the last ten years for day schools and 18.1% for boarding schools. However, this side of the box is pressured by a sagging economy, poor stock market performance, and competition for donor dollars. Can schools expect to fund the future based on continued increases in giving?
- *Using endowment income.* Schools use endowment income to keep the lid on the box. Schools also use capital campaigns to cover their deferred maintenance and to build new buildings. A lagging economic environment can have deleterious effects on the ability of schools to use income from investments or fundraising to achieve

certain goals. Additionally, many schools, particularly newer schools, have very few or no endowments that provide the luxury of the endowment management challenge.

The need to increase faculty and staff salaries and benefits to attract and retain the best staff possible in order to run the best school possible is pressuring the four sides of the box. Additionally, for so many schools, the increasing costs (and pressure) to build, manage, and maintain top-notch facilities are enough incentive for schools to deconstruct and rebuild the box strategically sooner, before its explosion forces them to respond later. Daignault encouraged the participants to rethink these issues in creative ways; perhaps to go so far as building a new box based on new assumptions and realities regarding quality, competition, and market-driven demand.

Overlaying such mundane, ground-level issues, it is important to recognize that schools highly value their independence. Whether driven by the mission-specific nature of schools or competition for students and/or donors, striving toward and preference for singular uniqueness inherently limits the willingness to reconstruct the box, cooperate with other schools, or visualize untapped potential.

Pricing and Revenue Issues

D. Scott Looney, director of external affairs at The Cranbrook Schools (MI), delivered a presentation designed to provoke discussion around school pricing strategies, touching on issues of demographic and economic trends, tuition discounting, and financial aid. Below are critical assumptions and considerations around how schools should approach the pricing and affordability issues they face:

- There are inherent difficulties in making changes to the way schools do business, and it is often challenging to communicate these difficulties to boards. Board members are often drawn from successful for-profit executives and they may not automatically understand the differences in the financial model in a school.
- In a for-profit business, a simple explanation of the pricing model is that Price = Cost + Profit. Consumers know that they are paying more for a product or service than the actual cost of producing it. Generally, price can be adjusted swiftly and there will be immediate changes in both demand and profit as a result. In a typical school, it costs more to educate a student than schools receive in tuition per student. Additionally, most schools do not aim to make a profit. As such, the school pricing model is: Price = Cost MINUS Financial Aid MINUS Subsidy (annual giving or other contributions, investment income, etc.). Price is adjusted annually (with mid-year adjustments being made only when changes in financial aid offers to families occur). However, changing the equation by changing financial aid ("tuition discounting") is a somewhat predictable process because most schools assume that aid, once awarded, is awarded at the same level for the rest of the child's stay at the school.
- What colleges have discovered as part of their pricing model is that tuition is not price-sensitive. That is, applications do not decrease even as tuition rises, and col-

leges just give more financial aid in order to get the students they want. Highly selective colleges have traditionally assessed high tuitions but have been able to extend significant financial aid. Now the less-selective colleges are increasing tuition and aid dramatically. This has turned out not to be a panacea, however. Some schools are losing enrollment even as they are increasing financial aid in order to fill the school.

- In looking to the future, schools are wise to consider two factors which have affected parents' willingness to enroll in private schools (because both factors may be changing):

    - According to the NAIS Public Opinion Poll of 1999, over 60% of parents say that they would prefer to go to an independent or private school if price were not a consideration. Schools cannot assume that this high degree of preference will never change, given political support behind school reform through legislation such as the No Child Left Behind Act. Even if it does, it is important to understand the growth in alternatives such as charter and home schools that may increasingly serve families' needs at no (or low) cost.
    - Also, NAIS enrollments correlate with the available number of school-aged children overall. In less than ten years, there is projected to be a steep decline in available children and this may affect the price sensitivity of tuition in independent schools. Some research Looney has conducted suggests that this dip in school-aged population is more likely to impact independent school enrollment than a dip in the economy would.

- Another demographic factor affecting pricing is that teachers are retiring and will be replaced by young people who are currently facing heavy competition for their skills. Not only will the pressures of a general teacher shortage affect independent schools' ability to be competitive with public schools, it is not unreasonable to assume that a younger generation may not be as comfortable with giving up pay for the other benefits of teaching. As such, more pressure to attract teachers away from other industries will be evident. According to the U.S. Census Bureau's Current Population Survey of March 2002, the median income of households where the householder has earned a Bachelor's degree is $67,165, $78,902 with a Master's, and $92,806 with a Doctorate. Professionals (with law or medical degrees, for example) earned a median income of $100,000. Compared to the median 2001–02 NAIS teacher salary of $38,500—and if current or potential teachers lessen the value of the "psychic rewards"—why stay in schools or enter into teaching at all?

Strategies for Addressing Pricing Models

In what ways can schools explore opportunities and strategies for re-evaluating pricing structures? Here are some thoughts emanating from the financing symposium discussions:

1. *Consider pricing alternatives.* Since demand does not generally appear to be price sensitive (i.e., applications, inquiries, and enrollments rising even as tuition growth outpaces inflation), rethink how and what schools charge for tuition.
   a. Eliminate the typical subsidy on tuition by charging what it costs; increase financial aid to those who cannot fully pay it.
   b. Price tuition based on core services and charge additional fees for supplemental services (e.g., charge a base tuition for a certain number of courses and an extra fee for courses above that minimum).
   c. Investigate sliding scale for tuition levels (based on income level) or the feasibility of locked-in tuition rates.
   d. Make cost affordable by extending more information and resources on financing strategies for families.

2. *Evaluate changes in program strategies.* Requests for extra instructional support or additional facilities are not always market-driven. As often, decisions on program enhancement are driven by internal desires to improve programs as a matter of leadership and/or perceived competition. Schools need to be prepared to go back to the community to discuss financial realities that drive programmatic decisions and/or to examine the true market demand for program enhancements.
   a. When adding programs, think first about substitution, not enhancement; consider whether adding programs is a market-driven response or a matter of leadership and mission; if adding a market-driven program, be equally prepared to eliminate one that is not in demand (having eight or ten students in a classroom is not *always* a positive).
   b. Incorporate distance-learning opportunities to "export" core curricular services to other audiences (adult learners, home schools, charter schools, public schools, etc.) and to offer broader service to core students at low cost.
   c. Use off-campus programs provided at lower cost to expand enrollment, allowing the school to over-enroll by a certain number of students; possibly target gifted and/or special-needs students, who tend to be underserved in the public schools.
   d. Pursue partnerships with other schools and/or higher education to jointly offer specialized courses.
   e. Consider the possibility of managing multiple campuses based on different value propositions; in other words, can one school operate a campus that appeals to one type of consumer (low student/teacher ratio, sprawling campus, new athletic field house) while operating another that appeals to a different type of consumer (higher ratio, one or two modest buildings, no athletics, but with world-class teachers)? Under one administration with different core values or level of "frills" on different campuses, economies of scale might be achieved through combined administration. One possible model of this concept is multiple lower-cost elementary school campuses, some located in urban areas where demand is high, becoming feeder schools for higher-cost suburban middle school and upper school campuses.

3. *Attend to cost containment.* The cost of schools can always rise to meet the revenue stream. As such, a significant part of the discussion on pricing must center on cost containment. Not only does this impact the price charged, but it reflects the need for schools to discipline themselves not to spend the entire revenue stream—being more fiscally responsible in ways that support the school's future financial health.
   a. Increase student/staff ratios and consider the ramifications of tying salary-setting more directly to evaluation of personnel (e.g., bonuses, pay for performance). The expansion of faculty and staff is creating lower ratios, making schools less "productive" in economic terms since 1992 (i.e., one teacher teaches fewer students now than ten years ago). As such, there was considerable energy around, and discussion of, reversing the trend to expand dollars for staff compensation and financial aid by rethinking the student/teacher ratio. That is, schools should seriously examine the possibility of moving the ratio from 9:1 to 10:1 or 11:1 in a day school or from 7:1 to 8:1 or 9:1 in a boarding school. Common sense concludes and some research confirms, particularly in grades PK–4, that students in smaller classes outperform students in larger classes. However, adding a few more students in independent school classes is unlikely to change the quality proposition significantly, whereas the additional revenue can have considerable impact on the budget. In any case, with public school ratios at 17:1, there is plenty of room for adjustment of the independent school ratio without nearing the public school ratio.
   b. Pursue cooperative buying of services to take advantage of economies of scale on a broader level; in other words, purchasing consortia with other area schools (or nationally) to get supplies, materials, or equipment at a discount.
   c. Create electronic marketplaces for schools to buy, sell, or exchange products and services (e.g., consulting, curriculum, computers, books, equipment, etc.) among each other.
   d. Structure schools to expand and contract similar to the college model of staffing: implement adjunct faculty positions to create flexibility in response to changing demands in program and curriculum while paying less in staff salaries/benefit; limit the number of full-time teachers and instead hire part-time or adjunct teachers for specialized courses, which may save benefits' costs and reduce salary scale.
   e. Save facilities and administrative costs by outsourcing or pooling resources with other schools on areas such as maintenance, custodial work, payroll, benefits administration, or food service.

Of course, there is no "one size fits all" answer to applying strategies such as these. In fact, the lens through which the suggestions listed above need to be viewed is that there are four basic kinds of school types to consider:

- High endowment, high demand
- Low endowment, high demand

- High endowment, low demand
- Low endowment, low demand

Certain opportunities and strategies concerning schools with low demand may not be sufficiently represented or proposed. Given such variety among the endowment/demand continuum (and other characteristics), it is important to consider that no magic bullet exists that would perfectly meet the needs for all schools—there will be different solutions for different schools. Where demand is concerned, however, it is important to consider how establishing programs within the community can impact demand. That is, demand for the less-selective schools could be increased by a broader presence in the community: change the image of independent schools within the greater community and impact the demand curve.

Clearly, school mission and values overlay all of these approaches. Therefore, it should be no surprise that another critical issue relative to pricing strategy, program evaluation, and cost containment is that schools have to evaluate the interplay between their "independence" (represented by their missions and core values) and the financial imperative. For example, entering into cooperative agreements will be counter-productive if it causes the school to erode its core values. Does being in a purchasing consortium or other collaborative venture mean giving up independence? Where is the fine line between functioning in the corporate and educational models of financing? Are there compromises a school makes by giving up the "culture of education" by adopting more approaches based on corporate models? Clearly, different schools may have different answers to these types of questions, influencing different strategies or approaches and/or making it more or less difficult for school leaders to propose or accept changes to the traditional models.

Because many of the ideas expressed generated more questions than they answered, neither NAIS nor NBOA have supported, endorsed, or recommended that schools take any of the above steps. In fact, it is important that further research be conducted to examine schools that have implemented or experimented with these ideas, develop benchmarks for optimizing efficiency, and better understand the market demands that the parent constituents have (what do they want, how much will they pay for it, how do they currently pay for it, etc.). This set of issues is clearly among the most complex to solve.

Fundraising Trends, Challenges, and Strategies

Another critically important variable in the financing formula is fundraising. Tracy Savage, senior consultant with Marts & Lundy, Inc., discussed the key challenges, issues, and opportunities that the future brings, offering observations and views on both external factors and internal procedures that impact schools' ability to raise funds effectively now and in the future.

The primary responsibility of the development professional is twofold: "get the dollars now" *and* position the institution to "get the dollars later." As such, schools must go beyond the surface tasks of what gift vehicles and methodologies to use, but they increasingly must inform and cultivate the members of the community in a strategic way that puts forth the school's image as a compelling and worthy institution, deserving of the gift (now and later).

Given this charge, it is not surprising that expenses related to fundraising have become important to consider in the financing model, not just the value of the funds raised. On average, Savage stated, fundraising costs between 7% and 8% of the operating budget, an expense that has doubled since 1991. And even this figure may understate the "real" cost, since it does not include costs such as the portion of the head's salary devoted to fundraising. On the other hand, some development offices are involved in activities (such as website development, marketing, communications, or public relations) that may have increased costs that are not directly related to raising funds. Nevertheless, the operational costs are not insignificant and the role of the development officer is changing. Clearly, it is fairly easy to measure the return on investment as "cost per dollar raised." Typically, the cost per dollar raised is between 12 and 20 cents.

The benefits from fundraising are also a small piece of the operating budget—9% for annual giving and a widely varying amount for restricted contributions and endowment interest. But it is fundraising that provides the buildings to the school through the capital campaigns. The percentage of budget to allocate for fundraising becomes essentially a risk management question, since spending the money doesn't guarantee that the donations will come in.

According to Savage, the "universe" of donors a school experiences can be depicted in a visually meaningful way: Take a triangle, intersect it with two lines horizontally and two lines vertically, producing nine compartments. Horizontally, the top of the grid represents close friends who give frequently, the middle portion represents acquaintances who give occasionally and the third portion represents unknowns who do not give. Of course, each of these segments gets larger as the "closeness" factor diminishes. Vertically, the triangle is divided to characterize the capacity of those mentioned above to give: those with large capacity to give, those with smaller capacity, and those with limited capacity. Over time, naturally, some of the people with smaller or limited capacity will develop greater capacity to give. It is the development office's responsibility to move these people from "unknowns" to "acquaintance" and from "acquaintance" to "close friend" so that this capacity to give will be realized. With limited time and resources, a critical and strategic challenge, of course, is to decide which few segments of the triangle are most cost-effective to cultivate. Where will the development dollars best be spent to achieve both goals of "money now" and "money later"?

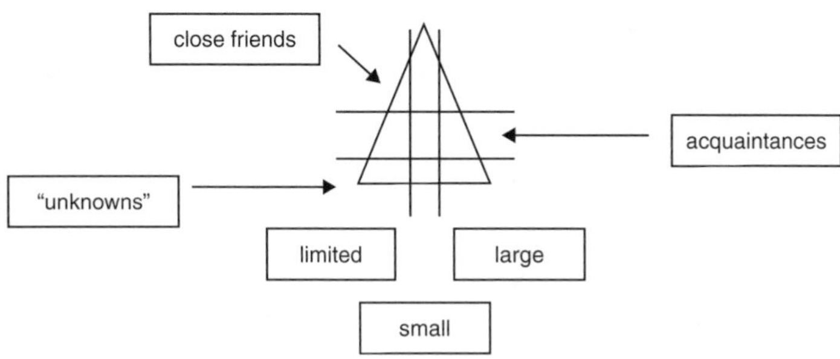

Savage also noted that there is an increasing trend toward soliciting unrestricted gifts. This is in part because schools are getting less conservative about debt financing and moving to new debt instruments such as tax-exempt bonds. Unrestricted giving history is helpful in improving credit assessments. Also, the cost of maintaining a relationship with a restricted donor is higher than the cost of maintaining relationship with an unrestricted donor. In both cases the donor must be cultivated, but there is a higher degree of specific reporting for the restricted donation.

What is the trend in giving for education and for independent schools specifically? Savage illustrated that, between 1992 and 2001, the growth in contributions for independent schools has outpaced growth for other educational institutions (specifically, public and private research universities and liberal arts colleges). This is particularly true for capital and endowment campaigns but not for operating costs. Savage was careful to warn that, generally, trends in independent school mirror trends in higher education philanthropy but on a five- to fifteen-year lag. If this is the case, she argued, it is reasonable to expect a significant decline in unrestricted gifts—and an increase in gifts for restricted purposes. This projection poses the fundraising issue in an important way—what measures can schools take to prepare for this possibility?

Another trend she noted is that this growth is coming not from the alumni, but increasingly from the current parents. NAIS statistics show that even among secondary schools, alumni participation in annual giving is at just 23.3%, compared to nearly half of current parents (49.9%). For schools of all types, alumni participation in annual giving is 17.1% and 57.1% of current parents. This pattern has an impact on the nature of fundraising. Current parents are more interested in seeing how their gifts affect their own child's education. If their child is in academic or disciplinary jeopardy, how will this affect their giving? Or how will their giving affect the child's status in the school (i.e., different standards?). On the other hand, if an alienated parent leaves the community, his/her impact may be diminished as he/she moves on to another school or community, while an alienated and vocal alumnae/us may be a thorn for a long time.

Although annual giving is increasing, the average 9% contribution to the budget from the annual fund is not changing over time. How can schools manage annual giving for greater impact? If parents are most likely to be contributors to the annual fund, is it reasonable to expect more from them? Should schools more aggressively pursue other potential donors (particularly alumni) or alternate fundraising vehicles (e.g., planned giving) in order for the annual fund to be a bigger player in the annual budget? Some suggest that the development of a coordinated, multi-year fundraising plan that includes planned giving is essential in this area. Perhaps the typical practice of constantly asking parents to give through auctions, bake sales, annual funds and the like might damage community-building by indirectly creating perceptions or anxieties around social segregation. Are there other intrinsic value propositions that annual giving provides? What about that most instrumental step of turning a non-donor into a donor (i.e., the first gift)? This step neatly exemplifies that typically an annual fund gift can be the best way to begin and cultivate the long-term relationship.

A third pattern to consider relative to fundraising is the potential impact the trend in tuition increases may have on donors, particularly parent giving. Savage argued that tuition hikes may not be relevant to philanthropy. The concern that a high increase in tuition rates will hurt annual giving or endowment does not appear to be borne out by the facts. While this may be true overall, it may have different impacts on different types of potential donors. One example might be the independent school "middle income" family—families that are wealthy enough not to qualify for financial aid but feel strapped financially to make the sizable contributions that schools might expect they can. By some accounts (depending on the school's location), these families might fall in the $120,000 to $200,000 income range. According to a 1999 survey by Independent Sector, families earning over $100,000 gave 2.2% of their income to charitable endeavors in 1998 (the most recently available data), down from 3.4% given in 1995. Arguably, there could be an effect on giving from families at this "middle income" level since they also are more likely to express feeling "squeezed" between being full-pay families while being expected to be sizable contributors to both annual giving and capital campaigns.

Endowment-building is also a critical issue in the development discussion. Building endowment takes a very long time and may be more difficult with current parents doing more of the giving. It was noted that parents are more likely to want short-term impact for their dollars, not being as committed to the long-term health of the school once their child leaves. Clearly there are many exceptions to this observation, but large endowments were built generations ago and the danger with endowment is to think that raising endowment will solve a *current* financial challenge. Both the long-term nature of increasing endowment size and advice to be conservative when drawing income from the endowment to support operations underscore this danger. Nevertheless, the important question of "how big an endowment is enough?" is a critical one to explore with further research and study.

Strategies for Rethinking the Fundraising Paradigm

Given these issues, how can schools rethink the role of fundraising now and in the future?

- Establish and articulate the school's mission first, internally and externally. Fundraising efforts and goals should unequivocally support the mission and core values of the school. Not every gift is a good gift if it creates conflict or misdirection in what the school is striving to achieve.
- Expand the job description of development and actively involve other school administrators in understanding and reaching development goals. The resources required to be effective and the fundraising goals themselves are both increasing at faster rates and are significant enough for the effort to be comprehensive and school-wide. Development concepts impact (and can be impacted by) admissions and financial aid, college placement, community outreach and advocacy, parent association, public relations, marketing, communication, and so on.
- Research the donor market. Focus groups, surveys, demographics, and trend analyses assist schools in understanding which segment to engage and cultivate and in better meeting the goal of matching interests between the school and the donor.

- Include operational/overhead costs in fundraising goals and establish an endowment line accordingly. This can include both the administrative costs of the campaign itself, and seeding the ongoing costs of maintaining the program or facility the campaign is supporting. For example, target 125% of the cost of the project as the fundraising goal.
- Consider how the school's creative programs and/or curricula can increase the school's attractiveness to donors. For example, Crossroads (CA) Community Foundation's arts outreach program in the public schools (funded by donors) also attracted substantial capital donations for Crossroads School's regular facilities from donors whose affection for the school was increased by this public-benefit activity.
- Think long-term. Development goals should be planned for 10 to 15 years from now. This makes researching demographic and economic projections extremely important—trends in population, income, technology, and other areas will create challenges that are likely to be different from the ones schools face today. It is imperative to foresee and plan ahead to avoid being reactive or caught by surprise.
- Consider explaining some portion of school's economics more broadly to the community. Parents need to understand that giving is part of the assumption in independent education, and that the high costs represent an investment in the future of the student and need to be a priority for the parent.
- Important to consider the mix of donors and "holders of the mission" in board membership. Wealthiest donors may value time above all and not want to be on the board. It may also be important that governance issues not be addressed solely by the wealthy.

Potential New Ventures for Non-Tuition Revenue

Another variable in the financing formula, of course, is revenue. Rethinking strategic ways schools can create income other than from traditional sources (e.g., tuition and fundraising) to support the overall financial health of the institution is increasingly important. Peter Stokes, executive vice president of Eduventures, Inc., a research and consulting firm specializing in education market development, neatly surveyed the education industry as a market for investors and its connection to possible ways that schools can create new products and services to enhance its non-tuition revenue stream.

Stokes' work involves in-depth scanning of the education industry as a market for companies (e.g., suppliers, publishers, testing organizations, technology firms). Since the education industry includes childcare, PK–12, colleges and universities, e-learning, tutoring, and education-related support industries, its impact on the overall economy is large (an estimated $106 billion generated by for-profit providers in 2002) and has grown by an average of 5.5% annually. The PK–12 sector and its support services represent more than half of this, at $58 billion (of which about $6.7 billion is education itself). Since 1990, almost $10 billion in venture capital has been invested in education businesses. More than half of that, $5.5 billion, came in during the years 1999 and 2000. Since then, venture capital has dropped precipitously, not just in education (largely due to the overexuberance of investors related to e-learning businesses), but across all industries. Over the past three years, education investments have accounted for approximately

2.3% of all private investment activity in the U.S. By contrast, fields such as health care can account for as much as a third of all private investment in a given quarter.

Stokes contended that while the education industry (like other sectors of the economy) may be suffering from a bottoming-out in private investment, it remains a viable, serious, and potentially lucrative business. He believes that independent schools can benefit from some of the successful strategies that companies like Edison and the Apollo Group (parent company of the University of Phoenix and University of Phoenix Online) have deployed to generate revenues.

Based on his observations and expertise, Stokes pinpointed three specific areas that provide interesting potential for schools to explore further:

Intellectual capital: Schools can take better advantage of capitalizing (literally) on the assets they possess that are directly related to their core competency: nurturing and growing human and intellectual capital. Home-grown curricula, testing and assessment tools, administrator and teacher recruitment expertise, pedagogy, and other assets can be packaged and resold to other organizations and individuals. Traditionally, public schools, home schools, charter schools, and for-profit schools are seen as competitors with independent schools. In this context, they can be seen as partners and/or new markets for programming, consulting expertise, and other vital areas.

Incorporation: Since schools do not always have the correct set of managerial skills to most effectively handle an entrepreneurial venture, forming a corporation might provide a better approach. Stokes shared the example of British Columbia, where school districts are able to form corporations as adjuncts to school boards. Instead of a school's faculty, staff, or volunteers creating and managing a particular venture, a school can restructure itself to create an incorporated offshoot that can be equipped with the resources to more aggressively explore, create, manage, market, and sell intellectual and human capital in ways that will enhance the revenue streams back to the school. This approach protects the traditional value proposition that a school brings with it while creating new opportunities to leverage intellectual property.

Internationalization: This opportunity involves leveraging the school's assets and entrepreneurial skills to reach foreign markets and bring content, technology, and services to new markets. These efforts can widen the targeted customer pool while creating opportunities to scale entrepreneurial activities for greater efficiency and return on investment.

Of course, there are a few critical risks that must be considered when evaluating these concepts and their applicability. These risks and obstacles include:

- intellectual property may not be truly unique
- it is difficult to manage the change in culture to think in more entrepreneurial ways
- corporate-based business development skills do not typically exist among the core competencies of school staff
- criticism or perception that the school is diluting its central value proposition

One way to evaluate the risks was to imagine a series of four concentric circles with the schools' core function and skill sets in the center (teaching, learning, etc.). The next outlying circle contains the core methods that schools rely on today to raise capital (e.g., tuition, giving, investments, and debt). The third ring represents opportunities to transfer intellectual capital into revenue (curriculum, assessment, tutoring, and recruitment). The fourth concerns reaching out to new markets and strategic realignment (internationalism, incorporation, distance learning, and reselling). As a school moves further from the center of the circle, the more risk it faces. As schools have found that delivering quality in the center (the first ring) has required increased resources, they have devoted more and more attention/resources to managing those activities outside of their core competency to maximize the ability to raise the funds needed (i.e., the second ring). As such, growth in the need for better business managers, professional development staffs, creative and aggressive admissions teams, and more effective communications and public relations experts has occurred. Similarly, the move toward the next two rings of the circle may be driven by the need to diversify income streams even more, requiring new skill sets and new structures to address them strategically and effectively.

The obstacles and risks notwithstanding, schools need to think provocatively about opportunities to explore new sources of revenue beyond the traditional focus put on after-school programs, summer camps, school stores, and renting facilities.

Strategies for New Revenue Opportunities

What are some of the opportunities for new ventures and non-tuition revenue streams schools might consider?

- Consider franchising and branding school name/reputation.
- Turn courses into products and sell administrative expertise to other schools, public or private. Identify and work with a for-profit partner that has the expertise to develop, deliver, and distribute the profit-making enterprise.
- Offer alternatives for adult learners in the community, such as remedial courses, night classes, and special series for alumni.
- Manage tutoring services for PK–12 learners in the community not attending the school.
- Seek more creative and aggressive use of facilities for rental—not just gyms and chapels, but also technology centers, meeting space, laboratory buildings, art/music studios, and performance centers.
- Consider change in the school model: perhaps job sharing or change in the school calendar that allows teachers to teach for part of the year at the "teaching rate" and then for several months of the year at higher rate in a for-profit job.

Suggestions for Additional Research

More than others areas discussed above, new ventures may be the area in which the group felt the need for external guidance through research and other support to better identify what is possible. As such, schools, in conjunction with groups like NAIS and/or NBOA, should consider engaging in research projects that

- Outline an inventory of critical assets (particularly human and intellectual capital) that schools have that might be sellable and then consolidate on a consortium basis and sell as a group. There is considerable caution and uncertainty over how schools can discern key issues like the uniqueness of its capital, the expertise/resources needed to develop and manage a particular venture, and the skills needed to match target audiences with what schools have to offer.
- Identify best practices/models on summer and after-school use of facilities. Determine uses not in conflict with the mission of schools. These are "overhead absorption." Goals are simultaneously to expand revenue, create additional demand in families not fully aware of independent school options, and to change the perception of independent schools in the community.
- Outline an inventory of consulting skills that schools might market and develop a "consulting bank" where services could be exchanged or sold from one school to another.

The rubric overlaid on these discussions was the importance of returning to mission. Admittedly, as a whole, schools are slow to be entrepreneurial and the anxiety of delving into areas far afield from the critical central purpose of the school can be restrictive. However, it does not have to compromise a mission to explore new ventures such as these. In fact, it may not be unreasonable to add a statement about the value of such activities as part of the mission statement. Furthermore, it is important to balance the school's mission by recognizing the increased costs of being a charitable organization and providing service to meet the mission. As such, schools must be more strategic about and diversified in how they meet or subsidize those costs in order to achieve the mission and remain affordable.

Conclusion

While acknowledging that the main goal of this chapter is to explore new thinking offered by key leaders in independent education, associations, and business, there is still more work to do before truly "box busting" strategies and ideas can take enough shape for schools to consider implementing them. Not surprisingly, the ideas and issues discussed above create more questions than answers and it is clear that additional work from schools and associations needs to be done to analyze the possibilities:

- Conduct market research on current independent school parents. What do they look for/value in independent schools? How can survey data support or refute assumptions schools make about parent demands (and their resulting effect on financing models)? Also, such research provides an opportunity to examine tuition elasticity and how parents finance school costs to help answer questions around affordability.

- Create task forces to study/further pursue three specific ideas:
  - Purchasing consortia. What are the opportunities for cost containment through joint purchasing? What are the risks or obstacles?
  - New revenue streams. Investigate the feasibility of packaging and reselling intellectual capital. Explore international models and markets.
  - Benchmarks for optimal performance. What operating ratios and other critical indicators can a school use to determine whether it is operating most efficiently? Consider variables such as school size and endowment in establishing different benchmarks for different types of schools.
- Collect and evaluate models from schools on two issues (including examples/models from for-profit schools):
  - Alternative tuition/pricing structures (e.g., 100% of cost, sliding scale, indexed tuition, fixed tuition)
  - Non-tuition revenue sources (e.g., summer school, after-school programs, spin-offs, intellectual property)

NAIS and NBOA look forward to pursuing these possibilities with the guidance and assistance from key leaders in independent schools, higher education, and business to provide feasible strategies for addressing these complex issues.

Mark Mitchell oversees the operation of NAIS's School and Student Service for Financial Aid (SSS) and provides support to schools and other organizations through workshops, writing, and resources. He offers consultative guidance in effectively administering financial aid programs, and is a frequent presenter at national, state, and regional association conferences.

How Much Endowment Is Enough?

By Sorrel R. Paskin

On the surface of it, the question seems silly. How can a school have too much endowment? After all, Harvard's endowment is well over $15 billion and campaigns for additional gifts to its endowment continue to prosper. And the presence of a large and growing endowment in universities and independent schools does not seem to have restrained tuition price increases, suggesting that trustees are not looking to endowment as a means to curtail the growth in fees necessary to meet increasing operating costs. What then is the function of endowment?

There are several reasons why schools and colleges seek gifts of endowment. Investment return earned on endowment portfolios can provide a financial cushion or safety net in times of fiscal stress. In this respect, endowment reduces the risk position of the school by providing a source of stabilizing revenue in the face of enrollment shortfalls or unforeseen environmental circumstances. Again, endowment investment return can provide "venture capital"—opportunities for program service enhancement and expansion beyond the resources that can be provided through tuition revenue—thereby contributing to the school's claimed "margin of excellence" and the "implicit scholarship"[1] that every student receives. It can support faculty compensation goals and professional development activities and underwrite visiting scholar programs. Finally, the presence of a substantial endowment portfolio can strengthen the school's balance sheet, thereby enabling the assumption of tax-exempt debt under favorable terms. Of course, a strong and growing endowment is also an expression of confidence in a school.

The question remains, however: How much endowment is enough? The question asks whether there is an optimum level of support that a school's endowment should provide to the operating budget (the primary function of endowment) and, if so, what level of endowment assets will provide that optimum level of support? If there is an optimum level of support, then a school should be able to identify it and, in concert with other policies, determine the portfolio value that will provide it. If there is not an optimum level of support and every dollar of endowment raised inures to the fiscal health of the institution, then it is clear that schools and colleges will seek to grow their endowments without limit.

We believe that the question is answerable and that it acquires strategic importance in light of the inherent competition that exists within a school's fundraising priorities for operating versus capital gifts and, in the case of capital gifts, for gifts to physical capital and for gifts to financial capital. Each of these types of gift has a unique form and, usually, a characteristic size range. Annual fund gifts for operations are typically smaller and support operating needs. Gifts for physical capital generally fund new construction or extensive renovation and upgrades and are typically larger than gifts to operations. The principal of gifts to the endowment is always restricted in perpetuity with the investment return earned on those gifts either unrestricted or, typically, restricted to operating items (financial aid, faculty development, chairs of distinguished teaching, etc.). Such gifts tend to be large and are of interest to a more limited pool of donors.

Clearly, as evidenced by practice, most schools seek all three kinds of gifts. Interestingly, schools set goals for the annual fund and for capital gifts to plant but only rarely state a goal for endowment unless gifts to endowment are included within a capital campaign. The level of support provided by the annual fund is usually prescribed by the budget and takes into account past results. New construction and extensive renovation have identifiable costs. The figure included for the endowment component is not constructed so definitively, however. It is sometimes founded upon what the school feels the campaign can achieve in total and the perceived interests and capacities of those benefactors likely to give to endowment. The inclusion of endowment also establishes a kind of "balance" among the beneficiaries of the sought resources. Even in this case, however, one senses that this particular burst of enthusiasm for endowment, even if satisfied, will not result in the creation of an investment portfolio sufficient to meet the school's judgment of its need for financial capital. That amount of endowment perpetually remains out of reach.

In most independent day schools, parents are the principal source of philanthropy. Not only are they asked to pay substantial tuition and fees, but they are also called upon to make gifts to the annual fund, to fuel additions to plant, and to secure the future well-being of the institution through the perpetual support provided by gifts to endowment. Alumni giving in day schools through grade 12 also supports these campaigns but becomes a more significant player in boarding schools.

In recent years, capital costs associated with technology infrastructure, installations, and equipment acquisitions have required substantial investment in plant. Additional plant investments have arisen from the need to retire deferred maintenance backlogs, to adapt existing space to new uses, and to add facilities desired by today's students and parents. At the same time, operating budgets have continued to rise, on average, about 1.5–2.0% above external CPI inflation[2], necessitating tuition increases averaging 5% per year and increases in the annual fund at about the same level. If parents are the principal source of gifts made to the school, then of necessity, the school must prioritize its fundraising goals to ensure the success of each of the components of its annual campaigns. It is in this context of defining fundraising goals and gift solicitation and allocation strategies that it makes sense to inquire into whether there is an optimum level of support a school should seek from its endowment.

In what follows, we will attempt to formulate a strategic decision framework sufficient to enable a school to rationally answer the question, How much endowment is enough? Along the way, we will investigate: (1) the nature of an endowment gift; (2) the link between total return payout/reinvestment policies and the growth in the school's operating budget; (3) the role of endowment in maintaining financial equilibrium; (4) types of payout policies with a recommendation for a particular "hybrid" model; and (5) the link between these factors and the determination of how much endowment is enough.

The Nature of an Endowment Gift

In a 1939 decision, the New York State Supreme Court provided the authoritative definition of endowment: *Endowment is "the bestowment of money as a permanent fund, the income of which is to be used in the administration of a proposed work."*[3] The definition makes clear the permanently restricted nature of the principal of the gift and the fact that only the income may be used in support of the donor's stipulated purpose. Prior to the adoption of the Uniform Management of Institutional Funds Act (UMIFA) in the 1970s, most states included endowments within the purview of trust law which defined income as the sum total of interest, dividends, rents, and so on earned on the underlying portfolio investments. Gains and losses were regarded as adjustments to principal and were not subject to appropriation.

By regarding net gains as a component of total return, UMIFA granted trustees the authority to appropriate this element of total return to an extent deemed prudent with respect to the exercise of fiduciary responsibility. Of course, the appropriation is also subject to any limitations on that use imposed by donor stipulation or state law.

A donor who makes a gift to endowment without further direction concerning the use of the investment return earned on that gift intends to enhance the level at which the school provides program services to students. The enhancement may result in the provision of new services, an expansion of certain existing service levels, or an increase in the quality of existing services. Most donors do not intend that their gifts should offset tuition increases arising from ordinary budget growth.[4]

A donor who makes a gift to endowment and stipulates a specific use for the earnings on that gift most certainly intends that the endowed function exist in perpetuity. The annual investment return supporting that endowed function must grow at a rate commensurate to the rate of growth in the cost of the endowed function. In this manner, the endowment supporting that function continues to provide a constant level of service in perpetuity. Thus, a donor who gifts a $1 million financial aid endowment to a school that spends 4.5% of the gift principal (and reinvests the remainder of the total return) expects that her endowment will annually fund two full scholarships if, at the date of the gift, the applicable tuition is $22,500 (2 × $22,500 = $45,000 = 4.5% × $1,000,000). *In effect, what is given are two full scholarships; the transferred assets function as the medium through which the gift will function.*

If this interpretation of an endowment gift is correct, the common practice of utilizing the endowment investment return as a replacement for budgeted financial aid, for example, is clearly inappropriate. If the donor's intent is to enhance the service level of a particular function, the replacement practice frustrates that intent. In fact, the freed-up, replaced funds are now available to enhance all other functions or to reduce the growth rate of tuition.[5]

It may be argued that service enhancement is a goal for some donors but not for all. Indeed, there are other reasons for donors to make and for schools to solicit gifts to endowment. Among these are the capacity of the return on the portfolio investments to contribute to earned surpluses which enhance the school's unrestricted financial capital and strengthen its balance sheet.[6] That increase in financial capital is then available to function as a buffer against adverse economic circumstances and unplanned declines in enrollment,[7] and to serve as a moderating factor in the need for future tuition increases. No doubt these reasons factor into the decision to solicit endowment gifts, the construction of reinvestment/payout policies, and the additions of unrestricted bequests and earned surpluses to the quasi-endowment.

Payout/Reinvestment Policies and the Operating Budget

The determination of the payout/reinvestment policy is usually linked to estimated long-term inflation, estimated long-term total return on the portfolio, and a "comfort factor" that attempts to balance the school's need for current operating support with the trustees' concern to "grow the portfolio" for the future. However, taking seriously the two points made above ([1] internal cost-rise over and above CPI associated with the failure to achieve productivity enhancements and [2] the intent of a donor to provide the increased service level in perpetuity) means that the payout/reinvestment policy must provide for annual increases in endowment investment return applied to the endowed function *at the rate of the growth of cost of that function.* For example, an endowment of $1 million that provides two full scholarships in 2000–2001 at a total cost of $45,000 must increase at the rate of 5% per year through reinvestment[8] in order to continue to provide two full scholarships if the school's budget grows at the rate of 5% per year.[9] That is, in 2001–2002 the endowment principal underlying the function must increase by $50,000 (5%) to $1,050,000 in order to provide $47,250 at a 4.5% payout rate. Note that if the budget grows 5% and the tuition price correspondingly increases by 5% (from $22,500 to $23,625), the $47,250 will continue to provide two full scholarships.

Of course, in order to meet these requirements, a 4.5% payout rate and a 5.0% increase in investment principal, the total return on the portfolio must have achieved 9.5%. This level of return dictates an investment strategy that can be expected to meet the requirement long term.

The Role of Endowment in Maintaining Financial Equilibrium10

At any point, the investment return on the school's endowment funds, whether unrestricted or restricted to specific operating functions, covers a certain percentage of the operating budget. Thus, a school with a $20 million operating budget and a $30 million endowment utilizing a 4.5% payout rate includes $1,350,000 of endowment investment return in the revenue stream of its operating budget. That level of endowment investment return represents 6.75% of the budget.

Maintaining long-run financial equilibrium with respect to endowment investment return means that absent new gifts, over time and on average, (in this example) 6.75% of the operating budget should continue to be supported by endowment investment return.

Alternatively stated, in long-run financial equilibrium, the growth rates of investment principal, investment return, and the school's operating budget are all equal. The equilibrium payout (or spending) rate that produces that result is the *equilibrium spending rate.*

Equilibrium spending rate = real total return – real cost-rise[11]

(Note that the relation can also be expressed in nominal values. Since external inflation (CPI) increases the real total return and the real cost-rise to the same extent, the CPI value simply subtracts out.)

In the example above, if real total return is 6.0% (nominal total return = 9.0% if CPI = 3%) and if real cost-rise is 1.5% (nominal institutional inflation = 4.5% if CPI = 3%), then the equilibrium spending rate is 4.5%. This is the payout rate from the endowment investment return that is sustainable in the long run and that maintains the endowment's share of the operating budget, a condition of financial equilibrium.

Source of Funds	*Growth Rate*	*Use of Funds*	*Growth Rate*
Inflation	3.0%	Inflation	3.0%
Real total return	6.0%	Real cost-rise	1.5%
		Spending appropriation	4.5%
Total	9.0%	Total	9.0%

Thus, for an endowment to support an activity or a function in perpetuity, the growth of the endowment fund must be matched to the school's cost-rise average (the annual growth rate of the operating budget). This is the meaning of *support in perpetuity*—an endowment that grows at the rate of budget growth maintains its purchasing power over time; in this manner, the real value of the endowment is preserved.

However, there is another reason to match the growth of the endowment fund to the school's cost-rise average. When the purchasing power of endowment funds is preserved, equity among past, present, and future generations of students is also preserved. In the words of Yale economist James Tobin,

> "The trustees of an endowed institution are the guardians of the future against the claims of the present. Their task is to preserve equity among generations. The trustees of an endowed [school] assume the institution to be immortal. They want to know, therefore, the rate of consumption from endowment that can be sustained indefinitely. . . . In formal terms, the trustees are supposed to have a zero rate of time preference.
>
> "Consuming endowment income so defined means in principle that the existing endowment can continue to support the same set of activities that it is now supporting. This rule says that current consumption should not benefit from the prospects of future gifts to endowment. Sustainable consumption rises to encompass an enlarged scope of activities when, but not before, capital gifts enlarge the endowment."[12]

Note that an overly conservative posture on the part of trustees, expressed in policies that require reinvestment of all endowment investment return or provide for spending rates that are less than the equilibrium spending rate, benefits future generations of students at the expense of the present generation. Given a balanced budget, less than the optimal allocation of endowment investment return to operating expense must result in an excessive tuition price if service levels are maintained or a reduction in service levels if growth in the tuition price is constrained.

Payout Policies

Payout or endowment return spending policies take a variety of forms throughout independent schools and colleges. Some schools spend investment yield (interest and dividends) only, reinvesting realized and unrealized gains; others spend a percentage of the ending market value of the endowment investment portfolio. In an effort to smooth the volatility associated with either of these approaches, many schools utilize a moving average technique, spending a predetermined percentage of a three-year or five-year trailing average market value of the investment portfolio. Another approach adopted by a smaller number of schools is to increase the amount spent each year by a preset increment (percentage factor) applied to last year's appropriation. Thus, if in 2000–2001, the endowment investment return included in operations is $1,000,000 and the preset increment is 5%, then the appropriation for 2001–2002 would be $1,050,000.

The amount of reinvestment delivered by a spend-only-yield policy bears no relation to the amount necessary to offset internal cost-rise; the actual amount reinvested may be more than or less than the amount required. Such a policy may also bind investment strategy to the school's need for current funds, thereby dictating portfolio management strategy.

The ending market value technique is based upon total return and has the advantage of separating portfolio management issues from current spending needs. However, the results of its application are also subject to volatility. Consider that a portfolio invested 70% in equities and 30% in fixed income securities has an expected nominal total return of 9% (expected real return is 5.5%); however, expected volatility for this investment sector allocation is 12 percentage points (i.e., there is a one in three chance that annual investment return will fall outside the range of 5.5% +/– 12%). Such volatility can produce unacceptable swings both in the annual amount spent for operations and in the amount reinvested in the portfolio.

The moving average technique dampens volatility but increases the divergence between actual and equilibrium spending levels as the number of years included in the average increases. Moreover, the effect of a large total-return deviation in one year remains in the moving average with undiminished weight until it is dropped at the end of the last year included, thereby producing a kind of "jerkiness" in the determination of the actual spending level for that next year.

Finally, while the preset increment method matches endowment return spending to the growth in the budget, it contains no "feedback" mechanism for deviations of total return from expectation and can result in spending levels in excess of the equilibrium rate and reinvestment levels below the amount necessary to maintain financial equilibrium. For example, if real portfolio return in a given year is –6.5% and the preset increment is 5% (i.e., the amount to be spent next year is 5% more than the amount spent this year), the amount spent as a percentage of ending portfolio value will significantly exceed the equilibrium spending rate.

It is possible to combine the moving-average and percentage-increment methods into a technique that exploits the strengths of each and minimizes their individual weaknesses. This hybrid method[13] is applied on a per-share basis, not to the overall market value of the portfolio. The procedure simultaneously takes account of the equilibrium spending rate and the desired spending increment based upon budgetary growth. The actual spending appropriation resulting from the calculation tends to converge to its equilibrium value.

The calculation formula is actually an exponentially weighted moving average; the influence of each prior year's total return declines exponentially. For example, the weight applied to the current year's market value is 0.33, that for last year's is 0.33^2, the one for the previous year's is 0.33^3, and so on. This avoids the problem with the simple moving average technique that a given data point may vanish abruptly. Spending growth is continuously adjusted in response to market results.

The method is applied through the following procedure:

1. Calculate per-share spending under the preset increment method, setting the escalator equal to the expected budget growth.
2. Calculate equilibrium rate spending, which is the product of the equilibrium spending rate and the beginning per-share market value.
3. Set next year's per-share spending equal to a weighted average of the preset increment and the equilibrium values. The weight applied to the equilibrium spending level usually runs between 0.25 and 0.4. A weight of 0.33 is used at Stanford and Yale.

For example, if last year's spending appropriation is 50 cents per share, this year's beginning market value is $10 per share, total cost-rise is 5.0%, the equilibrium spending rate is 4%, and the weighting factor is 0.33, next year's spending appropriation is given by the following expression.[14]

[(Weighting factor) × (equilibrium spending rate) × (beginning per share market value)] + [(1 − weighting factor) × (preset spending increment) × (prior year per share amount)]

$$(0.33)(0.04)(\$10.00) + (1 - 0.33)(1 + 0.05)(\$0.50) = \$0.483$$

In this example, per-share spending declined from 50 cents to 48.3 cents instead of increasing by the desired 5%. This is because the current per-share market value of $10 will sustain an equilibrium spending level of only 40 cents. The smoothing rule phases in the lower spending level a little at a time. On the other hand, if the total return on the endowment had been higher—so that the market value had been $13, for instance—the formula would yield 52.3 cents per share. This compares favorably with the desired value of 52.5 cents.[15]

The degree of smoothing is determined by the weighting factor selected for the calculation. At a value of 1.0, there is no smoothing at all and the calculation produces the equilibrium spending level with maximal variation in the amount spent. At a value of 0, there is no smoothing and the calculation produces the preset increment amount.

A Decision Framework for Determining How Much Endowment Is Enough

Managing the Endowment-Support Ratio

There is not a single, universal answer to the question, How much endowment is enough? Instead, each institution must make its own determination of the answer to that question. It is clear from the foregoing that a number of factors enter into that determination. The strategic construction of those factors into a decision framework enables a school to rationally identify its optimum level of endowment support.

Important to the decision framework is the endowment-support ratio, calculated as follows:

Endowment-support ratio = [(spending rate) × (beginning endowment market value)] / [operating budget for the year]

The endowment-support ratio is the strategic variable in the determination of the optimum level of endowment support. It reflects the fraction of the budget that is supported by endowment investment return. *The answer to the question of the optimum level of support to be provided by the endowment is the determination of the optimum value for the endowment-support ratio.* In concert with the other factors identified above, the optimum value established for the endowment-support ratio determines the answer to the question, How much endowment is enough?

Managing the value of the endowment-support ratio should be a conscious process; its value should not be allowed to evolve as an unintended consequence of other policies. Basically, there are three levers available to establish and maintain this value. Each of these levers marks a further point of strategic decision-making: (1) the real budget growth rate; (2) the spending/reinvestment policy and total return earned on the portfolio; and (3) gifts and other additions to endowment.

The greater the budget growth rate the more upward pressure there is on the endowment-support ratio. Using the equilibrium-spending rate is a sufficient condition for maintaining the endowment-support ratio only when the budget is not growing faster than institutional cost-rise. The budget growth rate will normally exceed institutional cost-rise when present service levels are expanded beyond ordinary inflation (increasing faculty and staff numbers or enhancing benefits programs, for example) or when new programs or services are introduced. Absent service expansion, the equilibrium-spending rate should maintain the endowment-support ratio over time.

The amount of income and net gains reinvested affects the numerator of the endowment-support ratio by changing the beginning endowment market value. Therefore, reinvested income can offset the effect of real budget growth and stabilize the endowment-support ratio even in the face of increased services and programs. Adjustments to the portfolio asset mix that do not lead to inappropriate assumptions of risk can achieve this outcome. Reducing the spending rate also increases reinvestment but at the expense of the initial endowment-support ratio.

A capital campaign is the most visible method of increasing the flow of gifts to endowment. As noted above, however, schools often add large unrestricted gifts and bequests to the endowment portfolio, and operating surpluses may also be designated for long-term investment as endowment. In each of these situations, the trustees must make a choice between sometimes competing goals. In the case of a campaign, the decision may rest upon the allocation of goals between physical capital and financial capital. In the case of unrestricted gifts and operating surpluses, the decision is between current consumption and accumulating operating reserves or investing for the future. If the path of investment for the future is chosen, then a further decision must be made between which form of capital, physical or financial, will benefit from that investment.

If a school is growing in size and its budget is increasing to reflect that growth, maintaining the endowment-support ratio requires that new gifts be added to the endowment or that additional total return be reinvested in the portfolio. This implies that in the case of a growing school any capital campaign (or private solicitation) should contain an endowment component. Again, if the board determines that the range or quality of services offered to students should be increased without a corresponding increase in enrollment or in price, an effective way to manage the added cost is to increase the endowment-support ratio over a specified period of years through an appropriate adjustment of fund-raising and resource allocation priorities.

Optimizing the Endowment-Support Ratio

A school has enough endowment when the accumulation and spending policies established by the trustees for the endowment portfolio maintain the value of the endowment-support ratio over time. The value of the ratio that is optimum for a given school is established by its long-range strategic plan. In constructing that plan, the trustees take into account the critical factors associated with the school's performance: enrollment change, planned initiatives (including new programs and services), facilities needs and responses, market constraints and opportunities, and institutional strengths and weaknesses. The strategic plan also models alternative futures based upon the different scenarios constructed.

The financial component of each future modeled includes estimates of revenue inflows derived from tuition, operating and capital gifts, endowment investment return, and other revenue sources, along with projections for each operating and capital cost center. Within each of these alternative futures, coverage (contribution) ratios describe the percentage of operating costs to be met by each element of the revenue stream. Thus, the endowment-support ratio describes the percentage of operating cost to be met by the component of endowment investment return applied to operations.

The optimum value of the endowment-support ratio is determined within the framework of the totality of circumstances a school faces. It is that value prescribed by the most desirable future described within the strategic plan. In modeling alternative futures, the board considers the consequences of actions that would increase or decrease the ratio, providing larger or smaller levels of endowment support for operating needs. In the context of the totality of resources available and their allocations to cost centers, the board can subjectively judge the resulting utility of each model. Thus is the optimum value of the endowment-support ratio determined and the answer to the question, How much endowment is enough?

When additional endowment gifts are received or large unrestricted gifts, bequests, or operating surpluses are added to the endowment, or as enrollment, facilities, or program expands, or service levels for existing programs are increased (more output and/or increased outcomes), the strategic plan is modified accordingly, new futures are modeled, and a new optimum level for the endowment-support ratio is determined.

Sorrel R. Paskin is President of Resource Associates, Inc., a firm specializing in providing business administration, accounting, and employee benefits administration services to smaller independent schools. Formerly the Associate Headmaster for Finance and Administration at Riverdale Country School (NY), Sorrel's career in schools and colleges spans 44 years and includes financial and business administration, investment management, and institutional strategic planning, as well as teaching. He presently serves as an adjunct professor in logic and critical thinking at Johnson and Wales University (RI). Sorrel is a graduate of the University of Pennsylvania (BA), New York University (MA), and the University of Missouri–St. Louis (MO), and is a Certified Management Accountant.

Notes

[1] The implicit scholarship measures the excess of value received over price paid (tuition) for the instructional and other services provided by the school.

[2] Characteristic of schools and other labor-intensive organizations in which productivity gains are difficult to achieve is the phenomenon of internal cost-rise. In schools, faculty salaries may comprise 50% or more of the operating budget. In order to attract and retain quality teachers, schools must compete in the broader marketplace against industries in which productivity gains often result in increased real wages for workers. However, "academic production" is sticky in the sense that student/faculty ratios are often perceived as surrogates for academic quality. Thus, in the case of at least 50% of the school's operating budget, the growth in cost is not offset by increased "production" and the school's operating budget—and its tuition price—increases commensurately. Economist William Baumol has labeled this phenomenon education's "cost disease."

If productivity increases in the United States average two percent over the long run and the goods and other non-faculty services purchased by schools are subject to economy-wide inflation, then the "cost disease" can account for about a one-percent over inflation internal cost-rise (50% × 2% = 1%). Thus, the limited ability to achieve productivity gains should result in school budgetary growth of at least 1% in real terms.

For the past many years, independent school tuitions have risen substantially more than can be accounted for by the "cost disease" explanation. It is likely that, exploiting both a favorable economy and strong demand, schools have increased tuition to improve faculty compensation and to increase program services, while at the same time adding to and upgrading technology holdings and adding to plant and facilities. These moves are market based, responding to the demands of customers, and reflective of the need to remain competitive as more and more families seek the advantages of private education.

[3] St. Joseph's Hospital vs. Bennett (281 N.Y. 115,118, 22 N.E. 2d 305, 306 (1939)).

[4] This outcome may, however, appropriately arise from the inclusion of past earned surpluses, unrestricted bequests and other large unrestricted gifts received in the quasi-endowment portfolio.

[5] It is of course true that donors often establish purpose-restricted named endowments to honor an individual who has played an important role in their lives or to recognize the work of an exemplary teacher or coach. Some donors who find particular merit in certain of the school's programs or services, may wish to endow some or all of the cost of those programs or services, thereby ensuring their preservation in perpetuity. While such motivations do not specifically address service enhancements, we believe that donors implicitly intend such gifts to provide benefit to the school through the augmentation of resources that can be committed to the endowed functions.

[6] An additional advantage of the strength that quasi-endowment adds to the institution is the resulting increase in debt capacity and the improved debt rating available for bond issues.

[7] It is noteworthy that endowment investment return is one of the few income streams available to an independent school that does not depend upon enrollment.

[8] Unless the donor or state law requires reinvestment of some portion of the total return as additional permanently restricted principal (permanently restricted net assets), all reinvestment must occur as unrestricted designated endowment (a form of quasi-endowment).

[9] We assume that the tuition price will increase at the rate of growth of the budget if school size remains constant.

[10] Financial equilibrium is identified with six specific objectives: (1) current operating revenues equal or exceed current operating expense; (2) the rate of growth of operating revenues over time equals or exceeds the rate of growth of operating expense; (3) financial capital is preserved or augmented (through prudent reinvestment); (4) physical capital is preserved or augmented (through planned reinvestment including the accumulation of reserves; ongoing renewal, replacement, and adaption activities; and retirement of deferred maintenance backlogs); (5) human capital is preserved or augmented (through professional development programs); and (6) the quality of the curriculum, program, and services to students is preserved or enhanced.

[11] This formula assumes that the spending appropriation remains in the endowment portfolio and earns a return for the full year. In that case, the ending value of the endowment is given by the following expression:

$$\text{ending endowment} = (1 + \text{total return} - \text{spending rate}) \times (\text{beginning endowment})$$

[12] Tobin, James. "What Is Permanent Endowment Income?" *American Economic Review* 64. 1974. Quoted in Massey, William F. et al., *Resource Allocation in Higher Education.* Ann Arbor, University of Michigan Press, 1996, pp. 93–94.

[13] Massey, William F. et al., *Resource Allocation in Higher Education.* Ann Arbor, University of Michigan Press, 1996, pp. 107–108.

[14] The first line of the expression represents an unsmoothed version of the moving average technique; the second line reflects the preset percentage increment method. The weighting factor (0.33

in this example) determines the relative "influence" of each of the methods utilized on the final outcome. Note that this approach provides important feedback to the determination of next year's spending level.

[15] In the face of a sustained and severe market decline, the hybrid approach promotes a "negotiated compromise" between the need for current spending to support budgetary growth and a decrease in spending designed to protect the value of the portfolio. In the above illustration, for example, suppose that the unit value had declined to $8.00, a loss of 20%. Then the payout would be calculated as:

$$(0.33)(0.04)(\$8.00) + (1 - 0.33)(1 + 0.05)(\$0.50) = \$0.457 \text{ per unit}$$

instead of $0.483 per unit, a 5% reduction. Note that the budgetary appropriation is not impacted by the full market decline in portfolio value but does take that fact into account in order to determine the spending rate. Of course, the extent of reduction is also dependent upon the size of the factor (0.33 in these examples). A factor larger than 0.33 would result in increased reinvestment in the portfolio and reduced support for the operating budget.

Strategic Financing: The Relationship Between Your Mission and Your Money

By Bill Lowman

School Finance, the Mystery of It All

Why is it that the strategic plan and the annual budget seem to be written in another language and the quarterly financial statements never quite seem to reflect either of them? Many of us in the educational community feel inadequate in this essential area. Financial decisions seem to be made by a closed circle of middle-aged men in dark suits who sit quietly at the back of the boardroom. With apologies to all those accounting majors and MBA students, practical financing is simple and interesting. Planning, budgeting, and reporting are some of the most important elements in our work, for they can produce the resources to achieve our educational dreams. Anyone can learn to use financing creatively to achieve an important mission in a non-profit institution.

From Strategic Financing to the Annual Budget, It All Starts with the Mission

Is it ridiculous to state that Financial Planning begins with a school's mission? The mission is a statement of the most important elements of your non-profit purpose. If it is not included or implied in your mission, how will you find the will to fund it? A few examples of missions which directly lead to funding follow:

(1) The Idyllwild Arts Academy is dedicated to pre-professional training in the arts and a comprehensive college preparatory education in an environment conducive to positive personal growth for talented students from all over the world. Any question about providing the financial aid and recruitment expense for the best young bassoonist from Siberia to play in the school's world-class youth orchestra and eventually go to the Juilliard School on a full scholarship? How about struggling with the alienated young visual artist with extraordinary academic potential who was thrown out of school for disinterested doodling (we call that drawing!) in the back row of his class? Would it be appropriate for Idyllwild to invest in a first-rate set of athletic fields or equipment for a football team and cheerleaders' outfits?

(2) The Thacher School combines a rigorous academic program with mountains,

horses, sports, and the arts to develop young people's minds, bodies, and character. In a time of significantly reduced resources from donations and increased need for financial aid, would you suspect that Thacher would cut its horse program or the expenses associated with its new student wilderness trip?

(3) The Webb Schools of California offer superior academic and athletic programs and residential experiences in a coordinate school structure. Will Webb decide to change from a boys' school, a girls' school, and a museum of paleontology to a more efficient, less expensive operation? Why bother with all that duplication of course offerings?

(4) Western Reserve Academy believes that its academic, art, and athletic programs educate young people and provide a solid values base for the future. Would you expect Reserve to cut back on its competitive sports teams to expand its environmental education program?

(5) The Cate School challenges its students intellectually and emotionally with high expectations for self-fulfillment and service to others. Would you expect Cate to start a program for developmentally disabled young people and cut its community service programs?

The mission sets priorities for the annual budget, including funds raised in support of the program, money spent on instruction, and extracurricular activities. Plans and funds for needed facilities and capital improvements are all derived from your purpose. What good is an excellent educational idea if you have no funds to implement it? You are what you fund! If you really don't care about an educational area, it will be simple to not fund it. If you really do care, it will be very difficult to exclude part of your mission from annual funding.

A Budget Is Just Like Your Checkbook Except with More Zeros

In 1974 I was offered an administrative position in the School of Performing Arts at the University of Southern California (USC). In my first week on the job, the Dean called me (a former musician, summer counselor, and rock climber with a dismal mathematics transcript) into his office and requested that I create a budget for USC's summer arts school in the mountains. I swallowed loudly and mentioned to this elegant man whom I greatly admired that I had never created an institutional budget before. He looked at me for a moment and said, "You have a checkbook, don't you?" I nodded my head. "Then make a column for expenses and a column for revenue and balance it at the bottom. It's just a matter of more zeros!" He was absolutely right. That was a $400,000 budget. That moment and the work ahead stimulated an intense interest in practical financing and strategic planning.

In 1977, two musical colleagues and I founded a community school of the arts and summer arts camp in Nevada, using the important mission of much-needed arts education combined with a knowledge of budgeting to secure sponsorships from the local schools, the university, and the county parks and recreation department. We started from scratch and, after eight years, enrolled 1,100 students from three-year-olds through high-school seniors. The program budget was over $300,000 annually and the publicly funded agencies provided much of the overhead, all the facilities expenses, and capital improvements. By combining tuition, a state arts council grant, and some community fundraising the Nevada School of the Arts was able to offer many excellent programs for young people, no matter their family's financial circumstances.

Following that stint in creative financing, I moved to Southern California to assist in the redevelopment of that original summer arts school formerly owned by USC and founded the Idyllwild Arts Academy in 1986 as the year-round incarnation of Idyllwild's artistic goals. In 1985, Idyllwild offered its summer arts program for ten weeks a year, raised additional revenue from Elderhostel Programs, and rented the campus for conferences on the weekends. The budget was over $800,000 and there were eight full-time employees. In 2003, Idyllwild Arts has an annual budget of $13.5 million and nearly 100 full time employees. The Idyllwild Arts Academy trains and educates the next generation of artists in its boarding high school for young musicians, dancers, artists, actors, writers, filmmakers, and interdisciplinary artists. The nine-week summer program offers 95 different workshops for students aged five to adult in virtually every area of the arts for students of all abilities.

Each of these tasks was accomplished by envisioning an important mission, developing strategic financial plans to maximize the resources available to achieve that mission, working with an extraordinary faculty and staff to offer the finest educational program possible, and working with philanthropically minded volunteer board members to ensure both resources and appropriate oversight. Later in this article I will illustrate a very simple financial planning tool and indicate what strategically important elements may be manipulated to assist in achieving a school's educational dreams.

Do You Want to Play Mozart or Mahler?

First, however, ask yourself why you would want to become deeply involved in the financial strategy for a school. The rhetorical question best used to illustrate the answer is, "Do you want to play Mozart or Mahler?" Why must we choose? Mozart composed beautiful music, representating the thoughts of one of the great geniuses of the classical period. Mahler composed at the turn of the 20th century, celebrating the cross-cultural forces which later produced the best of times and worst of times that now characterize the 20th century. Can't we play both? The truth is, we need a strategic plan: For those not familiar with classical music, a Mozart-sized orchestra is made up of as few as 36 players, including 25–36 string players, 10 wind instrumentalists, and one tympanist. A Mahler orchestra is usually made up of more than 100 musicians, including 70 strings, double winds, a full brass section, expanded percussion, harps, and may include a choir and/or vocal soloists. Even though the concert hall has the same number of paying seats, the cost of performance is many times more for the latter. The artistic leader needs to understand when the players are ready to play the more demanding Mahler and when the orchestra organization is ready to assume the expense. Who should make this decision? Whoever it is, he or she must understand the financial impact, the risks involved, and the importance of the decision.

As head of an independent school, I want to make every decision of this magnitude.

I need to understand how artistic/educational improvements will impact each student's education and the reputation of the school. Will these improvements call for additional financial resources? How will I recruit the additional talented musicians needed to play the Mahler? Can I sustain the added students, the needed funds, the necessary infrastructure (a larger stage, more instruments, and on and on)? I must not only understand but I must carefully prepare so that I can convince other important forces in the school community that this path is the right one.

At a typical non-profit school, the finance and audit committee of the board, made up of accountants and business leaders, in cooperation with the Chief Business and Financial Officer, take a hard look at the operations of the school and determine the tuition increase for the upcoming year, the enrollment goal, the amount of the faculty salary increase, and the overall budget increases or decreases. Sometimes, these all- important decisions are created in a vacuum, without considering all the strategic possibilities as well as the risks and opportunities. What happened to Mahler? Who gets to decide?

Operating a School without a Strategic and Financial Plan Is Unwise and Shortsighted.

Every five years, at least (every three years would be better), the school community should participate in a detailed evaluation of its purpose, its programs, its employees, its facilities, and its administration. This positive study should clearly indicate where the institution wishes to go and how it might get there! It is very helpful to request outside assistance from a professional consultant. Finding the right person is essential. A non-profit school needs dispassionate advice from a well-educated financial planner with an understanding of non-profit mission and finance. It is most important that this respected person work in concert with the Head of School, the business office, and the board planning committee/task force to produce a plan that will engage the entire school community.

In 1993, Bill Dietel, legendary former head of Emma Willard School, came to visit our school at the request of a foundation to assess the state of our operation. Our Summer Program was nearly fifty years old and chronically underfunded and our Arts Academy was seven years old with 140 students enrolled. Our budgetary operations were in the early entrepreneurial stage where every decision was financially critical and we were constantly being saved by major donations from two extraordinarily generous major donors. After reviewing plans for the school and its current situation, Dietel suggested that our school employ the services of Dr. Tom Clough, a sole practitioner in Strategic Planning who specializes in assisting non-profit organizations that have difficult funding issues. Tom received his Doctorate in Economics from Harvard and later was employed by Cambridge Associates. When his wife was offered the opportunity to serve as Dean of Carleton College in Minnesota, Tom hung out his shingle and began offering planning advice to non-profit organizations. The original plan created by the school and Tom Clough, and the subsequent updates, helped produce an extraordinary period of development at Idyllwild. Between 1993 and 2003 the Idyllwild enrollment grew from 140 to 265 students and annual budgets grew from $7.4 million to $13.5 million. Earned income grew from $4.7 million in '94 to $11.2 million in 2003. Our operations required annual donated income of at $2.7 million in '94 and we were able to reduce that to $2.2 million by '03. In 1994, 49% of gross tuition was spent on financial aid and by 2003 only 23%, but we increased the amount spent from $1.6 million in '94 to $2.3 million in 2003. Successful completion of a $9.5 million capital campaign provided the facilities and campus upgrades necessary to cope with the growth and expansion of the school. Every one of these statistics represents a strategic decision.

I have seen a number of plans, many of them lengthy presentations of educational philosophy, institutional values, and dreams. These ideas are faithfully gathered from faculty, parents, administration, and board. Plans produced from our educational dreams often mention the need for a world-class technology program or raising faculty salaries to the top 10% of the national average, or provide a moving rationale for new construction. In my experience, many such plans represent dreams without strategies and end up gathering a great deal of dust on an office shelf. An excellent plan presents a clear picture of the strengths and weaknesses of the institution. It makes assertions in words and proves them in numbers. As it projects a stronger, more effective future, it must be clear that successful realization of the plan will provide the necessary resources to solve the current problems and produce important educational improvements for the school. The consultant and the planning team must ask many important questions: Why is this our mission? Why do we achieve it in this manner? Can our purpose be accomplished by operating differently? Why are we important? What is unique and rewarding about a student's experience at our school? Why should students attend our school? What is the desirable outcome of our brand of education? Do we achieve that outcome? What is the value added for students that would encourage their parents to pay tuition rather than attend free public school? The answers must be clear and make sense. The heart of the plan is the statement of the goals of the school combined with a multi-year financial projection that indicates in clear numbers what the priorities are, for what purpose the funds will be spent, and where those all important resources will come from.

Such planning eases the difficulty of preparing the annual budget. In a typical school, competition for the resources available each year is intense. It is the mission and the plan that will help the school to make the appropriate decisions. If the plan has been properly constructed, the educational improvements every good school desires to make each year will have been generated by those closest to the program, evaluated by the management team, and adopted by the board. At the close of each year, the school's progress toward its goals easily can be compared to the projections of the five-year plan. As you prepare the new budget, past experience in meeting planning goals will assist in knowing where the risk factors are in each year's budget. When economic conditions, market issues, and development trends change, it's time to revisit the plan.

Over the years, I have observed that non-profits face financial issues in many different ways. A non-profit school is an educational institution, a humane organization that promotes personal growth and challenges students to achieve not only their dreams but to understand the accumulated knowledge of human history and to be able to critically evaluate the constant changes that we face each day. How, then, can schools operate in a strategic, businesslike fashion? Can we be both personal and businesslike? Can we fund those important elements that are essential to our beliefs? What follows is a simple model for constructing a school budget, some very specific opinions about the important categories in that model, and a series of suggestions and ideas about financing issues.

The Model:

Summary:
+Total Net Revenue
–Total Program, Support and Recruitment Expenses
–Total Overhead Expenses
+Total Unearned Income
+Net from total operation of your non-profit corporation

Model Detail:

Category	**Description**	**Comments**
Revenue	**Earned income**	
Gross tuition	*no. of students* × tuition fee	Note 1
(Financial aid)		*Note 2*
Net Tuition	*The most important source of income*	Note 1
School fees		Note 3
Interest income	*Tuition payment plans, invested excess cash*	
Net revenue		
Auxiliary services		Note 4
(Cost of sales and service)		
Net Revenue		
Other income	*Campus rentals and special programs*	Note 5
(Expenses)	*Cost of prep., maint., utilities, programs*	
Net revenue		
Total Net Revenue		
Program Expenses		
(The cost of achieving your educational mission)	*Salaries of all kinds, benefits, faculty development, instructional supplies, equipment, faculty travel, student travel, student enrichment, master classes*	Note 6
(The cost of extracurricular activities to achieve your mission)		Note 7

(The cost of measuring the outcome/effectiveness
of your mission) Note 8

College counselor/staff, testing services, etc.

(The cost of supervision, support, and safety: student services) Note 9

Dean, dorm parents, counselors, nurses, health center staff, transportation staff, security officers, food services

(The cost of recruiting students: admissions) Note 10

(Total Program, Support and Recruitment Expenses)
Program Net: Net Revenue minus Program Expenses

Overhead Expenses: (These expenses may be allocated on a per-student basis or a per-department or grade-level basis, but can be best envisioned and managed by analyzing them individually.)

(The cost of operating/maintaining school facilities
to achieve your mission) Note 11

Salaries, maintenance and custodial, equipment, supplies, training, utility expenses, depreciation expenses to ensure long-term viability of the physical plant

(The cost of improving/operating your 21st-century
technology program) Note 12

Salaries, campus technology in operations, admissions, finance, administration, student services, advancement, technology support for students and faculty, library, dorms, across the curriculum, purchases, upgrades, wiring, connections, hardware and software.

(The cost of advancement in support of your mission) Note 13

Salaries and benefits, director of development, staff, director of public/community relations, alumni relations staff, marketing and publications and staff, supplies, travel, equipment, consultants' fees

(The cost of overall administration of the school,
to support your mission) Note 14

Salaries and benefits, head of school, assistant head/s, chief business officer and finance staff, central office staff, human resources staff, legal advice, campus risk management

(Total Overhead Expenses)
(Net from All School Operations) – Program Net minus Overhead

Donated Income Note 15
Revenue from Endowment investments
Annual Fund donations—gifts from all sources

Total Donated Income
(Net from All School Operations)
Net from Total Operation of Your Non-profit Corporation

This short analysis does not include capital items, either the funds donated for such construction or purchase, the cost of such fund-raising or the cost of construction. If you want to see what a strategic change will mean, consider any action—short- or long-term—risky or practical, and its effect on the budget or plan. Some suggestions:

Revenue or net revenue considerations

1. Tuition revenue is the most important source of income for all necessary operations and improvements at a school. Should you increase the amount of tuition annually by more than the cost of living? How else will you provide increased salaries for your faculty, deal with the rising cost of technology, upgrade equipment, cope with surprises like utility cost spikes in California or refurbish your aging facilities? Private institutions have been increasing tuition annually in larger amounts than inflation for a number of years. It seems to be the only method of recovering rising costs and making improvements; that is, those families who can afford to pay tuition cover the increased costs. Those who cannot should receive some institutional financial aid. Foregoing tuition increases simply assists the affluent yet does not seem to help those who have real need in your financial-aid program. **Suggestion for creating more revenue:** Size your school to maximize revenue—determine the number of students who may be added to the student body without increasing the number of faculty or requiring new facilities. This revenue is the most important source of income for all necessary operations and improvements at a school. At the heart of these numbers is the student/teacher ratio in each classroom.

2. Financial aid has been a remarkable tool in independent education to provide access to extraordinary educational opportunity, but it has an economic base. Whatever your purpose in offering financial aid, whether it is to maximize the diversity of your student body, secure the enrollment of academically talented students, find a principal oboe or bassoon for the orchestra, or recruit the starting quarterback on the football team, you can achieve your goals. First, calculate the marginal cost of adding a student. If you wish to enroll this student and have open spaces in school or can add this person to the student body without adding faculty or facilities, you need to know what it actually costs. In a boarding school, the marginal cost is a total of the cost of food, school transportation, and any special supplies. When you calculate the impact of this enrollment, determine whether the fees paid (gross tuition minus the financial aid award) produce more revenue than the marginal cost. If the student will improve your program and produces net tuition in excess of the marginal cost, you will improve the financial operation of the school and add an interesting student to the community. Another way of understanding the economic power of financial aid is to visualize airline ticket pricing. My economic advisor calls this pricing along the demand curve. Without becoming too technical, this concept suggests that there is not sufficient demand for all the seats in an airplane at the full price. Therefore, the airlines offer some seats at discounts to maximize the income from that flight. Colleges have understood this concept for years and have increased institutional financial aid, calling the amount that remains unfunded in their annual budget the "discount rate." For those who are fortunate enough to have large endowments in support of their institution, the entire financial aid budget may be funded from investments. Also, those schools who are fortunate enough to have hundreds of students on waiting lists can decide how many scholarships (discounts) to offer to meet their educational mission and support their commitment to diversity. **Suggestion for increasing net operating revenue at the school:** As you increase the number of students to your optimum enrollment, carefully decrease the percentage of financial aid with relation to the whole. Financial aid amounts will stay level or increase but more tuition will be earned.

3. School fees: Businesses, cruise lines, vacation travel agents, colleges and schools all debate whether clients (in our case, parents) will be angered by adding a number of small fees on top of an expensive tuition, or whether the tuition should be all-inclusive. There are three answers: (1) Yes, they will be unhappy. (2) A school cannot afford to charge an all-inclusive tuition and cover every other expense. These expenses are a bit unpredictable and the sticker shock of current tuition is bad enough. (3) Charging additional fees is a time-honored tradition and so far, the best method of recouping additional expenses. **Here are some ideas for additional fees:** Charge a graduation fee for seniors (caps and gowns, invitations, grad speaker, and expenses for other ceremonies). Charge a fee for English-as-a-second-language students (ESL) that covers the cost of employing specialists in this field and the operation of an excellent program to transition international students to American school life. Charge a fee for specialized private instruction in music or private tutoring, commensurate with the cost of the lesson, the transportation, and the coordination required. Determine the amount of supplies in art classrooms that are covered by tuition and charge fees for additional photo paper, drawing paper, canvas and stretcher bars, oil paint, and so on. Charge transportation fees for students and families that cover the wages of drivers, gasoline expense, vehicle maintenance, and insurance costs. I recommend a per-mile charge for all elective transportation. Set up a fee program in campus dormitories that charges users an extra fee in addition to the telephone-company fees for using the campus phone system and a technology fee for Internet access in private dorm rooms. These fees will provide for the expense of staffing and hardware, software, and wiring problems. (Make certain you provide free and effective Internet access in classrooms, the library, and other appropriate places.)

4. Auxiliary services can be a very effective revenue producer for a school. Make certain to analyze the profitability in the bookstore (price versus cost of sales) with special attention to trendy student items such as clothing, water bottles, and souvenirs. Colleges have recognized significant revenue by branding their logos and allowing their commercial sale. What about putting a store on your website to accept orders and using a commercial company to produce and transport the items? How many Harvard sweatshirts have you seen? Does this represent a much-needed profit and good advertising, or the watering-down of your reputation? Perhaps it depends on your point of view! At a boarding school, the campus washing machines and dryers are major sources of revenue. If you charge for attendance at school events, the ticket price can produce needed revenue, as can the gallery percentage of sales from the campus art gallery. Depending on your commitment to health, campus vending machines can be helpful as well.

5. Other income: This broad category covers all the programs within your educational mission that you offer during vacations, off seasons, after school, and summer to maximize the productivity of your school. They can include leasing your facilities to a chamber music program like Encore! at Western Reserve Academy or Music Academy of the West at Cate School. You may wish to develop your own summer programs like the Idyllwild Arts Summer Program which offers 95 different workshops in the arts for students from age five to adult. This program has its own staff, tuition and fees, donated support, and traditions. You might consider developing a summer science camp to bring the best young minds in the area to your school. How about a series of summer Elderhostel courses taught by some of your inspirational faculty? Senior citizens make great students, ambassadors for your school, and possible future donors. Wouldn't it be terrific if a number of the excellent boarding schools across the country formed a consortium to improve teaching in American schools? Perhaps a foundation grant could provide financial aid for young teachers in the public schools across our country to learn from the best practices at independent schools. Summer ESL courses were all the rage in past years, but the market is quite competitive and the teaching of English continues to improve in the Asian countries that were the market for students. I'm sure you have heard of a summer program for students who have extraordinary potential to be excellent academic students but not much opportunity. Why not provide wonderful educational opportunities in your city for such students? How about developing a program for gay and lesbian students in your area? A summer course replete with acceptance as well as challenge and rigor can change a young person's outlook forever. All of these, along with your ideas, should be carefully evaluated with relation to the revenue produced (grant funds or fees), the direct expenses of the program, the indirect expenses with relation to the physical plant and coordination required, and the net revenue. This bottom-line approach should include for consideration the impact on your regular school-year admission and such intangibles as service to the field, community outreach, your reputation, the expansion of your fundraising contacts, and, of course, your mission.

Expense Considerations

6. Educational program: Now it gets really interesting—How do you count enrollments at your school? At the Arts Academy, we count musicians, dancers, theater majors, visual artists, creative writers, and interdisciplinary arts majors. These are the categories in which students enroll at our school. The academic program must cope with large numbers of juniors and seniors each year. (This enrollment pattern is identical at the other two independent boarding high schools for the arts in NAIS.) Each major has a number of skill positions such as violinists, violists, cellists, bassoonists, oboe players, percussionists, lead ballerinas, male dancers, male actors, theater tech students, and so forth. When we recruit students, each major has a numeric goal and specific talent requirements. I often characterize this yearly task as the equivalent of assembling a championship basketball team: a seven-foot center, a point guard, a power forward, etc. Actually it is much more complicated, but alike in the issue of potential versus actuality. Would it intrigue you to know that there are financial characteristics for each major? Music majors have the highest percentage of financial aid in the school, followed by dancers. Does is surprise you that these are the majors with the highest requirements for proven talent and previous training? When we made the decision to grow the Arts Academy in size we decided to hold the music and dance departments at then-current levels and expand the other departments. In order of the highest contribution of net tuition (gross tuition minus financial aid) visual arts is first, interdisciplinary second, creative writing third, and theater fourth. This was the most important element of our original strategic planning. Guess what? We decided to maintain our world-class chamber orchestra. We decided that the nearly $1,000,000 in financial aid necessary for a very high-level music department of 65 was all we could afford. So, we kept our Mozart-sized ensemble and WE DON'T FIELD A MAHLER ORCHESTRA! However, we bring in additional players for special concerts, offer master classes, and provide other large ensemble opportunities for our wonderful young musicians. That was a strategic planning decision!

At independent schools across this country some version of this strategic enrollment program plays out each year. (We know that selective colleges, universities, conservatories, and art schools work this system because our students are very successful at achieving admission because of their special talents in addition to their academic preparation.) So what is the makeup of the enrollment requirement at your school? Is it simply × number of ninth graders through twelfth graders or first graders through eighth graders? Or are you looking for a certain number of boys and girls? Do you need a certain talent in science and math to study successfully in your remarkable curriculum? Do you offer unusual outdoor education? Are languages a key element at your school? However you count enrollment, a careful study of your history will provide a recognizable financial pattern which can be projected and extrapolated to provide you with a plan for the student body that will address your financial needs.

One more arts example: When we decided that the Arts Academy needed to reach the enrollment of 265 students to maximize net tuition, offer the best artistic programs, make the academic class student/teacher ratio the optimum and provide funds for needed student support services, we realized that our current majors were unlikely to be able to expand in enrollment enough to meet that goal. In a business sense, we needed a new product. Enter our new film major. For many years, we had debated whether Idyllwild Arts Academy, only one hundred miles from Hollywood, should tap some of the expertise and interest in the movie business and start a new major. Strategically, it never seemed to work. On top of the cost, current arts department chairs saw the possible new department as a competition for resources and students. Some board members did not view filmmaking as art. In recent years, however, the cost of equipment had dropped drastically due to digital technology, a foundation became interested in an artistic film program for high-school students and we needed a new major. We assembled an advisory committee; announced our intention; and secured funding for marketing, faculty recruitment, and construction of a soundstage on campus. In seeking a board consensus, we were able to convince our planning committee that our educational mission to train the next generation of artists included not only the preservation of the best expressions of Western culture (classical music, dance, and theater) but also required a commitment to the creators who seek to expand our vision of the world with cutting-edge expressions (visual artists, writers, filmmakers, performance artists, choreographers, composers).

After a year's work, the new Department of Moving Pictures was operational in the new Bruce Ryan Soundstage. Even better, 12 students enrolled the first year and 23 the second. Most of the students were from affluent families and needed no financial aid. Despite the concurrent downturn in the U.S. economy, this influx of tuition took the pressure off the other departments and provided needed new revenue to support all the important elements of the school. A strategic decision succeeded.

What new idea is around your institution? Are you in competition with a fine public school in your area? Would it help to double the size of your junior and senior classes to be able to offer your most advanced courses for a final two years of college prep? If you are losing students to another school, should you enlarge the size of your lower school to minimize the impact of the enrollment changes between 8th and 9th grade? Can you think of improvements at your school that will produce net tuition, stimulate increased endowment funding, stimulate a development grant . . . develop interest in your community . . . serve a pressing educational need . . . improve the lot of your students . . . add net revenue that can be used to raise faculty salaries . . . provide outside support for new construction?

A number of new schools are appearing in the Los Angeles area. There seems to be a great need for independent education in the urban centers of the U.S. and bond funding is available for non-profit corporations. What will these new institutions bring to the table? I know of a very committed group of parents with excellent advice and good funding sources who plan to start a high school whose mission will be to educate the leaders of a new world, changed by globalization. I can envision world cultures classes, international study programs, inter-cultural partnerships, and a unique foreign language program. Is the bottom line financial or educational? The answer is yes—it's both financial and educational.

An idea to provide funds to increase faculty salaries:
Manipulate the student/teacher ratio in classrooms to determine the necessary number of faculty. Raise it from an average of 12 students per teacher to 13. Put a cap on any class of a certain number.

7. Extracurricular: Expenses in this area are based on the school's mission and the culture of the school. At Idyllwild, for example, the arts are not extracurricular. However, the calculus club is!

8. Outcome: Despite the fact that each independent school has a unique mission and a strong school culture as well as a special brand of education, parents are interested in the outcome of their child's experience. Their interest will be primarily in an accredited diploma and a wonderful college admission. Following this, they will focus on SAT scores and AP classes, and then usually end up thinking about whether their kids have become more mature, developed good values, and enjoyed school. I recommend that you spend some of your resources measuring the positive outcome of the experience at your school. At Idyllwild Arts Academy acceptances in the most selective conservatories and art schools are as important as SAT scores or class rankings. It is very difficult for us to measure the effectiveness of our work through a visual art portfolio, a violin audition, a theater audition, a student film. We have products that are not usually recognized for educational excellence. Whatever it is at your school, make certain that you can measure it, recognize it, and spread the word about it. A good educational outcome is the basis for paying tuition.

9. Student services: This area is a growth industry in schools as responsibility for student problems and behavior expands beyond our capacity to envision. Significant numbers of medicated students, complex psychological and physical issues for an increasing number of students, and rising parent expectations regarding institutional expertise are the major concerns. Prepare thorough admission materials that ask important questions regarding student problems. Require communication from professionals who have treated the student as part of your admission decision. Set up direct communications links to deal with problems. Make a clear agreement with parents regarding the limits of institutional response. Make agreements with parents that they pay additional fees for medication- or counseling-related issues that are beyond the normal responsibilities of your student support program. Add fees to provide for additional staff to respond to the needs of this growing element in your student body. Develop carefully crafted plans for a psychological counseling program which clearly explains your role and the point at which parents must assume financial responsibility. Make careful decisions regarding full- or part-time positions for counseling. Look forward to the dueling therapists/medical specialists game that accompanies every serious health and disciplinary decision.

Special support for students is just one part of student services. Rising parental awareness of more general health issues calls for consideration of all kinds of adjustments to school life that will expand our budgets. Welcome to the world of vegans, vegetarians, carnivores, supplements, vitamins, energy drinks, and on and on. Bid out your food service operation regularly—don't necessarily change it, but get competitive bids. While your academic faculty may believe that caffeine is a priority for late-night study and for early classes, the student services staff will expect you to ban that substance from all vending machines and the entire campus. The latest brain research indicates that teenagers go to sleep late in the night and should sleep until at least 8:00 to maximize rest and the learning processing that occurs in the brain. Starting classes around 9:00 or 9:30 will significantly impact the daily schedules of your faculty and their families. Not to mention the athletic program, early-bird classes, breakfast schedule for boarders, evening study-hall time, bedtime, orchestra and choir rehearsal, among many other things. Research also indicates that it would generally help each student if he or she had a water bottle handy all the time and ate plenty of fish. Also, faculty who wish to make the greatest impact on student learning should never carry on lecturing about a subject for more than 15 or 20 minutes without a physical or mental break to allow the brain to process the information. Easy to say that independent schools are student-centered in their approach!

10. Admissions: This office is the sales team for the school. It is not usually productive to cut the budget in this area. Brochures, website presentation, travel, and publications represent your unique school to the student and parents who comprise your market. More and better are the watchwords. If attendance at your school is expensive, your materials should reflect the quality that expense represents.

Overhead Expense Considerations

11. Physical plant: For many years, the amount of student financial aid, needed artistic equipment, the quality of artist/teachers, the orchestra repertoire, the number of male dancers, the number of pottery wheels in the studio, and the nature of the theatre productions was much, much more important to me, as headmaster, than the physical plant. I learned several lessons over the years at a boarding school: (1) Deferred maintenance will not somehow magically disappear and the campus maintain itself. (2) Utility prices are indeed unstable and can spike very quickly. (3) The size and general state of the water pipes beneath the ground have a huge effect on fire safety, water quality, food service, and the quality of dormitory life. (4) Plant staff do not generally seek work at your school because of their belief in its mission. (5) Parents and students who are willing to pay independent school tuition do not evaluate only the program, but expect that the school grounds will look like they are also worth the costs. (6) Leaky roofs are not an indication of bad character or management, but must be fixed or they are an indication of poor maintenance. Unfortunately, I have many more experiences with the plant that I could share with you. However, the important lesson is that, while plant expense may be carefully managed to help you save costs in the short term, adequate funding is a must for the long term. Both annual operating budgets and long-term depreciation allocations are essential for the future of your fine school.

12. Technology: Good luck. Returns on the massive investments schools have made in technology have not been realized. However, your school will be expected to develop and maintain a superior program to be competitive. Specific advice: If outdoor education or the arts are the major focus at your school, you may be able to get away with improving your technology program after the fact. In this way, you can see what works and what doesn't rather than investing in all that cutting-edge equipment and software which is out of date or can't be serviced because the company went bankrupt or was purchased.

13. Advancement: If your independent school can survive on tuition alone, you will not need an advancement staff. However, in the world in which we live and operate now, this area is becoming increasingly important. Most fine independent schools are fully enrolled or developing the reputation necessary to be that way. After that, there is no other reliable source of significant income than donations. These gifts are directly related to those who have experienced the excellence of your programs (parents, students, alumni), those who have read or heard about the reputation of your programs (public relations) or those who might be interested in future participation (marketing and publications). In most independent colleges and universities, the management of the advancement team is the province of the president or CEO and the operation of the school the work of the deans or provosts. Many independent school heads complain of the pressing needs they are required to attend to that are external to the school. They must keep one foot in the school community and one foot in the real world. Excellent professional staff and adequate budgets will provide the assistance and follow-through necessary for the head's success in this all-important area. By the way, this is the area that many school trustees and donors understand least. They believe that they support the school without expense attached (wrong!) and that marketing and PR funds are money down the drain.

14. Administration: Keep your administrative costs as low as possible and remember that everyone who works in this area is in service to your educational purpose. Ideas to save on expense: Bid out your health insurance and liability insurance regularly; check classifications for worker's compensation to determine whether a job reclassification will save you dollars.

Donated or Unearned Income

15. Development: Increase the annual fund goal. Better yet, analyze your development mailing list and current annual income to determine where the most potential lies in your donor base as well as the source of the largest amount of net donations. Focus part of your efforts on potential and focus professional efforts on expanding the successful area. For example, you may pride yourself on the percentage of participation by families or alumni in the annual fund, but it may be more productive to make 25 more major donor requests in a year than to allocate more staff time to family participation. Be careful to analyze any fund-raising events so that you understand clearly the net revenue (after all the costs) that comes to the school.

The Final Word

Financing a school, developing a strategic plan, and operating a non-profit educational institution is a challenge. I have often noted to the executive committee of my board that, if you really want to keep tabs on the important financial matters at the school, you should manage a few key elements:

1. Tuition and Fees—Require regular admission reports on the number of inquiries, the size of the applicant pool, the makeup of the pool, and the number of contracted students.
2. Financial Aid/Net Tuition—Review regular reports on the amount of financial aid budgeted, offered, accepted, and declined.
3. Development Income—Require regular reports on progress toward the annual fund goal in each category of donor.
4. Review the monthly reports on the performance of endowment fund investments.
5. Review the monthly reports of salaries for all employees compared to the annual budget (projected monthly).
6. Review the annual decisions, by competitive bid, for all campus insurance policies: general liability insurance, group health insurance, worker's compensation, and directors' and officers' liability insurance.
7. Review the food service budget and the monthly reports of budget versus expense.
8. Review the physical plant annual budget and the depreciation budget as well as the monthly reports of how those funds are expended.

All those people who worry about the number of pencils used, the office supplies, the class supplies, the audio-visual equipment—that can be delegated. Your school will succeed or fail financially because you planned well and managed the big pieces.

Good strategic planning makes for a great school and a continually vibrant mission. At Idyllwild, the Planning Committee is a standing committee of the board which reviews our progress against the current plan on a regular basis. It is essential to regularly review the dynamic relationship between mission and money.

Bill Lowman is the founding Headmaster of the Idyllwild Arts Academy in southern California. He received his A.B. in history, with related fields of music and civilization, from the University of Redlands. Prior to his tenure at Idyllwild he founded the Nevada School of the Arts, a community school for talented young people in Las Vegas. He was on the staff of the USC School of Performing Arts in the 1970s. Bill was a Klingenstein Visting Fellow at Teacher's College and was on the Faculty of the Salzburg Seminar entitled "The Future of Classical Music." He serves on the Board of the Pierson-Lovelace Foundation, the Yosemite Fund Council and the University of Redlands Alumni Association.

The Problem of Productivity in Schools

By James E. Buckheit

Not a Business?

My finance committee chair gave me another lecture on cost control last week. Tuition increases of more than twice CPI are not acceptable, he says. He keeps asking me why we can't run the school more like a business. This week that very same trustee, who also happens to be an alumnus, is upset because his favorite teacher of yore complained about feeling undervalued. How is he undervalued? I told him I had to drop his favorite elective and give him another section of U.S. history. The elective is chronically under-enrolled. I'll have to hire another part-time teacher if I keep it in the schedule. A school is not a business, this teacher keeps telling me. I wish he would tell that to the finance committee.

You might have heard such a lament the last time you invited a fellow school head out for a drink. Or you might have said something similar yourself, complaining to your spouse after a long day. There's a lot of it going around.

It could be worse. That thirty-year veteran could have given up coaching, forcing you to create a new "fifth assignment" for him, even though you didn't need it. He may be lecturing from the same yellowing notes he used twenty years ago when that trustee was in his class. He may be using the same sage-on-the-stage techniques with his elective of six students that he uses with a regular section of 18 (a number about which he complains bitterly). He may leave his e-mail unanswered unless a hard copy is placed in his mailbox. It's almost certain that his salary, inflated by decades of compounding percentage raises, is two-and-a-half times that of his junior colleague, who has just decided to leave the profession after only two years. Teaching four large sections, coaching two sports, and trying to do an attentive job as an adviser, despite the palpable disappointment of parents about not getting someone more experienced, turns out to be too much. And just when she was starting to be really effective!

What's a school head to do? Ask the trustee to underwrite the cost of his favorite teacher's favorite course? Drop a popular elective taught by a more pliant teacher and force the students into the under-enrolled one? Lock the trustee and the veteran teacher in a room and let them decide if the school is a business, once and for all? One thing that head had better do is become more conversant on the topic of productivity and how it relates to education. As a profession, we are in danger of losing credibility with our business-minded constituents on whom we depend for financial support. Furthermore, we need to do a better job of helping our faculties understand how their own interests are served by making our schools more financially viable.

It's hard to get teachers excited about lowering costs, but it's also hard to blame them. If an endowment gift of $100,000 arrived in the mail, it would be cause for celebration. The board chair would be asked to write a thank-you note. The head would invite the donor to lunch. The gift would get special mention in the annual report. Trimming $5,000 in recurrent operating expenses has exactly the same impact on the bottom line, yet we approach it with hand-wringing and apology. Improving productivity is tantamount to fund-raising. However, there are systemic reasons why it's more difficult to achieve in schools than in many other kinds of enterprise.

Baumol's Disease

Over thirty years ago, economist William Baumol explained the reasons for higher than average price increases in public sector and non-profit services, a phenomenon that became known as "Baumol's cost disease."[1] In a nutshell, he pointed out that some sectors of the economy are able to cash in on technology to increase productivity—that is, produce more units with fewer workers, who in turn are rewarded with better wages. Because of the effect of those higher wages on consumer prices and general standard of living, increased productivity in the one sector tends to push up wages in others, including labor-intensive services that aren't able to take advantage of technological advances, like schools and orchestras.

As Baumol illustrates, it still takes four musicians and 35 minutes to perform Mozart's Quartet in D-major, just as it did in 1786 when Mozart wrote it. You can't play it recognizably with just three musicians, and no one wants to hear the ten-minute quickie version. Meanwhile, today's cellists would like to earn at least as much as carpenters. The music metaphor is appealing, since good teaching is also an art that should not be rushed. Furthermore, it captures the financial challenge with a touch of irony, since every prima donna needs a patron or two in order to keep singing. What is a faculty's favorite solution to the annual budget dilemma? Raise more donations!

So, Baumol's disease explains it. The public is just going to have to accept the facts of life about non-profit economics, including inevitably accelerating costs of things like classical music performances and calculus classes. Parents are going to have to accept rising fees, and donors are going to have to step up to keep the band and the football team playing. Unfortunately, that's not how most of them see it. Not that many people have heard about Professor Baumol, and even fewer care. What they care about is relative cost and value for the dollar. To raise the stakes even more, productivity in some services is rising, challenging the theory of cost disease. Meanwhile, productivity in education, albeit poorly defined and difficult to measure, continues to plummet, at least according to economists who pay attention to such things.

Defining Productivity

Let's be clear about the definitions. If you can increase your output of a product or a service without increasing the labor input, you have increased productivity. That goes for quality as well as quantity. If you can increase the quality of a good or service, and thereby charge more for it or increase market share, without increasing the labor input, there again you have increased productivity. Maintaining a set level of quality and quantity, while decreasing input costs, is equally good. Profits go up either way, as long as demand holds.

Does this have any relevance to schools? Examples from manufacturing are a stretch, so consider a service: banking. The appearance of 24-hour automatic tellers dramatically decreased the labor cost of many standard transactions, while improving customer satisfaction. The proverbial "bankers hours" ceased to be a problem. Make your deposit or withdrawal at midnight if you'd like. That is a productivity improvement.

It's tempting to force an analogy with something technological, like course web pages, which students can access from home. Although not a bad idea in its own right, anything involving computers invites obvious rebuttals: You can't replace a teacher with a machine. There's more to learn than information. Students need the guidance of an adult who can respond to their particular needs. Kids spend too much time staring at screens already. All true, but these responses miss the point.

Banks initially attempted to increase their customer base and simultaneously meet demands for convenience by extending their hours. It worked, but the cost per transaction went up. The introduction of mechanical tellers was a risk, but one that was based on a sophisticated understanding of the customers' requirements, which varied significantly with different transactions. We're not likely to see drive-through loan officers in the near future. However, understanding the extent to which convenience contributed to the definition of quality in typical savings and checking operations enabled banks to capitalize on the available technology. That technology led to huge increases in capacity while allowing labor costs to go down. However, that was not simply about technological innovation. What made the venture successful is that banks understood and clearly defined quality.

Quality and Capacity

Efficiency experts base careers on the premise that there is reserve capacity in every system. Some of that is free for the taking once it's identified, like shortening the distance between steps in a process or supervising employees in a way that ensures paid time is fully worked. Productivity comes into play when capacity is actually increased by changing the way things are done. You can speed up the assembly line or increase the number of patients per hour coming into the office. The downside is that you can be virtually certain in both cases that the defect rate will also go up. Whether or not that increase in capacity will turn into increased profit depends on whether the higher defect rate is "commercially acceptable." Will the product or service still be marketable despite having more flaws? Only the customer can tell you. If the flaw is a secondary infection from a medical treatment, the quick-stop clinic may be in trouble. If it's merely a snippy response from a charge nurse, it will likely pass muster, if everything else goes well.

The really interesting examples involve a total overhaul of the process that increases output while decreasing the defect rate. The famous stories of production teams replacing assembly lines in Toyota plants are about changes in attitudes and practice that move quality control to the front end of the process. There is more than one way to build a car. There is more than one way to do anything.

Productivity is a function of capacity—how much you can produce or how many clients you can serve in a given time frame. Capacity is inextricably tied to quality, because quality affects demand. That's why you can't know your true capacity without first defining quality. In the educational arena, however, quality can be hard to define.

For independent school parents, there are some necessary conditions that must be met for a school to be in the game. Safety is fundamental, and depending on the clientele, some kind of status is usually essential, too. Test scores and college placement history are a shorthand way to rank schools academically, but once the league is defined, interest in those numbers diminishes. Interestingly, schools of very different size and per-pupil expenditure, and consequently different cost structures, can be comparable in terms of safety, test scores, and even college lists. One thing that's likely to vary is status, which seems always to rise with cost. A couple of other variables point to some especially important quality indicators.

Independent school families are willing to pay a premium for attention and opportunity. In the absence of lengthy explanations and esoteric dialogue, for which parents have little patience, the proxies for those two values are class size and curriculum menu. They are the complementary parameters of the quality discussion. At any given level of per pupil expenditure, you can decrease average class size or you can increase the program variety. But you can't do both, at least not without suppressing salaries. The analysis of productivity in schools has been further complicated by the way demand for both attention and program variety have risen. The "services" being offered today, at admittedly much higher prices, are considerably more diverse and customized than those of a decade or two ago. There is not a lot of evidence to suggest that such enhancements have had much effect on what students know or what they can do. But without reliable and broadly accepted measures of educational output, our default measures will focus on inputs, like the range of courses or the number of specialists on staff.

Expanding the menu seems like good business. Let's say I want to add Chinese to my program, but I can't drop French, despite shrinking enrollments. The senior French staff is entrenched in the school community, and a segment of the parent body considers French essential to a good education. I keep French to appeal to the tradition-minded, and I add Chinese to appeal to a new, more entrepreneurial set. I could pay for the suboptimal enrollments in language classes by increasing section sizes in math. But the math teachers, feeling entitled to the same average class sizes they've had in the past, cry foul. To be fair, why should a French teacher with a caseload of 40 students spread across four sections get the same pay as a math teacher with a caseload of 80? In terms of revenue production, the math teacher is actually doing more for the school. However, revenue production is an alien concept. The parents, perhaps getting wind of the math department's displeasure, might then raise concerns about the attention afforded their children in math. I turn to my trustees and tell them that I need some additional funding for the Chinese program. Then, that darned finance committee chair asks why. We're not adding more students, are we? No, so I guess what I'll have to do is cut the electives in other departments with enrollments below a certain number, or else cut the JV crew team. It's small but very expensive. Wait for the phone to ring. Those menu items have loyal fans, too.

The way we use input measures, such as class size and program variety, to market our schools sets a trap. The way we distribute the workload among faculty closes that trap tightly around our options. One way out of this bind is to differentiate the allocation of staffing dollars, according to what quality means in different contexts. That, too, can be a hard sell.

Changing the Staffing Paradigm

In the interest of equity and conflict avoidance, we tend to treat all instructional situations the same. A teacher is a teacher, and a class is a class. Four or five classes is a "full load," regardless of how many students that represents or their level of maturity or competence. A course is a course and confers the requisite units of credit, provided it meets a prescribed number of times. We know education is actually more complicated than that, and in those complications lie some interesting opportunities.

In the case of a beginning language class that needs to be highly interactive or an English class that emphasizes writing, the quality of the experience will be very sensitive to numbers. Smaller class size translates into more rehearsal time and more individual prompting for each student. On the other hand, in a science class that moves back and forth between whole group lecture/demonstration and small group lab experiences (including the increasing use of computer simulations), quality may depend less on the number of students than on the kind of assistance the teacher receives. A single class of 24 with a teacher and a paraprofessional lab assistant might be better for the teacher than two classes of 12 with no assistant. It will also be less expensive. In this case, in contrast perhaps to a discussion-based literature class, better for the teacher translates into better for the student, because of the importance of classroom setup to quality in lab sciences.

Caseload can be just as important as course load in terms of both equitable distribution of work and effectiveness. Sixteen eighth-graders in Latin I probably need to meet five times per week and get a lot of direction from their teacher. The five seniors in Latin V might well be ready for a tutorial approach. At the very least they can be expected to do more on their own. Furthermore, that Latin teacher with a caseload of just 45 students in four sections, compared to the Spanish teacher with 72, could be expected to pick up a fifth course to bring his caseload up to 60. How burdensome that additional course would be depends a lot on how flexible and imaginative the teacher is with his methods. An argument can certainly be made for having a minimum caseload as part of the criteria for full-time status.

Scheduling can be another damper on productivity. Take the humanities teacher who has three sections of civics and wants her students to watch a segment from the film "Twelve Angry Men." She schedules the media room for three different periods, and she sits through the film segment three times. Assume that media and lecture are regularly part of her presentation of material every week. A timetable that gave her one longer plenary session with all her civics students together could free up enough time for her to take on an additional role, such as mentoring an intern or supervising the student council.

Art teachers are sensitive about the status of their departments, and college admissions officers have aggravated the problem by discounting grades for art and other "soft" courses before they re-compute an applicant's GPA. In defense, art chairs vie for graduation requirements and equal representation in the schedule. Art is important. But how much sense does it make to schedule 45-minute art classes for an entire semester, just so it's treated like math or English? Effective studio time is more comparable to athletic practice than to math class, with preparation and cleanup requirements, as well as the need for focused feedback in order to refine performance. A sensible delivery system for studio arts might schedule it opposite athletics, rather than more standard academic classes, but run the course for only eight weeks. Is a two-hour studio art class equivalent to two one-hour English classes from which a teacher takes home thirty papers to grade, or perhaps a bit fewer? The simplest ways of thinking about workload are not necessarily the most fair, let alone the most efficient.

Instructional Models

The range of scheduling alternatives and delivery systems available to a school is limited in part by the range of methodologies available to the teachers. At the simplest level, while you might expect a lot of lecturing in a section of plane geometry with twenty students, you would be surprised to see the same instructor spending as much time standing at the board and expounding to a group of six advanced calculus students. The maturity of the students and the increased opportunity for collaboration and discussion would seem to call for a different method. Such refinements of technique could, in turn, affect student motivation and even performance. But how might they affect productivity as measured in gross economic terms?

The range of opportunities expands with our willingness to challenge the superstitions and sacred cows of traditional academic routines. How essential is direct instruction or discrete courses to every kind of learning? An experiment at an elementary school[2] where formal Spanish instruction began in fourth grade assigned one group of third-graders to a Spanish-speaking physical education teacher. She simply spoke to them in Spanish, using lots of modeling and visual cues, but otherwise did standard PE. The students, whose parents had agreed to the experiment, were a bit confused at first, but quickly took to the charm of the teacher and the fun of cracking the new code every day. By the end of the year, their Spanish listening and speaking vocabularies were on par with that of the fourth-graders, and their accents were generally better. The results should come as no surprise. Immersion and kinesthetic reinforcement enhance second-language learning. The following year, those children took an accelerated version of the fourth-grade Spanish class—higher performance at no additional cost.

Mixed-grade teaching is fairly common in elementary schools, but the same techniques can be applied at the secondary level. The two-year time frame of the International Baccalaureate allowed one international school[3] to retain a psychology elective despite low enrollments. The syllabus was redesigned to have two entry points, and a group of six first-year students was added to a group of eight second-year students. In their common year, they covered the same topics and were assigned the same work, although the grading standard was more stringent for the second-year students who were facing a rigorous external exam. The relative expertise of the second-year students raised the quality of discussion in the class and gave the first-year students a push. The occasional requirement to tutor and mentor their younger classmates in recurrent topics, such as research methods and statistics, ensured that the second-year students were relying on their own understanding and developing clarity of expression. The school got essentially two sections for the price of one, and the students earned examination scores above the historic trend in the course. The necessity for collaborative work, as well as the inevitable review as the teacher cycled back to earlier points to accommodate the novices, probably led to a higher level of retention of the factual material. The lively communal spirit in the class certainly did no harm.

Lots of schools advertise writing across the curriculum, but how many practice it effectively? Most writing happens in English courses, and much of that is literary criticism. The writing lab or writing studio model employed by some colleges and graduate schools might adapt very well to high schools. It could feature lots of coaching and peer editing at early stages of the process under the guidance of assistant teachers, with only polished, final drafts submitted to master teachers in literature, history, or science. Such differentiated staffing would remove from the workload of veteran instructors one of the more onerous repetitive tasks—editing student drafts—and allow them to focus more on explaining content and developing pedagogy. Properly designed, it could also save money.

None of these ideas may be broadly applicable to schools, but they serve to illustrate an important point. Some of the limits we place on capacity are artificial, dictated by habits and untested assumptions. Learning is not restricted to fixed groups of pupils, in a classroom, with a single teacher, for an assigned number of periods of specified length. However, our ability and willingness to experiment with potentially cost-effective alternatives is greatly limited by the paucity of output measures. How would we know an alternative method is effective, especially if it looks strange? You can't determine your capacity until you define quality.

What About Technology?

By putting its student handbook online, one school saved $5,000 in printing and mailing costs—just like getting a $100,000 gift to the endowment. However, that and many comparable savings would still not be sufficient financial justification for the hundreds of thousands that most schools have invested in equipment, software, and support personnel. It makes sense to try to recover some of the outlay. Opportunities can be found in publications, mailing, telephone charges, file storage, and even carbon paper. But so far, the use of technology has not made it possible for schools to reduce administrative personnel. In most cases, personnel expenses have gone up. Has technology been a bad bet?

There are a couple of different answers to that question, even in the for-profit world. One is pretty much based on faith. Computers have not helped us improve the bottom line yet, but a tool this powerful will eventually lead to breakthroughs. A second answer is that it's a moot point. Communications and marketing have evolved with the world-wide-web, and that is simply the new playing field for doing business. If it has changed the cost structure, so be it. It's done that for everyone. Figure out a way to make it work. The problem with these answers is that they are grounded in traditional cost analysis and ignore the paradigm shift that has occurred in organizational structures and cultures in many industries.

E-mail has sped up communications of all kinds. Interactive databases have provided a way to customize a wide range of services and greatly reduce the cost of direct marketing. Connectivity has obviated the need for some forms of travel, and wide-band, multimedia programs have revolutionized training. A growing number of smart companies are turning those developments into profits. However, the biggest single change affecting productivity so far, cutting across all kinds of businesses and organizations, is the lengthening of the workday. By investing in the mechanisms that allow employees to log in to the workplace from elsewhere, more work is being produced outside the normal workday and during absences, such as travel and sick days, without any increase in compensation. That's potentially unhealthy, but the flexibility and freedom are valued by many professionals, allowing them to take better advantage of their own schedules and work patterns. As long as there's effective quality control, worker autonomy will drive productivity.

Student Productivity

An interesting feature of schools is that our workforce is made up not only of employees, but also clients. Early in the reform movement he led, Ted Sizer[4] suggested that we should stop thinking about students as our product. We don't make them. Our output as organizations is student work, the production of which results in learning. That notion of teacher-as-master/student-as-apprentice changes the concept of instruction and assessment in exciting ways. In that context, it's reasonable to think about how to help our apprentices be more productive.

No one would suggest that video games and chat rooms have improved student productivity. Neither did the telephone forty years ago, when young people first started getting their own lines. The only fair analysis must look at students who are motivated and focused. Have members of that elite become more productive? Speaking of forty years ago, consider what it was like to write a term paper before the days of word processors. Consider what it was like to hike back to the library in the evening to read that article on reserve—an article now available online. The "workday" of diligent students has always extended into the wee hours, but technology has offered ways to improve the quality of that time. Some of the students now taking four or five AP courses in a single year, the wisdom of which should be open to question, would have had a very hard time getting it all done without the use of a computer and the Internet.

The anticipated hi-tech revolution in education has fallen short of the fantasies, so far. To have any substance within academic institutions, it will require the majority of teachers to achieve a level of technological proficiency approaching that of our best students. Nevertheless, schools have been irrevocably changed by computers. Course Web pages make it easy for students who have been absent to catch up and for parents who are interested to get some clue about what's going on in class. Many teachers now do online conferencing and editing with their students. Electronic sensors and interfaces have sped up science labs, and graphing calculators have sped up problem-solving in precalculus. Distance learning is still in its infancy but already expands the offerings at some rural schools. Such conveniences are attractive. However, the most significant changes ahead will likely be in the way students organize and process information in their brains as a result of the tools at their disposal.

In the 1970s, MIT professor Seymour Papert challenged conventional wisdom about cognitive development when he introduced five-year-olds to the computer language, Logo, which could control a drawing device called a "turtle." The children demonstrated mastery of a wide range of geometry concepts assumed to be beyond their reach. What they were lacking was not mental capacity or developmental readiness, but rather a communication tool they could manipulate. With a programmable turtle, new intellectual vistas opened up. This led Papert to criticize "our culture's relative poverty in materials" (for learning),[5] but his research was not embraced as a stimulus for reform. Six-year-olds who know a lot of geometry are an inconvenience. Likewise, there are college math professors who would prefer that students not take calculus in high school. It disrupts their routine.

The real issue is not about computers. We have long had a non-mechanical technology of instruction that is largely ignored. For instance, research on collaborative learning and its impact on cognitive rehearsal and retention is compelling. Yet the practice remains rare. The inquiry method utilized in middle-school science in Japan has been well publicized, as have the high test scores to which it contributes, but there has been very little cross-fertilization with Japan or any other country. Reform movements that focus on instructional practice, such as National Board Certification or Critical Friends Groups, have remained on the fringe, despite their demonstrated effectiveness. Instead, a great deal of teaching in American schools, including some of the best independent schools, is characterized by covering material and providing answers for which students have no questions. The productivity of our students remains low, largely because we can't make up our minds about what we want from them. Inefficient, at times even shoddy, practice remains commercially acceptable because our quality measures, such as SAT scores, are driven more by demographic and economic factors than by classroom instruction. Instruction, in turn, is driven more by the habits and aesthetic choices of teachers than by research on learning.

That could change. In time, the growth of cognitive science, hand in hand with computer technology, may well alter the entire concept of our work in schools—what we produce and why—thereby altering the definition of quality. With that will come a new set of productivity measures that will track how quickly teachers and schools catch on.

For Now

Meanwhile, at the national level, the convergence of political agendas and financial crunches virtually guarantees that standardized tests will remain the principal yardstick by which school quality is measured, at least in the near term. They're quick, they're inexpensive, and they have the appearance of scientific objectivity. Productivity will continue to be defined by economists in terms of test-score improvements against per-pupil spending. The attendant impatience on the part of elected officials will furthermore make it difficult for public school educators to address underlying problems that suppress academic achievement. So we will likely see school districts and for-profit management companies competing increasingly for small and probably meaningless differences in average test scores. While that development may add to the demand for private education in various forms, in the long run it will not be good for independent schools.

To thrive, institutions of genuine learning require a literate, civic-minded population and high level of economic prosperity, neither of which will be promoted by a devolving public debate on education or a growing disparity between rich and poor. At the very least, it behooves independent school educators to use our influence to improve the quality of the yardsticks. If teaching to the test remains the norm, then a smart test is better than a dumb one. Beyond that, it is in our interest to find ways to elevate the national dialogue about educational quality. Our credibility in that arena will depend on having our own houses in order and not relying on our reputations or endowments to sidestep the tough questions.

Within each of our schools, to the extent that we retain the ability to stand apart, we need to work continuously at developing a local consensus about the meaning of quality. It is the particular definition of quality that makes an independent school distinctive and generates enthusiasm among its constituencies. It is also a necessary condition for identifying reserve capacity and managing the institution as effectively as possible. To get support, tuition increases and annual fund goals will have to be backed up by credible business plans, and productivity will have to become part of our working vocabulary.

James E. Buckheit is the headmaster of Baylor School in Chattanooga, Tennessee.

Notes

[1] Towse, Ruth (ed.) and Baumol, William (ed.). (1997). *Baumol's Cost Disease: The Arts and Other Victims.* Northampton, MA: Edward Elgar Publishing

[2] St. Paul Academy and Summit School, 1989–90, under the direction of the author

[3] Frankfurt International School, 1994–1997, under the direction of the author

[4] Sizer, Theordore. (1984). *Horace's Compromise.* Boston: Houghton Miflin Co.

[5] Papert, Seymour. (1980). *Mindstorms.* New York: Basic Books. p. 20

Navigating the Rough Road to Effective Pricing

By D. Scott Looney

For many schools, the current economic recession brings, or threatens to bring, decreases in endowment, annual giving, auxiliary program income, student retention, and admission activity, while also heralding increased interest in financial aid. With the need to increase teacher compensation and manage escalating benefit costs it seems that both the expense and revenue sides of the ledger are concurrently under attack. For most schools, the greatest annual financial variable is tuition income. The members of independent schools' boards of trustees are usually well prepared for their financial and fiduciary responsibilities except, perhaps, for the task of setting tuition. The financial paradigm with which most board members are familiar is a tremendous advantage in managing endowment investments or analyzing the financial ledgers. However, these bright and dedicated people are often ill prepared to understand the potential results of their decisions related to the setting of tuition.

With consumer demand for independent schools affected by the complicated intersection of so many factors—demography, the economy, consumer preference, and public and private competition, to name a few—is it at all possible to predict future demand? How can we set tuition for our schools without knowing future demand? How do we set tuition to maximum financial advantage during times of favorable consumer demand, without pricing ourselves out of the market when demand falls? These are the fundamental questions with which boards struggle. I would add one other question which, unfortunately, boards seldom ask: How can the board learn the nuances of market positioning for not-for-profit organizations and learn how to price a luxury service, when the board's own background largely consists of for-profit marketing and the pricing of commodities?

Tuition as a Car

Imagine if you had a car (*independent school tuition*) that had no reverse gear and no brake, except for the emergency brake (*tuition discounting*). Also, the gas pedal in this car was set so that each time you stepped on the pedal you would accelerate incrementally more than the last time you increased the gas (*the compounding effect of tuition increases*). On an open, straight road (*great economy, great demographics*), this might not be such a bad ride; in fact you could simply keep a steady acceleration (*raise tuitions beyond the rate of inflation*). However, this road has twists and turns (*swings in the econ-*

omy and demography), some gentle, some severe. There is also traffic (*public schools, parochial schools and other independent school competitors*) to consider. The scenario gets even worse because the driver (*the Board of Trustees*) is only familiar with cars that have brakes (*the selling of commodities which can be advertised on sale*) and normal gas pedals (*sticker prices that can go up and down with demand*). In the backseat there is one passenger barking out instructions to go faster (*teachers who require significant salary increases*) and another passenger yelling to slow down (*the tuition-paying parents*). With this dysfunctional car and unfamiliar driver, how is it possible to reach your destination (*a balanced budget*) in time without coming out of a tight curve (*economic or demographic downturn*) careening out of control at a high rate of speed?

Supply and Demand

Board members are often from the business world and have great familiarity with setting the price for commodities. They know that if you have a short-term surplus you discount that surplus to reduce inventory. They know that if the surpluses continue over an extended period of time you must lower the sticker price and continue discounting. . . . perhaps even offering 0% financing. In order to maximize profit, when consumer demand later increases, sticker prices must go up and discounts are discontinued. In the business world, financial strategy decisions get made each financial quarter, so incremental adjustments to pricing strategies are frequent.

If the goal of an independent school were simply to fill *each* enrollment space with *any* student, without consideration of the match between the student and the school, then many business techniques would be more applicable. However, most independent schools have selection criteria that has an impact on and is effected by demand. If in a given year a school simply lowered its admission criteria it would have an easier time filling all the enrollment spaces for that one year, but the resulting decrease in student quality over time would diminish the reputation for this school and ultimately lower the demand for that school. If, in times of strong demand, a school were to work to stay affordable, the result would be the building of deep waiting lists for prospective students. That surplus consumer demand helps to bolster the school's reputation, which in turn helps that school weather hard economic and demographic times. If this same school were to simply raise their sticker price to maximize revenue, as a for-profit entity would, they would do so until there were no students on the wait-list. While they would be maximizing profits, they would be reducing their surplus consumer demand. Were hard times to befall this school, their only choice would be to discount tuition, whereas the school with surplus consumer demand would simply see thinner wait-lists, without having to resort to discounting to maintain full enrollment.

Commodity versus Luxury Service

Unlike discounting a commodity, it is difficult for independent schools to have a "sale," as any attempt to advertise that sale would be counterproductive (*Attention independent school shoppers, Cranbrook Schools is having a blue light special, one-time only, third-grade spots . . . 50% off*). When schools do decide to have a sale, using tuition discounting, it is complicated by the fact that most independent schools feel the obligation to renew financial aid awards for subsequent years. So, if a student has her tuition discounted when she enters ninth grade, most often that is a four-year commitment on the part of the school. Obviously, this makes tuition discounting a rather cumbersome tool for managing surplus enrollment spaces.

Businesses have the luxury of being able to reduce their sticker price, something that would not likely work well in the independent school world. While a consortium of schools could collectively decide to reduce their price, and this would no doubt be well received in the marketplace, an individual school which decides to reduce its price runs the real risk of being perceived as being in dire straits. Price reduction can be seen as an act of desperation. Given the insular nature of the community of independent schools and the fact that current constituents generate approximately 70% of admission inquiries from word-of-mouth, this is a decidedly risky move.

Some boards are blessed with businesspeople who understand the difference between selling and pricing a luxury service versus doing so for commodities. All of our prospective students have a free educational option; many of them have an excellent free option. While surveys have shown that about 60% of the public would send their child to a tuition-charging school if it were not for the tuition, only 1.5% send their children to independent schools, and only 10% send them to any kind of tuition-charging school. Make no mistake—tuition is *the* hurdle. With the exception of a small portion of our prospective student market, our schools are viewed as a luxury. Luxury items are more price-sensitive than necessities. When gas prices go up, people complain but keep on driving their cars. When finances get tight, people will wait before buying that new sailboat.

The Selection of Models

One of the appropriate ways in which boards educate themselves in trends relating to tuition pricing is to look for models in both the independent school and the college and university world. While this strategy is a good one, it is often tricky to interpret. In 1997, I wrote an article for NAIS titled "Lessons from Private Colleges: A Short Term Strategy and Long Term Solution?"[1] For a copy of this article go to http:www.nais.org/docs/htm/LooneyNTR.htm, which details the similarities between the enrollment and financial challenges of private liberal arts colleges and that of independent schools. In that article, I suggested that the colleges might lead the way for schools in both short-term strategy (tuition discounting) and long-term pricing solutions (keeping costs down and freezing or lowering sticker price). The 2001 report from The College Board, "Trends in College Pricing," clearly shows that my hope for the college world to serve as a shining example for independent schools was misguided. While I certainly predicted the usefulness of tuition discounting to liberal arts colleges, little did I know that the "short term solution" would not be followed by a sane "long term strategy"; private liberal arts colleges find themselves in an even more precarious position today than they did in 1997. During the last ten years, the use of tuition discounting in colleges, particularly private colleges, has skyrocketed, but so too has college tuition. The use of tuition discounting was not followed by an attempt to keep costs and tuition down, but rather by an aggressive increase in tuitions followed by even higher tuition discounts in order to keep enrollments steady. During what should have been the best of times for college enrollments and revenues (strong economy and record number of graduating high school seniors), most liberal arts colleges (with the exception of the Ivies and Little Ivies) say their net tuition revenue was either stagnant or actually declined.

In his 1999 report "Discounting Toward Disaster: Tuition Discounting, College Finances and Enrollments of Low-Income Undergraduates," Kenneth Redd thoroughly details this tuition-discounting arms race. Redd notes that, "between 1989–90 and 1995–96 institutional grants to students attending four-year private institutions jumped by nearly 70 percent in inflation-adjusted value, from $3.7 billion to $6.2 billion" (p. 2). Redd goes on to discuss how the schools with the greatest increases in discount rates did not see any real growth in net tuition revenue; in fact they saw small decreases in revenue. Although there was a rapidly increasing use of tuition discounting as a merit scholarship source, Redd notes that, "discounting strategies also do not appear to have significantly affected the academic 'profiles' of admitted undergraduates, when measured by changes in median admission test scores of entering first-year students." There were a few positive results from the increased use of tuition discounting. The most notable gain was that colleges did see increases in the numbers of low-income undergraduates able to attend college. However, as Redd points out, "for at least one quarter of the four-year private institutions, discounting has resulted in a substantial loss in net tuition revenue."

I still stand by my contention in 1997 that the net tuition revenue strategy, using tuition discounting, is an effective short-term solution for schools that are notably under enrollment capacity. However, it is only a short-term solution and must be followed by effective pricing and marketing strategies to sustain long-term financial health. The problems the private liberal arts colleges created were largely the result of following increased tuition discounting with higher sticker prices and getting caught up in a "merit" arms race using the additional institutional aid available from discounting as a way to leverage stronger students into enrolling.

Boards also look to their peer schools as examples for setting tuition, but even this can prove misleading. Among private liberal arts colleges only the Ivy and Little Ivy colleges came out of the era of high tuition/high discount in better shape; the rich schools got richer, and the poor, poorer. Their substantial endowments and markedly higher prestige allow these select schools to thrive with greatly inflated sticker prices, while their peers with less endowment and prestige suffer. Independent schools often follow this same path, using a handful of the most well-endowed and prestigious schools to set the pace for the rest of the independent school community. While it is difficult, perhaps somewhat demoralizing, for boards to acknowledge they are not among the elite in affluence and prestige, failure to understand their school's actual rank among peers is courting disaster. Most liberal arts colleges appear to have joined the elite colleges on the high tuition/high discount bandwagon, and have suffered for it.

Watching the Horizon

The last and perhaps most dangerous potential dysfunction related to applying a business paradigm to tuition setting is the tendency toward short-term thinking. Businesses review their financials each quarter and are often under great pressure to outperform the previous quarter. This emphasis on profit and short-term results is a powerful driver of the free market and capitalism. In a for-profit company, this drive can bring about efficiency to help outpace the competition. However, it is dangerous as a function of pricing an independent school for two primary reasons:

1. Independent schools cannot move their tuitions backward. Given that tuitions cannot be reduced, only increased slower than inflation, when tuition is increased beyond inflation it has a cumulative effect. As such, if a school decides to increase its tuition beyond the rate of inflation for several years in a row, the actual rate of that increase is compounded. As we all know, compounded interest over time becomes an exponential curve. The decision to raise tuition beyond the rate of inflation is not simply for that year, but for all future years as well. From 1955 to 1980, the tuition at independent schools increased at about the same rate as the consumer price index. That is, private school costs remained roughly the same, in real dollars, for twenty-five years. However, since 1980, tuition for independent schools has increased at a rate significantly greater than that of the consumer price index; attending our schools is becoming more expensive at an unsustainable rate.
2. Independent schools can't react to market forces (*fluctuations in economy or demography*) as fast as businesses can. To restore financial equilibrium, businesses can cut costs swiftly and dramatically in ways that independent schools cannot. The majority of the expense items for schools are fixed, contractually and culturally, for significant durations. Tuition at independent schools is set once per year and the resulting sticker price is the cumulative total of all previous increases. The economic tools available to businesses—quickly cutting costs, sticker price, or holding an immediate discount—are not possible for independent schools.

While navigating the pricing road, independent schools need to move forward slowly, steadily, and with an eye on the horizon. Looking at demographic forecasts, previous enrollment trends, and long-term economic projections must factor in the board's tuition setting decisions. While driving that dysfunctional car is a challenging task, looking into the distance to see the curves and dips ahead makes picking a traveling speed a little less risky. Speeding up to get to our destination faster makes sense when we are pointed straight ahead, but much less so when the road curves and we are launched off a cliff on the other side of the curve.

Trend Analysis . . . Is This the Road Map?

Population growth rates rise and then fall; the economy surges and recedes; private schools gain and lose favor; and so forth. Each of these cycles is formidable, and fully understanding their interaction is nearly impossible. Looking at historical data related to independent school enrollments, demographic trends, and economic indicators, however, does suggest some patterns which many boards fail to take the time to identify.

It was not long ago, the late 1980s to be exact, that market forces conspired against independent schools. The school-aged population was declining, recession was becoming a reality, and Americans in general saw reason for public school reform, led by a strong commitment in Chicago and elsewhere. The late 1980s witnessed a decline in private school enrollments and either coincident or concomitant drops in admission standards. Indeed, many less well-established schools went so far as to rewrite mission statements or even close their doors. The mid to late 1990s saw exactly the opposite phenomenon, with both population demographics and the economy booming. This current recession (late 1999 to 2003) is the first time since the early 1980s that the population and economic trends are in opposition. In order to understand how the current recession might affect enrollment health I want to answer the following question: Which matters most, population demographics or the economy?

Taking data from a variety of demographic and economic indicators during the time frame 1986 to 1999, I placed them on a common scale (using the Z-score formula). I analyzed trends in the following data: population of school-aged children, public school enrollment, private school enrollment (including parochial schools), NAIS school enrollment, the number of SSAT test-takers, the Gross Domestic Product, and the Average per Capita Income. While my research does not provide any concrete conclusions, it does suggest that NAIS school enrollments mirror demographic trends much more closely than economic trends. In other words ***the enrollment health of our schools is more likely to be related to the number of school-aged children in the geographic areas from which we draw students than from the fluctuations of the economy.***[2]

Fortunately for schools today, the population demographics for the next few years look as favorable as the current economic climate looks frightening. The population of school-aged children in the United States should continue to grow until about 2007 before leveling off for about three years and then beginning a ten-year precipitous decline starting sometime around 2010. Many economists and demographers cite a strong relationship between population demographics and the economy. The Harry S. Dent foundation studied the relationship between overall population demographics and stock market performance. They found there was a strong positive correlation between the population of people in the U.S. who are in their peak income-earning years (35 to 55) and the performance of the stock market. If this historical trend proves predictive, then we should see a relatively strong economic boom for approximately the next 18 years, given that the baby boomers are just reaching their income-producing years.

While the road ahead may have some short, quick turns, it is still advisable to look to the horizon while driving. Although it is nearly impossible to predict the economic future precisely, we can predict population demographics. Population demographics and their relationship to independent school enrollments and the economy suggest that independent schools should face good times for most of the next decade (the current recession notwithstanding), but also that we should be bracing for a return to the conditions of the late 1980s sometime around 2015. Since we need to be bracing for poor future conditions, should we encourage drivers to map the smoothest route through those conditions now, instead of crossing the proverbial bridge down the road?

The Boards of Trustees at independent schools have the nearly impossible task of trying to set tuition in order to maximize the revenue necessary to run the best possible program to achieve our missions, while not setting price beyond the means of our current and future customers. This requires our board members to be prudent financial managers, active listeners to program needs and private school market realities, and nearly clairvoyant interpreters of current trends. We should applaud their willingness to be our designated drivers; they have our schools' future in their backseat. We can only thank them for the ride and remind them to keep their eyes on the road.

Scott Looney is responsible for supporting the Director of Schools office, managing cross-divisional projects, website development, institutional research, parent communications, and co-chairing the all-school curriculum committee. His previous positions at Cranbrook include Interim Co-Head of the Girls Middle School, Director of External Affairs and Director of Admission & Financial Aid. He has been a frequent presenter and faculty member at conferences and workshops sponsored by NAIS, TABS, SSATB, ISACS, ERB and Crows Next Institute. He has published several articles in *Independent School* magazine. Scott lives on campus with his wife, Leslie Short, and his three sons, Ryan, Tyler and Zach, who all attend the lower school.

Notes

[1] For a copy of this article go to http:www.nais.org/docs/htm/LooneyNTR.htm

[2]For more information on this topic and my research, the PowerPoint presentation is posted at http:www.nais.org/docs/ppt/Demographics.ppt.

Financing Independent Schools for the 21st Century

By Patrick F. Bassett, NAIS President

NAIS surveying last year indicated that financing schools was among the top most pressing issues and challenges facing school leadership: How do we re-think financing independent schools for the 21st century so that we can remain solvent and accessible? In the fall, NAIS and NBOA collaborated to convoke a brain trust of school heads, trustees, business managers, and advancement professionals to begin to explore the possibilities of re-engineering school finance. Preliminary thinking from the Financing Schools Symposium led to the offering this summer of our first Financing Schools Institute, led by Harvard's Jim Honan and offering teams from several schools the opportunity to develop new models for their own schools. As we expand our modeling and experimentation, we will continue to publicize "what works" in publications like this *Independent School* magazine and on the NAIS website.

For any school prepared to do the work involved, there are two key steps:

1. Data-driven leadership: Exploring one's own five-year data and comparing those trends to the NAIS global trends reported on the NAIS website.
2. Financial modeling: Projecting forward five years, using the online NAIS Financing Schools Calculator, to produce differing financial scenarios in an attempt to develop the preferred script for the future.

Data-driven Leadership

Schools for the 21st century will surely pay more attention to comparative data and make decisions based upon projecting out over time the consequences of decisions made today. It is hard to believe, had we done that ten years ago, that we would have the ten-year trends we now see. The global NAIS independent school data is both fascinating and sobering. For the 900 or so schools in the NAIS database who have consistently provided data over the past ten years, we see the following trends:

1. ***Tuitions are up, on average, 30% in real dollars*** (i.e., adjusted for inflation). Thus, while the conventional wisdom in recent years is that tuition should rise at the rate of inflation plus 1 point (if CPI, the Consumer Price Index, goes up 3 per-

cent, schools would increase tuition by 4%), in fact for the last two decades, NAIS schools on average have raised tuition by a dramatic 3 points beyond cost of living/CPI increases, each and every year. This, of course, has not always been the case: In fact for the decades of the '50s, '60s, and '70s, the rate of tuition increase mirrored, roughly, the rate of inflation. So something has changed fundamentally and alarmingly about our collective thinking on tuition increases. The immediate questions this trend suggests include the following: Is this a sustainable trend for the next ten years? Even if it were in terms of demand for our schools, will what seems to be a virtuous cycle from a business standpoint (more revenue per customer) also be a vicious cycle from a mission standpoint (a narrower range of customers and the elimination of the middle class in our schools)? Do we risk what businesses in similar situations risk: lower-cost competitors entering the marketplace and seriously eroding our base of customers?

2. ***Demand is up in terms of inquiries, applications, and enrollment, overall:*** While enrollment is up 20% in the NAIS benchmark schools, inquiries are up 51% and applications 30%, so in fact independent schools overall have enjoyed the luxury of becoming more selective while raising their prices. What seems counter-intuitive is true, at least in the last decade, for the average independent school: price is inelastic, a very unusual and economically advantageous situation. Like medical care, high quality education so far has seen no limit to what people are willing to pay nor any limit to the sacrifices they make to do so in order to access the service. Interestingly, despite much higher prices, attrition is down (by 8% overall, averaging 9% for day schools and 15% for boarding schools) for the majority of schools, so one could argue that we have the ultimate "virtuous cycle" occurring: rising demand allowing higher prices and therefore more revenues, with a greater percentage of satisfied customers. Of course there are many caveats to this observation: that any individual school's situation can vary significantly from the trends, especially in "small markets" where there is no real price comparison to other independent schools, so the customer base compares the independent school tuitions to public schools (free) or parochial schools (very low cost). That being said, even in small schools in small markets, tuitions continue to rise and enrollment seems at least stable if not growing. The bigger caveat, of course, is that we may face an uncertain economic future: The only time in recent history when NAIS enrollments actually plummeted was when there was a confluence of events that is rare: a relative dearth of school-aged children (the baby boom and bust cycle) and a recession. We have just entered again at the elementary-school levels the first of these phenomena (depressed demographics), and we are precariously perched on the brink of the second (sustained depressed economy).
3. ***Faculty salaries have improved but only marginally,*** in inflation-adjusted dollars up only 1% a year (11% over the last decade). The good news is that the increases at the starting (around $30,000) and median (around $40,000) put NAIS schools as a group in a much more competitive place than we have been vis-à-vis public school salaries, which are, nationally, only about 10% higher. The bad news has

two components: first, that in terms of relative increases, our faculty are not better off than they were a decade ago; second, the national averages belie the fact that very high urban independent school salaries raise our averages overall but still our schools in urban, suburban, and rural areas struggle to close the salary gap with the most prominent public schools in their individual communities (an important consideration, since independent school teachers tend to benchmark their salaries against the highest-paying local public school system). From a systems analysis point, however, the most striking realization that data suggests is that average faculty salaries are not the culprit for the dramatic increases in tuition. When we ask school leaders and trustees, then, what is the driver for our price increases, they offer primarily two answers: the arms war in facilities and the ever-increasing investment in technology. While these two factors indeed are contributors, they are *not* the main issue. What is, then, our budgetary aneurism working its way through the independent school body politic?

4. ***Total staff has increased by 32% and the student/faculty ratio has declined by 7%*** (9:1 for day schools and 7:1 for boarding schools). While it is *not* true that salaries for faculty have grown substantially, it *is* true that the salary and benefits budget has exploded: The story is not better pay but rather many more paychecks, for essentially in most cases the same-sized school. So who are all these new employees we have hired? More teachers for new programs, more technology staff, and more counselors head up the list. Thus we have, some would argue, two factors at play here: expansion of program (more sports, more foreign languages, more technology, new courses) and expansion of services (more learning specialists, more student specialists—deans, counselors, diversity coordinators, etc.) What is driving this expansion? The first answer seems to be "parent demand," but NAIS wonders if this is in fact the case. We are conducting some parent research to see if the majority of parents want more services at higher prices, or rather, as we suspect, a vocal minority has captured the attention of our schools, and we have just found it easier to provide more programs and services than to moderate price increases. On the other hand, NAIS's recently published *Attrition Study* indicates through its study of low versus high attrition schools that low attrition correlates not with class size or school size but rather with student services provided (including having a diversity coordinator).
5. ***Financial Aid grants are up 38%*** (in inflation-adjusted dollars) but the number of aid recipients is flat (only up 1.8% in 10 years). Obviously, what schools have done, to their credit, is to match tuition increases by comparable increases in their financial aid budgets. What they have not done is to seek more socio-economic diversity and equity in their schools by expanding the number of students receiving aid (which is now about 20% of the typical student body: around 16% receiving financial aid and around 4% faculty kids receiving tuition remission). Furthermore, the data from SSS's statistics show a dramatic shifting of the income levels of those applying for financial aid: the near-middle-class applicant pool is headed way down and the affluent (over $100,000) applying for financial

aid is headed way up. The critical mission-related question for financial aid planning is this: Do we want middle-class families ($40–80,000 family income) in our schools? It is worth noting that while the median income for a family of four is in the $50,000 range (hence "middle class," as defined by demographers), independent schools tend to define the "middle class" in the $75,000–$125,000 range, what demographers define as "near affluent" ($75,000–$100,000) and "affluent" (over $100,000). So while we do want "middle class" families, we are having difficulty even defining what that means in terms of income, on the one hand, and entertaining increasingly meeting the needs of those over $100,000 in family income at the expense of the real middle class (those at $40–60,000).

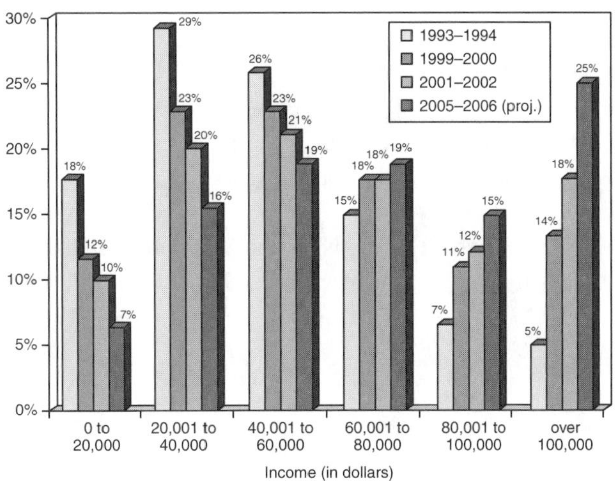

Financial Modeling

Leadership in the domain of financing schools for the 21st century will engage schools is serious financial modeling, projecting forward five years, to produce differing financial scenarios in an attempt to develop the preferred script for the future. *Independent School* magazine's fall 2003 issue is dedicated to some of the new thinking that is emergent regarding new sources of revenue, higher levels of productivity, and economies in expenditures. Reading those articles, and brainstorming with one's administrative team, faculty, and board will produce some new and better thinking for the future, helping us answer the most critical questions:

1. Why is a 9:1 student/faculty ratio a sacred cow in our schools? What could we pay faculty if the ratio were 10:1 or 11:1?
2. If we can't or won't downsize the staff size, why don't we at least freeze it for the next five years by disciplining ourselves so that we don't add a program without sunsetting something else: So you want Chinese? OK: Which current foreign language do we drop?

3. Let's declare an armistice in the facilities arms race, since new buildings are actually a "liability" in terms of expense rather than an income-producing asset. How many hockey rinks does a school need? So you want a new media center and field house? OK: We don't dig the hole until we raise the cost plus 25% to endow its operation and replacement. Conversely, how will you turn your facilities (an expense) into an income-generating asset by much more aggressive programming on evenings, weekends, and summers?
4. If our greatest untapped resource is our intellectual property (we actually do know what to teach and how to teach better than anyone else), why don't we capitalize that, literally, and enter into the online home school market?
5. If equity means in part a socio-economically diverse class and not just a racially or ethnically or religiously diverse class, what would it take to expand our financial aid to 25% or more of the student body with a large segment of the middle class enabled to access our school?

These and many more questions are perhaps the most important strategic questions a school could ask—and answer—in the coming years.

Patrick Bassett is the President of the National Association of Independent Schools. He writes and speaks frequently on subjects related to independent school life.

Capital Formation for Independent Schools

By Robert Fuller

Since 1985, not-for-profit independent schools have increased their use of debt financing to achieve important strategic goals. Both in commercial bank borrowing and increasingly in the tax-exempt bond markets, independent schools use debt financing to acquire capital assets that further their mission. For example, Moody's Investors Service, a bond rating company, maintains public market, tax-exempt bond ratings on at least sixty independent schools. Management and governance of these institutions learned to see judicious use of debt as a safe and cost-effective means to support the activities and legacies of educational institutions.

Yet, for many school executives and trustees, debt raises suspicion, and is sometimes seen as undesirable or even dangerous. For them, debt is seen as a means of mortgaging the future and perhaps limiting flexibility to meet the vagaries of an unknown future.

Whether debt is in or out of favor, most private school business and financial officers are familiar with debt in some form. Whether in the form of traditional bank borrowing, installment debt, leases or mortgages, debt is a feature found on numerous independent school balance sheets. Thus, the question is rarely debt versus no debt, but how much and in what form.

Many schools enjoy some combination of financial surpluses from operations, income from endowment, and significant ongoing philanthropic support. For managers and trustees the question of debt appears discretionary. If substantial financial assets, earnings, and philanthropy exist, why borrow? Other schools rely mainly on pay-as-you-go financing from operations. Yet all schools have multiple obligations, for improved campuses, new programs, and teacher compensation while maintaining or improving student diversity and tuition affordability.

This chapter asserts that capital borrowing (using long-term debt to finance long-term assets as opposed to using debt to pay for current or short-term expenses) is a safe, effective tool to achieve both current and long-term goals. Rather than let "capital" be a fuzzy term, I define it as physical, financial or even intellectual property (or asset) that can produce a financial return. In not-for-profit organizations, the financial return, by tradition and under law, may not enrich owners or investors. Rather, financial returns from capital sustain and advance the benevolent ends and means that the institution undertook when formed.

Whether a particular not-for-profit independent school benefits from surpluses, endowment, and philanthropy or not, many can better achieve their goals with some debt than without it. This is akin to taking a mortgage to buy a home. People who could easily afford the cash purchase of a dwelling rarely do so. There is more to this than expected long-term capital gains from such a decision. Rather, how a home is financed relates to many things, including preservation of capital that is otherwise and perhaps more productively employed. While mortgage debt cannot be taken lightly, most homebuyers opt for some form of debt financing to acquire a house (capital investment) in which their home (goal) is made.

The claim that a modicum of debt is a good thing rests on the ability of not-for-profit borrowers to conserve and invest operating surpluses and other financial assets (including endowment and philanthropic contributions) at a rate of return higher than the cost of a prudent level of debt. Unique among borrowers, not-for-profits may draw on their tax-exempt status to secure low-cost and flexible debt at a rate that, over any reasonable period, is almost certain to be less than investment returns from conservatively invested financial assets. Using this opportunity routinely produces cash inflows for tax-exempt borrowers.

In short, the difficult balancing of goals and constraints that independent schools face may be easier with debt financing than without debt financing because properly employed debt adds financial balance to an organization. Implemented carefully, debt can produce a financial return in not-for-profit institutions.

Why Borrow at All, Ever?

Independent schools face many complex strategic, operational, and financial challenges. A focus for schools is whether and how (and, not incidentally, how to pay for) renovating or upgrading facilities to meet current and expected life-safety codes or meet increasing demands from students and their sponsors. While academic excellence must remain the cornerstone of independent schools, the type of and quality of student facilities and amenities affects academic experience as well as the ability to attract students. This applies not only to renovating old facilities but also to building new structures for purposes not thought of when the school was originally built. For example, many private schools have recently built student centers, performing arts centers, or fitted facilities for modern computing and telecommunications technologies. Few doubt that projects like these improve the educational experience. Fewer still ever considered them essential in years past.

For schools with adequate resources, it appears simple to allocate existing funds to needed projects. For others, the financial burden is too great. Strategically valuable projects are scaled down, deferred, or cancelled.

Raising dedicated philanthropic funds for such projects is a viable alternative for schools if the time horizon from concept to completion is not critical. Alternatively, tuition increases and/or student headcounts can be raised to eventually cash-fund such projects, again lengthening the time to put new assets in place.

The constraints of depleting either operating financial surpluses or available funds from financial assets can be moderated by judiciously using debt to fund capital assets.

Fundamentals of Capital Management

The complexity of modern finance and accounting essentially flows from two questions: 1) What investments should an organization make? and 2) How should those investments be paid for? This is Corporate Finance 101 and it argues that the question of "what" should be separated from the question of "how," or for the separation of mission and financing the mission. This is good theory but only to the extent that the "what" question is not beyond the institution's "how" question. "What" and "how" interact no matter how theory operates. This is the "budget constraint," where desired investments are limited by the ability to pay for them. In corporate finance's profit motive, investment decisions should be ranked according to those with higher returns winning over those with lower returns.

But what about organizations where higher returns are not the objective? Not-for-profit and "public benefit corporations," including independent schools, can still make excellent investment decisions and financing decisions in the absence of a profit motive, with one caveat: For any investment decision does not allow for *both* the return of the capital investment and a return on that investment, the organization must provide for an *overall* institutional return of capital and return on capital that promotes the continuing purposes of the institution. Otherwise, the organization is making an "exit decision" to fail eventually to meet its purposes and perhaps to fail institutionally. This allows "mission-driven" investments to be made, even in the absence of a return of and on capital on that investment. However, it demands that investments that do not return their capital and offer a return be financed from some known source of funds.

The budget constraint can be modified with the decision to use debt financing for key investment decisions, and this can be done responsibly. Moreover, as mentioned above, debt financing by not-for-profit borrowers can provide a return on investment by borrowing at a lower rate while financial assets generate a return higher than the costs of debt.

What About Risk?

It makes no sense arguing that introducing debt into an organization does not increase financial risk. It does. The nature of debt repayment introduces fixed charges that, once undertaken, must be repaid. These commitments can be long-term and have serious consequences if not met. Further, fixed charges from debt, or any source, affect future decisions. However, equating debt with risk should consider what happens if needed investments are not made or are made later than needed to support or enhance the institution's purpose and staying power. Sometimes, the risks of waiting or foregoing needed investments outweigh the risk of fixed charges and when they do, debt can be an effective and responsible way to balance those risks.

What About Cost?

Debt expenses include both repayment of principal and the interest costs for borrowing. Interest expense, the cost of borrowing, is a market-determined cost. Debt markets for independent schools are broad and include traditional bank borrowing, leases and the like, as well as access to tax-exempt bond markets. There also exist a number of hybrid borrowing techniques available. These include "bank eligible" municipal bonds for single issues below $10,000,000 and private lending sources that lend on banklike terms that can be more attractive than bank loans or bonds.

For bank borrowing, commercial lenders have a familiar process to vet potential loans with customary loan covenants and terms familiar to most board members and business officers. The public bond markets have a similar process that, though more involved, can (though not always) offer lower cost with longer-term and more flexible repayment arrangements. The "brain damage" of a bond offering in initial and continuing effort and time is often worth it because the overall financing is both cheaper and on better terms than a bank loan. The goal is to secure the lowest-cost, most flexible debt available which, if done well, can make borrowing affordable and responsible, and therefore an effective tool to achieve institutional goals.

Debt Structure

"Debt structure" is a fancy term for two things: 1) how long a borrowing should last (its maturity) and 2) whether the interest rate should be fixed or variable. The first issue is straightforward, the second, less so.

Maturity

Maturity should match the useful (strategic use and/or revenue-producing capability) life of what is being "financed" with debt. Accounting guidelines are helpful in establishing useful life and essential to how financial statements will reflect "consumption" of the purchase. For schools and many other institutions, accounting useful life is not the whole story. Much character, function, and purpose remains in historical buildings that can be several hundred years old. Yet, accounting guidelines have much to contribute to conservative judgment of how long an asset may be productive. A quick example should suffice. A building may be "depreciated" over a 20-to-40-year period for accounting purposes even though it may remain economically and strategically productive for a multiple of its initial depreciation schedule. Computer equipment, which may be depreciated over five to seven years for accounting purposes, often is economically useless in as little as two years.

The prudent way to employ debt financing is to match a conservative useful life schedule against the repayment schedule for borrowed funds. That is, debt maturity should last no longer than (and possibly shorter than) the financed assets useful life.

Fixed Rate versus Variable Rate Debt

Earlier, I mentioned similarities between debt financing for independent schools and home mortgages. That comparison is valuable in looking at how interest rate–type figures into debt financing. Most homebuyers select fixed-rate mortgages as a conservative financing vehicle. This is especially appropriate when a homebuyer plans to own the home for a long period because it fixes the interest while allowing value growth over years. Yet, if a home purchase will be for a short term, it can be smart finance to use variable rate financing. Why is this? Because shorter-term interest rates are normally lower than long-term interest rates. Moreover, over longer periods (a year or more), the average interest costs of short-term financing are *always* lower than long-term average interest costs. This means that, if some volatility in interest rates is not troublesome, interest costs of variable rate debt, over time, will be less than that for fixed rate debt. The average cost of debt will be less with variable rate debt than fixed rate debt. Later, I will argue that some variation in interest cost is desirable for schools that want to stabilize net income and link it to investment returns.

Schools borrowing short-term may need "credit enhancement" to better "match" short-term debt with longer-term financing. Although this can be economic, it introduces risks that schools may not want, mainly the need to refinance short-term debt at a time not of its choosing.

There are debt instruments that have a long-term maturity and interest rates that "reset" periodically called "auction rate securities." Because auction rate bonds are not subject to refinancing risk, they require a long-term credit enhancement, economically available to financially stronger schools in the form of municipal bond insurance. For schools that can tap this market, auction rate securities are a very good way for independent schools to moderate and manage debt costs safely and economically. In general, for both debt maturity and fixed versus variable rate financing questions, the prudent and conservative course is to finance longer-term assets with longer-term debt and shorter-term assets with shorter-term debt. Yet, prudent (exercising good fiduciary responsibility) and conservative (staying with the familiar) can diverge. That is the topic of the next section.

Asset-liability Management

Bankers, investment bankers, and financial analysts look at organizations as a collection of operating and financial statistics that constitute a bundle of financial risks. This is a disconcerting view of things from the point of view of independent school trustees and management. Yet, there is merit to considering how this perspective can help a school to achieve its goals.

Asset-liability management is the way that financiers array and analyze organizations. A few definitions: *Assets* are what you own or control. *Liabilities* are how you finance assets. Assets and liabilities are recorded within an organization's financial accounting statements on its *balance sheet. Revenues* (earnings from assets and liabilities) are financial resources flowing into an organization as it performs its functions. *Expenses* are financial resources flowing out of an organization as it performs its functions. Revenues and expenses are reported within an organization's financial accounting statements on a *statement of operations. Cash flows* are how the interaction of assets, liabilities, revenues, and expenses causes increases or decreases in cash available to an organization. Inflows and outflows of cash are recorded within an organization's financial accounting statements on a *statement of cash flows.*

Businesses increase their value by increasing revenue faster than expenses, assets faster than liabilities, and cash inflows faster than cash outflows. This is for the benefit of business owners that believe that their wealth will increase faster in a particular enterprise than from alternatives. The goal is profit maximization.

The first sentence of the last paragraph applies to any organization that expects to survive, including independent schools. It is the second statement that does not apply to not-for-profit organizations. Increasing "profits" to owners, either in the form of distribution of profits (dividends) or increased value of the owners' interest (capital appreciation) is neither intended nor permitted in not-for-profits. The original "investors," the founders, want or wanted something different from wealth generation.

However, founders and those who serve the organization today (trustees, managers, and employees) want the organization to enjoy continued economic success, a continuing legacy. Therefore, the focus on managing assets, liabilities, revenues, expenses, and cash flow is on the return *of* invested capital and enough return *on* invested capital to assure that the organization continues to meet its purpose. It requires the return of and return on capital needed for sustained achievement.

Using debt to create return of and return on capital is consistent with sustained achievement if assets and liabilities are "matched": That is, short-term liabilities "finance" short-term assets and long-term liabilities "finance" long-term liabilities. Physical plant, equipment, and some educational programs are long-term investments and may responsibly be financed with long-term liabilities (debt) if the returns from the school's mix of assets and liabilities produce both return of and return on capital. Further, preservation and growth of financial assets (endowment and investments earning a market financial return) by employing debt to finance long-term assets instead of using those financial assets to purchase long-term assets can produce a financial return if the rate of return on the preserved financial assets is greater than the cost of debt. Not-for-profit organizations can borrow at lower rates than expected returns on financial investments.

The expected rate of return on a traditional (equities, bonds, and cash) portfolio of financial assets varies over time and may produce both positive or (as in recent years) negative returns. If organizational fixed charges (and here I mean all hard-to-modify expenses including salaries and program costs) cannot adjust to reflect lowered portfolio returns, net income will drop. But, if fixed charges moderate when portfolio returns moderate, net financial surplus (income) can be stabilized. This is what happens when institutions match assets and liabilities. Well-matched assets and liabilities achieve this because portfolio investment earnings tend to move directly with interest costs—when portfolio returns are generous, interest cost will rise and when portfolio returns decline, interest costs decline. Either way, net income becomes more predictable over time, improving operating budget performance and forecasting.

Schools that do not match assets and liabilities "bet" that, with fixed costs and variable portfolio returns, portfolio returns will rise to offset rising fixed charges. This mismatch causes unwelcome volatility in operating financial performance—in high portfolio return periods, they "win," in low portfolio return periods, they "lose." The winning periods are fun; more things can be done with the "winnings." Losing periods cause problems, including budget cuts and the delay or cancellation of desired investments. Over years, the effects of both winning and losing periods hamper both strategic and financial performance as well as planning.

Add to this the benefit of preserving financial assets using debt to finance long-term assets. A larger financial assets portfolio produces greater investment income than a smaller portfolio that can better "carry" operating finances. In addition, add to that the ability of not-for-profits to borrow at lower cost than expected portfolio returns. If expected portfolio returns are, say, seven percent and costs of borrowing are, say, six percent, the one percent positive "spread" exists between investing and borrowing. This further increases the financial performance of asset-liability management by creating positive "spread" between the costs of borrowing and expected portfolio returns.

Stabilization of net income, the benefits of "carry" and "spread" may seem like alchemy. But many tax-exempt organizations employ these methods to their benefit. The key here is to recognize that the portfolio is to be either preserved or grown. Any spending of principal reduces financial assets, which both lowers wealth and in turn lowers future returns to the portfolio.

How Much Debt?

I will assume that the above arguments are taken with skepticism and caution, as they should. If, however, you are now more inclined to consider debt, the obvious question becomes: How much debt? If the earlier discussion appears aggressive, on the question of how much debt I am more conservative. But in the context of asset-liability management, the question is more complicated, though its answer is more precise.

The concept is to employ the amount of debt that matches long-term debt to long-term assets *and* that preserves portfolio while supporting its growth. This means that debt and its related costs should be limited to promote stable and predictable portfolio returns and not consume unrealized capital gains or the investments themselves. For most organizations, this means that debt principal should be limited to the principal amount of fixed income (bonds, cash, and real-estate investment income) and preferred stocks. It is marginally more aggressive, and appropriate, I think, to include portfolio returns from dividend-producing equities. Remember that this excludes capital gains.

For a school with a $20,000,000 investment portfolio allocated to 50% equities (25% of which are preferred shares), 40% bonds, and 10% cash, debt could equal $12,500,000 ($8,000,000 attributable to bonds, $2,000,000 attributable to cash, and $1,250,000 attributable to preferred shares but ignoring completely stock dividends). It makes little difference whether the investments are permanent endowment or not. So long as the earnings are available to the school for general purposes or spent according to the endowment restriction, endowment restriction is not a barrier to this rule of thumb unless donors prohibited endowment earnings from supporting debt repayment.

Further, employing variable-rate debt, that lowers debt expense at the cost of the ups and downs of interest rates, "matches" portfolio returns to interest expense, and fixed income returns move with interest rate moves. Again, as interest rates rise, so will returns to investments, and as interest rates fall, so will returns to investments. And as the returns to investment vary with interest expense, net income is stabilized.

From this example, I tacitly argue that 100% of the debt has a variable interest rate, a concept many trustees and managers may find abhorrent. But the mathematics of the argument support this. To the extent 100% variable-rate debt is deemed too aggressive, fixed-rate debt is introduced into the variable/fixed debt mix at the cost of a higher cost of debt and more variable net income.

Notice that I did not address what the debt was used to finance. This too is important. To reiterate, if debt term matches the conservative and productive asset life, this improves financial and strategic management both in the near and long term.

Conclusions

All the above deserves more rigorous analysis than a book chapter can give it. The decisions needed to consider strategic and fiduciary obligations faced by independent schools require careful analysis and detailed discussion, especially when they involve committing to any action with long-term consequences. Yet, I know that independent schools have among their trustees and managements the ability to look at such issues and make very good decisions. Not-for-profit organizations make such decisions all the time: for example, with their curricula, student body count, student diversity, and financial aid decisions.

As to the many things that need thorough vetting—debt versus no debt, bank loans versus bonds, fixed rate versus variable rate, to name a few—there are many professionals ready to help in addressing the issues. Boards of trustees often have much of this expertise among their membership. The growing sophistication of independent school executives can contribute here too. As the school's resources are tapped for these important discussions, financial professionals that have detailed knowledge about how independent schools interface debt markets can augment these resources. While I caution against asking a banker if you should consider a loan, or an investment banker as to whether you should issue bonds, professionals from these fields can help, as can independent financial advisors that work directly for the school under the watchful eyes of experienced trustees and managers.

More and more independent schools conclude that debt financing is both prudent and conservative. Debt is not for the desperate; it is a tool for the responsible and the knowledgeable. It is a safe and useful way to achieve the missions of not-for-profit independent schools over the short and long run.

Robert Fuller is principal and founder of Capital Markets Management, LLC, a financial advisory firm specializing in providing "accountable advice" on external financing to not-for-profit and public benefit corporations. His prior experience includes seven years as managing director at Standard & Poor's, where he managed the higher education, healthcare and housing bond ratings departments. He was also a vice president of JP Morgan for six years where he headed sub-sovereign credit and securities research, gaining experience in institutional banking, investment banking, securities sales and trading, as well as investment portfolio.

Achieving and Maintaining Financial Equilibrium

By Sorrel R. Paskin, CMA

Among the several ways to measure the financial health of an independent school is the determination of whether or not the school has lived within its means over the past several years and can be expected to continue to do so for the near future, as indicated in its long-range plan. In addition to living within its means, however, measuring financial health also includes an assessment of the extent to which the school is meeting its stewardship responsibilities, that is, the extent to which its financial, physical, human, and program resources are protected from erosion in value over time and can be expected to maintain or even augment present service levels in future periods.

These measures of financial health can be "codified" into a set of six distinct criteria that identify financial equilibrium;[1] as criteria of institutional well-being, they should serve as essential goals to be sought in any long-range planning process. At the same time, each annual operating and capital budget should be informed by them and explicitly address their implementation.

1. **Annually, revenues equal or exceed expenditures, including operating expense, transfers to plant for routine renovation and adaption activities, equipment acquisition, and reserves funding, and transfers to endowment for reinvestment.**

Most schools plan for tuition revenues net of financial aid and revenues generated from fee-for-service programs, unrestricted annual giving, endowment investment return, and several other resource inflows to at least equal, if not exceed, operating expense. But it is essential that reserves funding to maintain the "value" of the plant and the endowment also be included in the planning for tuition pricing. Absent that effort, to the extent that revenues do not support reserves funding and the other components of total cost, the school permits the value of its physical and financial capital to erode over time. The inclusion of routine plant renovation and upgrades and equipment purchases in the tuition price ensures that these needs receive appropriate attention. Maintaining the value of the endowment through appropriate reinvestment of a portion of earned return ensures that the benefit it provides to the operating budget is maintained over time.

It is clear that students today enjoy both physical and financial resources that their parents did not provide; they benefit from the generosity of past donors and the stewardship efforts of the institution throughout its history. But in order to preserve the interests of future generations in the assets available today, those assets must be preserved and suitably enhanced in order that their service potential in future periods be commensurate with their contribution levels today. Present students must pay a pro-rata share of the cost of maintaining *intergenerational equity.*

2. **Year over year, the annual rate of growth in revenues equals or exceeds the annual rate of growth in expenditures, including transfers to plant and endowment, and reserves funding.**

It is clear that growth rates in revenue and expenditures inclusive of transfers must be in balance to ensure that, annually, revenues will equal or exceed expenditures inclusive of transfers and reserves funding. However, an unnoticed problem can arise in schools where enrollment is growing. In such situations, it is expected that both revenues and expenditures will increase annually. Unless the annual rates of growth in the components of each are carefully monitored, it is possible that once the school has achieved its target enrollment, it will have committed to a rate of growth in expenditures that exceeds the anticipated rate of growth in revenues through "marketable" tuition increases. This might happen through increased program services that become available through the revenue enhancement attributable to additional enrollment. Increases in numbers of faculty through expansions of existing programs and introduction of new programs, augmented administrative service levels, enhanced development and institutional outreach programs, and the addition of new facilities that must now be maintained are among the factors that can contribute to the problem. Each of these enhancements has its own rate of increase and thus drives total costs up. If the blended annual rate of growth in cost exceeds the rate of revenue growth at the point where target enrollment is achieved, the school is on the path to financial disequilibrium.

3. **The value of financial capital is preserved or enhanced.**

In combination, the permanently restricted, true endowment of the school and those unrestricted funds set aside to function as if they were endowment (quasi-endowment) comprise the school's financial capital. The quasi-endowment—including amounts periodically reinvested in the portfolio to preserve its value, bequests and other large unrestricted gifts received that are designated by the board for long-term investment purposes, and operating surpluses also designated for long-term investment—is unrestricted, that is, the funds are available for appropriation but intended to be held intact in perpetuity. This stated intent—the retention and investment of these funds in perpetuity—makes the label "financial capital" appropriate to the commingled aggregate of these funds.

The economic function served by financial capital is to provide a growing and lasting stream of income to fund the school's activities and operating budget growth. To the extent that the growth rate of financial capital exceeds the growth rate of the school's operating budget, it can provide increasing budgetary support over time and can serve as an expanding buffer against enrollment fluctuations, tuition constraints arising from market circumstances and increasing financial aid,[2] and lagging compensation programs. It is noteworthy that investment return from permanent capital is the sole source of income to the school that is not directly dependent upon enrollment.

New donor gifts to endowment augment the portfolio and enhance the utility of that resource in funding school operations and maintaining the school's claimed "margin of excellence." New gifts are *not,* however, a means of protecting the value of the endowment; instead, protection results from a disciplined program of reinvestment.

Of course, the determination of reinvestment amount is tied to the school's payout policy for endowment investment return. In turn, that policy reflects the school's use of a total return measure of investment performance, its investment sector allocation and market segment strategies, and prevailing economic conditions. In order to maintain the purchasing power of the endowment, reinvestment policies frequently use the level of CPI inflation for the calculation. In this manner, the portfolio is assumed to grow at a level that does not impair its value to future generations.

However, if the school's budget grows at an annual rate of 1.5% to 2% greater than CPI inflation (i.e., the *real* rate of growth in the school's budget is 1.5% to 2% over inflation[3]), reinvesting just CPI will erode the value of the portfolio. The erosion will become manifest in future periods as the proportion of total expenditures "covered" by endowment investment return declines. For example, if inflation (CPI) growth is 2% and this is the amount of principal reinvested in the portfolio, then we should expect that the investment payout in the next fiscal period will also grow by 2%. However, if the school's budget grows 4% per year, the endowment support provided to the budget will grow at a rate just half of the budgetary growth rate. In short, endowment support declines and other revenue sources must make up the growing deficiency or else curtailment of services will be the necessary result.

Thus, in order that the endowment support for the operating budget not decline over time, it is necessary that the reinvestment policy take into account the growth rate of the budget, year over year. This necessitates a long-term view of how to balance the competing needs—the need to grow the endowment to maintain its long-term support to the budget and the need for current funding to meet program service requirements.

4. The value and functional adequacy of physical capital are preserved or enhanced.

An important component of financial equilibrium for schools is the maintenance of the value and functional adequacy of the physical plant. Proper stewardship of facilities' assets includes an initial facilities audit, repeated at appropriate intervals, to determine both the physical condition and the functional performance of existing facilities. The audit should examine buildings, building systems, and interior functional spaces, as well as supporting exterior infrastructure to identify tasks that must be undertaken to restore the plant to good condition and to ensure effective facilities support for the achievement of institutional mission. A program of annual "reinvestment" in facilities maintenance and upgrades should then be mounted.

Resources committed to facilities under the annual reinvestment program accomplish three principal objectives:

(1) renewal, replacement, and special maintenance activities that retire the accumulated backlog of deferred maintenance over a short-term period and that bring the plant into reliable operating condition ("catch-up" maintenance);
(2) renewal activities and funding for reserves that maintain the good condition of the plant for its present uses;
(3) adaption activities and funding for reserves to alter the physical plant for changes in use (e.g., changes in instructional and administrative technology, changes in building use, changes for gains in efficiency and cost savings) and changing codes and standards (e.g., asbestos removal and encapsulation, Americans With Disabilities Act, other externally imposed laws and regulations).

Annual funding to accomplish the ongoing renewal activities necessary to maintain good physical condition (no. 2, above) and to provide for adaptation needs (no. 3, above) has been estimated at about 3% of plant replacement cost (plant renewal at 1.5%–2.5% of plant replacement cost based on facility subsystem lifecycles; plant adaptation at 0.5%–1.5% of plant replacement cost). Estimates of the "catch-up" costs to retire the deferred maintenance backlog are specific to each institution. Annual funding for these needs is usually accomplished by a transfer from operating funds into an account captioned, Provision for Plant Renewal, Replacement and Special Maintenance (PPRRSM).

While depreciation expense and the PPRRSM reserve both address costs associated with the deterioration and loss of economic value of facilities through use and functional obsolescence, these concepts are quite distinct. Depreciation is based on the *historical cost* of plant assets; PPRRSM funding is based on the *replacement cost* of plant assets. Depreciation is not a source of funds to accomplish renewal and adaption activities; PPRRSM funding establishes and annually funds reserves that are committed to these activities. Depreciation is usually not included in the annual budget; PPRRSM funding is accomplished through the transfer of unrestricted resources from current funds to plant funds and as such is a component of the annual budget. Since tuitions are established to recover operating costs (inclusive of reserves funding) net of investment income and other revenues, transfers for PPRRSM are reflected in the tuition price. Finally, the PPRRSM transfer is not an expense; it reallocates unrestricted balances to a specific use.

Inclusion of funding for PPRRSM in the annual budget (and in the tuition price) accomplishes several important goals. It ensures that annual resource inflows accommodate plant needs on a replacement-cost basis; it allows for the undertaking of renewal and replacement activities in an orderly and planned manner; it provides a source of funds for the timely correction of system failures when they occur; and it removes from operations (the current unrestricted fund) the costs of major plant work.

Few schools will be able to set aside 3% of the replacement value of their buildings and land improvements. Indeed, for most, this represents a very aggressive level of reserves funding. However, in both annual and long-range financial planning, it is critical that boards and senior administrators be aware of the full amount needed in their institutions and that planning processes accommodate that need in an amount that is representative of both the need and the institution's resources, and that increases annually to a realistic predetermined level.

5. The value of human capital is preserved or enhanced.

A school's human capital is comprised of its faculty, administration, and staff resources. While the quality of the student body is also an element of human capital, we exclude that constituency on grounds that its preservation and enhancement needs are met through the instructional and other program services provided by the school.

With respect to faculty and administrative employees, preservation and enhancement of value can be addressed through initiatives and programs designed to build on existing competences and skill sets. Annual personnel evaluation programs that are based upon and utilize generally recognized and research-based performance criteria and standards can assist faculty and other employees to improve their work performance. Professional development programs utilizing effective presenters and specially designed experiential learning for faculty can enhance present understandings and lead to the development of improved teaching methodologies. Formal graduate education, attendance at conferences and regional support meetings, school-supported curriculum development initiatives during summer periods, among other opportunities, can materially assist the school's efforts to preserve and enhance its human capital resources.

Oftentimes, recognition of the importance of these undertakings can serve as a significant marketing tool in the school's efforts to solicit endowment gifts to underwrite these experiences. A named professional development endowment fund can often meet the interests of both the school and the donors of that fund.

6. The quality of the curriculum, programs, and services to students is preserved or enhanced.

The reputation of a school is determined by the perceived quality of its faculty, curriculum, programs, and services to students. On that perception hang the outcomes of the school's student recruitment efforts, the support of its alumni, the continuing support of friends in the community, the commitment of its parents, the morale of its faculty, and even the performance and achievements of its students. Clearly the lifeline of the school is its people and its programs.

Through professional development activities to promote professional and personal growth, through competitive compensation programs to attract and retain the best faculty available, through aggressive recruitment strategies that identify and seek to enroll those students best served by the school's mission, schools can identify and build on their own distinctive competences and can convert these to competitive advantage in their markets. Beneficiaries of such moves are the children the school serves, their parents, the school's "presence" in its community, its reputation, and its financial future.

It is notable that faculty compensation programs in most schools comprise as much as 50% of the operating budget. Program services to students can require an additional 15% or even more. Thus, the importance of services to students is matched by the percentage of total cost such services consume each year. Boards and administrators recognize these facts but, in periods of fiscal stress, may be too willing to reduce the school's commitment to funding growing compensation needs (i.e., salary plus benefits), curriculum development, and materials and supplies budgets. Any economy gained through such moves, however, is a false economy. The future well-being of the school may be compromised by the savings resulting from such short-term measures.

Sorrel R. Paskin is President of Resource Associates, Inc., a firm specializing in providing business administration, accounting, and employee benefits administration services to smaller independent schools. Formerly the Associate Headmaster for Finance and Administration at Riverdale Country School (NY), Sorrel's career in schools and colleges spans 44 years and includes financial and business administration, investment management, and institutional strategic planning, as well as teaching. He presently serves as an adjunct professor in logic and critical thinking at Johnson and Wales University (RI). Sorrel is a graduate of the University of Pennsylvania (B.A.), New York University (M.A.), and the University of Missouri–St. Louis (MO), and is a Certified Management Accountant.

Notes

[1] Financial equilibrium was initially identified by Cambridge Associates as comprising four goals. The discussion in this paper modifies the original four and adds two additional goals, numbered 5 and 6 here, which, while not specifically financial in nature, can have significant impact on the school's financial condition.

[2] Note that the support provided to the operating budget by endowment investment return and operating gifts received provides each student an "implicit scholarship." This "implicit scholarship" measures the excess of value received over the price paid (the tuition) for the education.

[3] There is ample evidence to show that on average school budgets grow at rates that exceeds external inflation by 1.5% to 2% per year. This phenomenon is the result of the labor-intensive nature of school operations and the limited opportunities to gain productivity enhancements.

FACULTY

Re-recruiting Faculty and Staff: The Antidote to Today's High Attrition[1]

By Don Grace and Siri Akal Khalsa

In December 2000, the head's support committee here at Chapel Hill–Chauncy Hall School (MA) stared into the front entrance of a veritable labyrinth in our school life. The puzzle started with the loss of many faculty/staff members we had wanted to retain from the previous year. We had a 22% attrition rate. Our assistant head, responsible for recruiting all the replacements for those faculty/staff members, jokingly told me he had taken to asking strangers whether they had ever taught before and whether they had any interest in teaching ___________. The blank changed, depending on the response to the first question; the first question was always the same. He not only ate, drank, and breathed faculty/staff recruitment, he dreamed about it—and those dreams were not always pleasant. And he was not the only one. Others were responsible for doing initial phone interviews, scheduling candidate visits, coordinating evaluations of candidates, making offers, and integrating new people into the community.

We filled all our openings, but only after taking many unnecessary wrong turns, retracing our steps, and trying a myriad of new routes to get the job done. And it is not as if we did this work without an audience. Many of our current parents had sent their children to our school because of the outstanding relationships students had with faculty/staff members, and they were anxious to know when we were going to finish the hiring task, who we had hired, and how those new people could possibly measure up to the high standards of those they replaced. So we were trying to move through the staffing labyrinth in front of a critical, vocal audience. For the head's support committee, this was anything but a home-crowd advantage. This was a committee used to helping the head wrestle with nearly impossible tasks, but when it came to the conundrum of retaining teachers, it was stuck.

As we examined our staffing attrition and its powerful side effects, our assistant head had an insight that led to a key breakthrough. Given that we had to recruit several candidates at a time to replace one faculty/staff member we would have liked to keep, we should treat our current faculty/staff as if they needed to be recruited . . . in fact, re-recruited. As we talked about it, we began to understand that the labyrinth could not be negotiated by an action or two—in fact, we needed to create a whole re-recruitment system to reduce our attrition to a workable level and to move through the many twists and turns ahead. And so we began two years of work.

Year One

At first, our "re-recruitment plan" was more of a series of tentative steps. We had varied success. Some of our actions were powerful and replicable. In February, we created a panel of the board chair, a board member, a parent, a staff member, and a faculty member, each responsible for explaining to faculty and staff members in a meeting why they ought to sign up for the school again when contracts were offered a month later. We made that a tradition at the school. In contrast, some of our attempts were not easy to repeat. In December, we received a donation of $61,000 from an anonymous donor, to allow for each faculty/staff member to receive a $1,000 check at the holiday party, giving new meaning to "holiday cheer." Holiday party attendance skyrocketed after that, but we have yet to provide comparable surprises.

Some initiatives we didn't try to repeat. When the administrative team created a relief night for dorm parents, the drain on the administrative team was so large and the impact on the dorm parents was so small that we discontinued the practice. We continue to wrestle with the issue of workload in other ways. Occasionally, we tried something that unwittingly seemed to be part of an "un-retention" plan. For instance, when we staged an end-of-the-year celebration of faculty and staff by the Parents and Guardians Association, a number of faculty and staff did not attend. Afterwards, we asked people why and discovered that many people experienced social events with parents as open parents' meetings about their children. Not exactly the celebration of faculty and staff we had in mind.

One of the benefits of committing to a plan was that we began to notice when actions in other arenas had side benefits for retention. To orient the large number of new faculty/staff members in 2000–2001 to the values and practice of our school, we expanded the new faculty/staff orientation from one day to five. That not only provided new faculty/staff members with more vital life signs on opening day 2000; it also helped ensure a higher retention rate of that same group of new people the following year.

We tried a number of other effective initiatives that first year.

- We created a list of positive characteristics of our faculty/staff and distributed that list to the faculty/ staff on the day of our panel, to celebrate our strengths.
- We developed a brochure entitled "Why Teach at Chapel Hill–Chauncy Hall School?" and gave that brochure to current as well as prospective faculty/staff members.
- We devoted a board visiting day in January to the focus question of "How do we retain the faculty/staff most appropriate to our mission?"—ending the day with discussions between individual trustees and small groups of faculty/staff members about the focus question. We developed a set of low-cost/no-cost retention actions from that day.
- We started a three-year curriculum review process in the fall of 2000, suggested and designed by our Curriculum Committee (our academic dean along with de-

partment and program heads). This proved to be an engaging, important process for our whole faculty.

- We continued the prior years' structure of faculty-based summer work groups. The school funded the time of five faculty members on a summer work group that was asked to recommend solutions to a school-wide problem selected by the head and administrative team. We implemented approximately 80 percent of the ideas proposed from these groups and tapped faculty wisdom and creativity in new ways.
- We started an ongoing tradition of providing doughnuts and bagels to faculty/staff from one of the administrators on Friday mornings.
- We instituted a voluntary retirement policy that allowed veterans with long service to the school to leave with half pay and full benefits for the next two years after their last day. This meant some of our veterans—who may have wanted to retire but were afraid of the financial consequences—could then afford to leave.
- We realized that our tradition of ending faculty/staff meetings talking about individual student victories allowed faculty to balance the usual exhaustion of teaching with the rich emotional rewards of individual student turnarounds.
- We used a system of feedback loops (questionnaires and focus groups) with faculty, staff, and parents—about what was working in the school, what was not working, and suggestions for change—to make small, important improvements in the school each year.
- We started doing exit interviews with those employees who had decided to leave, asking them to outline their reasons for leaving to the dean of faculty, to a selected faculty member, or to a selected outside volunteer resource (a former head of school).

The results were striking: We cut our attrition rate in half, to 16 percent, going from the 2000–2001 school year to the 2001–2002 school year. Though there were factors outside our control, such as life decisions about going to graduate school or starting a family, our efforts did make a difference in heightening our retention rate.

Year Two

With the success of our first steps, we decided to expand our efforts, to begin forming more of a plan for entering the attrition/retention labyrinth and emerging with an acceptable attrition rate. We continued some initiatives with little change. The re-recruitment panel, new faculty/staff orientation, positive characteristics of faculty/staff, recruitment brochure, summer work groups, and student victory discussions all happened again in much the same way. At the same time, we made small but important adjustments in some other initiatives from Year One. The faculty/staff celebration was held without parents, and it was hugely successful in spirit and in attendance. The board visit day turned to the question of "What is the ideal student body for Chapel Hill–Chauncy Hall?," engaging students as well as faculty, staff, and board in new ways about a critical, substantive issue. The curriculum-review project moved into the second phase, boosted by our hosting the regional association's fall workshop on curriculum revision with curriculum guru Grant Wiggins (and allowing for our entire faculty to attend). We moved Friday's doughnuts and bagels to a more spacious, central location, leading a quarter of our faculty/staff to gather for a few minutes most Friday mornings for valuable social time. We adjusted our presentation of exit-interview results to include the national perspective on faculty/staff attrition and retention and to communicate the complexity of the problem and the multiple layers of our response.

We also started some new initiatives, many of them allowed by fund-raising done the year before. In consultation with a local corporation, we analyzed the needs of all our buildings, created a five-year plan, and began systematically tackling the most necessary building renovations. We landscaped the school's entryway and all of our major buildings and either painted or sided many of them. Classrooms, workspaces, and living spaces all benefited from our concentrated efforts. We paved the pathway to one of our major classroom buildings, answering the cries from students and faculty alike that they had to wade through a virtual swamp to get to class. We added 87 new computers, created a digital arts lab, provided a computer workroom for each dorm, and—most importantly—hired another staff member to keep up with all the needs of computers and humans alike. New signage went up this year around campus, and we are now in the midst of a pond reclamation project. One trustee said it was more exciting to come to campus because there was always some project in progress. Capping our fundraising results was a 6% raise across the board for the 2002–2003 school year, which was double the raise from the year before. By looking at low-cost/no-cost ways of doing things, we avoided pouring money down enticing but finally blind alleys.

We continued to find new low-cost ways to retain our faculty/staff members. To give faculty members new opportunities for leadership, and to address other school needs at the same time, we created an administrative intern position for each of two trimesters in the area of faculty/staff recruitment. Not only did we gain two faculty advocates for our school, we also connected those two faculty members more powerfully to our community. Our dean of students created a Host Family Weekend for two weekends a year, when all boarders were placed with local families in our school. That allowed for an important respite for faculty and staff, particularly for those living on campus, and led to potluck dinners and other relaxing social events. While faculty and staff appreciated these social bonding opportunities, they also valued the work we did with them following September 11, 2001. By moving announcements in faculty/staff meetings to voicemail, memo, or e-mail, we set aside time to check in with all faculty and staff members about how they were coping with the challenges of the tragedy of that terrorist attack, including bringing a principal of our Employee Assistance Plan to address the group about the free counseling services available to all employees at that time and throughout the year.

At the end of Year Two, we had a second straight year of under 20% attrition, at 19%. Though we had initially hoped to match the 16% from Year One, we gained valuable perspective from our assistant head's study of national statistics (small independent schools average 23% attrition, according to a University of Pennsylvania study, for example). The trustees' and the head's support committee celebrated ongoing progress in the labyrinth at the same time that they understood there was more work to do for the next year and beyond. The ball of string we needed to get out of the labyrinth was growing. Just as we benefited from the perspective of national attrition statistics, so we began to understand that we would gain much from connecting with other schools. We presented our attrition/retention story at the NAIS Annual Conference in San Francisco, and our audience of school administrators told us that we were exploring important territory. From that conference experience, we decided to poll other schools and to offer our re-recruiting experience in other conferences.

Year Three

Last summer, as we entered Year Three, we sent a poll to the heads of schools in the Association of Independent Schools of New England (AISNE) and in the Connecticut Association of Independent Schools (CAIS). We asked about their faculty/staff attrition rate and their opinions about the initiatives in their school that helped retain faculty/staff, the major obstacles to retaining people, and the steps they planned to take in the future. The high return rate of the questionnaires told us that this was an important issue to other heads and administrators. We were surprised by the greater frequency of professional development initiatives as compared to other categories. Of course, we understood that these questionnaires represented (1) administrators' best guesses on what makes a difference for their employees, just as our initiatives also represented our administrative estimates, and (2) the answers reflected what actions were best for the least expenditure, in most cases. We were struck by the range of initiatives, the differences from school to school, and the creativity of some of those actions. In December 2002, we did the first of our workshops on re-recruitment, this one at the annual conference for The Association of Boarding Schools (TABS). To present the workshop, we created the kinds of categories that emerged from the AISNE/CAIS questionnaire, and we organized our own actions over two years into those categories. In the course of the discussion with boarding school administrators, we were struck again by how different schools are, how distinct each faculty/staff culture is, and how much effective retention actions vary from one school to another.

As we shape our own Year Three retention program, we realize there is still much to learn about how to retain the faculty/staff most appropriate to our mission. Our first, tentative steps have grown into an imaginative program. We also lowered our attrition rate significantly two years running. At the same time, we realize even more clearly now than ever before that we need to keep checking in with our faculty/staff members about what will attract them back. From our own experience, we urge colleague schools to talk about faculty/staff attrition, to formulate re-recruitment initiatives and a retention plan, and to consult with faculty/staff about the potential impact of specific actions and categories. Having company in the labyrinth increases the chances of everyone re-emerging (and re-contracting) together.

Summary of AISNE/CAIS Survey Results on Notable Retention Actions and Programs in Member Schools (In order of frequency):

1. Professional development and support (including summer travel, sabbaticals) (51)
2. Salaries and benefits improvements (including housing) (31)
3. General working environment (11)
4. Appreciation/social events (8)
5. Leadership opportunities (8)
6. Logistical support (including facilities, equipment, buildings, and grounds) (4)
7. Extra pay/bonuses (2)
8. Personal/sick day flexibility (2)
9. Celebrating students (1)
10. Mission/values (1)
11. Hiring experienced faculty/staff (1)
12. Recognition programs (1)
13. Summer program opportunities for extra pay (1)
14. Student/teacher ratio (1)
15. Problem solving with faculty/staff (1)
16. Highlighting benefits of working at the school (1)

Innovative Programs/Actions for Faculty and Staff Retention From AISNE/CAIS Survey:

1. Professional development and support (including summer travel, sabbaticals)
   a. Ten-day orientation prior to start of school for all staff (Connecticut Friends School)
   b. Individual professional growth accounts—each teacher receives $500 to spend in accordance with individual needs (books, posters, travel, equipment) (Wooster School)
   c. Summer travel grants (competitive) (Canterbury School)
   d. Chair/sabbatical program (Holderness School)
   e. Experienced teacher reviews (Waynflete School)
2. Salaries and benefits improvements (including housing)
   a. Low-interest mortgages (Fairfield Country Day School)
3. Appreciation/social events
   a. A faculty meeting on Friday afternoons at a local establishment, with spouses (Oxford Academy)
4. Logistical support (including facilities, equipment, buildings and grounds)
   a. Technology training support dollars (Choate Rosemary Hall)
5. Extra pay/bonuses
   a. Pay for master teachers (Epiphany School)
   b. Dedicated head's fund for faculty enrichment (in addition to professional development budget) (Hopkins School)
6. Personal/sick day flexibility
   a. Faculty have unlimited sick days for themselves and for sick children or spouse—at no charge (Wooster School) (Pine Point School)

7. Celebrating students
   a. Faculty get to talk about students at graduation. This highlights the faculty while giving honor to the students (Community Prep School)

Notes

[1] This piece originally appeared in *Independent School* (Vol. 62, No. 3), 20–27. It is reprinted here with permission from the NAIS.

Don Grace worked in independent schools for 31 years and headed four of those schools over a period of 20 years. He is currently the chief development officer for All Kinds of Minds, an institute founded several years ago by Dr. Mel Levine and Charles Schwab to promote understanding of students' learning differences.

Siri Akal Singh Khalsa, the head of Chapel Hill–Chauncy Hall School, in Waltham, MA, holds a doctorate in educational administration from Teachers College, Columbia University, where he worked under Prof. Pearl Kane. Prior to that, he served as assistant head at Oakwood Friends School in Poughkeepsie, NY, and as vice-principal of two international schools in India.

Attracting and Retaining Qualified Faculty

By Dan Cohen

As independent schools refine their curriculum and improve their facilities in an effort to keep pace with the findings in educational research and the changes in technology, they had best recognize that the profile of the teacher is changing as well. The attraction and retention of qualified faculty demands that attention be paid to who today's teachers are and what they seek in choosing an independent school as an employer. Old standards and assumptions will no longer suffice. Independent schools must recruit actively, they must be open to innovative ways of matching and creating positions with desirable personnel, and they must seek innovative means for defining compensation.

Today's recruits are not necessarily second income earners. Today's recruits are not necessarily sheepish when it comes to negotiating job load or compensation. The fresh battalion of teachers today will not necessarily accept the traditional approach of standardizing salaries or assigning a conglomeration of ancillary duties. Today's teachers do not accept the notion of teaching as a second-class profession. Independent schools will need to recognize the new group of teachers' desire to be treated individually and to have their personal lifestyle or family concerns appreciated.

There remain some traditional concerns facing independent schools that seek to attract or retain faculty. There are also issues that will lead independent schools into relatively unchartered waters, particularly for those schools that have been grounded in tradition for many years. The following seeks to address some of the preliminary, long-standing concerns facing independent schools, while taking into account the nature of today's teachers.

Regarding Public Schools as Competitor

Candidates Interested in Public and Independent Schools

Recognizing that public schools tend to offer higher salaries and more complete benefits and that some offer comparable settings to independent schools provides the logical starting point when setting out to attract faculty. A competitive public sector becomes an immediate challenge when attempting to draw in the candidate who is open to both public and independent schools. Considering that one can, in the main, acquire a higher salary through public school employment, the independent school must provide tangible reasons for choosing the position with less pay. It would be safe to assume that those candidates who consider public and private schools as options are looking for reasons other than salary to sway their choices.

What should independent schools offer as motivation other than salary? All candidates will look at class load, student contact numbers, beyond-the-classroom opportunities, and access to professional development, community, and facility. A brief look at each concern is in order.

Class load is perhaps the single most important issue to teachers considering both public and independent institutions. The independent school must create a level of appeal that channels the candidates' focus toward the private school. I recall interviewing a career public school instructor for a math position at the middle school level. When I displayed a mock schedule, showing her duties as two sections each at seventh and eighth grade per day, with an advisory and club thrown in here and there, I noticed her widened eyes. She asked what the "numerous" blanks in the schedule represented. I informed her that they were prep periods. The quantity of these planning sessions clearly took her by a most pleasant surprise.

When candidates who are interested in public and independent schools discover that their student contact load may range, typically, between forty and eighty students, it is evident that this is quite meaningful to their decision process. The combination of smaller course and student loads speaks volumes about the differences in the expectations and environments between public and independent schools. These differences provide additional incentive for the candidate considering both arenas of work; the independent school assumes that there will be a closer relationship between faculty and students and that teachers will put their individual stamp on the classes they design. Smaller class and student loads deliver the same message found in most schools' brochures that the school values these relationships and the authenticity of its courses. More importantly, from the candidate's perspective, smaller class and student loads demonstrate to faculty that not only does the school value these aspects; in truth, the school actually enables its faculty to carry out this part of their mission.

The opportunities to do more than teach will be highly attractive to many candidates. (This will be discussed later as a potential hindrance to the retention of desirable faculty when it is a school requirement.) Many candidates are looking for responsibilities that will initiate student contact and experiences outside of their core teaching duties. This is especially true for younger candidates. The educator who is able to add dimensions to their campus life by leading or assisting in coaching interscholastic or club sports, joining outdoor education programs, designing and implementing electives, or playing the role of advisor, will find the independent school's openness to these endeavors as a definite attraction. The richness derived from these experiences can become a crucial ingredient to a candidate's choice of setting.

A school's notion of professional development expresses to faculty the degree to which the school believes a teacher's personal interests may affect the teacher's performance. It can also express the degree to which a school will work with potential deficiencies discovered to be a part of a teacher's profile.

I have seen a relatively wide spectrum of approaches to professional development. In its strictest sense, some schools mandate that for a teacher's "application" for a professional development experience to be approved (school to foot the bill), the teacher must show how the experience will be directly linked to the day to day life of the teacher's students. That is to say that faculty must show how the class(es) that constitute(s) the teacher's core duties will incorporate the results, findings, outcomes, or general experience had during the professional development program. Toward the other end of the spectrum are the schools who, when awarding professional development opportunities, ask "Will this experience charge a teacher's batteries?" "Will the teacher feel culturally rich or physically invigorated and therefore enthusiastic about their future work?" Candidates who perceive a school to model the latter approach clearly see the school as one that values the whole teacher.

The prospective teachers just beginning in the field will look for a different component in their use of professional development. Middle-school science is becoming less segregated based on biology, chemistry, and physics and more integrated, involving the instruction of all three sciences in any given year. Less experienced science teachers, who are perhaps skilled at instructing biology, may see professional development as a way to gain the knowledge and resources needed to branch into physics and chemistry. This resource would enable them to use their natural ability to become an excellent integrated science program instructor. A school's willingness to use professional development to enhance deficiencies will communicate to candidates the school's desire to work with and foster true growth in the teachers to whom they are committed.

Recruiting teachers with experience demands that the interview process take into consideration the school's role in communicating a sense of community. Experienced teachers know what to look for when gauging a school's community. This candidate will want access to students and teachers, preferably those with comparable experience and expertise, to get a true, candid account of what it is like to attend and/or work for the school. The experienced teacher will likely know what things they wish to be present when examining a school's community and climate. It would benefit a school to be cognizant of this and allow for casual discussion time between these candidates and the people who are already a part of the community.

In many cases, independent schools' facility will provide a meaningful and lasting impression in candidates who are considering both public and independent schools. There are exceptions to the rule, but generally speaking, the independent school holds the upper hand in terms of the campus it offers to students and faculty. This would include classroom quality (layout and equipment found in science labs or art rooms) and quantity (whether teachers share rooms), open spaces, athletic facility, commons, technology facilities, and all of the things that create atmosphere and a sense of one's environment. Facility will not be a small matter to many candidates and the independent school will do well to use their campus as a recruitment tool.

Candidates Interested Only in Independent Schools

There are several reasons why one might be interested in teaching nowhere other than at an independent school. Perhaps one does not possess the credential necessary to work in district schools. Perhaps one fondly remembers one's own experience as a student at an independent school. Or, as is likely the case, a candidate places a premium on one or more of the aspects mentioned earlier that enable an independent school to stand out from the public school. Suffice it to say that this group of candidates does not see salary or benefits as the only measure of a worthy profession.

Attracting teachers who are intent on finding an independent school position obviously pits one independent school against others. Usually, the competition would be regional, meaning the prospective teacher has chosen a geographical region in which to live and work and therefore seeks the best match within that region. Unless one school offers a salary that far surpasses others in the area, schools will vie for these teachers by offering the best combination of the aspects mentioned previously: class and student load, ancillary duties, facility, and the like. In some cases, candidates may be seeking a school whose philosophy includes the implementation of integrated curriculum or grade-level teaming of faculty. I have found that the latter two often will serve as a "tie-breaker" when independent schools seem to offer similar work environments and load.

There are, of course, prospective teachers who present themselves as flexible in terms of where they will locate. Again, attention will be paid to the crucial aspects of teaching in independent schools. But the elements found in living in a specific region can come into play as well. The desirable candidate who is open to a variety of geographical regions may be swayed by the recreational opportunities available in the Northwest or mountain regions, while another candidate may be swayed by the affordable living conditions found in the Midwest. In any case, schools wishing to attract this candidate will do well to highlight the positive aspects of living in the region of their school.

Regarding Myths, Misconceptions, and Negative Stereotypes

The question is "Why teach?" Why would one choose to work in a field that garners little societal respect? Why would one associate oneself with the group of "Those who can't, teach?" Why would one choose to accept the financial struggles associated with being a career teacher? Specifically, once one has decided to become a teacher, why would one choose to work predominantly with the wealthy and the inherent attitude of entitlement so often associated with today's independent school clientele?

I have previously addressed the notion of choosing the independent school as a destination for prospective teachers. But given the dramatic need facing schools today to find new teachers to replace the plethora of those reaching retirement or to meet the demand of an increasing population seeking independent education, schools may find themselves playing the role of recruiter in similar fashion to how the military, police, or nursing profession recruit: convincing people to consider teaching as a profession.

Some teachers would never have guessed as college students or young professionals that they might be interested in becoming a teacher. In addition to the steps necessary to attract teachers to their school, independent schools may very well need to develop their own recruitment strategies in an effort to attract younger people, or those choosing career changes, to the profession. Independent schools need to be comfortable publicizing the profession of teaching and the advantages of doing so in an independent school.

Schools will need to publicly celebrate the richness of the relationships had between faculty and students, the satisfaction felt by those who design and implement curriculum, the joy discovered in working in a close-knit group or team of teachers, and the opportunities available to grow professionally. These are, of course, the hallmarks of choosing to work in healthy independent schools.

Regarding Inflexible Compensation Systems

One of the negative stereotypes associated with the teaching profession involves the system for the compensation of faculty. Such systems are generally seen as those that reward factors (seniority and advanced degrees) unrelated to high performance and good attitude and thereby discourage talent from entering or staying in the profession. The general paradox is that the "across-the-board 4% raise" approach to compensation is generally accepted by faculty as fair but seen by others as both unfair and inappropriate in terms of serving as an incentive, rewarding individuals, and moving the organization forward.

I recall my early years of being a teacher in independent school settings. I echoed the latter portion of the description above: Flat raises across the board do little to motivate talented faculty to continue to produce and grow as teachers. Make no mistake that faculty members, as measured by students and parents, know their status within any school. The good ones know who they are; the ones who need refining know who they are as well. If it is true that in the "real world" the good ones are rewarded in a different fashion than those who are still developing, regardless of experience, why should teachers accept the standardization of compensation? As I recall my latter years of teaching and my current tenure in administration, I realize my attitude about this has not changed.

Independent schools have the opportunity to bring "real world" realities into the buffered world of academia. Needless to say, the nature of most teachers includes an inherent devotion to fairness. This manifests itself in their treatment of their students and how they wish to be treated. A uniform salary increase for an entire faculty, however, is not necessarily fair. It will be especially difficult to convince the next breed of teachers that this approach to compensation is appropriate. Not all teachers with seven years of experience contribute to a school's success to the same degree. Yet, for the most part, they are compensated in similar fashion.

One division head for whom I worked responded to my request for separate compensation treatment by asking me what I did to increase revenue for the school. The school was fully enrolled with a substantial wait list. Did my presence, she asked, bring in additional revenues compared to other faculty within our fully enrolled division? If not, she asserted, what would be the reason for offering more salary to someone with my experience than would be offered to a colleague with similar experience?

It was certainly true that I provided no extra tuition revenue for the school. I could not argue that if I were to leave, the school would eventually have some empty seats to fill. (The school has remained full in my absence.) I suggested a different reason. I suggested that my presence kept the desirable students present and increased the quality of applicants, as the community desired my instruction for their kids. I suggested that this is precisely what helps the school maintain an excellent reputation as a top-flight school. The division head agreed, but was quick to remind me that I still was not responsible for increased revenue, from which the notion of individualized compensation systems are born.

I recall understanding the logic of her argument. But more important, I recall how it failed to reflect an understanding of the changing of the guard. Perhaps I represented a breed of teachers who is unwilling to accept the old notions that teachers do not care about compensation, or that teachers do not have the fortitude to stand up for what they feel they deserve as individuals, or that if teachers express a desire for an increase in salary they will be seen as not being devoted to the profession or to being a team player.

Today's younger teacher is not the same as the novice from years past. Perhaps they seek "real world" treatment, both in compensation and in the evaluation process. Independent schools will need to look at this characteristic and work toward creating a compensation system that holds on to some of the historical values, yet recognizes who today's teacher wants to be. I recall a school some years ago whose system involved a pay scale in a traditional sense, with significant ranges present instead of specific numbers. This enabled the system to reward individual work, contributions, and worth, while maintaining a grip on standardized compensation. Today's recruitment pool may be looking for this type of opportunity for reward.

The Relationship Between Traditional Job Configurations and Dual-Career Young Families

Consider the "triple threat" model of teacher/coach/advisor or dorm parent. I previously referred to this as one of the positive aspects of working for independent schools. The variety of responsibilities and types of student contact are precisely what is integral to developing the relationships made available through the smaller communities of independent schools.

Perhaps today we are describing only our single faculty when we perpetuate the notion that independent school faculty play a multitude of roles. The hours demanded of teachers who live up to the triple threat's call are significant. Perhaps today the payout for full devotion to the teaching cause is not enough to keep the dual-career families satisfied, particularly if the partner in the family could do far better giving the same time commitment to a different profession.

It was standard during my first years to coach a sport, or the like, in addition to the classes I taught. Attending Outdoor Education programs was part of the picture as well. I still hold on to these values. Many of my ex-colleagues and charges that are younger than I, however, do not necessarily see things this way. While there may be people who are more than willing to take on the ancillary responsibilities as part of being a teacher, today's young family may not be capable of relying on the multifaceted, consumed teacher as their primary source of income.

Offering stipends is, of course, one method for keeping some young teachers involved in extracurricular programs. But it may be time to let go of the triple threat. I have seen this tendency unfold on campuses that "contract out" their coaching duties, usually hiring qualified off-campus personnel to coach. This is also a result of the craze for "expertise" instruction (implying the off-campus hire is more adept at coaching, say basketball, than is the seventh-grade math teacher) even at the middle school level. But it also shows a loosening in schools' willingness to expand their resources for maintaining highly desirable extracurricular and interscholastic programs.

The prospective teachers from dual-career families will be the most difficult group to attract if the assumption is that their duties must be multifaceted. This will be especially true in areas like San Francisco, New York, Seattle, and other cities or suburbs where the cost of living is extreme. This group of teachers may simply have less time that they can afford to give to their school even though they may be outstanding teachers. Perhaps they may be expected to do less outside of their classrooms if their presence on campus is truly important.

The attraction and retention of faculty from two-career families will be particularly tenuous for boarding schools. Boarding schools situated in metropolitan settings with significant cost-of-living statistics will suffer exacerbated versions of the difficulties satisfying the dual-career family. Even the rural or suburban boarding school will find it difficult to attract teachers from dual-career families, especially if the assumption of multiple duties holds true for these teachers.

The primary benefit of working in the boarding school environment is, of course, the possibility of attaining housing as part of compensation. This may be an area of focus for seeking creative means for dealing with today's teachers. Perhaps the desirable faculty member whose partner is devoted to his/her own career can be offered housing that is not within dormitory confines or is at least found on a portion of campus that is physically removed from the majority of campus activity. Within this scenario, a school may need to consider offering the more-isolated housing conditions in exchange for the teacher handling some duties usually associated with a dorm parent.

It is likely that the dual-career family would not wish to be such an integral presence on campus. It is quite possible that this prospective teacher wishes for the boarding school experience without the traditional degree to which such a position consumes one's life. In effect, some among today's potential teachers want a boarding school position without wishing to devote their entire existence to the job. These are the teachers who seek a balance between work and home, especially if their partner is devoted to a career as well. Perhaps a housing offer could include the possibility of off-campus housing, coupled with some degree of on-campus duties other than teaching classes. Playing the role of an advisor, or the occasional on-duty dorm tutor or coach may be appealing to this group because of the luxury offered through a housing compensation. As an off-campus housing scenario exemplifies the school's concern for the private life and values of today's teachers, boarding schools may find themselves appealing to a greater pool of teachers if they consider creative, less traditional approaches to bringing in devoted faculty who seek the benefits of boarding school without the commitment required in the past. A desire to have a more independent life may not describe the ideal motive that boarding schools have looked for in a prospective teacher, but it may be indicative of the wants of today's faculty members.

Can boarding schools address other concerns facing dual-career families? It would appear that the boarding school is in the unique position of offering some lower profile, yet crucial tangibles to which some dual-career personnel may be drawn. Such items may include the dual-career family's access to medical services, meal programs, day care or babysitting possibilities, and, of course, tuition waivers. The underlying message is, once again, that today's teachers are looking for meaningful ways for the school of their choice to exhibit concern for the faculty member's personal life and individual needs.

Regarding Retention

Strategies for attracting qualified teachers are varied indeed, but not to the extent found when considering the retention of desirable faculty. There is no magic formula. There may, in fact, be little evidence to suggest that even age divisions, or gender, or discipline of instruction provide patterns sufficient enough to establish generalizations about why a specific group of teachers chooses to remain with their schools. The retention of teachers can be a highly individualized process between a school and its faculty.

Generally speaking, science teachers prefer top-notch facilities and equipment and an endless budget. Foreign language teachers prefer to do their work in schools that value foreign language as they do all other core subjects. Younger teachers may have the time and energy to commit to a variety of responsibilities. More-experienced teachers may be less inclined to commit to new programs or classes, preferring to remain in the comfort zone they have worked for years to achieve. Middle school teachers may prefer to work in a school whose organization includes grade-level teams and an integrated curriculum.

Yet within each of these groups, variations exist. Classifying the wants and desires of any of these groups is one thing; assuming that such classification will provide insight as to what an individual member of the group values most is an entirely different, and inaccurate, exercise. As a science teacher, I cared about a good lab facility. A state-of-the-art lab, however, could not have prevented my move from a metropolitan area where the cost of living had left my family by the wayside and whose quality of life no longer was attractive. A veteran faculty member who does not believe advisory programs ought to be the responsibility of an AP History teacher may choose to depart if her school demands that she pick up that duty. A middle school teacher who wishes to have control over the entire English curriculum may prefer to teach grades six through eight, as opposed to devoting to just one grade level and its team of faculty. A foreign language teacher whose class load far exceeds that of other members of the faculty may value his relationship with his administration enough to "put up" with his unpleasant load.

Some independent schools in high market, high property value communities offer partner home purchases between "the school" and a faculty member. There are districts that offer comparable signing bonuses. These are the most generous and heartfelt gestures a school can put forth in expressing its desire for teachers to remain a part of their community. Yet a teacher turned down the opportunity for the home partnership because he and his family wished to leave the high market, high property value atmosphere and lifestyle. Can a school prevent this?

Perhaps a school cannot prevent the departure of those who seek some form of dramatic change. But schools definitely can play an active role retaining many of the desirable faculty members who hint at their potential departure. Schools have to be independent enough to handle as separate entities those teachers who are deemed invaluable to the community. There are several plausible issues that present themselves as critical to what teachers find attractive about their schools. Identifying the core values of faculty members and having the ability to satisfy them individually is paramount to a school's success in retaining its qualified faculty.

Dan Cohen instructed outdoor education programs for three years and middle school science for five independent schools over the past sixteen years. He has lived on the west coast for 25 years, enjoying its geographic variety while holding on to his Midwest upbringing. He is currently the middle school head at Seattle Country Day School.

The Faculty Search Process: Strategies for Recruiting and Hiring in Independent Schools

By Jay Underwood & Robert Berkman

Finding the right people to teach our students can be arduous and time-consuming work. According to a 2001 NAIS survey, many schools agreed that the greatest frustration of the faculty search process is the time it takes to identify and hire candidates. A search can also be costly in both financial and human terms; it is an expensive process that requires from participants tremendous energy, commitment, and emotional investment. Given these challenges, how do schools go about finding the "right" teachers? The NAIS survey offered the following information:

- 94% look to colleagues, both internal and external, to recommend teachers;
- 81% of schools place classified ads in local papers and other publications;
- 75% use professional search firms;
- 59% use online services;
- 52% attend job or career fairs.

Of these practices, recommendations and search firms yielded the best reviews for producing high-quality candidates. So what else can a school do to attract—and ultimately hire—the best teachers? We believe that an effective search process is built upon three iterative themes: *planning, cultivation,* and *collaboration.*

Before beginning our journey, we always chart a course; it is crucial to enter the search process with a plan in place.

- Identify the qualities you are looking for in a teacher. Begin by examining the school's mission and strategic plans. What does a mission-centered teacher look like? If the mission states explicitly that the school is child-centered, then you will want to attract teachers whose love for children is evident.
- Clarify the expectations that will be placed upon the teacher. Write a job description that details every aspect of the job. Make sure it is accessible to candidates at the outset of the search process.

- Take an inventory of your current faculty and seek to fill the gaps wherever possible. Does the school need to stay true to its diversity goals by hiring more people of color? Are there enough faculty leaders? Does the school need someone to offer fresh perspectives or to toe the line? Firms such as Independent School Management offer resources that can be helpful with evaluating the current complexion of your faculty and forecasting your school's needs.
- Try to stay ahead of the game by determining your needs as soon as possible. Along with a staffing inventory, identify teachers who, for whatever reason, may be on their way out. Are there teachers who have a significant other living far away? Have any teachers recently expressed a desire to retire or to explore a different career? Keep an open line of communication with these teachers early on to assess the likelihood and timing of their departure.
- Determine how much of a budget you are willing to dedicate to the search process. Include travel expenses for recruitment efforts and for candidates visiting from afar, payment of placement fees to search firms, career fair registration fees, and search firm memberships.

The concept of "recruiting" implies that a school is maximizing its exposure to potential candidates, identifying those who are likely to be a match, and pursuing them swiftly and confidently. Though we tend to use the term liberally, the approach we employ is often a passive "advertise-wait-and-hope" model. As in successful marketing, admissions, and fund-raising programs, effective faculty recruitment depends upon the ongoing cultivation and maintenance of strong relationships. Such efforts are also strengthened by the collaboration of individuals who offer expertise and have a clear stake in the hiring decision. Making contacts and maintaining relationships with people you trust, both from within and without, can yield outstanding leads.

Maximize print advertisements. While local newspaper ads may bring in scores of applicants, the quality of those applicants is often mixed at best. However, the wording of the ad can be instrumental in helping to attract the right candidates and repel the wrong ones. At minimum, it should list the position and give a brief overview of the school, where it is located, and whom it serves ("A private independent school for girls in northern Essex County serving students in Kindergarten through Grade Twelve"). The ad should always feature the school's website to offer resourceful candidates immediate access to information about your school. Also, think carefully about the timing of the ad's placement. For example, a holiday weekend, when many people are travelling, is not an optimal time to place a Sunday ad.

Use websites. Your school's own website is the ideal place to herald openings: It offers an inexpensive way to communicate whatever you wish. Maintain an employment section of the site that details position openings, job descriptions, and desired qualities of teachers. Some school websites list answers to a set of "frequently asked questions" (FAQs), addressing issues such as salary ranges, benefits, and professional development opportunities. Other websites, such as NAIS's Career Center (nais.org), isminc.com, and klingenstein.org, offer low- or no-cost Web advertising for independent schools. The NAIS Career Center features several articles and resources to assist both schools and candidates in the search process. There are also websites that feature position openings for both public and independent school teachers, such as usteach.com.

Produce a publication for the purpose of recruiting teachers. Such a publication can be as simple as a photocopied version of the FAQs from your website or as elaborate as a tri-fold, color-infused brochure. In any case, the publication should include accurate and timely data about your school, including information about current teachers, professional development opportunities, compensation and benefits, and the surrounding community. Focus especially on your school's culture and underscore the intangible benefits your school offers, such as the spirit of collegiality and a shared commitment to fundamental principles. When authoring such a publication, involve current teachers who are able to articulate the school's strengths with personal conviction.

Cultivate relationships with organizations and people who can help you recruit. Think about the people who recommend schools to families new to your area. Consider collaborating with your school's admissions office to present an open house for local realtors. Introduce yourself and your school to church, synagogue, and temple leaders in your area. Send them admissions material and a fact sheet giving general information about teaching at your school. Keep a list of e-mail addresses of contacts and inform them when a position becomes available.

Connect with local education pre-service programs and university career centers. Some independent schools have partnered with local colleges of education to offer teacher training programs, which often include coursework, practical teaching experiences with a mentor, and additional school-based professional development. Not only do such programs help schools to "grow their own" teachers, they also offer opportunities to empower current master teachers in new and invigorating leadership roles. Since the design and implementation of teacher training programs require careful long-range planning, consider in the interim offering your school as a place where education students can perform internships, serve as student teachers, or conduct field studies. Additionally, build relationships with the career centers and teacher placement offices at colleges and universities. Send them copies of all job vacancy announcements.

Cultivate prospects, even if there are no immediate openings. Invite exciting candidates to visit your campus. If you do not have a teaching position to offer them, probe to see if they are willing to get involved in another capacity, such as substituting, tutoring, coaching, or teaching an enrichment course. Many schools have had success in hiring teachers who were once teaching assistants, interns, substitutes, and coaches. Identify excellent internal candidates early on and do what you can to enhance their professional development.

Respond to every inquiry. A timely, personal response sends candidates the message that your school is a caring and responsive place. In a very real sense, recruitment is a form of marketing, and every impression your school makes affects the way it is perceived.

Share your wealth. If you meet strong candidates whom you are unable to hire, refer them to a sister school that might be interested in them. In the bigger picture, advocate on behalf of independent schools and the teaching profession in general. Direct potential teachers to resources that will be useful to them, such as NAIS's Career Center, or to a search firm that could assist them in finding a match.

Connect with other independent schools. In the NAIS survey referenced above, 84% of the schools responded that recommendations from colleagues were among the most effective of all recruitment strategies. Given this figure, nurturing the quality of relationships among schools pays great dividends.

Two years ago, we discovered a level of collaboration among sister independent schools that resonated well beyond the search process. In a conversation among administrators from eleven northern New Jersey schools, we collectively recognized that we each shared the challenge of identifying and hiring excellent teachers. For many of us, this challenge was fast becoming a hardship, as we lamented the difficulty of finding high-quality local candidates. Following the lead of six central New Jersey independent schools, we decided to pool our financial and intellectual resources to sponsor a "Career Forum" targeted at prospective independent school teachers. We chose a Saturday in late February and advertised in the local papers. We sent e-mails and reproducible fliers to colleges, graduate schools, churches, synagogues, and social organizations to promote the event. We rented a large university gymnasium in a central location as our venue.

Like our colleagues in central New Jersey, we began the morning by introducing a panel of speakers representing different schools, speaking on topics from school culture to compensation and benefits. After thirty minutes of presentations, we planned for two hours of "contact time," during which candidates could learn about individual schools and their potential openings. We set up a table for refreshments in the back of the space, chairs in the center facing the presentation area, and a six-foot table for each school lining the perimeter. Though we anticipated that we would meet prospects through the forum, we emphasized in our promotional material that the event was an information session rather than a job fair.

Given this, we had no idea what kind of attendance to expect. We were thrilled, then, to welcome over two hundred people. Attendees ranged from experienced public school teachers to career changers to recent college graduates. We were particularly pleased that a significant number of attendees were people of color, the hiring of whom was high priority for many of our schools.

Some of our schools yielded hires from the career forum, while others did not. But the shared sentiment was that the event was well worth the effort. First, it enabled us to cultivate a strong set of local candidates. Moreover, we agreed that it was an excellent way to spread the news about independent schools and the opportunities they offer. Perhaps the most significant outcome of the career forum was that it encouraged colleagues to forge lasting relationships. In fact, well after the forum was over, we continued to reach out to each other on matters of hiring, recruitment and other issues in our schools. The following year, our group welcomed two more schools—and over three hundred candidates to the career forum.

As in recruiting, having an established plan for the hiring process ensures accountability and consistency. In structuring our own plan at Far Hills Country Day School, we began with two resources: our mission and NAIS's "Principles of Good Practice for the Hiring Process." Both of these resources directed us to engage in a collaborative process, one in which a team of teachers and administrators works together to find the candidates who are right for our school. We recommend the following practices that have worked particularly well for us.

Establish a "point person." We found it critical to empower one individual to ensure consistency, coordinate communication, and maintain the integrity of the process. The primary responsibilities of the point person are to

- facilitate the authoring of a position statement or job description;
- manage the advertising and dissemination of information about the position;
- coordinate all recruitment efforts;
- assemble and chair the search teams;
- perform initial resume screenings;
- send response cards or letters to all applicants;
- coordinate candidate visits;
- communicate to candidates and team members;
- alert the school community when a candidate is visiting;
- provide relevant information to candidates prior to their visit;
- greet candidates upon arrival at the school;
- oversee the time horizon for each search;
- make the offer to the top-choice candidate;
- communicate with other finalists once the position has been filled;
- conduct a search summary and evaluation once the process is complete.

With this long list of responsibilities, we learned that the point person may be occupied with little else between January and May, so it is important to assign the role to one who can dedicate the time to do it effectively. At our school, the director of curriculum serves as the point person; other schools might choose a head of school, assistant head, dean of faculty, or divisional director to fill the role.

Construct a search team for each position. Along with the administrative members of our team, we invite teachers who have a stake in the decision, especially those who will be on the same grade level or department as the new teacher. Additionally, we invite teachers who are especially strong representatives of our school's culture; they may be particularly instrumental in "selling" the school to top candidates.

Once we have determined the team members, we define the team's responsibilities. It is important to establish unambiguous expectations for the team. We do not lead a team to believe that it will actually make a hiring decision when in fact it will make a recommendation to the head of school. The team meets as a group at least twice: once at the beginning of the process to establish a plan of action and again after all candidates have been interviewed to discuss final recommendations. In the interim, the point person coordinates all communications via e-mail to keep team members updated. We have developed a simple candidate evaluation sheet to facilitate communication and consistency among team members.

Working together to establish a game plan for a candidate's visit is absolutely essential. The process described here assumes that candidates are able to visit our campus more than once; at times, limitations of time and geography have compelled us to condense candidate visits into one whirlwind of a day.

Screen carefully. Once recruitment efforts have begun in earnest and the letters of application roll in, the point person performs the initial screening of candidates. He separates the clearly unqualified from the excellent and potential candidates. We employ a three-number ranking system to assess a candidate's viability. Once we determine a candidate is not a match (a "3" in our system), we do not revisit the application once a response card is sent. Candidates receiving the highest ranking (a "1") go directly to the next stage of resume screening (in our case to divisional directors) to determine whether or not to invite them to visit our school. Middle-range candidates ("2"s), those who have potential but do not stand out immediately, are placed on hold for further consideration if the "1"s do not pan out.

When we screen resumes and letters, we look for several qualities beyond the candidate's explicit experience and qualifications. As many schools do, Far Hills places a high value on a teacher's technological proficiency. Therefore, a candidate who does not include an e-mail address on her resume is somewhat of a red flag for us. We also pay close attention to the candidate who has done her homework: She has taken the time to learn about the school and respond specifically to our program and the job description. What schools look for should, of course, be a reflection their mission.

The phone screening is more than just a call to arrange an interview. We take the time to get to know the candidate by posing simple, open-ended questions such as "What you led to us?" and "How did you get interested in teaching?" We consider how parents, who have regular phone conversations with teachers, would react to the candidate.

The first visit. Upon a candidate's arrival, the first person to greet her is the point person. We always begin the visit with a trip to our dining room, where our teachers gather informally for coffee and breakfast each morning. This gives the candidate a brief but intimate glimpse into the culture of the school. After an interview with the point person, we give each candidate a complete tour. We use the tour to learn about the candidate. We listen carefully for reactions to what she sees. Does the candidate simply observe when we visit a classroom or does she talk to the children? What is the candidate most impressed by on the tour—the facility or the people?

On a candidate's first visit to the school, the point person and at least one other member of our search team, usually a divisional director, are available for interviewing. We conduct thirty-minute individual interviews. Prior to the interviews, we coordinate questions among search team members to ensure that we are hitting all of the bases and not overwhelming a candidate with the same questions. Interview questions speak specifically to three different aspects of the job and the candidate: *technical, personal,* and *cultural* (see fig. 1). The best interviews are conversations: We ask questions that lead to the telling of stories. We listen for talk about children and learning. We ask the candidate what appeals to her about our school. We ask questions that will give us insight into how she will relate to the culture and mission of the school. After these initial interviews are completed, the point person informs the candidate about next steps and when she can expect to be contacted. At this time, we often speak candidly about salary ranges and benefits. There is no reason to be secretive about such information. In fact, we have found that candidates feel more at ease when such details are on the table prior to the second visit, when the stakes have suddenly become higher.

The second visit. A candidate who reaches the second interview has become a finalist. When we call her for a second interview, we ask her to share her impressions of the school. We listen for an emphasis on people. The point person then arranges for the candidate to spend an entire day at the school, meeting with every member of the search team and the head of school, observing classes, eating lunch with colleagues, and teaching a sample lesson. While some may view sample lessons as superficial and inauthentic ways by which to evaluate a candidate's teaching potential, we feel that they provide us with vital information that is difficult to uncover in any other venue. How well did the candidate prepare? We always suggest that the candidate e-mail the teacher whose class she will be teaching; did she make to effort to do so? How does she relate to the children? After the sample lesson, we informally debrief the candidate. We listen for enthusiasm and excitement about the lesson and a connection with the students.

References. After finalists have visited for the second time, the point person collects feedback from team members and arranges for the team to rank the finalists. The point person then begins to call references. We require a minimum of three references that are recent and professional. One reference must be from the candidate's current supervisor. If the candidate is from another independent school, we always make certain that the head of that school knows that the candidate is pursuing a position at our school. We look for references to verify our impressions of the candidate. We inquire about her working relationship with colleagues and the degree to which she executes professional responsibilities. Additionally, we try to determine the candidate's need for supervision, her willingness to take initiative, and her ability to be flexible and to accept criticism. Does she require guidance and "stroking" or does she respond best to autonomy? Such information often proves helpful in designing the candidate's induction process and personalizing her entry plan.

The offer and beyond. When we make an offer, we are careful not to pressure the candidate. We try to gauge her level of interest by asking how she feels about the offer, and we ask her to please communicate about any obstacles to her accepting the position. Time frames depend upon the situation, but we are often in a position to offer a candidate a few days to consider the offer. We always follow the phone call with an e-mail and formal letter that details the specifics of the offer. If timing is an issue with other candidates, we will call them to explain the situation. We feel that this is not only courteous, but it is another opportunity to represent our school in a professional light.

Evaluation and reflection are important components of any program, and the faculty search process is no different. If a candidate turns down our offer, it is critical for us to understand why. We have found that most candidates have been up-front during the process about any misgivings, so non-acceptances are minimized. Once all searches are completed, we step back and evaluate how we did. We track the total number of applicants received for each position and from what source the applications derived. We further record the number of interviews, hires, and offers made from each source, giving us compelling evidence about how to spend our resources for the next search.

While an effective search process for teachers is undoubtedly systematic, we try to never lose sight of the fact that it is, ultimately, a human process. It is about finding people, not filling positions. Accordingly, the process must always be flexible, humane, and inclusive. One of our greatest hopes is that, in the end, everyone involved in the search process will feel positive about it. It is only then that we feel we have truly accomplished our mission.

Fig. 1 Questions to Ask Teaching Candidates

Technical

What was the most challenging situation you've dealt with in the classroom?

Tell me about any leadership opportunities you have undertaken.

What committees have you served on?

Do you have experience with ____________? (guided reading, investigations math, phonics, etc.)

What will be your greatest challenge in this position?

Cultural

Tell me about a success story with a student.

A student tells you that other students are making fun of him and he doesn't know what to do. What do you tell him?

How would students/colleagues/parents describe you?

If I were to walk into your class, what would I see?

Personal

What do you do to relieve stress?
What are your hobbies?
What gives you the greatest satisfaction as a teacher?
How do you know when you are being a good teacher?
Do you use humor in your teaching? Why or why not?
Do you want your students to like you? Why?
How did you decide to become a teacher?
If you could write your own job description, what would it be?

Jay Underwood is director of curriculum and faculty development at Far Hills Country Day School in New Jersey. He has engaged in extensive research and collaborated with colleagues from other schools to recruit teachers and to promote independent schools.

Robert Berkman is assistant head of school at Far Hills Country Day School. He is a veteran adminstrator with extensive experience in hiring teachers of all grade levels and subject areas.

Creative Compensation[1]

By Peter Gow

A 1989 NAIS video identifies independent school teaching as a "Profession at Risk," with aging, underpaid, and under-recognized members drifting into retirement or off toward more remunerative and prestigious work. The video was intended as a wake-up call, a plea to administrators and boards of trustees to bring salaries and benefits into line with those of other professions, bluntly stating that "if [independent schools] want a faithful, productive workforce, they must pay for it." Fourteen years and the detonation of a whole arsenal of dot-bombs later, the outlook is a bit brighter. Although salaries still lag behind those of public school teachers—and, in real dollar terms, behind rising tuitions—they are, in general, no longer laughably small. And benefit packages, along with job security, now make independent school teaching at least a plausible option for young people looking for stimulating work. But even with schools paying more and to-die-for jobs in cool start-ups growing thin on the ground, the challenge of finding and keeping great teachers remains.

NAIS president Patrick F. Bassett has identified the signs of a "crisis in recruitment," and hiring, in the words of Jim Dunaway, dean of faculty at The Kinkaid School (TX), is no longer a matter of "if you're lucky, we'll allow you to break in with us. Recruitment is changing, and now you really need to sell your school." And "selling" employment, as schools across the nation are discovering, requires both investment and creativity. Along with innovative thinking in the obvious areas of compensation and benefits, schools are looking harder at how their programs and policies can continue to entice teachers of various ages and career stages. At the center of the issue, of course, lies the simple but enormous question: How can schools afford to hire and keep the very best teachers?

New Recruiting Strategies

One area of changing practice is the recruitment of new faculty. Many school websites now have sections specifically devoted to employment, and some provide significant amounts of information on school culture. Kinkaid goes further, offering detailed data on the cost of living and quality of life in Houston. The more information, the better, in Jim Dunaway's opinion, as the "kind of information prospective teachers want varies widely by age and experience." Northfield Mount Hermon School (MA) carries extensive employment information on its website, and also prints a brochure focusing on the nature of the school community—something that applicants "can hold on to and read over before they go to sleep," says Mary Pleasanton, director of recruitment.

While the major placement services continue to do land-office business, specialized organizations, such as Stratégenius or the National Employment Minority Network (NEMNET), that place traditionally underrepresented candidates are also growing. By soliciting applicants through such organizations and aggressively working people of color job fairs, a school can send a powerful message about the type of community it aspires to be. Advertising open positions in ethnic, gay-lesbian, or other minority-community publications can also telegraph the sincerity of a school's commitment to diversity. In time, such practices build school communities whose shared values can be compelling in attracting and keeping committed teachers. More than ever, publications and the interview process should communicate a school's values and culture. Applicants are savvy cultural consumers, and so what a school says about itself should match real experience. As Kinkaid's Dunaway puts it, "I want new teachers coming to me in a year and saying, 'You didn't lie to me.' "

Applicants want and need to understand what kind of a community they will be joining and to have a sense of who their peers and students will really be. "What attracts teachers," says Stuart Remensnyder, a former faculty member at The Loomis Chaffee School (CT), "are faculty members who feel great about their school." School visits should include informal meetings not only with students but with other teachers, especially teachers at similar stages in their own careers; such meetings can serve as a reality check against the impressions made by formal interviews and ivy-covered buildings.

Internships and Orientation Programs

A growing number of schools sponsor internship programs. In general, these come in two forms: first, low-budget, part-time employment arrangements that meet short-term needs and second, more elaborate programs designed to prepare recent college graduates for teaching careers. Shady Hill School (MA) and Hawken School (OH) partner with degree-granting graduate schools, while many other programs, like those at Wyoming Seminary (PA) or Mentoring at Punahou School (HI) are contained within the school. Although internship salaries tend to be low, benefits such as housing (at Punahou, in expensive Honolulu) or the availability of flat-grants toward further education (at Wyoming Seminary) sweeten the pot. David Davies, dean of Wyoming's upper school, says programs should give interns "a sensible introduction to teaching, with the hope that the interns will stay in teaching, either with us or at another independent school," and he estimates that three-fourths of Wyoming's former interns are working full-time in independent schools. Past Punahou intern Jennifer Darrah, now teaching in a Boston-area school, calls her experience "the perfect balance between independence and support." Internships build competence and professionalism that lead to successful and satisfying entry-level experiences—and, ideally, to long careers.

Schools can also ease new teachers' entry by taking advantage of comprehensive orientation programs such as the pre-service or fall workshops offered by many regional independent-school organizations. The New England New Teachers Seminar is a week-long boot camp in curriculum and classroom management and includes workshops on such topics as assessment, diversity, the art of coaching, dealing with student wellness concerns, and "Managing Your Life as a Teacher." Schools' own orientation programs increasingly focus not only on "administrivia" but also on school values and culture. The four-day "Progressive Education 101" workshop at Beaver Country Day School (MA), for example, focuses not only on cognitive theory, curriculum design, and equity issues but also on the role of faculty in carrying out the school's overall mission and strategic goals—as well as library procedures and book ordering.

Housing, Bonuses, and Other Special Compensation

Internships and orientation programs are all to the good, and, properly managed, are usually affordable, but there remains the much larger question of how even the most dedicated teachers can sustain a career without falling significantly behind the standard of living of non-teaching peers and, perhaps more acutely, their own students. Joan Lonergan, head of The Castilleja School (California), points out that "no one expects to have to take a vow of poverty in order to teach." In initiating Castilleja's attempt to address this problem three years ago, Lonergan put the issue directly to families: "Teachers do not want to be second-class citizens in an increasingly homogeneous, high-end community. No teacher wants to make less in a year than what some families spend on a car for their 16-year-old or for a February vacation." At Castilleja, in the heart of Silicon Valley, the teachers' economic distress had become desperate by 2000. Annual faculty attrition approached one-third, as housing costs—which reached as high at 70% of some faculty members' take-home pay—drove teachers from the community. "We weren't developing a core of master teachers who could commit emotionally to being at our school," Lonergan says. "It was a crisis."

Castilleja's solution was direct aid. "We wanted," Lonergan says, "to impact retention immediately." Lonergan and the school's board initiated a fast-track, highly focused fund-raising effort to implement the "Special Compensation Plan," a multimillion-dollar diminishing-endowment fund to be "invested conservatively and spent aggressively" in the form of $10,000 per annum bonuses over a three-year period for all faculty and staff members earning over $40,000 a year (lower-paid staff bonuses are 25% of annual salary). The bonus program was designed to provide maximum flexibility to teachers. With the variety of faculty "ages and stages," says Lonergan, "there was no way to meet everybody's needs [with a single benefit in kind]. We did not want to be paternalistic or lock people into a long-term relationship with the school through a mortgage program. We should not be deciding for people what their financial needs are." Having made other adjustments to Castilleja's benefits package (including an expanded sabbatical program) and course load, Lonergan reports that faculty attrition has dropped ("We're suddenly very attractive to a lot of candidates, as well") and faculty morale is "bar none. Faculty members are no longer second-class citizens in our community." A campaign is now under way to make the "bonus" program permanent.

Other schools have been forced to address similar cost-of-living issues. Punahou has a small number of housing units for rent to faculty or as accommodation, gratis, for interns. In the past two decades, Brunswick School, in pricey Greenwich, Connecticut, has acquired or built over thirty housing units that are made available to faculty at submarket rates, and the school is currently constructing ten more units. Headmaster Thomas W. Philip says that housing can be used as "an attraction tool" or internally "for retention or to reward senior or highly valued faculty." Since most housing is on or contiguous to the campus, the community feel of the school is also enhanced. As for raising the money to support the program, "It's the easiest ask," says Philip. "People know it's the way to get the best teachers for their children." Neighboring Greenwich Academy is now following suit.

In New York City, The Browning School has instituted, with the help of an E.E. Ford Foundation grant, an "Indebtedness Reduction Benefit" to relieve younger teachers of an often-dispiriting burden by helping them pay down student loans. "It's a great way to target a certain group for retention," says Headmaster Stephen M. Clement III. Although the program most often benefits newer teachers, Clement adds, established faculty recognize that "it is in everyone's interest to attract and retain the best teachers"; a generous professional development program shares out the wealth in other ways. Other schools, such as St. Paul's School (MD), offer interest-free loans to faculty in a similar effort to ease financial strains.

Although merit-pay schemes have met with little enthusiasm in independent schools, other bonus or bonus-like programs have succeeded. At Browning, a relatively new program, funded by an alumnus, makes up to $5,000 (after taxes) available each year to one faculty member—as early as the third year of teaching—as a direct grant, with the recipient determined by fellow teachers. At St. Paul's School, a similar program benefits four faculty members per year. More broad-based bonus programs, like those at Oak Mountain Academy (GA) or the "pay for performance" compensation plan in use at Rohan Woods School (MO), reduce perceptions of favoritism while raising both pay and morale. Says former Oak Mountain head John Meehl, now at Cape Fear Academy (NC), the bonus "made people feel good about the year they'd just had, and it provided a significant [$2,000] bump in the salary of some younger teachers."

Bonus programs reward exemplary professionalism, but professionalism can be cultivated and recognized in other ways. At the simple-and-inexpensive end of the scale is the public recognition of service—for longevity at various stages, for example, or for particular achievements in other areas. "It's another emotional hook to help keep good people," maintains Robert Hallett, executive director of the Edward E. Ford Foundation. Similarly, many schools "midwife" gifts from donors to teachers of cultural or sporting event tickets, museum memberships or passes, and financial planning or other pro bono personal services, a practice that can strengthen family-faculty partnership bonds. "People still feel called to this profession," Hallett says, "and they want to remain in it. Schools need to be imaginative and look for ways that don't cost much to help them do so."

Endowed Chairs and Master Teachers

At the high end of the reward scale lie endowed chair or "master teacher" programs. Frank Jones, upper-school head at Holland Hall School (OK), has written extensively (most recently a doctoral dissertation) on such programs, which he says can "create enticing goals for outstanding young teachers, possibilities whereby they can realize, through dedication and hard work, the personal fulfillment, recognition, and financial reward to which we all aspire in our professional lives." The model that Jones favors involves the creation of endowed chairs to offset significant portions of the salary of true "master teachers," whose presence as mentors and role models can have a school-wide impact on the quality of teaching. Jones's own experience at one school with an extensive endowed chair and master teacher program showed him "the power of this program. It put the school in the catbird seat as far as retaining the best teachers, and it was also a big plus in overcoming some geographical limitations in recruitment." Perhaps best of all, it provided great teachers with a financial incentive to remain in the classroom and not feel compelled to "take the soup"—to give up teaching for the material rewards of administration.

Professional Development

Between public recognition ceremonies and endowed chairs lies professional development, a potent and probably underutilized recruitment and retention tool. Here, too, schools can maximize impact at little or no cost by encouraging teachers to apply for such high-prestige, funded programs as Fulbright and Klingenstein fellowships and National Endowment summer seminars, or to present at major workshops and conferences. Some schools, like Hawken, Browning, and Collegiate School (New York), designate an amount of money per teacher that can be spent on individual professional development and/or cultural enrichment, while other schools target professional development on school-wide goals. In some cases, schools have been successful in situating high-value professional development resources on their own campuses. Holland Hall's Kistler-Gilliland Center for the Advancement of Learning, for example, supports workshops and speaker programs for Holland Hall faculty as well as for parents and the larger Tulsa community. "It creates a sense of professionalism and a climate of professional development for faculty," says assistant head Robert Bryan, "and it also creates a sense of partnership with parents"—a sentiment echoed by several people interviewed for this article, who noted that a positive family-faculty atmosphere, based on the recognition of faculty professionalism, can itself be highly significant in teacher retention. Indeed, the building of the parent-teacher relationship is an extension of a broader effort in numerous schools to retain teachers by developing a collegial environment—looking at the total work situation to identify ways of making the adult experience in schools more meaningful, more satisfying, and, ultimately, more productive.

Quality Schools

Although educators can be reluctant to name it, another factor in faculty retention can be the enhanced self-esteem some teachers take in identifying themselves with an institution. Tradition and prestige can play a major part in this phenomenon, but so, too, can other factors. A distinctive school mission, for example, may inspire great loyalty among faculty, and teachers are not immune from the pleasures of basking in the reflected glory of unique or high-profile programs. Better still, schools can encourage individual entrepreneurial spirit and convert creative energy—even professional restiveness, perhaps—into successful practice. By supporting and celebrating initiative, schools can profit (and add to their own institutional prestige) by the synergy that a cadre of dedicated and energized teachers can create. The list of projects funded by the E.E. Ford Foundation (www.eeford.org/Pages/projects.html) is a testament to the potential of this synergy.

Conclusion

While highly funded programs can be very effective tools in recruiting and retaining teachers, the recent experience of Massachusetts, where $20,000 signing bonuses have had only mixed success in helping stabilize the public-school teacher population, shows that the advantage money confers is by no means absolute. Schools must become increasingly creative in developing practices and policies to attract and support teachers in every phase of their careers. Reflecting traditional school needs as well as the evolving expectations of members of the workforce, current best practices are focusing as much on the intangible aspects of job satisfaction as on the material conditions of employment. A teacher whose career began at a large boarding school listed all the things that the school had done to encourage and validate his work as a starting teacher: professional development, meaningful committee assignments, choice of classes taught, encouragement of his ideas. "In all," he says, by offering him what he needed most at the early stages of his career, "the school got thirteen years out of a young man who had only considered dabbling for a year or two." While money does talk, it is the entire quality of the work experience that ultimately tells a teacher whether to stay or go.

Notes

[1] "Creative Compensation" originally appeared as "Creative Compensation: What It Takes to Keep Good Teachers Today" in *Independent School* (Vol. 62, No. 3), 28–34. It is reprinted with permission from the NAIS.

Peter Gow was born and raised in the independent school world, and he is entering his fourth decade as a teacher and administrator. Passionately concerned with helping schools recruit and retain the best teachers, he is currently expanding the article included here into a book on best practices and teachers' stories. He is the academic dean at Beaver Country Day School.

Teaching Intern Programs

by David L. Davies

"Experentia docet." *Experience teaches*. There. Mrs. Mulhern, my ninth-grade Latin teacher, would be so pleased that I used a Latin phrase to open a piece of writing.

The expression is appropriate from a variety of perspectives when considering programs designed to introduce teachers new to independent schools and to the profession of teaching. Teaching Intern Programs, Teaching Fellowships—regardless of the name—these programs that bring enthusiastic, bright, young people into the work that we love mutually benefit the schools and the interns. Interns teach students, experienced faculty teach the interns, and, perhaps surprisingly, the interns teach the seasoned veterans.

My experience with an intern program comes from my years as dean of the Upper School at Wyoming Seminary College Preparatory School in Pennsylvania, where we created a program in 1991 that continues to flourish some twelve years later. The impetus for the program came from Jere Packard, whose tenure as President began the previous year. Shortly after taking office, he observed that our faculty was "quite long in the tooth." My response was that there were only three ways to alter the experience profile: fire seasoned pros, expand the school, or hire interns. The first was undesirable and the second unlikely in the short run, so we were left with option three. The Teaching Intern Program at Wyoming Seminary has introduced nearly forty individuals to the independent school teaching profession, and I am pleased that most have continued to teach after their internship experience.

Our goal was twofold: to provide the school with well-educated young professionals who would bring enthusiasm, energy, and new ideas; and to provide the interns with a more sensible introduction to the profession than many of us experienced when we were "thrown to the lions" as full-time teachers fresh out of college.

From the school's viewpoint, the rationale for hiring freshly minted baccalaureate degree-holders is clear. As the graying of independent school faculties continues and the projected teacher shortage looms, it is essential that we attract teachers who will have developed experience by the time the expected large-scale retirements occur. Although seasoned professionals are a staple of independent school faculties, the presence of younger role models for our students creates an entirely new and different dimension to the student/teacher relationship. For boarding schools committed to the "triple threat"—teacher, coach, dorm parent—we find more and more of our veteran teachers struggling with the lifestyle. Younger teachers bring enthusiasm for the multiple tasks that schools need to cover.

Schools with intern programs have an opportunity to "audition" prospective full-time teachers without the implied tenure that often accompanies a "permanent" hire. Although in many schools the majority of interns serve only their one-year term, unless a school's policy prohibits retaining participants in these programs, the possibility of keeping an outstanding intern for an appropriate full-time opening increases the odds of a successful match when compared to the vagaries of the open hiring process.

Interns also provide mentoring opportunities for experienced faculty. While the benefit of a constructive mentor/intern relationship to the intern is obvious, the relationship can be salutary for the mentor as well. Our seasoned pros may be excellent teachers intuitively, but explaining one's craft to a novice forces the teacher to reflect on his/her practice in ways many have not done in years. Further, a rookie teacher can raise some of the tough questions that a colleague might wonder but elect not to ask for political reasons. (Experentia docet—in both directions.)

Finally (and I have deliberately saved this reason for last, because I believe that this should not be the driving factor behind instituting an internship program), interns provide a source of less-costly person-power that can enable schools to weather the current fiscal pressures. However, if the perceived benefits to the interns—such as great mentoring, opportunities to grow personally and professionally, and a reasonable expectation of a full-time position in an independent school the following year—are few or absent, the program will die because of a lack of enthusiastic recommendations to prospective interns from the current year's group.

Benefits to the intern vary depending on the nature of the program. Most obviously, intern programs provide professional opportunities to individuals without full-time experience. If the school does not schedule the intern with full-time responsibilities, he/she will have the luxury that most of us did not in our entry-level position: time. Interns can actually prepare thoroughly for their two or three courses. They can visit other teachers' classrooms, both in their own department and in other disciplines, to observe master teachers at work. They will also have time to search for their subsequent position and visit other schools to interview without the disruption a school experiences when a teacher carrying four or five courses is absent.

Although salaries are lower for internships than for full-time positions, especially in boarding schools that provide an apartment and meals, an intern can actually fare better financially than a rookie full-time teacher living in a high-cost-of-living area. Finally, there is a real psychological benefit from the one-year commitment. Many college graduates are uncertain about whether teaching is their life's work. There is some comfort from the defined term of the internship, and if either the specific school or the profession in general is not a match, there is less trauma involved in walking away after the year.

A well-constructed intern program should enable the intern to teach approximately a half-load in his/her subject area. There is little value to having interns spend extensive time observing or aiding; after all, the interns have as much training and experience as many of us in our first year. Schools should not dump undesirable duties such as detention supervision, weekend campus monitoring, or driving duty exclusively on interns. Whether a school employs a structured mentoring program or not, interns should be introduced to and paired with experienced colleagues. I favor a multiple mentor approach, including a colleague who is also teaching some sections of the course(s) the intern teaches, coaches or advisors in each of the activities the intern supervises, and a dorm mentor in the case of boarding schools. There should be an extensive orientation program and continuing conversations throughout the year. Finally, the school should provide career counseling and help the intern with the job search process.

Although the program has been extremely successful, there are numerous pitfalls to avoid. I adopted a mantra early in the program: "Don't use the 'I' word." In other words, there is no benefit to be gained from designating the interns as anything but regular faculty, albeit with reduced loads. Students need to have confidence in their teachers, and they should not be allowed to think of interns as anything less than their other teachers. If a separate designation is used, parents will tend to think of interns as student-teachers, aides, or practice teachers.

Another problem lies with the number of interns in relation to the overall size of the faculty. There is a critical mass in a department or residence hall beyond which the benefit of interns diminishes. This number varies with the size of the school, department, or dorm. In many schools, two interns in a department would be the upper limit. If there is a likelihood of retaining one intern in a department the following year, having two interns vying for the one spot can resemble the "steel cage match" in professional wrestling and lead to hard feelings on the part of the intern not chosen. In a dorm, the number of interns should be lower than the number of experienced dorm parents. When the interns outnumber the veterans, transmitting the culture and ethos of the dorm is difficult.

Finally, although there are internship programs in schools with primary divisions, the self-contained nature of many elementary classrooms makes intern programs there risky, since in many schools the students' regular teacher is the main adult contact throughout the school day. Should an intern turn out not to be strong at the secondary or middle school level, he/she might represent only one-fifth or one-sixth of a student's school time. On the other hand, a weak intern teaching the majority of a self-contained class would be a nightmare.

A teaching internship/fellowship program can be a wonderful avenue for recent college graduates to enter the profession, or a source of cheap labor through which schools dump undesirable duties on young people. Simply hiring recent college graduates and thrusting them into the fray is a recipe for failure. A well-designed program requires planning and effort if it is to benefit the school and the intern.

Dave Davies created the teaching intern program in 1991 at Wyoming Seminary College Preparatory School in Kingston, PA. In 2003, Dave became the founding upper school head at Parish Episcopal School in Dallas, TX.

The Job Share: A Win-Win Proposition

By Kate Windsor

As educators, we would certainly all agree that our work in independent schools is focused on meeting the needs of children and families. However, I have more than once found myself in educational institutions with employment policies and procedures that are not supportive of the needs of faculty and staff with families. In my role as the head of school of The Sage School, I have attempted to realign the employment policies to better reflect the needs of working people with families. What began as an initiative to support working parents has 1) resulted in benefits to all of our employees, 2) directly enhanced the academic program we deliver, and 3) led us to create a job-share model where none existed before.

It is important for educators to recognize, through our story, that it is possible to make fundamental employment changes even within the confines of a limited budget. The Sage School is a small school (approx. 140 students) with a budget funded almost exclusively by tuition. When I came to The Sage School, the maternity leave policy consisted of two weeks' unpaid leave for the birth of a child. This unrealistic policy meant that virtually all faculty and staff who became pregnant left the school. As a small, young school with a small, mostly young group of employees, this meant that we were suffering significant and costly attrition. The first step was to convey to the Board of Trustees that, rather than thinking we could not afford a paid maternity leave, we needed to address the fact that we could not afford *not* to have a paid maternity leave. This fact was demonstrated by pointing out the significant costs related to the attrition and the subsequent recruitment of faculty and staff. Without much delay, we were able to implement a parental leave benefit, which was funded primarily through short-term disability insurance. The cost of the short-term disability was minimal and the exposure for the other portion of the parental leave costs was also minimal. In the end, employees acquired both a parental leave benefit and a short-term disability benefit, which resulted in increased commitment to the institution rather than the bitterness that resulted from the two-week leave. We were able to solve two problems with one solution.

The implementation of a viable parental leave policy became intimately connected with the next step in our organizational evolution—the job share—when, not long after the maternity leave issue was resolved, our music instructor came to me to say that she was pregnant. When we met to discuss her request for parental leave, she also stated that she would like not only to take the eight weeks to which she was entitled under the terms of employment, but that she would also like to work part-time when she returned. My first reaction to her request was ambivalence. Clearly, this teacher was interested in continuing her work at the school, and there was no doubt that I was interested in having her continue. However, I had worked hard to eliminate part-time positions, not least because I felt that they often became, in practice, full-time positions with part-time pay. Specifically, in my experience, part-time employees in independent schools were easily burnt out; moreover, they could be hard to supervise and schedule. Nevertheless, I agreed to begin a search for a music teacher who would be willing to cover the parental leave full-time, followed by a part-time teaching position for the conclusion of the year. To my surprise, even with quite a bit of lead time, we were not able to find a suitable candidate to fill the position. I was in a quandary. I knew that I would lose her expertise if I did not accommodate the teacher's request for part-time status. Moreover, in this particular case, she was deeply involved in the development and implementation of a new music program, and her departure would possibly create a significant curricular setback that we could not afford.

As the spring turned into summer, I became increasingly concerned. The dilemma was even more complicated by the fact that I, too, would be away in the fall for parental leave as I welcomed our second child. The hire needed to be made and time was running short. Eventually, I decided that perhaps we would need to abandon the original concept of hiring a music teacher who would cover the leave and continue on a part-time basis. We would focus, instead, on finding a substitute who would be both qualified and available to cover the leave. The teacher who emerged was a woman with extensive experience in dance and drama. She had taught dance and drama in our summer enrichment program, and had also worked as an assistant teacher in our prime (early elementary) division, but had left that full-time position at the end of the prior school year in order to pursue more actively her real passion for the arts.

Although I had no idea how she might respond to returning to the school in a substitute capacity, I approached her about the temporary position. She was intrigued, but made it very clear that she was not a music teacher and could not teach a traditional music program. I reassured her that I was not asking her to teach music, but rather asking her to provide a contained unit on dance and drama: I had decided to offer students a single unit on dance and drama during the music teacher's parental leave period, with the intention to return to the traditional music program.

The next step, and perhaps the turning point in my thinking and ultimately the move to a job share, came when I discussed the plan with the music teacher. Prior to meeting with her, I feared that her response would be dismissive or defensive. Would she feel vulnerable at the thought of bringing in a teacher who would be introducing a whole new content area? Would she resent the fact that her curriculum would be interrupted and thus she would not be able to complete her planned objectives for the year?

I was pleasantly surprised by her response and what later became the genesis of our performing arts program and the job share arrangement between these two professionals with different areas of expertise. The music teacher, now quite pregnant, was first and foremost relieved that, finally, I had a viable teaching candidate. Instead of becoming territorial, she began to think more globally about how she and the dance teacher might be able to create an integrated performing arts unit that might be appropriate not just for the maternity leave but rather for the entire school year. This meant that once the maternity leave was over, we could create a job share based on two different sets of expertise, instead of dividing the music classes in half and having two part-time teachers, each with half of the sections for instruction.

The job share differs from dividing a full-time position into two half-time positions in the following ways:

- In a job share, the two teachers each work with all of the students, rather than each working with half of the students.
- The teachers work together to plan and implement the learning objectives for the year.
- The teachers produce one curriculum, one set of assessments, and one set of progress reports.
- The collaboration results in two professionals contributing to the outcomes rather than just one.

We learned several important lessons from our first year of a job share at The Sage School. First and foremost, it was a huge success. Students, parents, and other faculty members raved about the new "Performing Arts Program." Second, we recognized that constant communication between the teachers who are job sharing is critical to the success of the overall effort. Third, although it is not necessary for the teachers to have the same style with respect to instruction, their styles must complement each other, and there must be mutual respect between the two teachers and their areas of expertise. The scheduling was not as hard as we had expected. The job share features actually provided more options for scheduling than would a single teacher. Finally, we did not struggle with finding substitutes or see interruptions in the course of study during the year due to teacher absences, primarily because the coordinating teachers typically covered for each other.

The progress reports were the most difficult component to "share" and finalize. After much discussion about progress report strategies, we decided to have each teacher write about their area of expertise. The student comment section included a piece written by the music teacher about the student's progress in music and a piece by the dance teacher about the student's progress in dance. On the one hand, I felt that this methodology respected the two very different disciplines involved in the program. On the other hand, I felt that the separate nature of the comments felt somewhat disjointed, particularly since the classes in the performing arts program were, in reality, much more integrated—a fact that was not necessarily revealed in the comments.

The winter and spring concerts became the venue for sharing with the entire school community the work that was done in the performing arts class. What was once a somewhat repetitious showing of singing with occasional instrumental solos became a schoolwide event with dancing, singing, acting, and beautiful costumes and sets. Moreover, the visual arts teacher was drawn into the mix. She saw opportunities for integration through the sets and costuming. By the end of the year, the arts department (performing and visual arts) had made a commitment to fully integrate their programs and was granted stipends for summer work.

Thanks to this pioneering job share effort, The Sage School will look at job sharing differently in the future. First and foremost, instead of thinking about job sharing as a solution for particular situations like the one described above, we will consider it for its own merit. Second, based on last year's job-share experience, any teachers with job shares from this point forward will have one day of overlap. As a consequence, the combined job share position will now exceed that of one full-time employee, but the rewards are worth it: Not only will the job-sharing teachers have common planning time, but they will have opportunities to team teach, observe each other teaching, and communicate face to face—none of which happens when the schedule does not have any overlap. Third, we will reconfigure the progress report to better reflect and integrate the total experience of the students in the performing arts program. Fourth, we will make sure that, in situations where we would typically allocate one resource per teacher, we duplicate for job sharers. (For example, the two performing arts teachers shared a single e-mail address, which was ineffective and confusing.)

The performing arts program has now formally replaced our traditional music program, and we are continuing with the job share in this curriculum area. Something that evolved from a desperate attempt to cover a parental leave has allowed us to provide more depth of content and experience for our students in the arts. The music teacher is grateful for the flexibility that the job share has allowed. She now admits that if she had not been able to work a reduced schedule she would likely have relinquished her duties altogether. Instead, she feels empowered by being able to continue with her professional work and care for her baby daughter. I believe that she is modeling for our female students that it is possible, and rewarding, to blend being a new mother with a professional commitment.

Both teachers feel that their teaching experiences are richer than they would have been if their positions were configured around a part-time employee model rather than the job-sharing model. In the end, they feel that they are able to achieve ambitious goals with the students and throughout the school, while at the same time they feel as though they are highly valued, in ways that part-time teachers unfortunately all too often are not.

One final note for school leaders: Job sharing can utilize two different sets of talents and expertise, as in the case just described, or it can be applied to one overall set of responsibilities. In the latter case—for example, a job share for the position of a science teacher in the upper elementary division—I would still recommend a day of overlap, primarily to plan and communicate, but also to optimize implementation of curriculum aspects that feature student sub-groupings with close teacher supervision. (This sub-grouping approach is a staple of our educational program.) In the case of job shares in which responsibilities directly overlap, whether among teachers or administrators, an emphasis on common goals, regular communication mechanisms, and agreed-upon procedures is paramount.

As the quality-of-life equation becomes ever more complex for families in today's world, the benefits of job sharing become potentially more attractive than ever. I encourage all family-friendly schools to think about the possibility of job shares and their impact not only on faculty and administrative job satisfaction, retention and overall costs, but on the achievement of institutional and curricular objectives.

Katherine Windsor is the graduate of an independent school. Directly from college she returned to prep school to teach history, coach women's lacrosse, and serve as the director of residential life before accepting her current position as head of The Sage School.

Endowed Teaching Chairs at Independent Schools

By Frank G. K. Jones, Ed.D.

How Can Endowed Teaching Chairs Benefit a School?

The purpose of establishing endowed teaching chairs at independent schools is to address a significant need, the need to recruit and retain independent school faculty of exceptional talent, training, and performance. This need has become more acute in recent years for several reasons, all of which tend to revolve around the issue of money.

The school-aged population in the United States is surging and likely will increase by 10% in the first decade of the twenty-first century. At the same time, there is a public demand for lower student-teacher ratios in public schools and for higher standards and better teachers. Because of the projected retirements from the teaching ranks, the small number of college graduates entering the teaching profession, and the 13% average attrition rate of those who do, the U.S. Department of Education has projected that public school districts will need to hire over two million teachers in the decade between 2001 and 2011 to meet the requirements of anticipated student enrollments (*NCES, October 2002*). This demand for new teachers will have an impact upon recruitment and retention of faculty at independent as well as public schools, for in many instances non-public and public schools will be competing for the same limited labor supply. Many public school districts are attempting to attract and retain teachers by offering signing bonuses, higher salaries, and better benefits. Such financial inducements put pressure on independent schools to remain competitive.

One apparent solution to this teacher shortage for independent schools is simply to raise tuition to a level at which schools can pay highly competitive salaries, and therefore can attract the teachers they prefer to hire. However, just as public schools are restricted in what they can pay their teachers by limited tax revenues, so most independent schools, even the elite independent schools that are in high demand and have waiting lists, are constrained in what they can pay teachers by what they can charge in tuition and fees. In fact, independent schools are limited by five factors, all of which must be kept in balance when a board of trustees determines tuition:

- First, independent schools must compensate the faculty at a level that will attract and retain the teachers they want to hire. If salaries are not sufficiently competitive, teachers will leave. In this computation, a school must also consider whether or not it will be adding or deleting any positions.

- Second, independent schools must maintain a low student/teacher ratio (approximately 9:1) to ensure a competitive market advantage. Individualized attention and the nurturing of a student's personal, social, and intellectual growth are reasons many families choose independent schools. A higher ratio entails hiring fewer teachers, thus reducing costs, but in raising the ratio the school loses a competitive edge in the marketplace. Third, independent schools must provide financial aid to expand access to more families and to improve student quality by making admission available to a wider range of students. Full-pay students are not always the strongest students, and the strongest students may need financial assistance. Some schools provide financial aid from designated endowment income, but many grant it through tuition discounts, an expense that must be funded by full-pay students or gifts to the school.
- Fourth, independent schools must keep tuition affordable. Few schools charge in tuition what it actually costs to educate a child, so all students receive a subsidy that must be made up through endowment income or gifts to the school such as the annual fund campaign. Increases in tuition reduce the number who can afford to enroll.
- Fifth, independent schools must consider any expenses, whether for capital items or for operations, that will not be covered by additional sources of income such as capital campaigns or fund-raising events.

Accordingly, independent schools cannot solve the problem of teacher compensation by considering tuition increases in a vacuum. Other factors complicate the issue. Nevertheless, in the decade between 1992 and 2002, median tuition at independent day schools, adjusted for inflation, did increase by 38% while in the same period the median teacher salary, adjusted for inflation, grew by just 11% (*NAIS Stats-on-line 2001–02).* What happened to the additional income? One explanation lies in the fact that during the same ten years, faculty and staff at these schools increased nearly 32%. Instructional support personnel alone—tutors, school psychologists, and learning specialists—increased by 53.5%. In addition, the introduction and expansion of technological resources, important both in teaching children and in marketing the school, required additional instructors and support staff. Thus, the data suggest that the tuition increases during this decade were used for purposes other than to compensate the faculty at a level commensurate with the higher level of revenue.

Although raising tuition is problematic, increasing faculty salaries to competitive levels is critical to independent schools, particularly small ones that pay significantly below their public-school counterparts. Annual teacher attrition at larger independent schools (over 600 students) runs about 10% a year. Smaller independent schools (under 300 students) lose many more, about 25% each year, probably because their salaries and benefits are well below market rates (*NAIS/NBOA Independent Schools Financing Symposium Summary Report, November 2002*).

Data from *Private Schools: A Brief Portrait* included in *Findings from the Condition of Education, 2002,* published by the National Center for Education Statistics, indicate that

> private-school teachers were more likely than public-school teachers to 'strongly agree' that they were generally satisfied with teaching at their school (66% versus 54%). . . . In four areas of school policy linked closely with teaching—establishing curriculum, setting student performance standards, setting discipline policy, and evaluating teachers—the sector differences were substantial.

Yet, if private-school teachers are so positive about their working conditions, why in the years under review was their attrition rate nearly twice that of their public-school counterparts? The most apparent answer is money.

How Do Endowed Teaching Chairs Provide Higher Salaries for Faculty?

Limited in their ability to raise tuition to the level required for significantly higher teacher salaries, some independent schools have addressed the problem of attracting and retaining outstanding faculty by establishing endowments either to supplement or to support entirely increased compensation for teachers. Borrowing the concept from universities, these schools have established endowed teaching chairs. The endowed teaching chair creates a career stage, in some schools designated "master teacher," that seeks to reward inspiring teachers *for their teaching*. By honoring these individuals with the title of the endowed chair and by compensating them at a higher level financially, a school makes a statement and demonstrates a value: Teaching and learning are the most important tasks that go on within these walls, and therefore our most accomplished teachers are worthy of our highest esteem. They are also worthy of salaries commensurate with that esteem.

Detractors have argued that creating a special category of teacher undercuts collegiality and encourages professional jealousy. Certainly there is a risk of these reactions among a faculty when endowed teaching chairs are introduced and chair holders are appointed. Distinctions that heretofore were only implicit become explicit. By according certain members of the faculty a prestigious title and awarding them more money, the differences in teaching performance that previously may have been only privately acknowledged among colleagues are now formalized and proclaimed publicly. Recruiting accomplished teachers from outside the existing faculty and appointing them to endowed teaching chairs can also ignite resentment. The typical argument made is that many on the current faculty have labored long and hard in the vineyard, and therefore they ought to be the first to be rewarded with appointments to endowed chairs. Some schools appoint only internal candidates to teaching chairs, and longevity of service to the school is an important criterion in selection. Some schools try to avoid collegial controversy by rotating the chair appointments on three-year or five-year intervals. Other schools consider both internal and external candidates, taking the position that there may well be outstanding teachers on the existing faculty who should be considered. However, the endowed teaching chairs are not simply rewards for longevity of service; they are recognition for exemplary teaching.

The use of income from the endowment that supports the faculty chair also varies from school to school. In some instances, where the corpus of the endowment approaches

$2 million, the income—usually 5% of a three-year rolling average of the value of the endowment—pays the entire salary and benefits of the chair holder. Any residue is added to the corpus to protect against inflation. This arrangement relieves the operating budget, so funds that would have been used to pay the master teacher can be "blocked out" and used to enhance the salaries of five or six other teachers in a significant way. Some schools cap each endowed chair at a designated level such as $750,000, and any excess accumulation in the corpus is redirected to begin another endowed chair. The chair holder is paid a stipend of $5,000 from the income of the chair's endowment in addition to his regular salary, paid from the operating budget. The remainder of the income from the chair is added to the instructional budget to support the salaries of all other teachers. Accordingly, faculty members have the impression that all teachers benefit to some degree from the endowed chairs. Other schools use the endowed chairs to support general operations. The chair holder receives a modest stipend of $1,500 that supplements his salary, paid from the operating budget, but the bulk of the income from the chair's endowment can be used to pay utility bills as well as teachers' salaries. This practice allows funds to be diverted from the instructional line item, so it is less reliable than the previous examples in ensuring a significant enhancement in teacher compensation.

Funding of Endowed Teaching Chairs

Clearly a critical factor in initiating a program of endowed teaching chairs is generating the endowed funds to support the chairs. One may well advise a school to go out and raise endowment dollars for faculty salaries, but what is the feasibility and likelihood that independent schools can attract the funds necessary to endow the chairs? Actually, the prospects are good. Despite the economic fluctuations of the past decade, philanthropy for independent schools has been strong, particularly for capital projects and endowment. In her study for NAIS, *Schools and the Quest for Philanthropy,* Tracy Savage compares philanthropic giving to independent schools from the period 1991–96 with the period 1997–2002 and finds that, despite some economic turbulence, independent schools not only have been able to raise large sums of money for both capital projects and endowment but also have been able to increase significantly the percentage amount of dollars raised.

Another finding of the Savage study is that the fundraising experience in independent schools mirrors, five to fifteen years later, the fundraising history in private colleges and universities. Accordingly, independent schools are now finding that donors are "significantly more sophisticated about fundraising than they were twenty years ago," and that the "number of 'major gift' donors who are young (and entrepreneurial) has increased markedly." These two observations may explain why independent schools, like private colleges and universities before them, are seeing a decline in unrestricted gifts and an increase in gifts restricted for specific purposes.[1] The rise in restricted giving is a trend that can help funnel major gifts to specific targets, targets that are priorities for the donors and the school. Those donors interested in supporting teachers' salaries or in enhancing faculty quality can be focused on endowing a teaching chair. Consequently, the teaching chair not only becomes the means to recruit and retain excellent faculty, but also the tool by which the endowment to support the faculty, can be raised.

To raise the necessary funds for an endowed chair will require a commitment by the leadership of the school to the primacy of classroom instruction and a dedication to compensating outstanding teachers at a sufficiently high level so that they will want to remain in the classroom. Some of the points that the head of school can make when soliciting gifts for an endowed teaching chair are as follows:

- Funds contributed for a teaching chair will have a direct impact on the quality of education students receive.
- By committing endowment dollars to faculty compensation, the school makes a statement that it highly values the quality of classroom teaching.
- The endowed position will be perpetual and therefore will benefit hundreds of students for many generations.
- The endowment income used to pay the chair holder will free up other dollars in the instructional budget, designated as "blocked-out" funds, to increase the salaries of other teachers on the faculty.
- An endowed chair affords a major donor a naming opportunity through which the donor may honor himself or others.
- The increase in endowment helps to put the school on a sounder financial footing by increasing its tangible assets.

How Have Endowed Chairs Performed at Independent Schools?

In a recent study at independent schools where endowed teaching chairs have been in place for at least 15 years, faculty identified problems and concerns as well as advantages with these programs.[2] The principal misgiving among those voicing concern is that endowed teaching chairs create a tiered system within the faculty that can undercut morale and threaten collegiality. This stratification may exist in any case between beginning or mid-career teachers and their older, more experienced colleagues, but the awarding of chairs, especially to external candidates, has the potential of sowing dissent among those veteran teachers who are eligible for appointment to chairs and do not receive one. There is also the prospect of disgruntlement between those departments or divisions that have a chair—in some cases several chairs—and those that have none. As one teacher said, "It's perceived by some departments [without a chair appointment] that we are the redheaded stepchild here." While there is this undercurrent of concern for morale and collegiality, the disquiet was expressed most strongly by those with administrative responsibilities rather than by the classroom teachers, who, one would think, were most directly affected. What seems to mute the potential discord is the recognized competence and/or commitment of the chair holders and the sensitivity of those teachers to the feelings of their non-titled colleagues.

That endowed chairs create a special category of teacher is an issue. A corollary to this issue is the concern, as one teacher put it, for all those "amazingly good teachers who labor in anonymity in the trenches, especially in the middle school" and do not receive recognition comparable to that of a master-teacher chair holder. One would like to do more to show appreciation for such teachers, but one cannot make everyone a master teacher or "master teacher" no longer has any meaning. What one can do, however, is to reward those deserving teachers financially at a significantly higher level by restricting the use of the blocked-out funds in the instructional budget to faculty salaries. Some schools do this; others do not. As the CFO at one boarding school affirmed, the income from the endowed chairs pays the $1,500 stipend each chair holder receives, but "the bulk of the earnings go toward running the school." One part of the "running of the school" is faculty salaries, so in an indirect way endowment income from the chairs does support faculty salaries, but the income is not restricted to that purpose, so the money can be used for other purposes as well. Unless there is a strong commitment by the head of school to improving faculty salaries, income from the endowed chairs could be used to replace a boiler or put a new roof on a building instead of paying teachers. Despite the endowed chairs, salaries at this particular boarding school, based on 2001–02 data, were not highly competitive among the other nine schools in its association, suggesting that the commitment to faculty compensation was restrained.

Another potential source of resentment among the faculty is the recruitment of endowed chair holders from outside the school. Yet, when asked, "Are the master teachers the best teachers in the school?" faculty members at schools that appointed external candidates overwhelmingly acknowledged that, in their perception, they were. Some qualified their statements and said the master teachers were "among the best teachers in the school," but none denied that they were in the top echelon of the classroom teachers. In each case, the selection process had been done carefully, and the master teachers lived up to expectations. Conversely, at some schools where all appointments were from among internal candidates, several knowledgeable respondents were firm in their assertions that not all the chair holders were among the best teachers in the school. There was a consensus that these chairs, largely honorific, were frequently a reward for longevity of service rather than for exemplary teaching. Moreover, the criteria for selection were idiosyncratic and some were awarded to faculty with administrative responsibilities. This practice has had a depressing effect upon those who believe the chairs should honor the strongest teachers. Setting forth clear criteria for master teachers and searching both within and without the school's own ranks for candidates seem to be the preferred procedures for appointing faculty to endowed chairs.

Understandably the endowed teaching chairs do not act as much of an incentive to younger teachers to stay in teaching when there are just a few chairs at each school, and the appointments are typically held for many years. The fact that one must compete against external candidates is also an impediment. However, indirectly the endowed chairs may advance the goal of attracting and retaining inspiring teachers because the endowments allow schools to increase the median salary for the whole faculty. Of course, continuing to add endowed chairs will increase the opportunities for all teachers either to hold a chair or to benefit from the blocked-out funds, so long as those funds are restricted to faculty compensation. Nevertheless, the beginning teachers who were interviewed do not see endowed teaching chairs as an alternative career path that could serve to keep them in teaching.

One goal of several endowed-chair programs is to have the chair holders mentor their younger colleagues, particularly teachers new to teaching. This initiative has had limited success, but the problem seems to be one that the heads of school can correct by formalizing the arrangement between the mentor and his charge with explicit assignments and obligations. If, as they grow older, master teachers yearn to turn over coaching assignments to their younger colleagues, mentoring seems to be an appropriate alternative for these experienced teachers. Formalizing the arrangement would reduce the anxiety of the less experienced teacher about approaching a "master teacher," and it would dispense with the concern of the more experienced teacher about imposing himself or his views on his younger colleague.

Despite expressing concern for certain features of the endowed teaching chairs, overwhelmingly the respondents at the schools surveyed saw more advantages in the programs than disadvantages and wanted to see the concept expanded and improved. Teachers recognized that endowed teaching chairs provide an attractive compensation package and professional prestige for the teacher selected. They also understood that income from the endowments enhanced the operating budget so that other teachers could be compensated at a higher level. The chairs essentially created "a bigger bag of money." Endowed chairs were also cited as a means to recruit and retain teachers for positions difficult to fill, or to bring them to a geographical location that was not in itself compelling. Using the chairs to recruit outstanding teachers improved the quality of the faculty and thus the reputation of the school. The chair holders are seen as impact players that elevate the performance of their colleagues as well, and potentially they can be very good mentors for less experienced teachers. Better compensation and distinguished colleagues are useful recruiting tools to bring other good teachers to a school. The higher level of compensation means the school can hire and keep the teachers it wants to employ. Endowed chair holders also provide leadership on the faculty as well as in the school community, in the region, and even in the nation. Because they tend to stay in their positions until retirement, endowed chair holders bring stability to a faculty. Moreover, the endowed chairs provide naming opportunities for donors and are an effective means of raising money to support faculty compensation in perpetuity. As a vehicle for raising money for faculty salaries, endowed chairs demonstrate the value that the school places on quality instruction, and this commitment to people is even more important when schools invest large sums of money in facilities.

Conclusion

Studies of the teacher labor market in private schools indicate that endowed teaching chairs are successful devices for recruitment and retention of faculty. Independent schools are susceptible to market forces and, therefore, if they are to attract tuition-paying students, these schools must employ teachers that are highly effective in the classroom. Independent schools do not offer tenure to their faculty, and typically they pay their teachers for performance. Those private schools that use a salary scale will, when necessary, go "off scale" in order to recruit or retain a teacher the school wants to employ. Very few independent-school teachers are represented by labor unions, so administrators have the flexibility to hire and fire faculty to meet the programmatic needs and performance expectations of the school.[3] Despite the fact that private-school teachers are typically paid less than their public-school counterparts, they report a high degree of job satisfaction owing to working conditions such as smaller classes, control of the curriculum, fewer discipline issues, and motivated students. Because independent schools typically use differentiated salaries and some form of merit pay, a merit award such as an endowed teaching chair would fit into the culture of these schools. Even those teachers who do not actually hold a chair can benefit from the endowed chairs because the income from the chair enhances the total instructional budget, and the status of the chair heightens the reputation of the school in the marketplace. The current data on fund-raising at independent schools indicate a propitious climate and a favorable trend for generating the long-range funding required to establish endowed chairs. Moreover, the development directors at these schools are becoming increasingly sophisticated in working with potential donors to raise the money. For independent schools the endowed teaching chair is a concept that holds much promise.

Notes

[1] Savage, T. "Schools and the Quest for Philanthropy." NAIS/NBOA Independent Schools Financing Symposium. (November 2002) [On line]. Available: www.nais.org.

[2] Jones, F.G.K. (2003). *Endowed Teaching Chairs at Independent Schools.* Unpublished doctoral dissertation, University of Kansas, Lawrence.

[3] For a discussion of these elements of the teacher labor market, see: Ballou, D. (2001, February). Pay for Performance in Public and Private Schools. *Economics of Education Review,* 20, 51–61.

Ballou, D. & Podgursky, M. (1998). Teacher Recruitment and Retention in Public and Private Schools. *Journal of Policy Analysis and Management,* 17 (3), 393–417.

Ballou, D & Podgursky, M. (1998). "Teacher Unions and Education Reform: Gaining Control of Professional Licensing and Advancement." Teacher Unions and Education Reform Conference. Kennedy School of Government. Harvard University. September 24–25, 1998.

Frank Jones's chapter is based upon research he did for a doctoral dissertation titled *Endowed Teaching Chairs at Independent Schools.* He is continuing this project beyond the scope of the dissertation and would be pleased to hear from anyone who has experience or knowledge of such programs. He is currently the head of the upper school at Holland Hall.

Developing School Leaders: An Intentional Approach

By Ellen Welsh

The leadership crisis in independent education is steadily moving from prediction to problem. NAIS research indicates that 70% of independent school heads will leave their positions during the next decade. As a person who finds herself, somewhat surprisingly, in the headship of a NAIS PK–12th grade coed day school, I feel personally invested in developing leaders for schools. Being head of a school was not an early dream of mine, but over the years it slowly became a possibility and now a reality, thanks to supportive and stimulating leader-colleagues.

I offer some observations to expand thinking both about leadership development and, perhaps, our reservoir of leaders. While I address my remarks primarily to sitting heads who are relating to faculty and staff in the early years of their careers, I ask other readers to modify their perspectives as needed in order to apply these principles to their own school leadership situations. Some of my suggestions are distilled from personal experience and others come from human development literature.

Traditional methods for filling the head of school's chair that have oft been tried are now proving to be less true. One well-worn method has been modeling.

Modeling Revisited

Modeling can be magical. Let all those aspiring school heads stop, look, and listen. Let them absorb the lessons to be learned from their local standard of excellence in the headship. But, lo: What if their head doesn't seem to be having any fun? What if the dimensions of the job seem gargantuan? I'm reminded of a recent faculty party where two female teachers echoed each other in a now familiar refrain, "I would *never* want *your* job!" There were no visions of sugarplums about school leadership dancing in their heads—more like a B horror film.

Notwithstanding a couple of fine-print disclaimers, I love my job as a head of school, and I believe strongly in the value of independent education. That's why I think heads should both develop skills to make us more effective nurturers of talent and be very intentional in our recruitment efforts. To rely on modeling, expecting our younger colleagues to be so inspired or so captivated by our lifestyle that they will simply step up to the leadership plate when it is their logical turn at bat is too random. Still, modeling can have impact. In the daily living of our jobs, many heads do inspire others to seek leadership opportunities. Therefore, let's not be silent about the sophisticated satisfactions of the headship. Let's converse authentically with freshmen colleagues about the personal meaning of our jobs. We should also articulate the stressors. Let's name those beasts, not as some Godzillian horror to be survived, but as forces to face with heart and mind and the accumulating wisdom of the independent school community.

The Talent Pool

Another musty approach to leadership development has been to expect the heir apparent to the headship to be swimming in the white, male, upper-division talent pool. As we seek to diversify the independent school community, let's hasten the process by diversifying its leadership—ethnicity and gender are obvious categories. I would add "career path." One of the "No, not me!" female teachers from the above-mentioned faculty party might be an extraordinary head: at the right time, in the right school, with the right development. Her current position as a fourth-grade teacher might shrink our vision as we fish for future leaders in the talent pond. Let's use the best bait. Not all schools have the same mission or leadership needs. A faculty member with a tremendous gift for teaching might be intrigued if her head helped her see the potential for using her teaching skills in varied ways, with parents, faculty, even trustees. Let us look at our very best people (our high potentials) in independent schools as promising heads, no matter their background, current position, aspirations or dreams.

The Gift of Time

Are we wincing yet? What time? This is where conviction comes in. When school heads believe that we have the responsibility of growing leaders and when we also help our board chairs internalize this value, then we may allow ourselves to legitimately schedule time for leadership development.

Sometimes we will enjoy the fruits of leadership farming at our own school's garden. But for the good of the independent school universe, let's not hold this as a prerequisite for tilling the talent field. The kindergarten teacher that I encourage to become a division head may eventually move to another school. So be it. The 21st century is increasingly populated by free agents, people not bound to one institution or career. I turn here to a series of truisms such as "a rising tide lifts all boats" or "what goes around, comes around." Our collective contributions to leadership development may benefit all schools, not just mine.

The gift of time enables us to offer the gift of relationship and interest in another human being. Interest is a powerful tool. I recall interviewing a young minority candidate for an independent school position. Another fine school was also interested in her. I asked a simple question, "What would you like to be doing in five years?," which prompted a rich conversation. The effect was persuasive. The candidate, who chose my school, said that no one had ever shown as much interest in working with her to achieve the future of her dreams.

The relationship might take different forms: perhaps more as a mentor, providing career guidance and support over a span of years, or more as a coach, here and now, one who helps another set goals, develop a plan, and practice the behavioral skills to blossom as a leader. Once a head is committed to growing other leaders and begins to invest time and energy in encouraging, trusting relationships, several strategies can help. I address just four: collaborative dreaming, personal excavation, goal setting, and rehearsing. Let us be mindful that we are not scheduling an event (there is no quick-fix workshop) but committing to a process.

Collaborative Dreaming

Because there seem to be fewer school people dreaming of leadership, I think it behooves current leaders to work with colleagues to develop various dream scenarios. Nudge people to mentally expand their "comfort zones"—those behavioral patterns that are psychologically safe and sound and often limiting. Practice collaborative dreaming. Our objective is to help others go beyond embellishing or expanding their dreams to consider inventing something different. If their dream begins to look like ours, then pause for reflection. The "independence" in independent education applies to leadership as well. I have found heads to be splendidly diverse in our journeys and styles.

Explore potential leaders' interests and passions and help them see how they might relate to and fuel the tasks of leadership. For staying power, goals should be uniquely tailored to the individual. Craft questions to provoke thought: What would you like to see yourself doing more of? Less of? What would it look like if you were a department chair? Through your ongoing conversations, create a series of storyboards to pick apart or polish. Help others imagine dreams of a different stripe. Another helpful strategy is to excavate within ourselves, seeking more detailed self-knowledge.

Personal Excavation

Several leadership development tools from the corporate world exist to fast-forward this process. They can help school people better understand their interests, preferred working styles, stress points, needs, and more. I have found that the most useful personal and organizational development tools go beyond describing observable behavioral patterns. They also address a person's needs, which can be invisible but extremely important since they drive behavior. Additionally, the best instruments also offer prescriptions or suggestions about how to work more productively. If both the sitting head and the aspiring leader use the same self-knowledge tool, their relationship will likely become more effective.

Goal Setting

Don't underestimate the power of written goals just because they are so commonly recommended. Goals may respond to problems one is experiencing or they may be focused on creating opportunities. My experience in leadership development moves me to recommend that the goals be focused on relational skills. As we analyze the leadership breakdowns in schools and other organizations, we learn that the problem often relates to what are sometimes called soft skills. Influential authors such as Daniel Goleman underscore emotional intelligence (EQ) as the sine qua non for effective leadership.

Ironically, in talking with aspiring leaders, I find that they often are more worried about learning to deal with the "urgent" rather than what I have found to be the "important." For example, financial, facilities, legal, governance, and personnel issues often intimidate potential leaders and perhaps scare a few off the track to headship. Conversely, they may spend their energies implementing a learning plan to fill in the "hard" information holes. But what is truly hard? Working effectively with and through other human beings to fulfill a noble mission tops my list. Here I appeal to the "just in time" training concept. When it is necessary to understand the audit process in a school or read financial statements, the knowledge can be acquired quite quickly. The kind of knowledge that cannot be snapped up so expeditiously is in the area of emotional intelligence. The good news, however, as Daniel Goleman so persuasively presents, is that even EQ can be developed. Therefore, I contend that defining and pursuing goals in this realm are the best investment in growing future school leaders who are comfortable and effective in their multifaceted roles.

Brokering

As sitting heads, we can deftly broker resources to help others achieve their goals. Once I approached an unsuspecting first teacher with the subtle insistence that she apply for the Klingenstein Summer Institute. She attended and the experience was transformational. Another future leader in the hopper! As heads we often have access to information and resources unknown to our faculties. Let us remain alert to brokering learning opportunities for growing leaders.

Rehearsing

When working with another to help her grow into school leadership, create lots of opportunities for practicing the "moves" of leadership. I worked once with a technology teacher whose dread of public speaking became a problem-solving goal. She faced her first "audiences" sitting down. Little by little, after working through her action plan which included "appearances" to share knowledge with technology colleagues, then parent groups, she was able to stand with confidence, figuratively and literally! The problem became an opportunity as she received more and more requests to make presentations in education circles.

Rehearsal can also take another form, that of mentally affirming and visualizing the new behaviors and feelings that we pursue. Research in cognitive psychology has been translated into can-do techniques for all to use to change behaviors, enhance performance, and achieve dreams. I greatly admire a colleague, a middle-aged non-athlete, who visualized and affirmed herself through a rigorous training program to the finish line of a marathon. This example underscores that fact that helpful rehearsing of leadership behaviors can successfully occur in non-school venues. As head, send a young teacher to participate in a Chamber of Commerce leadership forum. Broker an opportunity for her to join a non-profit board. These activities outside of a comfortable collegial group also help prepare growing leaders for the "weight of being watched." Leaders live under scrutiny, often producing a heightened level of stress for the novice. Opportunities for rehearsing leadership skills abound—pursue them with creative energy.

Conclusion

Several years ago I was principal of a lower school division. Now, as a head of school, I am keenly aware of the leadership gifts that I have received over the years from a large ensemble of leader-colleagues. One of my former headmasters helped develop over a dozen heads of school. To paraphrase Marian Wright Edelman, I consider leadership development the rent I pay for enjoying a career in independent education. With great intentionality and a commitment to building my coaching skills, I seek to return the gift to the rising generation of leaders.

Before assuming the headship at The Canterbury School of Florida in 2002, **Ellen Welsh** was head of Presbyterian School in Houston, Texas, for six years. She has also served as a division head at the Kinkaid School in Houston and as a division head at two bilingual international schools in Bogota, Colombia. Thanks to the Board of Trustees of Presbyterian School and The Klingenstein Center, Teachers College, Columbia University, Ellen was a Klingenstein Visiting Fellow in 2002.

The Administrator as Member of Your School Community

By Tom Hassan and Ty Tingley

Recently, Phillips Exeter Academy embarked upon a search for a new director of admissions. At most other independent schools, the process would be clear: Cast the recruiting net far and wide to find the best-qualified candidate for the job. At Exeter, the school's centuries-old traditions suggested a different approach. Most admissions directors at our boarding school in New Hampshire had come from our faculty. The community long reasoned that Exeter faculty already had an intimate knowledge of the academy because they had taught around the Harkness tables in our classrooms and have lived in our dormitories. Thus, they were the only ones able, most appropriately and effectively, to represent Exeter to prospective families and to make decisions about which students would attend their school.

Faculty attitudes toward the demands and desirability of administrative work vary over time, however. When no internal candidates at Exeter stepped forward to apply for the admissions director position, our search committee did what many other schools have done: We posted advertisements in the various educational journals, engaged a search consultant to help identify promising candidates from outside the school, and conducted a thorough screening of candidates both on paper and in person. Exeter's final choice of admissions director brought with him a number of years of experience recruiting and selecting students and has helped establish a new path at the academy as a key administrator from outside the school.

Finding the strongest candidates for top administrative posts at independent schools today may mean looking outside your own ranks. What has changed recently in our schools that compels us to look elsewhere for administrators? Clearly, independent schools have grown more complex in recent decades; consequently, some areas of their oversight may require particular administrative experience. Fostering large endowments and raising funds for an institution's continued growth, for example, take special skill and training. Also, students and their parents now expect ongoing support, beginning before they enter the school to the time they are applying to college. That kind of service may require adults with special training. Overall, schools are much more involved with issues facing society in general, such as risk management and the law, that call for expert administrative oversight. As a result, it is more difficult today to rotate a faculty member into a key administrative role and have that person learn on the job. The stakes are too high, the collective knowledge base too deep, and, frankly, our tuitions too costly not to get the most knowledgeable employees we can to care for our students, staffs, and overall institutions.

As we welcome administrators new to our schools, what can we do to ensure their successful transition? Connections are one good answer.

First, it is important that a school takes an introspective look at its particular culture and the ways in which it has—or has not—embraced administrators without a previous affiliation. Exeter's model of academic governance has often been described as the "faculty run school" with faculty rotating into administrative positions and bringing with them institutional history and experience. This practice has been a long-standing one at our school, clearly defined half a century ago in the Exeter Study of 1953:

> Whenever possible, administrative officers should be appointed from the Faculty. Such a policy can encourage teachers in their own work and keep alive their interest in the general policies of the Academy. It can increase the bond of fellowship among the administration, department heads, and members of the teaching staff. It is much easier, too, for a man to acquire a thorough familiarity with Exeter's standards if he has been a classroom teacher here.

Important decisions are often made in a full faculty meeting each week or through periodic standing committee meetings. We don't have much experience in settling in administrators without a significant history with our institution.

Furthermore, our school values collaborative conversation. Exeter's Harkness plan, instituted in 1931, encourages debate and dialogue among students and teacher around a large oval table. As one faculty member describes the Harkness approach, "the teacher is a guide on the side, and not a sage on the stage." Therefore, selecting an administrator willing to debate with and listen to his or her colleagues is critical at our institution. Equally as important is our own acknowledgment that we are relatively new at making these folks easily and immediately welcomed.

Second, schools must also engage in well-advertised searches for key administrators. We know legally we need to do this, but it is also a way for us to continue to diversify our adult population. However, we cannot lose sight of the fact that members of our internal communities need to know that an opening exists, even though the job may require specific knowledge and skill that are outside the area of expertise of most faculty or current staff members. Those whom we are ultimately asking to welcome and to embrace the final candidate don't appreciate surprises. Educating the community about the job and the candidates will go far in helping the ultimate choice succeed.

Third, once an administrator has been invited to relocate to your school, the school needs to have a sound orientation program. Most independent schools have refined orientation programs to include ways to meet others, absorb the nuances of the school's technologies, and quickly get to know the lay of the land, both figuratively and literally. Orientation, however, should not stop after the newcomer settles in. Connections should continue to be made throughout the first months of the employee's tenure. Even though their professional lives will be busy, are there ways for administrators to sit in on classes during the year and to attend special assemblies or programs that give them a true flavor of your institution? Some administrators may even take on other roles in the school—adviser to students and/or to clubs, coach of a sport, or even teach a course. At Exeter a member of the treasurer's staff works on finances with student clubs. Administrators are asked to join faculty and students in giving one of our Thursday morning meditations. Special assemblies that feature members of the community include an administrative presence.

We need to encourage, or perhaps even require, such immersion. Enjoying real life experiences at your school makes employees more effective spokespeople and overall workers. Since personal connections will likely increase the time they remain working at your school, the newest employees in our close-knit communities, as well as their families, need to be connected early on to the rhythm of our daily life. Inviting spouse and children to participate in appropriate social gatherings and certain extracurricular activities are rewarding ways to include them in the school's daily culture. This sometimes takes more of an effort than a simple invitation. New administrators may not feel comfortable joining an activity that they perceive reserved for faculty and/or students. It may take a direct invitation and perhaps a particular task to do at the event to make a new person feel included.

Fourth, new administrators appreciate having a mentor, a fellow administrator to whom they can turn as they adjust to their new surroundings, at least in the first year. While not a unique concept, mentorship is often cited by the administrators new to their schools as most helpful in making them feel welcomed and connected. Through a mentorship role, administrators can honestly ask questions and receive feedback about their work. One of our administrators offered this observation: "At a previous school, I recall vividly the feeling of isolation during my first year. There the feedback came well after a year after my start. As I manager, I vow never to do that."

Fifth, compensation that acknowledges the degree of expertise necessary for some administrative jobs is vital to a school that hopes to keep good administrators in the community. The issue of compensation of all administrators has taken on a new, and sometimes explosive, twist in our schools in recent years and may in some institutions be a block to the connectedness to which we aspire. Back in the 1950s, that Exeter Study Committee spelled out a simple, direct strategy: Administrative officers at Exeter would receive salaries "in line" with those of the teachers. They wrote, "If the yearly salary (of the administrator) is based upon an eleven month working year, it is reasonable to assume that their average remuneration should be about 16 percent higher than that of classroom teachers." The Exeter report of half a century ago also foreshadowed a trend we see today. They noted in 1953 that certain administrators, then the Exeter principal and the treasurer, were paid a salary higher than others because "of the special nature of their functions."

Within the last decade, the top salaries of many school leaders have not only increased substantially, but have also been made public through the Internal Revenue Services Form 990. The 990s, which can be found easily on the Internet, have turned what was once a hushed and speculative topic into full-blown conversation and debate. What we find today is that the salaries paid to top administrators vary greatly from Exeter's 1953 general rule of thumb; some administrators are paid more than teachers even taking into account that they work the full, versus academic, year. A few faculty have an understandably difficult time accepting a discrepancy in administrative and faculty salaries, even when it is argued that the administrators bring a particular skill set that requires specific training and experience. Today's reality is that in regard to many key administrative specialties—especially admissions, financial, and development—the marketplace has lifted the norms for compensation faster than for teaching faculty. We have found that the best way to diffuse concerns about this disparity is to be as open as possible about issues of compensation.

Finding the strongest administrative faculty today may mean looking outside your school, welcoming them over time, *and* compensating them competitively. Given that reality, though, we should not lose sight that developing internal experience and capability is healthy for the school and operationally useful. We need to continue to keep an eye on promising young faculty at our own schools and provide them with opportunities and encouragement to try out administrative roles. The part-time faculty administrative model that Exeter's faculty advocated in 1953 is still viable, but with the increasing complexity of the world in which our schools exists, we know we may find the best person to fill an administrative role from outside our school. It is then incumbent that we work to bring together those with the deep knowledge of our culture and traditions developed through a long connection to our school with our newest community members.

Tom Hassan is the assistant principal and a teacher of mathematics at Phillips Exeter Academy in New Hampshire. Prior to his current role, he served as the academy's dean of admissions as well as director of college counseling.

Ty Tingley has been the thirteenth principal at Phillips Exeter Academy, serving since 1997. Prior to Exeter, he served as the head of school at both Kingswood-Oxford (CT) and the Blake School (MN).

School Headship: 25 Years Ago and Today

By Stephen DiCieco

There is little doubt that the skills, talents, and experiences needed to be a successful independent school head have changed dramatically in the last quarter century. In this chapter, we will examine the "then and now" changes in light of four forces affecting heads of school. They are societal, legal, economic, and educational forces.

Why have things changed? Society, culture, and independent schools themselves have changed, and one must understand the nature of this change to fully comprehend the change in the nature of school leadership.

In the late 70s and early 80s, most independent schools more closely resembled their forbearers—that is, they were relatively traditional, and supported by families who understood the nature of independent education. Many of these families, and indeed, many of the members of the faculties of these schools had themselves attended such schools. Today, NAIS reports that well over 70% of parents who send their children to independent schools did not themselves attend such schools. This means that these parents are not inculcated with the traditional mores of independent schools. What are those mores? Twenty-five years ago (then), independent schools were seen as far less democratic than they are today—that is, the heads led the schools, making most of the major decisions themselves. The head evaluated teachers personally and s/he hired and fired pretty much at will. Right or wrong, this was the norm. Merit pay was common. Parent involvement was limited, and most boards truly left the running of the school to the head. Families understood the role of the head and of the board. Parents did not challenge school values, decisions, rules, or expectations. Kids did their homework on time, and parents rarely asked the school to let a student go early for a family vacation. Parents almost never took their kids out when the school said no to the early vacation.

The nature of the head's job 25 years ago was indeed different. Being a head of an independent school then meant being a leader with clear values and a strong personality. Most successful heads were generalists who became actual leaders as compared to managers (more on that later). Most were male; most attended independent schools and most knew each other. Searches were controlled by a very few people (men) who developed "stables" and put the same candidates into each search they carried out. Axiomatic for a successful head was a strong sense of self (appropriate self-confidence), relative sophistication and a sense of humor. Few heads had doctoral degrees and some did not hold masters' degrees.

So, how did we get to where we are now? The first force affecting independent schools and the nature of headship is a *societal* change. The breakup of the two-parent family and the double-working family created an interesting paradox for schools and heads. One would think that divorced parents would mean fewer mothers available for volunteer work in school activities. The same, one would think, would hold true for the married working mothers. Many of those mothers (and fathers), in fact, do not participate in school activities regularly, yet they do become involved in their children's education. For reasons that psychologists will someday unravel, today's parents have huge expectations for their children . . . and thus for the schools that are educating them. As we all know, extensive tutoring for kindergarten entry in Manhattan is more than common. Once accepted, today's parents expect that the school will ensure that their child gets in to only the "best" schools at the next level of education. If they do not, the school is blamed. Today's school head must have a thick hide to handle the parental firestorms that evolve from perceived poor placement (note that college placement offices are today called college counseling offices—no accident, that). Today's head must be willing to deal with this pressure. This form of parental pressure is one of the reasons that the number of candidates for head-of-school positions has diminished.

"With a tuition of $18,000 for the third grade, I am entitled to know what the school is doing specifically for my daughter." Another societal change, which is often linked to finances, is the sense of entitlement. Twenty-five years ago, such a statement of the tuition would be rare—today we hear it regularly. Another paradox—the same parents who bemoan the tuition are the ones who claim year after year that the teachers are the soul of the school. With schools working hard to raise salaries above embarrassing levels, parents should understand the need to charge a realistic tuition.

The entitlement issue is a crucial one, as it affects many aspects of school leadership. When schools were seen as true families or communities, heads were seen as father/mother figures that kept everyone together following the school's mission. With entitled individualists (and their plural, *constituencies*), the head must become a diplomatic politician, an ongoing developer of consensus, keeping diverse individuals and groups happy. Have you ever had to tell a mother that she cannot call her daughter on the cell phone during third period? This is not an easy task.

Legal forces are in play today. A quarter of a century ago, school leaders need not have had much understanding of the law. In today's litigious society, most heads understand contract law and risk management. School discipline decisions are now often made with consultation of the school attorney. Faculty termination has become a paper-trail task that often results in the retention of a less than effective employee. Almost all heads today have their faculty, parent, and student handbooks reviewed by the attorney. The head's own contract, once a simple letter of agreement or even a handshake, is now a lengthy compensation document, often developed with the help of a compensation consultant.

Many of the skills needed by today's heads are management skills as compared to leadership skills. Heads need technical knowledge in many of the legal areas that yesterday's heads never even considered. Can you imagine Deerfield's Frank Boyden worrying about the language in a faculty handbook (if he even had one)? Insurance companies, safety and security concerns, and litigation threats have had a real impact on the job of the head.

Economic forces are in a different place today as well. The state of today's economy compels school heads to be skillful budget developers as well as "green shades" in their overseeing of the school's resources. Few heads in the early '80s had to worry as much as today's heads about tuition increases, income streams, decreasing endowment value, and operating expenses. The dramatic rise in costs for all forms of insurance (particularly health) has caused chaos to carefully crafted budget plans. Even with top business managers (who are now very highly paid themselves), today's head needs a clear understanding of the balance sheet and its ramifications.

Of course, the economy affects the applicant pool. While the top-tier schools remain full, there is significant admission tension at some other schools. Heads must have a handle on admission processes to ensure that the school is filled with the right students (as defined as fitting the mission). A head who leaves the entire admissions program in the hands of the admissions office today is a head who may face an unfilled school.

The changes in *education* represent a force as well. A quarter of a century ago, students were pretty much taught in the same way—lecture and test format. Colleges and secondary schools followed similar practice, and it was up to the student to learn that which was passed on to him or her. Most heads of school were taught in the same manner; thus, their understanding of pedagogical practice was based upon teacher-centered learning. With the development of the theories of multiple intelligences and student-centered learning, how we teach and learn has altered (and many would say to the better). Heads today must be cognizant of these theories as well as their relationship to objective testing and the growing public cry for testing accountability. One head lamented to this writer "it is not a facile task to explain to a parent the excitement of portfolio use with weak ERB scores."

There is often a built-in conflict between that which is educationally sound for the student and the expectations of his or her parents. Being accepted at a highly competitive school or college may be prestigious, but it also may be a recipe for educational disaster. It would be interesting to study the high percentage of college transfers in light of the appropriateness, or lack thereof, of a student's acceptance to that college. This keeps school heads up at night.

So the forces combine and the nature of the position of head of school changes. Today's heads need a different set of skills and experiences to succeed at the job. Gone are the days of the autocratic head (I met a head who had never held a faculty meeting in two decades of leadership). Today's heads need to be consensus builders and diplomats who use charisma and compromise to form policies and direction. Systems are rampant in schools today and those systems require managerial expertise and understanding. Yet, do not assume that all of these changes are negative. There were problems, in some cases, with teacher-centered teaching and strong heads with little accountability.

Today's schools are, in many senses, better places. Faculty members are more engaged in the operations of the schools, the nature of learning is better understood, and students have personal involvement in their own educations. Today's heads are sensitive, more open and involved as chief *cheerleader* working with others to meet the goals of the school's mission.

Professionalism has replaced the generalist nature of the position. Aspirants for head of school positions today understand that building a career path, which strengthens their candidacies, is a wise route to follow. Most of the scores of superb candidates we meet have had strong administrative experience, and almost all have advanced degrees. Unlike 25 years ago, many of these degrees are in education rather than a particular academic field such as history or English. Many have participated in the efficacious Klingenstein programs, and a successful head has mentored many. All seem to understand the changes in schools and, happily, they see headship today as a powerful and positive challenge. So while the pool of top candidates may be smaller than in years past, we believe it to be an excellent one. Independent school leadership is in good shape.

Stephen DiCieco is the president of Educational Directions, Inc., a full-service consulting firm. The firm has carried out over 120 head of school searches as well as numerous planning and management projects for independent schools. A former school head, Mr. DiCieco is also a senior trustee of two independent schools.

Eating Our Young or Crafting a Profession? Transforming Schools through Effective Professional Development

By Sandee Mirell

It was two "R's" rather than the proverbial three that were uppermost in the minds of heads of schools as the 21st century dawned. An NAIS survey revealed that for a random sample of school heads, recruiting and retaining qualified faculty was the top "hot topic" concern.[1] The nation as a whole faced a teacher shortage of crisis proportions, we were told, needing between two and two and a half million new teachers within the first decade. Pat Bassett, executive director of NAIS, estimated that independent schools would need about 10% of that number, or 20,000 to 25,000 new teachers. As the millennium has unfolded, it is becoming clear that of the two "R's" mentioned in the 2001 survey, it is the second that is the real issue. The problem is not that there's a shortage of people qualified—or even interested—in teaching. The problem is keeping them in teaching.

Even in the best of times for recruitment and retention of teachers (which generally coincide with the worst of times for the economy) the rate of attrition for new teachers in the first five years of service has been 15–30%, averaging around 25%. These figures generally hold true for the independent school community as well as the public schools. Further, a report issued in February, 2003, by the National Commission on Teaching and America's Future, indicates that between the years 1984 and 1999, the number of new graduates from education programs actually increased by 50%, to around 220,000 annually. However, teacher attrition has been increasing at an even greater rate. In 1999–2000, for instance, 232,000 teachers were hired across the nation. By the next year, 287,000 teachers had left their jobs, a net loss of 24%.[2] And the number of retiring teachers is not as big a factor as has been suggested. The sad truth is that "the number of teachers leaving the profession for other reasons is almost three times larger than the number who are retiring." The report concludes, "It is as if we were pouring teachers into a bucket with a fist-sized hole in the bottom." Or to use another metaphor that's been offered, the sadder truth may be that education is a profession that "eats its young."[3]

Perhaps most alarming, it's the "best and the brightest" who are most likely to leave. A study boding ill for independent schools, because of the kind of young teachers we tend to hire, found that new teachers who scored in the top quartile on their college entrance exams were almost two times more likely to leave their jobs than new teachers with lower scores. Public school superintendents in the Midwest have reported that from 75 to 100% of teachers leaving their classrooms were at least "effective" and many were "highly effective."[4] The most common single reason for quitting that researchers from the New Teacher Center at the University of California at Santa Cruz heard from new teachers was that they felt they weren't good enough—and these were certified teachers whose districts were eager to keep them.

Why Do They Leave?

Are the twenty-somethings going into teaching less motivated and dedicated than earlier cohorts? This question was raised in 2001 by Public Agenda in a survey of 664 public school teachers and 250 private school teachers who had been teaching five years or less. Overwhelmingly, (96%) they reported that teaching is work that they love to do. However, only 68% said they get a lot of satisfaction out of it, and roughly 20% said that if they had it to do over, they would make a different choice.

When the new teachers were asked by Public Agenda to name what they thought were the most effective ways of improving teacher quality and retention, the top three responses were smaller class sizes, requiring secondary teachers to major in the subjects they teach, and increasing professional development for teachers. Ranking number five, behind salary at number four, was "requiring new teachers to spend much more time in classrooms supervised by experienced teachers." Salary was not as important as many believe. In fact, given a choice between two otherwise identical schools, one offering a higher salary and the other a school where student behavior and administrative and parental support were better, nearly 90% said they would forego the additional salary, while 73% of administrators believed they would make that choice.[5]

Also notable was the finding that although a higher percentage of private school teachers than public school teachers felt appreciated and respected in their jobs (86% to 63%) only half of them felt that morale at their schools was high, or that they could count on the support of the school community. Private schools may well be congenial places to work, but they are not necessarily collegial ones.

Clearly the first years in the classroom are overwhelmingly challenging and equally clear is the fact that the profession's response to this has been ineffectual at best and indifferent at worst. Researchers Stephen P. Gordon and Susan Maxey have outlined a few "environmental" difficulties new teachers face that are "grounded in the culture of the teaching profession and the conditions of school as a workplace."[6] They do nothing to dispute the inference of education's cannibalistic tendencies. And the conditions described are in some cases, like boarding schools, even more difficult in independent schools.

- *Difficult work assignments*

  New teachers are given at least as many if not more responsibilities than veteran teachers, and performance expectations are the same for new teachers as for experienced ones. The most interesting and best-disciplined classes are reserved for the veterans.

- *Unclear expectations*
  Aside from all the myriad rules and forms that are new to beginning teachers, there are the many informal aspects to school cultures that are seldom delineated, adding to a general feeling of being overwhelmed and incompetent among new teachers.
- *Inadequate resources*
  New teachers do not have filing cabinets full of last year's lesson plans and tests. Veteran teachers usually have commandeered the best equipment and classrooms for themselves.
- *Isolation*
  While many observers have commented on the isolated nature of classroom teaching for all teachers, the effects of it are hardest on new teachers. Experienced teachers do not often offer assistance to new teachers for reasons ranging from a belief that new teachers "need to go through their rites of passage alone," to not wanting to seem to be interfering, to thinking it's the job of the administration.

A recent study from the University of Wisconsin–Milwaukee compared the overall attrition rates of four professions in which the educational requirements were similar: teaching, social work, nursing, and accounting. Teaching was not the worst overall. Social work was. But teachers are more likely to leave their profession than nurses are, and leave as frequently as accountants do. However, when age distribution is factored in, the youngest teachers are much more likely to leave teaching than their age-mates in the other groups.[7]

To be sure, a review of the research reveals a fairly wide variety of opinion as to just how bad the teacher shortage and attrition rates are, but on two points there is widespread agreement. First, once young teachers get through their first years on the job, they tend to stay the course until they are near retirement. And second, while salary is certainly a factor in why some teachers leave, the real bottom line most often is, "it ain't the money, it's the working conditions."

And speaking of money, it's not only teachers who are being poured into the bucket with a hole in it—it's money. The financial cost of attrition is huge, and is incalculable in the difficulty in building and sustaining stable teaching and learning communities, it. A recent study in the public schools of Texas, for instance, estimated that that the cost of teachers leaving their jobs in Texas school districts is at least 20% of the departing teacher's salary.[8] In contrast, the cost of providing new teacher support programs is very small. Estimates from a number of independent schools in California indicate that funding such programs amounts to approximately one-tenth of one percent of the schools' annual budget.

How Do We Encourage Them to Stay?

Ironically—and sadly—it's not as if we don't know what to do about it. Research substantiates the results of the Public Agenda poll. Factoring out the smaller class sizes that independent school teachers generally enjoy, the availability of effective professional development and of experienced teachers willing and able to support new teachers in their first years is known to make a difference in retention. Evidence from independent schools is mostly anecdotal, but in the public sector, according to *No Dream Denied*, "Teachers who have no induction program are twice as likely to leave within the first three years."[9]

Ellen Moir, former director of the credential program at the University of California, Santa Cruz, relates that she became increasingly dismayed at the number of frantic phone calls she received from first-year teachers (many of whom wound up leaving teaching after that first year) who all said the same thing: "Why didn't you tell me it would be this hard?" In response, Moir became a founding member of the Santa Cruz New Teacher Project (SCNTP), a joint partnership between the university and nearby school districts in the county. The purpose of SCNTP is to provide first- and second-year teachers with mentors—exemplary teachers who have been released full-time by their districts for a two-year period to provide support for a small group of about 12 new teachers each.

An unexpected benefit occurred as the program evolved. Mentor teachers began gathering informally on Fridays to discuss and reflect upon their experiences in mentoring. They discovered that they often could not "deconstruct" what they did well. They had little experience in systematically identifying and inquiring into what and how students were learning—and the experience of working to support new teachers was giving them a wonderful laboratory in which to gain such pedagogical knowledge.[10] Selecting a problem to solve, gathering data, making and implementing a plan for action, then assessing results became the basis for their support of new teachers. It is also central to SCNTP's vision of creating teachers who routinely examine and reflect upon their practice. From this beginning project came the New Teacher Center, a first-of-its-kind resource for the support and development of teachers. (For further information see www.newteachercenter.org.)

The unexpected benefit came with the discovery that providing support for new teachers gave veteran teachers a new professional role. Not only did the experience of being a mentor lead to renewed vigor and enthusiasm in their own classrooms when they eventually returned to them, but also led to the development of teacher leadership capacities and responsibilities that, as Moir puts it, help "craft a profession." The practice of advising new teachers, she says, "is a powerful form of professional development that furthers these advisors' knowledge of pedagogy and helps them take apart what they know, ultimately producing ever more capable teachers."[11]

The New Teacher Center has formed partnerships with school districts in California and in four states across the nation to help build effective induction programs. These programs have not only positively affected attrition rates, but also increased job satisfaction, professional efficacy, and willingness to assume leadership roles in both the mentors and the new teachers they have advised. SCNTP retention data indicates that after nine years, 94% of the teachers mentored in the 1992–93 program were still in the classroom in 2001.[12]

Although most of the work of the NTC has been with schools in the public sector the collaborative model they employ, not only in their university-school district alliances but in the process and activities of mentoring itself, is one which translates easily into the independent school world. "Few of us," acknowledges Moir, "have lived in school cultures that demand collaboration, foster inquiry into teaching practice, and ask us systematically to collect and review data of our professional practice."[13] Yet this is just the kind of activity that research in adult development shows is most effective for adult learning.

One of the recommendations of the NCTAF report is, "We must develop and sustain professionally rewarding career paths for teachers from mentored induction through accomplished teaching."[14] A new teacher support program that simultaneously develops new and veteran teachers can be a place to begin.

The New Paradigm of Professional Development

Increasingly it is being acknowledged that teaching is a complex job, involving many skills. As Linda Darling-Hammond says, "an effective teacher is one who learns from teaching rather than one who has finished learning how to teach."[15] This idea of learning from teaching resonates with what research tells us about the ways adults learn best, and both have contributed to what amounts to a paradigm shift in what characterizes effective professional development.

The idea that adults continue to develop is a relatively new one. The word *adult* itself (being, as it is, the past participle of *adolesecere,* meaning to grow up) implies that adult development is an oxymoron. The dictionary, for instance, tells us that an adult is one who is "fully developed, mature." The return of fully developed, mature adult veterans to college after World War II provided impetus for the creation of the field of adult development, and began a trend that by the end of the last century had developed into one of the fastest growing areas in higher education. The proportion of older to younger students in the classrooms of our nation's colleges and universities doubled in a single generation.[16]

It became clear, as colleges and universities attempted to meet the needs of these older students, that neither raw intelligence nor chronological age guaranteed that any given adult was, in fact, "fully developed and mature," or was able to achieve the adult learning goal of becoming a "self-directed learner." Self-directed learners

- can examine themselves, their culture, and their milieu in order to understand how to separate what they feel from what they should feel, what they value from what they should value, and what they want from what they should want
- develop critical thinking, individual initiative, and a sense of themselves as co-creators of the culture that shapes them
- set their own goals and standards, with or without help from experts
- take responsibility for their learning, direction, and productivity
- exercise skills in time management, project management, goal-setting, self-evaluation, peer critique, information-gathering, and use of educational resources.[17]

Experts in the field of adult learning came to see that becoming a self-directed learner is a developmental task, and a new definition of adult evolved. An adult is one who is able to relate to, as opposed to being identified with, the life roles he or she plays. The submission of the student to the authority of the teacher, which is appropriate in the education of minors, takes on a different coloration when the student is an adult. Adult development researcher Laurent Daloz gives us a handy summary description of an adult learner when he says, "Authority becomes something we possess rather than something we defer to."[18]

Used in its psychological sense, identification is an unconscious state in which, without realizing it, we model ourselves upon our ideas about our parents, teachers, culture, religion, and any number of other formative influences we encounter as we grow. As noted above, for instance, veteran teachers often are not able to deconstruct what it is they do well. Many may not even be able to identify what it is they do well, much less deconstruct it, and may be unconsciously imitating the behaviors of good teachers they may not even remember. Likewise most adults would be hard-pressed to articulate why they parent as they do—except to be sometimes appalled at finding themselves sounding just like their mothers—or their fathers!

In contrast, through a process of learning one can come, at least to some extent, to consciously choose with whom to identify, and to recognize when unconscious identification might exist. Adults can "examine themselves, their culture, and their milieu in order to understand how to separate what they feel from what they should feel, what they value from what they should value, and what they want from what they should want."

Compare any two lists of what research reveals are the needs of the adult learner and the characteristics of effective professional development and, unsurprisingly, you will find remarkable resonance. Lois J. Zachery in *The Mentor's Guide* (which is based on Daloz's research) and Linda Darling-Hammond, in a report written for The Center for Teaching and Learning, agree that adults learn best and thus professional development is most effective when:

- they have a specific need to know and immediacy of application
- learning is experiential, engaging teachers in concrete tasks of teaching, assessment, and observation that illuminate the processes of learning and development
- they are self-directing, involved in diagnosing, planning, implementing, and evaluating their own learning
- learning is grounded in participants' questions, inquiry, and experimentation as well as profession-wide research
- their life experience is a primary learning resource and the life experiences of others are available for enrichment
- learning is connected to and derived from teachers' work with their students as well as to examinations of subject matter and teaching methods; it is collaborative, involving a sharing of knowledge among educators
- they are internally motivated to learn

- learning is sustained and intensive, supported by modeling, coaching, and problem solving around specific problems of practice[19]

The mentor teachers involved in the early days of the Santa Cruz New Teacher Project who gathered informally on Fridays to talk about their experiences as mentors were engaged in activities that fit all of the above criteria, and the inquiry-based new teacher support program they helped to create fit, as well. Responding further to the observation that veteran teachers often are not able to deconstruct what they do well, SCNTP added another mentor training program—for the mentors. In addition to receiving training in observation skills, effective use of formative assessment tools, adult learning theory, and ways to give feedback effectively, each new mentor is paired with an experienced mentor. New mentors set professional learning goals and chart their progress with their mentors over the course of the year just as they do with the new teachers who they are supporting.

Out of the ongoing collaboration between beginning teachers and their mentors, and among mentors, has come the New Teacher Project's *Continuum of Teacher Development.* Initially developed to be used solely to support the reflective practice of new teachers, it has evolved into a document that "provides a common language for setting and discussing goals for professional development within an environment of collegial support."[20] It provides a model for describing what effective teaching practice and professional development look like throughout an entire teaching career—a document in service of "crafting a profession."

SCNTP's model of collaborative partnership between universities and schools in which the role of the teacher is central is a 21st-century model. It is an example of the new collaborative model described by Robert Yinger, dean of the School of Education at Baylor University, when he says, "This is not the old collaboration model where the university came in and told the school what was wrong. Now the questions and problems to solve are generated by teachers, based on the data they're reviewing. They are asking hard questions on how to improve instruction and how students are doing."[21]

The Importance of School-Based Professional Development

Not only does this type of data-driven focus fit the criteria for effective adult learning and professional development, it is also, inevitably, collegial. While university-school partnerships can be important and valuable, it is the climate and culture of the individual school—the working conditions—in which new teachers practice daily that ultimately make the difference in encouraging new teachers to stay in teaching. Research from the Project on the Next Generation of Teachers at Harvard notes that new teachers need "sustained, school-based professional development—guided by expert colleagues, responsive to their teaching, and continual throughout their early years in the classroom."[22] The operative words here are *sustained* and *school-based* professional development. Add these to "collegial" and therein lies both the challenge as well as the opportunity for improvement.

Again, it's not as if we don't know what to do about it. Yet, as Virginia Richardson, professor in the School of Education at the University of Michigan, notes, most professional development in education does not match what we know about adult learning. It still "derives from the short-term transmission model, pays no attention to what is already going on in a particular classroom . . . offers little opportunity for participants to become involved in conversation and provides no follow-up."[23]

Harvard researchers Susan Moore Johnson and Susan M. Kardos describe three types of school culture found in their study: veteran-oriented, novice-oriented, and integrated. In the former, relations were often cordial and congenial and sometimes, between veterans, even collegial. It is these kinds of schools most often found in the independent school community, and where, as the earlier noted Public Agenda survey found, new private school teachers felt that they were appreciated and respected but could not depend upon the support of their community. In the Harvard study, researchers found that new teachers in veteran-oriented schools "generally remained on the margins, without induction into the professional life of the school. Respondents often said that veteran teachers were highly skilled, but new teachers who might work across the hall from those veterans had no access to that expertise."[24] In contrast were schools—generally start-up charter schools—in which "youth, idealism and inexperience prevailed." As can be imagined, little or no access to experienced teachers was available in such schools and turnover rates were high.

Johnson and Kardos describe the school culture most beneficial to new teachers as "integrated," in which "schools or subunits within schools, encouraged ongoing professional exchange across experience levels and sustained support and development for all teachers." Such schools had structures in place that enabled teachers to plan, study, assess, reflect, and work collaboratively and in teams. They were schools in which opportunities for professional development were built into the daily schedule.

Sadly, there are not too many schools that fit this model. Even sadder is the picture painted by Roland Barth, who sees in teachers a "passive resistance to teacher leadership [due to] the primitive quality of the relationships among teachers." Echoing the research of Stephen P. Gordon and Susan Maxey on the environmental difficulties of teaching, Barth asserts, "The classic hallmarks of collegiality—talking about practice, sharing craft knowledge, rooting for the success of others, observing one another engaged in practice—are simply absent" in many schools.[25]

Changing the Menu: The Key Role of School Leaders

Happily (or not!), the same people who have the power to eat their young and institutionalize the feast can change the menu. Leadership from administration and faculty working together can create the kind of school culture that benefits not only new teachers but veterans as well. Clearly the concern of the surveyed NAIS heads is well placed, for recruiting and retaining effective educators is a primary role of school administrators. Two things not often discussed in the crisis of the two "R's" might well point to possible solutions: the responsibility faculties have for improving working conditions for new teachers, and the responsibility school administrators have in facilitating and promoting teacher development.

Without strong leadership from the head of school, the kind of integrated school culture Johnson and Kardos describe cannot be created. Yet, one of the difficulties in creating one lies in the fact that independent school leadership is usually evaluated and rewarded less for its support for faculty development than by how fiscally sound the school is, how effective is the planning for long-term needs, and how well the school is thought of by consumers. Likewise, ability and willingness to collaborate, and commitment to their own professional growth are often not included in criteria for faculty evaluation, except, perhaps, indirectly. Yet, the menu-based cannibalism and lack of collegiality can only be redesigned in the ambiance of such an ethos.

Certainly there are teachers who may be "finished learning how to teach," as Linda Darling-Hammond put it, and teachers who are committed narrowly to their own disciplines and domains. However, the truth is that a love of learning is one of the things that draws many to teach in the first place. Virginia Richardson's work in professional development does not support what she calls the "recalcitrance model of change" many see in veteran teachers. This model of change "assumes that someone outside the classroom claims to know what teachers should be doing. And teachers—when told about these or trained in these other methods, curricula, approaches to students, or ways of thinking—simply refuse to implement them."[26] Often in independent schools, such teachers are brilliant, highly creative, and part of a school's institutional heritage. It is not immediately self-evident to such teachers that there is a need to change their behaviors.

There is a lot of evidence, however, that teachers change all the time. Whether they are reorganizing their curricula or changing texts on the basis of a summer's research or learning to integrate technology, Richardson found that teachers, in fact, tend to be highly pragmatic and experimental in their practices, constantly evaluating them on the basis of whether or not they "work." They were deemed to work when they engaged students without violating the teachers' need for control or philosophies and beliefs about teaching and learning. And, of course, when they produced student learning. Richardson found that a collective, inquiry-based approach to professional development that makes use of teacher experience and expertise can enlist and engage teacher support because it enhances what teachers most often are doing already on their own—in isolation.

Further, collaborative practices can have the effect not only of supporting new teachers, and deepening and enriching classroom planning and practices of both new and veteran teacher alike, but of renewing—and retaining—the interest of longtime teachers in their disciplines. One twenty-year veteran from an independent school in California spoke to this in saying, "My interest in math would have dried up long ago if I had not been collaborating with colleagues. I continually learn new ways of approaching a subject that, in some respects, has not changed for hundreds of years."[27]

Just as the model of collaborative partnerships between schools and universities is changing, so must our models of professional development and behavior. Collegiality and collaboration can neither be forced nor contrived, but it can be encouraged. Too often in education the cry for reform and change causes a "flavor of the month" approach to professional development, as well as to curriculum, pedagogy, and other aspects of the field. We need not abandon attending workshops and inspirational lectures, obtaining advanced degrees, and so on, as useful practices of professional development, but add to and implement them in a school-based climate that seeks coherence, integration, and gradual improvement over time.

The same ingredients in ourselves and in the job of teaching that drew us into education in the first place can, in new and innovative combinations, create new menus that could transform it. We can build on and "tweak" what we already do well—find new ways of using faculty and department meetings, restructure committees and school schedules to allow for collaborative teamwork. Administrators and faculties working together can create climates—"working conditions"—that make a school a meaningful and exciting place to work—and a difficult one to leave. Interestingly, in a survey conducted by AISNE/CAIS of retention programs in place in schools belonging to their associations, the top three in order of frequency were: professional development and support, salary and benefits improvements, and general working environment.

There is also evidence that not only can professional development support be a factor in retention; it can make a school an attractive place to choose to work in the first place. Increasingly, interviewers are reporting that one of the questions prospective new teachers are asking them is, "Do you have a mentoring program?"

Summary

The sad irony of the economic downturn of the early years of the new millennium is that many public school districts are facing a retention crisis of a different sort than anticipated. Shrinking budgets are causing the threat of severe teacher layoffs in school districts across the nation. How this situation will affect independent schools remains to be seen. While there are many reasons to be disheartened about the education profession today and undeniable financial and human resource challenges facing both the private and public school worlds, it's also an exciting time to be an educator. We have new knowledge about the plasticity of the learning brain, and about human development across the span of a lifetime that enlarges and supports the work we do with our students, our colleagues, and ourselves. We have important work to do, knowledge with which to do it, and the opportunity to change the status quo in our profession. Creating new teacher mentor programs and integrated school cultures isn't going to solve all our problems, but it is a place to start. We can continue "eating" our youngest practitioners, or we can create supportive structures, practices, and networks to work collaboratively with them to craft a profession. It's ironic that a profession whose mission is ensuring the future of our students has done such a poor job of ensuring our own. It's time to change that.

Notes

[1] National Association of Independent Schools (2001), *NAIS.ink* 2, 1 (September 2001). [Online] Available: www.nais.org

[2] *No Dream Denied: A Pledge to America's Children* (2003), National Commission on Teaching and America's Future (January 2003) 25. [Online] Available: www.nctaf.org

[3] Halford, Joan Montgomery (1998), "Easing the Way for New Teachers." *Educational Leadership* 55, 5 (February 1998). [Online] Available: www.ascd.org

[4] Voke, Heather (2002), "Understanding and Responding to the Teacher Shortage," *Infobrief,* 29.

[5] *A Sense of Calling: Who Teaches and Why* (2001), Public Agenda (April 2001). [Online] Available: www.publicagenda.org

[6] Gordon, Stephen P., and Susan Maxey (2000), *How to Help Beginning Teachers Succeed,* Alexandria, VA: Association for Supervision and Curriculum Development, 2–5.

[7] Keller, Bess (2003), "Question of Teacher Turnover Sparks Research Interest," *Education Week,* XXII, 33 (April 30, 2003), 8.

[8] "The Cost of Teacher Turnover" (2003), *Research Brief, 1,* 8 (April 15, 2003), Association for Supervision and Curriculum Development. [Online] Available: www.ascd.org

[9] *No Dream Denied.*

[10] Gless, Janet, and Ellen Moir (2001), "Teacher Quality Squared," 22,1 (Winter, 2001), *Journal of Staff Development*, National Staff Development Council. [Online] Available: www.newteachercenter.org/publications_articles.shtml

[11] *Ibid.*

[12] Moir, Ellen, "Supporting New Teachers During their First Years of Teaching," New Teacher Center, University of California, Santa Cruz. [Online] Available: www.newteachercenter.org/publications_articles.shtml

[13] Gless, Janet, and Ellen Moir (2001), "Teacher Quality Squared."

[14] *No Dream Denied.*

[15] Darling-Hammond, Linda (1999), "Professional Development for Teachers: Setting the Stage for Learning from Teaching," *Teaching and California's Future,* The Center for the Future of Teaching and Learning, 3. [Online] Available: www.cftl.org

[16] Daloz, Laurent (1999), *Mentor: Guiding the Journey of Adult Learners,* San Francisco: Jossey-Bass Publishers, 13.

[17] Grow, Gerald, "Teaching Learners to Be Self-Directed" in *Adult Education Quarterly*, 41, 125–149, quoted in Robert Kegan (2000), *In Over Our Heads: The Mental Demands of Modern Life*, Cambridge, MA: Harvard University Press, 274.

[18] Daloz, Laurent, (1999) *Mentor, 186.*

[19] Zachery, Lois J. (2000), *The Mentor's Guide*, San Francisco: Jossey-Bass Publishers, 4–5.

Darling-Hammond, Linda, (1999), "Professional Development for Teachers: Setting the Stage for Learning from Teaching," 13.

[20] *Continuum of Teacher Development: Teaching Practice and Professional Development* (2002), Santa Cruz: New Teacher Center at the University of California, Santa Cruz, 4.

[21] "School and University Partnerships" (2003), *Education Update* 45, 3 (May, 2003), Alexandria, VA: Association for Supervision and Curriculum Development, 1.

[22] Johnson, Susan Moore, and Susan M. Kardos, "Keeping New Teachers in Mind" (2002), *Educational Leadership* 59, 6 (March 2002), Association for Supervision and Curriculum Development, 13. [Online] Available: www.ascd.org/readingroom/edlead/0203/johnson.html

[23] Richardson, Virginia, "The Dilemmas of Professional Development" (2003), *Phi Delta Kappan* 84, 5 (January 2003), 401. [Online] Available: www.pdkintl.org/kappan/k0301ric.htm
[24] Johnson, Susan Moore, and Susan M. Kardos, "Keeping New Teachers in Mind," 14.
[25] Barth, Roland, "Teacher Leader" (2001), *Phi Delta Kappan* 82, 7 (February 2001) 446.
[26] Richardson, Virginia, "The Dilemmas of Professional Development" (2003), *Phi Delta Kappan* 84, 5 (January 2003), 403. [Online] Available: www.pdkintl.org/kappan/k0301ric.htm
[27] Howland, Jonathan, and Henri Picciotto, "Into the Province of Shared Endeavor: The Benefits and Challenges of Teacher Collaboration" (2003), *Independent School* 62, 3 (Spring, 2003), 18.

Sandee Mirell taught high school English for 17 years in various independent and public schools. Her postgraduate work is in English, psychology, and education. She is currently the director of professional development for the California Association of Independent Schools.

Collegiality: A Catalyst for Growth Through Teacher Evaluation and Professional Development

By Judith L. Gaston Fisher

Introduction

Those who direct independent schools know that good schools depend upon good teachers, teachers dedicated to the craft of teaching. But often efforts to improve teaching are themselves fragmented. Curricular initiatives, faculty development, and outcome assessments are often pursued independently, sometimes even serially, each becoming a kind of program *de jour*. This chapter develops the theme that collegiality provides the unifying context for pursuing teaching excellence. Currently, the benefits of collegiality, its integrative influence on evaluation and professional development, have not yet been fully recognized or acknowledged, nor have specific proposals been articulated that champion collegiality as a vehicle for enhanced professionalism and accountability.

A Brief History of Me

It has been over twenty years since I was given my first assignment as a teacher. I was one of those female educators who entered the field in part because it was a path well trod by other women. My mother was a teacher; my father was a professor. My husband was studying for his Ph.D., and thus I became the breadwinner. The awareness that I loved teaching, that I understood children and had the ability to motivate and challenge them, would eventually work itself into my self-concept.

It was the latter part of the seventies when I began teaching seventh- and eighth-grade English in a small midwestern school. I relished the earthy smells of this agriculture community that wafted through my classroom window.

But I was largely on my own. I set aside the newly purchased basal reading series for dog-eared books found in the closet, books with titles I recognized from my own days as a student. Short stories and poetry were read and discussed in my classroom, echoing those from my junior high years. Reading, writing, recitation, and grammar were all skills I instilled in my students.

There were no faculty meetings, no departmental meetings; there was no conversation among the faculty as to teaching technique and no real sharing of ideas. The grist of my own experience was milled into my daily lesson plans. This was teaching, I supposed. This would be my life: uncertainty aggravated by isolation yet also fulfillment in discovering I could learn on the job and do that job well.

Twenty years later, after a few layoffs and reassignments, after teaching in inner-city schools, university lab schools, and independent schools, my experience had spanned most grade levels from first through eighth as well as a few adjunct teaching assignments at local colleges and universities.

At times I was given advice by others when I became disgruntled or upset by the lack of collegiality displayed at the various schools in which I taught. Typically the counsel was the same: "Count your blessings. You are lucky to be able to close your door and teach what you want." No set curriculum, no teaching to the test, but at the same time no standards, no accountability. Freedom? Yes. But it was not enough to feed my thirst for the knowledge that I wanted and that I needed to meet the needs of my students. I sought collaboration, conversation, and collegiality. I sought help which would enable me to grow and learn and would, in turn, enrich the experience of my students.

Today, this lack of accountability has led many schools to high-stakes testing and demands for higher standards for teachers. But still, the path is uneven and the way uncertain as schools seek improvement. Is it team teaching? Is it a better evaluation system? Is it professional development?

It was at Community School in St. Louis (MO) that I learned there was indeed a school whose foundation fused collegiality, high academic standards, and professional growth. My thirst for a better way was quenched in this environment where the expectation for teachers and administrators was to collaborate, learn, and make knowledgeable decisions in the best interest of the child.

As an administrator at Community School, reflection and hard work on the part of the faculty and administration has led to a better way. When a school expects and supports collegiality, and incorporates a scaled evaluation system devised by teachers in conjunction with administration, guided professional development is born that benefits both the individual and the school. It is a system that works.

PART ONE
ESTABLISHING COLLEGIALITY:PROCESS COUNTS

Learning is the heart and soul of a school. It is the purpose, the function, the very ethos on which schools were founded. From one-room schoolhouses, to neighborhood schools, to large institutions, learning is epitomized as children enter and exit—books in hand, smiles on their faces, caught in the delight of learning. What school does not use these images on the cover of their latest publications? The smiles and books are an indication that, yes, here indeed is a school blending and balancing the social and the emotional, the academic and the athletic. At least that is the glowing vision readily accepted as the norm; it is the apparent reason many have entered the field of teaching: to impart knowledge into the minds of the students, creating happy, well-balanced children.

> "Almost everyone has had occasion to look back upon his school days and wonder what became of the information he was supposed to have amassed during his years of schooling." (John Dewey)

The task of education has indeed changed. Teachers are less likely to be conveyors of the evanescent information imagined in Dewey's quote, and more likely to be coaches encouraging their charges to become "lifelong learners," an oft-heard expression making its way into many educational mission statements. Fading in relevance is the teacher as fount of information, the transmitter of knowledge; replacing her is a new kind of academic arsonist who kindles the fire of the mind and blows on the embers of new knowledge.

Educational credentials are not enough to stamp an educator "Ready for prime-time! No more development needed here." Cooperation and teamwork will be key success requirements. Schools must be wheels of learning, each spoke representing a separate constituent: parent, teacher, student, administrator, and staff. Each flows to the center, to the hub of the wheel, to the heart and soul of the school, to learning itself.

Expectations of teachers and administrators have also changed. But how do schools formulate a road map which ultimately leads to that hub of learning? What is vital in creating a school where the phrase "lifelong learner" is a living, palpable reality? How can a school assure that the images of learning are matched by the reality?

Standardized tests are not the answer. Neither are annual teacher evaluations. The answer does not lie in the acquisition of the latest text series or the number of faculty meetings held. Instead, the answer lies in the underpinnings of school life: *collegiality and teamwork, evaluation and goal setting, professional development combining to establish growth for all constituents of a school!*

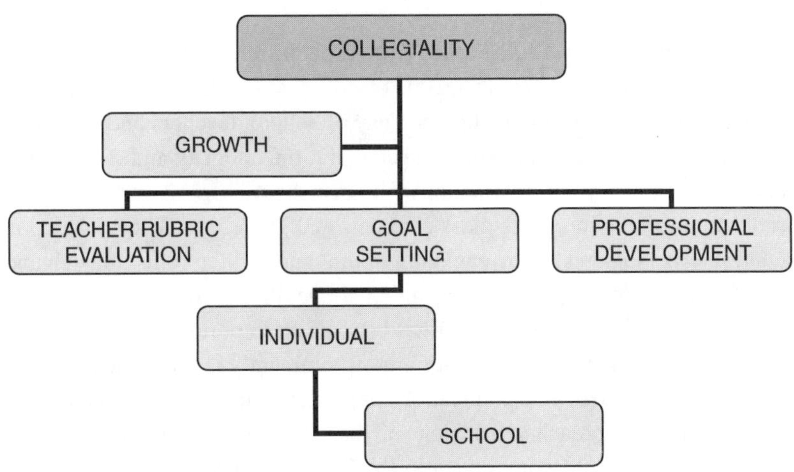

Premise #1

If growth and learning for all constituents of a school is to occur, collegiality and teamwork *must* be a part of that school's foundation.

Educational journals are filled with research and suggestions promoting solid professional development for teachers. There are even suggested budget and time allocations:

10% of the annual operating budget and 25% of teacher time are cited as benchmarks for maintaining teachers as learners (Kelleher 2003). Arguments are made for whole-school development centered on a given topic; for example, how to create a literature-based classroom, or how to establish a math program based on the National Council of Teachers of Mathematics (NCTM) standards and the Third International Mathematics and Science Studies (TIMSS) studies.

Justifications are offered for individualized models of development, allowing a teacher to target growth in a specific area; for example, how to encourage reading or how to establish cooperative learning. Implicit is the assumption by both administrators and teachers that the particular method will effectively improve student learning. But which among this myriad of approaches is most effective or most appropriate for the given context?

Perversely, too much focus on the desired end can cause us to neglect the means. Frequently in the field of education we are like a fledgling football team, confidently predicting touchdowns when we need to attend to our blocking and tackling. Perhaps professional development will feel more like moving the ball down the field than scoring dramatic touchdowns. Certainly the process must not be neglected. A school must understand the work that needs to be done to make evaluation and professional development succeed. The desire and demand for collegiality must first become the basis for school progress. Collegiality and teamwork must be the underpinnings on which evaluation, goal setting, and professional development rest.

Understanding Collegiality: Our Expectations for Children

We can best understand the nature and value of collegiality when we consider the daily rhythms of the classroom. From the opening day of school, teachers and administrators expect students to display consideration and cooperation, integrity and self-reliance, humility and kindness in all their interactions with peers.

Students are partners in setting class contracts and guidelines. They develop intrapersonal and interpersonal skills by engaging in oral and written reflection. Character is emphasized on the playground, at lunch, and in cooperative learning groups; it is noted on student report cards. Ethical behavior has become an important expectation at many independent schools; indeed, for many it figures prominently into acceptance decisions.

The Responsive Classroom, a publication supported by the Northeast Foundation for Children, provides an approach to teaching and learning that offers insight and guidance to teachers in developing the communication skills of students. The desired result is for students to learn together as they interact with purpose, as they organize to action, and as they reflect upon outcomes. As competition among children is diminished and self-understanding emphasized, children begin to risk more in social and learning situations. They unite for individual and group growth and in self-knowledge.

It is powerful to watch students apply the skills of character, collegiality, and teamwork to learning. Motivation, empathy, and achievement all grow. But this communication and cooperation does not occur overnight. Indeed, it is a step-by-step process. It is putting the ball in play and moving it down the field; the touchdown is an incidental reward. It takes goal setting, tenacity, understanding, cooperation, and reflection. It takes the teacher leading the offense with drive and spirit. Like the *Little Engine That Could,* determination breeds success.

Typical Teacher-to-Teacher Interactions

So why is it that many schools expect adult interactions to run smoothly, without laying the cultural groundwork that collegiality needs? Without understanding and practice, expectations and follow-through, teachers experience fear and competition among themselves. The symptoms include: a breakdown in school communication, an increase in competition among teachers, a lack of trust that one is valued and supported. It is one thing to expect trust and acceptance, cooperation and understanding, in children; it is another to expect teachers to accept and model this as a basis for collegiality among adult peers.

Too often, what is valued most—such things as student achievement, strong standardized test scores, parental happiness—comes at the loss of teacher teamwork. What happens between the openness of the classroom and the gossip of the teacher's lounge, or between the predictable and formal statements in the faculty meeting and the heated and animated conversation in the parking lot?

We have all watched the inexperienced teacher fresh out of school, filled with ideas and theory crushed by comments such as "Tried that, didn't work." Or, we have observed criticism and doubt as risk was taken in offering a fresh approach to a school dilemma. In two or three years, this new teacher often gives in and gives up and becomes isolated from colleagues. If the school is the sea, each classroom becomes a ship tossing and turning while trying to navigate to shore, the lighthouse offering sporadic beams of light to guide the way.

What Not to Do as a School Leader

But how does a school begin the process of developing collegiality and teamwork? Does it commence by displaying a list of rules for everyone to follow? *Excellent schools teach, promote, and expect collegiality. We are an excellent school; therefore, you will be collegial. Here is the list of desired behaviors.* (If this occurs, just watch the parking lot syndrome where subterfuge occurs while teachers discuss how to disregard each rule.)

Does an administrator pedantically detail the benefits of collegiality, citing all the indiscretions of the past that have thwarted teamwork? *We will be collegial. I expect all teachers to observe each other teaching. I expect you to talk about your practice in a positive way, not through criticism as in the past.* (Guilt only alienates, generating greater mistrust.)

Should a letter be placed in faculty mailboxes or sent via e-mail listing requirements and expectations for collegiality? *Please read the following memo regarding collegiality.* (Just watch the e-mail routings light up!) Administrators may use these techniques, paying lip service to the latest trend: "Did that. Check it off the list!"

For collegiality to occur, honest discussion and attention must be given to the nuances of its meaning and its implication in the school setting. The process cannot be rushed, as it lays the foundation for all future growth. It takes planning. It takes time. It takes commitment. When collegiality becomes a focus during in-service in August, the stage is set for all future growth and change.

Activity

Question before the faculty to be addressed in small groups: *What is congeniality, and what are its implications for the faculty of a school?*

Ten minutes later happy, laughing teachers will compile comments such as:

We like each other.
We have happy hour on Fridays.
We have a hospitality committee in charge of parties, birthdays, and special events.
We do things together outside of school.
We cover each other's classes when needed.
We share duties.
We joke and send funny (but appropriate) e-mails.
We have fun while working.

Underlying these comments may be internalized thoughts of acknowledgement about grouping and comfort. Beverly Tatum's *Why Do All the Black Kids Sit Together in the Cafeteria?* (1999) can be applied to groups everywhere: individuals seek people of like mind, of like age, of like experience, of like race. Congeniality is enjoying the company of those like you whom you choose to admit to your select group. Choice and likeness elicit kindness of action and deed. It is easy to notice the congenial groupings of the faculty by observing their choice of lunch partners. Congeniality may mean friendships forming by teachers with similar-age children, teachers teaching the same subject, teachers having experienced the same workshop or class, teachers planning for the weekend, teachers planning a wedding or birth. Like mind-set contributes to congeniality, the vagaries changing according to circumstance and experience.

Indeed, congeniality is the spirit the faculty is sharing at this very moment before the opening of school, the one that often gets lost with the stresses of the year. Too often, congeniality is confused with collegiality. While congeniality is a smile and a laugh, collegiality is a method of interacting and working with others.

Criteria for School-based Collegiality

What does collegiality look like? How do we recognize it in our schools? By what criteria shall we measure our modes of communication to see if they rise to the level of collegiality?

Activity

Here is a question for the faculty, which might be ideally addressed in small groups: *If you were retired, living in your dream home in your dream location, if you had enough resources to travel anywhere you wished, what would be the qualifications/description of the ideal school that would entice you back into teaching? Think in terms of all aspects of the life a school—teachers, parents, students, administration, materials, etc.*

Without a doubt the conversation will begin with money and space and building conditions. But as the conversation ensues, teachers will begin to describe qualifications needed to meet student needs and promote student and teacher growth:

Small class size.
The freedom to implement curriculum in a manner meeting student needs.
An integrated curriculum that flows.
A child-centered mission statement that guides all decisions.
Standards created and agreed upon by teachers.
A correct focus on standardized tests.
Time to learn. Time to share. Time to plan.
An administration that listens, and understands children.
A faculty that shares and grows and learns.
Teacher study groups.
Money for professional development and advanced learning.
Support to publish and present at conferences.

Why Collegiality?

"Things that matter most must never be at the mercy of things which matter least." (Goethe)

Teachers are great at brainstorming the ideal school. They are great at generating lists of essential elements of such a school. They understand singular passion and commitment. On the surface, this appears to be an excellent beginning to a school year, one filled with hope and promise. And it is! But as the year unfolds, the lack of collegiality can create a lack of follow-through. Vision without collegiality breeds stagnation. Passion without collegiality begets inaction. School outcomes without collegiality become unsustainable. Collegiality deepens and unites the qualities found in vision, vitality, and competence. It allows that excellent beginning to permeate the day-to-day activities of the school year.

Collegiality Defined

Collegiality can be defined as informed, skilled communication resulting in trust and risk-taking. It is founded upon

- belief, support, and advancement of the mission statement of the school;
- decisions made in the best interest of the child (or children);
- free, respectful, and productive communications in interactions with all constituents; and
- shared learning with and from colleagues.

Collegial Communication

For collegiality to take hold and grow roots, teachers must be educated in the skill of communication. First they must be taught and given time to understand each other's background, viewpoint, and learning style. Understanding leads to respectful and productive interactions, discussions where all voices are heard and decisions that are supported by a team.

1. Understanding each other

Just as congeniality emanates from affinity groups, developing an understanding of the colleagues with which one works helps promote collegiality. There are many quick "ice-breaking" methods and activities that benefit both existing and newly formed faculties and groups. Color-coded personality descriptions[1] and multiple intelligence indicators (2003) offer easy insight into the differences of personality and style. More advanced development is promoted in the low ropes skills of *Project Adventure*[2] and in-depth personality identifiers such as the Meyer's Briggs[3] and Enneagram Type Indicators.[4] One such activity offered by David Levine[5] significantly broadens understanding by engaging participants in gaining knowledge of generational imprints. (Teachers divide themselves into generational affinity groups. Each group is assigned the task to communicate to the whole the imprints of their formative years. For example, ages 40–50 may "produce" a Leave It to Beaver show referencing phrases, products, and expectations of the time period.) As teachers become more familiar with each other, the need to understand the essential elements of communication becomes more apparent, as does the benefits of applying them.

2. Skilled Discussion Techniques

Let the training begin! Whether working with a team partner, in committees, as a full faculty, or in parent/teacher conferences, communication skills are vital. Working to create a common language facilitates the direction and movement of a conversation. Have you ever tried calling "tech support" when having trouble with your computer? The conversation goes something like this:

"Yes, I'm having trouble with my computer. It is frozen." And after reporting the serial and model number, the store and date of purchase, whether you paid extra for a extended warranty (and they have all this on file as you frantically search the computer system and your paperwork for the answers), you receive instructions.

"Hit control, shift, and F7."

After searching the keyboard for the correct buttons you respond, "Where is control?"

"The bottom left of the keyboard. Now hit all the buttons together, at the same time. Nothing happens? Try again. Okay, now shut off the computer, or unplug it, or take the battery out or go to the start button, left click, right click on settings, and follow the arrows until you find . . . where you left click . . . are you with me?"

If you are fortunate, and after having spent much more time than you ever anticipated working with technical support, you achieve *success*! But too often you hear, "You will need to ship the computer to us. We'll have it back to you in ten days." With this comment comes admission of defeat. The project is doomed, and you now have to figure out how to disconnect all the cables!

But having a basic computer language of RAM, ROM, and gigabytes would have facilitated the flow of communications, reduced the time spent on the task of repair, and contributed to an understanding of the entire process that would also have held the added benefit of overcoming any attendant fear of technology. And, remember, we just want our computer to work!

> The single most important factor in maximizing the excellence of a group's product was the degree to which the members were able to create internal harmony, which lets them take advantage of the full talent of their members (Goleman 1995, p. 161).

Collegiality and skilled discussion allow communication and decisions to work! The work of Peter Senge, Robert Garmston, Lisa Lahey, Laura Lipton, Charlotte Humbard, and Bruce Wellman offer strategies and structure to facilitate such an endeavor. Their work contributes to:

- Understanding background
  - What you "hear" and how you speak is based on the background and experience of each group participant

- Listening techniques
  - Silence is golden (don't jump in and interject)
  - Summarization of others' opinions and ideas ("Is this what you are saying? I think I hear your position as. . . . " "Let me be clear about your point.")
  - Methods in sharing your ideas that allow for understanding ("I agree with you on ________; however, let's think about ________?")
  - Asking for further clarification ("I am a bit confused about this point. Could you help me understand?")
  - Perceptions of body language

- Debate
  - A command of skills to reach a decision
  - Use of hidden perspectives and loyalties to undermine the process

- Skilled discussion
  - Based upon a common belief or expectation, shared values and goals
  - Use of participants' background experience and knowledge
  - Disclosure and acceptance of all opinions
  - Inquiry and understanding resulting in a conclusion or group decision

Understanding skilled discussion techniques brings a faculty together through use of a common language. Practicing these skills in layers of situational difficulty energizes teachers! Instead of that lone ship on a turbulent sea, practice directs a crew to work in harmony to achieve the harbor of security and productivity.

Practice of skilled discussion techniques again takes time. It takes the allocation of faculty meetings distributed throughout the course of the academic year to practice technique. It is practice with purpose! Each session also takes reflection and sharing of what works and what doesn't. It takes trust. By first using simple questions for small non-affinity groups to address, a comfort level is established, permitting the implementation of newfound skills.

Activity

Here are questions for the faculty to address in small groups that will help develop skilled discussion techniques.

What is hard about change? This broad question can allow for the hidden issues of a school to unfold.

How important is community?

What role does teacher learning play in a school setting?

How important is a school's focus and commitment to a specific methodology such as Teaching for Understanding or Curriculum Mapping? As the questioning deepens and issues become more pointed, skilled discussion becomes vital!

How does diversity affect a community?

Combining Congeniality and Skilled Discussion to Create Collegiality

Using congeniality to understand background and experience coupled with skilled discussion and dialogue develops collegiality. When collegiality is taught, expected, and modeled by administration as a "way of life behavior," positive results happen! In Primal Leadership, Goleman (2002) explains:

> The "Group IQ," then—the sum total of every person's best talents contributed at full force—depends on the group's emotional intelligence, as shown in its harmony. (p. 15)

Understanding of self and others, possessing a common language of skilled discussion, results in visionary decisions being made and having their desired effect! Collegiality now unfolds at the very heart of the school as teachers create that ideal school where the growth of all constituents is a way of life. Teachers are now freed, as Roland Barth (1990) has explained, *to talk about practice, observe each other, work on curriculum, and teach each other.*

PART TWO
DESIGNING AND USING TEACHER EVALUATION THAT GUIDES GROWTH

Premise #2
Schools are about growth and learning for all constituents.

As a new teacher fresh out of college, evaluation scared and intimidated me. I found myself waiting for that "one time in the year" when the principal would come in, take a seat in the back of the room, script detailed notes, then call me to his office for my yearly review. All this was presumably required to renew my next year's contract. Not surprisingly, I became insecure and defensive in the face of this one-shot evaluation.

"What does he know?" I queried. "He hasn't taught in years! He has no idea what I do in my classroom." Or I joined in the lounge talk, "Isn't this a joke? She told me I needed to choose a better literature book! What does she do in that office all day?" And with each classroom and school change, the modus operandi for evaluation remained the same. Sometimes, the review came as a handwritten evaluation in my mailbox, only to be read at my leisure and then entombed in some file drawer.

I was alone in my classroom island, working to improve my singular practice. I knew there had to be a better way. My early desire for collaboration and collegiality, for discovery of a pathway for growth and development was not easily extinguished; indeed, my growing dissatisfaction led me on a quest for renewal. The journey led me to conferences and books; it led me to observing and talking with teachers and administrators of like mind. It led to Community School, where the mission and atmosphere invited a working system based on risk-taking and collegiality.

There are many evaluation systems available today. Strategic Performance Group has designed the 360 Performance Evaluation (taken online or in-house), which can be used to meet specific school needs. The Association and Supervision for Curriculum Development (ASCD) also offers guidance in designing a solid evaluation. There are numerous articles, videos, self-help programs, and promising new trends. It is generally agreed that evaluation is needed, that its purpose is quality assurance that recognizes, cultivates, and develops good teaching (Danielson 2002). Consideration is given to differentiated evaluation formulated on levels of experience: cyclical for the experienced teachers, yearly for the new teacher with five years' or less experience, self-directed with assessment driven by reflection for the vanguard teacher.

These systems have their respective strengths and weaknesses that become more apparent as they are applied to specific contexts. But there is, in my opinion, no off-the-shelf program or system that will meet the needs of each and every school—no one-size-fits-all approach. Designing an evaluation system that works is based upon:

- The establishment of collegiality: teachers talk and learn from each other using skilled dialogue and discussion.

- The belief in a shared identification of goals and mission: decisions made in the best interest of the child or children
- The need for growth: understanding that a school is about learning for all constituents
- The freedom to risk: identification of and desire to meet student need; a program based on research, experience, and reflection
- The advocation of accountability: for students, faculty, and administration based upon presupposed goals and standards

With these principles in place, full faculty participation in the creation of the system is driven by the process of dialogue and discussion. Just ask; teachers want to improve their practice! Teachers value input and feedback by committed, knowledgeable educators. Good "evaluation raise(s) the level of professional discourse within the school" (Clem, nd).

Activity #1

Scaled Evaluation Development (combined departments or full faculty)

As you acknowledge the mission and the strengths of the faculty, lead the teachers to brainstorm characteristics of "master teacher." With collegiality in place, the discussion and identification will be rich and validating as teachers focus on their own strengths or the qualities they admire in others, in mentors or in teachers from childhood that motivated or valued them in some special way. Before the group, chart or web each comment connecting to main ideas or center spokes. Upon completion, your web may look something like this!

Brainstorming Qualities of a Master Teacher

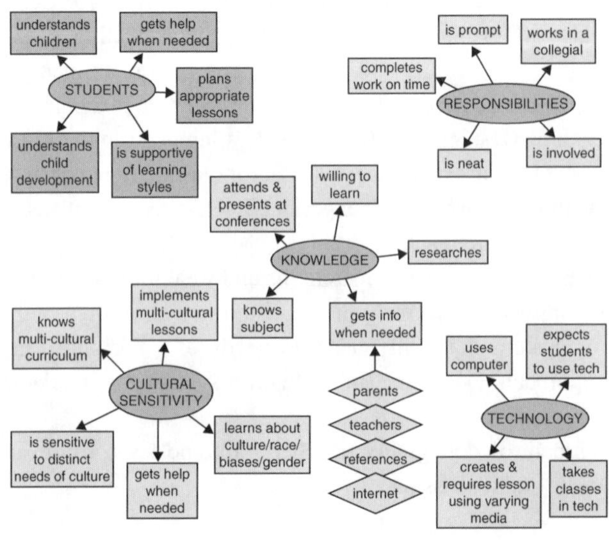

As teachers see the beginnings of their ideas, the list becomes long and varied, embodying subtle nuances of language. As the facilitator, your job is to accept and note *any* and *every* idea! When ideas are exhausted, fine tuning begins. As a group, center the ideas in approximately six fields. Organize all sub-topics under the appropriate field.

Activity #2

Creating the Scaled Evaluation

Divide the faculty into groups equaling the number of rubric fields. Hand out one field generated during the last activity to each group. Instruct the group to discuss and define the working field, creating a "title" that best describes the category (or accept the title listed). Next, have each group combine, delete, or construct field descriptors that best characterize the field. This process takes time as each group seeks to clearly represent the field's breadth and depth. Have each group then report, allowing for clarification and contributions.

At Community School, the teacher-created fields are as follows:

NURTURING THE GIFTS OF MIND, BODY, AND SPIRIT (*mission*)

Name___________________ Class Assignment___________________

Date________

Teacher Signature_________________ Division Director______________

Head of School______________________

Scale: 1.....2.....3.....4.....5.....6.....7.....8

needs improvement average exceptional

Curriculum Knowledge & Implementation

___has knowledge of subject matter and researches additional information if necessary

___uses a wide range of materials and resources

___projects interest for teaching

___is a risk taker: open to new ideas, approaches, & curriculum

___communicates clear expectations to students

___plans and implements lessons in a sequential manner

___develops interdisciplinary lessons

___has knowledge of and incorporates technology into curriculum

___keeps current on ideas and materials through readings, discussions, conferences, workshops and professional organizations

Collegiality: Inter & Intra Skills

(***adults talking about practice, observing each other, working on curriculum, teaching each other***)

___listens to and respects ideas of peers

___shares ideas and materials

___works collaboratively for the good of each child
___follows through with commitment
___works to achieve positive class and grade team interactions
___recognition of strengths and weaknesses
___commitment to personal excellence
___is supportive of new teachers
___demonstrates ethical behavior of thought in decision making and in interactions with colleagues, students, and parents

Student Relations

___respects development and individuality of each child
___develops and modifies programs to meet the individual needs of each student
___creates an environment supportive of developmental learning
___allows children appropriate levels of planning ownership of work
___promotes positive student interaction to develop self-esteem

Parent Relations

___communicates student progress accurately and sensitively
___returns communication in a prompt fashion (see faculty guidebook)
___initiates communication for positive student accomplishments
___understands the parent perspective of the child
___respects the uniqueness of each family and child
___actively listens to parents (is sensitive and responsive to parents)

Cultural Sensitivity

___has knowledge of multicultural curriculum as related to grade level
___revises, develops, and implements multicultural curriculum
___teaches from a multicultural viewpoint
___utilizes outside resources when applicable

Professional Responsibility

___fosters enthusiasm for lifelong learning
___takes advantage of professional development and uses knowledge in curriculum
___is involved in Community School committee work
___completes paperwork in a timely manner
___respects attendance by arriving for duties and responsibilities in a timely manner
___cooperates with administration and handles concerns via appropriate channels
___classroom management
___maintains classroom and personal space in an organized manner
___adheres to dress code (see faculty handbook)
___discusses students in a thoughtful manner

OVERALL EFFECTIVENESS

___Performance ___Attitude

(use numbers to indicate level of performance and attitude)

With the completion of the evaluation scale, the question becomes, "What now?" How does a school take that step from understanding the implementation scale to promoting growth?

Implementation of the Rubric

At Community School the evaluation scale is used yearly with each and every teacher. In April, each teacher completes the scale in pencil. The supervising administrator also completes an evaluation scale for each teacher. The power of the scale comes in the skilled discussion the administrator and teacher have regarding it. To begin this process, it is important to follow a few rules:

- As a supervising administrator, admit that you are scared and that sometimes, you will not have enough knowledge to complete a line item!
- State your criteria before discussion: (7,8,9 mean exemplary while 1,2,3 mean definite growth must occur! A 9 means there is no more room for growth!)
- Don't be concerned about leaving a field blank and asking for the teacher to enlighten you (which provides rich and eye-opening discussion).
- Change a number when you feel you understand and agree with the teacher's point of view.
- Don't let the teacher be too hard in their self appraisal.
- Start by giving lower numbers: If consistent in applying this with all teachers, understanding and acceptance occurs.
- Make notes and drawings on the scale as connections transpire between fields.
- Allow enough time for solid and thorough discussion. (Sometimes it takes forty-five minutes, sometimes two hours. The time is well worth the effort.)

Teacher/Administrator Evaluation Discussion

The unexamined life is not worth living. (Socrates)

After the initial greetings and explanation, the conversation between teacher and administrator may go something like this (A= administrator, T=teacher):

A: With which category would you like to start?
T: I don't really know (teacher is a bit scared and timid).
A: Ok, I'll choose Curriculum Knowledge and Implementation. You know, that is your real strength. Before even looking at the numbers I want to let you know your understanding and continual learning of the knowledge in your field is amazing. In fact, next year let's find a way to honor your work by allowing you to share specifics during our

lesson studies! We'll talk more about that later. Let's see, I put an 8 in knowledge of subject matter. What did you put?
T: I put a 6. I think there is always more I need to learn.
A: While that is true, given that you teach all day, the amount of information you acquire through reading, workshops, and by asking colleagues is amazing. Why don't you change your number to an 8? I did put a 7 in "using a wide range of materials and resources" because I find that you gather the most information in the areas you love: literature and expository writing. But I think you would benefit from understanding a bit more about how to teach creative writing. What do you think?
T: I didn't think of it that way but it makes sense. I think I need that to be a 6 though I had put a 7.
A: I put an 8 for being open to new ideas (just look how easily we are having this conversation!). But the next one, "communicates clear expectations to students," I think needs some work. I put a 5.
T: A 5! Ouch! Help me understand.
A: Well, sometimes your mind gets ahead of the explanation. You know what you want to say when you give assignments, but often, the details get scrambled. Let me give you an example . . .
T: You are right. How can I work on that?
A: The next time you give a detailed assignment, write the sequence of steps on paper. Itemize them and give each student a sheet. You can have this list on the SmartBoard and show one item to the students at a time. Better yet, the students can bring the list up on their laptop while you use the SmartBoard. When you explain the steps, the students can visually see the instructions (good for those visual and auditory learners). Leave space after each item for the students to take any notes they wish. We may want to consider this a goal for you to work on next year, though I believe you can accomplish this in record time!
T: Thanks for the help. Might I have you come in to see if I am on the right track next year?

And now for a difficult category!

A: Let's tackle Professional Responsibility next.
T: Oh, no. I know I need work there.
A: Do you want to start?
T: I have difficulty coming to meetings on time. I don't know, I always find something to do in the room or I get caught talking with someone.
A: I have noticed that. And when you come in late, what message are you sending your colleagues?
T: I didn't think of it that way, but I am letting them know that I don't think these meetings are important. I guess I need to give myself a 3.
A: I don't think a 3 is warranted. Let's compromise on a 4. Maybe we will make this category your main goal next year. I have noticed that you have difficulty coming to school on time also. What about your carpool duties? Are you on time for those?

T: I think time is my issue. When I think about it, I am sending a message to my colleagues when I am late for duties that my time and teaching work is more important. This sure doesn't help collegiality.

After all the categories have been discussed and signatures affixed, setting the next year's personal goal at this time, while the information and excitement is fresh, becomes vital. The conversation may proceed as follows:

A: Which category do you wish to make your personal goal for the next year? We have talked about your strengths and also the areas for growth.
T: I really think that in keeping with the spirit of collegiality, I need to make "timeliness" my overall personal goal. I am not sure how to do that. Any thoughts?
A: Let's start by stating concretely what you will do.
T: I will arrive to meetings five minutes early!
I will be the first to arrive to duties!
I will turn in all paperwork the same *day that I receive it!*
A: Now, that sounds like a plan! But how are you going to measure that?
T: I can keep a journal. When I receive our meeting and duty schedule, I will make a spreadsheet of dates and times. Then, on a daily basis, I will check off if I arrived on time or not.
A: I could help. Bring the spreadsheet to meetings and I will initial that category. Also, during our monthly meeting, we could review the spreadsheet and talk about what is working and what needs fine tuning!
T: Great. I am energized. I definitely want to be a team player.
A: You know, when you accomplish this, would you be willing to admit your goal to the faculty and share your plan: successes and failures?
T: Probably, though I will need a push from you.
A: Let's play that one by ear!

One final step before the end of school is the requirement of a self-reflection letter by each teacher, summarizing the growth they made during the year. The final paragraph should identify the personal goals citing measurable and incremental steps developed in a logical, sequential time frame which helps guide and accomplish that goal.

Collegiality and skilled discussion blend during the rubric discussion to create an in-depth and accepted self-reflection that benefits the teacher, the school and, most important, the students. The added benefit is that growth is projected by the teacher and then discussed with the administration. It is not dictated by the administration, a "You will do this or else. . . . " Collegiality coupled with the development and implementation of the rubric creates harmony. It allows for measurable goals to form. And it helps set clear expectations of performance.

PART THREE
PROFESSIONAL DEVELOPMENT

Premise #3

As the teacher learns, so too does the student.

In many schools, the approval of professional development goes something like this: It is mid-October. The director's desk is filled with requests for professional development: one-day seminars, half-day interest groups across the city, weeklong conferences on technology, on diversity, on curriculum mapping, on "Teaching for Understanding." There is a limited budget with funds being deleted in record time due to the excitement generated for continual learning. So, who receives what? Is it first come, first serve? What about the teachers who *always* want to attend conferences? What about those who *never* want to attend a conference? What about those who know if you turn a request in early, you are approved? And how is a teacher "debriefed" and information disseminated to others?

Professional development is the key to creating an unparalleled, successful school. Linda Darling Hammond (1997) explains this in terms of the student's experience:

> The single most important determinant of success for a student is the knowledge and skills of that child's teacher. (p. 689)

Good schools acknowledge that to acquire and develop knowledge is to keep learning in the forefront of teachers' minds and thereby directly benefit students. The question is, How? While a piecemeal approach to professional development may accomplish limited objectives, a focused strategy identifying individual and organizational goals, teacher requirements, and the school's future direction will guide and direct professional development in a purposeful way.

Consider the various teachers within your school. There are new teachers, experienced teachers, and crafted veteran teachers. There are teachers who are working toward graduate degrees and teachers planning weddings or starting families. There are empty-nesters and teachers overextended yet willing to take on any task presented. There are talented, dedicated teachers who can be counted on to lead with aplomb no matter what the assignment. And there are teachers afraid of leadership and learning. Since you now understand the nature, skills, and needs of each teacher, it becomes easy to focus professional development that is teacher centered.

Other considerations for professional development are the needs of the school indicated by the strategic plan, through standardized test scores, or through an agreed-upon theme or event (e.g., a school anniversary; education toward diversity awareness, acceptance, and celebration; adaptation to a new head of school).

INDIVIDUAL GOALS

New Teacher: The First Five Years

The summer before school begins, first-year teachers need to understand the focus and the operation of the school. If Teaching for Understanding or Multiple Intelligences is the stalwart guiding principle of the school, summer is a time for learning the basics. Generally, reading books on a set topic, then joining for discussion with groups of volunteer teachers and administrators, is enough to establish a solid foundation. At Community, new teachers read, discuss, and explore application from books such as *Improving Schools from Within* by Roland Barth (the focus is collegiality) and *The Teaching Gap* by Stigler (the focus is understanding the components needed to develop a solid foundation in math) to help ease their transition.

Come September, new teachers bring life and energy to the school setting. They are often idealistic, seeking to try new ideas and theories. They need guidance and nurturing to understand the culture and life of their particular school. School is often an exhausting yet energizing endeavor. Professional development in this stage should center on:

- Year-long participation in a focus group exploring the culture, expectations, and curriculum of the school—the group offers guidance in collegiality; in dealing with the students, colleagues, and parents. It becomes a sounding board for ideas, inspiration, and reflection.
- Outside of the school setting, development should center on half- or one-day seminars directed to the interest of the teacher to keep that excitement alive: literature books at a given level, positive discipline, cooperative learning strategies.
- Evaluation-scale goals should be concrete and easily attained through a step by step process.

Teachers from Year Five to Fifteen

This group brings stability and comfort in their adaptation to the particular school setting. They know and understand the school culture and have become comfortable in the classroom setting. Many are furthering their education at a local university or by taking courses online. Analogous to the months of January, February, and March showing increase in productivity and learning in students, the three- to fifteen-year teacher, when guided through appropriate professional development, now acquires more in-depth knowledge and the first inklings of leadership ability. Professional development in this stage should center on:

- Acquisition of an advanced degree or in-depth acquired knowledge in one particular area. Personal growth through workshops and seminars should center on individual rubric goals. For example, if a teacher identifies understanding and use of technology in the classroom as a goal, professional development should be approved which fulfills this goal. A first step might be identifying and observing a teacher in-house who would function as a guide and mentor. Next, two-hour workshops on programs such as Inspiration and i-movie. As skills advance, completion of a class on PowerPoint presentations for use for and with students could be considered. Finally, a three-day to one-week workshop covering all components of technology would further the teacher's knowledge. Each of these steps can be easily tracked by a teacher-developed spreadsheet or journal, then shared with an administrator in a monthly meeting. To further promote collegiality, respect, and learning, this teacher might use technology for a shared classroom experience during Lesson Study (discussed later).

Teachers from Year Fifteen and Over

As time and experience combined with guided professional development permeates a teacher's mind-set, growth takes the shape of leadership: teaching others. The spirit of the teacher must be honored and valued, then applied for the development of colleagues both within the school and without. Professional development in this stage should center on:

- Workshop presentations, articles written for publication, attendance and participation in national conventions, chair of school committees, mentor to younger teachers. As a sage is valued for her wise knowledge, a teacher in the fifteen-and-over group is looked up to and honored for those specific and unique attributes comprising the nature of excellence. Whether it is the acknowledgement of motivation, the use of technology, the skill in communication, the ability to write and teach writing, validation must occur. Just as it takes individuals with specific strengths of position—speed, quickness, strength for a football team to gel for that Superbowl victory—crafted veteran teachers offer depth and superior performance in a specific area.

Yes, these recommended time frames for the new, experienced, and crafted, veteran teacher offer simple guidelines. However, the vagaries of learning and life situations (e.g., marriage, parenthood, illness) offer much play and latitude as both teacher and administrator shift through the growth stemming from the evaluation scale and professional development. It is important to understand no one individual can and should achieve perfect 9s on a given evaluation scale. Just as teachers recognize and support the strengths, talents, abilities, and weaknesses of each student in a classroom, so too does the school identify and value individual teacher strength while supporting learning and risk for those abilities not as solid. Life is about continual growth; it is not about perfection.

GROUP GOALS

Just as particular, focused growth occurs for the individual, so too does group growth transpire that benefits the whole community. For example, if a need has been identified to further faculty understanding and best practices in teaching a diverse population, whole faculty learning on this topic must occur. As with the slow and steady development of collegiality, group goals take time to seep into the hearts and minds of a school body. A one-shot in-service motivational speaker or video generating laughs and determination is just that: a shot in the arm, the boost lasting until the memory of the event dissipates in the day to day classroom routine. Instead, group growth should follow a sequential year or two-year plan.

Process for School Wide Growth

The approach should be multifaceted:

- Begin by identifying purpose and mission as formulated by the strategic plan, standardized tests, parent initiative, and so on.
- Establish a committee of interested and vital faculty to research the latest findings, best practices, and recognized schools.
- Report the findings to the full faculty.
- Identify speakers and facilitators to work with the faculty throughout the course of the year.
- Promote small group or full faculty field trips to organizations, schools, or locations that further the goal.
- Establish time (using, one hopes, already established faculty meeting time) for study groups for dialogue, discussion, and debriefing of learning experiences.
- Establish book groups with a choice of book (not topic!).
- Allow monthly ten-minute teacher sharing of "what works in my classroom," centered on the group goal.
- Promote outside-of-school professional development on this topic.

The result? Deep and rich full-school understanding of a given topic.

Faculty Meetings

An added bonus to collegiality is the development of energized, enjoyable, and puposeful faculty meetings. When teachers arrive on time finding a comfortable setting, are greeted with snacks and an agenda, are solicited to tell classroom and personal stories for all to hear, focused work happens. Participation and input is generated in the decision-making process, causing faculties to become energized. The end-of-the-day blues are instead replaced with a sense of renewal in knowing that faculty opinion matters. At Community School, the tone and focus of each meeting is important, which further enables teachers to strategize, solve problems, and plan.

Lesson Study

At Community School, Lesson Study, a valuable program acknowledged in Japan that focuses on the perfection of teaching one particular skill, has been adapted to become small-group faculty study and sharing of a given topic. Meeting monthly, each session begins with an individual teacher sharing new insight, a particularly positive lesson, or information learned from a conference. Lasting up to ten minutes, congeniality and collegiality happen as respect is generated for adult learning. Lesson Study is then directed to the study and revision of curriculum and subject matter. In the past, the yearly focus has been Teaching for Understanding; working together to curriculum map a given subject via a computer program; or working together to identify, share, and revise best methods of teaching creative writing. Often research is shared or a book studied. But always, teachers are engaged in vigorous, thoughtful discussion directly affecting student learning. It goes without saying that as teachers share, peer observation occurs naturally! The halls and rooms before and after school are abuzz with teachers talking about their practice.

Action Research

A final word must be said about in-house learning generated through action research, which benefits individual teachers, small groups of teachers, and full faculty. As teachers join together to study their own classrooms using methods of action research, a genuine learning community forms in which issues are openly discussed. Teachers, by learning from the expertise of each other, feel empowered to take risks and bring scholarly innovations to their classrooms, their school, and to fellow teachers both locally and beyond.

In action research, the context of each teacher's study is vitally significant as teachers learn by doing. Individual questions are formulated and discussed. Each member of the team becomes a "critical friend," allowing the exchange to be sensitive, helpful, thought-provoking, and professional.

Specifically, "[a]ction research involves educators in: (1) identifying a concern, question, or problematic situation regarding the teaching-learning or schooling process; (2) focusing on existing practices or taking new actions to address the concern, question, or problematic situation; (3) determining and collecting the relevant data that will offer evidence of the success or failure of actions; (4) analyzing the data for new insights, understandings, and concepts; and (5) writing a report on their findings, including plans for new actions for oneself and recommendations for others.[6]

At Community School, the pivotal forming year of the action research committee chose a rather controversial issue, the value of homework, to explore. The goal was not to decide if homework was to be given, but how to make homework more meaningful and beneficial. Singular classroom questions were:

> How can I foster more effective communication with parents to ensure that there is a partnership in meeting students' homework goals?
>
> How can my actions in the classroom encourage children to incorporate independent reading into their daily routine at home?
>
> What strategies can I use to assist students to complete reading comprehension homework with better accuracy and greater understanding?

How can I develop a well-balanced program of homework that motivates the children to turn in quality homework and feel positive about the amount of time spent on their homework?

It was collectively, though, that these teachers united to study the overall summer homework policy. Through teacher and parent surveys, research, and an understanding of the history and expectations of Community School, the scholar-teacher group formulated an objective, purpose, and action plan accepted and implemented by the full faculty and greatly appreciated by the students and parents.

Conclusion

It has been observed that evaluation is something we do *for* people, not to them; the same insight should be applied to professional development. This chapter has maintained that the context for development—indeed, for personal and professional growth—is the key ingredient: This context we champion is collegiality. Collegiality depends upon informed, skilled communication that, in turn, promotes mutual trust and risk-taking.

My personal pathway and program and that of my school have been described in some detail. I offer it not as a detailed recipe—recognizing that each school is unique and must tailor its approach to growth—but as testimony to the possibility of creating an atmosphere of collegiality and educational excellence.

Bibliography

Barth, Roland S. (1990). *Improving Schools from Within.* San Francisco: Jossey-Bass.

———. (2001). *Learning By Heart*. San Francisco: Jossey-Bass.

Blanchard. K. (2001). *High Five! The Magic of Working Together.* New York.: Harper Collins.

Blase, Joseph (2000). *Bringing Out the Best in Teachers.* 2nd ed. Oaks, California: Corwin Press, Inc.

Bower, Bert, and Lobdell, Jim (2003). "Where Does Your Intelligence Lie?" *Social Studies Alive.* Palo Alto, CA: Teacher's Curriculum Institute. 95,96.

Clem, Steve (nd), "Evaluation and Supervision: Assumptions and Approached," http:www.nais.org

Danielson, Charlotte (2002). "New Trends in Teacher Evaluation," *Educational Leadership* 01 Feb. vol. 58. #5: 12–15.

Danielson, Charlotte (2000). *Teacher Evaluation to Enhance Professional Practice.* Alexandria, Virginia: Association for Supervision and Curriculum Development.

Darling-Hammond, Linda (1997). *The Right to Learn.* San Francisco: Jossey-Bass.

Drucker, Peter E. (1999). The *Drucker Foundation Self-Assessment Tool.* San Francisco: Jossey-Bass.

Fiegelson, Sheila (1998). *Energize Your Meetings with Laughter.* Alexandria, VA: Association for Supervision and Curriculum Development.

Gardner, Howard (1995). *Leading Minds: An Anatomy of Leadership*. New York: Basic Books.

Garmston, Robert (1995). "Adaptive Schools in a Quantum Universe." *Educational Leadership* 95 April. vol. 52, 7: 6–13.

Goleman, Daniel (1995). Emotional Intelligence. *New York: Bantam Books.*

———. *(2002).* Primal Leadership: Realizing the Power of Emotional Intelligence. *Boston: Harvard Business School Press.*

Garmston, Robert (1995). "Adaptive Schools in a Quantum Universe." *Educational Leadership* 95 April. vol. 52, 7: 6–13.

Goleman, Daniel (1995). *Emotional Intelligence.* New York: Bantam Books.

———. *(2002).* Primal Leadership: Realizing the Power of Emotional Intelligence. *Boston: Harvard Business School Press.*

Guskey, Thomas R. (2003). "What Makes Professional Development Effective?" *Phi Delta Kappan* 84 June: 748–750.

Kegan, Robert, and Lahey, Lisa Laskow (2001). *How the Way We Talk Can Change the Way We Work.* San Francisco: Jossey-Bass.

Kindler, Herbert S. (1996). *Managing Disagreement Constructively.* Menlo Park, California: Crisp Publication, Inc.

Kelleher, James (2003). "A Model for Assessment-Driven Professional Development." *Phi Delta Kappan* 84 June: 751–756.

Lipton, Laura, Wellman, Bruce, and Humbard, Charlotte (2001). *Mentoring Matters: A Practical Guide to Learning Focused Relationships.* Norwood, MA: Christopher-Gordon Publishers, Inc.

Morris, Meg, and Chrispeels, Janet, and Burke, Peggy (2003). "The Power of Two: Linking External with Internal Teachers' Professional Development." *Phi Delta Kappan 84* June: 764–767.

Osterman, K., and Kottkamp, R. (1993). *Reflective Practice for Educators: Improving Schooling through Professional Development.* Newbury Park, CA: Corwin Press, Inc.

Senge, Peter (1994). *The Fifth Discipline: The Art and Practice of the Learning Organization.* New York: Bantam Doubleday Dell Publishing Group, Inc.

Sweeney, Diane (2003). *Learning Along the Way.* Portland, ME: Stenhouse Publishers.

Tatum, Beverly (1999). *Why Do All the Black Kids Sit Together in the Cafeteria?* New York: Bantam Books.

Wald, Penelope J. (2000). *Educators as Learners.* Alexandria, Virginia: Association for Supervision and Curriculum Development.

ATTACHMENT
SUGGESTED PROFESSIONAL DEVELOPMENT

ORGANIZATIONS PROVIDING ONLINE/DISTANCE LEARNING

colearn@ncte.org (30-day free trial: $1,500 site license/academic year)

NCTE's CoLEARN: (Centers of Literacy Education Achievement, Research, and Networking) is a comprehensive professional development program based on teacher inquiry, teacher collaboration, and rich resources. The program's research and practice center on compelling, grade-level questions that invite teachers to observe and reflect on their students' learning and their own practice. Key to this process are tools designed to build a professional community so teachers can learn from the collective expertise of their peers. Included:

- online portfolios
- professional readings
- chats with leaders in the field
- network of experienced mentors

www.teachercreated.com ($129 personal growth, $229 professional growth, $425 graduate level)

- curriculum: reading, writing, math, science, social studies
- management: gifted students, multiple intelligences, inclusion, teaching strategies, testing, grant writing
- technology: integration, internet, digital media, Inspiration, Kid Pix, HyperStudio, Word, Excel, PowerPoint, Web pages

http:wideworld.pz.harvard.edu ($349 to $595)

- engaging students in deeper learning
- practical strategies to take your students to higher levels
- assessment strategies
- using web tools to support learning
- teaching to standards with new technologies
- looking at student work collaboratively
- using multiple intelligences as a tool to help students learn

Personalizing curriculum in an age of high-states testing

Understand by Design Exchange
www.ubdexchange.org
Understanding by Design templates and unit examples

ALPS
http:learnweb.harvard.edu/alps
Teaching for Understanding templates and unit examples

Association and Supervision of Curriculum Development
http:ascd.org/trainingopportunities/pdonline.htm
Examples:
Evaluation
Literacy and Learning Strategies
Understanding by Design
Crafting Curriculum

Student Portfolios
Surviving and Thriving in Your First Year of Teaching
Embracing Diversity
Conflict Resolution
Planning for Technology
Multiple Intelligences
Parents as Partners
The Brain
Effective Leadership

Summer Institutes

The Principals' Center at Harvard University
principals@gse.harvard.edu www.gse.harvard.edu/principals

- Focus on Accountability
- The Art and Craft of the Principalship
- Leadership: An Evolving Vision

Project Zero at Harvard University
www.projectzero.harvard.edu
The Thinking Classroom
Education with New Technologies
Teaching for Understanding

Ackerman Center Summer Institute
www.edci.purdue.edu/ackerman
(765) 494-4755
Ten-day institute for twenty teachers from across the nation of grades 4–9 to work at Purdue University with nationally and internationally recognized civic leaders.

Council for Spiritual and Ethical Education
www.csee.org
Adult Ethics Institute
International Institute

Milton Academy: (617) 898-1798
Cultural Diversity: Implementing the commitment in independent schools (brochures mailed to all NAIS heads of school in March)

Summercore
summercore@nobles.edu
weeklong technology training for all levels of knowledge

The Gilder Lehrman Institute of American History
(646)366-9666
Levin@gilderlehrman.org

NAIS
nais.org
workshops are listed according to season
Examples: Emerging Leaders Program, Experienced teachers, Curriculum Mapping

ASCD
www.ascd.org
Institutes (1–3 days)
Academies (5 days)

Klingenstein Center for Independent School Education
(212) 678-3156
www.Klingenstein.org

Project Adventure
www.pa.org/workshops.asp?workid=1
high and low challenge elements for all audiences

GRADUATE DEGREES

Examples of programs designed for distance learning with on site summer expectations:
Penn State
Columbia
Seton Hall

NATIONAL ORGANIZATIONS

National Council of Teachers of Mathematics www.nctm.org
National Council for the Social Studies www.ncss.org
National Council of Teachers of English www.NCTE.org
National Middle School Association www.nmsa.org

OTHER CONSIDERATIONS

Stipend for:
writing for publication
research
writing new curriculum
archeological dig!
designing Web Quest
designing web page

Notes

[1] The PACE Organization. Studio City, CA

Interpersonal Style Profile. The Pennsylvania State University, Management Development Programs and Services

[2] Project Adventure, Inc. Hamilton, MA: Kendall/Hunt Publishing Co.

[3] Meyers-Briggs Type Indicator, consulting Psychologists Press, Inc.

[4] Enneagram Type Indicator (RHETI). Enneagram Institute: Riso-Hudson.

[5] Presented by David Levine at a Community School workshop (exercises learned from Dr. Gerry Edwards, Adelphi Univ). For more information contact David Levine Incareofstudents.org.

[6] Dr. Marilyn M. Cohn.. St. Louis, MO: Retired Clinical Associate in the Department of Education at Washington University. Advisor to the Community School Scholar-Teacher Group.

Judy Fisher is the curriculum specialist at Community School. Judy has teaching experience in first through eighth grade as well as at the university level in both public and independent schools. She received a B.S. at Millikin University and an M.A. at the University of Illinois.

COMMUNICATION

Knowledge Discovery and Management; Streamlining Communication to Address Individual Student Needs

By Alan Bain

The promise of every independent school's mission statement is some form of student growth—academic, athletic, or social. The teaching and learning that enables this growth is the core activity of all of our schools. As such, it makes sense to consider the role of streamlining communication within this context by addressing the question: *What kind of feedback and communication serves student growth, and how can that communication be served by technology?*

It is impossible to address this question without paying attention to developments in the field of knowledge discovery/management that have revolutionized communication in the world beyond schools. In this chapter, I will explore what this field offers independent schools. We will see that an immense potential exists in the application of knowledge discovery and management to schools, although, as with prior technologies, this opportunity also poses significant questions and challenges for independent school communities.

Technology *Serving* the Individual

Technology advocates, information technology providers, and a host of commercial enterprises bombard us incessantly with the promise of sophisticated tools that can personalize our lives. These tools are "pitched" in a number of guises, including time saving and convenience, comfort/gratification, and knowledge acquisition, the latter frequently linked to some form of economic advantage. For example, the web commerce site Amazon.com profiles our interests and tells us about forthcoming books based upon our past purchases. The Xerox advertisement tells us we can assemble the desired features of a new car online, followed by the instant dispatch of a custom color brochure. We can bank and invest online, trade, spend and borrow faster and more expediently from any location. Online dating services mine personal information to find potential partners. College freshman and, in the future, independent school boarders, select their roommates through a fundamentally similar process and get to know each other before they actually meet on campus. Soon, we are told, TV viewing will be customized to our personal viewing preferences—"ME-TV," that only plays the programs and ads we want to see, or maybe in the case of the latter, none at all!

By way of comparison, the traditional bookseller stocks its shelves with those books it believes have broad or niche appeal. The car company makes one brochure that is more about the car and less about the driver. We go to the bank or brokerage house to make transactions on *its* time schedule. We see the programming and advertisements the television networks decide will sell successfully on their time schedule.

This is not to say that the end consumer was not considered in these more traditional approaches. Sophisticated marketing tools, ratings surveys, and various forms of field-testing are all used to establish our needs and interests. However, the net objective is to find the common denominator, the ideal time, the best place, the market niche and the most successful product, the one size that fits all, or the many, in a given segment or niche.

What we see in the Amazon, Xerox, and other examples is a very different approach, one that is focused on serving many by identifying the specific needs of the individual. Each example shares a common underpinning technology. They are built upon the capacity to manage and analyze massive amounts of information about each and every one of us. Sometimes, we volunteer this information; often it is acquired by more or less legitimate means, or is shared by others with or without our permission. This information is subject to fine-grained analysis to detect patterns and trends and then used to predict possible future behavior—our needs, interests, and desires. The goal—to discover more about who we are, what we need, and how we can best be served. From a consumer perspective, this is what knowledge management is all about.

What does/could all this information accumulation and sharing mean for schools and education? Reconsider, if you will, the statements—*learning more about who we are, what we need, and how we can best be served.* When we reflect on these remarks from an educational perspective, they actually sound a lot like the kind of words we use when describing the promise our schools make to teachers, parents, and students. We are seeking to build communities, where we better understand our learners in order to enhance their growth and better serve them. In doing so, we expend immense energy on personalizing the educational experience in a manner that enables our schools to fulfill their respective missions.

The rhetorical similarity between the rationales for knowledge management out of education, and the core purposes of our schools, begs the question—Is there a connection between the way knowledge is being discovered, managed, and used in so many aspects of our lives, and what schools do every day? Does the Amazon example, the Xerox brochure, or the promise of "ME-TV" have anything to do with the core activity of our schools—*teaching and learning* and, for the purposes of this discussion, how we communicate about them?

Data-Mining

To answer this question, we need to look more closely at what is going on in the Amazon, Xerox, and other examples. In every case, technology is being used to gather, organize, and interpret information that, in the pre–knowledge management era, would have languished, unreconciled, in filing cabinets or computers in different floors or maybe in different buildings of companies and public sector organizations. This data warehousing was largely justified for accountability purposes, ensuring that organizations had a record of important transactions.

The questions being asked and answered today, using this information, are: What do those transactions mean about the future and what can we learn from them? How can we turn large amounts of information into knowledge and manage that knowledge in ways that result in a significant advantage? This advantage can assume a host of forms or purposes associated with consumption, safety, and service, for profit or maybe not. Further, these knowledge management questions can only be asked and answered on such a massive scale with computer technology.

The specific technological tool that underpins our capacity to turn information into knowledge is relational database software that can warehouse and connect massive amounts of formerly disconnected information. In business, this means analyzing trends and patterns about what a business does, mining the data to find patterns and processes that can determine where future energy should be expended, who should receive the catalog, how to balance inventory more precisely, or where the sales force should pay attention; making changes in product; or finding ways to reach more consumers more effectively.

It is also a process being used extensively, right now, in the development offices of the majority of independent schools to establish the circumstances and giving capacity of their constituencies. We call this process data-mining.[1] It is the working activity that makes knowledge discovery and management possible.

The term *data-mining* is an apt combination of terms associated with the newest world commodity (information) and an allusion to a more traditional form of commodity extraction. We mine for data in a way that is similar to a gold-miner panning a stream. What may turn up in the process is information that can have a massive impact on the organization's future—a significant nugget or maybe many finely grained pieces of dust that together form a trend or pattern that will change the way an organization functions.

The key to successful data-mining is being able to turn raw data into metadata (big-picture data) to which we can assign meaning, and in doing so further articulate what an organization does; its key transactions; how its inputs, throughputs, and outputs are undertaken, and how that affects the current and future behavior of the people involved in all phases of the activity.[2] In doing so, we turn information into useful knowledge. For example, the school's development office is interested in finding out which parts of the country would be most appropriate locations for fund-raising events. It keeps extensive demographic data on the alumni body, past and current parents. By mining its database it can find those places where there is a convergence of sufficient numbers, interest, and giving capacity, and then compare those places, drawing more subjective and creative factors into the decision-making process but always building on a foundation of solid data.

Knowledge Discovery and the Core Activity of Schools

What, then, is the implication for schools beyond fund-raising? How do all these examples relate to their missions and purposes? Is there some advantage associated with being able to communicate information trends and patterns about the school's core activity—*student learning?* Absolutely.

Consider the traditional teacher-student learning interaction. A teacher grades a test or quiz showing that, despite classroom instruction, a student clearly does not understand a central concept. What options do we currently have at our disposal to address this situation? We might talk to the student or other teachers, or check the grade book and prior reports to look at past performance. We might, then, offer some form of extra help or tutorial support where the process can be broken down further or teach the concept more slowly or using a different approach. We know from research that the latter is a much less frequently used option.[3]

What If?

What if we had, at our immediate disposal, anywhere, any time, a compendium of essential information about the way the student learns best, the type of teaching that they respond to, and their ongoing performance in the curriculum? What if every teacher could log on to a relational database that contained a detailed history of the student's past performance, curriculum placement, learner preferences, and those teaching and evaluation approaches that have worked most effectively in the past? What if that database also afforded the opportunity for students to provide constant input regarding how they were progressing and what they feel is working for them?

Further, what if this was not some locked-down expert system pumping out formulaic prescriptions or solutions, but was an open-ended creative tool, transparent and readily accessible to a broad cross-section of the school community? What if every teacher could contribute new information to this repository and build upon it, sharing how things are going and those current approaches that work best? The result would be a dynamic tool that is customized not only to the needs of the student but the culture, values, and professional context of each school. Every teacher could mine the data for insights about how to create a truly personalized and adaptive learning experience for every student.

What if that database also provided feedback on how teachers were doing: engagement in class, classroom management, how well teaching approaches were used, and student performance and growth in the curriculum? Teachers, working in teams, could share this information, discovering new knowledge and insights about how to best meet the needs of all their students and how to engage in a process of constant improvement in their teaching. We could take the ethos and commitment to the individual that exists in all of our schools and leverage those strengths to a whole new level of professional sophistication.

Curriculum

The potential of relational database technology and knowledge discovery/management is not confined to managing process or evaluative data about what teachers and students do. This approach can be applied to the most critical constructivist tool in every school, the curriculum; specifically, to make the curriculum responsive to individual student needs. Individualization means, among other things, providing instructional materials adapted for different aptitudes and achievement levels, creating assessment tools that have differentiated expectations, and a range of teaching approaches that respond to different learning styles. While these curriculum components are widely acknowledged to be essential for genuine individualization, they rarely occur in substantive ways, and/or at scale in schools (i.e., for all students and teachers). The curriculum reality in most schools is "one size fits all" instruction accompanied by a genuine and effortful preparedness on the part of teachers to give extra help and support.[4] The latter should not be underestimated nor undervalued as it represents the essence of the independent school ethos. Yet it is a "low tech solution" in the broadest sense, not simply in terms of the potential to apply information technology to the challenge, but also with regard to all we know about teaching and learning. Further, without new ways to address the diverse nature of needs and aptitudes that exist in every class, questions of availability of time and practicality become resonant and legitimate concerns that further perpetuate the status quo. It is not realistic to ask teachers to do all that they do and add yet another new thing without thinking differently about the old things.

What we do know about the current condition is that if we were to expect teachers to do all those professional things that are required to address individual difference in the classroom, we would have a job that would be widely regarded as undoable. However, if the ethos of individualization was combined with a greater professional capacity to make a more personalized approach actually happen, the result could be immensely significant in terms of the capacity of schools to truly address individual difference.

Relational database technology can be used to reconcile ethos and professional capacity by helping to create curriculum tools that are flexible, more sensitive to individual difference, and capable of a deeper treatment of important subject matter. We can use such a database to store differentiated materials, to link lesson plans with assessment activities, assessment and evaluation activities with grade book, to develop assignments at different levels, and to plan and deliver instruction that is differentiated by achievement level on a day to day basis.[5] Further, we can use the same technology to interconnect all of these attributes in ways that make sense.

The grade book, the bulletin board, the day planner, the handouts, the books, and URLs can be reconciled in a single tool that connects the purpose and function of these sometimes disparate and unwieldy curriculum elements. Again, such a tool can be a place for teachers to create something that would have been immensely difficult without the technology. The same basic database approach that is used to find out who we are as consumers can be applied to the design, delivery, and evaluation of curriculum, making a truly differentiated curriculum an integrated classroom reality instead of a long list of things teachers need to do. With such an articulated curriculum approach we can go further in our knowledge discovery process, making connections between what is being taught, how it is being taught, and the learning that results. We can mine the data at different levels: student and teacher, team or department or whole school. In doing so, we can establish how we are doing as a learning organization.

Data Versus Intuition?

We should recognize that the essence of what is being described here is that which many intuitively gifted teachers do through a process of experience and connoisseurship. Those are the teachers we would have at the top of our lists of those individuals who really helped us over a learning hurdle, or made us see something more clearly or differently. A question might be, Would the type of knowledge management and associated tools I am describing unduly encumber the sophisticated intuitive process possessed by gifted teachers?

There is little doubt that knowledge management brings definition to an activity that currently occurs in a form ranging from the completely intuitive to more or less sophisticated efforts to use data in a logical process. As such, there is clear potential for such an approach to create a disturbance in the prevailing culture of any school. We can assume that disequilibrium will occur in a school or any organization when something that has traditionally existed in the subjective domain becomes the focus of a more objective process. This is especially the case if a school assumes the active participation of all teachers in the transition.

However, the history of change in schools tells us that such a disturbance may be more about the fundamental challenge of change than an incompatibility between objective knowledge and connoisseurship.[6] There is a strong precedent for reconciling the power of knowledge discovery with creative behavior in other fields, where data-mining empowers the creative process (including applications in music and creative thinking).[7] An intuitively gifted teacher working with a powerful relational database simply has more credible information at his or her disposal with which to create. In fact, providing those teachers with access to powerful relational database technology may enhance their abilities by providing evidence in places where they previously worked on assumptions. Knowledge empowers creativity in the generation of solutions for classroom learning. This is an emergent process less about reducing information to data and numbers and more about being able to manage and mine large amounts of numerical and non-numerical information for purposes that can be both inductive and deductive.

We also know that the gifted intuitive teachers are all too often the exception and not the rule in schools, inhibited in their capacity to communicate what they know because they have no professional language for doing so.[8] By capturing the essentials, the basics of a knowledge management process using technology, we can bring some form to this intuitive process. We can help all teachers to meet individual needs of students by having choices to pursue when learning is not happening.

Imagine a master teacher sitting in conversation with a beginning teacher about how to best meet the needs of a student who is having difficulty learning. They open a relational database that includes the information described previously and begin to discuss the teacher and student's performance at a whole new level of sophistication. The data combined with the expertise of the master teacher creates the conditions for a profound and substantive mentoring experience that provides the novice and ultimately the student with a genuine growth opportunity.

New Culture

When we consider the potential for many teachers to use knowledge management and discovery, it becomes possible to "re-vision" schools as more collaborative places where a common professional understanding helps to capture the collective intelligence that exists in every school. This is a condition where experts can mentor early career teachers, inducting them into a powerful professional culture that is more articulated and less mysterious and, in being so, can ultimately become more accessible for the novice.

For example, with such technology, we can begin to clarify what we really mean by learning and growth in a school. In doing so, we can bring greater clarity to those things that we believe contribute to the way teachers and students grow and develop. What it means to be master and novice can become something deeper, part of a shared understanding because we know what the terms mean. Further, when the processes of learning can be made clearer, students and parents can be invited into a conversation using language than can be understood by all.[9] Our beliefs about what our schools do and accomplish can be instantiated by what we find from our knowledge management tools. We can see whether those things that we believe constitute effective teaching or classroom management, actually contribute to student growth. What we find can either cause us to consolidate our current beliefs, modify them, or discard them altogether and investigate new approaches and potentials.

Challenge

It would be naïve to think that the kind of cultural shift that is implied by my description could simply be accomplished by introducing a relational database or any other piece of technology. There is a long and well-documented history describing the rejection of technologies in education that are not adaptive to the prevailing culture of schools.[10] Herein lies the challenge I alluded to at the beginning of this chapter.

A database is about fields and tables that contain information. In a school context, what we call those fields and tables and how we choose to define them would need, as an absolute requirement, a definition of common values and beliefs about teaching and learning. These fields need not always be filled with numbers but they do need to be filled with an articulation of what we believe. In the majority of schools, these values and beliefs frequently lack the kind of definition that could make them meaningful attributes in a relational database. Arguably they also lack the definition that makes them actionable in any collective, organizational sense. Few schools have decided what they are about, in this regard, with the level of clarity that could make for an easy transition to a knowledge discovery paradigm. *This is the challenge.* Revisioning schools as more-collaborative knowledge organizations requires that we bring sufficient definition to what we believe and do in order to create the knowledge management/discovery tools that can unleash the collaborative potential that exists in all schools. Working together requires, at a minimum, some common professional language and assumptions about professional practice.

Further, while many technologies represent a fairly benign automation of existing practice (PowerPoint instead of OHP, e-mail instead of mailbox, electronic grade book instead of hardcopy), what I have described in this chapter goes to the heart of what teachers and learners do every day in pursuit of learning. At present, in the majority of schools, this is, for the most part, a hands-off, "private practice" activity and not the subject of a commonly held view of professional practice. In fact, the prevailing disposition of schools in this regard is reinforced by one of the most widely held values of independent schools—teacher autonomy.[11]

However, the potential intrusion of knowledge/discovery on the autonomy of teachers should not be overstated. What is described in this chapter is the potential for any school to step up to a new level of professionalism by combining the widely held values of independent schools with more sophisticated professional tools. We know that such a goal can be accomplished without the result being a one-size-fits-all teacher.[12] Those tools require schools to bring greater definition to what they believe about teaching and learning. However, such a definition need not be imposed or externally acquired, just articulated in a manner that extends mission to a more specific articulation of what it really means in terms of classroom practice.

Herein lies the challenge that knowledge discovery presents to all schools if they are to realize the potential of the information age in ways that are revolutionizing life outside of schools. This is the opportunity to craft a true educational technology as distinct from the downstreaming of technologies from other fields. In doing so, it may be possible to create a synergy where technology helps articulate what we do in schools while that articulation helps to craft a more meaningful role for technology, one that extends far beyond the automation of current practice.

Notes

[1] Benoit, Gerald, "Data Mining." *Annual Review of Information Science and Technology* 36 (2002):265–310.

[2] "Middleware and Data Management Software." In Computer-Wire: Data Warehousing Tools Bulletin: Briefing Paper: What is Metadata? [cited 01 March 96].Available http:www.computerwire.com/bulletinsuk/212e_1a6html.

[3] See John I. Goodlad, *A Place Called School: Prospects for the Future* (New York: McGraw-Hill, 1984); Dan C. Lortie, *Schoolteacher* (Chicago: University of Chicago Press, 1975); Theodore R. Sizer, *Horace's Compromise: The Dilemma of The American High School* (Boston: Houghton Mifflin Company, 1984); Milbrey W. McLaughlin and Joan E. Talbert, eds., *Professional Communities and the Works of High School Teaching* (Chicago: The University of Chicago Press, 2001); see also Seashore Louis, Karen and Matthew B. Miles, eds., *Improving the Urban High School: What Works and Why* (New York: Teachers College Press, 1990): 3–14; Seymour B. Sarason, *The Culture of School and the Problem of Change* (New York: Teachers College Press, 1996).

[4] Alan Bain. *The Self-Organizing School in an Era of Uncertainty.* (Manuscript in review.)

[5] Bain, A. Curriculum Authoring Tools. (Wolfeboro, NH: Endeavour Group, 1997); Bain, Alan and Philip Huss, eds., "The Curriculum Authoring Tools: Technology Enabling School Reform." *The International Society for Technology in Education, Learning and Leading with Technology* 28 (fall 2000): 14–17.
[6] Seymour Sarason, *Revisiting the Culture of the School and Problem of Change* (New York: Teachers College Press, 1996).
[7] Siau, Keng. "Knowledge Discovery as an Aid to Organizational Creativity." *Journal of Creative Behavior* 34 (4th Qtr. 2000): 248–58. Conklin, Darrell and C. Anagnostopoulou. Representation and discovery of multiple viewpoint patterns. *Proceedings of the International Computer Music Conference,* pages 479–485, Havana, Cuba, 2001. International Computer Music Association.
[8] Alan Bain. *The Self-Organizing School in an Era of Uncertainty.* (Manuscript in review).
[9] Ibid.
[10] Cuban, Larry. "High-Tech Schools and Low-Tech Teaching: A Commentary." *Journal of Computing in Teacher Education* 14 (Win 1998): 6–7.
[11] Reil, Margaret and Hank Becker. "The Beliefs, Practices and Computer Use of Teacher Leaders" (paper presented at the American Education Research Association, New Orleans, April 26, 2000): 2. For a picture of the priorities in independent schools and autonomy in particular see "A Survival Guide for the Teacher Shortage." Norman M. Cobb, In *Independent School Magazine,* fall 2001—National Association of Independent Schools. Available from http:www.nais.org/pubs/ismag.cfm?file_id=932&ismag_id=1.
[12] Alan Bain and Peter T. Hess, eds., *School Reform and Faculty Culture: A Longitudinal Case Study. The effects of teamwork and collaboration on faculty culture in a major school re-engineering process* (manuscript in review).

Alan Bain served as the architect of the extensive school improvement and redesign of Brewster Academy conducted over the last decade, and is an international consultant to schools, systems, and industry on technology-based school reform. Now based in his home country, Australia, Alan is senior lecturer in the School of Education at Charles Stuart University.

On Meeting Well

By Lynne Brusco Moore

> . . . The biggest problem in any modern industrialized society, is loneliness. A great speech from a leader to the people eases over isolation, breaks down the walls, includes people: it takes them inside a spinning thing and makes them part of the gravity.
>
> —Peggy Noonan, *What I Saw at the Revolution*

First I should explain that I am an admirer of Peggy Noonan's writing. (*Who cares?*) We share similar perspectives on language and the way we make meaning. (*So what?*) Ordinarily, I write objectively, but not so today. (*Big deal.*) Meetings are about communication, and communication is the height of subjectivity. (*Is it possible there's a point to this?*)

A life in school includes, in no particular order, all-school meetings, faculty meetings, board meetings, staff meetings, advisory meetings, homeroom meetings, parent-teacher conferences, grade level meetings, curriculum committee meetings, college planning meetings, division head meetings, parent-teacher organization (PTO/PTA) meetings, department meetings, honor council meetings, club meetings, subcommittee meetings about meetings . . . and the list goes on. Meetings are an essential part of the way we construct community in school, but do we meet well? How can we make our time together, in student and faculty meetings, more effective? How can we overcome what is sometimes simply a basic failure to communicate?

The Well-Met Student Body

Some student bodies and faculty meet together every day, but this is rarer as schools grow. Others employ a 3–2 schedule, alternating an all-school meeting with small group advisories or homerooms. Some schools meet once per week in chapel or a similar setting. Auditoriums, gymnasiums, cafeterias, multi-purpose rooms, chapels, arbors, boathouses—wherever—students of all ages need a time and a place to gather, to see their peers and be a part of an esprit de corps that is larger than themselves.

In his celebrated literary portrait, *The Headmaster: Frank L. Boyden, of Deerfield,* John McPhee writes about Mr. Boyden's "art as a disciplinarian" and his ability to read and detect the mood of his students in the years (1902–1968) he served as Deerfield headmaster. According to Mr. Boyden, "You must have your boys together as a unit at least once a day, just as you have your family together once a day" (22). Studies conducted over the last decade chronicle the erosion of the family dinner hour. Distractions and fractured schedules are the culprits. Not surprisingly, the pattern is repeated in school. The academic schedule is tight enough for students and faculty, but then we factor in homework, grading, conferences, sports, clubs, projects, community service, and so on. Many schools that were once able to conduct daily meetings now meet twice per week.

Student body meetings have been eliminated almost entirely in some schools. Do not students and faculty see one another in class, between classes, at lunch, at games, etc.? Everyone is in the same vicinity after all. Information can be relayed in homerooms or cyberspace. The information age has prompted many schools to require that all students have laptop computers and Internet access. It becomes the responsibility of students and faculty to check for updates, but given what one head of school calls "the disabling effects of technology," this isn't always the best way to disseminate information. PDAs and high-tech toys cannot replace good old-fashioned face-time. Students may not always be as attentive as faculty would like, but they grasp a good bit of the information, especially when peers deliver the announcements, sports updates, prom theme teasers, and so on. They can be creative, slightly irreverent, and fairly entertaining—all in a well-spent fifteen minutes. Nevertheless, they should see their teachers and administrators together. One teacher mentioned the importance of seeing the head of school: "When she speaks, the activity center is quiet. They [students] understand and have a sense of the occasion that a lot of young people don't respect." Consider that twice-weekly meetings would be a gift in some Florida public schools where students meet in portable classrooms four days a week on a modified part-time schedule to accommodate school overcrowding (e.g., ABC High School Ninth Grade Annex). Grade level or all-school assemblies are practically non-existent—which means that if the school tracks or ability groups (academic, accelerated, Advanced Placement, International Baccalaureate, etc.), most students will not see or even meet peers in other tracks. Fortunate are the students and faculty in any school that places emphasis on meeting well and gathering as a community.

The Well-Met Faculty

When I surveyed several independent school teachers throughout the United States, they openly discussed their experience with various meetings. "They are *all* painful," was a reply from a teacher and coach at a Maryland prep school. He added that a department head referred to all faculty meetings as a forum for "consensual ignorance." An upper school head in the Carolinas sighed deeply, "A good meeting? That's a loaded question—I'll need all summer to think about it. . . . [laughing] What a cast of characters—the students and the faculty—and I'm one of the characters. . . ." He's right. Everyone has a role, but why the pervasive cynicism? Why does the topic elicit sighs and groans, but, ultimately, we laugh and show up? There's the rub.

Most faculty meet once or twice a month after school or during a scheduled break period. Some faculties meet for a weekly breakfast ("If you feed them, they will come," according to one dean). Then too, there are schools where faculty meet several times per week but with lapses in attendance. "The new teachers always need to be reminded, a few veterans choose not to go despite nudges from the main office—and of course there's always the absent-minded professor who never remembers. I sometimes wonder if they would be more apt to show if we didn't meet as often," said one department head. One new teacher said she attends because: 1) she feels it's her responsibility; 2) it's the best way to relay information that can fall through the cracks of faculty mailboxes both in and out of cyberspace; 3) they're amusing. "People can be very defensive. You can try to disguise it, but it comes through in discontented sighs, twitches and facial contortions that rival Cirque du Soleil. We're all in the hot seat at one time or another, but that's because we're in the business of taking things personally." Only in perfect relationships are things interpreted exactly as intended.

A frequently mentioned concern relates to those who speak without thinking. "Write down your thoughts before you jump in," said one department head after a meeting. "Listening to someone who knows exactly what to say would be refreshing." According to one administrator the best meetings always have an outline or agenda. "Let people know what you're going to cover—it's the only way they'll stay with you." Another teacher added, "Make it purposeful or please don't waste my time. It's good we meet frequently—but sometimes I just don't know what people were thinking in there." One new teacher keeps a separate notebook for faculty meetings. "Sometimes we get so stuck on an issue or argument that I'd forget everything else we talked about if I didn't take a few good notes."

In his book *The Fifth Discipline: The Art & Practice of the Learning Organization,* Peter Senge writes about systems thinking within organizations. Growth can only occur within a community that embraces choice. "One of the paradoxes of leadership in learning organizations is that it is both collective and highly individual. Although the responsibilities of leadership are diffused among men and women throughout the organization, the responsibilities come only as a result of individual choice" (360). Choosing to stay connected and to improve the way in which meetings are conducted are acts of community. Several years ago, a colleague summed up a Planning for Educational Change Conference he attended at Andover: "The headmaster said, 'Go. Find out what people are doing and how they're doing it.' It was great . . . lots of ideas and new people. When I got back, I thought they [faculty] were going to tune me out, but I was eager, so they were eager." Underestimation of faculty based on egos and quirkiness can be a deterrent to sharing community. Concord and discord always seem to be at work at the same time, but closer faculties seem to recognize and embrace this as part of the symbiotic nature of community. Dialogue allows us to make meaning. It enables us to clarify and create together. In the end, the choice remains: Say nothing and take no action, or go out on a limb and share our ideas because this is the essence of community.

What do most faculty members want from meetings? Some want facts alone. Others want Krispy Kreme Donuts ("only if the 'Hot' sign is on, otherwise forget it"), and others crave camaraderie. Connectedness is a recurring theme. As a full-time teacher and part-time administrator reflected, "Sometimes it's a lonely profession. Only other teachers understand the highs and lows. Meetings can be great and just the right support system if the mood is right. Though I probably feel closer to other teachers when we have events off-campus a few times a year—you know, holiday get-togethers and things. . . ." A new teacher added, "I never had a mentor, but I feel like the faculty adopted me in the meetings. I learned a lot—especially when they thought I wasn't watching." In this way, perhaps we did learn everything we needed to know in kindergarten: Listen, share, practice kindness, play nicely with the other faculty and, when necessary, take a time-out.

So at the close of the day many of the same questions remain: Did we meet our objectives? Did we invite participation? Have duties been delegated? Is everyone on the same page? Did we motivate? Are *we* motivated? Were we, as Noonan writes, taken inside the spinning thing and made part of the gravity? Have we, in fact, met well? One veteran department head said she looks forward to each meeting: "I really like my peers, and I work at staying organized and focused. Of course, some meetings with the kids and the teachers are more challenging, but I try to remember Anna Quindlin's mantra in *A Short Guide to a Happy Life,* 'I show up. I listen. I try to laugh.'"

Bibliography

McPhee, John. *The Headmaster.* New York: Farrar, Straus and Giroux, 1966.

Noonan, Peggy. *What I Saw at the Revolution.* New York: Random House, 1990.

Quindlin, Anna. *A Short Guide to a Happy Life.* New York: Random House, 2000.

Senge, Peter. *The Fifth Discipline: The Art and Practice of the Learning Organization.* New York: Currency, 1990.

Lynne Brusco Moore received her B.A. from Purdue University and her M.A. from Columbia University, where she participated in the Klingenstein seminar in Private School Leadership. She has worked as a middle and high school English teacher and upper school dean of students and currently consults with schools and corporations throughout the United States.

Capital Campaigns: Casing the Frame Before We Frame the Case

By Don Grace and Siri Akal Khalsa

Spring break ended with a bang and not with a whimper for faculty/staff at Chapel Hill–Chauncy Hall School. As we gathered in the theater for our first day back together, the audience quieted more quickly than usual. The expectant hush was filled with the measured, thoughtful voice of a design consultant. He confirmed what we had been told about this gathering: His team would spend the day working with the faculty and staff to begin to define the characteristics of classrooms in a new, proposed building. Along the way, the design team would also help figure out how we might retrofit other campus teaching spaces in order to best fit the work we do with students.

Our design consultant didn't begin conversation with faculty and staff with the expected question, "What does your ideal classroom look like?" In fact, he warned us away from visions of smartboards and wireless PCs at this stage. Instead he asked, "What is the work you do with students here? What is the work you want to do with students here?"

We had just been invited to step out of the box of traditional building design. We jumped at the chance and haven't looked back since.

The next six hours were filled with small, purposefully heterogeneous groups of faculty and staff exploring different perspectives of the questions posed. We regrouped, periodically, to share our thinking and, more quickly than would seem possible, a clear vision of what we do and what we would *like* to be able to do (given the appropriate facilities) began to emerge.

As we talked of integrating curriculum, of team teaching, of broadening methodology to address different learning styles and multiple intelligences, our design consultant guided us, wisely. When our thinking took us to envisioning a building of larger classrooms dripping with computer technology, he gently introduced the idea of what he termed "ethical thrift." Based on everything he had heard, our consultant suggested that we consider "clustering" teaching spaces. Taken together, for example, the classrooms serving ninth and tenth grades might offer all the facilities we wanted, though no one room would have them all. Teachers could then access the spaces best suited for the kind of lesson they had planned. We began to apply the same thinking to the classrooms serving eleventh and twelfth grades. We realized that this cluster would not necessarily look the same as the first cluster because the work we do with juniors and seniors is different from the work we do with the freshmen and sophomores—and requires different kinds of learning spaces to support it. Talk about a "Wow!" moment. . . .

It is impossible to describe the level of positive energy this day brought to faculty and staff. Our consultant (a veteran of decades of design work all over the globe) commented, "Maybe my cynicism meter is broken—but I haven't detected any here." We will continue these same brainstorming design conversations with students and parents, at appropriate times. The voices of all partners in this process we call schooling will have opportunity to be heard and, within the limits of time, space, and budget, reflected in the final design of a new classroom building. Interestingly, no one can say what that new building will look like—yet—and that's exactly the way we want it to be.

Most of us who have been through a capital campaign for a new building in a school know that although we may want it to be this way, it rarely is. The more common experience involves hiring an architectural firm that has 75% of a building's design already in mind. That firm might appear briefly to faculty/staff (never to students or parents) to ask a question or two about faucets and door handles in the building to be. It might even change a window or a storage closet after those conversations. But it would be loath to make significant changes in a new building from those conversations; it would not be charged with upgrading all campus teaching spaces; and it would not think of asking questions about ideal learning environments. Moreover, when a typical campaign for a new building is completed and the building is up, two classes of teachers/students are created—those who get to teach/learn in the new facilities and those who don't. Not exactly community building.

We are doing something different. In the parlance of capital campaigns, the administration and board need to frame a case for the capital campaign, to establish the need for campaign itself. As we have moved through this process, we realized that we needed to case the frame before we framed the case. We needed to understand how a new building might connect powerfully to other initiatives on campus that we had already made over the last few years. Here is how we arrived at the point of being able to plan for a new building that would be designed, from windows to doorknobs, to support the singular way we work with students at our school.

Casing the Frame

As we are building the case for a capital campaign to transform all teaching spaces on campus, we are realizing that we have made other powerful initiatives for the ideal—in faculty/staff, in students, in program and in buildings. This stemmed from our Long Range Plan, passed in 1998. That plan called for improvements in each of those four areas in order to serve the mission of the school more effectively.

Ideal Faculty/Staff

Three years ago, we decided that our attrition rate of faculty/staff was simply too high, at 32%. We committed ourselves to a program of re-recruiting faculty/staff most appropriate to the mission of the school. That program included four key components:

- creating a board focus for the year of how we might retain the faculty/staff most appropriate to the school
- making the faculty and staff evaluation systems more effective
- expanding our new faculty/staff orientation to five days
- publishing a list of characteristics we sought in a faculty/staff

All of these efforts helped us strive for the ideal faculty/staff to work with our students, program, and mission.

Ideal Student Body

The year before and the year after the board focused on retaining the ideal faculty/staff, trustees concentrated on answering the question of the ideal student body. We created board visit days around that question, with board exposed to seminars, class visits, student grade level reviews, debriefing, and small group discussions with faculty/staff on the issue. We came to clearer understandings about the best mix of our students:

- boarding/day
- domestic/international
- academic diversity within the student body

We realized that the question of retaining faculty/staff was tied to the question of the ideal student body in a number of important ways.

Best Curriculum

Three years ago, a summer faculty work group examined our curriculum and proposed that we commit to a three-year review, using Grant Wiggins' concepts (*Understanding by Design*, 1998). We began that work the next fall, exploring first the skills and understandings we wanted our students to have by grade level and by discipline. In the second year, we looked at the ways we assess whether or not our students have obtained those skills and understandings. This year, we are designing curricula and the daily schedule in consonance with our work of the first two years. This process has been driven by department chairs instead of a head's decision or outside evaluation.

Building Improvements

Four years ago, we did a complete theater renovation with funds raised through the parents and guardians association. The next year, we noticed that the assemblies we held in that theater space were more productive—in part because of the positive effects of those renovations. In the time since that renovation, we have completed over $2,000,000 in renovations of working, teaching, and living spaces and in the addition of 87 computers and five new computer facilities on campus. We have also created a five-year plan for catching up on deferred maintenance across campus, and we are into the third year of that plan. Vandalism and litter have decreased while the self esteem of our students has reached the heights of the new gym roof. The physical space can play a significant, positive role in the lives of our students and our teachers.

By working toward the ideal faculty/staff, student body, program, and physical spaces, we created a synergy of forces moving us toward the ideal. That synergy has led naturally to our taking on the unusual challenge of transforming all campus classrooms.

Framing the Case

Understanding our initiatives to the ideal, we have become more ambitious about a capital campaign and a building project. We are not satisfied with simply creating a new building, even if the new building might (alone) help us fulfill the mission. Instead, we hunger for renovating all of our classrooms on campus, so that no student and no teacher has to work against the physical space in their learning/teaching.

As we frame the case for the capital campaign, then, we will be able to appeal to our donors to help us change the way we learn across campus. We operate under the motto, "A School Without Labels. An Education Without Limits." A capital campaign to get all our classrooms up to an ideal will help us make dramatic steps in carrying out that motto and in fulfilling our mission.

Looking Ahead

We have yet to hire an architect to design an actual building. Our current design consultants will work with us through a couple of more phases before we are ready to interview architects. Design brainstorming meetings with parents and students are still to come. So is a utilization analysis of current space. This analysis will be placed over the ideas coming out of our brainstorming sessions, and whatever we want to do that can't be worked into current or renovated space becomes the new building. This is another aspect of ethical thrift.

While these design activities go on, we are in the quiet phase of the capital campaign, already having obtained some significant pledges in response to our synergistic case. Making the case, *especially without a portfolio of sketches*, couldn't be easier because we are asking donors not merely to help fund a new building, but more significantly, to partner with us in transforming the educational experience students will have.

How to Get Your School from There to Here

Are you frustrated by your school's conversations about capital campaigns, buildings, and ideal teaching spaces? Are you attracted by the prospects of more idealistic, inclusive, and synergistic dialogues on these topics? If so, we have a few suggestions for you:

- Look to the intersection of your long-range plan and your mission for opportunities to consider the ideal (whether that be faculty/staff, student body, program, facilities).
- Concentrate on one of those areas rather than all four. When you add a second area, look for synergy between two areas as you make progress on both.

- Find ways to treat your faculty/staff (and students/parents in your community) as the experts they are about what is working and what is not working in the school.
- Seek out capital campaign consultants and architectural consultants who are oriented to inclusive information gathering and to campaign/building designs that respond imaginatively to the community's wisdom.
- Talk to other schools about their best practices for capital campaigns, buildings and ideal teaching spaces. Include us on your list!

Success comes from casing the frame before you frame the case, and particularly in building teaching spaces that help your faculty serve the needs of your students.

Don Grace worked in independent schools for 31 years and headed four of those schools over a period of 20 years. He is currently the chief development officer for All Kinds of Minds, an institute founded several years ago by Dr. Mel Levine and Charles Schwab to promote understanding of students' learning differences.

Siri Akal Singh Khalsa, the head of Chapel Hill–Chauncy Hall School, in Waltham, MA, holds a doctorate in educational administration from Teachers College, Columbia University, where he worked under Prof. Pearl Kane. Prior to that, he served as assistant head at Oakwood Friends School in Poughkeepsie, NY, and as vice-principal of two international schools in India.

School Law: Trials, Tribulations, Confirmation

By Jim Leonard

About six months into my first year as head of school, I asked our physical plant manager if he could build me a small cabinet for an empty space along the back wall of my office. I found I was accumulating files to which I needed ready access—something closer than the closet that houses two big standing file cabinets—but which I could not leave piled on a corner of my desk. These were sensitive files.

The plant manager quickly obliged, and I have since nearly filled the top shelf of this cabinet with what I call "legal files"—those issues confronting the school on which I have either consulted our legal counsel or directly engaged him. The subject matter of these files would not greatly surprise any independent school head; they are the universals of school life. A student suspension challenged by the parents, who engaged a lawyer. A faculty member whose contract was not renewed for poor performance. An enraged parent who threatened litigation because her child had not received the positions or recognitions she felt were deserved. A prospective parent whose child was not admitted and who argued that the prior administration had effectively "guaranteed" admission. And more. When I checked the cabinet eighteen months into my tenure, I found ten files of varying thickness, import, and immediacy. Only one of these potential cases has landed in court, and I feel confident that the school has proceeded appropriately on each issue. Our lawyer feels equally confident but warns me that appropriate procedures do not ensure we won't go to court. In the American legal system, it takes only one to tango.

I did inherit one lawsuit when I took over as head of school: an age discrimination and wrongful dismissal case brought by a teacher released four years earlier. The court date had already been set, for October of my first fall, and I gradually came up to speed on the case over my first months. My interest, though, was initially quite academic. School employees were being deposed, the attorney hired by our insurance company briefed me on the details, and I kept the chair of the Board of Trustees apprised as various settlement offers were made and rejected. The morning I spent in court watching our former head of school testify seemed like an extension of the New Heads' Institute I had attended that summer: Here's what to avoid when terminating a longtime employee.

My interest shifted from academic to downright personal when the judge found for the former teacher on the contract claim—awarding her over $50,000 that I would need to find in a budget that had no contingency line item and a discretional account for me of only $2,500. (The judge did rule in the school's favor on the much more explosive and potentially damaging charges of discrimination.) The case is now under appeal, allowing us a couple of budget years to set aside the necessary money, and we may even overturn the judgement.

That first case has served as a useful touchstone for me as I encounter the inevitable conflicts and controversies of independent school life. School heads can serve for years, even entire careers, without ever seeing a case go to trial. I served for less than four months. The end game—hours spent preparing testimony, huge legal costs, damaging awards, potential negative publicity—was immediately made clear to me.

Common wisdom among school heads, particularly experienced ones, is that our increasingly litigious society has made it more difficult to direct school affairs. For that low-performing teacher who years ago could have been dismissed by the head because "everyone knows he is a poor teacher," we must now generate multiple documents cataloging his poor teaching and identifying steps to improved performance: Then, if he still falls short of the work, he can be released. Detailed campus security and safety plans must be crafted to appease board members, parents, and insurance companies when less comprehensive but more direct plans might better serve us in a crisis. Letters outlining a school's decision to require a student to withdraw for disciplinary or academic reasons are first run past the school attorney to be certain we're not sowing the seeds of a future lawsuit. And so on. In virtually every area of school life, from admissions to athletics to employment practices to, even, fund-raising, experienced heads descry the barriers to effective administration increasingly imposed by our litigious society.

I have great respect for that perspective, and even greater respect for anyone who has served as head of school over a period of years. But I would like to draw a subtle distinction. While threats of litigation—or the reality of a lawsuit—may generate extra work, anxiety, and even anger among school administrators, I am not convinced they force us to make decisions we would not otherwise have reached. School law impacts the *process* of decision making on complex issues within independent schools, not the *outcomes*. In fact, the cloud of litigation hovering always on the distant horizon may make us more compassionate, fair-minded, and effective heads of school.

That statement comes with one notable exception: the frivolous, baseless, wholly self-interested charges too often leveled at schools that swallow up huge chunks of a head's time and take us away from the essential duties of running a school. I have endured several of these charges already, and I fear they will comprise the majority of the legal issues I confront in the years to come. These challenges, often made by a frustrated party in the moments of initial disappointment, prove to be deeply distracting.

Rather, I am focusing on those many-sided issues that confront school heads several times each year on which we are urged by that inner voice to "check with the attorney" before a decision is reached. Each time I have listened to that voice—and then to the opinion of the school's counsel—I have gained a valuable perspective and, most importantly, *become more confirmed that the decision I was beginning to articulate was the right one.* Limited in years if not in cases, my experience suggests that school law reinforces rather than obstructs effective decision-making. I offer below several illustrations, but first, another caveat. Our attorney, while a current parent and thereby interested in the school's success, is, more importantly, the leading authority on school law in the state. He heads the school law practice at his firm, which represents over 90% of the school districts in New Mexico. Not only a good lawyer, he is a good school lawyer, and I would advise any head of school to begin a relationship with an attorney versed in school law—before that becomes a necessity.

Illustration #1

In my first year, we endured a disturbing amount of stealing—money, CDs from backpacks, jewelry, cameras, and so on. Ours is a school with lockers, but no locks; from office doors to bookbags to cars in the school lot, the expectation is the same: leave it unlocked; we can all be trusted. Yet over the course of several months, it became clear that one or more people within the school were preying on that trust. We took steps: Chronicling every item that was stolen. Calling in a detective to walk very publicly the campus with me and recommend several low-impact security measures. An all-school assembly that involved several adults and many students talking about the effect they felt this was having on the school.

And we called in any student who had been identified as potentially involved in one of the thefts. One young woman was clearly suspected by a number of students. We talked with her twice, once even involving her parents, but she was adamant she was not stealing, and we lacked any direct evidence.

In early January, her father called to tell me that he was planning to send her to a therapeutic school in a remote area of the west. She had run away from home, he could not control her, and he asked for my help in turning her over to him while she was at school, as he did not know how to locate her. He then planned to have employees of the therapeutic school take her into custody immediately and escort her away.

It was here that I called the school attorney (and the board chair.) We had not covered this type of scenario at the New Heads' Institute. . . . Our attorney advised that I had the right to cooperate with the parent—which I was inclined to do—and identified certain other conditions that he thought could help me in the scenario that was about to unfold.

Not everything went according to plan. The young woman was finally caught stealing late that afternoon but bolted from campus. When she returned the next morning, I confronted her with that information and expelled her from school but said I needed to turn her over to her father. She came close to bolting from the office but ultimately stayed to be taken to the therapeutic school, where she received help. She later attended a local public school.

My instincts—to support parents seeking help for a troubled, unwilling child—were reinforced by school law and by our attorney. Without that reinforcement, I might have told the father he would need to find his daughter somewhere other than on school grounds, expelled her, and moved on.

Illustration #2

In January, I informed a teacher that her contract would not be renewed for the coming year owing to poor performance in the classroom as identified by student assessments of her teaching, multiple visits by the division head, and lack of progress in the areas for improvement noted in prior evaluations. We spoke face-to-face on a Thursday, and I followed up with a letter to this effect on Friday. That Sunday, I left town for four days to serve on an evaluation team at another ISAS school. On Monday, I received a fax from this teacher, at the school I was visiting, informing me that she was planning to solicit letters of support for her teaching from colleagues, students, parents, and board members. I envisioned returning to a roiling maelstrom of discontent three days later, and felt it should be within my authority to preclude this teacher from generating an opposing force. So I called our attorney.

"You need to fax her something immediately stating that you forbid her from discussing her contractual status with parents, students or board members with the intent to disturb the operations of the school," said the lawyer. "New Mexico has a statute, #______, that specifically addresses. . . .

"One other thing," my attorney cautioned. "I assume you've got plenty of documentation on this teacher, her performance, and so on?" I responded that I felt pretty confident we did, then sent the fax, which quickly put an end to the teacher's plans to mount a defense.

Illustration #3

In April, a ninth grader who had been accepted for the coming fall at an eastern boarding school admitted to downloading a paper from the Internet and submitting it as her own work in an English class. Our approach to first offenses of academic dishonesty is to give a zero for the work, require a rewrite for no credit, place the student on disciplinary probation—and where the student is moving on to another institution (typically college), to inform the school that a disciplinary offense has occurred. We issued these consequences, and the parents went ballistic about our intention to inform the boarding school. "You'll send her there with a black mark against her," they said. "It feels like double jeopardy," said the father, a lawyer. "You punish her here, and then they'll punish her there." And finally: "If you do this, we're going to engage a lawyer."

By this time, our attorney was on my speed dial along with my wife, my best friend from college, and another local school head. "Fine. Let's meet with them," said our attorney.

First, we met alone to cover a few details. Having worked in eastern boarding schools, I felt pretty certain that this young woman's new school would not hold against her an initial offense—if she owned up to it fully and revealed that she'd learned from the experience. Unfortunately, her parents were sending exactly the opposite message. Nevertheless, I did want this young woman to have a clean slate at her new school and felt we could ensure that while remaining consistent with our policy of full disclosure about our students to succeeding institutions.

And so we met: the parents, their lawyer, the school attorney, and I. One of the first things about having an attorney versed in school law is that, *in every case,* he knows more about applicable statutes, case law, and school practices than the attorney from the other side. Since independent schools enjoy broad discretion in administrative decisions, our attorney's authority becomes even stronger. We ended up agreeing that I would draft a letter to the dean of students at the boarding school that would be reviewed first by our attorney, then by the parents and their attorney. We sent the letter *without changing a word* from the original draft.

*****

My father, a lifelong educator and president of a local teacher's union for 23 years, graduated from law school the same year I graduated from college. He was 53 years old. I think I know now what drew him back: The most intellectually and ethically challenging questions that confront educational leaders—board chairs, school heads, union leaders, superintendents—are not legal issues per se, but they invoke a legal dimension. To the extent that we can embrace that dimension and have it inform our resolution of these challenging questions—well, I believe that makes us more effective leaders.

Jim Leonard entered his fifth year as head of school at Santa Fe Preparatory School in the fall of 2003. Prior to his position in Santa Fe, he taught English and worked on the farm at the Mountain School of Milton Academy in Vershire, VT, for seven years. Jim and his wife, Story, also an educator, began their teaching careers at Pomfret School in Pomfret, CT.

The Courtroom in the Classroom: What We Should Talk About When We Talk About the Law

By Craig Thorn

Five years ago, I tried to put together a book entitled *The Courtroom in the Classroom: How the Law Is Influencing Independent School Life.* Many colleagues in independent schools were interested in contributing to the book. Educators offered to write about the law and sports equipment, the law and sexual harassment, the law and faculty evaluations. I heard stories by now familiar to everyone in independent schools about rickety fire escapes, asbestos, disciplinary decisions, and diploma requirements. Nearly fifty writers representing as many schools responded immediately to our call for writers with provocative stories and suggestions. Then, one by one, they called me back with the same story: "On advice of counsel, I have to withdraw my commitment to write for your book." The explanation was always the same: "The concern is that a piece that trades on our school's experiences with the law might be used in court someday against us." In effect, the early demise of the book was the book's best story about the law and its influence on independent school life. Over the course of my planning the book, however, I did hear several versions of the following joke:

> A small co-educational boarding school decides to focus its athletic program on a small selection of sports: lacrosse, field hockey, basketball, soccer, and tennis. Soon, the school becomes very successful in these sports, attracting students with fine academic records who excel in these sports and want to play them in good colleges. At a morning lacrosse game, a tennis star watching the contest slips on the aluminum stands and dislocates his elbow. The diagnosis is that he will be out for the winter. The parents sue the school, claiming that he cannot train in the winter and therefore his tennis career, in particular his national ranking, is jeopardized. The school, they argue, should have warned kids about the stands, made slippery because of the morning dew. The school knows that the claim is spurious, but they settle out of court. Because it is a small school, the liability insurance covers the settlement, but just barely. Two years later, the head of the school and the school's counsel are standing in the middle of an empty field. The head throws his hands up in the air.

"I have followed your advice every step of the way. We got rid of the sports programs. We got rid of coeducation. I turned the place into a day school. We closed most of the buildings. I've fired the faculty and the staff, we don't admit students anymore, and I don't even answer the phone. And we're still getting sued! What's left?"

The lawyer gazes across the empty field and regards the head of school carefully.

"Well, as far as I can tell, you only have two more problems."

*****

That the law increasingly influences the way independent schools conduct business is old news to most educators. However, I would argue that the law's presence in our schools is much more profound and troubling. Surely, the law has changed the three major areas in which essential education takes place: in our residential, academic, and athletic programs. As a consequence, the law is a major factor in changes that are taking place in independent school culture. Here are a few such changes that come to mind:

- introducing corporate models of governance into what we want to be communal environments
- formalizing what used to be informal relationships
- increasing the number of more specialized mid-level administrators and support staff in part to address potentially litigious issues
- cutting programs for which liability insurance is prohibitive
- responding to many individual situations with complex policy and protocol that attempts to comprehensively anticipate all possible future situations
- creating more work to protect the school against finely wrought charges of negligence: in particular, intensive coverage everywhere on campus and volumes of paper to document that coverage
- deputizing residential faculty with legal responsibilities as fire marshals, security officers, and officers of the court in conflict with formal and informal codes of confidentiality as counselors, advisors, and mentors
- codifying dormitory situations rather than relying on counselors' instinctive responses to specific dorm environments
- separating the administration from the faculty to protect both parties from contractual issues
- reducing physical plant to those areas that can be monitored, brought up to code, rendered impervious to accident
- standardizing all school communications—instructor reports, house counselor letters, college recommendations, and inter-office memoranda—so as to make them effective in court
- restricting student expression in theater, on the radio, in art, in student publications—effectively challenging the essential metaphoric quality of language so vital in the exchange of ideas because of the risks of misinterpretation

- shifting the way decisions are made from consensus to chain of command so as to have a clear line of responsibility
- redistributing allocations in operating budgets to address deferred maintenance that might run afoul of the law and to offset the cost of insurance
- establishing clear and much more uniform guidelines for the evaluation, assessment, and tracking of students in the curriculum

To many of us, this list might have seemed alarmist just a few years ago; however, if you have been involved in a lawsuit against your school, you know that the initial phases of a litigation are often limited only by an aggressive lawyer's imagination. The law defines itself by precedents and so lawyers look for them. Independent schools, with their pastoral communal traditions and quaint physical plants, are rich with potential precedent-setting cases.

In the three major areas of independent school life—the classroom, the campus, and the athletic field—legal cases have had a chilling effect on school culture. We educators have rightly added rules, guidelines, procedures, specialists, meetings, and protocols with which we hope to codify an ever-changing community of students and faculty from all over the world and every background on sprawling, sometimes aged campuses that are necessarily catching up here and there with still more codes. Of course, it is not possible to make an independent school safe from liability, short of eliminating most of what makes independent school life vibrant and challenging and ultimately worthwhile. Though a school may bring itself up to code, it cannot expect to protect itself completely from the possibility of lawsuits. Rather, a school hopes to demonstrate that it is not negligent in any aspect of its daily business. In order to demonstrate that it is vigilant, it must rely on its faculty and staff to do everything by the book. And that book gets bigger and bigger with each lawsuit. That sports can be made safer, crisis management in dorms more effective, and courses more sensitive to different learning styles and backgrounds are all indisputable. But the essence of a school environment—the students and the teachers—eludes uniformity.

A school's people and the relationships among them define a school's community. As long as there remains the possibility of two students on a swing set or colleagues in a dining hall, a school cannot reduce its personalities and relationships to the law. More important, what defines a school community is the essence of education: the messy, but rich business of learning. We do not produce a product that can be measured by codes, and we are not in the business of doing everything by a book. Our *business* need not be idealized, but it cannot be codified either. The law is pressuring schools into acting more like businesses and less like schools. It threatens to keep students and teachers from communicating honestly ("What if he reports me as a minor? I'd better just keep it a secret." "If I stick to this grade, might her parents accuse me of racism?" "Should I cancel the movie trip since I can't be sure that I will know where everyone is at all times?" "Should I write about this in my journal entry?"). The law also implies in its positivism when examining human relations that creativity, spontaneity, risk-taking, and unpredictability are less desirable elements in education. If a student says he's a little nervous about the trust fall, you respond with "give it a try" in 1980. After all, it is a few feet and there are eight kids waiting. In 2003, you probably pull the student out of the exercise, anxious that you may have isolated him/her by doing so, but unwilling to face the music if he twists a knee or breaks a finger. The law changes our understanding of accountability. Accidents do not happen. Someone must be held accountable. This rule has influenced the way schools organize themselves.

In addition to the three major areas of education, there is a fourth area that makes up the school's community and culture: namely, the school's governance. Schools must rely more and more on outside counsel and hired specialists when making decisions about their programs. Consequently, faculty meetings are more likely to feature speakers who are not directly involved in the day-to-day business of the school instructing those who are directly involved. More significantly, meetings about procedure (fire codes and room inspections, for instance) tend to outnumber meetings about pedagogy (how to coordinate writing across disciplines, for example). Faculty are expected to follow more rules more closely even as they have less influence over what those rules say about how to be a teacher. Administrators, meanwhile, have to formalize most meetings with a paper trail so as to protect themselves and the school when and if there is a problem with a colleague. What are the consequences of the law's influence on the way faculty view one another or the administration? What about the way the administration views its faculty? It is simplistic to see the administration of a large independent school as overly professional or ever more detached from the real business of education. Granted those who are forced to make the new rules may be threatening the role that instinct, intuition, creativity, and spontaneity play in an independent school education, particularly a residential school education, but a quick look around the real world demonstrates that the independent school administration is responding to sociocultural realities exacerbated by the omnipresence of the law.

Other pressures besides the law contribute to the culture of universal blame out there that threatens our culture of honesty and acceptance behind the stone walls and manicured yews: the cult of sentimentality that feeds into our desire to be blameless victims; the persistent sense that schools are the last community of any kind in the absence of family, neighborhood, town, or ordering principles in a shared folkloric, civic, religious, or mythic belief system; the development of languages that define the affectation of feelings, and not the feelings themselves; the strange mixture of moral conservatism and prurient curiosity that informs popular culture; and the puritanical liberalism with which we ourselves have sometimes embraced political correctness. The law, unfortunately, seems to be the last relatively clear measure by which we judge right and wrong, and it is arriving on school campuses with a vengeance. To experience as most schools have one of these protracted, contentious, frequently capricious lawsuits, is to have arrived at the awful realization that more often than not you have to be vigilant not just about the students, but about yourself and your colleagues as well.

*****

The overall scenario I have described of the law's influence on independent school life is still speculative. And yet schools need to recognize the inexorable progression of the law. For better and for worse, the law is a social science that develops by experimentation, trial and error. In civil litigation, that trial and error takes place at the expense of the defendant. Schools do not "win" litigation. They manage not to lose at great expense or they settle out of court, also at great expense. They are, perhaps, vindicated. In the meantime, they have suffered bad publicity, incurred expenses, invested time and energy, and most likely alarmed and exhausted faculty and staff who have found themselves embroiled in a battle that challenges their understanding of the idyllic educational enterprise. Furthermore, schools have struggled with the law in part because the free exchange of ideas is the essence of school culture. As educators, we see educational opportunities in challenging situations. Lawyers see lawsuits. The nature of the independent school, therefore, is to be the defendant.

To reverse this trend or at least slow it down, schools need to define the law's encroachment in our terms. Inventive collaboration and communication are the best ways to make the law's language into our own. First and foremost, schools should seriously consider collaborating by region and/or disposition. If they have not already done so, schools should consider pooling their resources to bargain with one insurance carrier for liability insurance and to retain as a group a well-placed law firm. As an association, schools should agree to draft statements that educate parents about how independent schools, day and boarding, operate and what "price" and "risk" comes with an open campus rich with challenges and opportunities. Of course, schools need not collaborate on mission statements or any of the programs or policies that make each school unique. But if schools presented a united front about what schools can and cannot do, then parents' expectations would be more realistic and reasonable. Parents need to understand that the ultimate price of litigation is the possible disappearance of the theater trip, the high diving board, the urban studies class, or room visitations. They also need to understand that schools respect the law and do everything in their power to bring themselves up to speed with the codes that define safe living, from handicap access to appropriate behavior.[1]

More important, administrators have to be frank with faculty about the law. Coaches, house counselors, and teachers need to know the worst-case scenarios on the playing field, in the dorm, and in the classroom. With respect to the law, your legal counsel will likely advise the risk of the gloom and doom Cassandra complex over the reality of an actual experience with the law in which there was no documentation about wet tennis courts, overly long room visitations, or special testing procedures for students with ADD. Teachers, coaches, and counselors must know when the school will support them and when it will not. Strong school leadership that offers a clear educational vision cognizant of but not beholden to remote legal ramifications helps preserve the give and take of a learning environment.

Most important, the school and the faculty must be forthcoming with students at the outset about the school's rules and about all the gray areas. Students need to know what might happen in certain situations *before* the situations take place. For instance, if the school has a sanctuary policy for substance abuse, then students need to "see" dramatized examples of that policy in practice. Students should know that if a sensitive conversation is about to develop, a faculty member might ask the student if there is another faculty member who might be present in addition to him- or herself for the conversation. In effect, the best way to deal with the subtleties and high stakes of the law is to embrace them, making them yet another part of the dialogue that defines the broad reach of a full education in a school community.

While a school need not make the law an enemy (in fact, Jim Leonard's piece, (pg. 205) also in this book, demonstrates how often the law can be an ally), schools need to re-position faculty, parents, and students so that they are shoulder to shoulder, looking at and learning about the law, as opposed to nose to nose, using it to establish winners and losers. Schools are handicapped in those situations not just because we are almost always the defendants but also because the language of our pedagogical culture tends to be metaphoric, expansive, and therefore malleable whereas the language of the law strives to be scientific, decisive, and therefore reductive. Perhaps the best way to make the law our own, therefore, is to find that place where the law and education are understandable to one another. Specifically, schools should consider studying hypothetical cases in the law based on the real experiences of schools with issues like student dismissals, sexual harassment, faculty evaluations, accidents involving the physical plant, grades and assessment, psychological counseling, learning disabilities, and off-campus trips and programs. The stories of other schools' experiences demystify the law and educate the school community—administrators, faculty and staff, students and parents. Working through these hypothetical stories of the law as well as the hypothetical situations that lead to them not only helps protect the school from costly mistakes, but also puts everyone back on the same side and puts law in an educational context.

If schools do not do so already, they should make sure that parents and students have read the school's rule book, its mission statement, *and* whatever documents counsel advises the school to create to inform its primary constituencies—faculty, parents, and students—about how and to what extent the school addresses potential legal issues. Time and energy invested preemptively reaffirms the school's overall mission and perhaps saves time and energy when the law comes knocking.

By collaborating and communicating both on and off campus with all our constituencies and our peer schools, independent schools are not reactive as potential defendants, but proactive as communities dedicated to learning through myriad relationships and challenges in and out of the classroom. If schools are always defending themselves against and/or settling litigation, they stand to lose a lot more than money.

Notes

[1] For an excellent discussion of parent-school communication, read Don Grace's piece "Parents, Boarding Schools, and Students: Time to Lay Down the Law," *Second Home: Life in a Boarding School,* 2nd ed. Ed. Craig Thorn (Gilsum, NH: Avocus, 2003): 280–285.

Craig Thorn has taught at Phillips Academy for 22 years, where he has served a term as chair of the English department. He has been the editor-in-chief of Avocus Publishing for seven years. He is the author/editor of six books on education.

Using Personal Electronic Communication to Increase Alumni Participation and Support

By Michael Kidd

Imagine reaching your constituents at home or at work in a manner that will inspire them to become more involved, provide you with personal data, or, better yet, make immediate donations.

Nielsen/NetRatings estimates that over 167 million Americans have home Internet access, and almost 51 million have access at work.[1] These numbers reinforce teachers' and administrators' intuition that the majority of independent school parents and alumni have access to the Internet. Our constituents live in a culture of instant, electronic communications, both in personal interactions and in business transactions. The growing electronic business and social culture will pressure schools to engage parents and alumni through e-mail and other electronic media.

In addition to the cultural shift to which independent schools are responding, an advanced electronic communications plan offers numerous opportunities. The escalating cost of printing and postage make e-mail a fiscally sound option. The last postal rate change increased the first-class mail rates up an average of 7.9%.[2] The cost of sending e-mail is negligible and reflects the price of software used to create and send the messages. In most schools, the organization's servers and internal e-mail software are up to the task and incur no further costs, website development is an existing line item in most budgets, and a refocusing of site contact should be an ongoing process. Additionally, there is no better way to get timely information to a large dispersed group of people.

Develop Relationships

For independent schools, broadcast e-mail and targeted websites serve two main missions. The first is to strengthen the recipient's relationship to the institution. Schools accomplish this in any number of ways. The most typical is to provide information about the school; after all, well-informed alums are supportive alums. Other successful strategies include offering interactive components to e-mail. Mercersburg has run several e-mails in which an online form invites recipients to submit a story, beyond simple class notes, for inclusion in the alumni magazine. This provides the magazine editor with fresh material, and, more important, it actively engages alumni. The subsequent use of these stories serves a stewardship role. It lets alumni know that their contributions are valued.

Philips Exeter Academy has received high marks for utilizing their teaching staff online. They offer online chat room discussions for their alumni. The value-added, continuing education that alumni and friends receive has helped solidify the loyalty people feel toward the school. Exeter cites the fact that chat room moderators are popular faculty members with whom alumni are familiar as one of the keys to the program's success. For instance, following the September 11, 2001, terrorist attacks, the longtime school minister led a successful discussion. Alumni were grateful for the opportunity to share their feelings with classmates and friends, in a discussion led by someone they knew and trusted.

Make Ask

Through the active use of the relationship-building e-mail and value-added websites, schools prepare to address the other main mission of specialized electronic communications—resource generation. Just as the relationship-building e-mail may have different foci and web applications may appeal to changing constituencies, the donation e-mail may be a means to generate financial commitments or may focus on donations of time or product. The specifics will vary based on the needs of the school and the philosophy of the development office, but many of the issues remain the same. Using e-mail to ask for donations is a scary thing for many development officers. E-mail by its nature is less personal than a face-to-face visit, or even a phone call. Additionally, e-mail eliminates many of the visual or auditory cues that a development officer uses when soliciting gifts. In order to compensate for these obstacles, e-asks need careful construction with emphasis on target demographics, content development, and a high degree of personalization.

Understand the Competition

In any marketing effort, there will be competition for customers and their support. Developing supportive alumni is no different, whether it is online or through traditional programs and initiatives. Most alumni have a fixed philanthropic budget and receive solicitations from more than one school, in addition to various community and special interest groups.

One of the greatest advantages an online philanthropy has is the short time from an emotionally charged event to the request for a donation. In the days following the September 11 terrorist attacks, the Red Cross and various other charity organizations launched high impact websites and placed banner ads to raise money for victims. They were able to tap into a highly emotional moment and motivate people to give. Regrettably, there were even organizations who used the tragic event to pose as charities and thus swindle money from donors. While these organizations can capitalize from major events, they do not have the long-term emotional tie to donors that one's alma mater does.

A fiercer competitor for access to online constituents is the sheer volume of e-mail people receive on a daily basis. Aside from business and personal e-mail, people also contend with other e-marketing efforts. Junk mail and *opt in* e-mails can quickly overwhelm anyone's ability to read everything they receive.[3] Many people never open, or merely glance at broadcast e-mail messages before sending them to the trash bin. When developing an e-mail communications plan for your institution, it is imperative to devise a way to get people to open your e-mail, and then read more than the first two lines.

The first challenge, to get the e-mail opened, can usually be addressed through a well-thought-out subject line and with thought as to the "from" address. Two schools of thought on the subject line are to either have a consistent title for all e-mail, such as a clever name for your e-newsletter. Many schools and universities have gone this route, as is evidenced by titles such as @ Stanford, Ed Cetera, and Proctor Academy Together.[4] An alternative route is to use the subject line to advertise some exciting content in the message, such as the headline of the lead story.

The first strategy assumes that constituents will be interested in a periodical from the school and will keep reading in order to see what is going on at the school. The second strategy can be effective if there is not a high interest rate and the school feels the need to generate interest in a specific story in order to get the e-mail opened. Once opened, the users of the alternating subject line strategy can use carefully crafted content to start building their brand loyalty.

Use Your Data

Independent schools have a vastness of data about their alumni that many colleges and universities only dream about. We know what sports and activities someone was involved in, we know about their parents and siblings, and many times, who their friends and roommates were. With this information, we can create extremely targeted, high-impact e-mail messages without a high degree of development complexity. Depending on the program used to create and send e-mail, you can create several "if then" scenarios that can easily generate hundreds of permutations of an e-mail message.

The essence of an e-mail message is the textual content. The only way to keep readers is to provide content that is well developed, relevant, and interesting to your constituents. If you cannot do that, your message will not get across and you will likely lose readers for future e-mails. Several key areas that are easily personalized are described below.

The initial area is the salutation. If you can call your reader by name, you will have started to build the relationship, and you hope this will lead to a more informed and involved alumni. The difficulties to be aware of in this instance are twofold. If you do not have a nickname field in your database, you should probably get one. The use of a formal first name, not used by an alumnus, can start the message off poorly. If William Smith has gone by Bill since birth, the attempt at increasing affection and building relationships through e-mail personalization can backfire if Mr. Smith receives an e-mail starting "Dear William."

As far as personalization goes, name usage is little more than a gimmick. Without further efforts, your readers will recognize it as a gimmick and not be impressed with your efforts. The mission of your e-mail will determine the specific personalization you can undertake. In a recent fundraising e-mail, Mercersburg used several areas of textual personalization to customize the message. We first determined if the person had made a donation in the past three years. If they had, we formatted the e-mail to thank them for their gift, including the year made and the amount. We then asked for a gift that was dynamically calculated by the program: $100 if they had given less than $100, and a ten-percent increase if they had given more than $100. If we had not received a donation from the alumni in the last three years, we asked for $25—just to get the person back in the habit of giving. A second bit of personalization included their class year in the challenge section of the ask. For example, one person's e-mail may have read "We are asking that every member of the class of 1990 give at the $100 level this year," while another e-mail may have said, "We are challenging every member of the class of 1968 to increase their donation by ten percent."

Proctor Academy in New Hampshire has one of the most advanced development offices in terms of the use of automation and technology. They use automated e-mails to solicit alumni during the same month in which they donated the prior year, for the specific fund that they gave to, and they make it easy to give by offering the ability to put it on the same credit card. In addition to their aggressive e-mail campaigns, Proctor provides individual web pages for each donor. These pages range from relatively simple pages that pull stories and information based on a donor's affinities and put them on a page, to very complex sites for their larger donors that profile scholarship recipients in detail. Through the aggressive use of their database, they tie their cultivation, solicitation, and stewardship of donors into a coordinated e-marketing program.

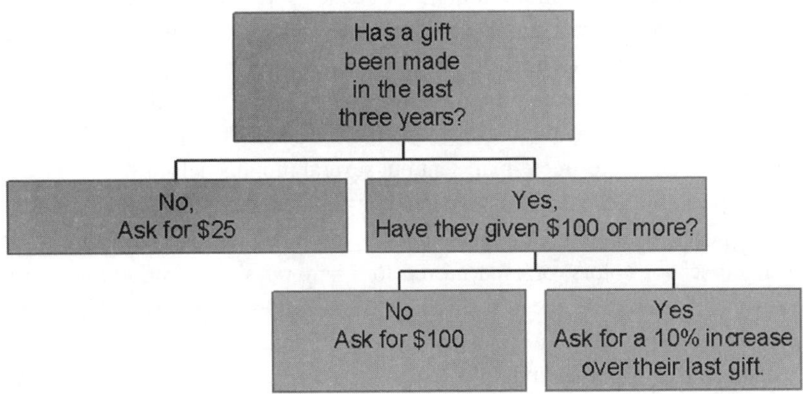

Other applications of textual personalization can apply to the stories that an e-newsletter displays for people. If a person was a star athlete while in school, it may be wise to lead with a story about the school's recent basketball success. Similarly, you may want not to include sports news when sending e-mail to an actor who had never played a sport in school. Like the decision tree above, this type of personalization can be accomplished with a relatively small amount of planning and programming. For schools without the access to programmers or the software to pull complex messages together, some of this can be done through some simple database queries to come up with several sets of e-mails. A look at your data may reveal some easy personalization that you can perform with some simple queries. For instance, Mercersburg found that 10 first names account for 30% of their alumni.[5] The school could conceivably send 10 e-mails out, referencing the recipient's name, and a general e-mail, and still be able to personalize the message to a sizable portion of their alumni with only a basic e-mail program. In this manner, you can send out several e-mails and obtain some level of targeting, even if you cannot send one command that will dynamically generate many permeations of a message.

While content will always be king in constituent communications, thoughtful use of graphical layout and images can reach people at an emotional level and significantly increase the effectiveness of an e-mail or web page. Two types of visual customization that should be considered are photography and general design. Of these, the most important is the photography.

A picture is worth a thousand words. If this is the case, you should be deliberate in your use of pictures in e-mail. In the annual fund e-mail described above, we inserted a picture into the body of the message. We hoped to find a picture that would speak to the recipient, generating happy memories of the school and putting them in a positive frame of mind. After some thought, we decided that if we can tailor the text to appeal to a specific profile, then we could do the same thing with images. We developed seven different criteria that we could test for in our database and then came up with pictures that appeal to each criterion. The activities/sports a student participated in, along with the recipient's age, determined the picture. Former wrestlers got a picture of Mercersburg wrestlers, while dancers got a photo from the last dance performance. We studied which activities attracted the highest number of students and took the highest participant groups for our customized sections. If an alumnus did not participate in any of the groups that we were testing for, the program inserted a generic campus photo. The extra work of dynamically inserting pictures paid off in the e-mail. The average gift per donor went up 67% from a picture-free e-mail sent out several months before.

A second option for graphical customization surrounds the general look and feel of e-mail or web pages. A major change such as when a school has gone from single-sex to co-ed, changed school colors, or even moved to a new physical location may warrant multiple designs. This may be one of the easier customization options available since it is in response to a binary decision cycle: only one field and two options are tested. The choice to change the format, including colors, navigation, and mascot images, often depends on which side of a specific date people were graduated. While this strategy may increase nostalgia in older alums, it may also hurt efforts to bring alumni into the new direction a school is taking. Alums who are also current parents may rather see the school as it is for their children, as opposed to how it was for them. For these reasons, schools designing the basic look and feel of an e-mail to fit a period-defined demographic should proceed with an eye to both the positive and negative aspects of such an e-mail.

As wireless communications grow, this type of customization will take on a more important role in communicating with alumni and friends. XML technology will allow schools to format e-mail and web pages to display not only various colors and designs based on a recipients' attributes, but will also reformat information so that it is displayed in a readable format, regardless as to whether it is being viewed on a desktop monitor, personal digital assistant, or cellular phone.[6]

Tracking and Analysis

Depending on the mission of the e-mail, there are several simple ways for independent schools to track the effectiveness of their e-communications. Many programs have sophisticated tracking mechanisms that allow you to tell who looked at an e-mail, when they opened it, and which links they clicked once they got in. This sort of data allows schools to focus future messages more successfully.

For schools that do not have access to more sophisticated tracking programs, the most obvious involves tracking gifts or purchases made in response to an e-mail solicitation. Unlike print advertisements or solicitations, which may spend some time on the desk or coffee table before being acted on, e-mail is usually acted on when first opened or shortly thereafter. If your number of online gifts increases in the 72 hours after an e-mail is sent, you can point to the increase as being driven by the e-mail. A second option is to request information within the body of the e-mail. Some schools ask people to respond to a question. This tracking method can serve a duel purpose. It lets you know if people are engaged in the message, and it can provide material for other projects. Whether through a reply e-mail, posting to a message board, or through a form embedded in the e-mail itself, this is a tool for obtaining alumni response to campus issues, or testimonials and class notes.

A third tracking mechanism that can indicate how many people are opening and reading your e-mail is a simple hit counter. Instead of sending the body of a message in the e-mail itself, you send a link to the e-mail. This way you can track the page hit through your normal website tracking software. This can tell you if people are opening and reading your message.

Success Stories

One of the easiest ways to create successful programs is to look at what others in your field are doing. While there are many examples of successful e-marketing campaigns that we can look to, I am including two that differ in mission and philosophy. The first example is a general alumni newsletter, while the second is an alumni relations campaign. Each institution is different in its culture, resources, and development mission. I hope that you will be able to use these examples to build successful campaigns that work for you.

Ms. Porters School—General Newsletter

The e-newsletter is by far the most used format of broadcast e-mails. Ms. Porters School in Farmington, CT, is experiencing success with this format, as expressed in alumni feedback. Like many other schools, Ms. Porters relies heavily on web news to provide content for its newsletters. Their newsletter has short feature stories based on campus and alumni news. Ms. Porters includes pictures in their e-mail, while some other popular e-mails are purely text and link based. The Council for the Advancement and Support of Education (CASE) e-mail publication, Flash Points, does a wonderful job of providing textual stories with links to get more information.

The newsletter format is often longer and more general than some of the more targeted e-mails discussed in this chapter. It is therefore advisable to make the individual stories as succinct as possible and provide, where needed, links to more in-depth material.

Mercersburg Academy—Alumni Relation

E-marketing programs do not have to be especially cumbersome. Mercersburg Academy has instituted a birthday e-mail program, which has won awards and allowed the school to touch alumni in a happy, non-threatening manner. Each day, a 25-line web-based program runs automatically. If an alumni's birthday matches the current date, the computer sends an e-mail with a short birthday wish from the school and a picture that is chosen for them, based on their activities as a student. The program also generates and e-mails a report to key staff members listing people who received e-mail that day, along with their class year and the picture that they received. "After a year and a half, we are still getting several responses each day from alumni, thanking us for remembering," says Lisa Heisey, Assistant Director of Donor Relations.

Notes

[1] http://pm.netratings.com/nnpm/owa/Nrpublicreports.usages Report run 11/26/2002, 10:57 AM

[2] United States Postal Office, http://www.usps.com/ratecase/first.htm 11/26/2002, 1:03 PM

[3] Opt does stand for option, in a round about way. *Opt in e-mail* is a term that has emerged to describe broadcast e-mails that you have given permission to be sent to you. Subscription e-mail is another term that means basically the same thing. However, *opt in* has been the term used among people in the marketing field in the legislation being introduced to control unwanted e-mail solicitations. It is generally accepted that if someone has given you permission to send them an e-mail, you have an affirmative defense against being labeled a "spammer."

[4] Stanford University, Maricopa Community College District, Proctor Academy

[5] John, Robert, William, David, James, Thomas, Richard, Charles, Michael and J.

[6] Extensible Markup Language (XML) is a markup language, similar to HTML, that allows programmers to display data in drastically different online environments with ease.

Michael Kidd is the assistant director of communications at the Mercersburg Academy. He manages the website, e-marketing, and new media for the school. Prior to his current appointment he worked as a lobbyist for the Maricopa Community Colleges in Phoenix, AZ, and has consulted with campaigns and special interest groups on data management and web issues. He has a masters degree in public administration from Arizona State University.

Marketing Our Independent Schools

By Lisa L. Bock, CFRE

We who devote our professional lives to independent schools know that the success of our institutions is increasingly tied to the proactive management of quantifiable resources. Those who are marketing professionals within independent schools cannot help but notice two significant dichotomies in our day-to-day existence.

To appreciate the first dichotomy, think back to your own school days. I am willing to bet that anything you recall in particular will underscore the point I wish to make: A school is a world unto itself. Students, teachers, coaches, administrators, and parents form the center of this universe, which is then encapsulated by those who interface at various times with the core—opposing teams, a yearbook production representative, a prom date who attends a different school, college admission officers, and the like.

A school is tucked away, literally and figuratively, behind its own gates. Now more than ever, our societal desire for security reinforces our appreciation of those gates. And yet, as marketing professionals, we realize fully the great benefits, and, indeed, the absolute necessity of bringing the good things that happen behind our gates out into the open for all to see. More than anything else, our job as marketing professionals is to tell our schools' stories.

The second dichotomy independent school marketing professionals recognize all too well relates directly to our nation's soft economy of late, and the fact that tuitions at nearly all our schools are rising at levels incommensurate with the national Consumer Price Index while salary increases barely keep pace with inflation. Further, socioeconomic studies point to a shrinking middle class in this country. As a consequence of heightened financial pressures on admission and development departments, marketing has gained credibility among our schools' senior administrators and trustees. The brighter spotlight, however, comes with greater scrutiny of our effectiveness and much greater pressure to perform in ways that are specific and measurable.

As marketing professionals, we are driven to perform. We want to do the very best we can by our schools. The objective of this chapter is (1) to speak directly to how we can increase awareness for our schools and engender greater loyalty among our key constituencies and (2) to spur some creative yet practical thoughts on how to go about achieving our worthy goals.

What Does Marketing Really Mean?

In its most practical sense, marketing is shaping and managing a school's image by promoting its intellectual, cultural, and physical assets. "Imaging" and "branding" are popular and alluring terms in the business world, and there is much about marketing for-profit companies that can be put to good use in marketing the not-for-profits. Yet, as John Ross and Carol Halstead have reminded educational marketing professionals, image is "transitory, temporal, and easily manipulated." A school's *reputation* or *identity,* on the other hand, is enduring. Thus, I would challenge the independent school marketing professional to consider as his or her primary responsibility promoting a school's reputation and projecting its identity in meaningful and memorable ways. Such positioning includes a continuous cycle of looking inward and reaching outward. As we look inward, we build coherence and consensus among those who know us best, including our teachers, administrators, students, parents, and trustees. As we reach outward, we establish a platform of stability to propel the school forward.

A school's character is arguably less tangible than a Coke, or a McDonalds, or a Mercedes, or many other consumer products that deliver immediate gratification. In our consumer-driven society, the returns on the investments we make in quality schools are not as immediate. Furthermore, schools mean different things to different people. Our schools fulfill different roles for the lead of the school play, the lacrosse captain, the Ivy League hopeful, the veteran teacher, or the involved parent.

The fact that there are different realities for different people brings unique challenges for independent schools. In this regard, it may be helpful to remember that the marketers of Coke, McDonalds, and Mercedes are utilizing their own specialized techniques to define not just their products, but the *experience* of consuming or owning the product. In a similar way, the independent school marketing professional is interpreting the experience students, faculty, and families gain by being part of the school community. It is the sum of the parts and their symbiotic relationship with each other that constitute the totality of the school's identity.

On "Identity"

"The identity of the institution must be so entrenched and so evident that it becomes the driving force behind all its services (products), behavior and actions. The ***services*** *the institution performs must project its standards and values. The* ***buildings and facilities*** *where the life of the institution goes on are compelling manifestations of identity. The* ***communications*** *materials must have a consistent quality and character that accurately and honestly reflect the whole institution and its aims. How the institution* ***behaves,*** *to its own members and everybody with whom it comes in contact, is a vital aspect of identity.*

—Carol Cheney, President, Cheney & Company
July 2000

While keeping *reputation, character, identity,* and *experience* at the forefront of our marketing initiatives, it is worth revisiting the more temporal subjects of "imaging" and "branding" if only briefly. Today as never before, we live in a brand-conscious society. Students are astute consumers, as are their parents. Thus, marketing professionals are on target in carefully analyzing and skillfully projecting what differentiates their schools.

As we tell our stories and state our cases, we must do so in ways that accommodate a society on information overload and consumers who process most of the information they receive as abbreviated sound bytes. Not surprisingly, then, we have but a few seconds to draw a person in so that he or she is willing to make the investment of time to delve deeper and to learn more about our schools. The five-minute "elevator speech," which is an essential arrow in the marketing professional's quiver, must now be distilled even further to a tag line consisting of a few sparse and well chosen words, inviting potential customers to investigate the substance behind our image.

Marketing customarily deals with the "4 P's": *product, price, promotion* and *place.* In the independent school world, I would add a fifth "P" for *perception.* While we carefully manage the messages we communicate about our schools, we must also realize that the personal experiences and interpretations of those on the receiving end underscore or detract from what we proclaim. Educating children is a human endeavor. Vis-à-vis factories that produce widgets, our schools produce confident, capable, and accomplished young adults. Our paying customers—parents of students or grandparents who pay their grandchildren's tuition—relate largely to our schools through someone else's lived experience.

While it may seem cliché, in our business *perception is reality*. A parent is only as happy as their child on any given day, generally speaking. Parent conversations that take place in the carpool lines are certainly as influential as our formal marketing messages, and many seasoned professionals would say they are even more so. Carol Cheney suggests that the overall identity of a school is often subordinated to a set of ***"sub-identities,"*** depending on an individual's personal connection to and experience with the institution. Conversations shared casually throughout our school communities, and especially the common elements of these conversations, routinely become part of our fabric. This is noted to underscore the fact that it is extremely important for us to know how satisfied our students and parents are with our services.

A Pressing Marketing Challenge

As mentioned in the introduction to this chapter, across the nation independent schools' tuition levels are rising disproportionately with the Consumer Price Index. This was less alarming when, only a few short years ago, the economy was strong and consumer confidence high. In 2003, however, marketing directors face unprecedented pressure to illustrate the ***value*** of an independent school education to prospective customers and to families already enrolled in our schools. In the book *Marketing Independent Schools in the 21st Century*, Jeffery T. Wack defines value as "a measure of the degree of balance in the exchange of benefits between seller and buyer."

As tuitions increase, the economy lags and our middle classes disappear, independent schools find themselves in constant competition with public schools, home schooling options, and other low-cost educational systems. Ideally, from a marketing perspective, any increase in our tuitions would coincide with new programs or greater services. This is simply not feasible, however. In the people-centered business of education, in which approximately 80% of our school budgets are allocated for salaries, benefits, and other personnel costs, tuition increases become cost-of-living wage adjustments, funds to cover ever-escalating health insurance premiums, and similar necessities.

Thus, as customers write larger checks for essentially an unchanged program, a psychological debate ensues in which one questions whether the product is worth the sacrifice. Emotionally, there is internal strife among many parents. On the one hand, they believe that an independent school education is an important investment in their child. On the other hand, because of the sacrifices made to pay increasing tuitions, they, as parents, are not able to give their children other experiences that make for well-rounded adults. Many families point to travel abroad as a specific example while others indicate that they are unable to set aside adequate funds for their children's college tuitions. These concerns are real for our families and translate into urgent challenges for us as marketing professionals.

To ensure that the value equation remains in balance and to compete in a consumer-driven society, independent school marketing professionals must continuously manage the perceptions, returning to our fifth "P" of marketing, of what our customers receive for the money they pay. Introspective marketing professionals continuously wrestle with their own fears that their schools are viewed as elitist. In some cases our work to avoid this label may make us overly modest. As storytellers, we must continuously celebrate the successes of our students, alumni, faculty, and institutions.

While we carefully and systematically articulate our case to prospective customers, we may become too casual in our approach with parents after they enroll their children. Those of us who work at day schools should take a lesson from our counterparts at boarding schools in not assuming that our parents, even those who volunteer in some capacity, are fully cognizant of the value our schools hold for their families. As parents try to accommodate the short-term wishes of their children, they may sometimes lose sight of lifelong benefits of an independent school education.

Consider the following example: Adam is a rising freshman at an independent school known for its academic emphasis. He works hard in his classes and his grades are evenly split between B's and C's. Adam's friends who attend public high school make A's and B's. Further, they spend little time on homework. The temptation for Adam's attrition is great as he would enjoy spending less time on assignments and facing less academic pressure. His parents are tempted because they believe Adam's grades would soar in the less rigorous environment. Through marketing's constant reinforcement, we hope Adam's parents and Adam himself will come to understand the value and long-term benefits of the independent school experience. Assuming families are inherently making these long-term connections is dangerous in a society geared strongly to immediate gratification.

Key Players and the Essential Triumvirate

Those in the marketing department are not the only ones actively marketing our schools. To the contrary, it is much more realistic and beneficial to recognize and to utilize faculty members, students, parents, and alumni as partners in our marketing endeavors. The key is getting these groups to embrace their role in a comprehensive marketing effort and to appreciate marketing for its ability to give our beloved institutions a position of strength.

Communications don't exist in a vacuum;
they are strands in the fabric of a unit's comprehensive life,
in which deeds always speak louder than words.
(Schoenfeld & Weimer 11)

An effective professional recognizes that a comprehensive marketing effort must include an internal marketing plan to augment the myriad external marketing activities. Most important, perhaps, faculty members must be solid partners. Years ago, teachers may have viewed marketing objectives, and, by affiliation, marketing directors, as unnecessary and, perhaps, less than noble. This is no longer the case, except in the rarest of instances. The National Association of Independent Schools (NAIS) and our regional associations have made direct efforts to assuage any previous misgivings. Schools have also become more sophisticated in their business operations in general in recent years.

Today, the marketing director who feels less than respected by their school's faculty would be wise to ask if she has done an adequate job in earning their faculty's respect. I submit that if we are truthful with ourselves, any disconnect will likely be attributed not so much to an active resistance on the faculty's part but rather to a more passive existence on our own.

Earning the faculty's respect and engaging their partnership is most effective when it's done one teacher at a time. This one-on-one approach may not be practical for larger independent schools—or at all, given the competing demands for a marketing director's time and energy. Thus, the savvy marketing professional will identify *opinion leaders* among his faculty and work most closely with those, facilitating their leadership and persuasion of colleagues throughout the school. To excel in a marketing capacity, one must know his school well. By attending faculty meetings, conversing with different teachers each day during lunch period, attending games, concerts, and competitions that our coaches, teachers, and advisors work so hard to bring to fruition, the marketing director should have ample opportunity to develop meaningful relationships with faculty.

Once these relationships are developed, teachers will more fully embrace our goals to position them as the spirit of our institutions. In fact, if done thoughtfully, such positioning can showcase expertise and recognize teachers as individuals. Keep in mind that not every teacher wants to be thrown directly into the spotlight. Indeed, one size does not fit all when it comes to the specific jobs we call upon our faculty to do. One science teacher might be delighted to present her latest research to your invited guests while her colleague may be much more comfortable writing an op-ed for your local newspaper on the use of the scientific method in daily life. Similarly, one English teacher may be the perfect choice to teach a poetry workshop at a local bookstore while his counterpart may be pleased to serve as a director on another non-profit's advisory board.

Scattered throughout a school's internal community are diamonds in the rough, so to speak, for a marketing director to develop into *school evangelists.* Trustees, in particular, should see themselves and want others to see them in this light. Evangelists are effusive in their views on the school's accomplishments and can speak to specifics because they know the school well. Evangelists are charismatic, articulate, and persuasive. They value the school as a community asset and are adept at sharing a school's finer points with general members of the community with whom they come into regular contact through social gatherings, professional affiliations, and the like.

A head of school is likely to be the institution's most persuasive evangelist. More than any other individual, a head of school is doubly important to a school's internal and external marketing efforts. Internally, the head sets the tone for the ways in which teachers, administrators, and others perceive marketing. Externally, the head is nothing short of an icon. He or she symbolically represents everything a school purports to be. Thus, it is imperative that the marketing director develop and maintain a close and trustworthy relationship with his or her head. Unless something is amiss, both parties will quickly find the relationship powerfully and mutually beneficial. The marketing director can solidify the head's position as leader and visionary, and the head can reinforce the marketing director's messages that the school is worthy of a closer look.

The most effective marketing professionals work closely with admission directors and advancement or development directors, forming an *essential triumvirate* for the areas that bring quantifiable resources to the school. Working closely together as a team benefits a school in several ways. First, while there is much common ground between the areas of marketing, admission, and advancement, there are subtle nuances that only experienced professionals within each department can truly appreciate. Second, each department relies heavily on the other two for maximum success. Fund-raising efforts are more successful if the admission department has filled the school to capacity and admitted students who are a good fit for the school's mission and are therefore thriving as students and fulfilled as graduates. Admission efforts are greatly enhanced if the school's financial coffers provide ample funds for financial aid, communication budgets, and so on. Marketing, while providing the necessary underpinnings for both admission and advancement, has a much more robust story to tell if the school is humming in both of these endeavors. Forming an effective partnership requires crafting and following an integrated plan, holding each other accountable for specific deliverables, participating in organized team meetings with specific agendas, and engaging in daily conversation as colleagues who enjoy working together.

Rights and Responsibilities of the Marketing Director

As the school's interpreter, promoter, and communicator, the marketing director must be well-informed and must have the privilege of access to necessary information. Working closely with the head of school, senior administrators, and particularly the admission and advancement directors, the marketing director essentially takes on the role of a walking encyclopedia.

With the blessing of the senior administration, the marketing director should serve as a clearinghouse for all significant print communiqués that go beyond the gates of the school. This is not to say that the marketing director should review every letter mailed to every individual, but it does refer to letters and other communiqués that go to groups. This element of control is essential for maintaining consistency in the school's graphic identity and is possibly the only way to ensure that marketing messages are consistent and continuous.

Our schools are continuously abuzz with activity and many events have marketing potential. Printed programs for concerts, drama productions, class plays and the like are read carefully by audience members while they await the performance. These printed pieces are often later shared with other family members or saved in family scrapbooks. Thus, though most of these pieces are produced inexpensively in-house, they are marketing tools nonetheless. Marketing directors must have a say in the design and content of such pieces to ensure that all include the school's mission statement and appropriate value statements.

Similarly, the head of school, division heads, and anyone who is called to make a presentation on behalf of the school to outside groups should always conspire with the marketing director to ensure that the presentation maximize its marketing potential. In each of these cases, the marketing director should be involved in the beginning of the process—rather than the end—to ensure adequate opportunity for input.

In most cases, marketing directors should be privy to things that happen behind closed doors. This includes board meetings, or at least certain segments of the meetings. Some schools invite their marketing directors to join their advancement and admission directors in taking part in board meetings. At some schools, only those staff members who report directly to the head are permitted to attend meetings of trustees. This may exclude marketing directors who are one level removed (and who usually report to advancement directors). If this is the case, it is incumbent upon the marketing director's supervisor to provide briefings, as appropriate, immediately following such meetings.

The marketing director's right to access comes with responsibilities, including confidentiality above all else. Maintaining confidences sounds remarkably easy. After all, marketing professionals build their careers on credibility and integrity. In reality, maintaining confidentiality requires constant vigilance. Marketing directors are in the business of cultivating friends, developing relationships, and gathering and exchanging information. And, while some matters are unmistakably confidential, others aren't so absolute. True marketing professionals are continuously cognizant in this regard.

Responsibilities also include loyalty to one's institution and particularly to one's head of school. In my opinion, loyalty equates to staunch defense of the head to anyone but the head. In private, behind-closed-door discussions, marketing directors owe their heads of school nothing less than complete candor. Candor does not mean disrespect. Rather, it means an honest appraisal of the situation at hand.

A final important responsibility is the marketing director's commitment to make good choices, to invest adequate time in high payoff activities, and to allocate an appropriate portion of each work week to research, reading, and thinking. In other words, the marketing director has the responsibility of striking the necessary balance between all things strategic and operational.

Marketing's Strategic-Operational Balance

Ever heard of the rifle/shotgun metaphor for marketing? It's frequently used, and for good reason. The more we understand our target, the more discerning and successful our marketing approaches will be. Given the sheer volume of work marketing directors do, it is easy to get caught up in the day-to-day operational necessities. True marketing professionals recognize the importance of planning and evaluating one's plan and results on a regular basis. Regarding the concept of the admission-advancement-marketing triumvirate, schools benefit greatly when these three directors engage in preparing an annual marketing plan, complete quarterly reviews, and share these reviews with the head and senior administrators.

Marketing plans typically address one year and are always built around clearly articulated, specific, and measurable objectives. Each objective is tethered to audiences or constituencies. The marketing plan specifies who must be reached in order to achieve the objective and how the audiences' behavior must change. Communication vehicles (brochures, special events, web), necessary for carrying the message to each constituency, are outlined in the plan. Finally, a calendar or timeline is included to provide contact dates for each audience.

Marketing, if done properly, is a careful balance of art and science. The scientific component—namely, the empirical data we are responsible for gathering through research—allows us to focus our resources where we most need them. Anecdotal evidence is important, too, if we are able to discern patterns and trends. Artistically, we then translate our data and information into compelling storytelling.

The admission-advancement-marketing triumvirate must create an integrated approach to collecting data and discerning information about the school's various audiences or constituencies. Records gathered early in the admission cycle, when families are most inclined to submit detailed and somewhat sensitive information, must anticipate future needs of advancement, admission, and marketing. Even something as simple as designing the admission application form to ensure that parents include their middle initial along with their first and last names will help further down the line if fund-raising research is conducted on the parent constituency.

Marketing directors are likely to utilize a combination of in-house surveying and profiling and professionally contracted services in order to better understand and respond to the real and perceived needs of the school's constituencies. In-house research projects cost little other than staff time and should be completed annually by the admission-advancement-marketing triumvirate and others as necessary.

Annual in-house projects include:

- analysis of the admission funnel (Which cities or geographic regions are major pockets of inquiries? What are our inquiries' major referral sources? At which point in the funnel do most people exit? Why?)
- phone interviews of a representative sampling of those who complete the admission process and are accepted but decline enrollment (Which school will the student attend? What were most important factors to the family? What role did price play in the decision?)
- feedback from "Your Opinion Matters" suggestion boxes, strategically placed across campus (Ask faculty and students what the school does best: What matters most? How can we improve?)
- Annual Fund parent participation analysis (What is the parent participation per grade? If certain grades or divisions are significantly behind the norm, at least a representative sampling should be contacted by phone to determine if lack of participation points to dissatisfaction. At the very least, the advancement office will learn which volunteers are more effective than others.)
- Annual Fund LYBUNT parent and alumni follow-up: LYBUNT refers to **L**ast **Y**ear, **B**ut **U**nfortunately **N**ot **T**his, and analysis is especially helpful if a donor with an established pattern of giving suddenly stops for no apparent reason (e.g., the student has not withdrawn or graduated; the advancement office is not aware of an alumna's divorce, loss of job, etc.).
- attrition analysis studies (Are there major exit points? Do teachers' input point to an "at risk" profile for students?)
- exit interviews of families whose children have withdrawn (Where attending? What role did cost play? Who at the school had a lasting impact on the student? It is important to note that many schools utilize outside sources to conduct exit interviews to ensure the greatest possible objectivity. If cost-prohibitive, it is better to proceed utilizing internal staff in lieu of forgoing the process altogether. The outreach is important and the data gleaned invaluable.)
- alumni reunion surveys (educational degrees and universities; professions; interests; affiliations, honors and awards; families)

The following research projects are also most worthwhile but can be conducted every other year unless a school's resources are great or a specific situation mandates otherwise.

- focus groups of first-year parents and students (Is the school living up to the family's expectations? What can the school do to better help families in transition?)
- current parent satisfaction surveys disseminated to the entire parent body or representative samplings large enough to be relevant (What does the school do best? What areas need attention? Similar surveys can be disseminated to faculty and students.)

Other projects, including the following, are feasible every few years and are best managed by outside professionals with specific expertise:

- alumni constituency surveys (similar to reunion surveys, but more extensive and conducted among all living alumni)
- demographic studies for your town or region (population trends, household income levels, race, education, age, etc.)
- Tuition Price Point Analysis (sampling of local competitors and comparable regional or national institutions; specific cost-of-living fluctuations and local economy must be taken into account)
- Marketing/Communication Audit (strategic analysis of systems comparable to SWOT analysis—Strengths, Weaknesses, Opportunities, Threats—specifically for the marketing/communication department)

How much of the above a marketing department can achieve depends upon staffing resources, level of expertise, ability to prioritize, and time management. The operational side of the marketing balance is rigorous and equally necessary. Producing publications, managing media relations, coordinating advertising placements, ensuring consistency in school communications, writing articles, taking campus photography, and maintaining visibility on our campuses are important components of a marketing professional's daily existence. The key is striking the appropriate strategic-operational balance.

One important caveat regarding constituency surveys, focus groups, and other polling instruments: A closed-loop approach is the *only* approach for schools that are responsive and respectful of relationships with parents, alumni, and others. Those who give of their time to help us analyze our marketing effectiveness should always hear back from us once the project is completed and results analyzed.

Ideas to Spark Further Creativity

Reviewing the myriad marketing techniques, including publicity, advertising, and media relations, is beyond the scope of this chapter. The objective of this concluding section is to leave the reader with thumbnail sketches of ideas that will hopefully spur further thought and creativity.

Positioning Faculty as Experts

- Include faculty bios on the school's website, including teachers' hobbies and interests.
- Showcase top faculty members through more in-depth profiles in the school's magazine. Include their teaching philosophy and career honors and achievements.
- As appropriate, recruit teachers to write "op-ed's" for the local newspaper. For example, a college counselor might write about the changing face of college admission. The head of school might write about how private schools serve the public good.

Bringing People to Campus

- Recruit a teacher who loves to read to lead a book review club once each semester. Host the club on campus and invite friends from the local community.

- Take maximum advantage of things the school is already doing, such as concerts, drama productions, and the like. Distribute free tickets to local museums and theatres and ask these other non-profits to share with their patrons.
- Host a Chamber of Commerce "Business After Hours" gathering.
- Position the school as an educational beacon by hosting a multifaceted lecture series on topics ranging from local conservation issues to business ethics. If feasible, partner with a local college or university and invite their professors to join the school's panels.
- Host a day-long education fair, and invite parents of all school-aged children in your community. Offer panels on various topics that might range from gifted education to helping children cope with grief. Include panelists from various social service agencies, local public schools, and so on to show collaboration.

Communicating Effectively

Experts who measure our reading habits tell us that America is an increasingly less literate society. As this chapter goes to print, the book publishing industry is in the midst of one of its greatest economic downturns in publishing history. Ken Miller of Ken Miller & Associates in New London, New Hampshire, encourages his clients to do the following in their schools' publications:

- Assume most people will not read text-heavy documents. Use more descriptive headings, "call-outs," and quotes.
- We are a visually oriented society. Invest regularly in obtaining quality, compelling photography. Build stories around photography.

Utilizing Objective Endorsements

Look to third parties to endorse the school and to lend a sense of objectivity to promotion and publicity.

- Capture information from business leaders who visit the campus.
- If the school has recently completed its re-accreditation process, review the in-depth accreditation for powerful quotes and attributes.
- Ask your college-aged alumni how well and in what ways your school prepared them for college.
- Ask the president of your regional independent school association for a quote on your school's strengths.

Through targeted and effective marketing endeavors, our independent schools carry their important messages directly to the individuals who bring vitality to our campuses. Through the work we do as marketing professionals, students come to our schools to learn, to excel and to acquire learning habits and competencies that will benefit them for the rest of their lives. Parents entrust our schools with their children. Teachers dedicate their lives to our institutions. Neighbors and civic leaders value our schools as community assets. Donors identify with us and invest financially. As marketing professionals, our work is met with these and other great rewards. Let's make the most out of our gratifying careers!

Bibliography

Cheney, Carol L./Cheney & Company. *Communications Audit Report for Saint Edward's School.* July 2000.

Miller, Ken/Ken Miller & Associates, LLC. *Marketing & Communicating the Saint Edward's Advantage.* August 2001.

NAIS. *Marketing Independent Schools in the 21st Century.* 2001.

Ross, John and Hallstead, Carol P. *Public Relations and the Presidency: Strategies and Tactics for Effective Communications.* CASE Books, 2001.

Schoenfeld, Clay and Weimer, Linda L. in collaboration with Jean Marie Lang. *Reaching Out: How Academic Leaders Can Communicate More Effectively with Their Constituencies.* Atwood Publishing. 1997.

Saint Edward's School is a co-ed independent day school on the Treasure Coast of Florida serving approximately 850 students in grades Pre-K through 12. **Ms. Lisa Bock** has served as the school's director of advancement since 1997. She is currently pursuing a Ph.D. in comparative studies through Florida Atlantic University's Public Intellectuals program.

Marketing: On the Anguish of Exciting and the Bliss of Dull

By Tim Blankenhorn

Stacks of Viewbooks

Twelve years ago, as admissions director of a large K–12 independent school, I accumulated independent school viewbooks, boxes of them. Now, charged with placing eighth graders in secondary schools, I'm accumulating boxes of viewbooks again. Then, as an admissions director, I collected them because we were getting set to put together our new viewbook, and we read stacks of them, trying to be duly diligent and up-to-date. Now, as upper school director in a K–8 school, I accumulate viewbooks for a different reason. They arrive unsolicited in the mail, from boarding and day schools interested in our eighth-graders. I place them in rough alphabetical order on my bookshelves, where they languish untouched.

As I leaf through them on their passage from the mailbox to the shelves, I note that the last dozen years have seen changes in the viewbook state-of-the-art. The current ones are obviously more expensive, for example. They feature heavy, glossy paper, more pages of earnestly edited and designed material—and they often sport color photographs worthy of national magazines or corporate annual reports.

But the old pile of viewbooks and the new share a deadly flaw—they are indistinguishable one from the other. The handsome students in front of the school sign, the campus in fall foliage, and the head's message—they are interchangeable, one book to the next—and they are dull. Now as before they seem inert. They seem ineffectual.

What's going on here? And what's *not* going on here?

A paradox, a paradox . . . most of these viewbooks will end up unread, unperused, unnoticed. They cost of fifteen dollars or more per copy, if you count the postage. (I received one that was Fed-Ex'd and enclosed an SSAT application for good measure.) And yet the schools are successful enough that they decide year after year, budget after budget, that this strategy works for them.

I have made presentations on school marketing in which I championed the qualities of attention-getting and excitement. But I have to acknowledge that playing it safe has its merits, and as I think about it, it makes sense to describe and give frank credit to dull marketing. "Show the flag" marketing I term it, and we must give it its due. It's not ever explicitly explained, but if it were, it would go like this: "This school wants to show that it is a respectable member of the independent school community, nothing more, nothing less." It's like my grandfather's advice to me: "Always have shiny shoes and a new wallet." It's a low-risk, low-effort strategy, and in it the viewbook becomes in effect a fat, expensive business card. "Here," and you hand it to the prospect, or mail to the feeder school. A sound solution in the pursuit of the status quo.

The Agony of Success

At a social event some years ago I saw a daunting matron whose children I had taught a decade or so before. We caught up briefly. "I must tell you something" she said then. "I have encountered your new brochure, and I find it garish."

Ah. Such were the rewards of the new viewbook that was born from the above-mentioned first pile of viewbooks. Those we'd seen from other schools were so forgettable that we decided to break the mold. Our consultant encouraged us to think creatively and we concentrated on thinking of the path the viewbook would take in the lives of inquiring families, on the impression it would make in the mailbox, in the eyes of the child, and after. We toyed with the idea of having it be something like a box of treasures, to be emptied joyously and fiddled with.

The consultant finally presented us with a concept that was way outsized, brightly ("garishly") colored (aqua, pink, blue-violet) and with a mere handful of spreads. It was printed on heavy, speckled matte stock. The consultant had made us bold. He was the one who had told the board at one college that his surveys had found that kids nationwide felt the college was a joke and a party school. The board members were not pleased. Nor was the board at a school when he presented the opinion that the school was full of "country-club alcoholics."

But when the printer was to deliver the books, I began to get calls from the feisty consultant, a few times a day. "Have they come yet?" His antennae were out. He had unveiled paradigm-breaking viewbooks before, and he knew what to expect. He was nervous. He admitted that the admissions director at the previous school had almost been fired because the viewbooks broke the mold so utterly. We began to worry.

But it could have been worse. Most of the horror was expressed outside my earshot. I had a deputation of mothers who marched into my office and voiced their dismay. ("Let's give it a chance," I counseled.) The office assistant found that metered postage wouldn't stick to the envelope, and she expected us to abandon the books altogether.

But we stood firm. The "first child-centered viewbook," I dubbed it to myself. The viewbook demanded to be seen, and each page turned. It worked. It was a coup. Our yield on inquiries rose to, and sustained, new levels. New as ever (although no one remembers the students in the photos), the book is in its fourth printing. Yet, while there were some pale imitations, there's been none like it. The consultant, who carries it among his samples, found that the piece attracts universal interest, but no other schools are willing to take so radical a plunge.

We had another marketing success that dealt out its share of punishment. Our boys' school assumed a leadership role in the boys' movement, and earned us a cover story in the Sunday magazine of our city newspaper. The paper's photographer wandered off to get some candid shots on a spring afternoon. Someone offered to escort him, but he suggested that since he'd been in Sarajevo and Beirut, he'd be fine. One of the pictures he took that day—unescorted—ran on the cover. Under a blooming tree, three seniors were playing whiffleball at lunch: a batter, a catcher, and an umpire. Shirt tails out, ties askew, animated ("Yer out!" one seems to say), having a good time.

Two results: First our inquiries went through the roof, and five years later, everyone in the city remembers the article fondly. It was wonderful to see boys being boys, they said. Second, it caused a firestorm of criticism because the boys were portrayed so informally, and out of uniform. "How could you do such a thing?" a teacher shouted at me in the front hallway.

Here's the bottom line: Controversy and conflict are part of the life of marketers. In every institution these have a tenuous status—they're championing outsider perspectives to insiders and insiders' perspectives to outsiders. This is tough duty.

Success entails risk.

The Promise of Marketing

In the early '90s, "marketing" was an exciting catch phrase among those of us in admissions. Thinking about "marketing" represented a real advance in institutional consciousness.

We became aware that schools were at the mercy of what were—in those days—negative demographic trends. Old and revered schools found themselves running large deficits because of enrollment declines that no one had foreseen—or could have.

"Marketing" came to mean several things to us:

- a field of expertise that promised mastery of our fate
- a source of professional pride that we were thinking about the same issues that business and colleges were, that we were, in effect, colleagues of big-time executives and consultants
- that it made sense to invest manpower and money in marketing, and to look through one lens at what had been disparate school enterprises of recruitment, retention, fund-raising, and publications

Nothing wrong with those feelings. The last decade was a good one for our schools. The surge of students, the boom economy, and our energetic pursuit of marketing served our schools well. But we have picked the low-hanging fruit. The challenges that face us—the costs, the teacher shortages, effective public school competitors, and stubborn insularity—require that independent school leaders develop a more sophisticated understanding of marketing, a more specialized expertise, and, most important, an understanding that marketing is far more than advertisements, viewbooks, and spiffy new stationery.

It has seemed easy, and we have been able to pretend that marketing is a pleasant, predictable affair. It is time that we embrace more sophisticated—and current—concepts of marketing. I think the current stack of viewbooks indicate we're not evolving at the pace required of us. To me, they are a clear indication that independent schools are stuck—confused about important marketing issues, issues they may not even recognize. This confusion has two results. One, lots of money gets wasted. Two, independent schools, in part because they are focused on, and were successful at, filling classrooms every fall, pay no attention to the large view, to the strategic marketing challenges that will affect us—and in my view could cripple us—in the coming decades.

Real-world Challenges

I had a tour of duty in marketing in the business world. Now I'm back in school—scheduling exams, calming parents, and adjudicating sock heights. (Sample: *Just touching the ankle isn't enough. They have to cover most of the ankle without having to be pulled up.*) I greet a hundred-plus people by name daily. We have spats and misunderstandings, but we love each other. I am happy. Life is good. It took a foray into the for-profit world for me to really "get it," to understand anew what independent school life really means.

I started teaching right out of college, and after thirty years, I needed a change. I had been the marketing/communications person at a large K–12 school. I thought of myself as something of an expert, and I took the opportunity to work as an editor/writer for a $230-a-year subscription newsletter for marketing directors in all industries. It was fun to learn, and it was nice to be able to work a whole day virtually uninterrupted. It was fun and go home and not to think of work until 8:30 the next morning. But it was strange. When I greeted people at the office with a warm, schoolmasterly "Good morning!" surprised co-workers dropped their eyes and scurried off. Vacation was earned at the brisk rate of .8 days per month.

The loud final bell rang in my head when the company owner walked in on a weekly lunch-break yoga group and broke it up. The issue, he explained later to his managing editors, was to nip in the bud any efforts to organize a union.

Gotta go.

I did, however, gather more valuable insights on my "paid sabbatical" that I want to share with independent school marketers and leaders. The fact is that that the marketing directors I dealt with regularly were uniformly intelligent, creative, and highly motivated. Theirs is a competitive world, where companies fail and jobs disappear every day. We need to listen to them.

1. The Challenge to Connect

It is human nature, especially in schools, to refer to what "everyone thinks" or "what everyone knows." This point of view unconsciously casts the market as a single unit. "The market thinks."

"Six Markets Theory" on the other hand, a British innovation, argues that business can be best understood as comprised of not a simple, unitary market, but a web of six different markets.

The concept can be applied and extended to our schools, where I count at least eight distinct markets:

1. recruitment of new students
2. retention of existing students

3. fund-raising
4. college placement ("selling" our school and students to colleges)
5. referral markets: nursery schools, K–8 schools, word of mouth
6. the community, including neighbors, zoning boards, and so on
7. retention of existing faculty
8. recruitment of new faculty

All must be taken into account. It is a balancing act, because the several markets have different criteria, points of view, and priorities. There are some clear conflicts, but they must be faced if your marketing efforts are going to be noticed and heard.

The Dull Solution: Address everything to everyone

The dull solution in many ways explains the current publications policy of schools, and it has its points. Avoid ruffling feathers. Don't diffuse your efforts. Trouble is, material that's meant for everyone gets read by no one, and is of especially little value as an outreach device, to the world outside of the school community. Indeed, the point can be argued that viewbooks are actually meant to appeal to internal constituencies, as a sort of yearbook.

This point of view is apparent when I am sent alumni bulletins from the various schools, as if eighth graders will be attracted to photos of seventy-year-old men standing with drinks in their hands. And it is apparent when faculty members resent the appearance of certain children in photos, because their behavior has not warranted such an honor.

It is human nature, especially in schools, to conceive of what everyone thinks or what everyone knows. And, as in our new viewbook controversy, there is the assumption in schools that current parents, past parents, alumni, English teachers, and a six-year-old should be addressed as a single body—and the result is a peculiarly obsolete, histrionic style of discourse that avoids offense and speaks to no one.

Exciting solutions

- Make good-faith attempts to target material at different groups. It won't be perfect. But it is a useful thing to think about—and avoid the most obvious errors.
- Construct child-centered materials. Children are the ones most likely to be left out of the loop in a single-audience strategy.
- Don't let development agendas drive everything else. It happens. Development directors tend to be driven and empowered, and that's what makes them good. Placing photos of large donors on newsletter covers, for example, will please eight people very much and cause hundreds, perhaps thousands of others, to toss the piece out unopened.
- Give materials to every college rep who calls and say a word or two about your school's direction. My experience is that this will shock and even flatter them. They won't be offended; they're in the business of doing that same thing.

2. The Challenge to Make Your Own Way

Branding is an expensive, difficult strategy. The essence of branding is to communicate a product's unique capacity to serve a customer, a capacity that differentiates it from competitors and that commands a premium over the price of the generic, *commoditized* product. Effective "branding" not only gives the buyer a distinct and favorable impression, but it lifts the product from the mire of price competition—and it matches the product well with customers, making them more likely to be satisfied and to maintain a buying relationship.

The problem with independent schools is that Ajax Farms Country Day thinks it's a brand when it's not. It's generic. It's simply the local private school in Greater Ajax Farms—and the marketing strategy for selling a generic school is distinct from selling a brand.

Indeed, there is a tendency in school "marketing" to project a generic identity: bland, undifferentiated. This is a safe but passive approach. We might call it the "show the flag" strategy.

The Dull Solution: Run with the herd

There's the one about the two guys and the bear. A bear runs into two men hiking, and it's clearly hungry and driven to succeed. The men run as fast as they can to get away.

"We'll never outrun a bear," the first guy pants to the other.

"I don't have to outrun the bear," the other one responds. "I only have to outrun you."

There's a strong tendency in independent schools to take the second guy's point of view. We only have to compete against you.

That's perfectly understandable, I have to say, but in the long run the herd strategy will hurt everyone. Why? Because schools are protected from daily marketing pressures in a hundred different ways, and they tend to grow more and more unresponsive to and remote from the real world.

Our schools have advantages:

- Parents are required by law to school their children—and care for them.
- Public schools are of uneven quality, and parochial schools are fading.
- Established, elite schools enjoy an oligopolistic position—because, for one thing, the cost of entry into the market is so great that founding a new school is a very expensive and difficult proposition.

Yet, independent schools offer more complex marketing challenges than typical businesses do. For example:

- The product is intangible.
- It affects a family's children—with daily reference to deeply held emotions and values.
- It represents a commitment of years.
- It represents an astonishing overall expense—with state-provided, cost-free alternatives in the wings.

- The best practices of schools are by no means settled; they're surrounded by controversy and ideological rancor.

These factors represent the vulnerability of independent schools.

We depend and always have depended on a seller's market, where there is large demand and few independent schools to meet it. We depend on a reputation for excellence that may or may not be warranted, and which we ourselves certainly never question. And yet, all of us in admissions understand just how vulnerable the independent school advantage is. Families can decide in favor of or against independent schools on a whim.

It's a strange world out there. Even as I talk to my eighth graders and their families, I notice that they make decisions about schools in ways that have nothing to do with what the schools do on purpose. In one school two kids in English misbehave in class during an open house. In another school, during a parent visit the admissions director stares at the feet of one of my mothers because (she swears) she was wearing sandals.

"What's School Y like?" parents ask me. "It's a good school," I say. "Sort of like X, but with coat and tie." They nod and write that down.

Or, they say, "I hear the kids at School Y don't like city kids." I scoff at such general statements, but the damage has been done.

Choosing schools is not as rational a process as we would like it to be, as anyone in admissions knows full well. I can remember the mother who moved from California. She planned to put their cars on blocks for the winter, so they wouldn't get snowed on. And she wanted her son to go to an eastern prep school. He was smart, we took him, but she took him out in less than a year. It was too hard, she decided. Too much work. I can remember the mother of a newly recruited soccer goalie who watched our opening assembly, wept uncontrollably, and left, with husband and son, for good. "We're not this kind of people," she said.

Exciting Solution: Explain what you do to serve your students for a mere $10,000 or $20,000 a year.

Typically we duck the question with platitudes, with cliches that we share in common: Independent schools are better, well, because they are better. We have lots of AP courses; we have good college admissions, our teachers care, we perform musicals and have lacrosse in the spring. At some point, if not now, we will have to explain what we do differently, and why it's so successful and worth investing in. We will have to explain ourselves in terms of "outcomes" and not "features." That is, rather than list our four foreign languages, we will have to explain to parents how we ensure that their child will be a better person as a result of this variety of languages.

3. The Challenge to Innovate

It's a fast-changing world out there. Doctors and lawyers are discouraging students from entering their fields. Only four in ten college graduates are boys—a stat that's even worse if you pluck out the technology fields that boys tend to dominate. The corporation has been declared dead by Peter Drucker, who virtually invented modern management, and the whole notion of job security became a myth when the phone company laid off 50,000 workers. What is it, exactly, that your school is doing to address these changes?

Dull Solution: Avoid rocking the boat by making any changes.
Exciting Solution: Do the best you can, but do something.

I know a school where the seventh and eighth graders were offered only Latin, and this was changed to allow a choice between Latin and Chinese. This engendered quite an emotional response on the part of the parents whose children were taking Latin, and there were heated exchanges between "Latin" parents and "Chinese" parents. The latter and the school leadership were accused of destroying the most valuable traditions, and, by the way, were ensuring their children's failure later on. The argument went that they would not know Latin roots, English words, and so on. There are reasons to consider changes in languages offered. In this case one and a half billion reasons, because the population of China is likely to be the focus of the world economy in the next hundred years. (Also, in this case, Chinese language proficiency gains a nice toehold on college admissions.) And it's the sort of decision that a school must make itself, without the customers.

The Innovator's Dilemma by Clayton M. Christensen sounds the alarm about customer-directed management trends. Christensen points out, in compelling form, a truth that is too often forgotten in marketing discussions: the customer and the institution have different goals, and an institution that listens too closely to its customers—and turns a deaf ear to its own experts—is likely to get into trouble. Why? Customers can leave at any time. The relationship isn't symmetrical. If schools end up being run by their own customers, they place themselves at great risk. This underlines the need for board training that emphasizes the long-term nature of the board role.

Let's take the example of the businesses that made power shovels in the 1950s. They all powered shovels with wires and pulleys—mechanically. Using hydraulic fluid to power the shovels had been tried, and it had failed. The shovel companies, the industry leaders, asked their customers, "Would you be interested in hydraulic shovels if we can get them to work?" The customers said, "No. Mechanical shovels are what we want." What happened? Hydraulic shovels were developed by fringe companies, and customers loved them and bought them in droves—and the leading companies, who took the customers at their word, went belly up.

It is the responsibility of the school, not the parents, to make the decisions necessary to compete in future years. Current families may like it, and they may not, but ultimately it is not, nor should it be, a decision that lies in their hands.

Two Guys and Two Bears

There was the board member who decided to do a marketing study. When I suggested that we would profit most from thinking what would happen if the courts declared open enrollment in every school district, an open issue at the time, he replied that there was no point in asking questions we couldn't know the answers to.

Seems to me, we're going to have ask questions we don't know the answer to. We ignore these questions at our peril.

If the bear chasing the two guys is joined by another bear, both guys are out of luck.

That is to say, if the market shifts in independent schools, and we're not prepared to explain ourselves in fresh, persuasive ways to people with whom we have not yet made contact, we could be in the trouble we were in back in the early 1990s.

Then, the unread, six-figure viewbooks will seem to represent a sadly lost opportunity.

Tim Blankenhorn is director of the upper school at St. Peter's School, a non-denominational N–8 school in the historic district of Philadelphia.

School and Community: The Case for Active Citizenship

By Peter Tacy

Why have community and government relations come to matter *so much* for independent schools? One of the most thoughtful scholars of this subject, Ed Burke of Boston College, puts it this way:

- Because the "psychological contract"—the "implicit expectation" that institutions and society have for each other—has *changed.*
- Because the "definer [of a school's] freedom to operate" has *shifted* to a more intimate site—away from distant entities, and toward local communities and states.

No one who has been involved for long with independent school leadership lacks stories about how the relationships of schools with neighbors, local government, and state legislative and regulatory bodies have become more difficult as the "expectations" held by these entities have changed. In some cases, such as those involving local regulatory bodies, school planning and operations have been negatively impacted. In others, such as the decision of the state of Ohio to mandate statewide achievement testing (and implicitly, a curriculum that's to be tested) for all of the state's non-public schools, an interaction may have had the effect of challenging independent education's "license to operate" by substantially constraining the ability of the state's independent schools to add the extra educational value that justifies payment of tuition.

Burke sees the changes cited above as ones that affect every kind of organization. But magnifying the nature of these changes for independent schools have been years of nonstop, highly publicized concern, debate, and political action across America regarding public elementary and secondary schools. Most polls show that schooling is either the number one or number two "hot button" political issue, no matter where in America a poll has been taken. And since we all know that "hot buttons" in a democracy must drive action, we should not be surprised to find that what we do and what every institution involved in education proposes to do can become enormously controversial.

Burke's proposed response has four main components. First, an organization must clarify what its own needs and goals are. Second, it must make it a part of its business to be continually engaged with and deeply knowledgeable about key outside entities—neighbors as well as local and state governments. It has to know these entities well enough to be fully aware of the needs each is experiencing and the goals each holds. The point of this endeavor is not just to gain information, but to become a "neighbor of choice"—a term that defines institutional behavior that not only shares knowledge, but creates and sustains *trust.* Third, the organization must take the initiative in its communication with the world around it: It moves out of a reactive stance. Finally, it assembles with allies to advocate for common aims. Why this last step? Because, for at least half a century, *that's the only way things will work.* As Burke points out,

> In the United States . . . with the exception of taxes, every major domestic policy program since the early 1960s has been set, shaped, and in some cases designed by organizations and citizen advocacy groups.

Closer to home, at the state, local, and neighborhood levels, this trend has been even stronger. If each of us wants to stay independent, then what we do on a school-by-school basis will be important, but it won't be the whole ball game. Our ability to work *together* skillfully and strategically, in towns and cities, states and at the federal level, will also be essential. So how can we turn such an analysis into a plan for action, both within a school and with peers in local and state associations? Here are a few suggestions.

A. Clarify Objectives.

For any school or group of schools, we can divide this task into two parts and processes.

First, identify *strategic community and government-relations objectives.* These should be seen in a long-term manner—say, over a span of twenty or so years—and will focus on the mission-driven conditions you believe must be attained for your organization to fulfill its core intentions. Probably the best way to describe strategic objectives is via scenario planning—envisioning the environment you *need* to have in order to succeed.

Then set clear *action policies.* These are written statements that describe what you intend to do, now and in the immediate future, regarding specific matters or issues affecting your strategic objectives—matters which are emerging in the larger environment, or that you wish to bring forward. Policy statements need to be concrete, unambiguous, and shorn of generalizations. A rule of thumb: Is the statement clear enough to ensure that a person representing the school/association will know *exactly* what you want her/him to do and not do? Is it both positive and candid enough that such a person can share the policy statement with allies and even, in some cases, with the media or opponents? If the answer isn't "yes" on both scores, it's time to revise.

Successful government relations demands clear objectives, and explicit policies.

B. Provide Resources

Assuming step "A" has been taken or is under way, then at the school level a variety of next steps will need to be taken. Here are a few.

- Appoint an appropriately skilled person to coordinate school advocacy and communications, local and government relations, and media interactions (such persons are often titled "Director of Communications" or "Director/Assistant Head for External Affairs." Whatever title is chosen is less important than the skill of the person selected, and the appropriateness of delegation, support, and supervision provided.

- Ensure this person reports directly to the head, as part of the core administrative leadership team. This status needs to be understood by the entire school community, including the board.
- Clarify that this person's role not only is one of initiating actions the institution needs and has planned, and managing communications regarding local/government relations issues that may arise, but also involves the general coordination of institutional communications, in order that a unified, policy-driven, strategically based school image can be maintained.
- Provide resources outside the school that the communications leader will need. These may include funding for research, or expert PR and marketing counsel. It will certainly mean ongoing professional development, and support for "networking" with peers.
- Educate *all* employees and, as appropriate, other constituencies (trustees, parents, students) regarding the community/governmental objectives and policies of the school, and how these are to be articulated. (Don't be afraid to be specific about do's and don'ts!)
- Ensure that the evaluation process for the communications coordinator is appropriately structured and data-based . . . and that some aspect of every employee's evaluation (and of the board's self-evaluation) references community and government-relations objectives.
- Celebrate *every* successful action! Celebration is vital to morale—and the creation and sustenance of positive morale may be the single most valuable investment you can make in future effectiveness.

The resources needed at the association are somewhat different. Assuming again that the association has taken step "A," then:

- Ensure that the association employs a skilled, effective spokesperson who can implement the organization's communications and government-relations objectives and policies proactively. Since for all but the largest associations this person will also be the executive director, ensuring that candidates have the relevant skills should be a top priority when a director is hired, and a core subject of her/his evaluation. This should also be a focus of at least a part of this person's ongoing professional education.
- Make it clear that public-policy objectives are a top priority for the time, energy, and activity of the executive director and staff, and of the board. This not only means ensuring there will be proper funding and that initiative-taking is encouraged and success appreciated, but that this part of the job is not "blocked" by other expectations, which, while customary, may be of less strategic value.

- Provide the executive director with access as needed to skilled guidance/backup. In all statewide (and some of the larger local) organizations, this should *always* include part-time or retained access to an expert consultant who can serve as a government observer and coach, a professional PR practitioner, and legal counsel.
- Ensure the association invests time and, where appropriate, collegial support in the development of allies. Examples might be relationships with the state CAPE, or with organizations of other non-profits, such as colleges and hospitals. Keep in mind that alliances of this kind need only be situationally useful—they need not reach to all subjects or be obliging beyond a specific shared interest. They are *not* apt to happen, though, if connections have not been created and nurtured in advance. My own State Department of Education has often been a valuable ally, in no small part because we and they have invested time and effort in building a relationship of shared service and trust.

C. Cultivate Relationships

It's been said that the most important word in "government relations" is "relations."

So let's assume that, for a school or a group of schools, steps "A" and "B" have been taken. Great! But these only yield capabilities—not action. You've created a direction, and have marshaled resources. Then . . . what? Imagine that you've made a plan for a trip you want to take, and have obtained a vehicle that can get you there. Here you are in the driver's seat. What else is needed? Fuel. *Relationships are the fuel of effective local/government relations.*

For many independent schools and associations, the pro-active building of direct personal ties that can open doors to those who will decide whether or not our strategic objectives and action policies will be achieved has been an area of weak performance. It isn't that doing this is expensive, but it takes time, humility, and patience; is wholly dependent on initiative; and doesn't yield an instant product. And the construction of key relationships has to be done *prospectively* and earnestly if it's to happen. You simply can't start a relationship when you need to ask a person for help or a vote of support.

So why do we under-perform in this area? Obviously, it takes time. And it doesn't demand to be done right now. Others may not see it as the strategic investment it actually is. And perhaps it may seem a bit *infra dig*—"beneath" us—to seek the counsel of neighbors or become friendly with state pols. Whatever the causes, though, a critical job for both school and association is too often done poorly, or not at all. Result? It shouldn't surprise us that, without an advance investment in the "fuel" relationships provide, we sometimes run out of gas when we most need to be speeding toward our objectives.

How do schools and associations ensure that they will have the relationships in place that they want when they most need the energy these relationships can provide? The principles are the same for both schools and associations. To make them have force, though, we must specifically expect leaders to do the following:

- Invest in building respectful, supportive ties and, over time, *trust* with key public officials. This must be done through the deliberate, sustained commitment of time, advice, reliability, and service, without regard to partisan allegiances and/or a person's prior "friendship" to your organization. The expectation must *always* be the development of mutually useful relationships and honest understanding. Never expect unwavering loyalty.

- Provide useful help wherever possible to those who lead local organizations, and to agency staff. Often the most valuable help you can offer will be information. Most public officials at the state or local level are understaffed, and often they lack some or all of the information they need to be effective. If you can provide solid, credible, unbiased, useful information, you can make a difference that will pay off—for them, and over time for your organization. At the local level, "help" may sometimes involve nothing more than providing a community leader the space to hold a meeting, volunteers for a service project, or a venue for a community event. If you can help leaders "deliver" in this way, over time you may create a lasting relationship. And by the way, open acknowledgement should be a standard part of such transactions. When your organization has been helped, don't *ever* miss the chance to thank the official who's aided you. This can turn a mere decision into a relationship. Similarly, *always* make it known that when you/your school/your association help an official or local organization, you expect an acknowledgement of what you've done.
- Take the initiative to develop a one-on-one relationship with members of the media who "cover" local/community news or, for an association, regional and state news. The goal should be knowledge-building as well as relationship-building. Trying to help a reporter understand what an "independent school" is, much less be sympathetic to the goals and culture of a particular institution, when a deadline for a story is looming, may be impossible. But you may be able to move directly to substantive issues with a reporter who knows the basics, and knows you. The result has a good chance of being a product you both will like. Associations can have an especially useful role in this area. Often an association executive is able to function as a sort of "research reference" for a journalist, leading a known and trusted reporter to sources at schools who can help him/her build a good story, and, not incidentally, a story that will fit in with the organization's objectives.
- Sustain alliances. The people who lead and staff allied groups and organizations are important to honor and nurture. Look back to the last item in section "C" and consider how leaders of a school or association might initiate the kinds of one-on-one actions with leaders of allied groups that will help turn a routine contact into a real relationship. The specifics are not hard to imagine. It's the initiative-taking that's the hard part.

Finally, two admissions.

Much of what I've been talking about as "communication" and "relationship-building" could just as well be called "lobbying." I haven't used the word until now—purposefully. I've wanted to avoid a term that has (for a mixture of good reason and political/media spinning) acquired a negative coloration. (*Lobbying? Isn't that what's done by those fellows Ross Perot described as liars wearing alligator shoes?*)

I know something about the bias regarding "lobbying." For fifteen years, by state law, I—like anyone else in a similar role with an association in Connecticut—have had to wear a badge whenever I am in our state capitol that proclaims, in bold letters, "LOBBYIST." You can imagine the looks this provokes from tourists and visiting groups of schoolchildren.

Well, having reasoned thus far while avoiding the word, let's—in the spirit of full disclosure—say it, and then demystify and embrace it.

Lobbying matters, and schools and associations must do it well. Lobbying, the process of employing developed relationships and sustained channels to advocate for actions that will serve the objectives and policies of an organization, is a *necessary* part of responsible community and government relations. If your school and your association don't see some of what they are doing on a regular basis as they deal with local and state governments as lobbying, and if they aren't ready to be judged on the effectiveness of this lobbying, then I'd suggest it's time to make some changes.

Marcia Avner, an authority on lobbying by non-profit organizations, presents the issue in this usefully blunt way:

> Non-profit organizations can and should lobby.
> It isn't difficult.
> It isn't mysterious.
> It isn't expensive.
> And it *is* a proper role . . . [as it] enriches a nonprofit's ability to fulfill its mission.

Lobbying is, in fact, a word that describes much of what I've been talking about. The difference is that using the word *lobbying* introduces a concrete notion of accountability. *Relations* is a word that's hard to link to outcomes. It seems pretty warm and fuzzy. *Lobbying,* even if you include its negative associations, certainly has to do with *results.* And since the results directly serve our missions, we should try to grow comfortable with this word.

If we see the process of setting objectives and framing policies, organizing resources, and cultivating relationships as one that needs to include accountability—in terms of product as well as process—then using the word *lobbying* in any discussion of this subject is vital. Yes, the game gets tougher when we expect results, but then it may also help to clarify that the investment a school or association is making in this area is important. I think that's in everyone's interest.

The second admission is that this subject—community and government relations and lobbying—isn't only institutionally important. It also matters in the context of educating students.

Schools that appear to be disconnected in the eyes of their students from the "outside world" and adults who seem to disdain an interactive civic connection may not be presenting a good educational model. Why? Most schools specifically mention "citizenship" in their mission statements; many associations do, too. Well what does that word mean, and where can it be observed in *action* by students? All of us could rebut doubters by citing expectations for kids regarding service and behavior, and do so with justifiable pride. But I wonder if the way our institutions and the adults who lead them are behaving in relation to neighbors, local communities, and larger levels of government is enforcing this model, or conflicting with it?

That is a question worth asking. The educational community that connects to, respectfully interacts with, and takes on a full citizen's role in relationship to a democratic society is accepting that its mission statements have a behavioral as well as a philosophical impact, and that this impact reaches beyond the world of a child to all of us. For leaders, it goes beyond the "talk" to the "walk." The school or association whose leaders fail to walk the talk is presenting a model, too . . . and the kids are watching.

Whatever words we use to describe our actions, whether or not we acknowledge the educational consequence of these actions, the changed and mounting community and governmental pressure on independent schools is clearly a fact—one we need to acknowledge and reckon with. Can we become "neighbors of choice"? Can we plan, resource, and cultivate the relationships that will enable us to be effective advocates for independence? Can we become good lobbyists, and at the same time exemplars of active, effective citizenship for our students?

Given the stakes, can we *not* do so?

Bibliography

Corporate Community Relations: The Principle of the Neighbor of Choice, by Edmund M. Burke. Prager Publishers, Westport, CT, 1999.

The Lobbying and Advocacy Handbook for Nonprofit Organizations: Shaping Public Policy at the State and Local Level, by Marcia Avner. Amherst H. Wilder Foundation, St. Paul, MN, 2002.

Peter B. Tacy, executive director of the Connecticut Association of Independent Schools from 1989–2004, is a graduate of Deerfield Academy and Williams College. He was the first chair of the 36-association Advocacy Initiative, and is currently a trustee of NAIS, where he serves on the public policy and government relations committee.

Communicating a School's Mission

By Joyce Gregory Evans

In 1993, The Town School, a coed, N–8 institution of 375 students on the upper east side of Manhattan was often referred to as "the best-kept secret in New York." The somewhat remote location, on East 76th and FDR Drive overlooking the East River, was one of several reasons for the reputation. Although historically well known among educators interested in innovative, carefully thought out approaches to teaching and learning, the general population was only somewhat aware of the school.

Board members, faculty, administrators and parents could articulate their deep-felt feelings for the school. All of them spoke eloquently about the experience their children were having at Town, yet to articulate the philosophy, mission, or educational program of the institution was nearly an impossible task. A mandate to the new head of school was to help Town articulate its mission and identify its niche in Manhattan.

At the time, Town was best known as a little, caring, and nurturing institution, one where children were happy and attended to individually, somewhere over near the East River. The students who were attending Town loved their school but they too had a difficult time saying why.

The process of communicating our mission to both our own constituents and the broader community began with a redesign of the school logo and then its liberal use throughout our publications. By retaining the prominent 1913 founding date and the old motto "Gaudeant Discentes," we were able to constantly remind the various constituencies that we were an old, solid, even somewhat classical institution with a Latin motto, yet the motto, loosely translated, means "Let there be joy in learning," emphasizing the importance of the social emotional component as well.

When reviewing and revising our mission statement to see if the "warm and fuzzy" message overshadowed the strong academic program, we discovered that by making it short and seeking to balance the use of words such as "academic rigor and nurturing environment," we were truer to our philosophy and clearer in our stated goals.

Shortly thereafter we recorded the curriculum in a printed booklet for parents and applicant families. By providing a curriculum outline that clearly listed the goals and the course content throughout the grades, we were better able to communicate a seriousness of purpose. We began describing ourselves as a school with a classical curriculum content delivered in a non-traditional way. Constituents were able to read course outlines that sounded similar to that which they had studied in school, yet they could see and sense, from the work displayed on the walls or done in class as well as from comments made by the students, that the approach made learning fun and full of excitement for the children.

We updated our brochure using pictures of students who were engaged and happy, and we carefully selected a limited text. We were careful to include photos of classroom work and daily activities, avoiding special events that occurred only occasionally, as we wanted the brochure to give a sense of the core program. Seriousness of purpose, along with obvious pleasure, was evident throughout the photos. The new brochure was then used for applicant families but was also sent with a "teaching" letter to all current families reminding them of the qualities of Town that led them to select the school for their children.

Several new publications were born out of our need to define and communicate more clearly the unique qualities of Town. "Questions and Answers from The Head" was a one-page interview that emphasized the three main characteristics that we determined best described Town: co-educational, ending in eighth grade, and an approach to learning that engages children.

Addressing the co-educational piece, we spoke of our efforts to make Town a great place for both boys and girls. We emphasized our work in bringing in outside speakers and assigning ourselves readings that would inform our faculty and administration about the unique issues facing both girls and boys. Early on we engaged the Sadkers to speak of their research, learned how to assess our classrooms for equitable learning environments, heard and read Michael Thompson's work on boys, and read Joanne Deak's book on girls, studied the AAUW reports, sent two faculty members to be trained to run a SEED group (Seeking Educational Equity and Diversity), and formed a standing faculty committee on equity and related topics. Overall we knew that each child, boy or girl, was unique and that our job was to discover that uniqueness, that giftedness, and make sure that it was developed. We acknowledged that at Town we had every kind of girl and every kind of boy: shy, aggressive, artistic, athletic, scientific, bookish. In order to meet our mission, each child needed to develop individually. One example of success that we often used was that fact that over a ten-year period with both girls and boys vying for the roles of president and vice-president of the student senate, we were equally balanced. Sometimes we had co-ed leaders, sometimes girls were presidents and boys vice-presidents, or vice versa. Both genders were always represented, serving together as leaders.

Ending our school at eighth grade was a conscious decision. The elementary years had been Town's forte for generations. We emphasized the advantage for middle school students to be "the seniors" leading the student government, editing the yearbook and acting as "big brothers and sisters" for the younger students. Another advantage to which we referred was the fact that without high school role models in their midst, the middle school and younger students seemed to remain "age-appropriate" in their behavior, not seeking to emulate their older classmates. By the time the students were ready for high school, as they graduated from the eighth grade, they had defined themselves as students, identifying their strengths and their interests, thus allowing for a high school choice that was a good "match." As well, they were ready for a change and often a larger school. By providing a placement program that included a "Decisions Class," meetings with students and parents, checklists and timelines and close communication with each family, Town students were sought after by the high schools that constantly reported that our students were both well prepared and self-assured. Faculty members from outstanding Manhattan independent high schools visited Town to "see what you are doing over here, and seek to discover your secret for solid preparation while at the same time turning out such nice, well rounded students!"

A new publication that was helpful for applicant parents, as well as our own, listed the schools to which our applicants applied and attended as well as a record of where they went on to university. (This information was acquired by initiating an annual alumni/ae dinner at Town for high school seniors and their parents. Not only did this gathering fulfill our purpose, it helped develop a continuation of the community that was so strongly felt by the students during their years at Town.) We carefully articulated that this new publication was not a "brag sheet" but rather an example of our mission, matching each student individually to the school that would best serve her/his needs. Applicant parents as well as current parents found it to be reassuring. It was evidence that our program was able to meet individual needs that would lead to appropriate educational opportunities for each student. Additional publications used mostly for admissions included a piece on Town's commitment to diversity as well as one directly addressing the choice of a school ending in eighth grade.

In defining the "approach" to education, we often referred back to the education that most of us remember when we were in elementary school. Rather than the rows of desks facing forward with the teacher serving as the "fount of all knowledge," students are grouped at tables with the teachers acting as facilitators, moving about the room and assisting as needed. Rather than an emphasis on competition, each student is encouraged to do his best, improving at their own pace and level. Grades are put off until fifth grade with low-key standardized testing beginning in fourth grade. Thus the emphasis was placed on the joy of learning and discovering, while at the same time making sure that the teaching of test-taking and other skills necessary for children in this test-driven society were included. Teaching children to think, to risk, and to push themselves results in strong, confident students. It was easy for parents to see this happening to their own children early on, particularly as reading and writing grew in importance in first and second grades.

The task of becoming more articulate in explaining our program and mission internally, to our own parents and faculty, was a unique challenge, one that often lacks focus in independent education. We somehow assume that once a family has joined our community, it becomes aware of our mission via osmosis.

In addition to the traditional curriculum evening or "Back to School Night," we added morning parent coffees, which focused on different areas of the curriculum at different grade levels. Every other year we emphasized our approach to language arts, alternating it with our approach to mathematics. We interspersed special topics such as science, values, and geography as well. Parent education evenings by grade level with the school psychologist, division heads, and teachers emphasizing the unique developmental and social issues of that particular age level were most helpful because they provided a forum for exchange among the parents. The school's philosophy and ways of dealing with issues, which reflected our mission, were emphasized and these evenings became teaching tools not only for parenting but also for the school's approach. Additionally, grade-level cocktail parties at the home of the head of school provided opportunities for the head to address the parents briefly and have them begin to articulate to one another the components of the program and mission that they liked and appreciated.

An annual three-part lecture series that addressed issues to the faculty and then to the parent body by prominent educators and psychologists such as Michael Thompson, Catherine Steiner-Adair, and Robert Evans provided the community with opportunities to discuss and examine the school's program and the ways in which parenting can be an extension of the same philosophy. The series brochure, a classy appealing piece, was mailed widely and was hailed by other independent schools, some of which sent groups of parents to hear the speakers.

Early morning "math clubs" were formed by the math coordinator, which allowed parents and young children to arrive in the library before school in order to work on math games, puzzles, and enrichment activities together. This provided an avenue for parents to understand the bigger picture about how math was taught at Town and what, in fact, a "conceptual grounding" actually looked like before the students became overly involved in computation. Once parents understood and experienced the process, they were most supportive and helpful with their children as they then learned and mastered the foundational math skills with understanding.

Using parent volunteers in admissions to lead round-table discussions with parents, during the hour that the parents were waiting while their applying children were being evaluated, proved to be an outstanding way of educating our own parents. The admissions director and the head of school met with the volunteers and discussed ways of articulating the mission of Town. Our numbers of articulate parents grew annually as these parents became supportive, well-informed, and well-spoken advocates for the school.

One of the ways that we were able to "teach" our own parents about the importance of being an elementary school that ends in eighth grade was by initiating an "All School Graduation and Promotion." We secured the use of Alice Tulley Hall at Lincoln Center where we had space for students in grades K–7 to sit together in long rows while the eighth graders were seated on the stage. (The sense of community when gathering the whole school together is powerful in and of itself!) After the processional, the division heads promoted each grade level, including the nursery three's and four's, describing their success for the year and announcing their advancement to the next grade level. As each class stood to receive their promotion, excitement and a sense of accomplishment and pride was evident among all. The entire parent body looked on and was particularly impressed by the two eighth grade student speeches, the personal words said to each graduate about themselves and their years at Town, and the emphasis upon the graduates attending a wide variety of schools. Parents were soon extolling the advantages of a school ending in eighth grade rather than being overwhelmed about the need to enter the somewhat daunting high school admissions process in New York City. Instead, they knew that their child would have the self-confidence, the preparation, and the powerful culmination of the foundational years on which to rely. The broad range of schools and the faces of happy, self-assured graduates helped to calm any worries and to abate an old issue of attrition at sixth grade because parents had previously become overly anxious about high school acceptances.

The Parent Association Council was asked to meet monthly with the head of school and often those discussions, which centered on events or concerns, were valuable opportunities to "teach" that group of leaders about school philosophy and policy such as birthday guidelines, evening events at school, expected behavior, and so on. Once the reasoning was understood, the council served as a valuable educational arm for the administration.

For some time, in an effort to save paper sending home "kiddie or backpack mail," we published *The Family News* once a month, encouraging parents, faculty, and administrators to use it as a primary means of communication. The monthly "Letter from the Head" on the front page was another opportunity to teach about the school's mission while at the same time supporting parents in their role as their child's primary educator. Since this publication was distributed to a wide audience of current parents, past parents, other school heads, and parent association presidents at other schools, it grew to become an effective avenue to tell Town's story, not only to our own families but also to the broader independent school community.

Just two years ago, we initiated "Caregiver's Coffees." Since so many of the children spent several hours each day with their caregivers, we realized that some time spent with them talking about homework, expectations, our methods of discipline, and our overall philosophy of dealing with children would be helpful. These meetings were warmly received and provided another opportunity for us to infuse our mission into an important constituency in the school.

When installing a new phone system throughout the building, we decided that we would continue to have the receptionist answer all calls in person, helping to communicate that we feel that each person who calls is important. However, we were able to add music to the "hold" button in order to communicate the importance of the arts at Town in a subtle way. We used a CD recording of Town students singing and have had an overwhelmingly positive response from our own parents as well as from those who simply telephone the school and are put on hold.

Through full faculty meetings, discussions, retreats, speakers, committees, and assigned summer reading, we as a faculty became more articulate in describing the educational process and philosophy at Town as well. At one full faculty retreat, values and behavioral objectives were agreed upon and written. These were hailed by the board and subsequently published annually in the parent handbook. They began with the words, "At Town we . . ." and included statements such as: ". . . show respect and civility for all members within our community" and ". . . acknowledge our differences with understanding and sensitivity."

Town's unique governance structure allowed for three faculty members to serve on the board of trustees. Thus, as the board struggled with becoming clearer and more articulate about the mission, faculty furthered those discussions.

Faculty summer study stipends played a role in further articulating our curricula and mission. Once granted a stipend, the recipients were prepared to report on their summer work to other faculty, the board of trustees, and to the parents at the Parent Association meeting in the fall. Hearing what faculty members were doing to enrich the curriculum and the classrooms was a great way to teach board members and parents about the program as well as giving faculty the experience of communicating the philosophy in yet another way. Not long ago, these reports were posted on our intranet site, which is accessed by our current students, faculty, parents, and often grandparents. When we began an endowment drive to support summer stipends and professional development, it became a favorite gift choice for many to support the teachers and the program. Donors and others saw that, as a result of such a summer program, teachers were able to deliver the curriculum with renewed enthusiasm, excitement, and creativity, modeling what the school felt was important in children's learning.

As we in our own community became more articulate, we were also able to state more confidently who we were not. "Do not choose to send your child to Town if you would feel uncomfortable with a productive 'hum' in the classrooms, children on the floor doing math or silent reading, or children progressing at their own levels, not learning to read in kindergarten but when they are ready." I often say that, "With all of the wonderful schools in New York City, your child will learn and progress in any one of them, basically covering the same content by the time they complete eighth grade. The difference is in the approach. Your children will do well in a variety of settings, but *you* may not! You are the ones who need to feel comfortable and trust the approach of the school you choose. If you are happy and supportive, your child will do well." I firmly believe that this is true. Problems arise when parents do not understand what they are choosing because we have not communicated clearly our mission and our approach in carrying out that mission.

Town's visibility in the Manhattan community was enhanced by the fact that senior administrators and faculty were encouraged to serve on boards, speak at conferences, invite colleagues to use our building for meetings, offer our space for New York State Association of Independent School workshops, and so on. Simply by bringing people into our building, we were able to "teach" about who we were and what was important at Town. By having our names listed as a member of a national, state, or local board followed by "The Town School" gave us name recognition and awareness that we were more than a "nice little school over by the river." Many of us were asked to speak on panels, be interviewed for articles on education, to serve as master teachers for student teachers, or serve on committees for conferences and accreditation teams. Also, as a result of our associate teacher program, numerous independent schools throughout the City hired Town-trained teachers; thus, Town's story was broadly told. As well, we were fortunate enough to receive a glowing write-up in the best-selling *Manhattan Guide to Independent Schools* written by two women who, several years ago, went through the admissions process and recorded their impressions.

How does one measure success in communicating one's mission? Although a sign of the times is the competitive admissions market in New York City, we determined that our long-term emphasis on becoming more articulate in communicating our mission was largely responsible for our 200% increase in applications for kindergarten at Town.

Town was no longer a "well-kept secret!" With such an increase in numbers, a new challenge arose: the task of determining which of the families believed in the mission and wanted their children at Town for the program and philosophy rather than the popularity of the school on the New York independent school grapevine. Probing during the individual parent interviews by the director of admissions has been successful in family selections, resulting in the acceptance of families that have been engaged in and supportive of the mission.

It is my firm conviction and experience that a clear and concise mission that is articulated by the broadest constituencies of the school is one of the most important tasks of all independent schools in this current educational climate. When a school is able to acknowledge that it cannot be all things to all people but instead has a clearly stated philosophy with goals and objectives, we are fairer and more honest to all of our constituencies. This articulation needs to be shared by the entire community but it is up to the leadership to educate, explain, emphasize, repeat and clearly state the vision that marks the institution. This is work that is never complete because schools that are alive are constantly redefining themselves in more precise and often exciting ways. As educators, in administrative roles, we are passionate about teaching. Our challenging teaching assignment, then, is to "teach" our philosophy and mission in creative and responsive ways.

Joyce Evans retired from The Town School, Manhattan, in July of 2003, after 10 years at Town and 39 years in the field of education. She served for several years on the National Association of Independent Schools' board as well as the New York State Association of Independent Schools' board.

CURRICULUM

Vision: A Path to Change and Innovation

By Mark Crotty & George N. King, Jr.

At an August 1998 retreat, The Greenhill Upper School Leadership Team[1] reflected on the state of the upper school. By almost any measure we were flourishing. However, life had become overwhelming: as George King, then head of the upper school, put it, the container was overflowing. Previous attempts to deal with the issue—discussions about trimesters versus semesters, schedule adjustments, blank campus exercises—had not rectified the problems. Trying a different tactic, George organized the retreat. There we reframed and unified all our concerns to clarify the real question: How do you take a great school and make it even better?

Before the retreat, George had the participants read Robert Evans's *The Human Side of School Change.* Clearly he expected the retreat to prompt some changes. Furthermore, rather than lead the retreat, George stepped aside so as not to influence the proceedings too much. He contracted David Grant, whom he had met at the Independent School Innovation Consortium. David led us through Ted Sizer's "Picture of the Graduate" exercise—a crucial launching pad.

In this exercise people imagine the ideal graduate of their school. What key knowledge, skills, and attitudes would that person have? Which are particularly crucial? After working in small groups, everyone re-gathers. Naturally, discussion buzzes about the school, the implications, and the possibilities. The exercise energized the leadership team, particularly because of the consensus that emerged; and they quickly agreed on two points: have everyone in the community complete the exercise, then form an ad-hoc committee to study the implications of the results and recommend responses. Thus was born the Vision Committee.

During orientation week the entire upper school faculty completed the exercise, and on class trips all students did so. Then approximately fifty parents participated. George also formed the committee. Because he recognized that any meaningful results must bubble up from the community and not cascade from the top down, he decided to ask Mark Crotty to chair it.

Immediately we determined some key first steps. We devised ways to help committee members get on the same page. We wanted to involve the larger community in key ways. We brainstormed on potential pitfalls and desirable outcomes. We reminded ourselves to remain patient. First, we needed to boil down the results of the picture of the graduate exercise. At this point we had hundreds of pieces of data. While we saw some general patterns, someone had to distill all of it into a succinct, coherent package.

Mark set to work on the data. After tallying the responses, he categorized them and identified threads. He then produced a seminal document for the ensuing work: "The Picture of the Graduate—A Composite View." The document was organized as follows:

- The Exercise and the Process
- Findings
  - Knowledge
  - Skills
  - Attitudes
- A Response to Concerns with the Exercise
- Basic Principles Which Emerge
  - The Type of School We Should Strive to Be
  - The Ideal Graduate
- Possible Implications for Greenhill School
  - Curricular issues
  - Graduation requirements
  - Co-Curricular Programs
  - Use of Time and Space
  - Character Development
  - College Placement
- Link to Greenhill School Mission Statement
- Appendices of POG Data

The committee approved this document, and then the journey really started.

The first challenge involved unifying the Vision Committee. While excited by the challenges, we also felt anxious. No one knew quite what to expect, and we each had ideas about the implications and possible fallout. After some tentative meetings, we had a working dinner party on a Saturday evening. For four hours we ate and brainstormed and dreamed. When the evening ended, we had a rough draft of ideas for recommendations. More important, we had a stronger sense of purpose and teamwork.

Of course, we still had to involve and excite the rest of the community. We knew we should operate as openly as possible. We gave regular updates at faculty meetings, shared Picture of the Graduate information, and published a Statement of Purpose. We aimed to thus establish common ground for all future conversations. Committee members kept the issues in front of people. In mid-November, George asked the faculty: "Based on what the Vision Committee has told you so far, do you want to continue this process?" They responded with an overwhelming "yes."

To channel this enthusiasm, we took some key steps. We formed four subcommittees comprised of VC members and other faculty: College Admissions, Graduation Requirements, Use of Time and Space, and Relationship of Parts to the Whole. We focused on these areas because we wanted to deal with the larger picture, then focus on particulars. For example, we did not want any changes to jeopardize college admission. Graduation requirements should reflect the program aims. To supplement Picture of the Graduate data, we surveyed students, faculty, alums, and trustees about issues highlighted. George asked four parents to join the Vision Committee, and later we added five students. We held a parents' evening to share our direction with them.

Meanwhile, the full Vision Committee kept meeting weekly, with people giving up their lunches and other free periods. We began viewing the situation as a Gordian knot—incredibly complicated, but solvable with decisive action and leading to great rewards. Mark challenged the group not to allow our work to become a time "when all is said and done, more is said than done."

That year raced by in a blur of various meetings—the full committee, subcommittees, random conversations, presentations. Several key questions kept rising: How far should we go? Which issues first? How do we present our ideas to the community? How do we deal with the individual responses to change? How do we convince skeptics? Can we ground our ideas in research? Do they fulfill our mission? Would they really help us to fulfill the Picture of the Graduate?

Pondering these questions also emphasized another challenge. As Wells McMurray, our college counselor, kept saying, "We're talking about the heart and soul of education." We wanted to address intangible, non-quantifiable elements in the quality of life in the upper school. We couldn't point to any test results or statistics, nor could we offer any quick fixes and guarantees. We even had a hard time articulating exactly how we would know when we had achieved our goals. Plus our target audience had not benefited from our extensive collaboration.

That spring the Vision Committee had agreed on our recommendations (see Appendix 1 page 267). First we presented them to the faculty, then students, and then parents. With each recommendation we included three sub-points: the benefits, some implications, and possible implementation. Afterward, we provided several means for people to respond by holding town meetings and broadening inclusion as other sub-committees formed. Overall, most people supported the recommendations, at least in theory. The real test would come when changes impacted them directly.

At this point, we had numerous subcommittees working on various recommendations. Some key ones were Statement of Values, Advisory, Schedule, and Student Voice. Each consisted of some full committee members, including faculty and student co-chairs, along with other faculty and students who applied. We strove to include different perspectives in the groups. They regularly updated the full committee, who maintained the penultimate decision on any plans for implementation. Once they finished with a proposal, it went to George and the head of school—first Peter Briggs, then Scott Griggs—for approval. This process enabled us to attack several fronts at once, to include a high percentage of the community, and to control how the pieces fit together. Math teacher Pam Bockbrader called the system "an excellent way for all of us to keep in touch with the entire process." Without it, the Vision Committee may not have achieved as much as it has.

In 2002–3, our search for a new division head forced us to reflect on our accomplishments. Scott Griggs asked committee member and math chair Barb Currier to report on the progress. She was "uplifted to see how many real changes have actually come about." So far those include the following:

- New graduation requirements
  - Our graduation requirements now make the ninth and tenth grades a core program, and the eleventh and twelfth grades a more choice-oriented program. The former include more traditional survey-type courses. In the latter, courses delve more deeply into narrower topics and emphasize student learning. These classes also meet less frequently for longer periods. We believe this makes for a better transition to college.
- New integrated and traditional courses
  - We determined to design courses that help students make connections rather than leave that to chance. Similarly, courses should reflect the way knowledge really works, not leave it departmentalized in convenient containers. In just a few examples, we have a Spanish service learning course in which students serve as translators for local agencies; an exercise physiology course that merges with physical education; math courses structured around real-world applications; and an epistemology course that examines all the traditional disciplines.
- New schedule
  - Classes now meet for different lengths of time and at varying frequency, based on need. For instance, upper-level science classes meet less often for longer periods to allow for the most productive labs. This schedule has had many benefits. Students and teachers have more unscheduled time. This facilitates extra help sessions, group work, research, reflection, and down time. Teachers feel students come to class better prepared, and daily life feels less hectic. More professional collaboration is possible. The change also is forcing teachers to rethink coverage and pedagogy.
- Capstone senior thesis project
  - We hoped to offer seniors a unique experience that would invoke many of the intellectual qualities cited in the Picture of the Graduate. The Capstone project—named for the final stone put in place on a structure—is an optional, student-designed, independent research project. Guided by in- and out-of-school mentors, students work for a year on the project. The final component must include a written portion, a public exhibition, and serving as a peer evaluator.
- More projects involving independent work and public speaking
  - As we asked students to do more independent work (particularly in upper-level courses) we also wanted them to present their findings. We also had concerns about poor public speaking skills. Our debate and speech teachers gave the faculty a workshop, and a year later we had a colloquium in which several teachers shared their successes in this area. Many teachers have followed their lead.
- Extended honor code
  - For years our honor code applied only to academics. Many of us worried about signals that may have sent about our values. Now the code covers academics, lying, stealing, and other character issues.

- Plans for extension to building
  - One goal involved looking at the relationship between facility, program, and purpose. Vision Committee work has greatly influenced the plans for an extension to the current upper school building.
- Greater student representation and voice
  - Standard practice now involves student inclusion on committees and projects that often comprised only faculty. Students serve on the leadership team, ad hoc committees, and various councils. Their input has proven invaluable.
- Helen Fulton awards
  - Special awards, named after the founding head's wife, honor those seniors who the faculty feels best embody the qualities outlined in the Picture of the Graduate.

Work remains. We wish to invigorate our advisory program and to have the upper school gather more frequently in meaningful fashion. We must discuss assessment and excellence. Naturally, some departments and individuals have moved further ahead than others. While the official Vision Committee disbanded in June 2001, a steering committee exists to keep us on track.

Beyond the obvious changes, the process has strengthened us as a community. It confirmed our quality. Simultaneously, we gained greater courage to take risks and even return to our roots as innovators. Toward the end of the process, Scott Griggs became head of school. He says, "It took great courage to step back and ask the questions that were addressed through this process. . . . This desire to continually strive for improvement is indicative of Greenhill's culture and one which was particularly attractive to me as a candidate." Parent committee member Nancy Brajtbord adds, "The most important aspect of that experience was the sincere dedication, persistence, and determination of the faculty to take a hard look at themselves and find a way to do it better. Not for themselves but for the betterment of the student body and the Greenhill community at large." Modern and classical languages chair Mary Tapia concurs: "I think an important part of the legacy is the confidence that we have the responsibility to constantly review our program and to suggest change as needed."

Meanwhile, daily life remains energetic and exciting, yet feels less stressful and frenetic. Pam Bockbrader asserts, "I truly believe that the pace of the school has changed for the better, and with more tweaking, the schedule will become stronger." The relationships strengthened while serving on committees have helped combat departmental isolation. Mary Tapia explains, "It was very refreshing to bounce ideas off my colleagues from other departments who were struggling with the same issues and to discover that we had so much in common." More than anything, the process deepened and broadened our conversations while giving them direction. As Barb Currier points out, "Rarely are we able to take/make the time to reflect on what would constitute an ideal learning environment." Wells McMurray adds, "I enjoyed the give and take of our meetings, the willingness of people to push ideas and challenge each other's thinking; I also enjoyed working to convince the faculty doubters, the ones who thought we were just more talk."

Such a fertile atmosphere cultivates professional growth. Going through the process also has helped individuals grow as educators. Mary Tapia calls the entire experience "one that transformed me as an educator.... The reading, reflecting, and sharing that I did truly helped me rethink my approach to teaching language and what direction to take for the future." More particular changes have had more pointed effects. The new schedule, for instance, has forced teachers to reconsider how they cover material. Christine Eastus, a veteran of over thirty years, tells about having her students read all of *The Adventures of Huckleberry Finn* rather than sections and how much better they grasped the novel. After a workshop on teaching in longer periods, several teachers tried out some of the techniques and raved about them. Barb Currier says "I build in more time for students to work together in groups on problem solving—both to encourage team learning and to encourage them to communicate better mathematically." She uses "a lot more wait time in all my classes" and totally reconfigured her AP Calculus AB classes.

Of course, not everything has gone perfectly and smoothly. Some teachers have struggled greatly with the changes; a few even have left. People worry about long-term consequences of changes in program, and we mourn what we have given up. But the Greenhill upper school faculty deserves immense credit. Early on, they could have stopped the process when George gave them the chance. Certainly they had doubts and fears, and not everyone felt the same urgency. However, they ventured forth because of their commitment to their students and their determination to provide them with the fullest education possible.

Before a school embarks on this adventure, it must be strong and confident. Although you highlight strengths, you must address weaknesses. Similarly, there is great risk. You don't know exactly what direction you will follow; despite great moments when pieces crystallize, often you feel as if you're groping through a cavern. Giving so many people a voice in the process also is dicey. Voices of skepticism may dominate conversations, and you may alienate those whose ideas are not accepted. You gamble some past and present success—that which is working—for the hope of an even better future.

So what do we recommend, based on our process and reflection? Books by leadership experts such as John Kotter and Michael Fullan provide excellent guidance about fostering change. Along with their advice, we stress some key points.

- Clarify the vision and keep it in front of people, with a clear rallying point. We had the Picture of the Graduate, to which people still refer quite regularly. At the same time, do not expect automatic buy-in or unanimity, no matter how well you believe you have clarified and sold the vision.
- Involve as many people as possible, even those who may derail the process. They are often influential voices, and they may see things you miss in your zeal. Don't forget parents and students. Parents have invested greatly in the school. Students know best what does and does not work for them. Listen to them. If we were to start over again, we would have involved students much sooner. Wells McMurray says, "What sticks out in my mind was the high quality of student participation after they picked up on how much we wanted to hear their ideas." Many times the students

reminded us of our ultimate goals. One key moment occurred at a summer retreat, when we were struggling over graduation requirements. The students stayed up all night, and the next morning told us they were taking over the meeting. Their proposal became the framework for our new requirements.

- Accept that the process is messy and complex. While you may be tempted, avoid quick fixes and fads. Instead, ground your decisions in your mission, school culture, research, musing, and dialogue.
- Finally, realize that finding the necessary time will be a great challenge. People gave of themselves incredibly—extra meetings at lunch, before and after school; daylong sessions; dinners; school visits; a retreat; extensive research. Rather than drain us, the sacrifice energized us.

Members of the Vision Committee often referred to a cartoon shown at that initial retreat. A family was traveling by camel, the father saying, "Stop asking if we're there yet. We're nomads." At times we often wondered if we would get there. But we are getting there. As Barb Currier says, "How we came through this delicate dance is a miracle." We know the journey of school improvement never ends, yet we are fueled by hope and idealism and a clearer vision of our destination.

Appendix 1

1. Create a statement of values suggestive of Greenhill's commitment to helping students foster all parts of their lives.
2. Enhance the advisory program to emphasize total student development.
3. Extend the honor code to all areas of school life.
4. Emphasize the value of interdisciplinary study, and provide more such opportunities.
5. Provide more opportunities for independent student and self-directed learning.
6. Develop a senior/upper class scholars program.
7. Reexamine the purpose, type, and amount of daily homework.
8. Reexamine the purpose of all activities and the subsequent expectations.
9. Restate our graduation requirements to match more closely what we say we value. Find ways to emphasize achievement rather than seat time.
10. Study methods of alternative assessment.
11. Increase the emphasis on public speaking.
12. Provide more opportunities for public exhibition of student talents and work.
13. Integrate digital technology better.
14. Reconfigure the schedule (daily, weekly, monthly, yearly).
15. Provide time for meaningful daily town meetings.
16. Emphasize the importance of school service.
17. Empower students with a stronger voice.
18. Carefully analyze the relationship between program, enrollment, and upper school facilities.
19. Create a structure for continuous review.

Notes

[1] At that time the upper school leadership team consisted of the head of upper school, assistant head of upper school, dean of students, director of college counseling, director of learning assistance, director of community service, department chairs/coordinators, and grade-level team leaders. It now includes a student representative from each grade.

Mark Crotty teaches English, coaches soccer, and serves as director of curricular programs PK–12 at Greenhill School in Addison, TX. He is married to Sallie Smither Crotty and has two children, Kate and Stephen.

George N. King, Jr. is an educator and administrator with over twenty years' experience in independent schools; he is the former head of upper school at Greenhill School and was recently appointed headmaster of Wooster in Danbury, CT. George is also an accomplished musician and an alumnus of The New England conservatory of Music, where he earned a Master of Music in jazz studies.

Mapping into the 21st Century

By Mary Ann Hoffman

Curriculum is the backbone of a school's program. It is the very foundation that teachers and administrators use to guide them in the education of children. This chapter will explore what will be needed for the curriculum of the 21st century and will provide examples of tools and strategies to help create it.

During the 80s and 90s, waves of educational reform spread across the country. Sizer,[1] Boyer,[2] and Goodlad[3] were leading the way to bring change to schools and part of the change was the development of new curriculum. The public schools embraced the movement in far greater numbers than in the independent school world. Change was needed in the public sector.

Conversely, independent schools were reluctant to jump on the reform bandwagon. Why should independent schools change when they were preparing students well for college and for life in general?

However, the world was changing at an exponential rate. Independent schools stood still on tradition while the world was whirling forward into the 21st century. With the demands of the new millennium, independent schools will need to determine and then implement new curriculum and instruction to meet the needs of the children they teach. Those needs should become the guiding light on the journey towards academic excellence.

The 21st-Century Student

With change as the only constant, today's students need to be challenged by a different approach to learning to prepare them for this new world. They need to be flexible and agile learners. Students need to know how to find and assimilate information, not to just memorize facts that may only be good for a quiz. It is impossible to learn all there is to know in today's world, because knowledge doubles in a matter of months rather than years. Therefore the ability to access and assimilate knowledge is paramount to succeed.

Students need to be creative problem solvers. They should know how to use their minds well. They are facing a world where there may be many answers to a problem. Education is not about *what* to think as much as it is about *how* to think. For a majority of a student's education, the lower level thinking skills that include knowledge, comprehension, and application from Bloom's Taxonomy[4] have been emphasized in the classroom. The upper levels of analysis, synthesis, and evaluation have been given less attention. This process should be inverted with the latter stressed to a greater degree for our students to develop into divergent thinkers.

The United States has led the world with innovation, risk-taking, creativity, and inventiveness, and the need for these qualities has grown even greater with the challenges of these and future times. The working world is crying out for different thinking. Business, government, and the like do not need students who simply regurgitate information.

Ted Sizer stated that the new fundamentals of the 21st century will reach beyond the reading, writing, and arithmetic we now consider the basics. Students will need to be well versed in technology and foreign languages, be practiced in cooperation, understand diversity, and be literate in all verbal modalities.

Ernest Boyer in his book *The Basic School* suggests that an educated person needs to have an understanding of "core commonalities" that include: the life cycle, the use of symbols, membership in groups, a sense of time and space, response to the aesthetics (expression in the arts), connections to nature, producing and consuming, and living with purpose. These basic concepts are "universal experiences that are shared by all people, the essential conditions of human existence that give meaning to lives." Boyer implies that all of these themes can be taught through the academic disciplines so children will see their connection with the world.

The students of the 21st century will need educational institutions that will be able to provide them with new skills and attitudes to be successful in a challenging world. Schools need to know in what direction to proceed, and the curriculum can be that guiding light.

When schools begin to write or revise curriculum, several considerations should be in place. Good thinking and reflection should precede action. Knowing the ages and developmental stages of children is essential to providing activities and materials appropriate for teaching them. Realistic expectations for each grade level are necessary for successful learning. An understanding of the new brain studies should be considered, as well as a background in national standards. These two areas will be explored in the following sections.

Brain-based Learning

In Renata and Geoffrey Caine's book *Making Connections, Teaching and the Human Brain,* the authors determine that an understanding of how we learn should determine what kind of curriculum we develop. The Caines studied the current brain studies and then advocated for curriculum that is focused on three areas: *Orchestrated Immersion, Relaxed Alertness,* and *Active Learning.*

Orchestrated immersion develops curriculum that is thematically based, integrating many of the academic disciplines. The brain loves to make connections, and integration of various subject areas keeps the brain engaged in learning. When preparing curriculum, connecting the different disciplines helps students to find patterns in their learning. The connections and patterns help us assimilate and accommodate learning. This is what Piaget suggests in his studies of children's cognitive growth.

The brain learns best when in an environment of *relaxed alertness.* The Caines propose that classrooms should be safe places to learn yet have a healthy challenge. There needs to be positive tension between what is challenging and what is too much pressure for a student. We have accelerated learning to the point that what was once taught in college is now part of a regular seventh-grade curriculum, and being mindful of this fact will help to develop more age-appropriate curriculum. Emotions play an integral part in how well someone learns. Safety, regardless of whether it is physical or emotional, is essential to successful learning.

Confucius said, "I hear, I forget. I see, I remember. I do, I understand." Most humans learn best when actively participating in the learning. The Caines call this *active processing,* and they recommend developing curriculum that fully engages children in their learning. Many hands-on activities should be used to emphasize important concepts. Reflection is another key component of active processing, and time should be set aside in the curriculum to give students opportunity to think about the work they have done.

Orchestrated immersion, relaxed alertness, and active processing are elements to make curriculum more meaningful for students, and as more research is done on how we as humans learn, there will be even more to consider in educating young people. Gaining greater understanding on how the brain works and then using this knowledge to create curriculum to enhance learning can make a real difference in teaching children.

National Standards

Another fundamental step that schools should consider when they prepare to write or revise curriculum is a solid understanding of national standards. For independent schools, reviewing the standards gives them an opportunity to see what is being done in the public school sector and is a resource for determining new direction for curriculum development.

Content Knowledge—A Compendium of Standards and Benchmarks for K–12 Education by John S. Kendall and Robert J. Marzano, an Association for Supervision and Curriculum Development (ASCD) publication, is an excellent resource for listing all the national standards for the various disciplines.

ASCD also publishes *Curriculum Handbooks.* This subscription system highlights the various disciplines with in-depth information about each one. The system runs around $400 annually. With the program, schools receive handbooks on curriculum renewal and planning and organizing curriculum, as well as language arts, mathematics, science, social studies, foreign language, visual and performing arts, health and physical education, career and technology education, and family and consumer education. Additional case studies and current articles relevant to curricular areas are included with the service. Subscribing schools can also go online to investigate a particular discipline for a deeper study of it. Materials are updated continuously and are forwarded to participating schools. A wealth of curriculum information is available to schools, and the subscription keeps schools current with curriculum trends and issues.

Omnibus Guidelines from The Work Sampling System is an additional resource for elementary teachers (K–5) to use national standards in their curriculum writing. The *Guidelines* gives specific examples of what each standard means for a particular grade level for each of the disciplines.

The various governing bodies for the disciplines, such as the National Council for the Teaching of Mathematics, publish guidelines of their standards, and they are good resources for schools to get information about a particular discipline. There are websites that list the standards as well. (The website—www.edStandards.org/Standards.html—lists all the disciplines and related websites for standards, and all the state standards for the disciplines.)

It is important also to check locally what is being done for the state standards. For example, the state of Virginia has Standards of Learning (SOL) that detail objectives for a certain grade that must be accomplished in a particular discipline. Often there are just too many objectives listed for anyone to accomplish for a given year, but SOL and other state standards do offer guidelines for curriculum that is being developed.

These initial steps are imperative prior to beginning curriculum work. Curriculum mapping is the next step, and it is a way for schools to learn more about themselves and see what is actually being taught in the different grades.

Curriculum Mapping

Curriculum maps are overviews of what is actually being taught in a school and when it is taught. Curriculum mapping is a vehicle for schools to determine duplications and gaps in the education of children. The Association of Supervision and Curriculum Development has stated that curriculum mapping is the most useful tool in the recent educational reform movement.

Often teachers have no idea what is taught before or after the grade they teach. In some cases, every grade in an early childhood program ends up teaching teddy bears and dinosaurs, and upper school English classes may all teach *Romeo and Juliet.* When schools take time to see what each grade and each discipline are teaching, they can become stronger schools for knowing what everyone is doing.

Heidi Hayes Jacobs' work with curriculum mapping has led the way in this country for schools to get a handle on their curriculum work. Her two books, *Interdisciplinary Curriculum: Design and Implementation* and *Mapping the Big Picture, Integrating Curriculum & Assessment K–12* are essential to study prior to developing a school's curriculum map. If the opportunity avails itself, Dr. Jacobs often conducts workshops throughout the country that take you step-by-step through the process. Currently, she has a program where she can answer curriculum questions via conference calling. Her website is www.curriculumdesigners.com.

The components in Dr. Jacobs's process are content (what is being taught), skills, assessments, and essential questions. Essential questions are anchors for the topics being studied, and they reflect what students are expected to remember in the future.

When a school undertakes the curriculum mapping process, teachers are asked to write down what they actually teach, not what they say they do or what a current curriculum manual says they do. It is a time to be honest. Referring to previous lesson plans is a good way to document this. For each month of the school year, teachers record the content units they teach, the skills that are taught for the units, the assessments for the units, and then the essential questions for the units. Maps are then collected, and copies are made so the editing stage can begin. All teachers then receive copies of the various maps, and they begin to read them to find gaps and duplication of content, skills, assessment, or essential questions. This part of the process is crucial for a school. It allows everyone to see what is really happening in his or her school. That knowledge is powerful when taking the next step to write or revise a curriculum. Curriculum mapping is an excellent way to find connections within the disciplines to develop interdisciplinary units of study. It gives a visual picture for faculties to rearrange or realign sequence of study to make understanding of materials more meaningful for learning.

The original mapping and editing process is going to take time, and schools will need to provide opportunities during in-services or during the summer break to do this kind of work. Another method schools can take to lessen the time crunch is to adopt an anecdotal approach to mapping by documenting each month's work as the year progresses. This process has less pressure for teachers and is helpful with the time issues concerning most schools. At year's end, the faculty can meet to edit. Then teachers and administrators will know where they are going, so they can provide the best education possible for their young people.

Once the faculty determines gaps and duplications, the hard work begins of deciding who is going to teach what and where it is going to be taught. Curriculum wars can start because teachers are very protective of what they teach, and claims are made about their territories, whether it is a devotion to *Tom Sawyer* or a weather unit. What everyone has to keep in mind is what is most important for the children they are teaching, not what is important to the individual teacher. Every child deserves to have fresh, new topics presented to them each year. That doesn't mean that basic skills are not taught, but the vehicle in which these skills are taught needs to be new for the students. Imagine studying dinosaurs every year. It would be just a matter of time before students would cease to be engaged in the learning. Challenging new topics should be the least we do for our students.

Curriculum maps systems can be purchased through companies such as Atlas so that teachers can document the data directly on the computer. These are expensive yet have excellent features, such as time-saving search engines. If you have a good technology person, templates can be made in Word or Excel that essentially do the same thing.

The following section is one school's story about its curriculum mapping journey.

One School's Story

Heathwood Hall Episcopal School, a coed day school of 750 in Columbia, SC, educates children from three-year-old nursery school to the twelfth grade. As a regional leader, the school has a history of thoughtful reflection about school improvement. Many of Heathwood's faculty members have developed exciting and innovative curriculum. For example, English and history were combined into humanities classes to deepen the study of various time periods. With such a creative curriculum, questions loomed about the continuity of the school program as it spiraled through the grades. When new faculty came on board, how did they know what skills to teach, and what were the expectations of the school?

To address these issues, the school underwent an intensive curriculum mapping review at the end-of-the-year in-service. Independent schools that encompass pre-K programs through the twelfth grade can find it difficult to coordinate the education of children in fifteen different grade levels. This is why curriculum mapping can be a meaningful tool for them. It can be a challenging undertaking but a necessary one if a school wants to do the best by its students. The mapping process was broken down in the following manner.

The process, involving every faculty member, took three full days to accomplish. On the first day, the faculty met in the morning to go over instruction for the initial phase of documenting what is taught. The faculty was reminded to keep what was best for their students foremost in their thoughts—this would become their guiding star. Curriculum work is about the students. The faculty was then asked to meet by the various grade levels and to fill out content, skills, and essential question calendar charts for their disciplines. The early childhood division documented by units of study, and lower school had to fill out charts for each of the disciplines. Each group returned its sheets to the curriculum coordinator, who copied them for the next phase.

In the afternoon, the groups returned as a full faculty for instruction for the editing process. The faculty was asked to circle duplications and check areas where gaps were apparent. To involve everyone in the editing process, Heathwood broke it down into two parts. First, the group met as divisions and edited the various disciplines in their areas. After the divisions completed their work, they turned in a copy for each of the disciplines to the coordinator.

The next morning in the check-in meeting, the group was divided into teams from all disciplines and divisions for a good cross-section of the school. The teams were given copies of all the disciplines and were asked to edit them. Many pairs of new eyes were looking at all aspects of the curriculum. The groups also filled out worksheets with suggestions and observations for each of the disciplines. The insights would be helpful when the departments and divisions met later to begin the revision process. At the end of the morning session, a copy of each discipline's map and a worksheet were returned to the coordinator, who divided all the returned maps by departments. This way each department would have input from the entire school.

In the afternoon of the second day, the faculty met for a check-in for further instruction. The faculty would then meet with their departments to begin looking at the big picture for revision. Each department had copies of all the edited curriculum maps and worksheets with ideas and insights for improvement. The data provided information for further discussion and initiated the dialogue needed to begin making changes. On the third day, the faculty met in the morning to debrief the experience and to spend the entire day working in grade-level meetings to make the necessary changes. The administrators worked with the grade levels to discuss the work that needed to be done on the curriculum and to help negotiate territory issues between grade levels.

This entire curriculum mapping experience was powerful for the faculty because everyone was involved, and everyone was then informed about what was taught to all of the students at Heathwood Hall. Each step of the way, coordinators and colleagues offered encouragement and instruction to help faculty master each part. This was essential for the success of the endeavor. Some faculty members were wary that this process was a waste of valuable end-of-the-year in-service time, but after the process, they felt it was a valuable experience for everyone.

This was only the beginning of the school's curriculum work. The faculty in later years worked on skills charts, essential questions, and assessment charts. The entire map was put on the school's intranet system so changes could be made as needed from anywhere in the school. Time has been allotted during the school year to continue the curriculum work, and periodic training is given to keep everyone abreast of school expectations and to bring new people up to speed with the school's curriculum work.

Curriculum mapping is a tool that allows schools to assess what is being taught in them. It helps to determine gaps and duplications, as well as seeing new possibilities for schools interested in developing new programs that include the integration of the disciplines. These possibilities can lead to curriculum that will be challenging to the students of the 21st century.

Benchmarking Curriculum

Curriculum is a dynamic process—the work never ends. Curriculum can always be made better, but how does a school determine if it is continuously improving? Is there a way to benchmark a school's progress with its curriculum and move the school to a new level of excellence?

Borrowing from the business world, schools could adapt a process called 20 Keys to benchmark their progress with curriculum. The Kaufman Consulting Group, implementation specialists who help companies benchmark manufacturing progress, developed 20 Keys. It is an assessment tool to help sustain and standardize sets of measurement for companies to compare growth in specific areas.

For example, a company selects 15 to 25 key areas of concern and establishes performance levels. *Traditional, learning, leading, world-class,* and *currently invincible* are terms used by some companies to determine where they are and where they want to be in the future. The company will then mark itself in each of the keys and determine where it is on the performance level.

Schools are not factories making cookie-cutter products but instead are places where children are handcrafted. Yet schools are systems that have curriculum areas that could be benchmarked. Schools are not dealing with inventories or equipment maintenances in the sense that companies deal with them, but they are working with English, math, science, fine arts, and so on.

Faculties could determine what each of the performance indicators might be for a particular discipline. For example, if the term *world-class* were used for English, it might mean that 80% of eighth grade students knew all their parts of speech and could apply the rules to their writing, and *currently invincible* might be 100% of the grade. The performance level could be customized for each school, and the areas of concern might vary as well. Faculties could then develop goals from the placement of current marker and determine what is needed to reach another level or that invincibility level. The goals would be measurable, and a school could compare itself to standardized benchmarks.

Accountability, strategic management planning, and the continuous improvement movement have been strategies the business world has shared with schools to help them be better places for children to grow. The 20 Keys process and other like tools are other ways educators can learn from the business community to improve their schools.

Summary

Curriculum is the backbone for creating school environments where children grow and flourish. Schools should provide curriculum that is engaging and fresh for its students. With the 21st century upon us, students will need a new kind of curriculum that includes the basics but incorporates new methods about *how* we think and *what* we learn.

Schools should consider developmental levels, have an understanding of how the brain-based learning can affect curriculum, have background about national standards, and incorporate curriculum mapping as a tool to create and revise curriculum for students. The 20 Keys process from the business world takes curriculum work to a new level of benchmarking a school's progress with its curriculum work.

Each school will take its own journey with its curriculum, each finding what works for them and what does not. Keeping what is best for children as a North Star, a school will find its way and be stronger for it.

Bibliography

Boyer, E. (1995). *The Basic School, A Community of Learning.* Princeton: The Carnegie Foundation for the Advancement of Teaching. (Copies available from: California Princeton Fulfillment Service, 1445 Lower Ferry Road, Ewing, NJ 08618, 1-800-777-4726)

Caine, R.N. and Caine, G. (1994). *Making Connections: Teaching and the Human Brain.* CA: Addison Wesley.

Jacobs, H.H. (1989). *Interdisciplinary Curriculum: Design and Implementation.* Alexandria, VA: Association for Supervision and Curriculum Development.

Jacobs, H.H. (1997). *Mapping the Big Picture: Integrating Curriculum & Assessment K–12.* Alexandria, VA: Association for Supervision and Curriculum Development.

Kendall, J.S. and Marzano, R. J. (2000). *Content Knowledge: A Compendium of Standards and Benchmarks for K–12 Education,* 3rd ed. Alexandria, VA: Association for Supervision and Curriculum Development.

Various editors*(1998–present). *Curriculum Handbooks, A Resource for Curriculum Administrators.* Alexandria, VA: Association for Supervision and Curriculum Development.

*Career and Technical Education—Ruth Loring

Family and Consumer Sciences—a chapter of the Curriculum Handbook

Health and Physical Education—Shirley Ann Hole/Hale, Gene Ezell, and Murray Mitchell

Language Arts—a chapter of the Curriculum Handbook

Mathematics—John A. Dossey and Sharon Soucy McCron

Planning and Organizing for Curriculum Renewal—Allan A. Glatthorn
Science—Dennis W. Cheek
Social Studies—Gregory Paul Wegner
Visual and Preforming Arts—a chapter of the Curriculum Handbook

The Ten Common Principles of the Coalition of Essential Schools

1. Focus
2. Simple Goals
3. Universal Goals
4. Personalization
5. Student as Worker
6. Diploma by Exhibition of Mastery
7. Attitude of School
8. Staff
9. Budget
10. Diversity

Notes

[1] Dr. Theodore R. Sizer and colleagues studied successful high schools throughout the United States. From those studies he found certain characteristics that later became the "Ten Common Principles of Essential Schools." Using the common principles as a foundation, curriculum can be developed that is student centered, will help students to use their minds well, is simple, and can be demonstrated.

[2] Dr. Earnest L. Boyer spent his life studying various levels of schooling. *The Basic School,* his last book, concentrated on elementary schools. School as community, curriculum with coherence, climate for learning, and commitments to character are the four tenets of this work. Boyer believed that curriculum should focus on the centrality of language, the core commonalities (discussed in detail later in the chapter), and measuring results. He believed that we needed to build a better world rather than just a better school.

[3] Dr. John L. Goodlad's in-depth study of American schools resulted in the book *A Place Called School: Prospects for the Future.* Goodlad looked at all aspects of schooling and analyzed what was being done within them. The text also looked at ways to improve schools, and there are several observations and insights regarding curriculum.

[4] Dr. Benjamin Bloom's work involved the formulation of a hierarchy of cognitive skills that range from basic to advanced levels. The types of thinking include knowledge (remembering), comprehension (understanding), application (solving), analysis, synthesis (creating), and evaluation (judging). The value of using these levels helps teachers to plan curriculum and instruction for their students.

Mary Ann Hoffman has a B.S. in elementary education and an M.Ed. in early childhood education and has been an educator for 25 years. She is the lower school head at Heathwood Hall Episcopal school, where she also is the curriculum coordinator for nursery through the twelfth grade. She loves teaching creative problem solving to her students.

Bloom and *Gardner*: Understanding as "Going Deeper"

By Chris Schoberl

I tried hard to come up with a wordplay using the names of two of the most influential thinkers in *the field* of education. I imagined I would extend the pun throughout this chapter, using words such as *germinate,* and calling forth images such as "the fertile ground," but the more I tried, the more contrived and distracted it seemed. After all, were any visual to stick with a reader, I would prefer if it were that of "going deeper," and if that conjures images of roots, then so be it. For it is the image of roots, or being rooted, that fully embodies what I think of when I consider a student's healthy growth in understanding: at first superficial and just scratching the surface, our initial thoughts about a topic are tentative, and we are unsure of ultimate survival of this seed, even with its tremendous potential. Eventually the seed is nourished as it synthesizes from its environment all it needs to find purchase and then flourish, pushing roots ever deeper and ensuring viability, ongoing connections, and offspring. How does one create a curriculum that allows a student to "go deeper," and what does deeper look like outside a flowerpot? In these thoughts, as well as others, I am indebted to many researchers who have inspired my thinking along these lines, but in particular, I am grateful to Benjamin Bloom, Howard Gardner, and the folks at Harvard University's Project Zero for helping me to see the good sense behind this convergence of thought.

Are We Teaching for Understanding . . . or Merely Covering Material?

It is perhaps axiomatic that "among the agendas of education, surely understanding must rank far up on the short list of high priorities" (Blythe, 1998). However, the traditional lecture or *chalk-talk* format is still the staple of teaching in many modern classrooms, despite the fact that researchers working in the area of learning theory have demonstrated that student understanding improves when teaching includes authentic or performance-based lessons and assessments that allow students to explore, apply, and hypothesis test (Gardner, 1991). With an eye on summative, high stakes assessments, a modern curriculum and pedagogy driven by what has been termed *the tyranny of coverage* may leave little room for students to inquire, discover, and gradually untangle initial misconceptions.

Combined with the value placed on performance-based instruction and assessment as advocated by the folks at Project Zero, many educational researchers working in the area of cognitive science advocate a movement away from the longstanding definition of intelligence as a single IQ measurement (Gardner, 1999; Perkins & Blythe, 1994). In fact, Gardner has identified at least seven "intelligences," or learning strengths through which people process the world around them (1993). In this context, lessons delivered through exclusive reliance upon the chalk-talk or lecture method may reach only those students with a strong linguistic intelligence, while remaining largely inaccessible to those who learn best through problem solving via visual, musical, logical-mathematical, inter- or intrapersonal, bodily-kinesthetic, or naturalist intelligences (Gardner, 1983).

How Do We Know When Our Students Understand?

A multifaceted definition of intelligence, in tandem with the widespread value placed upon authentic learning-by-discovering experiences, has compelled educators to create lessons by which students can learn through solving problems and fashioning products in a context-rich setting (Armstrong, 2000) that allows accessibility by a fuller array of intelligences. In contrast to what is generally perceived as the more traditional methods of training for the sake of coverage, currently employed in many of today's classrooms, a TFU or "teaching for understanding" methodology applies Gardner's MI (multiple intelligences) theory as it provides students with deeper and long-term conceptual inroads by affording them the time to apply to novel or wholly unfamiliar problem-solving scenarios unique and "thoughtful" solutions. Rather than relying solely upon an ability to recall abstract algorithms or to identify previously identified patterns, students who possess *true* understanding will *also* be able to extrapolate from a strong fund of essential knowledge and manipulate information in distinctive ways, in order to solve *tomorrow's* problems, problems we cannot currently solve, teach to, or even anticipate today. Unfortunately, where training for coverage is *terribly* efficient and, as such, may appeal to leaders at the helm of large school systems, the more effective methods of TFU, as inquiry and discovery based, are time consuming, resource critical, and costly.

Though the TFU model points to the importance of MI, performances linked to instructional goals, and ongoing assessment as important resources for teachers, teachers might still miss the mark of teaching for understanding, absent a definition or standard for "going deeper." Far from original thinking, I have come to appreciate the power of combining the relatively new thinking connected with TFU with the time-honored work of Benjamin Bloom and his taxonomy because, simply stated, it provides teachers with a clear standard for what it means to "go deeper." In this way, performances designed around MI theory via the TFU model are more likely to be both hands-on *and* minds-on and lead to our students' ability to demonstrate understanding through performances requiring them to apply, analyze, synthesize, and evaluate.

Benjamin Bloom's Work

In the mid 1950s, Benjamin Bloom and a research team of educational psychologists set out to define learning as represented along a continuum rather than as an absolute end state. When a thing is learned, such a theory would argue, a student might "know it" on one of several distinct "learning levels," depending upon how it was taught and how they are able to manipulate what has been learned as a resource to learn other things. Bloom's array of six learning levels came to be known as "the Taxonomy." Though each level of learning in the taxonomy was important, and each made possible the next deeper level, Bloom discovered that upwards of 90% of the questions that students were asked to answer existed on the lowest level of the taxonomy, knowledge or recall, rather than on the deeper levels of comprehension, application (the level upon which many define true understanding to begin), analysis, synthesis, or evaluation. Though many educators may embrace the work of Howard Gardner, seeing it as an answer to this great imbalance, it is likely that many an MI lesson has done little to work against Bloom's 90% observation. Used in tandem, MI as applied through the TFU framework along with the taxonomy can help students reach enduring levels of learning such that true understanding is the result.

Not Going Deeper

It is likely that the illustration below plays itself out countless times in classrooms led by teachers relying solely upon MI theory in an effort to teach for understanding.

Following a class discussion on plant anatomy, a teacher asks his students to trace a tree branch on a large piece of paper and to label all of the parts in this life-size drawing. Students are energized and many who may not have been engaged via a more typical assessment feel invited, fully connected to this performance, and are therefore more connected to the material itself. Students have fun and are likely to recall the experience as one they enjoyed. The teacher has worked hard to provide information in a nontraditional way, and has tapped at least three different intelligences by asking students to work together, to get up and move around, and to create a drawing representing their knowledge. This performance has taken much more of the teacher's time and creative energy than a more traditional method of instruction, and is most likely a more difficult way for him to "cover" the curriculum, but he has weighed this against the educational value of providing students with a chance to demonstrate what they know through such a performance, and has judged the added benefit of what he believes to be his students' greater degree of understanding as worth the extra effort.

Performances like the plant drawing above are indicative of teachers working hard to pitch lessons to a fuller range of student abilities, rather than relying upon more traditional methods that most readily reach students who learn best through the linguistic intelligence; this is clearly a step in the right direction, especially as an introductory performance (as distinct from inquiry/mid-course or culminating performance). In the case of the plant drawing, however (ignoring, for the time being, that all students do the *same* performance), though the lesson is a performance, and seems to pass muster according to the TFU model, the lesson is little more than direct recall of facts presented in a class discussion, a lecture, or a textbook. Even though the teacher has been thoughtful enough to include room for several intelligences, it is unlikely, according to the taxonomy, that students were given access to deeper levels of knowledge or ever reached a level of genuine understanding.

What Does "Going Deeper" Look Like?

Despite this teacher's efforts, the plant lesson is not much different than if the teacher had held a discussion and then asked students to parrot back what they heard . . . or if he had read a passage and asked students to represent the facts in a narrative or multiple-choice assessment. Such a lesson, though thoughtful in its design, falls short of *understanding* because of the fairly shallow degree of thinking it invites. It's a nice little project, and probably a lot of fun to do . . . and the kids will be able to *recall* the names of each plant part . . . to *know* them . . . but has this teacher left room for the deep conceptual knowledge characteristic of true *understanding*? For example, will these students be able to *apply* what they have learned to novel scenarios, *analyze* or draw conclusions, *synthesize* by recombining information into a new whole, or *evaluate* by supporting opinion with reasons, each a hallmark of deeper learning or understanding?

Though the TFU model suggests that "understanding is a matter of being able to do a variety of things with a topic, such as explain, find evidence and examples, generalize, apply information, create analogies, and represent the topic in new ways . . . ," the model does not:

- provide teachers with any codified qualitative tool by which to gauge whether any of this is happening in either introductory, guided inquiry, or culminating performances;
- differentiate gradations of "going deeper" by defining, quantifying, or weighting "deep," "deeper" or "deepest"; or
- provide a timetable or mix of such gradations in a curriculum designed to reach ever deeper levels of understanding from the beginning through the end of a unit of study.

Howard Meets Benjamin

Below is a simple graphic for which I am indebted to many other researchers and which represents thinking I have learned to embrace fully as I advocate for its use among my faculty members. By arraying MI against Benjamin Bloom's *Taxonomy,* while keeping the importance of understanding performances in mind, such a graphic might provide teachers with a valuable lens through which to consider their lessons as they design performances for understanding. In short, this chart can be the touchstone by which teachers, over the course of a unit, might assess the *depth* of their lessons: it can help teachers balance the time spent pitching a lesson to a broader range of intelligences *while* accounting for the depth of understanding their lessons are inviting.

Howard Gardner's *Multiple Intelligences*
Arrayed against Benjamin Bloom's *Taxonomy*

	Linguistic	Musical	Logical/Mathematical	Bodily Kinesthetic	Interpersonal	Intrapersonal
To Know						
To Comprehend						
To Apply						
To Analyze						
To Synthesize						
To Evaluate						

Bloom's Taxonomy Defined

To Know: remembering or recall of previously learned material, facts, or whole theories; bringing to mind (to define, describe, identify, list, match, or name)

To Comprehend: grasping the meaning of materials; interpreting; predicting outcome and effects (to convert, defend, distinguish, estimate, explain, generalize, or rewrite)

***To Apply:** the ability to use learned materials in a new situation, to apply rules, laws, methods and theories.

To Analyze: to be able to break down into component parts, to reorganize, or to make conclusions, to see related order, to detect relationships and perceive patterns, and to clarify.

To Synthesize: the ability to put parts together to form a new whole or to articulate a set of abstract relationships; to combine, create, design, and rearrange.

To Evaluate: to judge value as based upon a criteria, and to judge with a reason vs. guessing; to appraise, critique, compare, support, summarize, and explain.

To the TFU model, Bloom brings a sort of scale of understanding by which teachers can plan their lessons among all six levels in his taxonomy, from the shallower *knowing* that is reflected in a student's ability to merely recall, through *application,* the first level of true understanding, and deeper, through *evaluation,* the deepest and most enduring sort of understanding a student will reach.

*A widely accepted definition of "understanding," and the one advocated by Project Zero, application is the level on which true understanding begins.

During curriculum design, a teacher can assess a unit in terms of the number of intelligences it hits and the level of thinking it reaches by "checking the boxes" in this combination Bloom-Gardner graphic. In using Bloom in concert with MI, the goal is not to avoid shallower or lower-order thinking. In fact, there is a clear need in every unit of study for the early imparting of pure information. The ability to recall, most readily delivered through a lecture or linguistic mode, especially earlier in the year when a teacher spends time establishing a fund of content knowledge from which to draw during subsequent skills lessons, is the common (and effective) basis upon which to build. Rather, the goal here is to *deliberately* balance the use of time by ensuring that the greatest range of intelligences is invited into the lesson *and* that successive performances provide room for deeper and deeper thinking over the course of a unit of study.

If TFU/MI provides a framework within which to deliver a lesson to a variety of thinkers, Bloom provides a framework by which to ensure that the lesson *leaves room for* the deeper or higher order thinking that facilitates *true understanding.* As a lesson begins, it is likely that a teacher will rely most heavily upon lecture, "chalk talk," and introductory performances, but as the journey continues, teaching for understanding would necessitate that performances become less about mere knowing and that they leave as much room for Bloom's levels, if not more so, as they do Gardner's intelligences. If an introductory performance following a lecture required students to demonstrate their ability to recall information, this foundation should be built upon in subsequent lessons to the point where, at unit's end, the teacher has designed a performance experience that requires students to exhibit their ability to analyze, synthesize, or evaluate, skills that will require recall of the pure information imparted early on and in lecture.

Bloom as a Resource to Timeline a Lesson Plan

To teach for understanding is time consuming and may require, to some extent, a reordering of priorities. Time: there's the rub. For a school marching to the beat of a top-down mandated curriculum framework or for which covering material is the curriculum driver, such a shift will require quite a leap of faith. For such a school exploring these waters, it is important to know that the teaching for understanding framework does not discount the importance of content and the need to deliver a comprehensive and carefully wrought curriculum according to a deliberate plan; nothing could be more misconstrued. Rather, the TFU framework takes the focus off content and places it more squarely upon method, where performance and assessment become critical instructional tools as well as a means of generating the quantitative information necessary to account for what a student knows and is able to do. Such a shift towards method is time consuming, and to do it justice may require a schedule shift to provide teachers with the larger blocks of time necessary to allow students the time they will need to "muck about" and learn by inquiry, discovery, problem solving, and error, rather than from a scripted framework delivered, top-down, from someplace outside the very classroom in which it is delivered.

From another perspective, however, the TFU framework might be of use to teachers interested in ordering their limited time, even if block scheduling is not in the offing, as it points to the importance of introductory, guided/mid-course, and culminating moments in a unit. By compelling a teacher to reflect upon and articulate a beginning, middle, and end-point to each unit, the TFU framework may actually help teachers work more efficiently. Even if a mandated content is the fare, such efficiency may help a teacher find his or her way through it all, thereby covering material *while* ensuring opportunities for deeper understanding. To this end, a resource such as the chart below may provide teachers with a way to gauge each unit *on the front end* prior to delivering it, to balance the use of their time among the intelligences and Bloom's categories. By "paying out the rope" as a student journeys through a unit, a teacher would make room for instruction that includes a fuller range of Gardner's thinking while students moved from @, through #, and eventually through $ performances.

The TFU Framework
Arrayed Against Benjamin Bloom's *Taxonomy*

Course:	
Dates:	
Unit/Topic:	
Essential Questions	
Content	
Skills	
Performances	
Introductory (@)	
Mid Course/Guided (#)	
Culminating ($)	

	Linguistic Performance	Musical Performance	Logical/Mathematical Performance	Spatial Performance	Bodily Kinesthetic Performance	Interpersonal Performance	Intrapersonal Performance
Know	@	@	@	@	@	@	@
Introductory Assessment							
Comprehend	@	@	@	@	@	@	@
Introductory Assessment							
Apply	#	#	#	#	#	#	#
Mid/Guided Assessment							
Analyze	#	#	#	#	#	#	#
Mid/Guided Assessment							
Synthesize	$	$	$	$	$	$	$
Culminating Assessment							
Evaluate	$	$	$	$	$	$	$
Culminating Assessment							

Ultimately, it may be helpful to think of MI/TFU as inviting eaters of all types to the table and Bloom as a way of making sure they all eat their vegetables . . . as well as dessert.

Going Deeper: A Reprise

Informed by Bloom and making use of a resource such as the Bloom-TFU graphic, above, a teacher might modify the plant drawing lesson to include room for several multiple intelligence performances *and* deeper thinking.

Following the recounting of the plant anatomy lesson through their drawing, students are then asked to trace their hand on this same piece of paper, adjacent to the plant drawing, and to compare and contrast the human anatomy they learned in an introductory lesson with what the mid course plant lesson has taught them. Given this information, they are then asked to assess the efficiency of each model and attribute differences to dissimilar elements of their comparative study. Some will choose to make this report in a paper, some will deliver it orally, and some will do a skit. Students have fun and are likely to recall the experience as one they enjoyed. The teacher has worked hard to provide information in a nontraditional way, and has tapped at least three different intelligences by asking students to work together, to get up and move around, and to create a variety of performances to represent their knowledge. He has also ensured that this mid course lesson goes deeper than an introductory lesson by asking students to demonstrate understanding in a novel scenario, apply what they know in an unfamiliar exercise, and support their ideas with evidence they will draw from several sources.

Like the simple recall required of the earlier plant drawing, this performance has taken much more of the teacher's time and creative energy than a more traditional method of instruction, but has also afforded students a chance to demonstrate what they know through application, analysis, synthesis, and evaluation, and has given them an opportunity to explore what they are less sure of, to explain and support their thinking, and to represent what they have learned.

In applying such a convergence of the work of Gardner and Bloom, a teacher stands to optimize the value of both for his or her students. Furthermore, it is likely that this sort of teaching will be more inherently interesting to a teacher because it is never predictable, sometimes messy, and always leaves room for levels of revelation not possible through less *fruitful* teaching.

A doctoral graduate from Columbia University's Teachers College, **Chris Schoberl** is currently the academic dean at Fay School. Over the course of his 15 years in independent schools, he has been a teacher and department chair at Delbarton School School in Morristown, NJ, and Foxcroft School, in Middleburg, VA, respectively. He was the program coordinator for the Klingenstein Center, and was the founding head of school for the Ben Franklin Charter School in Franklin, MA. Chris lives in Southborough with his wife, three young children, and two Labrador retrievers.

"Hello, Writers": Teaching As a Work in Progress

By Nancy Fox

I imagine this midnight moment's forest:
Something else is alive
Besides the clock's loneliness
And this blank page where my fingers move.

Through the window I see no star:
Something more near
Though deeper within darkness
Is entering the loneliness:

Cold, deliberately as the dark snow,
A fox's nose touches twig, leaf;
Two eyes serve a movement, that now
And again now, and now, and now

Sets neat prints into the snow . . .
Ted Hughes, "The Thought Fox"

"Hello, writers," I'd say as students entered the room, often with only a notebook in their hands. "What's the story today?" The room did not resemble any class I had ever seen. The writers and I had composed it together out of a spare room in the library that contained the school archives and antique book collection. At the time we inherited it, the room had the atmosphere of an attic—dusty, unvisited, possibly moldering—with a hint of secrets or stories to be discovered. It was an off-hand offering, this room. Nobody wanted to teach in it, and my class—writing—was too undefined, too experimental, to warrant the use of classroom space. We would come to view this room as an integral part of the work we were doing: it was our "nerve center," the muted covers of century-old volumes a source of calm or inspiration, and when our successes gave rise to room choices, we felt too much at home to give it up.

Tables lined the walls, chairs were facing in, and students sat with their backs to the middle of the room: the classic seminar circle, but inverted. In the center of each table was a green library lamp: often, as students toured the school in their admission interview, they felt drawn to those green lamps, determined to join the people at those tables, side by side, notebooks or papers (or, later, keyboards) in front of them. It was, most of the time, a place of serious business. At quiet times I could hear the scrapes and taps of pencils and pens as writers pursued a thought. Sometimes I heard the words of conferring: "Yeah, I see what you're doing," or "That is awesome," or, at an impasse, "Try this." The focus in my classes, like the circles of light from those green lamps, was intense, directed down to the words on the pages: What were they saying? What did they mean? Where, if anywhere, could they go? We called this place "The Writing Room," at once simple and complicated.

> If I had to label those things that made (my writing) class work so well, it would be an atmosphere of trust, respect, and seriousness—that we were there to become a part of the greater community of writers, and even more so, the greater act of writing. It was that sense of being part of something so personal and at the same time so important as to transcend the individual that made it, I think, a real turning point for many of the kids. (Maynard)

It was writing itself that led me to teach it in this unconventional manner. Through writing, I had learned to think in ways that I could not know otherwise, ways that I could see, physically trace, and train for any use I needed. "I can't overemphasize how important it is for teachers of writing to write themselves," notes Alan Ziegler (1981) in his Writing Workshop series:

> Albert Einstein once said regarding science that "the years of anxious searching in the dark, with their intense longing, their alterations of confidence and exhaustion and the final emergence into the light—only those who have experienced it can understand it." Or, by implication, pass it on to others. Teaching writing, like teaching science, involves more than formulas and procedures. (5)

Language is the human territory, and I had entered instinctively, without conscious decision, the trail that writers use as they pursue their thought, the "body that is bold to come across clearings . . . coming about its own business." So Hughes in his poem described what we in schools have come to call "the process of writing."

I'm not sure anyone has parsed the process of writing as the physical act of thinking as deliberately as Peter Elbow in his 1973 *Writing without Teachers*. From his writing experiences he concluded that meaning in language occurs "in the middle" (153) of creativity and control. Creativity allows the words we use to flex and play as we struggle to express a thought; control allows our words to be understood. Writing is both imagination and structure, private and public, the "movement" that "sets neat prints" in Hughes' poem. Movement is not linear: ("now/And again now, and now, and now"). It makes its track, doubles back on itself, blurs its marks, picks up a trail again: It is, in Elbow's word, "recursive," fumbling, stumbling, finding and making its way as it goes. That it can become clearly a body that "sets neat prints," so that a poet like Hughes can reflect its motions in his piece, and we can read his creation with a sense of illumination and wonder, is the work of the rulebook: the mathematics of language we as readers, speakers, writers, understand.

"In the middle": Fourteen years after Elbow printed those words, Nanci Atwell reimagined them in terms of her classroom teaching. *In the Middle: Reading, Writing, and Learning with Adolescents* applied the equation, that writing = thinking, to a middle school program in Boothbay Harbor, Maine. The years preceding her workshops had seen the burgeoning of a pedagogy: Elbow was joined by John Gage, Dixie Goswami, Donald Graves, Jane Hansen and others who traced the patterns of thinking they found in writing. Of course the distinction between writing as a process—a mind's adventure over time—and writing a specific product—article, essay, story, or poem—became clear to those who studied it. Elbow's words of balance, "in the middle," also describe the place of Atwell's work between the research of these pioneers and the practices of every teacher who encountered her, including me, whose classroom she transformed.

I'd come to Atwell ready to read her, but at the time I didn't know that. I was aware that a program she'd piloted in Maine had closed, badly—not because its research was friable ground, or its students had failed to thrive, but because the school's constituencies had resisted it. That we both were involved with writing workshops was a serendipitous discovery when I read her book:

> (There is) an unusual way of talking about writing, about thinking, about knowledge, and about teaching that could be said to belong to writing teachers—a shared set of key terms and concepts, of examples and interpretations—that defines the order of things in this particular pocket of the academic community . . . Writing teachers, or teachers who care about writing, are strange. There are not many of them. They tend to teach differently from other teachers, even in their own content areas. (Bartholomae 1)

I read the book to see what the flap in Boothbay was about. I didn't expect that my classroom procedures would change utterly, that I'd throw away my red pen for good, that I'd never again rework a student's paper or place a mark on it without the student's permission, that I'd never require a teacher's desk, or that, like Atwell herself, and despite the success of teaching writing in this way, I would in my journey through schools encounter resistance of many sorts—that the days would come when I would recall her experience in Maine, and what had engendered a casual interest would serve me well as consolation.

I started a writing class because it seemed to me that no one, in the assigning of papers, was teaching *how* to write them, *how* to develop an original idea, *how* to deepen an argument. Nor was anyone teaching what writing really was—the concrete physical acts of creation and discovery. Moreover, I was interested in kids who liked to write, who maybe hid diaries, notebooks of stories, poems, songs, and arguments in their closets (as I had done), who might be said to have a professional enthusiasm for an hour in which it was okay to be a writer. The Writing Room was a place that encompassed *all* writing pursuits. I'd teach The Thesis Statement, discuss enjambment in a poem, present my theory of run-on sentences, and leave the novelist in the corner alone. I'd read a poem on the scents of a marketplace in India, or on the desertion of a father; an analysis of the Bill of Rights, or a bottle of Snapple tea, or a snowflake, or a black hole in space; the introduction of a five-paragraph theme on point of view in "Araby"; the text of a 4-H cattle project; the storyboard of a video project; and many lines of rumination:

> Different tasks will pose different problems and require in turn somewhat different writing processes. Some tasks require much planning and organizing before the writer can begin; some require careful editing before being shared with a critical audience. . . . Indeed, the universe of writing tasks, both in and out of school, is large and diverse. (Applebee 102)

A former writing teacher, Claudia Gallant, who is now the Vice President for Professional Development at NAIS, concurs: "On the whole, I'd say that what made the difference was the opportunity to do lots of writing using different methods, approaches, and topics." Essentially, we were writing across an entire pre-collegiate curriculum, and then some, in one tiny room.

The introduction of writing pedagogy, unique in a college preparatory school old enough to have a podium in some classrooms, was tolerated—then swiftly affirmed. In two words: *it worked.* By the end of its first term, the subject teachers of writing students discerned a development in writing they could measure. Grades in writing assignments increased exponentially the longer that the students stayed in the course, and the more experienced they became. More students enrolled and were able to learn not only from me, but also from writers who'd sat at those tables for two or four, or more years. It was the workshop's success that led to the students' ability to "loop" with me and stay in those seats for multiple years, pressured as students are for college-prep transcripts, and by those colleagues who did not view writing as integral to thinking itself, who saw science and math as more weighty. But students themselves exerted their own pressure: not only was The Writing Room a pleasant place to work in, but writing as we pursued it was a comfortable human act, one of the ways we think and make meaning. And grades were moving up; students were winning awards.

My aim was not "collect and correct": I didn't do that anymore. Rather, I taught each student *how* to write the chosen manuscript. The research paper writers, for example, did not use long lists of ready-made topics. They wrote to discover the area that seemed most compelling to them, read a bit, then wrote again to get a topic to pursue, out of a tangle of assertions, notions, and queries, their minds engaged in the act of thinking. The method we used was akin to Elbow's "looping," a slow process of leading a student from many ideas to one, beautifully formulated (Dye). The remarks I repeated, as I stood "in the middle" of that room, were, "Write your way to it. Your writing brain is in your hand." When I moved from one student to the next, I carried nothing except my belief in the integrity of their work, which informed what I had to say to them. And I never knew what I'd say until I'd read what they'd written. This style of teaching is described by Paul Connolly as an "ecology of learning":

> Elsewhere in school writing served principally to display and test knowledge, defined as information acquired from teacher and textbook. But in what is now widely described as a "process approach" to teaching writing, the classroom is less a lecture hall for an Authority than it is an intricate ecological system where organisms interact with one another and their environment. . . . In a "process" classroom, teacher and student are mutually responsible for the habits of writing that develop, the composing processes that become "second nature." The teacher moves physically from the front to the middle of the room, as learning that had been data-based now becomes task-oriented. (3–4)

I came to believe that no matter what the academic content and context were—English or math, science or history or tech—the writing experience needed this "ecology" to thrive.

In my particular class the source of all writing "products" was the process of writing that students pursued in a notebook. Students might find themselves transferring whole passages from their notebooks to a drafting paper for an essay, short story, poem, or article that they intended to present publicly. Or they might use only a phrase or spirit of a phrase. In the motion and play of their minds, the notebook was the necessary ground, as in Hughes, "this blank page where my fingers move." They could not tell the world what they knew until they were aware that they knew it: Their notebook spoke most eloquently to them, as writers. They needed to feel free to grow, erase, cross out, reword, imagine a sentence a third or thirty-third time (Fox 7). When products like papers or reports were required of them, they knew how to use writing to make these pieces original, powerful, startling—as thought is.

For example, even the standard five-paragraph essay can be a work of creative thought so that the structure becomes invisible (like a body's spine) behind an elegant argument: It need not be inert. But it will be inert if it's taught as a structure primarily, and composing is done in stratified pieces. This activity is not writing because it's not thinking:

> Students are not being asked to write ideas at all—they are being asked to write sentences. Such approaches are usually defended on the ground that writing is a competency, that is, an ability to construct written artifacts that have certain definable, formal attributes, such as subject-verb agreement or, at a higher level of sophistication, topic sentences for every paragraph. In effect, this technical approach to composition assumes that writing can be mastered by learning what the attributes are and by practicing them in exercises, apart from real writing situations. (Gage 13)

Thus, conventional writing instruction effectively teaches students what writing is not.

In fact, a Dartmouth study of student writing in 1963 (qtd. in Elbow 109) discovered that composing specific products (e.g., an essay on theme in a novel), even improving them with a teacher's corrections, did not necessarily benefit writing beyond that one endeavor. Once we come to understand that writing is "thinking on paper," (Howard), we see the futility of such discrete and disconnected practices in a student's writing education. I'd repeat the advice that the avenue to this understanding is not a rubric or text, but the teacher's own experience of writing. We need to observe what we do when we compose, not only letters and reports or, if we're inclined, poems and stories, but also sentences to clarify our thinking, and apply those lessons to our lesson plans. This backstory is not only mine. I have never heard or read the account of a writing teacher who is not also a writer in this way, who has not sat "in the middle" of imagination and structure, the "push and pull" of language Elbow describes (153), and tried to make a piece make sense, risk it and fail, pick up the pen, risk it again—"Till . . . It enters the dark hole of the head./ The window is starless still; the clock ticks, / The page is printed" (Hughes, "The Thought Fox").

Would that our profession were as fully realized as this poem. But writing teachers often cannot practice what they know. Writing instruction today, thirty years after the infusion of energy and heft of thought that Elbow and his companions brought to it, resembles nothing so much as the rough draft of a writer trying to capture an idea on paper. I sit surrounded by a circle of pages and reference books. I often stop writing, scribble a name, a query, a word. Sometimes I draw a diagonal line through a paragraph, or a page, and start the topic over, or drop it. My pages always look like this, as does my writing place. This wild landscape is the way I think: I am "in the middle" of imposing logic, order, printing tidy lines that lead to lines that led me now to here, the words I'm writing now, so they'll be understood beyond the circle that encloses me. Writing education, too, is "in the middle" of a multi-layered process, a profusion of philosophy, practice, and pressure.

As I compose this paper, my colleagues in independent, private, and public spheres assist me. It seems we share an awareness of our pedagogy as a problematic one that is not, at this moment, coherent—much like my paper as I sit composing it—replete with reversals, revisions, competing voices, and words of altering meanings. That there is a line of argument—a way of teaching writing that works across all disciplines and develops a student's mind—is clear to us. But as a profession we are far from seeing our pedagogy practiced in a way that seems to us conclusive and effective. Our profession is as much a work in progress now as at its inception—but not for lack of bravery or success.

These passionate words of Tom Romano are as true today as they were in 1987 when he wrote them:

> We English teachers sometimes seem surrounded by madness—demands for competency-based tests of composing ability, minimum standards, ludicrous quantitative measures of writing skill, a vain clamor for objectivity in assessing the inherently idiosyncratic, subjective act of writing. Amid this madness we too easily lose sight of our primary goal. We must encourage, beckon, urge, even incite every one of our students to write—not occasionally and not in proper paragraphs or five-paragraph essays or some other artificial rhetorical mode, but often,

> and in their individual voices, each cut loose, each growing, changing, and maturing by the very act of writing, and "each," to quote Whitman again, "singing what belongs to him or her and to none else." (14)

Schools and teachers do interpret this "act of writing" in profoundly different ways. As a result, the very term we use to describe the pedagogy has lost its depth and meaning. "'Writing process' is not used anymore," Donald Graves explained in an interview ("Answering"). "It got so misunderstood that now we simply just say 'writing.'"

I came to the writing of this piece with some sense of these misunderstandings. After over a decade in The Writing Room, I moved to the West Coast with my family and spent time in schools that seemed, on first meeting, to welcome a writing teacher: "Our writing scores are low," I heard. "Our students don't know how to write." But like Atwell on the eastern shore, I found a paradox: My students thrived, their writing visibly improved, but the school refused to accept the writing class "ecology": "It makes other teachers too uncomfortable." Erin Augusta, a writing teacher in California, describes the instructional level of writing at such a school precisely: "Teachers give a topic, students write, teachers fix, students copy over. There is no conversation or 'teaching' of writing."

Further, I encountered standards identical to those defined in 1894 by the authors of one of earliest curriculum guides, "The Committee of Ten": exercises in sentencing and usage, paragraph structure, and descriptive and narrative essays (Lundsteen 8–9). The schools required teaching grammar out of context, which in 1894 was held to be obsolete (Lundsteen 9). I found a school that followed a textbook chapter called "The Writing Process" which presented five discrete and linear stages in the expository essay, and classes "wrote" the same sections on the same calendar day. I learned for the first time in my teaching life what a rubric was, a tool for assessment since 1923 (Hudelson's scale in Bartholomae 3). I found that the absence of a teacher's red pen on a student's paper means, to many school constituencies, the absence of valid instruction—even if the writing is better than any the student achieved previously. Despite the easy frequent use of "writing process" as a term, its practice can be suspect—impossible, if the program is lockstep. I'd run up against a hard reality I later found stated succinctly in Graves: "This is a very definite minority of teachers (even though) things are happening with their kids that we've never seen before."

As many past and current writing teachers and I sit in our writing rooms and share our stories electronically, I hear these conflicted strains. The few who practice writing know their rarity. They know their schools might advertise their use of "writing process," when in fact the teaching is constrained to be conventionally grammar-and-mechanics based. Even George Hillocks, no ally of the process writing class, agrees that "we know that the teaching of traditional grammar has virtually no impact on the quality of writing and cannot be expected to have" (90). His statement has been reinforced by the Report of the National Commission on Writing:

> Writing extends far beyond mastering grammar and punctuation. The ability to diagram a sentence does not make a good writer. There are many students capable

> of identifying every part of speech who are barely able to produce a piece of prose. While exercises in descriptive, creative, and narrative writing help develop students' skills, writing is best understood as a complex intellectual activity that requires students to stretch their minds, sharpen their analytical capabilities, and make valid and accurate distinctions. (13)

But writing teachers are too often lost or marginalized in the practice of their own pedagogy: "I think writing teachers know a lot about what works," says Ms. Gallant of NAIS, "but their knowledge is pitted against the tide of all kinds of other issues and requirements." One of the causes of the scarcity of writing teachers is perhaps the frequency with which they encounter the word "No."

This word has many guises, and one effective "No" is lack of time. Says Diane Dye of time: "We are not given enough to focus on what is important. We have to cram in material every nine weeks without pausing for reflection. It is this reflection that is most useful in developing thinking. Thinking is writing." Time for reflection is a key factor in writing improvement that a British analysis of writing classes has noted specifically: "When writing prompts urged students to reflect on their learning processes—the challenges they faced and the strategies they employed—the educative effects of writing were substantially improved" (Bangert-Drowns, Hurley, Wilkinson 1). Studies in the United States have noted that "writing is a prisoner of time" (National Commission 20). Writing is recursive, as thinking is; sometimes it does not come. How many teachers have the freedom to wait out the stilled pens of student writers? Even when, because of their own writing experiences, they have the wisdom to do it? How many teachers have the time to allow their students to ruminate, "noodle-about," peck and poke and prod an idea, possibly discard it, in the course of writing a curriculum-required essay or research paper? However artificial our school calendars might be in terms of limits we impose on learning, thinking, and writing, they are real enough in the straits of teachers' lives, and writing teachers strain against this constant threat of deadlines.

"Writing is so complex an activity, so closely tied to a person's intellectual development, that it must be nurtured and practiced over all the years of a student's schooling and in every curricular area," says Barbara Walvoord in her guide for teachers across the disciplines (1). A longitudinal study of undergraduate writing by Harvard University concurs with this analysis: "Writing is learning. Writing is thinking" (Shen 1). Yet writing teachers know that behind a façade of "writing process" lies enormous pressure to conform for the sake of scores on standardized tests, which makes the nurturing of writing a quixotic goal.

Teachers see their writing time diminishing as they must focus on teaching mechanical tasks for tests. One teacher who asked to remain anonymous was "called on the carpet," she reports, because her school expects 90th percentiles in the SAT9's: "I am going to have to cut into writing time to teach to the grammar section of that test," she says. The use of writing time for such topical teaching has a deleterious effect on student success: "It should be realized that there is no evidence that writing quality is the result of the accumulation by students of a series of subskills" (White 23). But subskills remain the focus of schools that require the teaching of standardized test procedures (and many schools that don't).

Writing instruction "flies against all movement toward standardization," notes Mark Crotty of Greenhill School. Independent schools are not governed entirely by test scores—although this cannot be said of independent schools in California, where SAT9's are common occurrences, and at least one independent school markets its "writing" courses as test preparation for the ISEE. Writing teachers know, and keenly feel, the differences between this sort of rote instruction, which might require them to use a script, and teaching writing in a way that sticks beyond the deadline of test day.

Nor are tests the only tools a school can use to militate against the learning of writing. Pressures are often brought to bear on writing teachers by the school cultures themselves. Although a school might value writing as the act of thinking and a means of constructing knowledge (Schwartz), there might be within the school "standardized thoughts about education" (Crotty). Such standardized thoughts can define classroom conventions and customs: "We do what we do because we do it." Writing teachers know that they might be the only ones whose classes learn by writing: They are the anomaly. Sometimes the other teachers reject this pedagogy even though the school might permit it. ("I am the only English/reading/language arts teacher in my school who even attempts the writing workshop," says Natasha Warsaw. "I have no one to observe and help me adjust in problem areas. The others teach in a rigid format.") Teachers suggest the classes are too hard: "Perhaps I'm just jaded," says Sonja Schulz. "But in my school most folks just want to get it done and go to the house."

It is, perhaps, the unconventional structure (and stacks of works-in-progress) in a writing classroom that can make its pedagogy seem daunting. And it is true that writing teachers rely on everything they've written, read, or done, rather than on a script, or text. In this respect they do as "good teachers" always do: They teach themselves (Palmer 11). But the field of writing instruction is perhaps unique in that its philosophers and researchers have been people who practice in everyday life the methods they advocate: Their work is filled with advice to ease the trepidation of the teacher. Most particularly, subject teachers who engage their students in writing-to-learn will not, and need not, know what writing teachers know, nor of course are we talking about "grammar across the curriculum" (Connolly 5). Elbow speaks directly to this point: "Even though low stakes writing-to-learn is not always good as writing, it is particularly effective at promoting learning and involvement in course material, and it is much easier on teachers—especially those who aren't writing teachers" ("Writing for Learning" 1). And specialists in writing-to-learn assure teachers that "content writing can be integrated within the existing day. . . . Even theme evaluation, which is often perceived as a task so large as to discourage teachers from teaching writing, can be integrated naturally into the content teaching of a class" (Tchudi and Huerta 7). Finally, to dispel the misconception that a writing class itself is hard to conduct, this workshop can be a teacher's dream: the class that runs itself (Calkins14–15). Nevertheless, a standardized school culture will breed a species of teacher who is immune to innovation, who will teach the same way year after year, uninformed about developments in the profession. Such a culture, such a teacher, can be hostile to the writing teacher, who is unconventional by virtue of his calling.

Perhaps a more insidious problem because it is less easily articulated than the outright "No" is the effect of teachers who purport to teach "the writing process"—and maybe believe they do—but who teach a course programmed by kits and rubrics and textbooks, as standardized as writing instruction ever was:

> I have noticed that many teachers say, "yes I do writing workshop," but then upon closer examination you will find that the "writing workshop" only occurs *if* there is "extra time" in the day, doesn't allow choice, doesn't focus on writing for real reasons and real audiences, doesn't have real purpose, and doesn't involve any inquiry or in-depth study into real writing. (Kingsley)

One writing teacher refers to these methods as "curriculum in a box"; another calls it "the little box of comfort." Teachers who, without prior experience with writing, find themselves assigned to lead a workshop class rely on these books and kits to teach them how to teach writing. They speak of scripted lessons, all sequential, which their students follow in a clearly structured way to reach a certain product. "When I meet with teachers to talk about curriculum-related issues it sounds like they're doing what we've all contracted to do, but on a closer examination (asking probing questions) you realize that what they say they are doing is not what they actually do," says writing teacher Elisa Waingort. The ideas that writing pedagogy let loose in the territory of language, within the world of schools—that such conventions as grammar, mechanics, and spelling are not writing; that composing a piece in separate steps is not writing—are absent from these standard packages. The students write in rote response to teacher-given, often teacher-read, directions: There is little room for free, original, complicated thought.

And, subtler, perhaps, but no less powerful and real, is the absence of comfortable, natural writing that comes only with practice. Just as by reading we learn how to read (and the more we read, the more readily we understand questions on tests—all tests, not only those our schools admire), we learn writing by doing it. Given my writing education and experience, I was astonished when I heard that writing was *okay,* but the real business of teaching language was a program of book reports, comprehension questions, grammar, posters, role-playing, and vocabulary lists. I have come to believe that this sort of program defines the language education of most students. Very few may encounter teachers who encourage them to flex their minds and freely write.

According to writing teachers, however, students enjoy writing, and their work improves measurably: "I have successfully implemented both reading and writing workshops in New York City," Naomi Smith remarks. "I cannot quote research, but I have seen it work." Meg Krause, who works with low-income minority eighth-graders in New York, reports a similar success:

> This is definitely not research-based information but . . . my kids' writing has really improved this year because they choose what they will write about. So if you

> can get kids invested in a topic then it is so much easier to teach them how to improve their writing. . . . In the workshop structure kids know that they will be writing and that not all writing is "high stakes" writing. Kids just get used to writing and using writing to express themselves—and for me that's the crux.

(And who, Atwell has always contended, is more aware of the "research" more than the classroom teacher, who gathers the data every day?) "I love the writing workshop and believe in it," says Natasha Warsaw. "I've experienced the sheer joy of seeing it work exactly the way I imagine it's supposed to, it's incredible, and I see my students bloom." These teachers hear their students speaking of themselves as writers; they observe their students conferring, working cooperatively, without being formally directed (Augusta); and they see the writing grow, improve, become remarkable. "Truth be told," writes Mr. Maynard, "though they weren't real big on grammar or spelling, their stories were often more compelling and real than much of the stuff I had read from my fellow grad students." There are no distinctions I have yet found among writing teachers in public or private or independent schools, suburbs or the inner-city, classes of gifted or remedial students: All report the same good experiences.

And there is irony in these success stories. On 26 April 2003, *The New York Times* reported: "Writing in Schools Is Found both Dismal and Neglected." To writing teachers, these findings of the National Commission on Writing were not news. They know writing does not occur in schools. They know, without reading the report, the processes of writing it describes:

> If students are to make knowledge their own, they must struggle with the details, wrestle with the facts and rework raw information and dimly understood concepts into language they can communicate to someone else. In short, if students are to learn, they must write. (9)

And they know the truth of the commission's recommendations: that writing time be doubled and that writing be pursued in all subjects (28). "As for the national study," Mr. Crotty remarks, "I don't think most people use the workshop method—at least not correctly. . . . Plus there is still the idea that some people hold that you can teach writing by grammar rules and formulae. *I've never understood why some people believe taking apart sentences will automatically lead to putting them together effectively*" (emphasis mine). And the report itself reinforces this statement: it notes that students may respond correctly to a sheet of grammar exercises, and be unable to compose a piece of prose (13).

How is this failure possible, given the wealth of literature in writing pedagogy, the proliferation of "writing process" programs? Because, with few exceptions, "writing process" programs are no different from the conventional course in composition they claim to replace. They're standardized and uniform, from "brainstorming" to "final product," and they work on the most basic level of writing: The study is clear on that point (17). Further, the results of the National Assessment of Educational Process' 2002

Writing Assessment, released on 11 July 2003, support this conclusion (16; also Persky). In a room away from a teacher's correcting pen, most students are unable to express themselves coherently, with creativity and drive: One percent achieved advanced standing. The overwhelming majority had settled below "proficient," in other words, "precise, engaging, coherent prose" (16). In this context Ellen Berg expresses the worry of the writing teacher as she watches her students exit the class—their last experience, perhaps, with writing:

> While it is gratifying to see them begin to view themselves as writers, I am finding it difficult to let them go. I wonder what will happen to my readers and writers if they return to a "traditional" environment of worksheets and answer-the-questions.

Those of us who have seen our writing instruction reversed by that very event know the reality—and at this moment in schools, the futility—of her concern. Given the fact that both national reports are squarely allied with writing in all disciplines, it seems that the time has come for schools and their constituencies to stop saying "No" to the writing teachers.

These teachers already know how to address a group of inexperienced writers: "Pick up those pens and write something with them. Let's see what you get"—a different task entirely from the typical one, with maps and rubrics and topics, teacher-controlled, school-decreed, in very expensive packaging. It is its inverse: fractious, risky, topicless (the seminar circle turned inside out). It requires resources that teachers never knew they had. It asks them to think. It does not generate a tidy stack of sequential worksheets, corrected neatly and sent home in timely fashion. The teacher never knows exactly what she's going to get in those notebooks, and when she'll get it. But that's the story of writing. Instead of a certainty, the teacher starts with an open mind. But she can guarantee—the research supports her, as does the research of her own experiences—that the writing will get better over time. How much time? Who can say. That's in the nature of language: the more we practice it, the more adept we become. And the conclusion of my paper, and the draft that writing pedagogy is? Students are unable to write because they do not have the opportunity to write.

As a writing teacher, I would like to see these studies make the lives of writing teachers easier. I'd like to think that schools would grant them time and room to help their students' writing grow. I'd like to believe that more teachers might learn more from their own writing experiences, and as a matter of course withdraw from their reliance on rigid conventions and programs. It would be wonderful if students were allowed to learn the power of language, rather than answers to a test. I'd like to hope that schools would focus on the education of people instead of contentious percentiles. I would like to see writing extend outside the walls of a place that's fixed in space and time, like The Writing Room, and travel class to class, in the vehicle of the student's own notebook—the book of that student's mind. I would like to think that teaching writing could not only push its way beyond the text, but beyond the test—even that of the National Assessment—as well.

Experience is a cautionary tale: What I have seen and heard reported, outside a small number of writing teachers, is either pretense or resistance, and I worry that the radical changes suggested by the recent study will be met by customary means.

> It is the continual reformulation of what we know in the light of what we perceive that matters: and the hardening of what we know into a formula that we apply ready-made instead of reformulating—that is the danger. . . . (Britton in Rose 16)

I think we would do well to recall these words of James Britton, one of the early thinkers in this field. I worry that the writing program recommended for adoption will be another standardized package, that now writing will be perceived as another test to teach, and because it's so specifically taught, will become yet another score whose worth we can't in truth believe. But perhaps as securely as Nanci Atwell founded a school from the model of her workshop, (in the same area of Maine where she had once been unable to teach it), writing teachers may, with the publication of this study, see their practices settled on firmer ground. Nothing is sure—but then, with writing, nothing ever is, until the writer thinks it out, and in the process, learns.

Bibliography

"Answering Your Questions About Teaching Writing: A Talk with Donald H. Graves." University of North Carolina at Wilmington. 22 May 2003. http://people.uncw.edu/rivenbarkk/348/graves.html

Applebee, Arthur N. "Problems in Process Approaches: Toward a Reconceptualization of Process Instruction." In *The Teaching of Writing,* edited by Anthony R. Petrosky and David Bartholomae. Chicago: The University of Chicago Press, 1986.

Atwell, Nanci. *In the Middle: Reading, Writing, and Learning with Adolescents.* Portsmouth: Boynton/Cook, 1989.

Augusta, Erin. "Re: [MWPROJECTS] Writing." Online posting. 29 May 2003. MiddleWeb Reading and Writing Project. MWPROJECTS@Milepost1.com

Bangert-Drowns, Robert L. Marlene M. Hurley, and Barbara Wilkinson. "How Does Writing Affect Learning? A Review of the Research." Center on English Learning and Achievement. 22 May 2003. http://cela.albany.edu/newslet/spring03/howdoes.html

Bartholomae, David. "Words From Afar." In *The Teaching of Writing,* edited by Anthony R. Petrosky and David Bartholomae. Chicago: The University of Chicago Press, 1986.

Berg, Ellen. "Re: [MWPROJECTS] Writing." Online posting. 5 June 2003. MiddleWeb Reading and Writing Project. MWPROJECTS@Milepost1.com

———. "Re: [MWPROJECTS] Writing." Online posting. 13 July 2003. MiddleWeb Reading and Writing Project. MWPROJECTS@Milepost1.com

Britton, James. *A Note on Teaching, Research and "Development" in Prospect and Retrospect: Selected Essays of James Britton.* Edited by G. M. Pradl. 1982. The Conference on English Education. 23 May 2003. http://www.ncte.org/cee/britton.shtml

Calkins, Lucy McCormick. *The Art of Teaching Writing.* Portsmouth: Heinemann, 1994.

Connolly, Paul. "Writing and the Ecology of Learning." In *Writing to Learn: Mathematics and Science,* edited by Paul Connolly and Teresa Vilardi. New York: Teachers College, Columbia University, 1989.

Crotty, Mark. "Writing." E-mail to Nancy Fox. 29 May 2003.

———. "Writing." E-mail to Nancy Fox. 2 June 2003.

Dye, Diane. "Re: [MWPROJECTS] Writing." Online posting. 29 May 2003. MiddleWeb Reading and Writing Project. MWPROJECTS@Milepost1.com

Elbow, Peter. "Writing for Learning—Not Just Demonstrating Outcomes." National Teaching and Learning Forum. 22 May 2003. http://www.ntlf.com/html/lib/bib/writing/html

———. *Writing Without Teachers.* New York: Oxford University Press, 1973.

Fox, Nancy. *The Writer's Notebook.* Santa Barbara: The Learning Works, 1998.

Gage, John T. "Why Write?" In *The Teaching of Writing,* edited by Anthony R. Petrosky and David Bartholomae. Chicago: The University of Chicago Press, 1986.

Gallant, Claudia. "Writing." E-mail to Nancy Fox. 28 May 2003.

Handbook for Planning an Effective Writing Program. Sacramento: California State Department of Education, 1986.

Hillocks, George, Jr. "The Writer's Knowledge: Theory, Research, and Implications for Practice." In *The Teaching of Writing,* edited by Anthony R. Petrosky and David Bartholomae. Chicago: The University of Chicago Press, 1986.

Howard, V. A., Barton, J. H. *Thinking on Paper: Refine, Express, and Actually Generate Ideas by Understanding the Processes of the Mind.* New York: William Morrow & Co, 1988.

Kingsley, Laura. "Re: [MWPROJECTS] Writing." Online posting. 28 May 2003. MiddleWeb Reading and Writing Project. MWPROJECTS@Milepost1.com

Krause, Meg. "Re: [MWPROJECTS] Writing Workshop Focused and With Low-Income Minority Students." Online posting. 11 June 2003. MiddleWeb Reading and Writing Project. MWPROJECTS@Milepost1.com

Lamott, Anne. *Bird by Bird: Some Instructions on Writing and Life.* New York: Doubleday, 1994.

Lewin, Tamar. "Writing in Schools Is Found Both Dismal and Neglected." *The New York Times* 26 April 2003, nat. ed. sec. A:13.

———. "New Report on Students' Skills Reinforces Good News and Bad." *The New York Times* 11 July 2003, nat. ed. sec. A-9.

Lundsteen, Sara W., ed. "Research Then and Now." In *Help for the Teacher of Written Composition: New Directions in Research.* Urbana: National Conference on Research in English, 1976.

Maynard, Norman. "Writing." E-mail to Nancy Fox. 30 May 2003.

National Commission on Writing in America's Schools and College. *The Neglected "R": The Need for a Writing Revolution.* The College Board, 2003.

Noskin, David Peter. "Teaching Writing in the High School: Fifteen Years in the Making." In *Teaching Writing in the Twenty-First Century.* NCTE, 2000.

Palmer, Parker J. *The Courage to Teach: Exploring the Inner Landscape of a Teacher's Life.* San Francisco: Jossey-Bass Publishers, 1998.

Persky, Hilary et al. *The Nation's Report Card: Writing 2002: The National Assessment of Educational Progress.* U. S. Department of Education: National Center for Education Statistics, 2003. Available at http://nces.ed.gov/nationsreportcard

Petrillo, Lisa. "Report says students need to get the lead out and learn to write." *The San Diego Union-Tribune* 26 April 2003, A:7.

Romano, Tom. *Clearing the Way: Working with Teenage Writers.* Portsmouth: Heinemann, 1987.

Rose, Barbara. "Writing and Mathematics: Theory and Practice." In *Writing to Learn: Mathematics and Science,* edited by Paul Connolly and Teresa Vilardi. New York: Teachers College, Columbia University, 1989.

Schulz, Sonja. "Writing." E-mail to Nancy Fox. 28 May 2003.

Schwartz, Sherry. "Just Wondering." E-mail to Nancy Fox. 2 June 2003.

Shen, Andrea. "Study looks at role of writing in learning." Harvard Gazette: Science, 2000. http://www.news.harvard.edu/gazette/2000/10.26/06-writing.html

Smith, Carl B. "Writing Instruction: Current Practices in the Classroom." ERIC Digest D156. 19 May 2003. http://www.ericfacility.net/ericdigests/ed446338.html

Smith, Naomi. "Re: [MWPROJECTS] Writing Workshop Focused and with Low-Income Minority Students." Online posting. 29 May 2003. MiddleWeb Reading and Writing Project. MWPROJECTS@Milepost1.com

Tchudi, Stephen N. and Margie C. Huerta. *Teaching Writing in the Content Areas: Middle School/Junior High.* Washington: National Education Association, 1983.

Thorn, Craig, ed. *A Very Good Place to Start: Approaches to Teaching Writing and Literature in Secondary School.* Portsmouth: Boynton/Cook Publishers, 1991.

Waingort, Elisa. "Re: [MWPROJECTS] Writing." Online posting. 30 May 2003. MiddleWeb Reading and Writing Project. MWPROJECTS@Milepost1.com

Walvoord, Barbara. "Helping Students Write Well: A Guide for Teachers in All Disciplines." Marshall University Writing Across the Curriculum. 28 April 2003. http:www.marshall.edu.wac/html

Warsaw, Natasha. "Re: [MWPROJECTS] Writing." Online posting. 31 May 2003. MiddleWeb Reading and Writing Project. MWPROJECTS@Milepost1.com

Ziegler, Alan. *The Writing Workshop, Vol. 1.* New York: Teachers & Writers Collaborative, 1981.

———. *The Writing Workshop,* Vol. 2. New York: Teachers & Writers Collaborative, 1984.

Nancy Fox designed and directed the writing program at The Pennington School. She is currently pursuing graduate work in rhetoric and writing studies at San Diego State

University, where she is a writing tutor. Her publications include the text of her course, "The Writer's Notebook," as well as poetry and essays in such publications as *Poetry* magazine, *Four Quarters, The Princeton Review,* and the anthology *In My Life: Encounters with the Beatles.* She and two writing students are credited with the discovery of three new puns in *Alice in Wonderland,* and that paper was published in the journal of the Lewis Carroll Society in Oxford. She lives in San Diego with her husband, Stephen Edele, head of Harborside School, and their children Nicholas and Chloe.

A New Synonym for Learning Is "Fun"

By Wendy Sunderman

Prologue

Eight years ago while I was completing my student teaching at a middle school outside of Buffalo, New York, a veteran teacher happened by my room while my students were participating in an activity called "Traffic Jam." Desks originally arranged in neat rows had been pushed to all sides of the room, leaving the middle empty for students who were standing in two equal lines facing each other. A piece of paper representing a blank "spot" was positioned between the two lines of students. Twelve more pieces of paper rested beside each student, representing their "spot." The objective was to have each line trade sides with the opposing line. The challenge was that students could only move forward to an empty spot, and students could only pass someone if they were facing them face-to-face. A student leaving his/her spot to occupy the empty spot would leave a new empty spot for someone else. When students found themselves unable to make any more legal moves and had not completed the objective, I would say, "Traffic jam. Start over."

I can imagine the scene from my colleague's eyes—complete chaos—students all trying to talk at once, one student yelling so his voice could be heard over everyone else, arguing, and groaning at having to start over. I watched the veteran teacher shake his head and disappear past my door down the hallway.

If only he had stayed to see the rest of the chaos. After five initial tries, students started collaborating, listening to each other and complimenting the new ideas of their peers. "That's a good idea. Let's try Sam's idea." Everyone was silent as Sam gave the instructions. Traffic Jam.

Kim exclaimed, "Matt hasn't been saying anything. Matt, do you have an idea?" Matt shrugged his shoulders.

"I think I have it." Amy hadn't been saying anything either. Just watching. Everyone listened to Amy. She told everyone when to move and as a result the class solved the challenge. Everyone erupted into cheers. High fives, smiles all the way around the room. One student proclaimed, "That was fun." I cringed a little. Having "fun" in the classroom is often synonymous with taking a break from learning. I wanted my students to realize they had not taken a break from learning. We proceeded to sit down and figure out exactly what it was that we were learning.

That afternoon when I was leaving school, I ran into my veteran colleague again. "Interesting English activity you were running. Don't forget we have a curriculum to cover."

"Right, thanks." I wanted to defend my activity. I wanted to tell him that before I could teach a short story and expect my students to open themselves up in front of the class with their ideas and insights, I had to develop trust within our group. I wanted to tell him that I wanted my students to have fun learning. I wanted them to work together analyzing literature, and critiquing peer writing. I wanted to, but I didn't. I threw my book bag and my worn-out copy of *Silver Bullets* into the backseat, climbed in the front and drove home.

Eight years later, I find myself teaching middle school English at Maumee Valley Country Day School, and I am proud to say my colleagues and I have embraced the 1984 copy of *Silver Bullets* and the 1995 copy of *Quicksilver* and have developed a curriculum around it to enhance our learning community by having "fun."

My colleagues and I have come to agree that fun can be synonymous with learning. Steve Butler, co-author of *Quicksilver* (an adventure leadership book like *Silver Bullets*), defines fun as "a feeling and therefore somewhat hard to describe. Fun is laughter, energy, imagination, sharing, risking, challenge. It's spontaneous, focused, delightful, unpredictable. . . . Fun is contagious. . . . Fun is the invitation toward active involvement. It's the welcome sign that indicates it's OK to relax. Fun creates an immediate sense of togetherness and camaraderie that is essential to the group process" (13): A personal definition of fun that I think could also be used to define learning.

Learning should be laughter, energy, imagination, sharing, risking, challenging, spontaneous, focused, delightful, unpredictable, contagious, an invitation toward active involvement, a welcome sign that says, "relax." The group process should create an immediate sense of togetherness and camaraderie that is essential to learning.

Our Advisee Curriculum

Before the year begins students are divided into "Advisee Groups." Advisee groups include a seventh/eighth, male/female mix and one faculty advisor. The advisory program is not a new concept. Many schools have advisory programs. Our advisee curriculum is designed to engage and encourage students to become active members of the community willing to participate in enhancing their learning and social environment throughout the school year. There are many facets to our advisee curriculum. We go through goal-setting exercises. We have advisee projects. We do community service and we conference with the parents of our advisees in between each semester. The one element I want to focus on, however, is the initiatives and problem-solving exercises we have just recently started implementing. These exercises have been responsible for our creating an immediate sense of togetherness and camaraderie within our groups—the key elements for learning and having fun.

Ice Breakers

At the onset of the school year middle school students embark on a walk to Swan Creek Metro Parks for a picnic and orientation. This walk represents the first organized activity aimed at building a community of respectful, responsible, and kind adolescents. Advisee groups divide into pairs as they begin the mile trek to the park. Each pair is expected to ask questions of their partner to try to find out their likes, dislikes, hobbies, and so on. After a couple of minutes groups switch partners and the process repeats itself until everyone in the advisee group has talked to every other person in the group. This is a great way for students to be afforded the opportunity to connect with every single person in their group, not just the one or two they already know.

After each group has arrived at Swan Creek we all convene and begin the second activity, "Human Treasure Hunt." Each person receives a list of identity traits, (e.g., Find someone who is born the same month as you) and a pencil. The object is to find a different person for each trait on the list. After a set amount of time (time varies depending on the size of the group) we all reconvene and share our results. For example, we ask who found someone that could walk on his/her hands? Students raise their hands sharing names. All of the "named" enter the circle to show the whole group their special skill. One question may be, "Find someone who can speak another language." These students then get to share their language with the rest of the group. These treasure hunts lists can be tailored to fit any groups' needs and time constraints. Our orientation has proven to be a great kickoff to our year. (After a picnic lunch, we spend the afternoon relaxing and playing games.)

After orientation the advisee curriculum activities take place once or twice a month during an elective time in our middle school schedule. Whereas the activities at the beginning of the year are icebreakers and getting-to-know-you exercises, the rest of the year activities are initiatives.

Initiative Exercises

Karl Rohnke, author of *Silver Bullets,* explains initiative exercises:

> Initiative exercises offer a series of clearly and often fancifully defined problems. Each task is designed so that a group must employ cooperation and some physical effort to gain a solution. Some problems are more cerebral than physical and vice-versa. This problem-oriented approach to learning can be useful in developing each individual's awareness of decision-making, leadership and the obligations and strengths of each member within a group. Participants engage the problem in groups to take advantage of the combined physical and mental strengths of a team. These initiative problems also can be employed to promote an individual's sense of his/her own competence, and they also serve to help break down some of the stereotypes which exist so comfortable in our social network. Finally, initiative problems are a non-pareil for building morale and a sense of camaraderie (Rohnke 95).

Silver Bullets also includes detailed instructions for presenting group initiative problems and initiative problem debriefing topics. These instructions are essential in helping faculty members become facilitators for these activities. Many of the activities require the teacher to relinquish control of the activity over to the students. It is sometimes difficult not to offer advice to your students. It is hard to stand on the side simply observing. We're teachers. We *need* to be involved. I am often awed by the progress and conversations that take place during the initiative exercises.

Throughout the year each advisee group completes several initiatives. The following are examples all found in *Silver Bullets.* There are many variations and a plethora of other examples in *Silver Bullets* and *Quicksilver.* The best characteristic of these sources is the flexibility, flexibility, flexibility.

All Aboard—Objective: to see how many people can get on a 2' × 2' platform at one time. Each person must have both feet off the ground, and the entire group must be able to remain on the platform for at least five seconds.

T P (telephone pole) Shuffle—Objective: the group divides in half and forms two single file lines facing each other on the telephone pole (a log or tree will work). Each line then attempts to "shuffle" to the opposite side exchanging ends with the other line. This entire procedure should be timed. A 15-second penalty should be assessed for each touch off the pole. After one attempt, the group can then discuss how to improve their time.

Knots (Tangle, Hands)—A classic objective: A group of 10–16 people form a tight circle. Each person holds the right hand of one peer using their right hand, and the left hand of another peer using their left hand, and then proceeds to untangle the group without breaking any grip within their group.

Outcomes

What happens as a result of these activities? We find that students are more inclusive socially, more willing to take risks in the classroom, work well in learning teams on class projects, are more supportive of one another, and are better listeners. And they accomplish all of these things and have fun at the same time.

We end the year just as we begin it, with a picnic and hike through the woods right behind our school. However, on this walk no buddy chats need to be organized. All of my advisees walk and talk to someone for a while, then someone else joins the conversation and starts a new thread. Someone else jogs up to another trio of chatterers. No one is walking alone. Everyone is talking, laughing, and sharing. The activities in *Silver Bullets* and *Quicksilver* have enhanced our advisee curriculum in our middle school and, more important, they have strengthened our community at Maumee Valley Country Day School.

Epilogue

Silver Bullets and *Quicksilver* reside in my classroom right beside literary classics and the pedagogy of Louise Rosenblatt and Nancie Atwell. Much of my pedagogical style reflects the reader-response theory of Rosenblatt and the reading and writing workshop of Atwell. However, I credit much of my success in creating a safe, open environment for my students in the classroom to the activities from Rohnke and Butler. Before you can ask your students to create a circle of discourse, you have to help them learn how to trust each other. Before you can ask them to edit a paper written by a peer, you have to help them learn how to respect the voice of their peer.

In her book *In the Middle,* Nancie Atwell explains, "When we invite readers' minds to meet books in our classroom, we invite the messiness of human response—personal prejudices, personal tastes, personal habits, personal experience. But we also invite personal meaning, and the distinct possibility that our kids will grow up to become a different kind of good reader, an adult for whom reading is a logical, satisfying, life-long habit, someone who just plain loves books and reading" (1987). *Silver Bullets* and *Quicksilver* have helped my students and me appreciate all of our differences, enabling us to learn from each other in a safe environment.

Bibliography

Atwell, Nancie. *In the Middle: Writing, Reading, and Learning with Adolescents.* Portsmouth, NH: Boyton/Cook Publishers, 1987.

Butler, Steve, and Karl Rohnke. *Quicksilver: A Guide to Initiative Problems, Adventure Games and Trust Activities.* Dubuque, IA: Kendall/Hunt Publishing Company, 1995.

Rohnke, Karl. *Silver Bullets: A Guide to Initiative Problems, Adventure Games and Trust Activities.* Dubuque, IA: Kendall/Hunt Publishing Company, 1984.

Wendy Ebinger Sunderman resides in Findlay, OH, and has been commuting to Maumee Valley Country Day School in Toledo for the last seven years. She holds a Bachelor of Arts in English literature from the Pennsylvania State University and a master's degree in education from the State University of New York at Buffalo. She has fallen in love with the tradition and philosophy of independent schools as well as the energy and attitude of middle school students.

From Lakes to Rivers: The Independent School Library Looks Ahead

By Dorcas Hand

Thoughts of vacations at lakes elicit images of placid bodies of water where visitors can sit to absorb peace and quiet while relaxing in the sun. Many people have felt that libraries resembled lakes: They are traditionally quiet places where patrons sit to read while the staff works to keep the books in order on the shelves. The stereotypical librarian loves to read, and that is primarily what she does on the job. Little could be further from the truth. This traditional image is no longer valid—especially in schools where students are *not* by nature quiet and *are* by nature demanding of cutting-edge resources for information and recreation. These students require a library staff to be energetic and current in outlook and knowledge. Independent schools have a particularly strong tradition of excellence in education that requires high standards in all areas, including their library programs.

Still, while looking to the future, the library must remain aware of its history and the importance of print materials (aka books); students of today will only learn a love of reading when allowed access to plenty of books, for pleasure and research. Readers of literature generally are not comfortable reading long sessions on a screen, ebook, laptop, or otherwise. Libraries will remain centers of print resources for many years to come. Some older resources will never be digitized; our students need to know how to locate information and literature in a traditional library print environment as well as in other formats.

But they *also* need a variety of electronic resources—beyond mere Internet access and the world wide web—resources that are carefully indexed and monitored for quality by other librarians. Independent schools and their libraries must increasingly integrate electronic research tools and skills into the core curricula so that our students can become informed consumers of the information disseminated in their culture. Only some of that information is authoritative; only some of that information is useful. Mike Eisenberg, co-founder of the Big 6 Information Problem Solving approach, mentions that information is doubling every 5.5 years; the computer power doubles every 18 months; that the number of websites doubles every 40–50 days. Further, "When the class of 2000 graduat[ed], in that year alone the graduates [were] exposed to more information than their grandparents were in a lifetime; knowledge will increase 32 times by the time these graduates are 50." [http://www.ala.org/Content/NavigationMenu/AASL/Professional_Tools10/Information_Power/1, slides 8–9 : Information: Building Partnerships for Learning . . . Because Student Achievement IS the Bottom Line, Ala, 1999] In the face of such statistics, independent school librarians must use their professional expertise to provide students guided and age-appropriate access that allows them to locate useful information without being overwhelmed by the glut of erroneous or inappropriate material. The professional art of modern librarianship involves the selection of useful, appropriate, and cost-effective subscription databases that come with the authority of an established author, publisher, or university. These databases are the electronic extrapolation of traditional indexes (e.g., *Readers Guide to Periodical Literature*) on which generations of students in less information-glutted eras depended.

Independent school librarians must be extremely knowledgeable of the existing library collection so that they can build it—and weed it—appropriately to support the individual school's curriculum. To do that, they must also be extremely knowledgeable of the school's curriculum. This requires that they step out of the library frequently to collaborate with faculty and administration and to be aware of trends and changes within the school. The American Assn. of School Librarians and the Assn. for Educational Communications and Technology have collaborated to author *Information Power: Building Partnership for Learning* (1998), which includes the "Information Literacy Standards for Student Learning" that will help students become skillful producers and consumers of information. There are nine goals, but a major thread is to identify links in student information needs, curricular content, and library resources. According to *Information Power,* school librarians should share with teachers the responsibilities of planning, teaching, and assessing student learning to offer a truly cohesive curriculum. While librarians have always been teachers, they have not always been recognized as such or accorded equal teaching status in the process of curriculum design. Such a change from traditional practice does not come overnight, and requires the librarian to reach out repeatedly and determinedly to the academic teachers to begin to design collaborative units that imbed information literacy skills into academic projects and assessments so that students recognize throughout their education that information is a product to be consumed and produced carefully to assure accuracy and authority. There are several information and problem-solving models in wide use, including Big 6, Flip-It, and IIM, which many schools are finding most helpful as they work to imbed *Information Power*'s goals into the school's curricula.

The concepts of information literacy are based on an assumption of comprehensions skills, an assumption that students understand the material they are reading. Ellin Oliver Keene, co-author of *Mosaic of Thought* (Heinemann, 1997), discusses the difference between comprehension as generally taught, at a very surface and factual level, as compared with comprehension, which is built on substantive questions about the material under discussion. Libraries support this deeper kind of comprehension as they support students who question their world. Library resources offer a wealth of opinions and information for students to use as they consider their own opinions, and this perspective lends further support to the idea that strong libraries are essential to strong schools. Students from schools with strong libraries have demonstrably better test scores (1st Colorado study: "Impact of School Library Media Centers on Academy Achievement," by Keith Curry Lance, Lynda Welborn, and Christine Hamilton-Pennell, 1993; 2nd Colorado Study: "How School Librarians Help Kids Achieve Standards: The Second Colorado Study" by Keith Curry Lance, Christine Hamilton-Pennell, and Marcia J. Rodney, 2000 http://www.lrs.org/ documents/lmcstudies/CO/execsumm.pdf); these students are also better thinkers when they have access to such a variety of resources. Better thinkers will be better able to contribute to our democratic society when they reach adulthood.

These same librarians must be knowledgeable of their facility and how to maximize its use and maintain its functionality to support growing electronic and AV needs, as well as ongoing needs for current print resources, while maintaining adequate seating for students, teachers, and library staff. There is never enough space in schools, and libraries by nature require large amounts of space. If we accept that books are not going away, and that computers and other electronic media are also here to stay, we see a challenging recipe for facility size and design: space for traditional shelves; space for displays, space for computer workstations and for projection displays; space for research and space for recreational reading; space for students to sit to study, to view electronic images, and to listen to audio recordings; space for classes to meet, individual study, and faculty needs; space for library staff to manage library functions. Other issues that require consideration include lighting, humidity controls, sound management, electrical outlets and computer connections (wireless or cabled), and sightlines to easily supervise students. Maintaining existing facilities to support the most effective use of space is as challenging as planning a renovation or new facility. Frequently, librarians must defend existing space when other school needs impinge. Knowledge of current technology and likely future needs and trends is essential, and a building program sitting in a file in the librarian's office can be an ace in the hole when quick response is needed.

To do any of this, these same librarians must be masters of budgeting, to make every dollar count for the most value possible in these many directions and to demonstrate to the administration the need for adequate funding to support plenty of materials in all formats and the staffing to maintain them. The exponential speed with which the amount of information is increasing is made more overwhelming for libraries as we consider the variety of new formats available and the lack of standardization among these formats. Smartboard technologies and a variety of other new ideas are coming available almost monthly for schools to sort according to need. In many schools, the library has been the default AV department, as the school department most prepared to manage circulation of equipment. However, as the technologies increase in sophistication, librarians are less able to manage even minor repairs. Schools are beginning to have technology departments staffed by computer folk who manage the now essential digital networks that hold our data. These tech departments are happy to manage and maintain computer hardware that remains fairly fixed in location, but not peripherals like digital cameras that circulate. Their reluctance is understandable, but the issue undeniable. The library's job continues to grow, especially in schools where additional staff is not an option.

But the thread that holds all these elements together is a passion for teaching through the library's resources and facilities. That passion allows the librarian to infuse interactions with students, faculty, administration, and the wider community with a life-long love of learning. The independent school librarian who is excited about teaching will successfully navigate the rapids of information, technology, and curriculum with the best interests of the students at heart. The shoals along the way will provide additional challenges that focus the community in the short term as they look to the longer-term choices. A librarian who is not at heart a teacher will not completely succeed in providing a school community with a well-rounded library program, one that navigates the rapids ahead and notices the shoals as they develop in the river that is independent school education as it moves forward.

Outstanding independent school librarians are modern-day renaissance personalities. They enjoy a huge variety of challenges, and address them with great success. Administrative details underlie their efforts, but people skills predominate as they work with students, faculty, and administration to stay at the nucleus of the atom that is a school community. Teaching skills and library training are a powerful combination at work for the independent school community.

Think of these issues as crosscurrents in a river. Visualize librarians following the various currents as they cross, intermingle, and split apart again around obstacles. Skilled librarians manage to use the currents to best advantage, sometimes forcing them into a particular channel, other times allowing them their natural course. When a library finds an area of rapids, the librarian must exhibit great patience and skill, even art, to see the best course through the boulders, or even the shoals between rapids. This first decade of the new century offers all school librarians, and particularly those in independent schools, challenging rapids that seem to get steeper—until we remember that we are trained and experienced, trained to extrapolate new applications of old skills and experienced at managing change.

Dorcas Hand has been librarian in several independent schools in Houston, TX, since 1978, and came to Annunciation Orthodox School 13 years ago. She grew up in a family of independent school teachers as they moved from Virginia to Florida via North Carolina and Georgia, and back to New England; she attended Wellesly College for her B.A., then SUNY Albany for her M.L.S. She particularly values the variety and strength of the independent school community, and continues to think that libraries are an essential underpinning of an excellent educational institution.

Where Have All the Students Gone? Immersion and Learning

By Barbara A. Cleary, Ph.D.

To track down Miami Valley School (MVS) upper school students in late February, you'd have a challenge. Science labs are empty; classrooms seem to be deserted.

Some students might be at the controls of a Cessna. Others, tracing Caesar's footsteps from Rome to Hadrian's Wall. Still others might be taking photos of barns near Dayton, composing poems in their journals, or simply reflecting on a view from the Great Wall.

Far from being a misplaced summer vacation, this period is known as "Immersion," when students in grades 9–12 immerse themselves in a variety of interest areas for four weeks, led by upper school teachers who share their interest. They investigate, acquire practical skills, travel, write, paint, and pursue a host of other activities. The innovative program offers experiential learning opportunities to upper school students from late February to late March. Ninth graders explore leadership experiences together as a class, but those in grades 10–12 select from a variety of group or individual learning opportunities.

The program began in 1974 with language immersion for grades 7 through 12. Teachers from the Experiment in International Living in Vermont came to the campus, and under their guidance, students found themselves surrounded by language and culture representing the school's two major modern languages—French and Spanish. A café provided morning croissants, with the school's physical education teacher serving pastries and speaking French.

A few students chose instead to pursue Appalachian studies in that first year, traveling to Kentucky to learn crafts and pursue community study, and it was this model that prevailed in the formation of the program that was known from the beginning as Immersion. What became clear was that students would leap at a chance for learning in an interest area, and this formed the basis of the "new" Immersion. And MVS teachers wanted to be more directly involved in the learning, rather than standing by while "outside" teachers took their students through the language program.

The model invites learning together, since it is not based on teacher expertise, but rather derived from mutual interest, and provides opportunities for appropriate risk-taking as part of the learning process.

"If we hadn't introduced this concept in the '70s, we'd never have it today," says Miami Valley School headmaster Tom Brereton. "I doubt that many schools today would have the courage to surrender four weeks of Advanced Placement and honors courses so students could hike in Big Bend National Park or study theatre in New York." Too many factors would get in the way of introducing such a program to today's more intense generation of parents and students. Nonetheless, the current MVS community embraces it wholeheartedly as a way of life in grades 9 through 12.

Because the program models lifelong learning, teachers, too, become learners in the courses, often approaching areas of interest with little background or experience. Current headmaster Brereton (a former Cornell linebacker) led a dance Immersion with another teacher when he was a faculty member. Dayton Ballet, a leading regional dance company, provided class instruction. But the learning itself was often led by students, who patiently worked through steps with their teacher-learners and rehearsed strings of movement for an eventual recital offered to parents. "Performing in a leotard and tights before a group of parents, fellow teachers, and students gives you a feel for real risk-taking," Brereton says of his experience. The two teachers also developed an appreciation not only for the athletic demands of dance, but also for alternative learning styles. The instructor often admonished the adults, "You're thinking too much; let your body lead."

Some faculty members—like students—take smaller risks than others, providing, for example, travel Immersions to places whose history or art they may know from their own study. Even these, however, demonstrate to students what it means to push outside the comfortable classroom to examine implications and meanings. Science teacher (and director of Immersion) Bryan Czarnota frequently repeats an Immersion that examines ocean species on San Andros Island in the Bahamas. Although that study lies within his curricular interest, the Immersion also involves SCUBA instruction and study of island culture that creates a multidisciplinary learning experience, exploring not only the sea but the local culture and undertaking community service as well.

Immersion provides three learning models: the large-group experience for freshmen, independent learning, and small-group pursuit of interests. Ninth graders are engaged in a program currently themed as "Stepping Out" that examines individual values and group goals. Students learn about risk-taking by flying Cessnas (under the watchful eye of instructors), in tae kwan do training, and by a group camping experience at Hocking Hills State Park. (Yes, it's still winter in Ohio in February and March.) A concluding project is the sharing of their autobiographies, created throughout the Immersion period.

As students become juniors and seniors, they can pursue independent learning rather than the group experiences that characterize the first two years of their involvement. Some explore career options, shadowing physicians or architects; others pursue community service, seeking placement with homeless shelters or halfway houses. A young man who sought an experience with an IMSA auto racing team during a junior-year Immersion, just because he liked fast cars, later found himself in a career writing about racing. A student with a serious interest in music might study continuously throughout Immersion, discovering the challenges of the intense focus. Donning a white coat and entering the operating theater with a cardiac surgeon will give a student a clear idea about whether or not a career in medicine is for her.

The program remains among alumni's fondest memories of their experience at the school. Immersion offers a blend of the school's goals of rigorous college preparation and the experiential learning that contributes to broader life successes. It was the inspiration of David O'Dell, then principal of the upper school, who brought a rough concept of experiential learning from his prior teaching position at the Purnell School, Pottersville, NJ. A number of colleges offer immersion-type opportunities, including Hartwick College and its J-term program, and while the MVS model has some of the same components, it has been developed especially for the school's own students. At an overnight retreat that took place on a farm outside Dayton in the mid 1970s, faculty and administrators hammered out the expanded details of an immersion-type program as well as of Walkabout, another experiential learning program for the school. Unwittingly, the group was creating its own kind of "immersion," combining the camaraderie of singing around a fireplace and preparing a meal with friends with the serious business of problem solving.

A memorable moment, recalled in the school newsletter, recounted a student's experience with teaching. She was working with Sharyn Jackson, physical education teacher and later athletic director. After several days of leading seventh and eighth graders in gym classes, the student told Jackson that she had headaches every day when she went home. "Well," Jackson responded, "Teaching's not as easy as it looks." The young women later went into the education profession.

Another student, after a language Immersion in Spain, summarized his learning in a journal entry: "I have learned one thing that I believe is just as important as language or culture. This is that everything is what you make of it. If you say, 'I'm not going to like this museum,' well, then, you won't. But if you feel that everything has potential for special learning, then it will." While this may have nothing to do with conversational Spanish, it represents a life lesson that applies to most learning.

While travel programs remain predictably popular, "travel" can be defined in a variety of ways through Immersion. Students pursue world travel, to be sure. But other experiences, such as creative writing or the visual arts, offer opportunities for inward travel as well. One group of young women, with two female teachers, spent the Immersion away from school in an unheated camp in Vermont. They learned practical skills that were necessary for survival, such as keeping a fire going and skiing across the lake to gather drinking water from a spring. But they also explored through creative expression: photography, creative writing, film, storytelling, folk dancing.

"We don't want Immersion to be perceived as a chance for a luxurious trip, or 'time off,'" Brereton says, "but rather, a way for students to find out about themselves," sometimes in challenging living accommodations or tedious train trips. Brit Rail passes provided a way for one group to interact with people, engage them in discussion, and accumulate experiences for creative writing that culminated in a published work of photos and written expression.

Of course, not all Immersion experiences are successful, at least as measured by immediate experience. But the learning model for the program encourages the kind of learning that can come with so-called failure. One young woman who had always thought she wanted to be a social worker, for example, worked closely with an agency throughout her four-week independent learning experience, and discovered that she hated it. What better learning, than to discover this before entering a serious program of professional preparation?

In addition to built-in opportunities for reflection about the Immersion experience, another opportunity is the annual evening open house, among the best-attended events of the year. Parents and other students are invited to see the highlights of students' Immersions two weeks after their return, manifested in film, poster-board exhibits, photo albums, creative writing, PowerPoint demonstrations, and even T-shirts. "It's important to be able to process the experience of Immersion," says Czarnota. By talking about their experiences, students are not only helping others gain insight into what they learned, but they are also giving themselves opportunities to pull these experiences together. Most students also keep journals of their experiences, either as a required part of the program or on their own. Independent learning participants write reflection papers that become part of the school's library collection.

Clearly, Immersion experiences cost money. Parents and students make plans for the four-year Immersion opportunities, perhaps saving for "one big trip" or seeking ways to fund the added financial burden. Often students seek summer employment just to pay for their Immersions. In addition, however, the school has set aside an endowment fund for financial aid. The Thomas N. Elmer Immersion Fund is a source of help for students who apply for aid. About 7 to 10 percent of students receive aid from a growing fund, and about $10,000 is distributed each year. Established in honor of former principal Tom Elmer, the fund has grown partly through the enthusiasm of parents and alumni for the Immersion program itself.

Intensive learning in a focused area of interest supports the opportunity for what psychologist Mihaly Csikszentmihalyi identifies as "flow." In this experience, he says, "people enter a flow state when they are fully absorbed in activity during which they lose their sense of time and have feelings of great satisfaction." Csikszentmihalyi describes flow as "being completely involved in an activity for its own sake. The ego falls away. Time flies. Every action, movement, and thought follows inevitably from the previous one, like playing jazz."[1] Certainly, the reflections that students have had, both immediately and even years later, support the sense of creative flow that they experienced in Immersion.

A "Destination America" Immersion offered a group of students the chance to see "blue-highways" America. Eschewing interstate highways and big cities, the group meandered around the country from Baton Rouge to Venice Beach in a Winnebago, cooking on campstoves or eating in small-town cafes, taking pictures and engaging in conversation. "Talk about being able to slow down and think," one of the participants said in his journal.

A student kneading bread or throwing a pot on a wheel or focusing a lens on a waterfall or looking at a Scottish loch from a highland trail might say the same thing. What one rarely hears about Immersion is that pervasive, all-purpose adolescent damning judgment: "Boring."

Note

[1] Csikszentmihalyi, Mihaly. As cited at http://www.brainchannels.com/thinker/mihaly.html

Barbara Cleary earned a Ph.D. in English from the University of Nebraska and has taught English from seventh grade to university levels for the past 35 years. She is a co-author of three books on education (*Orchestrating Learning with Quality* with David P. Langford, 1995; *Tools and Techniques to Inspire Classroom Learning,* 1997; *Thinking Tools for Kids,* 1999 with Sally J. Duncan), has contributed to *Learning by Heart: Contemporary American Poetry about School* (U. of Iowa Press, 1999), and is currently writing a history of The Miami Valley School, to be published in May, 2004.

The Amit Community School Program: A School Within a School

By Linda Zimmerman

The Amit Community School Program began as the Special Needs Department of Jewish Educational Services in Atlanta, Georgia. This department was created in 1995 to provide consultative services and professional development opportunities to the Jewish preschools, synagogue supplementary schools, and day schools in the community. However, this added service was not enough for the parents whose children were still being asked to leave the Jewish day schools because of their learning difficulties, or for the parents of children who were never accepted in the first place due to the severity of their learning disability.

The Atlanta metropolitan area has four Jewish elementary day schools for students in kindergarten through eighth grade, and four Jewish high schools. Yet, in order to attend these schools children must be able to survive in a highly competitive, advanced learning program.

Year after year, children have been asked to leave the day schools due to their inability to flourish academically with the high standards required by the school. These children often end up in other private "clinical" schools or in public schools that may or may not be able to accommodate their specific learning styles, but do not provide the Jewish component that their parents so desperately want for their children.

The students who leave these day schools generally have only mild to moderate learning disabilities. But there is another population of students who have never had the opportunity to attend a Jewish day school: namely, children who have severe learning disabilities and/or developmental disabilities. For this population the doors to a Jewish day school education in Atlanta have never been opened.

How Does the Amit Program Plan to Meet This Need?

Staff and lay people from the Amit Steering Committee visited and contacted many programs around the country that provide support services to children with mild to severe learning disabilities in Jewish day schools. The information that was collected nationally, as well as data from a locally conducted survey, helped lay the foundations for a unique program that addresses the needs of the Atlanta metropolitan community that previously went unmet.

The Amit Community School Program focuses on four areas: *support services, modified self-contained classrooms (Gar'inim), teacher education,* and *disability awareness.*

Support services are available to children with moderate learning disabilities whose needs are not currently being met in the Atlanta day schools. These services, to be offered on site at participating schools, will include one or more of the following: a learning disabilities specialist on site to provide pull-out services in an Amit Learning Lab, a facilitator to attend class with a student, a modified curriculum to meet the individual needs of the student, available speech and occupational therapy services on site, resource materials, technological assistance, adaptive equipment, and general information and referral.

Gar'inim, the Amit *"School Within a School"* is a modified self-contained class housed in a day school in which eventually a wing will be designated to allow for the growth of the program from kindergarten through eighth grade. In kindergarten all academic and Judaic subjects are taught in the classroom, while the children attend all non-academic classes with their peers in the regular school program. Starting in first grade, children who show strengths in specific academic areas are able to mainstream into typical classes in the host school. The target population for the Gar'inim classroom includes children with severe non-specific learning disabilities and developmental disabilities.

An extensive *teacher education* program is being established to teach the faculty of the schools hosting the various Amit programs how to include children with different learning styles in their classrooms. In addition, classes will be offered on a regular basis to teachers in all Jewish day schools on how to teach material creatively in order for all children to benefit.

Through the *ability awareness and sensitivity* program, teachers, parents and students are learning to remove the social barriers which are regularly faced by people with disabilities. This program teaches that it is not the disability itself which inhibits individuals, but the attitudes and lack of acceptance by others, caused by ignorance, indifference, or discomfort. Through the sensitivity program, Amit staff and volunteers hope to work toward removing these barriers—this will help *all* children reach their full potential. The understanding and support of differences can help create a climate that values each individual's worth and abilities.

Menu of Options

As a fledgling program, Amit was asked by a granting organization to begin work on formulating a strategic plan. Due to the unique nature of the services provided, the Amit planners decided to create a "Menu of Options" which would guide the future growth of the program. We are not just a school that can plan for future growth by knowing that each year we will add a grade with one or more classrooms. Our main goal is to allow as many children as possible to remain in the school of their choice by providing the necessary supports in order for them to be successful. This "menu" includes a variety of services that are either currently available, or ones that the agency hopes to provide as the financing becomes available. The menu items are listed below with the fee for the service in parenthesis:

1. *Consultation Services* ($100.00/hr)—An experienced Learning Specialist is available to provide consulting services to school administrators and teachers in curriculum modification, case management, individual student planning, purchasing of resource materials, adaptive equipment and teacher mentorship.
2. *Staff Development/Parent Education* (fees vary)—Workshops and seminars for schools, parents and the community.
3. *Resource teacher* ($50.00/hr)—Amit will provide a teacher to offer remediation/tutor services for identified individual students who would benefit from assistance with a frequency of 30 minutes once a week to one hour five days per week.
4. *Learning Lab* ($5,000/yr full program; $2,000 to $3,000/yr transition program)—Students enrolled in the school of their choice will receive one to two hours per day of individual and small group instruction in the areas of language arts and math. In addition, the Amit teacher works with classroom teachers of all subjects to monitor the children's academic progress and advise on modifications as necessary. The teacher conducts an after-school homework hour twice a week.
5. *Facilitation* ($5,000 to $18,000/yr)—Amit provides a trained instructional aide to "shadow" one to three students on site. The classroom teacher maintains responsibility for all academic programming. Amit supervises and trains the instructional aides.
6. *Technology/Adaptive Equipment* (fees vary, if any)—Amit will provide adaptive equipment as specified in a child's learning plan or as needed for the child to participate fully in the school.
7. *Therapies* ($75/hr)—Amit will facilitate the planning, scheduling, and implementation of speech/language and occupational therapy services.
8. *Gar'inim (Amit's "School Within a School")*—A self-contained full-day program housed at a Jewish day school for children with severe learning disabilities and/or developmental disabilities. Students will receive secular and Judaic academic instruction in the Gar'inim classroom and will integrate into the host schools' program as appropriate.

The rest of this chapter will focus on three areas of direct service, which we are currently offering parents and schools.

What Is Facilitation?

A facilitator is a trained instructional aide hired to "shadow" one to three students in the child's own classroom. The classroom teacher maintains responsibility for all academic education while the facilitator oversees the child's ability to stay on task and learn.

In addition to reading, writing, and arithmetic, there are many learning opportunities throughout every day at school. They include reinforcement of academic skills, social skills (working in groups, intrapersonal relationships, self-motivation, etc.) and the building of self-esteem. A child with disabilities often misses out on the subtle cues given off by other children and adults that allow them to become socially adept. The facilitator ensures not only that the child stays on task and is able to learn academics, but also works toward helping the child to fit in among his/her peers.

The facilitator also works closely with the parents and with the therapists that the child sees during the week in order to carry over behavior modifications and therapeutic techniques into the child's schedule throughout the school week.

In a private school setting, facilitation is a costly endeavor. However, our hope is that this service will be more widely available in the future through establishment of an endowment fund and by working with the local public school districts to share resources.

What Is a Learning Lab?

The Amit Learning Lab is an innovative approach for teaching children with diagnosed learning disabilities. Amit piloted the learning lab concept with children in fourth through seventh grades at The Alfred & Adele Davis Academy, a Reform Jewish day school in Atlanta. The students are enrolled in the host school and pay full tuition. In addition, Amit charges a fee for the services of the lab.

Students are referred to the Amit lab after being identified by teachers and/or parents as having difficulties in the classroom. If the school feels that the child's needs are more than can be handled by the school's resource program, then the family is referred to the lab. The admissions process for the lab requires the parents to submit an application including: background information, school reports, a psycho-educational evaluation, therapy reports, etc. This material is reviewed by the Amit admissions criteria committee, and if it is determined that the child's learning needs can be met in the learning lab they are admitted into our program.

All of the students in the lab require assistance in reading and language arts instruction. Some also receive support in mathematics. The students come to the Lab when their classmates are receiving instruction on the same topic so that they do not miss their other subjects. The lab teacher uses a variety of teaching methods and materials to instruct the child and to help him/her develop techniques to compensate for their learning weakness. The teacher also follows the child's academic progress in their other subjects by meeting regularly with teachers and offering advice and assistance when necessary. The lab teacher is also available twice a week for an optional homework hour after school as well.

Creating the Gar'inim Program—The "School Within a School"

Gar'inim (Hebrew word for seeds) is the name given to the Amit modified self-contained program, our *school within a school.* Although the current trend in education is full inclusion, this is not always feasible in the private school setting. First of all, many private schools have designed a college preparatory curriculum that often pushes the average child to perform above typical grade standards. Secondly, the costs involved in hiring sufficient staff to ensure that each child reaches their ultimate potential is often prohibitive to the school and the families involved. During our visits to other locations we noticed that children who were supposedly "included" in typical classrooms were often alone in another room with their own instructor in order to learn the material at their level. If they were in the classroom they were in the back of the room learning alone with their facilitator.

Gar'inim was created to provide as much inclusion as possible in a typical private Jewish day school program while also addressing the individual learning styles and needs of children with severe learning problems and other associated sensory difficulties.

Many of the local day schools were approached to house Gar'inim. Atlanta's Jewish schools are fortunate to have the problem of full capacity, and unfortunately this means a lack of spare rooms. One of our schools was in the process of a capital campaign that would result in a new middle school building within the next two years. This school, The Alfred & Adele Davis Academy, was very excited over the prospect of offering Amit space for many reasons, the main one being the impact it would have on its current student body. The head of school, Rabbi Steven Ballaban, needed no help in seeing the many benefits to his school and his students. He understood that having children with developmental disabilities in his school would not only open the doors to a Jewish day school experience for the children but would help teach his current student body acceptance of all people. In addition, he had the foresight to see that families would want to enroll the siblings of the Gar'inim students into his school.

With a location secured, Gar'inim was born. An agreement was written between The Davis Academy and the Amit Community School Program outlining the financial obligations of both schools, staff concerns, and other administrative issues. Due to the lack of space at the current school, while the new building was being built two modular units were rented and installed on the school campus. The Davis Academy assisted in the costs of setting up the units and Amit pays the rental fees. Each unit has two classrooms. The Gar'inim program is currently using one full unit and The Davis Academy uses the other. The first kindergarten class began in the fall of 2002 with three students.

The Gar'inim students are not officially Davis students. The families pay tuition to Amit and Amit hires and supervises the staff, equips the room, and oversees all aspects of the program. The Davis Academy has been very accommodating, allowing our students to participate, accompanied by our staff, in all non-academic programming in the school such as physical education, music, art, lunch, recess, Shabbat programming, and field trips.

The Gar'inim students are divided and assigned to a Davis Academy classroom of the same grade. They attend all non-academic programming with that class and participate in other activities including "center time." The children are made to feel that they are an integral part of the classroom. If a Gar'inim child shows strength in a particular academic area, the child is permitted to go to the Davis Academy classroom when that subject is being taught. For example, a child who will be age-appropriate for first grade next year will attend math class in a Davis Academy classroom. An aide from the Gar'inim classroom will be with him until it is determined that he can function on his own.

A Typical Gar'inim Week

The curriculum and scheduling of the Gar'inim class is designed to meet the individual needs of the children as well as to allow for maximum opportunity for mainstreaming into the classes of the host school. The Gar'inim teachers meet weekly with the host school teachers to adjust the class schedule as needed in order for the children to participate in all extracurricular activities with their peers in the host school.

Sample schedule (M = mainstreaming with host school)

MONDAY	TUESDAY	WEDNESDAY	THURSDAY	FRIDAY
Prayers/Calendar	Prayers/Calendar	Prayers/Calendar	Prayers/Calendar	Prayers/Calendar
Reading/LA	Speech/Lang. Therapy	Reading/LA	Speech/Lang. Therapy	Kabbalat Shabbat (M)
PE (M)	Reading/LA	Music (M)	Reading/LA	Reading/LA
Lunch/Recess (M)	PE (M)	Lunch/Recess (M)	PE (M)	Lunch/Recess (M)
Math	Lunch/Recess (M)	Math	Lunch/Recess (M)	Host school buddies visit
Occupational Therapy	Math	Occupational Therapy	Math	Library
Themed activities	Themed activities	Themed activities	Themed activities	Themed activities
Center time (M)	Center time (M)	Center time (M)	Center time (M)	Center time

The above schedule is a general overview. The children we serve thrive on structure and repetition. Although there are set times of the day that the teachers put aside for academic instruction, the reality is that this occurs throughout every day. The teachers take advantage of every activity, planned or unplanned, to reinforce what the children are learning.

Children with developmental disabilities are also unpredictable. On any given day, one child may enter the room in a hyper state, the other children react to the behavior, and the best-laid plans of the teacher go out the window. The teachers must be flexible and have the ability to take any situation and make it into a fruitful learning experience.

The Gar'inim class uses an integrated curriculum. In addition to the daily prayers, the children learn about their Jewish history and the holidays through their daily academic activities. For example, when the children were learning about the holiday of Tu B'shevat, the Jewish New Year for Trees, they learned the customs associated with the holiday and also learned the letters *T* (trees) and *S* (seeds). For a science project they planted grass seeds and for math they collected nuts and used them for counting exercises. The students then went on a field trip to the park with the students of the host school.

Continuum of Services

There are two main issues involved in providing services to children with learning disabilities and/or developmental disabilities in a private school setting. One is the ability to meet the individual needs of each student in a cost-effective manner, and the other is the desire of most private schools to provide a highly competitive college preparatory educational curriculum.

The Amit Community School Program was designed to help the schools meet the unique learning needs of children with diagnosed learning disabilities in a cost-effective manner and without compromising the academic standards of the school. This is done through a continuum of services that allows each child to receive the support they need in the least restrictive environment possible for a private school.

Gar'inim is the *school within a school,* for children who need highly structured small group instruction with small teacher/student ratios. A classroom will have no more than 10 students with one lead teacher, one assistant teacher, and one para-professional. The children have the opportunity to mainstream throughout each day with students in the host school. This is an ideal program for children with developmental disabilities or severe learning disabilities with associated behavior or sensory problems. Some children will remain in the Gar'inim program throughout their academic career. Others will mainstream out of the program to the day school of their choice.

The learning labs provide support to children who are able to remain in a typical classroom with their peers; however, due to their moderate learning disabilities, they need the assistance from a special educator to be successful. They spend between one to two and a half hours per day in the lab and may return after school twice a week for "homework hour." And a facilitator allows for the child to remain the entire day in a typical classroom.

Special education is very expensive. The Gar'inim program, when full, will break even financially, but will not bring in the extra funds needed to provide additional services or cover administrative costs. The learning labs actually bring in additional funds due to the number of children that can be served by each teacher and the lower overhead costs. Facilitation is the most expensive service offered and is not covered by tuition alone. By offering a wide range of services the overall cost of the program is more manageable.

In addition, through combined services most children, regardless of the severity of their learning or developmental disability, can be successful in a Jewish day school environment. As students' needs change, they are able to move from one "menu option" to another, thereby allowing each child to reach their ultimate potential.

Where did the original funding come from and how will it be funded in the future?

The start-up funds for the Amit program and the Gar'inim classroom came from individuals in our community and a grant from the Partnership for Excellence in Jewish Education. The research had shown that the cost of a "school within a school" program would probably never be fully covered by tuition. This is why the Amit Community School Program was developed. By offering a variety of services to many different schools, joint purchasing, sharing staff and administration, and increasing the number of children receiving some type of support services, the money raised through fees would increase while expenses would be streamlined.

In addition the Board of Directors has developed a fundraising/income/development strategy that is broad, long-term, multifaceted and creative. This way the program will always be able to keep pace with increasing needs. The fund-raising committee has developed a plan that includes five fund-raising programs: Annual Membership Campaign, Special Events, Endowment/Planned Giving, Foundations/Grants, and a Capital campaign.

Closing Thoughts

The first few years of any new program are difficult. The community has to be convinced that the program is needed. Parents have to have trust in the school in order to send their children to a new program that has yet to establish a history. And foundations and individuals have to share the dream of providing equal access to all children in parochial and non-sectarian private schools.

The other factors that the Amit program had to deal with were the attitudes of the parents of the host schools whose children do not have learning problems. They feared that the highly academic program would be "watered down" once children with more severe learning difficulties were allowed to attend the schools. And the teachers of the schools had to be convinced that their workload would not increase with the new students.

Both of these issues were addressed through open forums and community education. Within the first few weeks of the school year, all initial concerns seemed to be forgotten. The teachers realized that the Amit learning lab and Gar'inim teachers were readily available to answer their questions and to give advice on all of the children in the classroom, not just those receiving support services. By the middle of the year, the host school teachers would routinely come to the Amit classrooms to borrow material or to ask for advice on a particular student. The parents were also more at ease when they came to realize that the classroom teacher now had more time to spend with their child. And their child's teachers began making changes in their teaching styles that benefited the entire classroom.

Linda Zimmerman is the executive director of the Amit Community School Program in Atlanta, Georgia. She established the Special Needs Department of Jewish Educational Services in Atlanta from which the Amit program was established.

Re-engineering Schools for the 21st Century

By Patrick F. Bassett

Twenty years after the publication of *A Nation at Risk* and three years into the new millennium, we seem to be in jeopardy again.

Of concern to educators who pause to contemplate what school is really meant to prepare students *for* is the dawning realization that schools seem ill-equipped to bridge the gap between what employers and universities are indicating will be the skills needed to succeed in the future with the values and cultures of schools in the present. In a recent assessment by The Manhattan Institute, research indicates that only around 70% of students graduate from high school with their class, and only about one-third of those are equipped to complete 4-year college programs.[1] Visionary school leaders are needed to confront this chasm of 21st C. expectations on the one side and seemingly permanent 18th C. school values and practices on the other.

What is ironic, of course, is that there is a growing consensus among the corporate community, the university world, *and* informed educators regarding the skills needed for success in college and in the marketplace. According to *Building a Nation of Learners—The Need for Changes in Teaching and Learning to Meet Global Challenges* (2003) from the Business–Higher Education Forum, "Today's high-performance job market requires graduates to be proficient in such cross-functional skills and attributes as leadership, teamwork, problem-solving, and communication" (listening, speaking, reading, and writing) as well as time-management, self-management, adaptability, analytical thinking, and global consciousness.[2] These same proficiencies and skills are also identified specifically in the new study by twenty of America's most prestigious research universities in their assessment of "Standards for Success": what's needed for students not only to matriculate to college but to succeed there.[3] Likewise, at the pre-collegiate level, we have now articulated standards of learning, state by state and nationally, all of which are remarkably similar in what we know students should know.[4] The issue, then, is not that we have any lack of clarity about what to teach, but rather that we are stuck in antiquated means of thinking about how to teach, and more specifically what exercises and experiences best produce proficiency in the skills and attributes that are critical. What we also know is that the legislative mandates ("high stakes testing") and slavish allegiance to traditional teaching practices and to one's own discipline of study are a diversion from serious attention to developing the more global mind-set and the skills and attributes our children truly need to succeed.

A New Framework for 21st C. Schools

All over the world, we see examples of schools resolving to resolve the contradictions between our vision of quality education in the future and our past and current practices. Reggio Emilia schools, Coalition of Essential schools, Montessori schools, Waldorf schools, Multiple Intelligence schools, environment- or farm-based or expedition-based schools, core-curriculum schools, technology charter schools with mid-week/full-day apprenticeships in the tech industry, and individual schools with no specialized philosophy or common theme but a will to experiment are experiencing amazing success in redefining what to teach and how to teach. That commitment itself is a 21st C. attitude.

It is likely the new definitions will comprise four universal expectations for students, that we will divide the school day, week, month, or year accordingly, and that promotion will depend on whether, not when, a student meets the expectations.

One will know when one is in a 21st C. school by the hallmarks of four recognizable expectations:

1. *Proficiency* (in literacy, numeracy, the empirical method and technology—as demonstrated by assessments in various and complementary forms: tests, portfolios, demonstrations).
2. *Fluency* (in communications, ethical decision-making, leadership and teaming—as demonstrated in project-based and experiential activities and products).
3. *Multicultural Literacy* (conversant familiarity with one's own native canon, language, geography, and ecologies plus that of at least one other place—as demonstrated by common intercourse in real and/or virtual exchanges with students of another language and culture).
4. *Performance* (in the fine and practical arts and athletics—as demonstrated by recitals, exhibitions, and competitions).

Samplings of all of these achievements will be captured in each student's digital portfolio, marking progress points across each of the four continua at successive stages in school. These four expectations will become in a 21st C. school the four hallmarks of how the school organizes itself, its program, and its assessment system.

Hallmark #1: ***Proficiency*** *(in literacy, numeracy, the empirical method, and technology—as demonstrated by assessments in various and complementary forms: tests, portfolios, demonstrations).*

The first hallmark will be the proficiency curriculum that is, in the words of Grant Wiggins, "backward designed" so that preferred outcomes dictate program and assessment. A student well-educated for the 21st C. would be technically proficient vis-à-vis

- literacy (including skills of reading with comprehension, writing with accuracy and cogency, and speaking in public with confidence and persuasiveness);
- numeracy (mathematics skills and mathematical reasoning through advanced levels);

- empiricism (the scientific method, as applied in scientific inquiry);
- technology (not only computer technology but expanded to include other tools as well: digital imaging, laser operations, robotics, etc.).

It is likely these proficiencies will continue to be taught as subjects in classes, but increasingly by customized "high tech" means so that assessments themselves are instant feedback loops that allow students to progress according to their developmental readiness. Promotion from level one proficiency to level two or three or four proficiency will be dependent upon demonstrations (tests, performances, electronic portfolios) of successively sophisticated indicators, and students may "graduate" from school at a stage rather than an age, when they have the level of proficiency required for the workplace, the military, or the university.

Hallmark #2: *Fluency* *(in communications, ethical decision-making, leadership and teaming—as demonstrated in project-based and experiential activities and products.)*

The second hallmark will be the understanding that a number of "fluencies" stretch students beyond the technical proficiencies. Fluency is developed less by instruction from the teacher and more by habituation of the student via practice and coaching by a mentor. A student well educated for the 21st C. would be fluent in leadership because he or she would have had leadership experiences inside the classroom (taking leadership for one task in a division of labors in a team project) and outside the classroom (on the athletic field or on the stage or in the editorial offices). A student well educated for the 21st C. would be fluent in ethical decision-making because he or she would have been trained to use principles to resolve real ethical dilemmas (the "teachable moments" that inevitably arise in the messy business of schools), since ethical behavior is ingrained when the young begin to develop the habit of acting ethically. "We are what we repeatedly do. Excellence, then, is not an act but a habit" (Aristotle). A student well educated for the 21st C. would be fluent in writing persuasively and speaking confidently because he or she would have done so *weekly* in the various presentations of the project-based learning environment, whether it be the puppet show on nutrition for the homeless shelter kids or the water quality PowerPoint presentation to city council. Teaming happens in physics class when the project, building a solar-powered vehicle in teams of three, is evaluated by seeing which team's vehicle goes the farthest around the track, which one produces the least waste and has the lowest impact on the environment, and so on. Indeed, as students and their teacher-mentors develop the various experiential projects and products they will pursue, each of these fluencies will be built into the design and outcome: leadership, ethical decision-making, communication.

Hallmark #3: *Multicultural Literacy* *(conversant familiarity with one's own native canon, language, geography, and ecologies plus that of at least one other place—as demonstrated by common intercourse in real and/or virtual exchanges with students of another language and culture)*

A student well educated for the 21st C. would be, in the words of education reformer E.D. Hirsch, "culturally literate." For U.S. students, for example, that would mean first being conversant with the often conflicting "idea of America" and the themes that have emerged from our collective history, literature, and art. These themes of course include the idea of "the experiment in democracy"; the idea of the "rights of man" borrowed from the French philosophers but codified by the American Declaration of Independence, Constitution, and Bill of Rights; and the persistent tension in America between individual rights and communitarian responsibilities (the latter a value much more prominent in most other cultures, for example). The other dominant themes of being a "land of immigrants," the idea of the "frontier," the idea of the land, the idea of the "American dream," the idea of the "melting pot" vs. a "mosaic" are all manifest in what should be basic in teaching about America. As controversial as the notion of "canon" may be, in fact its persistence suggests how important it is in the process of identification of one's "cultural fingerprint": There is a reason why in school we study the American Revolution, the Civil War, the Depression, the Civil Rights movement, placing a man on the moon, and other watershed and iconic events in the American experience. There is a reason why we continue to read in school English classes *The Scarlet Letter* and *Huckleberry Finn* and *The Red Badge of Courage* and *Walden Pond* and *The Great Gatsby* and *Death of a Salesman* and *A Raisin in the Sun* and the poetry of Emily Dickinson and Robert Frost and Langston Hughes. They embody those key stories and themes that define us. At the same time, the 13-year span of school before college affords plenty of room for the canon to flex, to become more inclusive, embracing the voices of Amy Tan, Maya Angelou, Chinua Achebes, Isabel Allende, and many, many others.

It is equally critical to say that a student well educated for the 21st C. would be fluent in globalism in general, multiple perspectives on world events (the British vs. colonial vs. Chinese interpretation of the American Revolution as a context for the competing world perspectives on the war in Iraq), and the interrelationships of the global economy and sustainable environments. At the same time, a student well educated for the 21st C. would be fluent in at least one other culture in depth (steeped in a non-English-speaking country's geography, religious beliefs, language, art, and political viewpoints). We know that immersion in another language begun at pre-school is the gateway experience for the acquisition of the language skills but also for interest in another culture. We know that experience with peers in another culture via exchanges, virtual and real, is what produces the empathy requisite for deeper appreciation and understanding.

Hallmark #4: ***Performance*** *(in the fine and practical arts and athletics—as demonstrated by recitals, exhibitions, and competitions).*

A fourth hallmark will be the "high touch" commitment to the centrality of the arts and their place in giving meaning to human life and experience. A student well educated for the 21st C. would be practiced in the practical arts (woodworking and paper-making and computer-assisted design, for example) and fine arts (graphic and performing). A student well educated for the 21st C. would be practiced in "teaming" by participating on teams in athletics, debate, theatre, the school yearbook or newspaper, or online publications.

All of these endeavors will be measured on a "performance basis," literally: It is evident to all when one's jazz band is mediocre and when it is exceptional; likewise one's literary magazine, cross-country team, sculpture exhibit, annual declamation or extemporaneous speech, and the like. Literally, the exhibits and performances and competitions will be captured, over time, via video and added to each student's electronic portfolio.

Re-engineering Schools

As schools evolve, we will redefine our goals in terms of the four hallmark expectations and re-design how we achieve them, allowing *time* to be the flexible variable and *learning* the fixed variable. In a re-engineered school program, the academic disciplines of middle school and secondary school will succumb at last to a much more thematically based and project-oriented program, much like that already in place in the best elementary schools. While the technical proficiencies will be taught and tutored in more skill-oriented formats of instruction, assisted by technologies available to customize and give feedback to students as they progress, the fluencies will be taught as teacher-leaders co-define with students units and themes related to real-world challenges and tasks.

One might imagine the day or week or month or year divided into thirds:

- one-third for customized coursework in the technical proficiencies;
- one-third for arts and sports and leadership development activities;
- one-third for academic team projects that require and develop cultural literacy and several of the fluencies simultaneously, in the context of active experience. Examples might include
    - scientifically and operationally assessing the town's waste management system and its impact on the local environment, studying how the political system works, and making a PowerPoint presentation to local authorities in an attempt to influence policy;
    - undertaking a "Habitat for Humanity" service-learning building project in a poor Latino part of town (or in Central America for that matter) where students utilize their Spanish language skills, develop literally "hands-on practical skills" and provide a commitment to the community, then study the issues of the community back at school;
    - filming a documentary based on oral histories and folktales that develops American themes across history and literature and art and compares them to themes from other traditions (e.g., a study of universal stories and varying cultural perspectives: creation and resurrection myths across cultures; the portrayal of women and "outsiders"; the relationship to the land).

How and Where to Begin

Find the individuals in your school who want to create the next iteration of your school and invest in them. Experiment at first, reducing the structure of "5 courses 5 days per week" for middle and secondary school students and teachers to "5 courses 4 days per week" to liberate one day per week for experiential learning, or take all of January to do so between semesters. Create an experimental school-within-a-school to involve only those students, parents, and faculty eager to try something different and willing to commit their energies to do so. Above all, remember Margaret's Meade's dictum: "Never underestimate the power of a handful of individuals to change the world. After all, it's the only thing that ever does."

Notes

[1] "High School Graduation Rates in the United States," Jay P. Greene. The Manhattan Institute, April 2002. http://www.manhattan-institute.org/cr_baeo.pdf

[2] *Building a Nation of Learners* (http://www.acenet.edu/bookstore/pdf/2003_build_nation.pdf), Business-Higher Education Forum, pp. 9 –11. 2003.

[3] See *Understanding University Success* (http://www.s4s.org/) for a substantial study commission by twenty research universities on what students who matriculate to college need to know in order to succeed at the university level. While the study proposes standards organized by academic disciplines, its introduction indicates the "proficiencies" these standards are meant to develop: "habits of mind including critical thinking, analytical thinking, and problem solving; an inquisitive nature . . . ; a willingness to accept critical feedback . . . ; openness to possible failures from time to time . . . ; the ability to express oneself in writing and orally . . . ; to discern the relative importance and credibility of various sources of information; to draw inferences and reach conclusions independently; to use technology as a tool to assist the learning process rather than as a crutch" ("Introduction," University of Oregon, 2003, p. 8.).

[4] See, for example, the concise statement of Standards produced by the AERO Project, a collaboration between NESA (Near East South Asia Council of Overseas Schools) and CBE (The Council for Basic Education): http://www.nesacenter.org/AERO/AEROhomepage.html.

Patrick Bassett is the president of the National Association of Independent Schools. He writes and speaks frequently on subjects related to independent school life.

Student-Centered Learning in the Knowledge Society

By Jerry Larson

The Changing Society

As we move further into the 21st century, it is clear that the Information Age is upon us. It is difficult to comprehend that the computer is fifty years old, and while it certainly has had an impact on certain areas of living, we still live much the same way we did fifty years ago. However, it is apparent that we are on the edge of some significant changes because of information technology. The Industrial Age has declined dramatically since the invention of the computer. In the 1950s, around 35% of U.S. workers were engaged in manufacturing; today that number is around 10%, with employment dropping rapidly as corporations move their production plants to inexpensive labor markets. Noted business visionary Peter Drucker, author of *Managing in the Next Society,* states that the Information Age and the computer will usher in a revolution of unimaginable changes and transformations, as knowledge becomes the primary resource of the next economy.

Drucker states that knowledge workers will be the dominant group in the workforce. Knowledge "products" such as software, consulting, research and development, and education will become the most valued commodity. We have already seen the dramatic increase in the amount and sophistication of knowledge needed for success in today's emerging global economy. Just as the railroad mastered distance in the Industrial Revolution, the Internet and e-commerce will also eliminate distance, opening up vast opportunities for new markets, distribution systems, industrial designs, and customer behavior. Corporations with monumental buildings and personnel structures as we know them today may vanish, replaced by teams of "portable" knowledge workers. These workers will be contracted by a small management team to complete a project, then they will move on to the next challenge when the project is up and running or the solution implemented. The "Knowledge Society" will provide unprecedented opportunities for all people, regardless of their background, because unlike a business, knowledge cannot be inherited; it must be acquired anew with each generation. Of course there will be shifts in society and work patterns as well, some of which we can already see, with the ability to locate knowledge technology anywhere in the world and transport it to another location rapidly. Thanks to the Internet, a knowledge worker can live in the mountains of New England and work for companies in London, Hong Kong, and New York simultaneously.

With the Knowledge Society clearly poised to dramatically influence this emerging economy, there will be certain demands upon the educational system, and most certainly independent schools. Teaching today uses the agrarian calendar in an industrial setting for an age of information and knowledge. Our schools, and their philosophies, are understandably embedded in a hierarchical model where self-sufficiency and security are characteristics of an autocratic, homogenous society based on the old economy. In the Knowledge Society it will be vital for our students, and for us, to understand and work within a diverse, global community where we will work with networks to build interdependent relationships based on information, knowledge, and most certainly technology.

The acquisition of information and knowledge will be ongoing as we all continue to be lifelong learners. Without the promise of lifetime employment, and in fact with an aging society, as we all live longer lives, we can expect our work lives to extend well into our 60s and 70s. This new, "portable knowledge" working economy will create a demand for schools to develop graduates who can self-market and brand their own "knowledge product line." They will, in effect, be their own boss, dedicated to lifelong education, research, and development in support of their own employability. In the future, the individuals who will be actively sought out by businesses, corporations, governments, and all types of organizations will

- possess creative thinking and strong organizational skills;
- be effective communicators both orally and in written form;
- have the ability to research, plan and make effective decisions; and
- be armed with a strong understanding of team building, business, and financial management.

These skilled workers will have developed what Peter Senge, author of *The Fifth Discipline,* calls personal mastery: *"learning to expand personal capacity to create the results we most desire, through mission, purpose and goals."*

21st-Century Independent Schools: Constructing an Educational Model for Effectiveness

There have been many types of educational reform initiatives. Many schools, certainly more independent schools than we care to acknowledge, limit access to knowledge. In an extreme example, they focus on content; the "expert" teacher shares what he or she feels is important to students seated individually, who in turn often fear a mistake or wrong answer while trying to comprehend the theory or idea that is the lecture topic for the day. While that may be a bit overstated, it is probably fair to say that most teaching practices in the United States are comfortable with their established success and do not yet see the need to acknowledge and accommodate the Knowledge Society.

Many of us teach as we have been taught; however, things are not the same as they were when we were students in the classroom. Subjects are carved up into discrete units and students move from English, math, and history to science, foreign language, arts, and athletics with little thought of crossover or transferable skills. One could argue that writing, solving equations, and reading cross discipline lines, but how often has it been intentional? Through brain research and multiple and emotional intelligence theories, it has become understood that learning is not an isolated or static process, nor does it occur in a vacuum. We enter classrooms and learning situations, in fact all situations, with our prior experience and knowledge as powerful factors in our ability to assimilate or learn new material. Over time, the tools available for that assimilation have changed and advanced greatly in sophistication. The world has changed and it is evident that computer technology is with us for the foreseeable future. By examining our practices and investigating much of the research available to us with a few keystrokes and clicks of a mouse, independent school administrators and educators alike can respond to the "Next Society" as foreseen by Drucker and many others.

In a time when most public schools continue to be caught up by state standards and specific mastery outcomes based upon an industrial paradigm, independent schools are in a position to adapt to the new requirements of the 21st century through innovation and the use of well established educational theories and practice. It is important to take a few moments to review some of the theory and research available.

Carl Rogers, founder of person-centered therapy, distinguishes two types of learning: cognitive and experiential. The former corresponds to academic knowledge, such as learning vocabulary or multiplication tables, and the latter refers to applied knowledge, such as learning about engines in order to repair a car. The key to the distinction is that experiential learning addresses the needs and wants of the learner. Rogers lists these qualities of experiential learning: personal involvement, self-initiated approach, and ongoing self-evaluation. To Rogers, experiential learning is equivalent to personal change and growth, which, in schools, is demonstrated by such things as internships and senior "capstone" projects. Rogers feels that all human beings have a natural propensity to learn; the role of the teacher is to facilitate such learning. According to him, learning is facilitated when

1. the student participates completely in the learning process and has control over its nature and direction;
2. it is primarily based upon direct confrontation with practical, social, personal or research problems; and
3. self-evaluation is the principal method of assessing progress or success.

A major theme in the work of Jerome Bruner is that learning is an active process in which learners construct new ideas or concepts based upon their current and past knowledge. The learner selects and transforms information, constructs hypotheses, and makes decisions, relying on a cognitive structure to do so. Cognitive structure (i.e., schema, mental models) provides meaning and organization to experiences and allows the individual to "go beyond the information given"; it is what Bruner has described as "Discovery Learning." His idea of Discovery Learning is not that students are to discover every bit of information by themselves, but that they are to discover the inter-relatedness between ideas and concepts by using what they already know.

Figure 1

A Comparison of Instructional Practices Adapted from Brooks & Brooks (1999) *In Search of Understanding: The Case for Constructivist Classrooms*	
Traditional/Industrial Classrooms	**Constructivist/Student-Centered Classrooms**
Curriculum is presented part to whole, with emphasis on basic skills.	Curriculum is presented whole to part with emphasis on big concepts and ideas.
Students are viewed as "blank slates" onto which information is etched by the teacher.	Students are viewed as thinkers with experience and emerging theories about the world around them.
Textbooks and workbooks are the primary source of curriculum information.	Curriculum development relies heavily on primary sources of data and hands-on materials.
Strict adherence to fixed curriculum is highly valued.	Pursuit of student questions is highly valued and sought out.
Teachers seek the correct answer to validate student learning.	Teachers seek the students' points of view in order to understand students' present understanding of concepts for use in subsequent lessons.
Teachers generally behave in a didactic manner, disseminating information to students. The sage on the stage.	Teachers generally behave in an interactive manner, facilitating and mediating the environment for students. The guide on the side.
Assessment of student learning is viewed as separate from teaching and occurs almost entirely through testing.	Assessment of student learning is interwoven with teaching and occurs through teacher observations of students at work and through student exhibitions and portfolios.
Students primarily work alone.	Students primarily work in groups.

As far as instruction is concerned, the teacher should try and encourage students to discover principles by themselves. The teacher and student should engage in an active dialog, such as the Socratic method, which is advocated in the Harkness Table approach, and implemented by many independent school faculty. The mission of the teacher is to interpret information to be learned into a format appropriate to the student's current state of understanding, and they should try to instill within their students a sense of confidence in their own ability to learn. Bruner's constructivist theory is a general framework for instruction based upon the study of cognition. Bruner's views are very similar to Piaget's in the sense that he, too, believes that the students can construct knowledge, if they are presented with appropriate chances to learn. Over time, Bruner has expanded his theory to encompass the social and cultural aspects of learning, which take into consideration the whole person. This theory is easily adapted to the independent school philosophy. Finally, Bruner believes that curriculum should be organized in a spiral manner so that the student continually builds, or constructs, upon what they have already learned.

As David Perkins of Project Zero at Harvard's Graduate School of Education tells us, *"No one can live in the world of education long without becoming aware that constructivism is more than one thing."* This can be frustrating for educators, who need to explain a complex practice to a public used to hearing arguments formulated in either/or statements. Constructivism has been identified as an approach to teaching based on research about how people learn. Many researchers say that each individual "constructs" knowledge instead of receiving it from others. Jacqueline Grennon Brooks and Martin Brooks, in their book *In Search of Understanding: The Case for Constructivist Classrooms* (1999), define constructivism as "a theory of learning that describes the central role that learners' mental schemes play in their cognitive growth." They go on in their introduction to articulate five overarching principles considered to be in the constructivist classroom: Teachers seek and value students' points of view, structure lessons to challenge students' suppositions, recognize that students must see relevance in the curriculum, plan lessons around big ideas, and assess student learning in the context of daily classroom investigations. Learning is assessed through performance-based projects. Traditional paper and pencil testing is not the preferred method of assessment. One could conclude that teachers coach and facilitate learning, while expanding on the principles of Ted Sizer's *Essential Schools:* the student is the worker and the teacher is the coach and also a learner. Teachers provoke a student's critical thinking, analysis, and synthesis through the learning process.

Constructivism is both a philosophy and a theory of learning. The key concept of constructivism is that learning is an active process of creating, rather than receiving, knowledge. In so many ways the independent school is a perfect environment for constructivism to take hold. Our mission and philosophy has at its heart the student's experience at each of our schools, for we strive to be deeply concerned about the individual and their education. We are, by our very nature, fundamentally student-centered, even though there is a preponderance of evidence to suggest the traditional classroom is alive and well in independent schools. Now is the perfect time for all independent schools to reflect upon their instructional practices and be responsive to the Knowledge Society and the competition it will bring in the educational marketplace in order to center our focus on our students and the knowledge and skills we all will need for the 21st century.

What Is a Student-Centered School?

A student-centered school is one that recognizes that a student's needs are the driving force behind the development and implementation of all the experiences or activities that make up the learning environment. It is the realization that "education" is an experience that students are directly and personally involved with themselves, rather than thinking of education as something that is done to students. A student-centered culture is focused on students' needs, not on their wants. These needs include a healthy learning environment that nurtures their personal growth, quality afternoon and community activities that increase their learning in a number of dimensions, personal experience that leads to feeling "connected" to the school community, and service-learning opportunities that develop them as responsible citizens. Of course, we must remember that students' needs are not necessarily vast, but they do vary among both individuals and groups of students.

The transition to a student-centered culture does not mean divorcing ourselves from the essential and valuable aspects of the current way we do business (small classes, individual attention, high expectations and behavioral standards, college-preparatory, individual extra help, caring and diverse environment); it does mean a fundamental change in perspective and actions to keep students' needs constantly at the center of our attention. The need to connect big ideas across the traditional discipline lines is a crucial component in the constructivist classroom. Consider exploring the connection between English and history more thoroughly through a course on women in history, where an intense study of the impact of influential women could be complemented by reading selected works about those women along with important works by women authors. The link between science and math could be demonstrated by a study of the parallels between the concepts of pH in the former and number scales in the latter.

An organization's culture is shaped by its attitudes and beliefs, and is embodied in its norms of behavior, structure, and systems. We will need to nurture a willingness to confront and overcome our discomfort with fundamental change, and the potential loss of control associated with letting go of our current paradigm.

Student-centered learning is a learning model, which places the student (learner) in the center of the learning process. It is distinguished by the following characteristics:

- Students are active participants in their learning rather than passive recipients.
- Students have opportunities and increased responsibility to identify their own learning needs, locate learning resources, and construct their own knowledge based on those needs (rather than having a standard or identical knowledge base imparted to all students).
- Students are provided with clear expectations and desired outcomes before lessons are begun.

- "Learning how to learn" skills are emphasized, such as problem-solving, critical thinking, and reflective thinking.
- Learning is considered in the context of differences, which accounts for and adapts to the different learning styles of students.

As educators, we are guided by what is best for the students when assisting or making decisions. Working with our students, we strive for outcomes that are fair, prompt, responsible, user-friendly, and caring, and that leave them with the sense that we truly value the privilege of serving their needs. We are committed to creating an environment where learning takes place anywhere, at any time, in many forms and by diverse means. A student-centered learning environment also supports the development of values and character in students by making them active players in their learning experience and, ultimately, by connecting them to the learning community through a variety of meaningful experiences.

Student-Centered Learning and Technology

The computer is transforming our society. We have immediate access to more information and a wider variety of methods to receive it than was even dreamed possible a decade ago. Technology has provided opportunities for experiential, real-world learning for students and it allows us to communicate with learners around the world in an instant. It can be handily incorporated into both student-centered learning and the Knowledge Society in a variety of ways. For example, in order to help prepare our students, teachers might establish an Internet relationship with schools located in other countries. A middle school social studies class in America might link up via e-mail and Internet video technology with a middle school in Brazil, or a high school economics class might link up with another school or an American businessman in the Middle East. This exact experience was implemented at our school, connecting history and economics classes with a current parent who is an economic advisor in a Middle Eastern country.

Teaching and learning are evolving to use these technology opportunities to prepare us for the world, which is emerging around us. While technology has the potential to transform classroom instruction, it does not drive this necessary change. In many classrooms, and schools, computers sit quietly much of the time, have become costly word processors, or are used primarily as a substitute for telephone communications. This doesn't have to be the case. In some classrooms, and schools, computers have become valuable tools to collect, organize, and analyze data. At the Kent Place School in New Jersey, use of a database program has replaced research "note cards." In addition to highlighting the importance of proper citation, this also provides an excellent opportunity to reinforce the need for ethics in proper crediting of research sources. Technology is also often used to conduct experiments or simulations, enhance presentations, and solve complex problems. In these classrooms situations, technology is transparent and learning is apparent.

Student-centered learning is all about inquiry, individual involvement, creativity, and personal expressions of knowledge in pursuit of big concepts and ideas. Computers are great tools for the construction of knowledge, as they allow the student the ability to be creative and to individualize both self-expression and learning. When used effectively, technology allows the student to be more autonomous, reflective, and collaborative—especially when one considers the application of technology in a distance learning experience, which is becoming more prevalent at the college and university level. The Internet is providing a tremendous number of opportunities for learning outside the classroom via online discussions and web-designed projects. It also allows students to take more responsibility for their own learning, as an increasing number of teachers are posting class notes, assignments, and supplemental information on the web in lieu of handing it out in class or incorporating it into a lesson plan.

Moving Beyond the Classroom

Just as Bruner expanded his theory to include the social and cultural aspects of learning, independent schools must expand the current process of education to evolve into constructivist/student-centered schools. They must move to bring these constructivist and student-centered philosophies and practices beyond the classrooms into the hallways, parking lots, dining halls, athletic fields, stage, clubs, and community at large—as well as into dormitories, if you are a boarding school. In this social context, theorists such as Albert Bandura emphasize the importance of observing and modeling the behaviors, attitudes, and emotional reactions of others. Bandura states:

> Learning would be exceedingly laborious, not to mention hazardous, if people had to rely solely on the effects of their own actions to inform them what to do. Fortunately, most human behavior is learned observationally through modeling: from observing others one forms an idea of how new behaviors are performed, and on later occasions this coded information serves as a guide for action. Social learning theory explains human behavior in terms of continuous reciprocal interaction between cognitive, behavioral, and environmental influences.

Social learning encompasses observational learning and includes attention, modeling, symbolic coding and rehearsal, as well as including self-observation, self-regulation, and motivation, vicarious and self-reinforcement. Because it encompasses attention, memory, and motivation, social learning theory spans both cognitive and behavioral frameworks.

Independent schools, and specifically boarding schools, have long held the assumption that teachable moments and good teaching occur in a variety of contexts; in the classroom, in the dormitory, on the playing field, and at the meal table. Anywhere students and adults interact with each other provides the opportunity for a lesson to be shared. While the philosophical statement is straightforward enough, the challenge comes in structuring a learning community, which consciously sets out to create an optimal environment where learning occurs in a variety of community situations. The challenge is a compelling one, but fully obtainable with caring, knowledgeable adults who are supported in their work.

The shift in social practices since World War II has been well documented. There has been a decline of the traditional family unit, as well as social fragmentation within neighborhood communities. Upwards of 50% of students are from non-traditional families. These changes in social practices have pressured traditional curricula to the breaking point. As this shift has grown and expanded, various educators have struggled to keep up, first by trying to gain a clearer understanding of the impact it has had on children, and secondly by trying to develop new curricula to meet their needs. Research has been conducted in various total-communities, attempting to identify strategies that encourage social and moral learning in a variety of settings, including schools. Popular figures like William Bennett have written extensively on these efforts, as have Ted and Nancy Sizer. The issue then, is not that the problems and the required teaching strategies are unknown, but rather that the educators have not been trained to utilize what has been learned from these studies. In short, teachers, for the most part, continue to teach as they have been taught, and while there have been new strategies and technologies introduced into the school, pedagogy has not been dramatically altered since the industrial revolution.

Our students today enter a world that is vastly different from the world their parents grew up in. The home computer is still relatively new, yet broadband and DSL connections are growing by leaps and bounds. Today children, their parents, grandparents, and friends communicate in real time by Instant Messenger (IM). Twenty-four-hour access to news, weather, and a variety of information on the Internet and television have gone a long way toward erasing cultural boundaries and the separations imposed by distance and time. Today our "neighborhood" doesn't just consist of the street we live on; it may include the friends and family that live halfway around the globe, or our "buddies" in our digital community, some of whom we may never have met in person.

Today's global community requires schools to move beyond the traditional industrial instructional model. Our students, as young as kindergarten age, arrive at our schools with a set of experiences unlike any other generation. Children today expect connections and integration between information they are exposed to and the world they live in. It begins with networks like Nickelodeon and PBS, where they can watch their favorite shows and then be invited to log on to an interactive experience. Research has shown that learning is enhanced when connections are made and disciplines are integrated. Theorists such as Howard Gardner (multiple intelligence and creativity), Daniel Goldman (emotional intelligence), and Robert Sternberg (successful intelligence, creativity, and wisdom), all point out that learning and knowledge go beyond books, lectures, and standardized test scores.

While Benjamin Bloom, Jerome Bruner, John Dewey, Lev Vygotsky and others have always advocated integration of information, few school curriculums have worked toward that end. It is not unusual for a student to learn about ethics in a "life-skills"–oriented class such as health or physical Education, as well as in history or English class, yet the disciplines are rarely related. Nor are subjects such as scientific discovery linked to history or mathematics theory. Additionally, many curriculum "extras," such as character education or student activities, are often present in a vacuum as "add-ons"; thus, little integration and reinforcement occur outside of that specific context. In recent years, however, more and more schools—such as Cheshire Academy, Culver Academy, New Hampton School, and Montclair Kimberley Academy—have successfully integrated character and ethics education into the whole school program.

In this age of ever expanding information and theory, the need for integration is stronger than ever, yet oftentimes educators resist intrusions into their own discipline area for fear of diluting content. As independent schools look toward the future, it will be critical to move beyond traditional departmental, hierarchical organization toward being a true learning community where knowledge and information cross disciplines and content areas.

As we move forward, we must recognize that we all bring our own unique experiences to the classroom, the lunch table, the athletic field, and our community. A constructivist/student-centered approach to education considers prior experience and looks to build bridges to new experiences for a deep understanding of knowledge and a recognition of differences. In a truly pluralistic society, a student-centered approach makes sense; we strive to develop responsible citizens who not only possess intellectual knowledge, but also have the ability to assess information, communicate empathetically and effectively, think critically, and make sound decisions based on principles. In a world with challenges that include ethics, values, and misunderstandings, we must move beyond the assembly-line educational approach of tradition and prepare our schools, our communities, and our society for the next revolution: the Knowledge Society.

Bibliography

Bandura, A. (1986). *Social Foundations of Thought and Action.* Saddle River, NJ: Prentice Hall.

Brooks J.G. and M.G. Brooks (1999). *In Search of Understanding: The Case for Constructivist Classrooms.* Alexandria, VA: Association for Supervision and Curriculum Development.

Bruner, J.S. (1997). *The Culture of Education.* Cambridge, MA: Harvard University Press.

Bruner, J.S. (1990). *Towards a Theory of Instruction.* Cambridge, MA: Harvard University Press.

Carkhuff, R. (2000). *The Art of Helping in the 21st Century.* 8th ed. Amherst, MA: Human Resource Development Press.

Drucker, P.F. (2002). *Managing in the Next Society.* New York, NY: St. Martin's Press.

Gauld, L. and M. Gauld (2002). *The Biggest Job We'll Ever Have: The Hyde School Program for Character-Based Education and Parenting.* New York, NY: Scribner.

Goldman, D. (1995). *Emotional Intelligence.* New York, NY: Bantam.

Nykl, L. and R. Motschnig-Pitrik (2001). *Uniting Rogers' and Vygotsky's Theories on Personality and Learning.* Retrieved on October 20, 2002 from http://www.saybrook.edu/crr/papers

Senge, P.M. (1994). *The Fifth Discipline: The Art & Practice of The Learning Organization.* New York, NY: Doubleday & Company.

Sergiovanni, T.J. (1994). *Building Community in Schools.* San Francisco, CA: Jossey-Bass Publishers.

Sizer, T.R. and N.F. Sizer (1998). *The Students Are Watching: Schools and the Moral Contract.* Boston, MA: Beacon Press.

Sternberg, R. J. (1997). *Successful Intelligence.* New York: Plume.

Jerry Larson has served as head of school at Cheshire Academy since 1999; before that he served as an administrator, teacher, coach, and dorm parent at Tabor Academy, MA, for 14 years. He has graduate degrees in business, counseling, and developmental psychology.

CULTURE AND COMMUNITY

Conundrums of Creating Diverse and Supportive School Environments

By Jeremy Packard

Some would say that diversity and, perhaps, supportiveness as well, begins with numbers. Healthy schools can function very well with a small number of selected "diverse" students—indeed for many years in independent boarding schools that was the hallmark of diversity. Small numbers of racial, ethnic, socioeconomic or international students can flourish submerged in a sea of white, upper middle or upper class American students, provided those "diverse" students have two or three of the following characteristics: 1) realized academic ability at or above the average of the school's norm; 2) socioeconomic standing at or above the norm; 3) social skills and confidence above the school norm; 4) tremendously strong and supportive familial or extra-familial support structures outside the school; 5) individual adult teachers or administrators, of any race or group, with whom they can establish supportive rapport; 6) the opportunity and the ability to develop supportive peer relationships with at least a few of the majority students.

The schools that could most effectively function for the benefit of both a small minority of diverse students and the school as a whole were the most prominent institutions, attracting both a national and international clientele, or, conversely, other schools that could count on particularly sensitive faculty and student support, as well as, perhaps, a strong local recruitment and outside support groups. But this model is barring a catastrophic deepening of current fiscal trends, an outmoded one. "Meaningful" diversity is the grail—with more than token numbers and percentages of non-Caucasians, non-upper or upper middle class students, internationals, and also some with physical, sexual orientation, and learning differences.

For all but a few nationally or internationally known boarding schools, or day boarding schools located in affluent metro-suburban areas, meaningful diversity of the racial-ethnic and class sort is going to be directly related to financial aid. Without one third or more boarding students on financial aid of 40% to 100%, American boarding schools in most locales are not going to achieve "meaningful" diversity. It is possible, with strong international recruitment efforts, to enroll a significant percentage of international students without a generous financial aid program. For all but the best internationally known schools, that international component will be narrowed to Korean, Japanese, Hong Kong, and Taiwanese s'udents who can "pay the full freight." Meaningful diversity in "international students" can only be accomplished by generous financial aid, in order to attract most European, African, and, increasingly, Latin American students, as well as non–East Asian Asians.

Likewise, racial diversity, particularly that which includes African-American or Latino/Hispanic elements, is stunted without serious financial aid commitment. This starts with the board of trustees, and demands a persuasive and ingenious school administration that is committed to diversity, stretching beyond the 10–12% level, which many would regard today as tokenism. Furthermore, recruiting "diversity" students with academic/intellectual ability at or above the school norm is, in most schools, only possible with significant financial aid. Can that aid be supported by endowment as well as a modicum of operating budget funds? At what point, at what percentage/amount of operating budget funds devoted to "diversity financial aid," do parents or boards say "halt!"?

A similar question concerns the fairness of distribution of funds to support domestic and international diversity: charity often still does begin (and end) at home. Schools with a significant number of financial aid internationals know this when it comes time to get them enrolled in U.S. colleges, most of whom give limited or no funds to internationals, particularly in this time of shrinking market value of endowments. My own school has recently, because of endowment market value shrinkage and unbalanced debt/asset ratios, had to cut financial aid, and the first group to be targeted for contraction was internationals receiving more than 60% aid.

Every school's mission, resources, and situation are different, and it is impossible to say that a 35%, a 40%, or a 50% enrollment of students on financial aid is necessary (or possible) to achieve meaningful diversity. I could say that I think that an American boarding school needs *at least* a 20–25% racial minority enrollment, and 15–20% international student body to achieve the kind of diversity that is healthy for our early 21st century times; and that 75% of the racial minorities and 35–40% of the internationals will need to be on financial aid—but that is a subjective and highly personal opinion.

In any event, how do we make our schools supportive for a diverse student body? To some, obvious support would be:

1) *Enroll a critical mass of diverse students,* so that each student feels "supported" by peers who in some way(s) share background and culture. But this is difficult to quantify. Enrolling a significant number of domestic minorities *and* non-white international students will provide skin-color diversity that looks good in the catalogue and may delightfully mirror "global diversity" but is not necessarily strongly supportive for individual students. Asian and African-American students usually have much less in common than white and black Americans. Black Africans and African-Americans are not necessarily mutually supportive. It is interesting for African-American students to observe that students, domestic or international, of South Indian background often have darker skin color than most African-Americans—but that is not necessarily supportive. Upper middle class blacks may not always be support for or be supported by full-scholarship blacks from welfare backgrounds. What the critical mass is will vary tremendously from school to school in terms of size and type of dormitory rooming (e.g., large dorms vs. small houses).

2) *Hire faculty of color and of other diversities (gay/lesbian, disabled, etc.)* to provide role models and friendly support. This ideal runs into difficulty, given the variety of diversities "needed" and the relative shortage of many types of diverse faculty, at least in the economic times of the past decade, who can meet normative expectations for teaching, coaching, and dorm living and can flourish on an often isolated boarding campus. Such faculty not only have to "represent" diversity but also model academic excellence and advising/ support sensitivity for a variety of adolescent backgrounds.

3) *Incorporate a multicultural and/or diversity coordinator into the administration to ensure that someone has as a prime responsibility the support of diversity students and who can help other faculty to help them.* Problems with this approach (beyond the expense of another administrator whom some schools can't afford) are that such an administrator cuts across whatever traditional lines of responsibility exist in the school, and needs not only sensitive counseling skills for adolescents but highly tuned talent for bureaucratic maneuvering. Such a person must have credibility as a faculty member and a worthy administrator with students and peers. In practice there does not seem to be a direct correlation between having a "diversity coordinator" and a more supportive environment for diverse students. Appointment of a diversity coordinator probably should not happen just to "sweeten" the financial pot to attract a minority or diverse faculty member. And, how well can a domestic diversity faculty member with a mandate for multicultural and diversity "coordination" serve the interests of both domestic minority students and internationals, who usually have very different support issues?

4) *Provide organizations that can function in part as support groups, partly as educational organs, and partly as enjoyable social extracurricular "clubs."* International or Diversity Clubs with effective faculty advisors can be very supportive. All schools today must have some group that provides support for and education about sexual orientation. This does not have to be labeled a gay-lesbian-straight alliance, and it does not have to be affiliated with an extra-school organization like GLSEN (Gay, Lesbian, Straight Educational Network)—though for some environments that may be fine. One school has a "Social Issues Club," which has held forums on sexual orientation issues ("Coming out and out and out . . . !") but also on body image issues, and most recently a very interesting open forum on "Socio-economic Issues." Black student unions or African-American societies can flourish constructively, though as with multicultural coordinators, there seems little correlation between the presence or absence of such groups and a pleasant, supportive school environment for black students. Thoughtful, sensitive faculty advisors with committed enthusiasm (not driven just by fulfilling an "extracurricular responsibility"), together with empowered and in some ways rewarded strong student leadership are essential for the success of such organizations.

5) *An administrative organization that facilitates able faculty/administrators making meaningful regular contact with students, comprehending both their academic and personal/social and extracurricular lives, and being empowered to have an impact.* Well-trained and sensitized (and supported) dorm faculty and the time-honored faculty advisor are the foundation blocks, and it is almost impossible to place too much emphasis on professional development of dorm faculty and advisors. But in a school of any

size, a meaningful support structure beyond the basic level is also necessary. Whether this is achieved by a strong "heads of house" system, a "form or class dean" setup, or the residential clusters that decentralize some of our largest boarding schools, there needs to be a strong backstop and support layer between the individual dorm faculty member and advisor and the "dean of students." Strong, experienced and sensitive deans, and heads of school are vital, but the days of a "Mr. Chips"-like dean who knew all things about every student are gone, at least in schools of three hundred or more.

6) *And finally, a) effective personal counselors who can work cross-culturally (not easy to find!); b) an English-as-a-Second-Language program with academic credibility (in which some of the faculty may be able to function quite effectively as multicultural coordinators for international students); c) some sort of "learning support program," even in the most selective of schools, to go beyond the academic conferencing with classroom teachers, for some able students with specific learning differences; and d) a strong student proctor/prefect/house counselor/residence assistant with effective sensitivity training.* Fortunately the stigma attached to learning support is past; even schools desperate to avoid being labeled as "schools for kids with learning disabilities," (or too arrogant to admit that they had any students with learning differences) have set up some extra support systems.

More than anything else, we need to generate constructive discussions among our faculty, informed by our students, on "what works."

Jere Packard has been head of Wyoming Seminary, an 870-student PK through 12 day/boarding school in northeast Pennsylvania, for 13 years. Prior to 1990 he was headmaster of Ridley in St. Catharines, ON, Canada's largest coed boarding school, and a teacher, coach, department head, dean and vice-principal at Choate and Choate Rosemary Hall.

Race and Ethnicity at an International School

By Tina Thuermer

A few years ago, when I was principal of our lower school at the Washington International School, two first graders were hauled into my office. Usually very good friends, Julia and Alex had flown at each other on the playground, and both ended up in my office in tears.

"What's wrong? I thought you two were best friends?"
"Alex hit me!" Julia sobbed.
"Alex, what's the problem, why did you hit Julia?"
"Because she's different!" wept Alex.

At this point I was rolling my eyes and getting ready for trouble—Julia was a Korean adoptee and Alex was a blonde American child. Were they about to play the race card? I gritted my teeth.

"Okay Alex, how is she different?"
"She wears glasses!"
"Well, I wear glasses."
"Yeah, but you're a grown-up," Alex scathingly dismissed me.

Well, Julia had worn glasses last year while they were still friends, so probing further I managed to figure out that now that Alex was hanging out with a bunch of tough guys, it was no longer acceptable for him to have a girl as a friend, and he had to demonstrate that somehow. We talked it over and they parted on good terms, understanding more about their conflict, and reinforcing the impression I had developed over my time at WIS that kids are not born with racist attitudes—they're taught them by adults.

WIS is an international, independent school in Washington, D.C., home to 825 students, approximately a third with two American parents, a third with one American family member, and a third non-American. Founded in 1966, the school has always had a curriculum based on international sources, and features all three levels of the International Baccalaureate Program (primary years, middle years, and diploma programs). As a result of the nature of the school, we run into race and ethnicity issues all the time, and in this respect we are no different from any other school except in one regard—we have the privilege of living every day in such a diverse community that we *have* to talk to each other in order to just make things work. The school's student body represents ninety different countries, the teachers thirty. To add to this potential Tower of Babel, all the students learn in two languages throughout their careers, starting as three-year-olds.

We have many privileges because of the nature of the school, but we have just as many responsibilities. One of those responsibilities is that we must negotiate the meaning of *everything* with teachers, parents, and students who hail from a myriad of cultures, and who may hold opinions about education 180 degrees different from one's own. To do that, we have to be willing to communicate. My assistant principal, who was French, kept thinking I was out in the hall saying "For having sex!"—her first introduction to that useful American idiom "for heaven's sakes!" When we talked about it, we had a good laugh, but learned that we needed to be more careful about listening to each other. She speaks French and I speak English, but we both had good comprehension of each other's language, so we decided that in order to maximize our potential to both communicate and understand, I'd speak to her in English and she would speak to me in French.

One of the privileges we have is that most of the people who come to our school come because of an idea. Those of us who are international in our orientation, who believe in bilingual education, or who are part of mixed-race families know that there are very few other opportunities like it in Washington D.C. We are drawn to WIS because we feel that it's a place like us, a place where we can express all dimensions of our "different-ness" in a way that would not be possible in a more monocultural setting. Therefore, we are fiercely committed to making it work. We have no other choice.

And so in the faculty room we have the English and the French arguing with the Americans as to whether someone can be "excellent" in the first marking period. We have African parents who believe that respect means dropping the child at the school door, and American parents who want to have a say in every single decision the school makes. We have students from Arab and Jewish families in history classes together. On the same day we have a Muslim teacher bringing in pastries to celebrate the end of Ramadan and a Burmese teacher running around with a sprig of mint and a glass of water spraying her students in celebration of Thingyan, the Festival of Water. And, possibly, the most difficult time of all occurs when the World Cup is being played, and people are remembering the last time, in 1966, when their two countries squared off and *somebody* cheated.

Students who have spent any time in the school become part of its conscience. When new students come into the school and express any kind of racist attitudes they are immediately put straight by their peers: "We don't talk like that around here." And yet, a group of eleventh graders was telling me recently what I have observed often in watching and listening to them, that they enjoy hurling what might be called racist or nationalist insults at each other as part of their daily banter. Recently our head of school was talking to two students, congratulating one on his prowess in soccer. The other said to him, "If his skin weren't so dark, he'd be blushing!" The discourse has moved so far beyond the normal bounds of what most in other schools in the U.S. can do that we are in another place altogether. We seem to be exploring new boundaries as to what it means for those from a variety of races and cultures to live together.

It is a delicate place, however, and the students know that. One eleventh grader articulated to the rest that she understands such banter when it goes on around her, and yet she cringes when she hears it because she is afraid someone will be hurt. I'm sure we do have children who are hurt, and that troubles me. Usually, when someone has crossed the line, the students can be trusted to call each other on it, but I'm sure there are times when we don't catch it, when the student who might be hurt doesn't say something. The students claim that they know with whom they can play with in this way and with whom they can't, but none of us is wise and sensitive all the time, and we have to be wary of abusing our privilege. Is there any guarantee that this kind of banter will not be carried beyond comfortable bounds and no one will get hurt? No, we are a human community, but what *is* guaranteed is that it will be talked about, and some agreement will be reached.

The same eleventh graders told me a story of a couple of last year's twelfth graders: Dean, who is from Benin, and Anna, who is half Japanese and half Swedish. Anna was eating M&Ms and when she opened her hand at one point she was holding a brown M&M and a yellow one. "Look, Dean," she said, "there's me and there's you." That reminded me of a visit I made a few years ago to a local independent school's kindergarten. The teacher had cut out silhouettes of the children and they were decorating them with yarn, buttons, and fabric. The thing that puzzled me was that the silhouettes were cut out of green and blue paper, so I asked her why that was. The teacher replied that she did that so the students didn't have to deal with "the skin question." I felt sad for those kids as I thought about one of the exercises our art teacher did every year, where she doled out paper of various colors for the second graders to make cutouts of their faces and decorate them. The kids inevitably argued about what color they were—"no, you're browner than that. . . . I think I need a different yellow. . . . you're pinker," and so on.

How Does It Happen?

How did we get to the place where kids take their variations in skin color so casually that these kinds of dialogues take place naturally and with little or no constraint? How can other schools with a less diverse student body approach this comfort level? I think there are several points worth examining here.

- We got where we are by hard work. Our diversity is by no means a guarantee of cross-racial comfort. Difficult issues exist as they would in any other community. I believe that the difference lies in how they are dealt with—frontally and in every context where they arise—and in the fact that over the years the weight of this experience creates a momentum that sustains itself. New students, teachers and parents are drawn in by the magnetic force of the existing ethos, and conform to it. Once that ethos is established, people who are like-minded are attracted by it, so the community, in a sense, is self-sustaining and self-renewing.
- Part of the comfort comes from the interpersonal relationships of individuals. And this means the relationships of teacher to teacher, teacher to student, and student to student. And we do have an occasional outlier, either among the students or among

the teachers, who simply cannot see past his or her own history without anger at another group.

- We have seen groups occasionally divide themselves and stay apart from the others. When this happens, it usually can be traced to one strong-minded, persuasive, informal leader who is bringing an agenda that she or he has imported from outside the school. Although there are ripples in the pool during their reigns, we find that when this student leaves, the groups settle back to the common denominators that are the norm. The lesson for us has been that it's not all sweetness and light; rather, it takes work and persistence. Communities do take two steps forward and one step back. Keeping the faith keeps you going through the difficult times.
- Stereotypical remarks or behavior are viewed as opportunities to educate, rather than to chide or mock. When we hear stereotypes, we are getting an insight into what information a student does have about another person, as well as information about what he or she needs to know. Many times when a stereotype is uttered, the reaction is so strong that a wall is put up and the person who needs better information shrinks away and learns not to ask more questions. This happened once when we were sitting in a Theory of Knowledge class one day and a student asked a question about someone white dressing "ghetto." Immediately two of our nominally "black" students (one of them has a father from the islands and a mother from South America, the other an African-American mother and an African father) confronted him for using a stereotype. The student who asked the question was genuinely looking for information; however, the other two were reacting to their own histories of being subjected to stereotypical views. We spent some time together as a class working on why the first student had asked the question, what information he was signaling he needed to know, and why the two girls reacted so violently. I hope they left the class feeling that, rather than being shut down when an opportunity came up to look at stereotypes more deeply, they were encouraged to understand each other and then explore the meaning of that stereotype to each of them. In another exercise our school does, we sometimes ask the kids to break into racial groups (as they perceive them) and sit down and come up with stereotypical names, words, and actions that they object to that are often used to characterize them. A group of African-American kids asked the others to "please stop feeling our hair!"

How Does It Apply?

What are the lessons that can be extrapolated from one international school that might apply to other independent schools? Given that most schools don't have our range of cultures, is there something instructive about our 36 years of attempting to make the mixture work? I hesitate to offer ideas about how others can come closer to the principles of creating a home in our schools for the diversity for which so many of us long. Obviously, WIS is in a special place, and we've got where we are today by reason of our nature. Because we are where we are in our development, perhaps we have something that can be extrapolated from by others, and can hold out a hope that joyful diversity does work. In a spirit of humility, here are ideas for schools to ponder:

- First, you have to *want* the diversity, and want it so much that you are willing to give up some of what is "yours" in order to acquire some of what is "theirs." It is only when you have to face giving up part of something you believe is basic to your definition of self that you find out what practicing true tolerance means. Diversity is not a binary system where you either have it or you don't. It's there already, and all our communities have it one way or another. The questions are: What kinds of diversity feel comfortable and supported in our school? Are we ready and willing to expand that universe?
- And on that subject, we have concluded in my twelfth grade Theory of Knowledge class that one of the first things we look for when we are trying to identify bias or bigotry is the splitting of the world into "we" and "they." "Those people" vs. "us" is what humans seem to get down to whenever our own values are questioned or challenged—there's a quick retreat into a smaller community, which may make us feel protected but does not allow for the bringing in of others. This will only be exacerbated with the growth of globalization, but folks, it's here and we have to deal with it if we want to grow. As a famous Arabic proverb says, "The dog barks, but the caravan moves on."
- Diversity can't and won't be done all at once. A plan to diversify a school must be so long-term that it's part of the definition of the institution, and like all change, it will look for a long time like a two-steps-forward, one-step-back progression. If you want it, people outside the school community, who might like to become your constituents, will eventually know that desire. And while it would be wonderful to be perfect each step along the way, what is probably most instrumental in achieving success in building diversity and tolerance is a persistent will to make it happen.
- Diversity committees are a good step, but they are only a step. The diversity committee is not going to be around when the children they attract come to school each day, or suffer their first setback, or find themselves in need of support. In a school that is identifiable by a majority of one culture, those who are "different" need to have a support system that will carry them right from the beginning through to the end. This may take the form of a community within the community which finds "first friends" for children, a fund for helping children from lower socioeconomic backgrounds buy uniforms, calculators or glasses, go on trips, and so on. This is most helpful when the support community comes from the child's home culture. And when your faculty mirrors your student body, part of your job is already done.
- I believe that the underlying lesson we can bring to the table is that communication is key. The lack of it gave rise to the problems of the Tower of Babel, and it's key to people from divergent communities attempting to live together. This does not mean expecting everyone to speak the same language, but that we are willing to learn the languages of others—when one learns in another language one participates in another culture and another way of thinking, and when we do that, we participate in the growth of both ourselves and our worlds.
- On communication: We have to be willing to talk about difficult things. We need to establish communities where we trust each other enough to listen to and talk about

the hard things, and places where we know that, because we're going to keep living next to each other, it's in our interests to figure out how to keep that dialogue going. Creating a safe haven for open conversations about race and ethnicity is an all-school thing. A commitment must come from the top, the middle, and the bottom. If the commitment is missing at any of those levels, children are the lonely victims of our good intentions. Topics of race and ethnicity can't be hidden; the conversation has to take place at every level, in every classroom, and among all the constituents of our schools. This takes courage, and it's not always comfortable.

- It's my belief that the new Golden Rule is "Do unto others as they would have you do unto them." How do we know what that is? How about asking? Poet and author Randall Jarrell once said, "If a pig wandered up to you during a bacon-judging contest, you would say impatiently, 'Go away pig! What do you know about bacon?'" (Jarrell, 74). Maybe a pig is not the best example in our multicultural school; let's change it to "chicken" so I don't offend anyone whose culture does not hold pigs in high regard. So let's ask the chickens about laying the eggs. Let's not guess what the "minority" members of our communities want; let's ask them. Let's ask them to share the lessons we all need to learn to be whole, to be "we."
- It doesn't just happen; you have to teach it. Conflict resolution, woven into the fabric of a school's life, is an obvious and effective method that works wonderfully, not only to make students more accountable for themselves, but also to help them mature morally, develop empathy, and value integrity and truth. Teachers at our school who have used conflict resolution techniques with children as young as three have been astounded at the fruits of it, and they have also been changed in the process. And as a trainer in conflict resolution told our teachers once, conflict resolution can't work if the community is not a true community. Along with conflict resolution, a wonderful program called "Teaching Tolerance," out of the Southern Poverty Law Center, helps schools take a student-by-student approach to developing trust in our schools.

So life goes on in our small, international, multicultural environment. We cannot afford to become complacent just because it's worked in the past. We need to be watchful, thoughtful, and hopeful. Sitting in class each day with our students allows us to believe that the model can work elsewhere, that the students will take what we practice together with them into their families, their cultures, and their worlds. As teachers the reward is to observe them doing the daily work of getting along together—they give us the strength and the inspiration to keep trying.

Bibliography

Jarrell, Randall. *Poetry and the Age.* NY: Knopf, 1953.

Tina Thuermer is a global nomad of American and other origins who has worked as a teacher and administrator at the Washington International School for 17 years, where she is alumni coordinator, Theory of Knowledge, and an English instructor.

Diversifying the Faculties of Independent Schools

Pearl Rock Kane & Alfonso J. Orsini

Why is it so challenging to attract and retain teachers of color? This question was at the heart of The Altman Foundation's inquiry and work with four programs they were funding to increase faculty diversity in independent schools. While each program was directed by a committed, idealistic, and hard-working leader, results were meager. Independent schools were attracting only a few teachers of color and only a few of those who were recruited decided to stay longer than a year or two. Between 1988 and 1999, the DeWitt Wallace Foundation invested $12 million in the Independent School Opportunity Program, which offered schools multi-year grants of $200,000 to $400,000 to schools in the northeast to increase racial diversity of students and faculty. The results for increasing faculty diversity fell short of expectations. Throughout the country, efforts at diversifying faculty yielded similar results. Despite millions of dollars invested, hard work and good intentions, independent schools were achieving minimal success in attracting and retaining teachers of color.

The year was 1997 and the NAIS reported teachers of color constituted 7.3% of the teaching force.[1] But when the NAIS data was disaggregated by schools, the findings were even more troubling. Fully 27% of independent schools had no teachers of color and 17%had one teacher of color.[2] This meant that almost half of all children graduating from independent schools might never interact with a teacher of color over the course of their pre-collegiate education. Further analysis of the NAIS findings indicated that the 7% reported figure shrank to 4.7% when data from independent schools in Hawaii and Puerto Rico were removed. Schools in those regions had higher percentages of teachers of color, inflating the overall results.

These initial findings provided the impetus for an extensive four-year study on teachers of color that included various research approaches, including case studies on schools with different levels of faculty diversity, on-site interviews with heads of schools, diversity directors and teachers of color, a national survey of 691 teachers of color, and the solicitation of personal stories from 25 teachers of color currently employed in independent schools. A full description of the study and the findings are reported in *The Colors of Excellence: Hiring and Keeping Teachers of Color in Independent Schools.*[3]

While conducting the study, and even after the book was published, we received numerous phone calls and e-mails from school administrators inquiring about what they could do to attract teachers of color. Many administrators expressed frustration with their schools' efforts. They were seeking solutions to the challenge of attracting and retaining teachers of color that might be offered in a short conversation. The findings of our study offer solutions but they are not quick fixes. Making schools more receptive to teachers of color requires a change in school culture, and changing the culture will also make schools better educational environments for teaching and learning. In a nutshell, that was the major finding of our study. In this chapter we provide specific recommendations for fostering cultural change that emerged from our findings. We begin by discussing why diversity is important to independent schools and then focus on recommendations for attracting, hiring, and keeping teachers of color.

Why Diversity Is Important

Diversifying independent schools is not simply an issue of political correctness or social justice. It is essential for fulfilling the very purpose of independent education. The mission of most independent schools is to prepare students to live, work, and improve the world they will inherit by making it a more just world. The racial and ethnic composition of the world our students are being prepared to enter is changing dramatically. People of color constitute 31% of the U.S. population and they are exercising increasing influence on politics, economics, and cultural life.[4] Most recent Census Bureau figures project that people of color will constitute 32% of the population by 2010, 38% by 2025, and 47% by 2050.[5] We need to prepare our students of all races and ethnicities to function effectively in a diverse world by creating a microcosm of society within our schools.

Diversity during the formative years of schooling provides the precondition for deepening student awareness of the feelings and perceptions of others and holds out the possibility of achieving greater understanding. Engagement with culturally diverse teachers helps students develop a sense of tolerance toward difference and may assist in breaking down negative stereotypes that students have about people different from themselves. Students of color, as well as white students, benefit when adults of color are part of the power structure of the school and provide positive role models. Independent schools increase their educative effectiveness when they reflect the demographics of the larger society.

Attracting Teachers of Color

To meet the philosophical imperative of diversifying independent school faculties, a school must consider what practical steps it can take. The recommendations that follow summarize the most salient pieces of advice that were gathered from the various studies.

Recruit Alumni/ae of Color

Both our surveys and the personal stories submitted by teachers of color suggest that many teachers of color took their first job at their alma mater. Independent schools that clearly value, respect, and honor diversity and the work of teachers are likely to entice alumni/ae of color to return as teachers themselves. Our national survey indicated that teachers of color are twenty times more likely than white teachers to have attended independent schools themselves. As the number of students of color increases in independent schools, so does the promise of increasing faculty diversity from the pool of alumni/ae already familiar with the culture and job expectations of independent schools.

Schools may consider creating prestigious "chairs" to attract alumni/ae from their own school or other independent schools for a limited number of years since alumni/ae may not want to make a long-term commitment. These initial opportunities may encourage many talented alumni/ae to make a future commitment to a role as an educator. Teach for America claims that 63% of their recruits have chosen to remain in the field of education.[6]

Network with Parents and Faculty

The study suggested that networking within the school community, particularly with parents of color, may be a vital step in finding candidates of color. Our survey indicated that a high percentage of teachers of color found their jobs through a previous association with the school. In their affiliations with churches and other community and cultural groups, parents of color can connect the school with a number of people it otherwise might never know.

Significantly, when parents and teachers are invited to become partners in the schoolwide work of fostering diversity, the values of the school are made explicit, offering an opportunity to educate the entire school community about the importance of diversity. Rather than pay search firms, schools might follow the lead of law firms and other businesses that pay a finder's fee for successful hires.

Open the Door to the Wider Community

Independent schools are often seen as exclusive, gated communities; indeed, many schools are surrounded by walls that give them a veil of mystery and exclusiveness. Since many teachers of color found their way to the school through a previous association, a school with open doors to the community is more likely to attract diverse teaching candidates. Offering summer programs and year-round cultural events that bring people of color from the surrounding community into the school may alter the image of the school and deliver the message that the school values diversity.

Cast a Wide Net in Advertising

Recruitment efforts must move beyond placing openings with placement agencies and hoping for the best. Schools can place ads in local newspapers focused on African American, Asian, and Latino audiences. Teachers can also be encouraged to reach out to graduate classmates and acquaintances they make at conferences to help generate more candidates of color. In sum, the more people involved collaboratively in the work of diversity, the better. Even if initial efforts do not immediately succeed, a collective, visible, and genuine effort may result in increasing the pool of students of color, as well as teachers of color.

Revive Face-to-Face Campus Recruiting

A key step in the process of diversifying a faculty is to know how and where to seek teaching candidates of color. Before independent school teaching agencies existed, representatives of independent schools went to colleges to recruit firsthand. While agencies may succeed in recruiting able candidates generally, the recruitment of teachers of color will require a more concerted, and more personal, effort. The agencies and recruitment organizations consulted in this study expressed their sense of frustration, both with finding candidates of color and with convincing independent schools to recognize the candidates' talents and credentials. Our explorations in this study clearly have suggested that face-to-face recruitment by independent school administrators and teachers may be the most effective means of finding candidates of color.

Candidates of color, particularly those unfamiliar with independent schools, need to be assured that they will be welcome and valued in independent schools. Schools might follow the lead of business organizations and successful endeavors such as Teach for America by having teachers, particularly young teachers of color, involved in campus recruitment. Teachers, to be effective at recruitment, require firsthand knowledge about the mission and culture of their school, in addition to its aims, values, and curriculum, to be spokespersons for their school. If potential recruits, unfamiliar with independent schools, feel some trepidation at entering alien environments, they need firsthand assurances and candid information from current employees with whom they will work.

Hiring Teachers of Color

Beyond efforts aimed at attracting teachers of color, the study shows that thoughtfulness in the hiring process is likely to make the school more appealing to prospective candidates of color.

Look Beyond Superficial Qualities

The teacher recruitment agencies consulted in this study clearly expressed their sense of frustration with convincing independent schools to recognize candidates' varied credentials and talents. The recruitment agencies noted that those responsible for hiring at independent schools often look for an Ivy League degree and middle-class background, or a diploma from an independent school.

While little research has been done on the educational backgrounds of independent and public school teachers, the sample in Kane's 1986 study suggested that 60% of independent school teachers attended colleges classified as "very competitive" or "most competitive."[7] That means 40% of teachers did not attend such competitive schools. Are candidates of color required to meet more stringent criteria for employment?

Many young people of color choose to attend colleges close to home so that they may be near their families, and some choose colleges based upon the financial package offered. Additionally, there is no data to indicate that one has to be a graduate of a highly competitive college in order to successfully teach in an independent school, even if parents do scrutinize such issues in their choice of independent schools.

In addition to credentials, appearance may be a consideration in hiring. A neat, clean appearance is important, but does not mean it is necessary for everyone to look alike. A quality teaching staff is crucial to the success of independent schools, but quality should not be equated with superficial characteristics.

Communicate Genuine Interest in the Individual During the Interview Process

Candidates need to feel they are entering a welcome, humane environment. If the interview process is conducted as an inspection of whether candidates fit a predetermined prototype of "the independent school teacher," then candidates will sense that they are not being valued for their unique, diverse talents. The implicit question in such narrowly conducted interviews is not, "What can you bring and add to what already exists here?" but rather, "How will you fit in with what already exists here?" That implicit question can be the first and fundamental denial of diversity that the candidate experiences. It can be the one that irrevocably and understandably turns the candidate away from the school. If schools can only feel comfortable hiring middle class candidates of color with all the right credentials to satisfy nervous parents, then the groundwork for true diversity has not been successfully laid.

Involve Teachers, Students, and Parents in the Interview Process

The interview process should include meeting other teachers, especially teachers of color, to understand what daily life is like at the school. Interviews by administrators and department heads may mask a very different daily experience seen by teachers, especially teachers of color. Candidates should meet students and parents, especially parents and students of color, during the interview process as well. If the school cannot freely invite teachers, parents, and students to talk with candidates about the culture and daily life of the school, then perhaps the fundamental work of honoring diversity at the school has not yet been done.

Offer Attractive Financial Packages and Tuition Scholarships for Children

Two-thirds of graduating college seniors incur loan debts averaging $16,928, often precluding the possibility of taking a job in teaching.[8] Enterprising schools may attract a diverse teaching force by offering to pay a portion of the loan for each year of service. Such a benefit would make teaching a viable option to a broader pool of college graduates.

Ensuring wages and benefits that are at least competitive with public schools may attract more people of color to teaching in independent schools. This is particularly important at a time when, perhaps more than ever, capable people of color are being sought by public schools and other professions eager to diversify.

Tuition scholarships for children of teachers appear to be another financial incentive. In our study, many teachers of color took their jobs in independent schools because they wanted to provide an excellent educational experience for their own children. This path serves to both attract and retain teachers of color while helping to diversify the student body.

Retaining Teachers of Color

Increasing the numbers of people of color in schools is simply not sufficient. Schools must provide an environment to which teachers of color are drawn and in which they are willing to *stay*.

Ensure that Leaders Openly and Clearly Commit to Diversity

The board and head must make evident to the school and the larger communities that they value and are actively engaged in building diversity. When parents express complaints about teachers of color, department heads and administrators must be skillful at sensing discrimination and be ready to defend good teachers who are being questioned because of race or ethnicity rather than ability. Indeed, all members of the school community must be ready to stand up to inappropriate comments and behavior from anyone in the community.

Involve the Diversity Coordinator in Decision Making

A diversity coordinator, if such a person is designated, should be part of the head of school's "cabinet" and have influence in decision making. In addition, the diversity coordinator should not become the only person in the school working to foster diversity and embrace difference. The work of diversity should be everyone's work, involving the diversity coordinator as the point person, in conjunction with school staff involved with admissions, hiring, curriculum development, academic affairs, and even the board of trustees.

Set Measurable Institutional Goals and Communicate on Progress

The head of school and board of trustees, after taking the time to educate themselves about diversity, should honestly confront the issue of how diverse they are willing to allow the school to be. They then need to set measurable institutional goals that they can communicate with the entire school community. The board can begin by looking at the composition of its own membership. The head of school can look at the composition of the administrative team. Clear communication of the school's agenda and goals is crucial because more often than not, a void of information and communication is filled with suspicion and cynicism. To maintain the integrity of the school's commitment, statistics on openings, interviews conducted, and positions filled should be made available at least to the faculty. The school community needs to know what efforts are being made to hire a more diverse faculty. A school's goals must be realistic, with progress toward those goals benchmarked and evaluated. The school's commitment to diversity and intercultural understanding should be clearly expressed in all of its literature, at open house presentations, and in every facet of daily life. Any outsider or visitor should know the schools' stance on diversity. As we shall see below, this commitment is also evident in the way a school allocates resources.

Provide Comprehensive Orientation

All teachers, and particularly teachers of color and others who are new to independent schools, benefit from having a thorough orientation to the school's mission and culture, and to the idiosyncrasies of its everyday life. This orientation needs to be followed up with structured, comprehensive mentoring, even with experienced teachers who are new to the independent school world. Comprehensive mentoring programs, such as the one established at the Lawrenceville School in New Jersey, provide mentors with training and guidelines for their work, define the relationship between mentor and new teacher, state the connection of mentoring to the evaluation process, and provide adequate time and compensation to mentors.

Don't Overburden Teachers of Color

If independent schools hope to retain teachers of color, they need to ensure that dealing with diversity is part of every teacher's responsibilities. The one or two teachers of color on staff, as is often currently the case, cannot be called upon to handle every racial issue, to deal with the problems of every student of color, to be the main line of communication to parents of color, and to organize every multicultural assembly and club. Young teachers of color are already faced with the struggle of trying to hone their skills in a new profession. If diversity will be a lived part of a school's mission, it must become part of the lives of all members of the school community, not delegated to the few teachers of color in the school.

Scrutinize Curriculum for Inclusiveness

Effective schools treat curriculum as a live document, one that is continuously being reviewed in terms of meeting the school's objectives. Part of the school's ongoing assessment should be a consideration of the extent to which the curriculum is inclusive and the extent to which it fosters intercultural understanding. At least one school visited systematically "mapped" the entire school curriculum for the degree to which it was genuinely multicultural. Self-reflective, ongoing, and honest assessments of the explicit and implicit messages of school curriculum are a necessary part of school diversity.

Make Exposure to and Awareness of Diversity a Way of Life

Through activities, trips, and service learning , students need to be exposed to people different from them, especially the people of color who statistically make up such a large portion the broader communities that students are part of. As important as this is, no amount of exposure to diverse people outside the community can counterbalance a glaring lack of diversity among the people within the community who most seriously influence and affect students: their teachers.

Make an Ongoing Commitment to Anti-Bias and Diversity Training

All teachers, administrators, students, and parents need to be exposed to diversity training on an ongoing basis, not just through one-time presentations that presumably put the matter to bed. They also need to be made aware of what it means to be a student or teacher of color in a largely white environment. People's voices from every part of the community need to be heard; nothing speaks more strongly than the firsthand sharing of experiences and perspectives from people both within and outside the community. As one interviewee stated, "recognize difference; don't pamper it." Until the school is truly a multicultural environment that acknowledges and honors diversity, one cannot expect teachers of color to enter independent schools or to stay in them if they discover a grim reality.

Devote Resources to Financial Aid for Students of Color

Boards of trustees and heads of school must also make a priority raising money for financial aid for students of color. This is a major step in the effort to diversify faculty, in that it builds a critical mass of students of color, expressing to candidates that the school values diversity in fact, not just name. Candidates of color feel that they have an important role to play in a school with a diverse student body, and feel that there is at least a community of students and parents with whom they can feel a more immediate affinity. In our study of NAIS statistics, the percentage of faculty of color correlated most strongly with a school's percentage of students of color and percentage of financial aid given to students of color.

Fund Professional Development

Independent schools need to offer support for graduate study that permits career building and enhancement, as well as support for culturally relevant professional development for all teachers. Schools should consider offering a bonus to teachers who spare the school's professional development budget by finding outside funding for professional development through scholarships or grants such as those provided by the National Endowment for the Humanities or the National Science Foundation. Independent schools need to show that they make diversity a priority by devoting resources to it, even scarce resources.

Conclusion

Many people reading this chapter may regard money as the essential component to diversifying schools. Certainly a school's financial resources allow for a response to our recommendations by providing generous financial aid for students of color, attractive remuneration packages for faculty, and professional development opportunities. But our data revealed a surprising finding. Some of the most well endowed NAIS schools in our study were among the least diverse, and vice versa. Having money is only part of the solution.

Our findings suggest that diversifying independent school faculties requires a great deal of thought and planning coupled with commitment and action. The key seems to be getting beyond having only one or two faculty members of color (or none, in a tragically large number of schools) to reach a critical mass into which more students and faculty of color can enter with assurance and hope. Perhaps the greatest care must be taken and the most serious work done by every member of the community in the early phases before the time when diversity begins to beget diversity.

By their very nature, independent schools have historically cultivated their exclusivity through their pursuit of excellence. This has tended to make potential clients want them more, clients who have traditionally been white people with resources. The question in the decades ahead will be whether independent schools can change with a demographically changing America. Can independent schools alter their conception of excellence and their complexion to match a nation and a world which is poised to become one of many faces and many cultures? If they do not change as such, they may soon find that their missions are antiquated and they are no longer meeting their promise of preparing young people to excel in and contribute to the world at large. In this regard, a diverse independent school is the best school for everyone: for those immediately connected with it, and even for the many millions of people who will never even visit an independent school, but will certainly work and live beside those who have attended independent schools.

Notes

[1] National Association of Independent Schools, NAIS Statistics, 1999 (Washington, D.C., 1999), Table 13.

[2] These figures are based on an analysis of the 1997–1998 National Association of Independent School database. Editor's Note: Data from 2002–2003 indicates significant progress, with teachers of color now representing a greater percentage of the teaching force.

[3] Pearl Rock Kane and Alfonso J. Orsini, *The Colors of Excellence: Hiring and Keeping Teachers of Color in Independent Schools* (New York, NY: Teachers College Press, 2003).

[4] Last date for which data is available; U.S. Census Bureau, Statistical Abstracts of the United States (2002), No. 15, Residential Population by Race, Hispanic Origin, and Age: 2000 and 2001, includes people of Hispanic origin of any race. http://census.gov/prod/www/statistical-abstract-02.html

[5] Last date for which data is available; U.S. Census Bureau, Statistical Abstracts of the United States (2002), No. 16, Resident Population by Race and Hispanic Origin Status-Projections: 2005-2050; includes people of Hispanic origin of any race. http://census.gov/prod/www/statistical-abstract-02.html

[6] Teach for America, Alumni Survey, 2002, reported in a phone conversation with Lauren Glick, marketing associate, Teach for America, 19 September 2003.

[7] Pearl Rock Kane, *Teachers in Public and Independent Schools: A Comparative Study* (New York: Esther A. and Joseph Klingenstein Center for Independent School Education, 1986), pp. 22–23.

[8] In 1999–2000 64% of college students graduated with student loan debt; the average loan debt has nearly doubled over the past eight years to $16,928. See Tracey King and Ellynne Bannon, *The Burden of Borrowing: A Report on the Rising Rate of Student Loan Debt* (State Public Interest Research Group's Higher Education Project, March 2002), http://www.pirg.org/highered/burdenofborrowing.pdf

Pearl Rock Kane is associate professor in the department of organization and Leadership at Teachers College, Columbia University, and director of the Klingenstein Center for Independent School Education.

Alfonso Orsini is the director of Emirates National School in Abu Dhabi, United Arab Emirates.

Toward a More Inclusive Community

By John Waters

In the summer of 2003, the Supreme Court ruled on the importance of diversity to the educational system. The dichotomy of opinion has been striking as some feel the pace of change has been been at a snail-like pace while others believe it is moving at the right speed. So much has been spoken and written about the concept of diversity that the word has become undefinable for many. The resulting confusion has become, in many settings, an impediment to change. By changing the focus from diversity to inclusivity, it has been our experience at The Pike School that the conversations have been much more productive.

Independent schools will need to be persistent in their efforts to convince many in the outside world that it is our mission to create inclusive environments that welcome and embrace children and adults from a variety of backgrounds and experiences. High tuitions and competitive admission markets make it easy for people to believe that our schools are only interested in perpetuating the "old boys'" networks of the past. Therefore, we will need to explain the value *for all* in creating inclusive communities where our children will have the opportunity to interact with and learn from others with a variety of traits and beliefs as we prepare them for the future.

Creating an inclusive community is difficult work that requires a long-term commitment by the school and its many constituencies. The first step is to evaluate honestly the current school culture. At The Pike School, we began by identifying an outside consulting group who would work with us by doing some training of faculty, staff, and trustees. The training included ways to create a climate where candid discussion can take place. Also, there were a variety of exercises that helped us identify issues about our identities and values as individuals that impacted our perceptions of the world. Our consultants then conducted a series of 23 focus groups involving 224 parents, faculty, and students (out of a school community that includes 428 students) as the basis for a multicultural assessment report for our school. The report was intended to serve as a "map to guide the community forward."[1] One of the lessons we learned in this work was that there is no final destination. It is the journey that is important, and we believe that every institution must undertake its own trek.

One of our first steps was the creation of a diversity action committee (DAC) that included faculty, staff, administration, trustees, and parents. It was evident that the work would be demanding as we struggled to come to consensus on the name for our group.

Conversations about the definitions of diversity and multiculturalism and the appropriate role for this group took a significant amount of time. The group met approximately once every four to six weeks during the school year and was charged with making recommendations to the head of school. The work was exhilarating at some times and frustrating at others. The exhilaration came from finally addressing an important issue that had been bubbling beneath the surface while the frustration was the result of the struggle to identify the concrete action steps required to move ahead. The frustrations were the result of the breadth of the topic and the difficulties in building clear consensus in a diverse group that had very different opinions about where we were and where we needed to go.

After one year, the committee had had many important conversations, but it was unclear where those conversations were taking us. We decided to hire an outside facilitator who could help develop clearer agendas and keep us on track. This decision and the perspective of someone from outside the community allowed us to regain some momentum that had been lost.

An important turning point for us was giving ourselves permission as a school to look at some aspects of building an inclusive community and leave other aspects to be addressed at a later time. Too often, we found ourselves blocked by guilt because some important issue had been omitted from the conversation. Someone asking if we were equally concerned by the challenges faced by families whose children had learning-style differences could bring a discussion about the challenges faced by families of color to a halt. In our desire to support everyone, we found ourselves overwhelmed and unable to act. We responded by listing many areas of concern and then choosing some to work on in the short term while others would be addressed in future years. Building an inclusive community is a task that is never finished, as there will always be ways to improve. The topic has to become an ongoing one in the life of the institution, which in turn allows the school to take the long view.

Before a school begins the process of examining itself and its ability to create an inclusive environment, it must make clear its willingness and intention to make changes in its culture. The values that are part of our mission statement and serve as the foundation of our strategic plan state the following: *We believe that by recognizing, respecting, sharing and appreciating our similarities and differences, we grow and flourish.* This statement, which had the full support of the board and administration, was a source of strength when we encountered the resistance that can and should be expected as part of the process of instituting change. Independent schools are proud of their traditions of excellence. Families make large commitments of time and money to our schools because they see the value in our schools for their children. Therefore, it is inevitable that a significant number of families will express concern over any initiative that could result in fundamental changes. We have all heard the refrain, "When I was in school, we did it this way, and it worked." Therefore, as programs change, there is a sense of loss that needs to be acknowledged. However, that sense of loss cannot be allowed to stand in the way of reacting to the realities of today's world.

We learned that even though we believed we had made it clear that to live up to the values of our mission statement Pike needed to be a more diverse and inclusive community, we had to do more to get that message out and to hear more opinions on that matter. The board had already made the decision that the school was committed to being an inclusive community where all members would be welcomed and valued for the many contributions and perspectives they would bring to the school. Therefore, we wanted to be clear that we were not conducting a referendum on whether or not the community wanted change. Rather, we needed input on the nature of the change that would be required.

At Pike, we met significant resistance and learned some important lessons in the process. We live in an era of instant communication, which has created insatiable appetites and expectations for more and timelier information about all that we do. On the one hand, we felt the need to allow our DAC enough time to discuss and consider the myriad possibilities and challenges ahead of us as we sought to find ways to make Pike a more inclusive community. The diversity of the committee members and their perspectives meant that we needed to spend several meetings to come to consensus on areas of focus and processes we would use to move forward. However, while we were having these important conversations, those who were not on the committee wondered what was being discussed. The lack of information created some anxiety in those who were worried that the school might be considering fundamental changes in a program that they supported and did not want changed.

A concerned and vocal group of parents began to voice concerns that in an effort to become more diverse and inclusive, Pike might lower the standards and expectations that had attracted their families to the school. While some of the concerns were being voiced behind the scenes in private conversations, we were able to deal with them more directly because of two structural features of our school. When we created the DAC, we made the conscious decision to include members of the community who had voiced concerns about the direction of the school. Those members aired their feelings as well as those of others who shared their opinions. Also, as head of school, I chaired the committee for the first two years so there could be no doubt as to the priority of this issue. Therefore, parents sought me out to share their interests, hopes, and fears as we moved forward. In one instance after I had heard from a group with concerns, I convened a meeting of that group with the chair and vice chair of the board and me. While there were differences of opinion at the end of the meeting, there was more clarity about where everyone stood and what the priorities of the school were.

The creation and implementation of a web-based survey that asked students in grades five through nine, all parents, and all faculty, staff, and administration to share their perspectives on school culture and climate represented the next step in our evolution as a school. The goal of the survey was to identify more closely the concerns and hopes of our community to help us set our course in the most effective way. Respondents were asked to describe their personal experiences at Pike with a particular focus on the degree to which they felt the community was welcoming and inclusive to all. A majority of the community responded to the survey and we are in the early phases of evaluating the data. A major agenda item for the coming year will be to share that data with the entire community and use the responses as a way to consider the need for change. We are pleased that several issues that have always bubbled below the surface have been brought into the light of day, which, in turn, will give everyone permission to address them. Our goal is not to create unanimity in the school community, for such a goal is unrealistic in such a complex area. Rather, we hope to create an environment where all feel comfortable in sharing their views because they know the school supports each member's right to speak his or her mind without fear of being shamed, blamed, or attacked.

What have we learned that might be helpful to others interested in creating a more diverse and inclusive community?

- The commitment to becoming more diverse and inclusive must be strong and shared by the board and administration from the start.
- Change in a school that is thriving can be threatening to people who chose the school because they like it as it was.
- People need to be reminded that the possibility of change does not represent a condemnation of what came before since times and circumstances change as well.
- Consistent communication is essential to minimize fear of the unknown.
- Outside facilitators can bring a neutral perspective that can be very helpful.
- Training for faculty, staff, administration, and board is important to help them examine the opportunities and challenges any institution faces as it tries to become more inclusive.
- All voices must be welcomed in discussion (including those who may oppose an initiative to be more diverse and inclusive).
- Managing the pace of change is an inexact science at best, given that some feel not enough is happening soon enough while others voice the need for more caution.
- Understand that this work will never be finished and that the journey is more important than the final destination.

We believe that all of our students will not be prepared for the ever more connected world they will inhabit as adults unless they understand the range of the human experience and have the skills to see and value the possibilities inherent in that diversity. By teaching them to appreciate how others see the world, we are preparing them for a more productive and fulfilling life. The work is often hard and painful, but the end result for our students and families makes it more than worth it.

Notes

[1] Editor's Note: In 2004, the NAIS developed a new diversity tool, AIM (Assessment of Inclusivity & Multiculturalism) for schools. For more information, see the NAIS website: www.nais.org.

John Waters is the head of school at The Pike School, a co-educational independent elementary school in Andover, MA. He has been a teacher and coach for all of his 29 years in education and is the proud father of three teenagers.

Solomon, Thoreau, and the Queen of Sheba: Fostering Spiritual Literacy in School

By Patricia T. Hoyot, Susan B. Altan, Patricia Orr Stephens, Linda Swarlis, & Anne Dilenschneider

> *"How do ethical and spiritual issues become a part of a student's life?" "How can schools make students aware of our heritage of rich, multiple spiritual and ethical beliefs?" "Do God and worship belong in our diverse school communities today? If so, How? Where?"*

Many schools struggle with these issues only to put them aside because they are too difficult to address, too controversial, or just too much to add to the already overloaded schedule. The faculty and students at Columbus School for Girls (CSG) found themselves forced to tackle these issues as they began revising the 1984 edition of the school's chapel *Book of Services*. This revision project became a complete re-envisioning of the role of chapel and religion in the institution. A six-year process of research, reflection, writing, collecting, and editing resulted in the publication of *Meditations of the Heart: A Book of Interfaith Services,* to be used during the first part of traditional and weekly assembly programs. The services are designed to provide a time that:

- encourages and instills a sense of wonder, the basis for all spirituality
- provides a challenge to grow in intellect and spirit
- preserves the moral and spiritual ideas that have traditionally governed the school
- opens hearts and minds to the diversity of the world's great moral and spiritual traditions
- fosters respect for diversity through spiritual and cultural awareness and literacy
- presents thoughts and writings of great religious leaders, spiritual guides, poets, and philosophers
- preserves the traditions and history of the school
- builds community by providing a timeless bond within the school community, past, present, and future

The journey from revision to publication was often arduous, but CSG was fortunate to be able to build on a rich tradition of chapel services that had begun in 1904. The original services included prayers, hymns, scripture readings, and usually a short lesson offered by the head of school. Each service provided an opportunity for both students and faculty to reflect on themes such as character, service to others, or wisdom, thereby promoting the moral and ethical standards that governed the school. Because CSG was founded on Judaic and Christian principles, the content of the services during the school's first century was primarily from those two faith traditions.

As CSG became more inclusive and more diverse, it became clear that the chapel programs as well as the *Book of Services* needed to reflect the changing school population and the world outside the doors of CSG. The tenth revision committee, brought together in 1997, included alumnae, parents, faculty, and students. Many of the early meetings were spent developing a common vision and unity of purpose. The questions the committee considered included: "Are our chapel services actually worship services?" "Is worship even appropriate in a secular school?" "How do we present the beliefs of each religion without offending anyone?" "Is the service format too Christian?" When the committee reached an impasse over these questions, the head of school wrote a letter that allowed the committee to move forward with unity of purpose. The following excerpts are from that letter, written by CSG's former head, Dr. Patricia Hayot:

> As I have spoken with my colleagues who lead and teach in other independent schools across the country about our project. . . . [and] as I examine mission and philosophy statements of independent schools without specific faith connection (Jewish, Catholic, Episcopalian, etc.), it is clear that virtually all—regardless of region, size, day or boarding or organizational structure (coed, all boy, all girl) acknowledge the centrality of attending to the moral and spiritual dimensions of the children they serve. This is often framed in the context of providing education of the "whole child," just as it is at CSG.

Part of the CSG mission statement includes promoting "the social, academic, physical, emotional, spiritual, and aesthetic development" of students, and faculty often speak of respect, honesty, fair play, justice, and honor for the opinions of others. This implies that we are open to different ideas and that we will provide opportunities for students to learn of these as well as to have a place to offer their own opinions, whether they have a strong faith tradition or none at all. Dr. Hayot continues:

> . . . The central question facing our committee is *how to preserve our commitment to educating the whole child, to promote our strong moral climate, and to advance the spiritual and moral development of each of our girls in our diverse school community, while being respectful of our own tradition and history.*
>
> . . . By insisting that our chapel services (or gatherings or convocations) be considered either worship or not, we lost sight of our commitment in our mission "to promote the social, academic, physical, emotional, spiritual, and aesthetic development of every child," regardless of her faith tradition or absence of a faith tradition. I do not believe that we can dictate worship for anyone; calling a gathering

> worship hardly guarantees that everyone will actively participate in worship. Likewise, avoiding the term *worship* hardly ensures that no one will engage in worship.
>
> Our challenge I believe is to create a book that will invite dialogue about those behaviors that heal, that reconcile, that uplift and transform; behaviors such as mercy, forgiveness, hopefulness, charity, and tolerance, while at the same time educating our community about major faith traditions—traditions which recognize and hold dear universal values we wish every CSG child to embrace.
>
> Education that is meaningful begins and ends in reverence. So does moral reflection and moral behavior. We do not hurt or destroy that for which we have reverence. How can our services, or gatherings or convocations, serve the purpose of promoting reverence thoughtfully and decidedly . . . leading perhaps some to worship and others not, (but) that will provide all with an opportunity to understand the values of our community and to experience the reverence of the moment.

It is difficult, if not impossible, to revere or respect that which is not understood. The '84 revision committee of the *Book of Services* showed great foresight by breaking the long tradition of using only Judaic and Christian selections and adding secular readings as well as some from other faith traditions. There was, however, often a lack of understanding from the school community of what was being read, and why. Using various religious and cultural readings in any setting might show a *tolerance* of the diversity, but *understanding* others is a higher goal that leads to respect and reverence.

Dr. Hayot summarized as follows:

> We speak often and passionately about context in our school. We are constantly challenging one another to articulate context for our ideas about curriculum, projects, programs and requirements. How then, can we provide a context for our discussions of spiritual and moral values—for what some of us recognize as "educating the heart of a child"? How can we erase the ignorance about faith traditions of the world in support of our commitment to educating the whole child?
>
> I believe our committee has an outstanding opportunity to create grand and significant meaning for our weekly gatherings. We have the opportunity to build upon our rich history, which was grounded in Judaic and Christian tradition; to embrace and be enlightened by the diversity of faiths of our present school community; to promote universal values associated with the world's great religions; to provide sanctuary in our over-charged lives, for strengthening our community, while demonstrating our loyalty to our mission of educating the whole child.

Following this letter, there were discussions from which emerged four principles that governed the process of selecting the materials for the book. These principles were presented in another letter from Dr. Hayot just a few months later:

1. *Reflection upon and strengthening of the human spirit:* The primary focus of the services will be to inspire participants to (1) reflect upon the meaning of spiritu-

ality, (2) deepen an understanding of the human spirit, and (3) instill a sense of wonder as we celebrate the gift of life in all its joys and sorrows. Joining together to reflect upon higher purposes and to develop an ethical and spiritual literacy will give living expression to our mission and deeper meaning to school life at CSG.

2. *Context:* A context should be provided for all services. This may be in the form of historical or religious information that will serve to educate and enlighten participants or it may be in the form of explanation as to why a particular selection has particular meaning to our school.
3. *Participation:* All services will provide participants with an opportunity to respond: Faculty or students may be asked to come forward and offer personal reflections. The sharing of music and readings, in common voice, is another aspect of the rituals that strengthen the bonds of community.
4. *Ritual:* Rituals that bind us together as a community should be incorporated into every service: the flag ceremony, the pledge, the school prayer, and a minute or two of silence or reflection. This quiet time will provide each participant with an opportunity to reflect upon how the particular service relates to her own experience and faith tradition; it will serve to deepen our ties as we realize that both our common beliefs and our diverse views serve to enrich our school family.

Once these guiding principles were in place, the committee began a discussion of *spiritual literacy* under the guidance of the late Dr. Howard Wilson, professor of religion and philosophy at Capital University, Columbus, OH. He stressed the importance of global spiritual and cultural literacy and the necessity for schools to "engage in the significant work of deepening students' knowledge of the world's sacred texts."

The committee of faculty, students, alumnae, board members, and parents divided into groups and, meeting throughout the spring, chose readings from which the new services would be created. The process included reading and using a number of books, as well as studying the latest revision of the *Book of Services* to decide which traditional readings to keep. The result was a list of more than 250 possible readings that were categorized by faith tradition and also by keyword and theme: character, community, joy of life, life experiences, natural world, peace and justice, sense of wonder, service, traditional school, wisdom, and knowledge. The committee also noted for each selection whether the author was female or male, the piece religious or secular, or the source ancient or modern. This information was crucial in maintaining balance.

A reference section, unique to this edition, grew out of the committee's desire to focus on spiritual literacy and educate at a deeper level. The key questions that guided the work of creating this section were:

- Where does one include sacred writings necessary to understand a faith, but that are too holy or specific to the beliefs of one religion for an interfaith service?
- How might the book address the specific interests of an all-girls school?

- Where was the place for the remaining significant selections too numerous to include in the basic services?
- How could one provide an understanding of unfamiliar religions?

From these questions grew a reference section consisting of essays on the world's major faith traditions, each including a section on the role of women as well as extensive sections of additional readings organized by theme. The essays were shaped and edited by leaders and members of the various faith traditions. CSG was fortunate to have present in Columbus the religious diversity that allowed the committee to draw on a wide variety of insights, information, and perspectives.

The Rev. Dr. Anne Dilenschneider, a CSG alumna now working in California, contributed her experiences and expertise in various faiths, as well as her knowledge of the history of the school, to suggest additional readings and to develop the format of the services. Using her doctoral work, which traces spiritual development from soul, to heart, to mind, to strength, the committee worked with a uniform service template based on a "call and response" flow. Thus, each service opens with the traditional CSG invocation from Psalm 14, and includes, at a minimum, the following: a responsive or unison reading, a hymn or song, a moment of reflection, and a conclusion with the traditional school canticle.

The committee then turned its attention to sifting through the overwhelming number of subjects, sample services, and readings to bring them into a manageable order. Intense editing sessions resulted in the creation of 24 services; an additional 25th service offers a pattern for creating an original service using the reference section or other resources. The themes of the services were organized using the same progression of soul, heart, mind, and strength that was used for the format of the individual services. Thus the themes were consolidated and organized into the following nine major headings with individual services as follows:

1. NATURAL WONDER
   Spirituality, like all personal growth, begins with our response to nature and life. Services include *Appreciation of Life, Beauty (Awe) of the World,* and *Environment.*
2. LIFE EXPERIENCES
   Spirituality deepens through reflection and relationships. Services include *Love, Friendship,* and *Loss.*
3. CHARACTER
   We hone our spirituality through the challenge of understanding other viewpoints. Services include *Inner Qualities, Right Thoughts, Right Actions,* and *Courage.*
4. KNOWLEDGE
   We reach a new understanding. The service is *Value of Learning.*
5. WISDOM
   We begin to move into and live our new understanding. Services include *Seeking Wisdom* and *Perspectives.*

6. CREATIVITY
   We make our experience, reflection, and understanding uniquely our own. The service is *Harmony of Soul.*
7. COMMUNITY
   Based on our experience, reflection, and understanding, we choose to become agents of change in the wider community. Services include *Honoring Parents, Respect for Others,* and *National Community.*
8. SERVICE
   Each individual's contribution can make a difference. Services include *Serving Others* and *Compassion for Others.*
9. PEACE AND UNITY
   We choose lives of compassion and respect, and we celebrate our world community. Services include *Common Good, Non-violence,* and *Peace and Unity.*

These services flow from the strong traditions and standards that have been the essence of school life at CSG since its founding in 1898. These values and ideas are explained and preserved in other sections of *Meditations of the Heart:* History of the School, CSG Philosophy and Mission, Traditional School Services, Songs and Hymns, School and Class Songs, School Prayer, and School Traditions, the latter one giving details of cherished CSG traditions.

In summarizing the work, Dr. Hayot states, "In today's world where religious tenets are sometimes used to divide and oppress, a tremendous opportunity exists to inform, inspire, and ignite the spirit of those we are privileged to serve by bringing into focus teachings that have guided humanity throughout the ages. This book will serve as one way to enlighten and educate young people and faculties about the myriad ways the sacred has been made accessible for more than 4,000 years. . . . I am confident that Meditations of the Heart will continue to guide CSG's journey in seeking to enhance our understandings of one another's spiritual journey."

Spiritual literacy is more than knowledge—it's also about wisdom and wonder and engagement!

Dr. Patricia T. Hayot is currently the head of school, The Chapin School, New York City. **Susan B. Altan** is the director of upper school, co-chair of the revision committee, Columbus School for Girls. **Patricia Orr Stephens** teaches lower school music, co-chair of the revision committee, CSG. **Linda Swarlis** is director of information services and library director, CSG. The **Rev. Dr. Anne Dilenschneider**, CSG '73, is a national spirituality and leadership consultant in San Mateo, CA.

Emergent Diversity: Beyond Accommodating Learning Differences

By Ann Kennedy

The need to increase diversity in independent schools has been prominent during the past ten years or so, and progress has been significant, including more inclusivity for children with varying learning styles. Mission statements and strategic plans reflect this change, the financial planning processes in our schools are changing, and boards, administrators, and faculty are expected to seek professional development opportunities that enhance their sensitivity to, and awareness of, difference. Marketing practices have shifted from the reliance on word of mouth, to deliberate recruiting of specific students, in some cases, from specific neighborhoods and schools. Additionally, our schools are doing a better job of committing to, and successfully providing services for, children with changing needs.

Independent schools have long been sustained by reputations of academic rigor embedded within caring and nurturing environments. Characteristics of fine schools have always included a well-defined mission and value system, sensitivity to whole-child growth and development, and academic excellence. The reputation of independent schools' success with preparing young people for higher education is unmatched and in the best of the best, the commitment to the families of those children is fierce. Preservation of a school's academic and social culture, enlightened and enriched by changing enrollments, which now include students who might not have been admitted previously, presents an invigorating challenge as independent schools continue to maintain excellence.

Adhering to a school's stated and implied mission, as well as being willing to let it evolve as necessary, is critical to moving forward with success, especially in the face of changing populations. To recognize that diversity can occur through carefully planned admissions actions as well as through the changing landscape of children's individual learning styles and experiences is crucial to defining community. As a school communicates its mission to families, it must continually and firmly reinforce that mission through program, curriculum, facilities, and support services. Faculty commitment and mutual acceptance of the school's strengths as well as its limitations is important. Even highly touted, premier schools should not claim or expect that their admissions policies and standards create the perfect match for every student enrolled, for that student's entire educational experience at the school. For all of the skill and excellence that exists, eventually the needs of some students will exceed the school's expertise and ability to serve. While this does not occur often, it is an inevitable outcome of broadening a school's cultural base.

The very human resistance to change—the sense of loss over what life used to be like in some of our schools—and complicating soul-searching by the decision makers places schools in vulnerable positions as they attempt to approach the whole issue of diversity. Each school faces a series of crucial questions as it defines diversity in the context of its current and "future community." For administrators, facing parental fear that increasing diversity may actually diminish the learning experience for their children has not been an easy task for, sadly, that fear has been widespread in some schools. It is this vulnerability that ultimately strengthens the community of the school, for it forces the development of a process to look at a critical issue—and one that, if approached with sensitivity and intelligence, will serve all children well. The gap between the nondiscriminatory statements published in schools' viewbooks and what happens in practice is narrowing. Schools that maintain a very public, outspoken, and aggressive optimism about their decision to diversify are finding success, as are those who face head-on the needs of all children in their midst.

The task of academic preparation is relatively simple for schools enrolled with bright, high-achieving children who learn in similar ways, talented faculties, and appropriately involved parents. Those are among the components that schools have historically sought, and community demand for those characteristics continues to be high. The task of additionally providing a diverse and supportive social learning environment has been viewed as much more complex. The question of whether or not to increase the diversity in our schools no longer exists as schools move forward in preparing students for success and active participation as global citizens in an unstable world. The question now is, How to do it best? The literature is replete with strategic planning advice, anecdotal reports about how schools have succeeded in diversifying, and what schools must do to compete in a global economy given their changing populations. The call is to embrace diversity and to teach and empower each student for whom we have responsibility in the school setting. This must occur regardless of ethnicity, gender, religion, or socioeconomic status.

Within our existing school populations there is a natural diversity that takes place in subtle yet significant ways. In the public schools, many classrooms are already complex cultural settings created by bringing together groups of children who share a similar chronological age, yet vary in intellectual ability, ethnicity, race, socioeconomic status, and religious background. That type of learning environment has become valued in independent schools as we seek ways to broaden opportunities and connections to the "real world" for our students. While we expect students new to our schools who have been admitted because of their ethnicity, religion, or race to bring, by their very natures, positive and challenging opportunities, we often overlook the emergent diversity that exists in classrooms already. All children bring diversity into the schools as a function of how they learn and behave. Siblings of enrolled children may enter the school with learning and behavior styles and needs that are different than their brothers and sisters.

In some cases, students who enroll from other programs into grades above the primary level may do so without the academic experience provided over the years for our existing students, particularly if local public schools have been in crisis. And most common, there are the young students who present with mild to moderate learning problems as they enter those critical learning-to-read years and who, in all likelihood, may need special help beyond the classroom. Additionally, schools should not overlook the social adjustment of a child as creating an immediate special need. Cultural unfamiliarity can be a liability for a new student coming into the learning environment for the first time as well as for existing students already in the environment. All of these children contribute significantly to the more tacit diversity of the school.

Recognizing signs that emergent diversity is occurring in a classroom is not difficult for an experienced teacher. Teacher instinct that "something seems different" often brings the first indication. Of course, observations such as a child's consistent and/or increasing difficulty mastering basic concepts can be an early warning sign of a learning problem. A widening gap between a child's general progress and that of his or her classmates should be cause for concern and action as overall class performance sets the norm. Obvious discrepancies between a child's potential as perceived by the teacher and that child's day-to-day achievement, or discrepancies across subject performance, should be noted. Additionally, a teacher may discover that changes in instructional pace or content are necessary for student success.

Not all signs of impending emergent diversity come from students. Noticeable changes in parent feedback such as more frequent concerns about quality and quantity of homework assignments, testing frequency, and grading policies may occur. Parent discussion about certain children may increase, and comments about classroom dynamics may indicate parental awareness of what teachers also recognize.

In Mel Levine's book *All Kinds of Minds,* a chapter dealing with the right to differ offers ways in which our awareness of diversity of minds can help to better serve our students. His self-described obsession with helping all children finds success in school leads us to three critical goals:[1]

- eliminating harmful practices
- preserving student accountability
- easing social pain

Each of these serves as reminders that our response to human diversity cannot be one of "fit in or leave," but one of compassion, success orientation rather than failure avoidance, and commitment to the unique qualities and richness that each child brings into a classroom. These goals should cause careful scrutiny of existing curricula and academic policies and procedures that impact our students.

With some sadness on the part of educators, the decline of many of our nations' public schools has become one reason why parents look at independent education as an option. Many of those parents have been long-term strong supporters of public education for their children. Thus, they come to independent schools with the expectation that their children will not only have an excellent academic experience, but one rich with the diversity that is readily available in much of the public sector. For these parents, new to independent school education and their involvement in the school's culture, the learning curve can be frustratingly high and cause them to view the independent school as one of default. Schools must provide for their needs and recognize that successful inclusion for their children is at least somewhat dependent upon successful inclusion for parents themselves.

The National Association of Independent Schools reminds us that we are engaging in a continual journey from awareness to action in serving diverse populations. Diversity requires a school to reassess its resource allocations, hiring practices, admissions policies and procedures, and curricula on a more frequent basis than previously practiced.[2] This most typically occurs when a school has a very deliberate and purposeful plan to increase its diversity in terms of ethnicity, race, and religion. Ongoing institutional self-assessment must include careful scrutiny of faculty professional development that broadens teachers' expertise in human development, learning, behavior, and special needs. For even the most experienced of teachers, the emergent diversity within a classroom as well as that which occurs through changing admissions plans require adjustment and accommodation in order to create an appropriate and inclusive learning environment.

In searching for teachers to serve inclusive and gradually changing classroom environments such as those created by emergent diversity, care must be given to exploring each candidate's gifts. Not only are experiences and mastery of subject critical, but also curiosity, challenge seeking, flexibility, and willingness to be an active *learner* as well as teacher are necessary skills. In a dwindling market of teachers, this is not an easy task. Schools that encourage and reinforce open-mindedness, risk-taking, and thinking outside of the box are often skilled at attracting teachers who are passionate both about enriched curriculum and about embracing each and every learning style and need as unique and valued. Finally, central to a teacher's success with diverse learners is a strong familiarity with normal child development. All too often, a limited perspective of normalcy occurs when a teacher's experience has been confined to homogeneous groups of high achievers!

Developing Support Systems

Schools need a support process by which a child's behavioral, social-emotional, and academic needs can be best served. Interventions might be required for short-term difficulties with certain assignments or unfamiliar tasks. Ongoing interventions might be necessary for problems that require special attention from the teacher, such as difficulties encountered by a child struggling with learning to read. On occasion, certain problems might be beyond the expertise of school personnel and will need intervention outside of the school setting. Including teachers in the development of support systems and in determining the varying needs of the students is crucial to the system's success.

As administrators and faculty have dialogue about resources and support, a common language will evolve that often reflects the sentiments of those involved in the planning process. Recognizing and accepting that diversity exists within each classroom and using positive terminology will assist any group in effective planning. Positive terminology referring to diversity might include, for example, *variety, multiplicity, assortment, heterogeneity, positive challenge* and *opportunity.* Negative connotations come frequently with terms such as *inconsistency, disparity,* and *dissimilarity.* It sometimes requires an outside facilitator to lead these discussions in productive ways.

"Management by profile" is a non-labeling model for educational care developed by Dr. Mel Levine and colleagues at the University of North Carolina. Rather than a single focus on a child's deficits, this system allows teachers and parents to develop a balanced profile that encompasses the student's needs and weaknesses, gifts and strengths. Each school's unique culture can help to guide decisions about implementing support systems for its students and families, but the following phases of management by profile as a means of supporting children warrant serious consideration in our schools:

- demystification, which helps children understand themselves
- accommodations, which can sometimes help in bypassing a child's weaknesses
- interventions at the breakdown points, which help to remediate and "repair gaps"
- strengthening strengths and affinities, which cultivates students' gifts
- protection from humiliation, which helps in preventing public embarrassment
- other services, sometimes outside of the school setting, which provide professional therapies

Guided by these basic tenets of support, schools can move forward in developing and implementing a safety net for all its students. To these fundamentals we should probably add:

- implementing a curriculum that allows for open discussion, practice, and instruction in life skills, conflict resolution, acceptance of human differences, and strategies for peaceful coexistence among different cultures (i.e., a "peace" curriculum)
- regularly scheduled, collegial discussion opportunities between faculty and parents, and faculty and students, regarding adaptation to change
- involving students in mixed-aged buddy activities in order to provide student role models to children of similar interests and cultural backgrounds
- providing a variety of positive extracurricular and social experiences for all students
- developing a system of volunteer peer-pairs to help children sense community inclusion
- implementing a descriptive, shared vocabulary that speaks to the ways in which the school wants to be perceived (e.g., "We are a learning community of peace and acceptance.")
- establishing a "Gently Read" library of donated easy readers, age appropriate novels, and textbooks that teachers can give to any student who may need support materials to keep at home

- considering a "Grand Helpers" program of grandparent volunteers to tutor, assist, and mentor students
- using older students as "Ambassador Tutors" to offer support to younger students
- soliciting the school's most creative thinkers to serve on a solution-seeking task force
- committing to appropriate expectations and high standards of behavior
- seeking programs that enhance social competence
- providing opportunities for students to form attachments to diverse adult role models in school and in the community at large
- providing ongoing parental support

The first step in developing support and implementing any adaptation of this model for emergent diversity is to identify the personnel responsible for advocacy for the student/family and for monitoring the student's progress. This can be as simple as designating the child's teacher or advisor to this role. In the case of students with more complex social, learning, or behavioral issues, a group of helping adults and/or professionals may serve this function. An effort should be made to have an individual assist parents with communication and understanding the helping process whenever possible, and schools need to reach beyond their own communities to provide this aspect of support if necessary.

Whether or not a school has a counselor, learning specialist, psychologist or other designated coordinator of support services, careful documentation of help requests should occur. As a file is established for a student, it should include, at minimum, the following information:

- a brief narrative description of the concerns expressed and submitted by the teacher, parents, or student
- a list of the observed behaviors and issues of concern
- a description and log of parental contacts regarding the concerns
- information received from other teachers regarding the concerns
- a description of the child's strengths

Once this information is recorded, a decision needs to be made regarding what action to take. A reasonable first step is to observe or interview the student, and begin collecting information to create a profile.

If a student is going to be under observation, as is often the case with a young child, or interviewed in the case of an older student, parental permission should be obtained. The rationale for this action should be carefully explained to the parent and provided in writing as well. When permission is acquired, the child's teacher and others can begin the process of developing a student profile, which will ultimately guide whatever actions need to be taken in order to provide help.

Each teacher who works with the student should participate in the descriptive process, thereby providing ownership and accountability for all involved in the child's success. In addition, participation by all or most of the child's teachers ensures an accounting of representative learning and behavior across the entire school day. The following types of forms or questionnaires will be helpful for this purpose:

- school behavior/situations questionnaires
- social skills assessments
- behavior rating scales and inventories
- early warning signs checklist for learning disabilities
- general academic assessments
- warning signs checklist for potentially troubled teens
- developmental milestones checklists
- readiness skills checklists

Although the primary goal of collecting this information is not for diagnosis, it may be the end result in some cases, particularly if professionals qualified to do so are involved outside of the school setting. Parents must authorize the way in which this information may be shared.

When input from all sources has been gathered, a designated individual prepares the descriptive profile, being sure that it provides the desired representative picture of the student's strengths and needs. The decision regarding the selection of individuals who will serve as the advocacy team on behalf of the student is critical and should take place at this time if it has not already.

The next step is to begin service decisions by asking these questions of the advocacy team:

- What does the student need?
- What does the family need?
- What do the teachers need?
- How can we get these things?
- Where can we get these things?

When this process is completed, a final action plan may be developed and, one hopes, implemented.

The plan might include seeking outside professional assistance and/or evaluation, as in the case of suspected major learning, behavioral, or attention difficulties. Determination of such disabilities needs to be made by qualified professionals following appropriate assessment in conjunction with regional and federal guidelines. While a specific diagnosis may seem to be a statement of the obvious to the child's advocacy team, its purpose is to lead to improved instructional programming. In addition, a formal diagnosis may sometimes qualify a child for special services through his or her public school district at no charge to the family. The more common situation, however, is that the struggling independent school student does not have serious enough problems to qualify for services at state expense, but still experiences difficulties in an enhanced curricular program.

In the case of students presenting with problems of impulse control, hyperactivity, and attention issues, it is never appropriate for teachers to recommend treatment with medication. That determination must be left to a physician. The role of the advocacy team is to develop a profile and describe behavior, not prescribe medication. For some students, medication may ultimately be part of the treatment and improvement plan, but it will not negate the need for careful educational or other interventions.

Any effective action plan must include suggested strategies for supporting the student across a full day of classes and activities as well as home suggestions. This process requires strong initiative on the part of faculty as they research methods and techniques that might be unfamiliar to them. There should be, however, no doubt that the capability exists in every fine teacher to identify support strategies for their students. If it doesn't happen, it's likely a matter of choice. Helping teachers to acknowledge their own expertise and excellence, supporting their efforts, and encouraging their creative problem solving is empowering. Their participation in and ownership of emergent diversity often yields many positive and unexpected benefits.

Communicating Plans to Parents

Since meeting parent needs is crucial to helping a family follow the path to inclusion and satisfaction at school, careful consideration must be given to ongoing communication. Families who are new to the school or whose children experience difficulty for the first time need mutual trust and good fellowship as the school manages its emergent diversity. Reminders of good conferencing technique assist the teacher's role in this process, so often taken for granted. Though schools need to develop and internally publish conferencing guidelines in the context of its own environment, the following format can easily be adapted for articulating support plans to parents:

- State the conferencing goals to the parent at the beginning of the meeting.
- Begin the conference with a positive, factual statement about the student.
- Tell the parents what is being done to assist the child in feeling as if he/she is a valued part of the community.
- Make a commitment to the parent to be an advocate for the child and his/her family.
- Describe the collective profile of the child and solicit further input from the parents.
- Support comments with specific examples and work samples when appropriate.
- Try to represent the range of performance observed in a child in order to present a balanced and positive perspective.
- If relevant to the particular student, ask if there is any culture-specific information that would assist the school in better serving the child.
- Suggest ways in which the parent can be an active part of the classroom and school community and offer to contact another parent to help with the process.
- Listen carefully and ask for clarification in any matters of confusion.
- If the parent is new to the environment, ask if there are questions about policies, procedures, special events, and activities.

- End the conference by a quick review of the action plan; promise and schedule follow-up communication.

Finally, to assist in his or her accountability, the student needs to know what has transpired, who is available to help, what changes might he/she expect in the course of the school day, and what his or her role is in the success of an action plan. This dialog can occur one on one or in the presence of several helping adults. In the latter case, the student should be told ahead of time what will occur in the gathering, who will attend, and why. It should be mandatory that at least one caring adult or parent be present with the student for the purpose of reassurance and support. Careful age-appropriate considerations should be given when planning this phase of assistance and student participation.

I am thankful that, in the overwhelming majority of cases, plans for success create success. However, in certain rare situations, advocacy teams may find themselves facing the very real question: What if we can't adequately and ethically serve a child's needs? In reality, there will be some children whose needs over time may exceed the expertise of both teachers and support personnel within the school. It is often difficult to determine when this is happening. When a child consistently requires a significantly disproportionate amount of teacher time and effort, and when a student no longer benefits from the mission-driven program, it may mean that it is time to reconsider the school's service value to that child. When consideration is given to withholding a re-enrollment contract, discussion should include these questions:

- Are there better services and support systems available that are within reach for this family?
- Have all in-house options for service, including personnel and class assignment changes, been exhausted?
- Have combination services (i.e., in-house as well as outside agencies) been tried?
- Would a temporary withdrawal from the school for the purpose of remedial assistance and a transition plan with the cooperating service provider allow for a possible re-entry in the school in the future?
- What course of action is in the child's best interest?
- Is the child regressing as a result of inadequate support services?

However difficult it is to communicate this information to parents of struggling students, it must be done early in the decision-making process, and with gentle but firm diplomacy.

In the long run, it is worth reminding ourselves that the dread of our forefathers that a multicultural society would prevent the development of a unified American culture has been unfounded.[3] As the major institutional entity responsible for the socialization of children, schools, the ways in which schools respond to human diversity, and the resulting practices they employ will set the course for what's to come, and what's to be, for our world.[4] Accepting individual differences as legacies by which we adjust and improve educational practice seems a better course to take than preservation of a dominant independent school culture from which many social learning opportunities may be absent. Focusing on the emergent diversity within our schools, in whatever form it may take, will once again affirm the distinction and eminence of independent schools and their capacities to prepare students for true citizenship now and in the future.

Notes

[1] Levine, M. (2002). *A Mind at a Time.* New York: Simon & Schuster.

[2] Bassett, P.F. (2002). *The Inclusive Independent School.* National Association of Independent Schools. [Electronic version]. www.nais.org/docs

[3] Stevens, E., Wood, G.E., & Sheehan, J.J. (2002). *Justice, Ideology, Education.* New York: McGraw-Hill.

[4] Spring, J. (2001). *Deculturalization and the Struggle for Equality.* New York: McGraw-Hill.

Ann Kennedy is the learning specialist and intermediate division head at St. Paul's Episcopal Day School in Kansas City, MO. She received her Ph.D. from Temple University and has been teaching or working with children and their families in schools since 1973.

Values Education in a Multicultural World

By Richard P. DiBianca, Ph.D.

What is the role of the secondary school in promoting values among its students during the first decade of the twenty-first century? In a time in which young people are confronted with an ever-widening range of cultural values, this question is an essential one for all who work with students and who seek to provide for them even the most rudimentary guiding ethical and moral principles. It is also provocative in that its exploration—if conscientiously pursued—might cause the contemporary educator to re-evaluate both the nature of his or her profession and the mission of the institution for which he or she works. In this essay, I will consider the role of the school in the teaching of values, examine the problem of deciding among those values to be taught in a "multicultural" world, and offer some strategies for the promotion of values in modern secondary schools.

If one were to read diligently newspaper articles, pay attention to present-day judicial decisions, and talk with most contemporary public school administrators, one would likely get the impression that the tenor of the day is to remove morality, or values education, from school curricula—at least, from those of the public schools. In part, due to vigilant sectors of society who demand that church remain separate from state, who believe that the sole domain for values education is the family, or who have convinced themselves that school teachers and administrators are neither equipped nor prepared to instill values in the children of society, there is a dominant feeling that the school experiences and curricula of today are expected to be value-free. I submit that this view is simplistic and it underestimates the range, scope, and power of the moral influences inherent in schools.

Following their extensive observations of eighteen elementary and high school classrooms, Jackson, Boostrom and Hansen (1993) identified eight spheres of moral influence in schools (figure 1). One set of influences are grouped as "moral instruction," even though only one of them—which, ironically, was nearly absent in their two-and-a-half years' worth of observations—relates to the explicit moral instruction of students. The other set, grouped as "moral practice," reveals the moral influences inherent—albeit usually invisibly so—in the routine practices of educational institutions and of teachers themselves.

Figure 1. Moral Influences in Schools (Jackson, Boostrom and Hansen, 1993, p. 42)

Moral instruction

- moral instruction as a formal part of the curriculum
- moral instruction within the regular curriculum
- rituals and ceremonies
- visual displays with moral content
- spontaneous interjections of moral commentary into ongoing activity

Moral practice

- classroom rules and regulations
- the morality of curricular substructure
- expressive morality within the classroom

Although one may quibble with these categorizations and may propose areas that the researchers may have omitted,[1] it is my conviction that anyone who has worked in schools would be compelled to agree that moral influences are inherent to these institutions and professional practices. Note that the purpose of presenting this research is not to argue on behalf of the power or efficacy of such sources of moral influence. It is merely to propose their existence, assert their *potential* for influence and expose the futility of ignoring them when undertaking the promotion of values in schools. Given the existence of moral influences in schools, it seems both irresponsible and illogical for them to be ignored by teachers, administrators, parents, and society at large. At the very least, these vehicles should be seen as opportunities to convey the most fundamental of our positive principles of behavior and attitude.

John Dewey (1897) took this a step further and regarded such vehicles for influence as more than opportunities, but as a "moral responsibility" that schools "and those who conduct [them]" have to society.[2] In the present educational context, however, one seems justified in demanding of Dewey, "To *which society* are today's schools morally responsible?" This is a serious question. In fact, it is the "rub" of this essay. Are American secondary schools morally responsible to the world-at-large, to a particular cultural or political heritage, to the nation, to their more intimate community or to some other "society?" Dewey's answer appears to be straightforward, "The society of which the child is to be a member is, in the United States, a democratic and progressive society."[3]

Whether this answer, given over a century ago, is still applicable is the issue before us as educators in the twenty-first century. It is before us because we live on a planet that is inconceivably more intimately interconnected than it was twenty, much less one hundred years, ago. On their televisions, on their computer screens and, for many, in their classrooms, American students visit and are routinely visited by representatives of other nations and other cultures. It is a daily occurrence. How can an even moderately reflective adolescent not suffer from "value confusion" when he reads that most Europeans believe that America is dangerously insular and too conservative but that much of the Arab world believes it is dangerously imperialistic and too liberal? Or when she hears conflicting messages from adults who encourage her to be open-minded and tolerant of others, but who admonish her to be wary of "those kinds of people." The current world context, the ever-shrinking global village, the rampant stimuli of divergent values all put Dewey's original definition of "society" to the test. More importantly, they are putting schools and their decision about promoting values to the test.

Let us say that a responsible secondary school formulates a strategic plan in which it commits to the promotion of values in a more explicit way than it has done in the past. What next? The school's first task might be to identify which values to promote. Here, it runs smack into a set of moral decisions, most of which appear to be rooted in *culture*. Thus, we come to problem #1: *Whose* values demand promotion? Four responses occur to me.

a) *One's own values*. This approach might be called *autoculturalism*. The potential benefits of emphasizing the values of one's own culture include self-knowledge, connectedness, an appreciation of heritage and tradition, and allegiance to and fraternity with others who are like you. The potential dangers of promoting exclusively the values of one's own culture include lack of awareness and understanding of others, intolerance, closed-mindedness, ethnocentrism, xenophobia, self-righteousness, and a sense of superiority.

b) *The values of others*. This approach might be called *heteroculturalism*. The potential benefits of emphasizing the values of other cultures include open-mindedness, awareness and understanding, empathy, cultural humility, and kinship with others who differ from you. The potential dangers of promoting exclusively the values of others include loss of self, an absence of frame of reference, and relativism—both cultural and moral. Of course, an additional danger lays in wait for the discussion about *which* of the countless cultural traditions and their values to emphasize . . . and which to ignore.

c) *Universal values*. This approach might be called *metaculturalism*. Does human culture emerge from universal, human notions of value or do values emerge as by-products of specific cultural contexts? If values beget culture, then perhaps there are values which transcend culture, those that all cultures hold in common? If these universal values are more than biological instincts and could be articulated, this would be a helpful, if not necessary, place to start. If on the other hand values emerge from and are inextricably bound to specific cultural contexts (history, traditions, and rituals), then a metacultural values quest would be in vain.

d) *A representative number of values, including one's own*. This approach might be called *multiculturalism*. At first, this seems to be a simple, sensible, and responsible compromise of the first two approaches—one which urges students to be equally propelled by two wise and ancient principles: "Know thyself" and "Do unto others. . . ." The danger that lurks in this golden mean of approaches to values education is the initial ascription of "one's own" and "other" cultures. Not only is it impossible to identify a single, or even dominant, cultural heritage represented by the student body at my own school, I couldn't do it in any of my classes. Thousands of other American secondary school educators would find this task similarly impossible. As any United States history teacher knows, there is not and never was one perspective on U.S. history. To represent it as such is to leave out many voices, many histories. So, if this is the approach is to be taken in an attempt to promote values, there is a caution about not starting the whole thing on the wrong foot with "us" and "them" ascriptions and predispositions.

If I seem to have slipped into a discussion of culture amid an essay on values, it is not accidental. It is my contention that the two are inextricably bound. Researchers have often suggested that one way of understanding the complex nature of culture is to recognize that they are composed of many different levels and contain both visible and hidden elements (Larcher, 1993). The visible elements of culture are those that reflect more conscious behavior, while the hidden elements are those that reflect more unconscious behavior. Any line proposed to separate the two kinds of elements would have to be a dynamic one. Fennes and Hapgood (1997) proposed a refined model of an "iceburg of culture" the visible elements of which are *laws, rules,* and *customs* and the hidden elements of which are *traditions, routine behavior,* and *unconscious habits*.[4] Where would one find values in this dissection of culture? Everywhere.

Before moving on to the question of *how* a school promotes whatever values it decides to embrace, it might be helpful to discuss some examples of values. I will offer a few that reflect my own educational philosophy. They may be general or intellectual or tame enough to be embraced by many readers as well. If the source of these values requires a categorization or an historic label, it might be called, simply, the tradition of liberal education.[5] Specifically, they are drawn from the principles of two organizations, the National Association of Independent Schools (NAIS) and the International Baccalaureate Organisation (IB). Below is a sample list of values that I would feel comfortable with and expect from a school with which I would be associated.

- respecting, affirming and defending the dignity and worth of each member of the school community
- developing in students a sense of responsibility for equity and justice in the broader community
- modeling integrity, curiosity, responsibility, creativity, and respect for all persons as well as an appreciation for racial, cultural, and gender diversity
- engaging students to develop a critical capacity to evaluate beliefs and knowledge claims and understand the strengths and limitations of individual and cultural perspectives
- helping students to identify values that underlie judgments and demonstrate an understanding that personal views, judgments, and beliefs may influence their own knowledge claims and those of others[6]

I am aware of and apologize for that fact that these "values" are a little on the wordy and heady sides, but they are simply meant to serve as examples of values that an educational institution might choose to stand for. (Incidentally, if values of this sort seem to be culture-free, then perhaps there is hope for the metaculturalists out there. More likely, I'm afraid to report, our "own culture" glasses are so powerful that we don't recognize that we are looking through them.)

I have presented some difficulties and complexities that a responsible secondary school is likely to encounter in its effort to complete the initial and seemingly straightforward task of selecting which values are to be promoted. Regardless of whether this task has been sorted out, it seems appropriate now to turn to the implementation of values education. Problem #2: *How* might a school promote values?

In a recent article published in the *Journal of International Education,* Michael Allan proposed a process that may be of service in addressing this problem. The process is called the "intercultural learning spiral."[7] In effect, this process is a blend of two earlier theories of cross-cultural learning. The first theory presents a process of intercultural learning wherein an individual progresses through a continuum of up to four stages of *attitude*.[8] If the individual moves in a healthy, reflective, committed and positive way—transcending the inevitable moments of cultural dissonance[9] in which alienation is experienced and felt—he or she can progress from an attitude of "awareness" to one of "appreciation and valuing"(figure 2). The sociological phenomenon identified with each of these stages appears alongside each of the "attitudes."

Figure 2. An Intercultural Learning Continuum (Hoopes, 1979; reprinted in Allan, 2003)

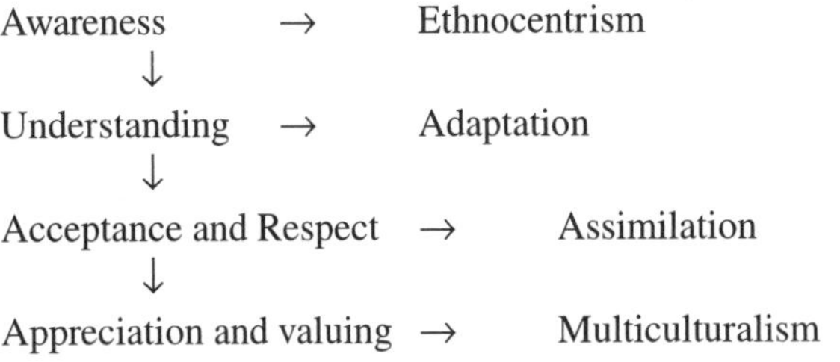

The second theory is that of intercultural learning *styles* (Kolb 1987, Cushner 1990). It proposes four styles of learning: concrete experience, reflective observation, abstract conceptualization, and active experimentation. It is suggested that each of these learning styles comes into play at various times throughout the process of experiencing another culture. Unlike progression through a continuum, movement among these styles is more haphazard. That is, one might go back and forth many times between concrete experience and reflective observation before returning to a phase of abstract conceptualization.

Allan suggests that a synthesis of these theories might be at work when an individual experiences deeply another culture. He suggests that in order to progress through the intercultural learning continuum, an individual must spend meaningful and reflective time spent in each "attitude." It is during these periods, when he or she experiences the full range (in whatever order) of the learning styles. Because it can be modeled as a progression, both "vertically" from the attitude of awareness to appreciation and valuing, and "laterally" among the learning styles, the process is modeled as a spiral of intercultural learning.[10]

Reflective cross-cultural research such as Allan's can be of service to the school that wishes to promote values. It offers a window into the nature of what might truly be involved in such a commitment. It also reveals what is at stake—attitudes and experiences, not just curricula. Armed with what is involved and stake, I return to the second problem: How might a school promote values?

My unadorned, two-step suggestion for addressing this problem is one that should come naturally to a reflective educator: 1) have students *do it;* and then 2) *assess it*. Schools assess what they value. After all, isn't this precisely what a teacher would do if the board or administration wanted students to learn civics or use microscopes or improve their basic grammar?

In an attempt to ease the way for educators to promote values—and, while I am at it, to make learning experiences engaging for students[11]—I propose a new vision of curriculum for secondary schools. I believe that most academic high school teachers are tethered. They are tethered by curriculum and by the demand of time necessary to *cover* it. Whether one is a teacher of an AP course who is required to *cover* a vast amount of content in order to prepare her students for the standardized exam in May or a teacher of a ninth grade course who is required to *cover* a requisite amount of content in order to prepare his students for the content they will confront in tenth grade, one can hardly find time to reflect,[12] much less innovate. However, I believe that is the school that is willing to untether its teachers from the unrelenting demands of content that may finally discover[13] other curricular opportunities.

In order to begin this shift in the vision of curriculum, the long-held and long-practiced convictions of student-as-listener, student-as-recaller, and student-as-mimic must make room for a new one: student-as-*doer*.

> The intellectual and moral will remain separate in our schools. . . . as long as there is a divorce between learning and doing. (Dewey, 1897)[14]

Values which educators wish to promote and wish to have instilled in the attitudes and habits of their students must be practiced. Simply "teaching" about values—whether overtly, via direct instruction, or covertly, via announcements, assemblies, displays, speeches, and so on—is not as effective as providing the opportunity for students to *do* them. If a school wishes to promote the value of "service to others," then it must first provide the opportunity, the time, and the support for its students to serve. If a school wishes to promote the value of critical thinking, then it must first provide the opportunity, the time, and the support for its students to think critically. If a school wishes to promote the value of multiculturalism, then it must first provide the opportunity, the time, and the support for its students to encounter-understand-accept-appreciate the cultures of others. If a school is committed to promoting values at all, it must adopt a new vision of curriculum, one that de-emphasizes content coverage and begins to emphasize experience.

A school that is interested in promoting values but which changes merely its curriculum—that is, the content or subject of study—in order to do so will likely find its mission incomplete. Therefore, I also propose a new vision of assessment.

Traditionally, what gets assessed in schools are the content knowledge and academic skills that compose the formal curriculum. Assessments of all forms—tests, quizzes, papers, reports, presentations, projects, and so on—are extremely familiar to students. Learning content and mastering some skills are what students believe they are responsible for in school. From their perspective and in their experience, academic skills and content are what schools truly value. Schools might declare that they promote other, non-curricular principles or skills such as tolerance, open-mindedness, or conflict resolution. But students know the difference. They know that they won't be held back, be admonished or fail if they don't practice tolerance, demonstrate open-mindedness, or apply the skills of conflict resolution. They do, however, know that grades, comments to parents, promotion, and graduation may be affected if they don't meet the traditional curricular expectations of content knowledge and academic skills—that is, learning civics, using a microscope, improving their basic grammar.

A school that has committed itself to promoting values by committing opportunity, time and support for its students to practice these values is on its way, but won't complete its mission until it appreciates the real purpose and power of assessment. A school values what it assesses. Therefore, it must learn to assess any changes it is willing to make to curriculum. A student who has been given the opportunity, time and support to *experience* those values its school wishes to promote (e.g., to serve others, to think critically, to appreciate other cultures) should expect some accountability for these experiences. Without an assessment which is connected to a student's final grade or permanent record, a tangential school requirement ultimately won't be embraced or taken as seriously as those which have always "counted."

But how can teachers assess *experiences*? While a multiple-choice test might not be an appropriate or useful assessment for a service experience, writing a journal or making presentation might be. Similarly, the use of clear, fair, and pre-established rubrics to assess the pursuit and acquisition of more complex values, such as critical thinking or appreciating the cultures of others, would seem to be appropriate.[15] Pre-establishing the rubrics to be used in assessing any task is critical. Not providing rubrics to students ahead of time is like telling them to go play a game without giving them the rules, and then, when it is over, informing them whether or not they won. Unfortunately, this is the model for many traditional assessments as some teachers find it necessary for students to guess or predict what will be on a test. If the experience with or acquisition of specific knowledge, skills and attitudes (whether values-based or not) is what is expected from one's students, then their chances for success will be greatly improved if they are made aware of the objectives, the rules, and the strategies from the beginning. Open communication and the use of clear, fair, pre-established, and relevant assessments are critical to this end.

I have offered some new visions and challenges to the secondary school that seeks to conquer the second problem in promoting values: *how* to do so. I am convinced that, in order to succeed in this endeavor, it must embrace its commitment to values education as it did with its commitment to content. To do this, it must—at every level, from board room to classroom—put "its money where its mouth is." That is, it must re-establish priorities for curriculum and assessment and then it must implement them. Without these steps, its commitment is a hollow one. It will not "get done," especially when the substance of the commitment is something as ineffable as values.

The implications of these challenges are significant. They include the importance of buy-in from all factions of a school community. They entail financial commitment—for research, planning and the development of new curricula and appropriate assessments. They require a shift in the technology of teaching, wherein: teachers are untethered from content-driven, standardized curricula; there is a de-emphasis on knowledge-based assessments; and in which time is made available so that teachers and administrators may cogitate and communicate.

To have a meaningful and lasting effect, the acceptance of those challenges does not call for a simple alteration of the status quo. As long as promotion means more than cheerleading, it is a commitment to making the changes necessary to promote values for students during the first decade of the twenty-first century, which was the purpose of this essay. In a time in which young people are confronted with an ever-widening range of cultural values, I believe that this pursuit is essential.

Bibliography

Allan, Michael. (2000). "Border Crossings: a study of cultural dissonance in an international school," M.A. dissertation, Oxford Brookes University.

———. (2002). "Cultural Borderlands: a case study of cultural dissonance in an international school," *Journal of Research in International Education* 1 (1): 63–90.

———. (2003). "Frontier Crossings: cultural dissonance, intercultural learning, and the multicultural personality," *Journal of Research in International Education* 2 (1): 83–110.

Braun, Eva. (1979). *Paradoxes of Education in a Republic*. Chicago, IL: University of Chicago Press.

Cushner, K. (1990). "Cross-cultural psychology and the formal classroom," in R.W. Brislin (Ed.) *Applied Cross-Cultural Psychology,* p. 98–120. Newbury Park, CA: Sage. Cited in Allan, Michael (2003), p. 102.

Dewey, John. (1897). "Ethical principles underlying education," *The Third Yearbook of the National Herbart Society,* University of Chicago Press, p. 7–26, reprinted in Pai, Young and Myers, Joseph, eds. (1967) *Philosophic Problems and Education*. Philadelphia: J.B. Lippincott, p. 394–410.

———. (1966 [1916]). *Democracy and Education*. New York: Free Press.

———. (1975 [1909]). *Moral Principles in Education*. Carbondale, IL: Southern Illinois University Press.

DiBianca, Richard. (2000). "Teaching Adolescents: Relationships between Features of Instruction and Student Engagement in High School Mathematics and Science Classes." Ph.D. Dissertation, University of Chicago.

Fennes, H. and Hapgood, K. (1997). *Intercultural Learning in the Classroom.* London: Cassell. Cited in Allan, Michael (2003), pp. 91–92.

Hoopes, D.S. (1979). "Intercultural communication concepts and the psychology of intercultural experience," in M.D. Pusch (Ed.) *Multicultural Education,* pp. 9–38. Chicago: Intercultural Press. Cited in Allan, Michael (2003) p. 101.

International Baccalaureate Organisation (1999). *Theory of Knowledge Subject Guide.* Geneva, Switzerland: IBO.

Jackson, Philip, Boostrom, Robert, and Hansen, David (1993). *The Moral Life of Schools.* San Francisco, CA: Jossey-Bass.

Kolb, D. (1987). *Learning Style Inventory.* Boston: McBeer. Cited in Allan, Michael (2003), p. 102.

Larcher, D. (1993). *Das Kulturshockconzept, ein Rehabilitierungversuch.* Klagenfurt: Institut für Interdisziplinäre Forschung und Fortbildung der Universistäten Innsbruck. Cited in Allan, Michael (2003), pp. 91–92.

Lortie, Dan (1975). *Schoolteacher: A sociological study.* Chicago: University of Chicago Press.

Moore, G.E. (1959). *Philosophical Studies.* Paterson, NJ. Reprinted in Pai, Young and Myers, Joseph, Eds. (1967) *Philosophic Problems and Education.* Philadelphia, PA: J.B. Lippincott, p. 394–410.

National Association of Independent Schools (2001), *Principles of Good Practice for Member Schools, 2001.* NAIS.

Pai, Young and Myers, Joseph, Eds. (1967). *Philosophic Problems and Education.* Philadelphia, PA: J.B. Lippincott.

Wittgenstein, Ludwig (1980). *Culture and Value.* Chicago: University or Chicago Press.

Notes

[1] Perhaps this is so because the majority of my own intersections with students these days is as an administrator, but I would assert the existence of a fourth kind of "moral practice" in schools: administrative policies and procedures. A moral tone is certainly conveyed in any worthwhile student handbook whose published content includes everything from the criteria that places students on academic probation to the rationale for a dress code.

[2] Reprinted in Pai and Myers (1967), p. 397.

[3] Ibid, p. 398.

[4] Cited in Allan (2003).

[5] I confess to a certain degree of irony, if not blatant inconsistency, by using the phrase "liberal education"—a classically un-ultilitarian notion of education (Braun, 1979, p. 20)—to refer to what I hope will be a plea for a more progressive—that is, utilitarian—model of education.

[6] The first three are taken from NAIS' *Principles of Good Practice for Member Schools* (2001). The final two are from IB's *Theory of Knowledge Subject Guide* (1999).

[7] April 2003, Vol. 2 (1), pp. 103–4.

[8] This is my term for the stages. It was not used by the researchers.

[9] Cultural dissonance refers to a (usually temporary) state of disconnectedness between an indi-

vidual and a culture that he or she is confronting, a period where withdrawal not integration (Allan, 2003, p. 104).

[10] Ibid, p. 103.

[11] In my earlier research, I demonstrated the powerful influence that student perception on the real-world applicability of an academic task has on their engagement with a classroom lesson. (DiBianca, 2000, p.136)

[12] "The first practical activity for a teacher is not planning and projection, but reflection." (Braun, 1979, p. 5)

[13] It is hard to resist pointing out that, at least in a curricular sense, the opposite of *cover* might be *discover*.

[14] Reprinted in Pai and Myers (1967), p. 403.

Dr. Richard DiBianca's primary research has focused on the process of engaging adolescents in high school classrooms; and his current interests are international education and the role of nontraditional assessments. He has degrees from Colgate University, St. John's College (MD), and the University of Chicago, and is currently the upper school principal and International Baccalaureate Coordinator at Newark Academy in Livingston, NJ.

On Creating a Culture of Honor

By Willie MacMullen

Note: The following, now with some minor editing, is a talk given to parents at Mothers' Day in the winter of 2003; and as such, it assumes an audience that knows the school.—WM

On Creating a Culture of Honor

We all read the papers, and occasionally you see a piece which ends up like a pebble in your shoe: you can't get rid of it. Such was the case not long ago with me, with an article in a major newspaper. The issue was cheating. A number of students at a private school had been disciplined after they admitted to cheating on the SATs; several were suspended, and others were expelled. The family of one student brought a suit forward against the school, charging, among other things, that the punishment was unfair since the Honor Code at the school defined cheating as unauthorized help on a "written assignment"—and the SAT was held off campus and, we are left to assume, did not constitute *writing*.

The article bothered me more than a little, and so I have been thinking about how schools impart values as well as information, and about how schools create a culture where honesty is a value of such fragility and importance that it is handed down over the years with almost ministerial care. And this article was deeply disturbing, in particular given the number of students who were involved and the parents' astonishing, sad parsing of the language. So recently I have been looking at all the places we do our teaching and wondered, "How do we teach values, especially the importance of personal integrity, at a private secondary school?"

*****

I hardly need to tell you the challenges faced by the faculty and administrators in our nation's schools today. Many families seek private education in part because the culture of many public schools, including some very good ones, is inconsistent with what they believed. And here I don't intend to take part in the all too common bashing of American education: I know full well how lucky we are here, with no state mandated curriculum and performance standards, with singularly motivated students, and where we can create an explicitly moral educational experience. We are fortunate indeed.

But life in many secondary schools is not a pretty picture, especially when we look at the issues of integrity. For years I conducted an informal survey in my classes, asking students to raise their hands if they came from schools where cheating was common. Inevitably, at least half the hands would go up. In 1998, a poll conducted by Don McCabe, the president of the Center for Academic Integrity at Duke, surveyed 4,500 students and found that 80% admitted to cheating in high school. Sadly, this is not news, as we know from newspapers across the nation. The notion that honesty matters in schools, much less is essential if they are to function, seems alien. Plagiarism and cheating have become the focus of faculty meetings, trustee boards, parents' committees, IT departments, counseling offices, and educational journals. How easy is it to cheat? Just log onto the Internet. It's a frightening exercise. Cheathouse.com is only one of many such sites. Boasting of their thousands of essays and millions of visitors, the website explains its intention to create a community of students and cautions users to cite sources—odd advice indeed, the fox telling the hens to close the door behind them on the way in. There are scores of other such sites. In response to sites like these, some schools have subscribed to Turnitin.com., an online service that scans student papers to find matching passages and determines whether the student has plagiarized. The catch-me-if-you-can game, once confined to the classroom, has moved to the laptop.

Much of this I know from my wife, who came to Taft after a decade of teaching at a large public high school. Of the many differences she observed between the two schools, the most significant was the culture of dishonesty that prevailed at her previous school, and how honor seemed to be part of the air we breathed here. At her former school, students routinely cheated on tests and completed major assignments with a cat-and-mouse approach, both teacher and student implicitly agreeing that this was the way things had to be. When a student was caught cheating, the consequences were minor: a failing grade, or a detention. Now, there are no villains here: I will not cast the first stone at an overworked teacher with a class of twenty-five, a principal worried about litigation and with little leverage he or she can bring to bear on such behavior, or at the student studying state-mandated material assessed with multiple-choice tests. But it is a terrible culture.

It is tempting to look out on that ethically pitted landscape and simply surrender—to concede the impossibility of creating a culture where honor, in and out of the classroom, is so valued that acts of dishonesty are the exceptions that prove the rule.

But it is not right, and we must never surrender. In fact, perhaps nothing matters more to the faculty here than the moral lessons that occur each day on the campus, at the odd hours and dark corners. It is a cultural legacy that has been past down to us by the thousands of alumni and teachers who came before us, especially school founder Horace Taft.

Everywhere in Horace Taft's writings, you find reference to what we today call moral education, or even a values-based education. He was not alone, of course, but he was unwavering in his belief that a school was obligated to impart certain values in its students, and he had a long time to develop these ideas as he headed the school from 1890 to 1936. His themes are ones you hear today: working hard, respecting others, serving the greater good, and above all, being honest. Letters, speeches, and remembered conversations often focused on his conviction that a complete education was only so if it spoke to the education of character, and most important, to honor. His letters to Sherman Thacher, his Yale classmate, lifelong friend, and founder of the Thacher School in California, are filled with the details of running a school: bills, tuition, lawyers, discipline cases—and the challenge of creating graduates with the moral stuff to serve the world. You read these letters and you cannot help but sense how profoundly Taft felt about the mission of a school, as he does in 1920, writing with his typical humility:

> Yet I do feel that the boys get a pretty good development of character and respond pretty well to the influences here. The result of it is plain and humdrum, but not to be despised, and the good of it in some cases far-reaching.

Horace Taft's legacy is obvious, and we have made his words part of the landscape. They are etched in glass in the Belcher Reading Room of our library: "For me, truthfulness or honor is the foundation. Whatever else a student is, if they tell the truth, there is hope, there is something to build on." It's hard for a student to walk into the library without seeing the quotation. I love that statement, solemn and lofty and yet so unpretentiously phrased.

And honor is more than an abstract legacy; there are policies and practices that affirm the importance of honesty. In 1914 the students created an honor agreement that focused on written work. By the 1940s, the honor code was in place, written by the school monitors and essentially putting all matters of honor in the hands of the students. Amended slightly in the early 1960s, it was changed in 1982 when the school monitors argued that faculty perspective needed to be added in the deliberations. In today's *Student Handbook,* you find a clear articulation of the values we care most about here. The honor system appears first, followed by the academic honesty statement, and then the preamble, a brief series of explicitly moral statements. My opening addresses to the school invariably speak to these values, but my last point always is this: without integrity, the school cannot function. Or as the honor system says, in wonderfully noble language: "This we believe: that personal honor in word and deed, integrity in thought and action, honesty in every facet of life, and respect for other people and their rights are the essence of a student at the Taft School." And I believe that in an era when the Internet provides quick answers, when the pressures on adolescents make dishonesty tempting, all schools, and certainly this one, have an importance that cannot be exaggerated. I would never claim that Taft students are honest all the time, and nor can I say that in my two decades here I have never seen acts of deceit, stealing or lying. Of course these things have happened and will so again. But I would say that nothing is more clear and non-negotiable than the notion that we should be honest in all we do.

*****

But acting honestly is not easy, especially for adolescents, and how young people make moral choices is very complex. Psychologists have pointed out how challenging it is for an adolescent to evolve to the point where internal principles govern behavior more than external factors like laws and punishment. But they remind us that it is possible. Like many schools, we have made this a critical educational objective, and part of a document—a portrait, in a sense—which describes what we want a graduate to look like when he or she graduates. For us, this is a very important document, a mission statement. Among about ten habits of mind and skills we identify, we write; "A Taft graduate will have cultivated moral thoughtfulness through exposure to various ethical perspectives and ways of thinking." Our placing that statement in that document is our way of saying it is crucially important. Our placing it first is not accidental.

It is not an easy task. Numerous other psychological studies have shown that people will be dishonest when given the chance. You may know of Hugh Hartshorne's and Mark May's famous 1928 study of moral responses in over 10,000 children, which demonstrated that when given opportunity, children and adolescents will lie, cheat, and steal in a variety of contexts. Behavior was linked to the specific situation: A child might be honest in one situation, dishonest in the next. What this tells us is that if we are going to help students not simply behave honestly *occasionally* but also internalize the value we place on honesty, we need to create a culture completely saturated in moral questions, where they *practice* honesty often.

This is what we try to create, knowing that we won't succeed with every student and every situation. Walk around the halls and you will see what I mean. Four times a week, students walk out of Bingham Auditorium after school meeting and find their packs in the hall where they left them. New students find this amazing. Few students lock their dorm rooms—indeed many have lost their keys by October! When a faculty member is giving a test, he or she thinks nothing of leaving the classroom to go to the Xerox machine for ten minutes—and on returning speaks to the class about what this meant to him or her. When a boarder signs out a weekend permissions card at the dean of student's office, he sees his signature as a profound, contractual statement; and the dean speaks explicitly of this. When a girl writes the "Pledge of Honor" at the end of her research paper, she understands full well what she has done; for she has had a class discussion on academic honor in the first week of class and she has signed her pledge on every assignment. Students are asked *to practice honesty* repeatedly. Again, Taft students are as human and flawed as any; at times, they err and fail to meet the standards. That is why there is an honor court made of students and faculty—to deal with those failures. But we begin with the two twinned beliefs: nothing is more important than honesty, and we should engage students in the habit of honesty. Can you imagine what the place would feel like if these things did not occur?

But how specifically do you create the conditions, the transparent as well as hidden curriculums, which convey the moral atmosphere of the place, especially when we seem to be swimming against the cultural tide and when psychological studies tell us that most adolescents demonstrate dishonest behavior under different conditions? These things a school must do:

As I have said, a school must have a *culture heavily steeped in honor—that is, the value placed on personal integrity is unquestioned, forcefully expressed, and continually reinforced.* We offer a clear definition of integrity in writing and in speeches and confront even the smallest violations of honor. We speak of the honor code in depth with new students and ask all students to read, discuss, and then sign a statement on academic integrity. Over and over we remind students that we treasure them being honest. They sign in at breakfast or a weight training class on an honor system: we trust that they will cross out only their own name. Small acts matter: we praise the student who hands in the lost wallet to the dean's office, confront the student who said he was going to the library but ended up at the student union. It takes enormous institutional energy to do this: faculty have to care deeply enough to teach in every available moment.

A school must *have students, especially leaders, who understand that the culture is to a great degree shaped by them; and they see it as a duty to uphold the central values.* Students do just that here, and the elected school monitors especially, as they have for decades, protect these values. For that reason, faculty come out of Honor Court deliberations awed at the courage of students who are willing to make recommendations that strengthen the school but may cause pain for a peer. Students created the honor code many years ago, and today they protect it passionately. We have entrusted them with it.

A school *must know its students very well* if it is to encourage honorable conduct. Numerous studies have pointed to this, and students at places where the faculty know their charges less well remark that they would be less inclined to cheat if their teachers knew them better. In the classroom this means knowing student work very well. A student is much less likely to hand in work that is not his own if his teacher has seen a dozen of his writings already—and if he feels a meaningful relationship with his teacher developed in the dormitory, playing field, classroom and elsewhere.

A school must construct major assessments in such a way that the student shows her teacher *the work as a process.* This, of course, was a luxury my wife, with her five classes and 130 students, could not afford. Here, though, and in most private schools, major works are often handed in only after the English teacher has seen a free writing, an outline, a rough draft; the math teacher has checked homework every other day; and so on. Teachers work so closely with students every day, and especially on major tasks, that handing in anything but your own work is all but impossible.

A school needs to create *opportunities for unique exercises,* where topics reflect the idiosyncratic passions of our students. Topics generated by students—and here I mean the widest array of eclectic interests—are much less likely to be found on the LazyStudents.com website. Forty page essays on acute respiratory distress syndrome, the socioeconomic and environmental reasons for dams on the Snake River should be breached to help the salmon migration, and integration of schools in St. Louis in the early 1970s may not have made it to the Internet database.

A school needs to *create a variety of ways students can show what they have learned.* Students can exhibit their skills and understanding in many ways, and tests and essays are only two of the more common. We ask students to show us what they have learned in ways that encourage independent work and make academic honesty a given. What they say unprompted in class, the skill with which they teach an idea to classmates, the mastery they reveal in a formal debate, the defense of a thesis given in an oral presentation, the self-reflection in a portfolio—all of these are ways students show their learning, and it is hard to cheat on them.

And finally, a school must have a faculty with a concern for the whole of the student, a faculty overflowing with *passion, patience,* and *power*.

I think schools that create cultures of honesty have done some or all of these things, and perhaps others as well.

*****

What I have described is not easy at all, and we have no simple solutions to a world where students often receive the message that half-truths and fabrications are pragmatic means to an end, where the Internet's siren call beckons them to founder on the rocks of plagiarism, where politicians all too regularly fail to meet the ethical criteria which accompanies high office, and where the corporate world has been shaken by scandals that dwarf even the stupendous ones of the late nineteenth century.

It is tempting to concede defeat in the face of all this, but educators should not, and we should refuse even to negotiate. Moral education happens at the most profound cultural level, in our stories, myths, rituals, practices, and heroes. It takes huge energies and intentional design and leads to the inescapable conclusion that nothing matters more than personal integrity. Like all great schools, we are shaped by our past. We owe a debt to the thousands of Taft students and teachers who passed through here before us and shaped this culture and made our present possible. I open yearbooks, some brittle-spined and yellowing, and faces stare out at me—from the earliest years of the school, when Horace Taft was forming his educational ideas; from the early 1940s, when the honor code was first created; from recent graduates, so many of whom I know have a story to tell. You see their faces and lock eyes with each of them, and you realize what they gave all of us here—something at once astonishingly durable and terribly fragile.

I have a literary hero, Thomas More from Bolt's great play, *A Man For All Seasons,* a play I have taught many times. More faces a terrible moral dilemma: Should he sign an oath of allegiance to his despotic king though doing so runs counter to what he believes and has stated, or maintain his integrity and refuse to sign? No one would blame him for signing; he will be executed if he does not. More refuses to. Tragically, his wife's love for her husband is rooted in the very virtues that will condemn him: his moral clarity and courage. She cannot make him change his mind, and she knows it. Their daughter Margaret's feelings may be even more heartbreaking. She is the child of both parents, intelligent and strong-willed; and she too sees that her father's stance will be his destruction. Can't he say one thing but mean something different in his heart, she pleads to him in his jail cell? He responds:

> When a man takes an oath, Meg, he's holding his own self in his own hands. Like water. (*He cups his hands.*) And if he opens his fingers then—he needn't hope to find himself again. Some men aren't capable of this, but I'd be loathe to think your father one of them.

It is one of my favorite lines in all literature, one of the few moments of unqualified heroism, and reluctant heroism, which is always the best kind. Not long after, More is beheaded. His seems an impossible standard, of course; and like all readers, I measure myself and see how much I am wanting. But that is the catharsis of more great works of art than I can count, and out of that wanting comes elevation and desire.

Think of his hands cupping that imaginary water. It is an image helpful for us here and in like schools, knowing that we have a legacy that was given to us by those who came before, and which we must bequeath to others. Ours should be a place where honor is deeply valued, fervently taught, and zealously guarded, knowing as we all do, that nothing matters more, and knowing we must never let it slip through our cupped hands.

Willy MacMullen, the son of two college professors and brother to two private school educators, graduated from the Taft School in 1978, attended Yale University where he majored in American Studies, and completed his masters at Middlebury College. After teaching English, coaching, and serving in various administrative positions at Taft for 17 years, he was appointed the school's fifth headmaster in 2001.

Countercultural Schools

By Patrick Bassett & John Watson

For the past thirty years the American culture has experienced repeated waves of nostalgia for better times, simpler times, different times. Our children listen to much of the same music we did. We don't like Eminem much, and they may despise Jan and Dean, but we can agree on Cream and Joni Mitchell. Clothes during the '70s were bizarre the first time around. They are, perhaps, even more weird today as the teenage culture of our youth comes back to haunt us once again, on the backs of our children, and sometimes grandchildren, no less. What was countercultural then is grease for the wheels of commercialism today.

But much of what we might label as countercultural was, in truth, quickly assimilated by popular culture and the commercial interests of the day. Music and movies were separate but equal driving forces of popular culture in the '60s, and they were certainly as commercial then as they are today. Fashion was then what fashion is today; forever changing itself in order to be the same as it once was. If fashion, music and movies drove popular culture then, it was the values of certain singers, poets and writers that drove the countercultural movement. What was most frightening to parents of the day was what the music, movies and fashion represented; a turning away from the traditional values that were handed down from their grandparents, to their parents, and then to them. That smooth transition of values stopped with the baby boomer generation.

The rejection of the values of the '50s by the teenagers and young adults of the '60s was an attempt by the hippies of the day to return to what they saw as a simpler, more pure version of what their parents once believed in, but had allowed to become corrupted. They felt that they were returning to the values of a true "American Dream" where honesty meant truthfulness in all things, where fairness meant that all humans were truly created equal. They championed a value system that trumpeted stewardship of, and living with the environment rather than exploiting it for mere money. They longed for a world where people live according to principle rather than exist as small cogs in the giant machinery of capitalism. They first sought to change the values of our country, and failing that, to change only their own.

Today, one could say we live in an incredibly similar world. Popular culture quickly sinks to the lowest common denominator in order to make headway in the marketplace. Consumption in all things is promoted as the public good, driving the GNP ever higher, and helping all of us to over indulge in even those things that are good for us. The individualism that helped to build our country has morphed into "me-ism" where opportunities for individual gratification intrude on our lives every minute of the day. We ceaselessly compete to the point where everything must be quantifiable, and there must always be a winner. Whether it is as superfluous as the popular TV show *Survivor* or as critical to the well-being of our society as the education of our children, we see competition and ranking as the only solution. We watch the evening news where "if it bleeds, it leads" creating the impression on those less discerning that our neighbors are dangerous folks to be wary of, and we should be even more fearful of those we don't know. We are fast becoming a nation of gated communities and places we know we don't visit or think about.

Honesty has become "flexible honesty" wherein plausible deniability, spin doctoring and what the meaning of "is" is play a more important part in public commerce than simply telling the truth. Fairness typically means "fairness to me," and if you are not fair to me I will sue you. The natural resources I want to steward are mine, and what happens to yours is your concern. Living by one's principles is an exercise in cost/benefit analysis, whether we are a corporation cooking the books for a higher stock price, or a taxpayer with an opportunity to hide a couple of thousand dollars. While baby boomers were certainly not always civil in their parents' eyes, they rarely if ever reached the heights of incivility of many of our athletes, and entertainers today. The purpose of professional sport outside of wrestling was to win, not necessarily to humiliate your opponent. Spectators went to events to support their teams and sometimes to "boo" their rivals, but they rarely beat up the referees or the opposing coach.

The "devolution" of culture has brought about the curious and encouraging situation where the cultural institution usually slowest to change has become countercultural despite years of trying to be with it. Effective elementary and secondary schools, whether independent or public, tend to be countercultural institutions that embrace many of the values that popular culture, clearly the dominant culture today, abandoned long ago. Those values make up the mission statements and lists of shared values our schools developed, and they are in clear opposition to those supported through popular culture.[1]

Values of Popular Culture	*Examples*
rationalize dishonesty	prevarications by presidents (Monica Lewinsky & Enron)
worship individual success	lionizing the individual; star-worship
excuse violence	bullying at all levels
accept incivility	vulgarity of everyday language, rock & rap lyrics
sexualize imagery	exposure, literally, of everything a la Victoria Secret
Win at any cost	cheating to win, if necessary
Consume conspicuously	status of cars, clothes, extravagances
assert differences	preoccupation with one's own tribe

Values of Effective Schools	*Examples*
expect honesty	honor codes
build team and community	collaborative efforts in academics, sports, extracurriculars

Values of Effective Schools	*Examples*
eschew violence	conflict resolution
expect civility	standard of "respectfulness"
expect modesty	prohibitions on "PDA," public displays of affection
expect fair play	sportsmanship codes
conserve the environment	ecological stewardship
build on commonalities	communitarian values while respecting differences

Beyond values and the will to promote them, what is it that these effective schools share? Effective schools share exceptional teachers, men and women who have undertaken with intelligence, joy and humor the critical task of educating our children. You find them in all schools to be sure. But in more effective schools you find them in greater abundance, both in the classroom and the administrative offices. Effective schools also share meaningful and appropriate moral climates. The administrators, teachers, and parents have agreed upon those things that govern the moral climate of the school and are willing to uphold them. Experience and observation tell us that effective moral climates tend to attract exceptional teachers and in a "virtuous cycle," exceptional teachers tend to support and help build effective moral climates. And that moral climate is most often in clear opposition to the dominant culture.

In our work with independent schools, we see literally hundreds of schools whose leaders know that "school climate" is the most critical element in developing both the academic and spiritual or character side of the youngsters in our charge. What follows are vignettes of schools committed to the "countercultural curriculum" of inculcating salutary moral values.

Darrow School is a small, almost entirely boarding school in upstate New York in the "far western" Berkshire Hills. Located in a former Shaker village, the school has taken to heart the Shaker motto, "Hands to Work, Hearts to God." For three hours every Wednesday morning all normal activities come to a halt as everyone from the school head to the newest student, joins for Hands to Work. They chop wood, prune trees, paint buildings, care for gardens, clean out sheds, maintain woods trails, shovel snow, plant trees, and do community service. Faculty, staff and students work side by side, and sometimes the student is the more skilled at a particular job. It is a lot of work to organize and maintain such a program, but the values are clear. Students learn humility and the value of physical work. They learn teamwork and how large tasks can be accomplished through consistent effort. They learn how individual efforts maintain and support communities. They learn how to give of themselves for the betterment of all.

Many schools sponsor overseas trips, but some take the concept much further. George School is a Quaker boarding and day school located outside of Philadelphia. Many of the qualities of a George School experience are rooted in Quakerism which has always been countercultural in some ways. But as happens in all schools, the values the community adopts are changed over time to become uniquely their own. Community service has always been an important feature of a student's life at George School. Each year a group of faculty and students travel to Cuba to work in a Quaker mission there.

The school had to advance their request to undertake the trip all the way to the Supreme Court just to get permission to begin the program in Cuba. Countercultural values abound in both the act of providing community service to "an enemy of my country" and also in demonstrating how citizens, even world citizens, can disagree on principle and still remain proactive and peaceful in action.

Some schools are creating countercultural norms with great intentionality. Cheshire Academy is pioneering the CASCLE (Cheshire Academy Student Centered Learning Environment) program. CASCLE is a planning process that seeks to improve academic performance through increases in student efficacy brought about by filtering all curricular planning through the core values of the Academy. Character education will not be a "program" at Cheshire Academy, but rather the glue that coheres all of the various programs of the school. The process focuses on professional development for faculty and takes the stance that in order to change student habits, we must first change our own habits. The CASCLE program will move to West Nottingham Academy beginning with the 2003–04 school year.

Community service programs abound in our schools. The Peddie School is situated in central New Jersey with a burgeoning immigrant population from Central and South America. For years the school has participated in a program to tutor immigrants in English through a local Catholic church. The students travel to the church one night per week to help children and adults with assignments from the English as a Second Language courses offered by the church. At West Nottingham Academy in rural Maryland the middle school has partnered with a local public elementary school to tutor students in mathematics, spelling and reading. In both cases the programs cross boundaries, both real and imagined, and in that crossing the programs become countercultural and multicultural at the same time.

Countercultural programs aren't necessarily new or different. An incredible array of programs has existed for many years in all of our schools. It is the recognition that these programs run against the grain of the dominant culture that is significant. The recognition makes them countercultural, and it makes them even more important than we imagined. We are all so inundated with cultural information every day that it is difficult to see that some of the things we do in our schools clearly defy the norms of the dominant popular culture. Once we see that, how can we not ask what else could we do to help our students see that there are different choices than the ones they see on TV or hear on MTV? What could we do to create a countercultural body image alternative for young women? What could we do to help boys understand that manhood does not equate with aggression? What could we do to reduce the incredible pressure to get into the right college by any means at one's disposal? What could we do to help make our country more sensitive to, and knowledgeable of, the wide variety of cultures and societies that make up our world? How do we teach the subtle distinctions we must make while we are at war that it is important to be patriotic and supportive of our troops and at the same time equally important to be preparing for peace and seeking peaceful resolutions in the future? All of these things, and a myriad of others, are squarely in the countercultural court.

So what's a teacher or school leader supposed to do, if he or she feels committed to these "countercultural" values that represent the most essential virtues?

We have just a handful of modest proposals.

1. Subscribe to the publications produced by the Council for Spiritual and Ethical Education (www.csee.org) and by the Institute for Global Ethics (www.-globalethics.org), where you will find penetrating ideas, case studies, and curricula for your school.
2. Become a storyteller. The best leaders (in all institutions and from all time) tell the best stories, stories that give flesh to the bones of generative ideas and moral lessons. Develop your repertoire of ten or so stories that capture the essence of the moral nature of your school community, then tell them every year.
3. Hire someone for who he or she is, not what he or she knows. We can and do mentor people with no teaching experience to become good at pedagogy, but no amount of "guidance" will change an adult's posture and character, once formed. While it's important, of course, that someone majored in math to teach math, the more important questions in the interview stage reveal "who I am." As William Bennett (former Secretary of Education and author of *The Book of Virtues,* an excellent resource of stories to use in school classrooms to teach ethical "precepts") indicates, there are three ways to teach virtue: i) by habit (the Aristotelian imperative to teach virtues by having students undertake virtuous acts), ii) by precept (the Ten Commandments, the principles of democracy, the Golden Rule, etc.), and iii) by example. Of the three, the last may be the most effective, since, as James Baldwin noted, "Children have never been good at listening to their elders, but they have never failed to imitate them."
4. Share with kids the moral dilemmas you face in your decisions at schools, and the values that dictated your decisions. It's important for teachers to know that they are, in the words of Charles L. Glenn ("Educational Freedom and Accountability") the cultural mediators between a school's mission and values and the received understanding of it by the students. It's important for school heads to share with kids, for example, why one may have expelled a student, especially when there are competing ("right vs. right") ethical considerations at hand, "what's right as a community that cares about a individual student who has made a mistake" vs. "what's right *for* the community that must uphold standards to protect the community and its values."
5. Confront your colleagues (this is the hard one) on the tough questions that permeate schools and that send the wrong signals to kids. As one wise school head said once, "The kids are the hypocrisy police." What are the rules for the adults and why are they different from those for the kids? Why do we treat kids more harshly than adults when they prevaricate, use illegal drugs, offend community standards, live promiscuous lifestyles, or behave boorishly on the sidelines of an athletic event?

Since everyone knows "school climate and values" are the most important factor the for success of schools and the kids within them, let's do, today, your quick inventory of time and resources allocated to that topic in your classrooms and at your school, and make an adjustment, if necessary, to spend more quality time, energy, and discussion on it: Attention to school climate and values is the most important thing we could possibly talk about in faculty meetings, making debate on faculty parking or parent drop-off routines or starting the day at 8:00 AM or 8:10 AM pale in comparison.

Note

[1] "Why Good Schools Are Countercultural," Patrick F. Bassett, *Ed Week,* Feb 6, 2002.

Patrick Bassett is the president of the National Association of Independent Schools. He writes and speaks frequently on subjects related to independent school life. **John Watson** is the headmaster at West Nottingham School.

Multiplicity
Radical Acts of Empathy in the Integrative School Community: A Survey of How Conversations about Knowledge Come Logically to the Idea of Story

By Craig Thorn

Justice Powell's Challenge

When Justice Powell wrote his famous opinion on the Bakke decision regarding affirmative action, a majority opinion that no one on the Supreme Court actually embraced, conservatives and liberals questioned his use of diversity as a goal for educational institutions. Liberals feared that, by not tying affirmative action explicitly to race and specifically to the idea of reparation for racial discrimination, schools might define diversity in such a way that would allow them to avoid "repairing" America's history of racism with American Indians, black Americans, and Hispanic populations. Conservatives feared that educational institutions might broaden Powell's idea of diversity to include all kinds of quota systems to serve all kinds of populations, effectively shutting out the mainstream population.[1] In effect, both sides disapproved of Powell's "majority opinion" because it defined a process, not a goal. Introducing "diversity" to the social science of school communities, Powell's opinion represents an awareness that affirmative action might not be the sole solution to the plight of minorities in America, but also that it might be a small part of the process by which social communities can be created.

Powell's strange and wonderful opinion represents an understanding of what Peter Senge calls dynamic complexity, the apprehension of interrelationships rather than linear cause-effect chains, of a meta-story about educational institutions and American culture. Sandra Day O'Connor's curious and hopeful opinion in the Michigan Law School case (Grutter v. Bollinger) that affirmative action might be "unnecessary" in 25 years represents a preoccupation with what Peter Senge calls detail complexity: In effect, eventually minorities will enter schools without any discretionary attention and so the schools will be multicultural communities and our work as reluctant social engineers will be done (71–73). The genius, however, of Powell's language is that it invites schools to rise above what has become the monologic of multicultural politics to the dialogical complexity of a more comprehensive diversity. To use Ken Wilber's and Jerome Bruner's helpful language, Powell's opinion continues to challenge schools to embrace cultural pluralistic relativism (Wilber 58; Bruner CE 3). Moreover, Powell's expansive language challenges us to take his opinion further than he could go as a Supreme Court justice navigating the politics of the bench. We have to imagine schools as ideal communities. We have to embrace Bruner's idea of students' creating communities as thinkers about thinking and Wilber's idea of universal integralism by reevaluating our curricular programs, perhaps even redefining what a curriculum is (Bruner CE 19; Wilber 53).

Powell's opinion was not polemical; on the contrary, it was an encomium to the essence of education as dialogical in intention. Writes Justice O'Connor of Justice Powell's opinion in Bakke in her own majority opinion on Grutter v. Bollinger, No. 02-241:

> We have long recognized that, given the important purpose of public education and the expansive freedoms of speech and thought associated with the university environment, universities occupy a special niche in our constitutional tradition. In announcing the principle of student body diversity as a compelling state interest, Justice Powell invoked our cases recognizing a constitutional dimension, grounded in the First Amendment, of educational autonomy: "The freedom of a university to make its own judgments as to education includes the selection of its student body." From this premise, Justice Powell reasoned that by claiming "the right to select those students who will contribute the most to the 'robust exchange of ideas,'" a university "seek[s] to achieve a goal that is of paramount importance in the fulfillment of its mission." Our conclusion that the law school has a compelling interest in a diverse student body is informed by our view that attaining a diverse student body is at the heart of the law school's proper institutional mission. . . . The law school's interest is not simply "to assure within its student body some specified percentage of a particular group merely because of its race or ethnic origin." That would amount to out-right racial balancing, which is patently unconstitutional. Rather, the law school's concept of critical mass is defined by reference to the educational benefits that diversity is designed to produce. . . .
>
> These benefits are "important and laudable," because "classroom discussion is livelier, more spirited, and simply more enlightening and interesting" when the students have "the greatest possible variety of backgrounds. . . . "
>
> . . . The skills needed in today's increasingly global marketplace can only be developed through exposure to widely diverse people, cultures, ideas, and viewpoints.[2]

In her clear reliance on Powell's reasoning about the university's educational mission, we can conclude that O'Connor endorses the fundamental role of dialogue in contemporary education and the creation of leaders in modern culture. Even our smaller independent schools are now serving students who represent diverse geographies, socioeconomic backgrounds, religions, and sociopolitical views. I would argue, therefore, that schools need a fresh approach to creating an integral school community that goes beyond race and culture (multiculturalism) or even varied backgrounds (diversity), toward celebrating the endless variety of kinds of knowing itself, what I am calling multiplicity. I would argue, furthermore, that embracing multiplicity will not lead to Bruner's acute relativism in which everything means something or the endless deconstruction that Wilber feels besets our academic culture in which everything means nothing (Bruner CE 8; Wilber 23).

There is a curricular choice that is integrative and leads to a unified constructivist vision that is moral, intellectual, and emotive: an approach that corrects the fragmentation in our curricular culture that currently separates the physical, spiritual, communal, and academic curricula of our schools. I would argue that all relevant discussions about education lead to storytelling as a way to create a dynamic school community that is intellectually rigorous, emotionally demanding, and morally subtle. By storytelling, I do not mean to conjure up campfires or fairy tales, although Bruno Bettelheim might correctly argue that they have great promise in the curriculum that focuses on multiplicity. And by embracing multiplicity, I certainly do not mean that schools must anxiously add more staff to their residential offices or more special events recognizing the multiplying perspectives and constituencies they represent. On the contrary, the emphasis is not on stories, but storytelling. And by storytelling, I mean the Bakhtinian dynamics of teller, story, audience, the contexts of each, and the immanence of language when teller and listener find the meta-story of themselves in the vibrant space between them (Todorov 57).

Neil Postman, John Dewey: Fragmented Knowledge and Early Reconstructions

In *Teaching as a Conserving Activity,* Neil Postman's pessimistic evaluations of television as the enemy of language-centered learning might be applied to information technologies today:

> In an environment in which nonlinguistic information is moved at the speed of light, in non-hierarchical patterns, in vast and probably unassimilable [sic] quantities, the word and all it stands for must lose prestige, power, and relevance. . . . (Postman, TCA 75)

In the presence of the television media, students give up trying to order a coherent view of the world because the world is presented to them in fragments, discreet images in a non-linear, non-narrative fashion (Postman TCA 78). He also anticipates, however, the promise of information technology. Fearing that the formulaic nature of television's simplified narratives subsumes the content, Postman writes:

> We come to reify our procedures: to believe that procedure supercedes purpose, that in fact procedure is more real than purpose. (Postman TCA 92)

Postman's diagnosis of television culture and his lament that schools played into that culture by quantifying and technicalizing learning in formulaic codified learning sequences that flatten individuality is still true today. He echoes Ken Wilber's assessment of educational curricula as postmodern, reductive, and deconstructionist (Postman TCA

94–106).[3] Postman offers what remains our best response, a language-centered curriculum that recognizes discourse communities. He argues that students need to learn the rhetoric of a subject. Every subject's language, he argues, is a kind of literature. In order to understand a subject, students need to learn the language by which inquiry, discourse, and argument is made in that subject: if a student is to adequately speak the language of a subject, he must change his personality, his manner of thinking, feeling and believing, to suit that subject's language, its way of looking at the world. (Postman TCA 165-167) This kind of linguistic empathy is very close to what most schools hope to accomplish in what has become our residential curriculum. In this way, Postman argues, students can contextualize meaning and therefore see multiple meanings at once. His comment on the word "law" nicely summarizes this point:

> To read the phrase "the law of diminishing returns" or the "law of supply and demand" requires that you know how the word "law" is used in economics, for it does not mean what it does in the phrase "the law of inertia" (physics) or "Grimm's law" (linguistics) or "the law of the land" (political science) or "the law of survival of the fittest" (biology). To the question, "What does 'law' mean?" the answer must always be, "in what context?" (Postman TCA 163)

Postman's arguments about language in a social context—the idea that by placing language of learning at the center of a curriculum we place students in an active relationship with the information swirling around them—echoes the father of educational theory in America, John Dewey, who, in *Experience and Education,* saw early on the importance of students' *experiencing* the acquisition of knowledge.

In response to his sense that students received static knowledge without context or personal relevance, Dewey adopted a scientific approach to learning by summarizing the dialectic process by which we gather information in which students observe phenomena, compare these observations with previous experience and the knowledge of others' previous experiences, and assimilate the resulting body of information in a more inclusive understanding of the original phenomena based on previous and present experiences. At the heart of this endeavor is a dialectic between student and teacher; student and other students; and student and contexts, past and present (Dewey, 69 and 85).[4] In short, Dewey's emphasis on experiential learning bridges classroom education with social and cultural experience:

> In the case of education, modulation means movement from a social and human center toward a more objective intellectual scheme of organization, always bearing in mind, however, that intellectual organization is not an end itself but is the means by which social relations, distinctively human ties and bonds, may be understood and more intelligently ordered. (Dewey 83)

That Dewey sees this movement as a dynamic relationship between interior and exterior systems (the student's accumulation of knowledge through personal experience and the potentially static bodies of knowledge that schools impart to the student) accounts for his continued relevance, today and to our discussion of a dialogic education based on continuous analysis and creation of stories about knowledge that redefines how we look at curricula:

> [W]hat has been said is organically connected with the requirement that experiences in order to be educative must lead out into an expanding world of subject-matter, a subject-matter of facts or information and of ideas. This condition is satisfied only as the educator views teaching and learning as a continuous process of reconstruction or experience. This condition in turn can be satisfied only as the educator has a long look ahead, and views every present experience as a moving force in influencing what future experiences will be. (Dewey 87)

Postman and Dewey suggest a process of learning that is collaborative, meta-cognitive and continuous. Though Postman is responding to media culture and Dewey to nineteenth-century traditions of authoritarian teacher-centered education, they both turn to language-centered dialogues as the way to reform schools.[5]

How does the relatively simple idea of dialogue in the school community rise to the level of a school's pedagogical philosophy, perhaps even its central mission? A brief look at Jerome Bruner and Mikhail Bakhtin offers us the philosophical underpinnings of multiplicity.

Bruner, Bakhtin, and the Risk of Relativism

Both Mikhail Bakhtin and Jerome Bruner struggle with the idea of a central moral stance because they both brilliantly argue the contingency of all language-based inquiries into a *subject* (something that is ephemeral, changeable) as opposed to an *object* (something that does not change), and they distinguish the human sciences or narrative mode from the scientific or paradigmatic mode of thinking so that they cannot avail themselves of the reifiability of science (Bruner AM 11–25; Todorov 23). So both thinkers understand religion to be a construction of language and therefore relative to and contingent upon shifting realities of speaker and audience and of historical, cultural, and social contexts. And they argue persuasively that science, on the contrary, is to be distinguished from the narrative mode of thinking or human sciences because it finds truth "by eventual appeal to procedures for establishing formal and empirical proof" (Bruner AM 11). Underlying both Bruner's theories of cultural psychology and Bakhtin's theories of inter-subjectivity (based as they both are on an understanding of story and dialogue) is an anxiety about creating a hopelessly diffuse relativism absent some absolute moral truth. This challenge is important to schools because what we argue here is that independent schools along with colleges and universities have the ability and responsibility to create "perfectly" diverse communities. Simply put, if your school is rich with countless perspectives representing endless contexts, how do you develop a unifying mission that all can embrace that is not hopelessly vague and difficult to apply in programmatic, productive ways?

Before we address the challenge of finding coherence in true diversity, we need to fully appreciate the richness of Bakhtin's basic philosophy of rhetoric and Bruner's brilliant vision for school community.

For Bakhtin, all understanding is dialogical (Todorov 22). That is to say, all meaning as we understand it is a negotiation through communication between the perceiver and an other. There is no meaning independent of language. Furthermore, a speaker represents a colloquy of voices from a series of concentric, fluid circles of influence starting with family and ultimately including historical and geographical contexts. Because the speaker is in constant dialogue with these contexts, shaping them through perceptions and being shaped by them, these contexts are both centripetal and centrifugal. This same inter-subjectivity or heterology defines the spoken word and the spoken to (Todorov 56). In fact, the self does not exist save for its communication with and relation to an other:

> The very being of man (both internal and external) is a *profound communication. To be* means to *communicate*. . . . Man has no sovereign territory; he is all and always on the boundary; looking within himself, he looks *in the eyes of the other* or *through the eyes of the other*. . . . I cannot do without the other; I cannot become myself without the other; I must find myself in the other. . . . (Todorov 96)

Consequently, understanding itself is an act of creation. One must first identify with another through his or her speech, imagine his or her worlds of experience and influence, and then one must place perceived meanings in the context of one's own worlds of perception. Bakhtin refers to this "double movement" as a rigorous act of discipline (Todorov 99). He recognizes that the contingency of meaning itself, its relativity to contexts, stems from the move in western culture from a monological values system to a much more complex dialogical condition in which there are a polyphony of voices in the absence of one ideological discourse that connects language to absolute meaning (Todorov 103).[6] So the Self must contain a plurality of consciousness. For Bakhtin, the absence of a central language to which one refers when gauging the meaning of a communication is both a burden and a blessing:

> There is no first or last discourse, and dialogical context knows no limits ([as] it disappears into an unlimited past and in our unlimited future). Even *past* meanings . . . can never be stable (completed once and for all, finished), they will always change (renewing themselves) in the course of the dialogue's subsequent development. . . . At every moment of the dialogue, there are immense and unlimited masses of forgotten meanings. . . . Nothing is absolutely dead: every meaning will celebrate its rebirth. The problem of the *great temporality*. [sic] (Todorov 110)

So Meaning is never realized, and no dialogue is actually finished. As a result, the Self and the Other are never "resolved," but they are also never limited. Perhaps because of his own situation in Stalinist Russia, Bakhtin defines "death" as the absence of a listener, the absence of the ability to be heard when speaking. Bakhtin also recognizes, however, the great energy required in order to compensate for the absence of an overarching language/meaning. While there are discourse communities (communities in which everyone shares a particular linguistic code that signifies meanings—a church, an academic discipline, a profession, a political party, a township), the individual must make up for the impossibility of the "objectivation of completion" (Todorov 106). Bakhtin comes up with what amounts to his own definition of empathy to define how one fills the absence of an absolute meaning: "The most important moment of this surplus is love . . . then, confession, forgiveness, finally simply an active understanding, watchful listening" (Todorov 106).

Jerome Bruner sees the Self similarly because he embraces Nelson Goodman's idea that "no one world is ontologically privileged as the unique real world" (Bruner AM 96):

> [S]elf as a text about how one is situated with respect to others and toward the world—a canonical text about powers and skills and dispositions that change as one's situation changes from young to old, from one kind of setting to another. The interpretation of this text *in situ* by an individual is his sense of self in that situation. (Bruner AM 130)

Relying on Vygotsky's zone of proximal development in which the child develops multiple perspectives based on perceived scaffoldings of meaning in turn based on perceived responses to actions (Bruner AM 73–75), and Piaget's idea of initial constructed "cultures" between child and mother (Bruner AM 96–98), Bruner offers a compelling definition of education's role in the development of the responsible individual:

> It follows from this view of culture as a forum that induction into the culture through education, if it is to prepare the young for life as lived, should also partake of the spirit of a forum, of negotiation, of the re-creating of meaning. But this conclusion runs counter to traditions of pedagogy that derive from another time, another interpretation of culture, another conception of authority—one that looked at the process of education as a *transmission* of knowledge and values *by* those who knew more *to* those who knew less and knew it less expertly. (Bruner AM 122)

In effect, Bruner argues that education's job is to train students to think about meaning-making even as they are making meanings themselves. He has, in effect, arrived via his cultural psychology at Dewey's conclusions a generation before him. He argues that "the child must [not just] make his knowledge his own, but that he must make it his own in a community of those who share his sense of belonging to a culture" (Bruner AM 127). Bruner's educational program, furthermore, is very similar to Peter Senge's learning organization in that he perceives the most successful school as one that invites negotiation and speculation, that creates an "amenableness to imaginative transformation" (Bruner AM 127). And his adding to Michael Halliday's functions of language the idea of metalinguistics, argues for something very much like Ken Wilber's higher states of consciousness as the culminating stages of that theorist's growth hierarchies in which the self embraces particular meanings even as it acknowledges other meanings to which it contributes and by which it is corrected (Wilber 52–57).[7] Echoing Bakhtin's aforementioned double movement, Bruner speaks of the "immediate implication that follow from the 'two-faced' nature of language" when he describes the discipline required of the student in the school community:

> *How* one talks comes eventually to be how one *represents* what one talks about. The stance and the negotiation over stance, by the same token, become features of the world toward which one is taking stances. And in time, as one develops a sense of one's self, the same pattern works its way into the manner in which we interpret that "text" which is our reading of ourselves. . . . Reflection and "distancing" are crucial aspects of achieving a sense of the range of possible stances—a metacognitive step of huge import. The language of education is the language of culture creating, not of knowledge consuming or knowledge acquisition alone. (Bruner 131–133)

However exciting this prospect is, Bruner like Bakhtin senses the anxiety inherent in a world of multiple stances. "Once an aboriginal reality is given up," he writes, "we lose the criterion of correspondence as a way of distinguishing true from false models of the world. Under these conditions," Bruner continues, "what can protect us against the galloping relativism that threatens to ensue?" (Bruner AM 98).

This is the question with which we began our discussion of Bruner and Bakhtin and if anything the question is still more delicate. In a school that embraces their perspectivalist, constructivist approaches to knowledge and meaning, are we not asking students to believe and not believe at the same time? Isn't this approach on some level fundamentally sacrilegious?[8]

Throwing Out the Baby with the Bathwater: Reuniting Thought and Emotion in Story

Ken Wilber rightly observes that liberal humanism inadvertently abandoned religious thought or spirituality in its suspicion of all traditional hierarchies. In other words, the modern mind rejected spiritual inquiry when it dismissed the trappings of specific religions and in particular, the use of religious, political, and socio-economic systems to oppress others (Wilber 25). Wilber attempts to reunite science and religion by showing that they both rely ultimately on similar, speculative modes of thinking, which he defines as a basically dialogical process leading ultimately to a higher state of consciousness that is integrative.[9] The three steps of inquiry are:

1. a practical injunction or exemplar
2. an apprehension, illumination, or experience
3. communal checking (either rejection or confirmation) (Wilbur 74)

Simply put, we engage in the world, we record and process our experiences, and then we share our conclusions in a community that has accumulated a body of perceptions about similar experiences. The resulting modifications of personal and communal perception account for culture. He goes on to dismiss the specific iconographies of religion as emblems of narrow religion and so exclusionary and even potentially fanatical. The iconography of religion is, in effect, monological. "Narrow" religion as he calls it is to be distinguished from spirituality or deep religion because the latter continues to change, embracing the integrative ideas of growth and inquiry (Wilber 78). I take exception to this last distinction because it misses the essential creative act that truly binds religious and scientific thought, and even more importantly thought and emotion.[10] The way in which objects and actions are transformed into signifiers of a physically absent meaning is through *story:* The Talmud, the Bible, and the Koran are all meta-stories that are "true" in that they have survived and evolved through countless interactions in countless discourse communities, but they are still stories.[11] So they are essentially dialogical in their creation. Their application may sometimes be monological, oppressive, even violent, but the initial act is speculative and communicative.[12]

Likewise, science relies on stories as well as it speculates new avenues of inquiry and possible explanations for seemingly disjointed bodies of information.[13] My own research of student writing at the higher end of our curriculum at Phillips shows that students across disciplines use basic forms of narrative expression to write about the law, biology, literature, physics, even math. More importantly, they *think* about narrative as they are consciously writing in the discourse of that particular discipline. They are, in short, conscious of the nuances from discipline to discipline even as they are aware of deep patterns in the rhetoric of thinking and writing about the subject at hand.[14] So while Wilber is careful not to throw out the baby (spirituality) with the bathwater (specific religious rituals and icons), I argue that the baby is the narrative means by which a spiritual sense is achieved, and the bathwater the way in which a believer might see the story of his or her faith and not the story's resonance with other stories.

Stories and storytelling engage all the intellectual and emotive elements of the individual. In order to understand a story, one must be able to apprehend the constitutive and intuitive elements that go into the making of a story and one's understanding of the story. Furthermore, if we understand the individual or ourselves as a composite of stories in the evolving story of that individual or our self in his or her or our development as a person in a community of persons (the person as text), then we have achieved an understanding of the spiral dynamic that is at the heart of a community: the endless relationships between the part and the whole. Our ethics stem from a rigorous discipline about how we understand, create and communicate stories. At the heart of our endeavor is our awareness of ourselves in others stories and our ability to see in our story others. This is radical empathy and it requires great passion in our intellectual pursuits and intellectual rigor in our full experience of compassion. It reunifies ratio-logical thought with intuitive, creative feeling. It has profound implications for our fragmented contemporary curriculum.

Bruner would argue that the way we resist rampant relativism is in the crucible of exchanges between self and others in which we find patterns that define certain codes of behavior. In its broadest sense, that patterned space between self and other is what Bakhtin calls translinguistics (an awareness of evolving generic patterns in language and thought that unite various ways of making culture), what Bruner calls meanings incarnate (Bruner AM 159), and what Ken Wilber calls universal integralism where meta-narratives return after being maligned by his long list of evils: "pluralistic relativism, extreme egalitarianism, antihierarchy furies, deconstructive postmodernism, fragmenting pluralism" (Wilber 28).

In *The Culture of Education,* Bruner offers a series of tenets he feels are essential to a psycho-cultural approach to education. These tenets serve a storied community well as they insist that the student is capable of thinking about thinking; maintaining and cultivating multiple, even seemingly contradictory perspectives; embracing belief systems even as they can intellectualize their provisional, contextual status; understanding the "minds of others" (Bruner CE 20); collaborating with peers and adults to formulate and reformulate ideas based on experiential learning; developing in entirely different ways depending on varying learning styles and settings (Bruner CE 26); recognizing the historical, socioeconomic, geopolitical contexts in which their education takes place; questioning the institutions of which they are a part even as they respect the serviceability, even elegance of those institutions in facilitating the questioning; contributing to their own educational program and evaluating themselves in ways that are rigorous, rewarding, and culturally relevant. All these abilities inhere in the early stages of any child's development, but few are utilized explicitly in our modern curricular agenda. To these abilities implied in his tenets, Bruner adds the narrative mode of thinking. He offers these thoughts, which I cite in full:

> None of us know as much as we should about how to create narrative sensibility. Two commonplaces seem to have stood the test of time. The first is that a child should "know," have a "feel" for, the myths, histories, folktales, conventional stories of his or her culture (or cultures). They frame and nourish an identity. The second commonplace urges imagination through fiction. Finding a place in the world, for all that it implicates the immediacy of home, mate, job and friends, is ultimately an act of imagination. So, for the culturally transplanted, there is the imaginative challenge of the fiction and "quasi-fiction" that takes him or her into the world of possibilities. . . . Obviously, if narrative is to be made an instrument of mind on behalf of meaning making, it requires work on our part—reading it, making it, analyzing it, understanding its craft, sensing its uses, discussing it. (Bruner CE 41)

Bruner invites us to do what Powell's decision does: create a truly diverse community in progress in which dialogue constitutes the meeting and endless evolution of stories in a kind of meta-story about storytelling.

Models for Multiplicity in the Modern School

Before I turn to models for multiplicity in the modern independent school, I want to address the matter of trust. Implicit in these arguments is the sense that a school will cohere despite the relativism a story-oriented approach might invite. "Students need more direction than multiplicity offers" might be the argument. One need not study the research extensively to note that students are well versed in the basic premise of multiplicity already. The information revolution and globalization together present the student with multiplicity in crude, telegraphic form. Postman would argue that students are exposed to visual images only, bereft of story and the moral implications of sound narrative structures. He may be right, but the innate abilities and, I would argue, sensitivities are there for us to nurture.

Consider that our students are presented with multiple narratives daily inside and outside the classroom. We just do not talk about them that way, nor do we suggest that they are rich with nuances that create conversations among them, deeper narratives that rise above the individual point of view. The very premise of the independent school—a community defined by some more general sense of excellence or special interest—creates more informal dialogues of the kind I have been describing than our occasionally clumsy formal constructions could possibly hope to recreate. How many students, for instance, embrace a religious faith and a scientific discipline simultaneously? How often must a student internalize differences between the stories implied in the architecture of this intentional campus and the municipal designs of a former school? My own research notwithstanding, I am always momentarily surprised to learn that the students in my advanced English classes have well-developed perspectives in disciplines not related to English, and moreover that they sometimes compare our ways of thinking to the mathematician's or artist's way of thinking. This happens because invariably I discover this ability in students while knee-deep in the interior rules of my own discourse. It is hard to climb out. Students are much lighter on their feet than we are, less set in their ways than we think.

So schools should start a reevaluation of their curricula by listening to their students and getting them to talk about what they already know, but perhaps do not know they know. They have astonishing things to say about the way academic disciplines comment on one another; the way community service reminds them of biology class; what they would really want to do with an all-school meeting schedule; what they really think of your residential program or community affairs office; how a campus with twenty outdoor tennis courts feels different from a city with twenty outdoor basketball courts; how different the Korean-American experience is in the Silicon Valley from the Korean-American experience in South Korea, and how it is similar. Schools should show students how stories work, what dialogue means. Schools should talk about how they work complexly. And schools should recognize that doing so means creating time and space in the curriculum and the daily schedule. Remember, however, that multiplicity does not mean more workshops, more staffing, and more curricula in and out of the classroom.

An underlying theme in any approach to multiplicity in a school community is that *less is more*. We have too many requirements, too many meetings, and too many discrete parts to a school day. If we want students to *experience* the idea of multiplicity, then our first move is paradoxical: Expose them to less information. In our rush to honor every ethnic group, every academic discipline, every possible extracurricular and co-curricular possibility, we have mimicked the very culture of images sans narrative that invites superficiality and cynicism. Schools know this, but internecine politics cripple any effort to change the pace of life. However, the reasons for doing so are compelling, and not just in the context of my arguments for the storied community. Here, in brief, are the most provocative advantages to a simpler curricular plan:

- directed time for reflection about the process of learning, the experience of it
- increased focus on what is left behind so that students can think about the process of acquiring, assessing and assimilating new information in more depth
- more freedom and responsibility for students to develop programs with teachers that represent their "story" in the sense I have described here
- opportunity to compare developing stories around them as students pursue some interests in great detail as opposed to many interests superficially
- creating a culture in which what is dealt with is cared for by the school community and not merely glossed over
- making the space necessary to put presently fragmented programs into meta-programs that represent more comprehensive approaches to learning and truer assessments about the way knowledge is acquired

Now here are some practical suggestions that may seem dramatic, but work when perceived as a whole, especially when the students are apprized of the meta-story a school community is trying to tell:

- Create six diploma tracks: arts and humanities; math and science; language; history and social science; religion and philosophy; and a core curricular track. Students take a core curriculum that exposes them to all the disciplines through ninth and tenth grade. Then, in the eleventh grade, they are invited to take one extra course (in effect, two courses) in the discipline of their choice, dropping one discipline as a result. Or they can continue to take the core curriculum. In the twelfth grade year, students may continue to take two courses in the discipline of their choice, but they will be expected to produce a major project in their discipline. All students in the senior year have the option of taking inter-disciplinary courses instead of a core curriculum.
- Cut syllabi back to allow more time for practical, transactional applications, extensive collaborations among students, alternative modes of assessment, inquiry-based problem solving models, opportunities to introduce other forms of meaning-making (disciplines, modes of thinking and learning outside the classroom) to the subject at hand, and *discussion of the interior rules of rhetoric—methods of inquiry, definition and exposition—of each discipline* (Postman TCA 148–168).

- Make sure that the school allows the opportunity for opposing views on political and social issues to be expressed in speakers' forums, publications, and all school meetings. Make a point of having students and faculty tell stories about their passionate interests.
- Explore alternative teaching spaces and alternative class sizes. Students can and should learn in large classes as well as small ones, and some students will thrive in electronic classrooms. Consider lecture-style courses with small study groups, weekly tutorials with small groups, seminar-based courses in which different teachers monitor self-study, and students as assistants in skills-based courses. These course dynamics anticipate work environments in which they will have to learn how to learn in the real world.
- Require that each student has at least one of the following experiences during his/her tenure as a student at your school:
  - a team-taught course
  - a course with multiple visiting teachers in which there is a faculty coordinator, but the only real constant are the students who "put the material together" themselves
  - an inter-disciplinary course on any subject: the photography, math, poetry, physics and history of the Brooklyn Bridge . . .
  - an independent project
  - a performance-based assessment
  - a transactional/pragmatic course as in a course that leads to direct application in the world off campus
  - a course that focuses on another culture
  - a research-based course
  - a course about a current political or social issue

Knowing that these courses exist is in itself an education for students. By offering them, the school is offering the possibility of new kinds of conversations among students outside the classroom about different ways of experiencing knowledge, different ways of knowing something.

- Create opportunities for faculty to attend classes in other disciplines.
- Use local businesses and the community whenever possible, inside and outside the classroom.
- Create student publications beyond the school newspaper and the literary magazine: magazines with political biases and social agendas; magazines that feature scholarship by faculty and students based on academic work, art, and photography; a general magazine that reviews art, music, movies, television, current trends, and popular culture. They do not have to be fancy. They just need to be everywhere. No student should be denied the opportunity to write outside the classroom.
- Develop a team of teachers across disciplines who research and create programs for writing across the curriculum.[15]

- Whenever and wherever possible, maintain and create off-campus programs. These need not be overseas. The Merrimac River may as well be a thousand miles wide between Lawrence and Andover, MA, where Phillips Academy is located. A foreign place in the storied community can be Malaysia or the local barbershop.
- Expand the work-duty program to include more than menial cleaning, even if it means complex release forms.
- The co-curriculum or life issues curriculum is coordinated with the whole school to focus on fewer subjects each year, alternating year to year to insure that the four-year student is exposed to a variety of perspectives on a variety of issues. So, for instance, one year the focus might be on Hispanic cultures in America. Academic disciplines, co-curricular programs and extra-curricular activities would all devote some time throughout the year on this broad subject, which other years could be the environment, civil rights, African-American history, the Pacific Rim, the Middle East, or helping the local town with the senior center.
- Redefine multicultural education more broadly so that it openly explores the ideas of dialogue and perspective so that:
    1. minority students do not feel as if they have to "represent" their minority
    2. there is a school-wide understanding that many factors define perspective
    3. academic and social curricula are re-combined and seen as working in concert to foster in students a sense of multiplicity
- If it has not done so already, the athletic program shifts its focus from inter-scholastic sports to physical education and development. Students are offered the opportunity to have one term off from sports in the eleventh- or twelfth-grade year, but otherwise are expected to participate in athletic activity every term. Sports teams reduce their schedules slightly.
- The school develops collaborative learning experiences in the classroom; more inter-disciplinary (combined disciplines on a general subject) and multi-disciplinary courses (distinct courses on parallel subjects); more opportunities for experiential learning; alternatives to class sizes including team-teaching, lectures and sub-groups, student-centered classes in which the teachers rotate from week to week to address the subject from their discipline's point of view.
- Reduction in the output of extracurricular activities on a cycle. For instance, one term/semester/year the paper comes out once a month and the next it comes out once every one or two weeks, so that students experience the challenge of hard work outside the classroom, but also the opportunity to think about what they are doing as opposed to just doing it.
- Create funds for house counselors to spend time with their students socializing, not just "discussing" life issues. In general, shift the focus in residential life from talking about how to live life to living it.
- Consider collaborations with other schools: peer schools in which students share projects; younger schools in which students work as assistant teachers.
- Involve "real world" adults in classroom and community service education.

One of the great ironies of our current curricular programs is that they look like multiplicity run amok. As a consequence, what we say we do and what we are really doing are actually contradictory. We say we are exposing students to a variety of disciplines. We are, in fact, teaching them how to hustle. We say we are sensitizing students to many cultures. We are, in fact, training them how to handle themselves and others correctly. We say we are teaching the whole student. We are, in fact, breaking him or her up into parts, but not putting them back together again. Visit any contemporary independent school and multiplicity reflects the excesses of our enthusiasm, our good intentions. Look at the daily schedule. We are teaching students how to read that Rubik's cube of squares and colors. That excessively complicated compartmentalization is the product of our current education.

Because we are good teachers, we sense this and across the country in school after school. One hears the complaint that there is no time to talk, no time to reflect. The most frustrating complaint is also the most telling: students say that we do not spend enough time with them. And yet we seem to spend all our time with students: in classrooms, dorms, playing fields, stages, and meetings upon meetings upon meetings. We are less likely to spend time with them on porches, in backyards, on paths, at dining halls, movies, plays, museums, on streets, in living rooms and kitchens. We talk about community incessantly because we have tried to create one out of parts relying on the bureaucratic constructions of an old and tired model for schools. We have specialists who are in charge of community. We hire professional coaches. We hire professional administrators to run our schools. We bring in experts to talk to us about talking. This fragmentation and specialization has happened because schools are in a dialogue with our contemporary culture that has ceded the idea of community to professional talkers and listeners, professional managers.

In the absence of neighborhoods, towns, and city blocks, we have for kids organized sports, play dates, pre-professional camps, a nearly stupefying litany of testing and exercise-taking, and codified lesson plans inside and outside the classroom through middle school, and for adults we have talk shows featuring reductive narratives, sensationalized and *psychologized* in mock forums that are more Roman than reflective; "reality television" in which people are put together in clever houses, races, and islands and then, in an extraordinary exacerbation of the dialogical dynamic between individual and community, told to work together but know that ultimately it will be one on one for a single prize; and a news media that presents a monological point of view on the world not because it wants to be political so much as it wants to be popular, and one point of view is a lot easier to absorb than two or three, or more.

In the dialogues between culture and school, however, we must remember that all dialogue has two speakers and two listeners. It is time for us to respond to a fragmented culture not by becoming fragmented ourselves but by embracing the very multiplicity that threatens to overwhelm us. Doing so is a challenge. All communities tell a story and stories take time to tell because we are the storytellers: the students and teachers. We are what make this community. You cannot instruct students about different points of view ad nauseum and expect students to internalize an expansive understanding of a polyphonic, many-voiced world. You have to create an environment in which students and teachers *experience* stories inside and outside the classroom. That takes time.

Stories are curative, communal, collaborative, corrective, collective, and essentially cognitive in that they require a simultaneous awareness of self and other. Stories arrange your experience in an order that makes sense to you and, you hope, makes sense to others. Because a story must be shared, it is organized, but it is also changeable. You, the storyteller, are the authority, but you can also change the story because it is made up of relationships between people, places, and things that are openly subjective—*particularly the relationships*—the product of your feelings and thoughts. Stories are relative in their truth, but true nonetheless. The only contract between the teller, the story, and the listener is mutual respect. Storytelling is fundamentally an ethical act, both a leap of faith and a scientific experiment.

What I propose requires a reduced curriculum and, yes, a smaller "physical" landscape of choices, but a grander "theoretical" landscape of possibilities. It requires telling students about what we're teaching as we're teaching it and asking them to tell us what they're learning as they're learning it. If we want students to understand and find a place in the global village, then we have to show them how to see interrelationships rather than linear cause-effect chains, see processes rather than snapshots (Senge 73). If you want students to appreciate the idea that quantum theory is as mysterious and elusive as the life of insects, that the life of a Peruvian woman can instruct the choices a farm girl from Kansas makes, that neutrinos approach the poetry of Wallace Stevens, and that the music of Mahler can inform architecture or numbers theory, you cannot just tell them that it does. They have to experience it. Multiplicity cannot just be thought. It must be felt. And that happens reverently in the fluid, polyphonic, and unifying worlds of stories.

Bibliography

Bloom, Lynn Z., and Edward M. White, eds. *Inquiry: A Cross-Curricular Reader*. Englewood Cliffs: Prentice Hall, 1993.

Bruner, Jerome. *Actual Minds, Possible Worlds*. Cambridge: Harvard UP, 1986.

———. *The Culture of Education*. Cambridge: Harvard UP, 1996.

Britton, James. *Prospect and Retrospect: Selected Essays*. Ed. Gordon M. Pradl. New Jersey: Boynton/Cook, 1982.

Castillo, Ana. *So Far From God*. New York: Plume, 1994.

Connors, Robert J., Lisa S. Ede, and Andrea A. Lunsford, eds. *Essays on Classical and Modern Discourse*. Carbondale: Southern Illinois UP, 1984.

Corcoran, Bill, Mike Hayhoe, Gordon M. Pradl, eds. *Knowledge in the Making: Challenging the Text in the Classroom*. Portsmouth: Boynton/Cook, 1994.

Dewey, John. *Experience & Education*. 21st ed. New York: Collier Books, 1979.

Everdell, William R. *The First Moderns: Profiles in the Origins of Twentieth-Century Thought*. Chicago: The University of Chicago Press, 1997.

Gordimer, Nadine. *Writing and Being*. Cambridge: Harvard, UP, 1995.

Gould, Stephen Jay. *Dinosaur in a Haystack: Reflections in Natural History*. New York: Harmony Books, 1995.

———. *The Hedgehog, the Fox, and the Magister's Pox: Mending the Gap Between Science and the Humanities*. New York: Harmony Books, 2003.

Hall, Kermit L., ed. *The Oxford Companion to the Supreme Court of the United States*. New York: Oxford UP, 1992.

Holquist, Michael. *Dialogism: Bakhtin and His World*. New Accents. Terence Hawkes, ed. New York: Routledge, 1994.

Kinneavy, James L. *A Theory of Discourse*. New York: W. W. Norton & Company, 1971.

Moffett, James. *Teaching the Universe of Discourse*. Portsmouth: Boynton/Cook, 1968.

Morrison, Toni. *Song of Solomon*. New York: Plume, 1987.

Murakami, Haruki. *A Wild Sheep Chase*. Trans. Alfred Birnbaum. New York: Kodansha International, 1989.

Nussbaum, Martha C. *Upheavals of Thought: The Intelligence of Emotions*. Cambridge UK: Cambridge UP, 2001.

Piaget, Jean. *Language and Thought of the Child*. Trans. Marjorie Gabain. New York: New American Library, 1974.

Piaget, Jean and Bärbel Inhelder. *The Psychology of the Child*. New York: Basic Books, 1969.

Postman, Neil. *The End of Education: Redefining the Value of School*. New York: Knopf, 1995.

———. *Teaching as a Conserving Activity*. New York: Delacorte Press, 1979.

Senge, Peter M. *The Fifth Discipline: The Art & Practice of The Learning Organization*. New York: Currency Doubleday, 1994.

Silko, Leslie Marmon. *Ceremony*. New York: Viking, 1977.

Steiner, George. *Grammars of Education*. New Haven: Yale UP, 2001.

Straw, Stanley B., and Deanne Bogdan, eds. *Constructive Reading: Teaching Beyond Communication*. Portsmouth: Boynton/Cook, 1993.

Tan, Amy. *The Bonesetter's Daughter*. New York: Putnam's Sons, 2001.

Thomas, Lewis. *The Fragile Species*. New York: Scribner's Sons, 1992.

———. *Late Night Thoughts on Listening to Mahler's Ninth Symphony*. New York: Viking, 1983.

———. *The Medusa and the Snail: More Notes of a Biology Watcher*. New York: Viking, 1979.

Todorov, Tzvetan. "Mikhail Bakhtin: The Dialogical Principle." Trans. Wlad Godzich. *Theory and History of Literature* 13. Minneapolis: University of Minnesota Press, 1984.

Vygotsky, Lev. S. *Mind in Society: The Development of Higher Psychological Processes*. Eds. Michael Cole, Vera John-Steiner, Sylvia Scribner, and Ellen Souberman. Cambridge: Harvard UP, 1980.

———. *Thought and Language*. Revised Edition. Ed. Alex Kozulin. Cambridge: MIT Press, 1986.

Wilber, Ken. *A Theory of Everything: An Integral Vision for Business, Politics, Science, and Spirituality*. Boston: Shambhala, 2001.

Young, Art, and Toby Fulwiler, eds. *Programs that Work: Models & Methods for Writing Across the Curriculum*. Portsmouth: Boynton/Cook, 1990.

———. *Writing Across the Disciplines*. Portsmouth: Boynton/Cook, 1986.
Zebroski, James Thomas. *Thinking Through Theory: Vygotskian Perspectives on the Teaching of Writing*. Portsmouth: Boynton/Cook, 1994.

Notes

[1]Alex Thorn, "The Precedential Value of Justice Powell's Opinion in Regents of the University of California v. Bakke 438 US 265 (1978)," unpublished (2003): 8–10.
[2] From excerpts from Justice Sandra Day O'Connor's majority opinion in Grutter v. Bollinger, *New York Times* 24 June 2003: A24.
[3] When Postman expresses his fear that schools will be called upon to right social and cultural wrongs, he echoes Wilber's shrewd observation that political correctness, though morally idealistic, can encourage a cult of sentimentality, adolescent rebellion or worse, a cynical facility with codified language because multicultural programs are too often presented as snapshots and not stories. Colleagues of mine call the risk that we might be teaching students not to be sensitive, but to be shrewd, "waving from the motorcade." Indeed, in his book *The End of Education: Redefining the Value of School,* Postman refers to multiculturalism as one of the false gods (along with economic utility, technology, and consumership), offering five constructivist narratives as the new gods of the modern era: the unfortunately titled Spaceship Earth, Fallen Angel, American Experiment, Law of Diversity, and World Weavers/the World Makers. This last is identical to Bruner's idea of a constructivist education.
[4] Dewey's scientific approach parallels Ken Wilber's argument in *A Theory of Everything,* that science and deeper spirituality rely on similar rules of inquiry: a practical injunction or exemplar based on the actor's desire to know a pattern; an apprehension, illumination or experience, and; a communal checking with the discourse community or "community of the adequate" (75). It also nicely coincides with Peter Senge's mental models in *The Fifth Discipline* that require balancing reason and intuition, observation and generalization, espoused theories and theories-in-use (186). Both authors agree with Dewey that objective and subjective (exterior and interior) knowing must be united.
[5] An excellent introduction to basic discourse theory as it applies to academic disciplines is James L. Kinneavy's book *A Theory of Discourse*.
[6] Bakhtin describes what William Everdell in his book *The First Moderns* called discontinuity, the revelation in all disciplines—George Cantor and numbers theory, Seurat's pointillism, de Vries and the gene, Einstein's theory of relativity, Whitman's free verse, Schoenberg's experiments in music—that the space between the individual and the absolute could not be bridged, and in fact might become the subject of art and science itself.
[7] Wilber's holarchic quandrants of development, based in part on Clare Grave's spiral dynamics, are remarkably similar to Mikhail Bakhtin's intersubjectivity, his theory of endless contexts spiraling out from and into the self, the communicated/perceived, and the other. Writes Wilber in *A Theory of Everything:* "It appears that the self is not a monolithic entity but rather a society of selves with a *center of gravity,* which acts to bind the multiple waves, states, streams, and realms into something of a unified organization . . ." (Wilber 54).
[8] George Steiner's most recent book, *Grammars of Creation,* addresses this anxiety directly, but does so in a way that anticipates our answer to this concern: namely in a nearly musical return to and embrace of first narratives of creation, the actual forms of creation myth to which, I would argue, many important ethnic-American writers such as Toni Morrison, Leslie Marmon Silko,

Ana Castillo, and Amy Tan have returned in some of their works and about which many writers from around the world have mused, writers as diverse as Haruki Murakami, Gabriel García Márquez, Milan Kundera, and Nadine Gordimer. Gordimer's book *Writing and Being* offers a fascinating perspective on the close relationships between factual observation and fictional renderings.

[9] It is interesting to note that the most popular shows on television tap into our culture's apparently deep need to unite the two basic modes of thinking: scientific and narrative. The main drama in the *X Files* was the tension between Mulder's interest in finding the mythic narrative embedded in unexplained phenomena and Scully's need to find a scientific explanation for the same phenomena, curiously manifest in the sexual tension between the two FBI agents. *Law & Order* and all its derivatives play on the dramatic tension in multiple dialogues between forensic science and sordid human stories. Notice that these shows work hard to keep the personal narratives of the regular protagonists out of the show, their wavering ability to keep their own stories from intersecting with the human drama of the story becoming the poignant closing minute of each episode, as they attempt to use the "science" of their professions as a shield (literally) from the empathy they cannot afford to feel for the tragedies playing out before them. *CSI* and *Jordan's Crossing* have simply made these dialogical dynamics more extreme. Medical dramas like *ER* rely on a similar tension as the measure of doctor's professional success seems inversely related to his personal success, the sudden shifts in point of view, from chaotic personal narrative to sharp, focused scientific narrative and back again, are part of the thrill of the show.

[10] Bruner shows that feeling is an essential part of knowing by following Piaget's explanation of how a child first comes to know things by experimenting with action and his or her feelings about the consequences of those actions. For Bruner and for Piaget, the resulting dialogue between the developing self and the world around it is the first cultural experience a child has. Martha Nussbaum's latest work, *Upheavals of Thought,* has as its central premise the proposition that emotions are "part and parcel of the system of ethical reasoning."

[11] Surely Chaucer understood this when he introduced the Wife of Bath's argument that women do not fare well in the Bible because the Bible was written by men. Of course, she then goes on to interpret the Bible in a way that justifies her outlook on life. This is no different from the retellings of creation one finds in Leslie Marmon Silko's *Ceremony* or Toni Morrison's *Song of Solomon*—two novels that are *about storytelling and storytellers as the enactment of stories themselves*—or in the essays of Lewis Thomas or Stephen Jay Gould, scientists who rely on combinations of narrative and science to retell stories of creation and death.

[12] Wilber points out as have many observers that religion accounts for most of the world's violent conflicts.

[13] Thomas has devoted much time in a number of books to his concern that science has hurts its own cause by placing itself in opposition to the humanities. Essays at the end of *The Medusa and the Snail, Late Night Thoughts on Listening to Mahler's Ninth Symphony,* and *The Fragile Species* are preoccupied with the contentious debate between scientists and humanists. Stephen Jay Gould addresses this concern directly in his posthumous book, *The Hedgehog, the Fox, and the Magister's Pox,* in which he argues that true inquiry must use the tools of both the scientific and humanistic methods of inquiry.

[14] I asked five teachers from five disciplines to pick the best senior writer in their respective senior electives. I then invited the five seniors to share their papers with each other and the five teachers. We then met as teachers, students, and students and teachers. In each of these three meetings, we all talked about the papers, the disciplines (biology, philosophy, English, history, chemistry), the courses, the teacher-student relationships, and writing in general. I am currently halfway through the second part of this study. In the second part, I am following 12 students for four years

through our curriculum. Each term (we have three a year), I interview them twice about their writing and thinking about writing. I also collect papers they have written for various subjects each term. The 12 students have just finished their tenth-grade year. Independent of the courses and the curriculum, they are developing a nascent understanding of the multiple ways of knowing things and multiple ways of expressing that knowing.

[15] Actually, of all the elements of a curriculum that embraces multiplicity, writing across the curriculum and writing theory are the most widely researched and developed. Some texts that study both writing across the curriculum and attendant ideas such as discourse communities and dialogism are *Essays on Classical Rhetoric and Modern Discourse,* edited by Connors et al.; *Thinking Through Theory: Vygotskian Perspectives on the Teaching of Writing,* James Thomas Zebroski; *Programs That Work* and *Writing Across the Disciplines* edited by Toby Fulwiler and Art Young; *Constructive Reading: Teaching Beyond Communication,* edited by Stanley B. Straw and Deanna Bogdan, particularly the essay "Beyond Actualization" by John Willinsky; and *Knowledge in the Making: Challenging the Text in the Classroom,* edited by Bill Corcoran, Mike Hayhoe, and Gordon M. Pradl, in particular Corcoran's essay "Balancing Reader Response and Cultural Theory and Practice" and Mark Faust's essay "Alone but Not Alone: Situating Readers in School Contexts." One of the best anthologies of essays that feature multi-disciplinary writing is *Inquiry: A Cross-Curricular Reader,* edited by Lynn Z. Bloom and Edward M. White.

Craig Thorn has taught at Phillips Academy for 22 years, where he has served a term as chair of the English department. He has been the editor-in-chief of Avocus Publishing for seven years. He is the author/editor of six books on education.

"Everything We Do Is Moral!" Moral Education in the Curriculum

By Judd E. Kruger Levingston

What makes a school a moral place?

"But everything we do is moral!" exclaimed a teacher at the outset of a day's workshops on moral education. She pointed to the debates about the treatment of slaves in history classes, the consideration of pollution in biology classes, the community service activities, and the one-semester health classes that sophomores take. From the mission of the school to inspire students to live by a set of values that will make them responsible citizens to the athletic program that aspires to teach sportsmanship, a typical school day could be filled with opportunities for moral education.

At the same time, it was necessary to point out that some might ask, "Whose morals are being taught?" At our school, we may emphasize community service that directs students into the larger community, while another school with a religious affiliation may emphasize the development of inner piety to the extent that one's individual moral formation takes precedence over social service projects. Some schools may emphasize the building of social relationships within the school community, while others emphasize the importance of academic rigor, reasoning that academic rigor is the surest way to combat ignorance.

In the classroom, teaching about the Civil War or environmental science does not guarantee that students will wrestle with moral issues: It is possible that the history teacher will maintain a tight focus on names, dates, and battles to the exclusion of discussions about states' rights, self-determination, and Lincoln's moral leadership. The environmental science teacher may focus more on chemistry and biology and less on human decision-making that led to pollution. A math teacher is correct in pointing out that the geometry of a triangle or the formula for parabolic or sine curves have little to do with morality. Does this mean that moral education cannot take place in a math class? For a math teacher, it may even be the case that a broad discussion about a moral issue might distract a student and impede her ability to recall specific information that will be useful on a standardized test such as the SAT-II or an Advanced Placement exam! It is not necessarily enlightening or even practical to bring moral issues into the classroom.

Is everything indeed moral, or should we be more reserved, regarding moral issues as belonging on the periphery of our work as educators? Should we save moral issues for freeform discussion once the most important content has been mastered? Can there be a middle ground in which a school acknowledges its role in the moral formation of its students while also acknowledging that moral issues and moral content may not pervade every aspect of a school's curriculum?

It would be difficult for a school to escape its inherent moral purpose. Public schools were founded to inspire educated citizens who could participate in civic life. Even in places where educational leaders may be motivated less by idealism and more by the need to train children for the workforce, as Philip W. Jackson and his co-authors write, "schools tacitly subscribe to a broad policy of acting in the best interests of the students they serve." Some schools may be more innovative than others, and some schools may be limited by economic constraints, but "the adults within our schools are basically good people who are out to serve as best as they can" (Jackson, et al. 1993, p. xvi).

Many schools have founding statements and mission statements that include a moral component. Phillips Exeter Academy, for example, received a deeply moral deed of gift from John Phillips in 1781. In the deed, Phillips wrote that his gift should make possible a school that teaches both goodness and knowledge: "Knowledge without goodness is dangerous, and goodness without knowledge is weak and feeble, but combined they form the noblest character." At the school where I presently serve in the administration, Chestnut Hill Academy, there are five core values that are symbolized in five light blue stripes on the forearms of the lower school student jerseys: courage, honesty, integrity, loyalty and sportsmanship. Middle and upper school students easily recall the five values because they are part of the school culture. These five values are invoked on a wide variety of occasions, from reminders about spirited play in gym classes to discussions about literary characters in English classes and discipline committee meetings evaluating a student's conduct.

Religious schools and schools from different movements pride themselves on the moral element in their statements of mission. The Solomon Schechter Day School of Greater Boston identifies a different set of five core values that are displayed on their website homepage: "Nurturing the soul, Inspiring the mind, Developing potential, Building community, and Continuing the tradition." In New York, the Rudolf Steiner School, a Waldorf School, has a deep moral mission coming from secular values. The school philosophy includes academic and moral goals for its students: "Through our rich curriculum and innovative teaching methods, we address the whole child, working to develop clarity in thought, balance in feeling, and conscience and initiative in action." While the rigorous academics at the school foster intellectual development, the statement continues, "Most of all, the close human relationships at our school help students develop a strong sense of themselves and an awareness of others." Mission statements with a moral angle are not limited to independent schools. A New York City public high school on the Upper West Side of Manhattan, The Beacon School, includes a statement about moral education in the school statement of mission: "The Beacon School students will participate in a curriculum which supports the development of character integrity and healthy lifestyle habits."[1] Schools with a moral element to their mission may be guided by a variety of factors: a set of core secular values, certain religious values, and a commitment to include moral issues in the curriculum.

John Dewey contends that a teacher's purpose is to impart ideas that will lead to moral behavior. In the opening paragraphs of his essay, "The Moral Purpose of a School," he writes:

> The business of the educator—whether parent or teacher—is to see to it that the greatest possible number of ideas acquired by children and youth are acquired in such a vital way that they become *moving* ideas, motive-forces in the guidance of conduct. This demand and this opportunity make the moral purpose universal and dominant in all instruction—whatsoever the topic. (Italics original. Dewey, 1959, p. 2)

While it would be hard to dispute the moral role of the institution in promoting civic values and in following through on its mission, many may bristle at the moral role of the teacher who is charged with shaping the values of young people. Dewey acknowledges that moral issues cannot always be at the forefront of a class discussion, but he does claim that moral thinking can be taught actively:

> It is not out of the question to aim at making the methods of learning, of acquiring intellectual power, and of assimilating subject-matter, such they will render behavior more enlightened, more consistent, more vigorous than it otherwise would be. (Dewey, 1959, p. 3)

Dewey's challenge to schools has reached into the second half of the twentieth century and into the new century as educational thinkers have continued to probe moral education and moral life in schools.

James Davison Hunter's *The Death of Character* (2000) considers the ways in which moral education has been furthered in recent years from the focus on "Values Clarification" in the 1960s to "Educating for Character" in the 1980s. In contrast to some of these more psychologically based approaches to moral education, the privately produced curriculum entitled, "Facing History and Ourselves," focusing on genocide in World War II and on rebuilding society in its aftermath, takes historically based material as its point of departure for moral education. Hunter concludes that in our day, society is too diffuse for a consensus about values, so it is not realistic to expect that reasonable people will share the same set of values. Such a consensus would require a greater degree of shared religious beliefs about what it means to be good and about consequences or sanctions for behavior that has fallen short of the good (Hunter, 2000, p. 200).

Coming from a different angle, the journalist Patricia Hersch writes that schools and parents have abdicated their responsibility to provide moral guidance. Her exploration of adolescent life in and out of "South Lakes High School" in *A Tribe Apart* portrays well meaning but ineffective teachers who lack sufficient time to focus on moral issues. Whether in regular classes or in special theme-based days on topics from honor to racism, students often understand what may be expected of them, but they are more likely to eschew a moral course of action and pursue compromising behavior in order to find benefits in the short term. As part of her study, Hersch meets parents who admit that they cannot seem to stop their children from risky behavior, and she meets students who know what they *should* do, but who don't always act according to their conscience. She cites a student poll that indicated that 90% of the student body said that they cheated "once in a while, to some of the time, to anytime I can get away with it" (Hersch, 1999, p. 99–100). Many of the young people she meets seem to be living in a moral vacuum, needing the guidance of an adult who can set limits and establish the grounds for positive moral behavior (Hersch, p. 296).

The Explicit and Implicit Curriculum

Goodlad, in *A Place Called School* (1984), describes the "explicit" and "implicit" curriculum in a school. The "explicit" curriculum is based in the rules and program that can be described in handbooks, course catalogues, and in the things said out loud at assemblies or in other settings. As part of the explicit curriculum, a school may provide Advanced Placement courses that lead students toward the annual College Board examinations each May. Other elements inform the "explicit" curriculum from state curricular requirements to budget and enrollment parameters that may determine the breadth of offerings. Certain teachers' loves also may affect curricular offerings: Ms. Smith loves to teach an elective on East Asian history, but not on South Asian history; Mr. Smith teaches satire, but not poetry. Traditions may also guide and inform the explicit curriculum: the holiday assembly requires that music classes be given over to preparation of holiday music, or the tenth-grade trip to Boston means that colonial history is emphasized in tenth-grade English and history classes. Sometimes, long-standing traditions such as that trip to Boston may continue to inform part of the curriculum even after the tenth grade history program has shifted to a focus on world history. Other elements in the explicit curriculum affect the education outside of the classroom: assemblies and religious services, community service days, athletic contests, and "ism days" (focusing on racism or ageism, etc.) have the capacity to transform student awareness about themselves and about the world outside of their school boundaries.

The "implicit" curriculum, though more elusive, pervades a school's moral climate as well. Some call it the "hidden" curriculum (Simon 2001, p. 53). Clues to the implicit curriculum can be found on a walk through the hallways of a school where one can observe whether students learn to "work alone or competitively or to work cooperatively in groups, to be active or passive, to be content with facts or also seek insight and on and on. Architecture, funding priorities, and even the administrative structure of a school have implications as well on the implicit curriculum. In brief, writes Goodlad, schools implicitly teach values" (Goodlad 1984, p. 30, quoted in Simon 2001, p. 260 n. 1).

Some of the more cynical critics of independent schools may view social and economic advancement as a hidden curriculum within an independent school, and it is not unusual for critics to accuse independent schools of treating moneyed students or parents differently from their less wealthy peers. The history of independent schools shows that many independent schools in the first half of the twentieth century remained homogeneous enclaves. This began to change after World War II when many, including

Harvard University president James Conant called for independent schools to become more diverse by welcoming youth from different economic, racial, and social backgrounds. As Arthur G. Powell points out in his book, *Lessons from Privilege* (1996), although 8% or more of a school's population come from families who face economic difficulties, the typical independent school student continues to come from wealthy or moderately wealthy suburbs and has little or no contact with fellow citizens who are low-achieving (Powell, 1996, pp. 108–9). While the implicit curriculum of the past focused on preparing student for the privileges of membership in the upper classes, the implicit curriculum today in independent schools focuses on preparing students for excellence in their academic work (Powell, 1996, p. 110).

When Philip Jackson and his co-authors embarked on a unique project to explore the ways in which moral values are conveyed in schools, they spent countless hours in classrooms, hallways and offices. Speaking with members of the school community and observing classes at all levels, they came to describe their findings in *The Moral Life of Schools* (Jackson et al. 1993). In this book, they identify eight different "expressions" of morality as the most telling indicators of a school's moral climate. The first four of these eight expressions of morality are based in the "explicit" curriculum, such as:

1. moral instruction as a formal part of the curriculum (e.g., courses in specific religious teachings or courses in citizenship)
2. moral instruction within the regular curriculum (e.g., debates in history about the abuse of power, or discussions about the impact of industrialization on the environment in a biology class)
3. rituals and ceremonies (e.g., opening day ceremonies, citizen(s) of the week; weekly assemblies; most improved player awards; Cum Laude or National Honor Society inductions; headmaster's essay projects; community service days thoughts of the week)
4. visual displays with moral content (e.g., library posters that urge, "Grab life by the covers!"; displays about exemplary alumni; posters urging students to "Be cool, stay in school!")

The fifth expression of a school's moral stance relies on teacher initiative and less on curriculum, but it is quite explicit as well:

5. spontaneous interjections of moral commentary into ongoing activity (e.g., "Pick up that paper, please." Or "That's no way to treat your friend; how would you say that differently?")

Administrators and teachers may urge students to behave themselves when students are assembled together, but their messages may be heard most clearly when they interject themselves into a conflict taking place in the midst of the regular day. When asking a student to pick up a piece of paper, for example, the teacher could make the request empty or full of moral meaning. Consider two approaches: "Please pick up that paper—

even if you didn't put it there, it helps to keep our school clean!" and "Why is that paper on the floor?" The first emphasizes a shared sense of responsibility; the second approach puts the student in a defensive stance in the initial salvo in a power struggle between the student and the teacher-authority figure.

Jackson and his co-authors identify three other ways in which schools communicate views about moral life that may have deep reverberations. These three areas include:

6. classroom rules and regulations (e.g., listen to your peers, cite the works of others)
7. the morality of the curricular substructure (e.g., English 9 focuses on leadership and power; science 10 requires independent research; history 11 emphasizes foreign cultures; all twelfth-grade students deliver speeches about subjects important to them)
8. expressive morality within the classroom.[2]

There may be ways in which moral relativism seems to operate in these three areas. In some classrooms, for example, students may be required to raise their hands to show their respect, patience and an ability to listen to their classmates ideas; in other classrooms, students may be told *not* to raise their hands in order to learn how to participate in an adult-level seminar. In some schools, ninth-grade English may focus on leadership and power while other schools may focus the curriculum on the quest for truth. Whether in rules and regulations or in curricular choices, choices are being made by adults with a vision for students' well-being and with a vision for the community they seek to create within their classrooms.

A thoughtful reading of *The Moral Life of Schools* might lead one to conclude that however a school may determine its guiding values, it will only be successful if the teachers at the school accept the institutional values and agree to teach them. Nel Noddings, an educator with an interest in school culture and moral education, offers a thoughtful response to this critique: schools need to foster an ethic of caring. In *The Challenge To Care in Schools* (1992), Noddings writes that schools are inherently moral places, grounded in the importance of caring about each student. Children are not interchangeable, Noddings writes, so teachers need to use different teaching methods and content in response to their students' interests and motivations (Noddings, 1992, p. 8). In their relationships with students, teachers need to be individuals who care, and they also need to teach their students, in turn, how to become individuals who care (p. 18).

Noddings describes the four dimensions to moral education that emphasizes caring. These dimensions include modeling, dialogue, practice and confirmation. Modeling involves educators being caring, themselves and showing what it like to care for and to be cared for. Dialogue involves a commitment to open-ended conversations between teachers and learners in which both hear each other and seek understanding. Practice involves a commitment to action, to respecting differences in background and gender, and to community service and other opportunities to show caring. Confirmation involves the ways in which adults provide feedback to students, affirming or seeking to correct behaviors they observe (Noddings, 1992, pp. 22–7). The fulfillment of this vision of a caring educational environment requires a commitment on the part of a school to fostering caring among the teachers and to possible changes in the academic program to allow for dialogue and practice to take place.

Attention to Moral Education in the Media

The vast literature that exists concerning moral education probes many different angles, including the possibility that moral development takes place in stages (Kohlberg, 1984), the possibility that gender may affect one's approach to moral issues (Gilligan, 1982; Gilligan et al., 1988), and even the moral narratives of children (Tappan and Packer, 1991). Robert Coles explores the moral lives of children from the perspective of a psychiatrist seeking insight into the moral choices that children make (Coles, 1986). In recent years, educational thinkers and participants in policy debates who are critical of "values clarification" approaches to moral education have instead focused on ways to promote what they call character education (Lickona, 1991, Hunter, 2000). Educational researchers have looked at moral education in religious schools (Ingall, 1999; Simon, 2001) and schools have been founded to focus on promoting academic integrity beyond a simple honor code (Gauld, 2003).

A sampling of articles from daily newspapers and from *Education Week,* the periodical concerning secondary educational practice and policy, reflects a popular interest in moral education. In the pages of the Philadelphia *Inquirer,* Susan Snyder explores a program in Delaware County, PA, in which students are engaged in the study of six areas of character: wisdom and knowledge, courage, love, justice, temperance and transcendence. The district, in partnership with teams from nearby universities, seeks to help students to develop and strengthen their moral character (Snyder 2002). In the education section of the Boston *Sunday Globe,* Laura Pappano explores the newly renovated Phillips Church on the campus of Phillips Exeter Academy in New Hampshire. At Exeter and at other schools in the Boston area, she finds that student interest in religion is strong and that students see religion as a positive force for building cross-cultural understanding. Pappano quotes a Protestant chaplain at Phillips Academy in Andover, MA, Michael Ebner, who comments that a religious gathering of students allows them to consider issues of justice, righteousness, aggression, and compassion (Pappano, 2003, p. B10).

Character education continues to appear as an important issue in the pages of *Education Week.* Essays occasionally call for programs of character education to become part of the foundation of an academic education. Howard Good,who teaches in New Paltz, NY, calls upon schools not to lose sight of their role in character development. Drawing from the four major characters and their respective quests in *The Wizard of Oz*—the Tin Man who seeks a heart, the Scarecrow who seeks a brain, the Lion who seeks courage, and Dorothy, who longs to return home—Good writes that a thoughtful program of character education could help students to develop a sharp intellect without sacrificing their hearts; help students to develop moral courage in the face of contemporary dilemmas; and help to provide a sense of connection and community so that students feel that they are at home (Good, 2002).

In an essay entitled, "Cheating, Honor Codes, and Integrity," Joseph W. Gauld, the founder of Hyde Schools in Maine, writes that character development needs to be a priority in schools because it can create a sense of community among faculty and students and because it can stimulate "a superior level of academic excellence" (Gauld, 2003, p. 41). In a third essay about the advent of a "virtual schoolhouse," Gene Maeroff of Teachers College cautions that an increasing focus on cyber-learning could jeopardize the quality of character education. He writes, "Character takes shape within the crucible of personal interaction" (Maeroff, 2003, p. 28). Online learning offers new frontiers for students in the realm of what Goodlad calls the "explicit curriculum," but the loss of personal interactions would deplete the effectiveness of the teacher-student relationship in the "implicit curriculum."

In recent years, psychologists have studied the ways in which children develop moral reasoning. An article in *The New York Times* health and fitness section reports that psychologists have found many schools offering and requiring programs in character education to combat the perception among two-thirds of Americans believe that morality has declined. The psychologists with whom the reporter has spoken believe that morality is a psychological "triad of emotions, thoughts and actions" (Gilbert, 2003, p. F5). Researchers have found that community service programs help to create a positive climate in schools. Jerome Kagan has identified three core moral emotions that lie "At the foundation of morality." These core emotions are empathy, fear and guilt. Cultivating these emotions and teaching moral character may be difficult to achieve because in the crux of the moment, an individual might only choose a moral course of action if she or he has time. If he is in a hurry, he might not stop to help someone, even if he knows that he should (Gilbert, p. F5). Like the writers in *Education Week,* Gilbert shows that classroom talk is insufficient to teach moral education and that moral character can be cultivated, even if it cannot be guaranteed, through performing service to others, by visiting artistic and athletic events, and by seeking activities that provide inspiration and a sense of achievement (Gilbert, p. F10).

New Directions in Moral Education

With schools paying increasing attention to moral education, it is fair to expect that new approaches to moral education and new studies will emerge. The work of Philip Jackson and his co-authors (1993) shows that field-based research could portray the ways in which morality is lived or emphasized in schools from ritualized ceremonies and activities to the ways in which teachers teach their students to become accountable young adults. Carol K. Ingall explores the unique setting of Jewish schools as places not only to transmit history and culture, but also as places to cultivate a new generation of thoughtful participants in an ancient dialogue about obligation and responsibility (Ingall, 1999, p. 69). She clarifies the role of moral education: Regardless of a school's formal affiliation, moral education "includes the realms of thoughts, feelings, and action, or knowing the good, loving the good, and doing the good" (Ingall, 1999, p. 82). While traditional programs of moral education sought to teach what is good in order to promote good behavior, present programs cannot expect to impart information and values in a traditional style. Instead, the values need to be explained, and not merely imparted, as authentic and relevant.

The challenge, as school people are likely to know, is that an authentic, instructive, and open-ended approach to moral education would require a great deal of time, something sorely lacking in schools. In her field research conducted in schools, Katherine Simon (2001) found that many well-meaning teachers lack the pedagogical skill to help students to develop their own moral character, or they lack sufficient time. A class in American history, for example, typically needs to "cover" nearly four hundred years of American history between September and June, so a twenty-minute digression into the moral implications of a particular law or policy might take the class too far afield. Simon describes a class looking at the United States during the New Deal, and she observes the teacher posing the question on a worksheet, "Do you consider social engineering a valid function of government?" Students become animated as they begin to raise their hands, but the teacher says that the class is "going to let it alone now." In a similar situation in a literature class based on a study of Elie Wiesel's novel *Night,* a student asks about the challenges to Jewish faith during World War II. The teacher maintains her own focus on symbols in the novel, preferring not to confront religious questions and deflecting the question to the school's rabbi.[3] If these teachers were to heed the call of many of the authors cited in this essay, if they had another chance to respond to their students, perhaps they would have seized the moment and helped to facilitate a discussion about the moral dimensions of history and literature.

After reading writers such as William Bennett (1996) and James Davison Hunter (2000), we might conclude that without attention to moral education, children will grow up with a form of moral relativism. Social philosophy offers reason for optimism. Charles Taylor's book *Sources of the Self: The Making of Modern Identity* (1989) suggests that each of us is part of a community already, and that our "web of interlocutors" gives us a language with which we define our identities and establish our moral perspectives. We are not free from others: Taylor argues, "We cannot do without some orientation to the good" and that our identities are determined by where we stand in relationship to the good (Taylor, 1989, p. 33). It would be difficult to imagine a school community that runs without a value system that praises, at the very least, good personal conduct and academic progress. By the same token, a school can foster character education and moral development through attention to the important messages in statements of mission and in other components of the explicit curriculum from curricular units on moral issues in different departments to service learning programs, student and faculty recognition, and through the cultivation of a corps of adults who are willing to serve as role models and advisors.

Returning to the faculty meeting in which the teacher contended that everything at a school is moral, it is clear that she is partially right. Everything has the potential to be moral, because moral education takes place not only through the explicit curriculum but also through the implicit curriculum. By paying attention to the implicit curriculum and to expressive forms of morality, a school community can become a moral community. Symbolic representations of the school's mission statement, training adults to be thoughtful leaders both in and out of the classroom, and cultivating a student leadership that is empathetic to adult concerns can all help to create a strong web of discourse about moral issues, ultimately shaping the moral lives of young people.

Bibliography

Bennett, William J. (ed.). (1996). *The Book of Virtues for Young People: A Treasury of Great Moral Stories*. Parsippany, NJ: Silver Burdett Press.

Coles, Robert. (1986). *The Moral Life of Children*. Boston: Atlantic Monthly Press.

Dewey, John. (1959). *Moral Principles in Education*. New York: Philosophical Library.

Gauld, Joseph W. (2003). "Cheating, honor codes, and integrity." *Education Week*. 2 April, p. 41.

Gilbert, Susan. (2003). "Scientists explore the molding of children's morals." *The New York Times*. 18 March, pp. F5, F10.

Gilligan, Carol. (1982). *In a Different Voice*. Cambridge: Harvard University Press.

———, Ward, J.V., et. al. (Eds.). (1988). *Mapping the Moral Domain*. Cambridge: Harvard University Center for the Study of Gender, Education and Human Development and Harvard University Press.

Good, Howard (2002). "Off to see the Wizard: What does it mean to be educated?" *The Education Week*. 11 December, p. 29.

Goodlad, John I. (1984). *A place Called School: Prospects for the Future*. New York: McGraw Hill.

Hersch, Patricia. (1999). *A Tribe Apart*. New York: Ballantine.

Hunter, James Davison. (2000). *The Death of Character*. New York: Basic Books.

Ingall, Carol K. (1999). *Transmission and Transformation: A Jewish Perspective on Moral Education*. New York: Jewish Theological Seminary.

Jackson, Philip W. et al. (1993). *The Moral Life of Schools*. San Francisco: Jossey-Bass Publishers.

Kohlberg, Lawrence. (1984). *The Psychology of Moral Sevelopment*. New York: Harper & Row.

Maeroff, Gene I. (2003). "The virtual schoolhouse." *Education Week*. 26 February 2003, pp. 28, 40.

Noddings, Nel. (1992). *The Challenge to Care in Schools: An Alternative Approach to Education*. New York: Teachers College Press.

Pappano, Laura. (2003). "Academy welcomes believers, nonbelievers." *Boston Sunday Globe*. 2 March, p. B9.

Powell, Arthur G. (1996). *Lessons from Privilege: The American Prep School Tradition*. Cambridge: Harvard University Press.

Simon, Katherine G. (2001). *Moral Questions in the Classroom: How to Get Kids to Think Deeply About Real Life and Their Schoolwork*. New Haven: Yale University Press.

Snyder, Susan. (2002). "Assignment: Learn to be happy." *The Philadelphia Inquirer* (10 December), pp. A1, A14.

Tappan, M.B. and M.J. Packer (eds.). (1991). "Narrative and storytelling: Implications for understanding moral development." *New Directions for Child Development,* 54. San Francisco: Jossey-Bass Publishers.

Taylor, Charles. (1989). *Sources of the Self: The Making of Modern Identity.* Cambridge: Harvard University Press.

Notes

[1] Each of these school's websites includes information about their core values and mission: www.exeter.edu; www.chestnuthillacademy.org; www.ssdsboston.org; www.steiner.edu; and www.beaconschool.org.

[2] In Jackson et al., 1993, p. 42, these eight categories appear in list form. The entire first chapter, pp. 1–44, "Looking for the Moral," describes the approach the researchers took in examining the many dimensions of the moral life of schools as participant observers seeking to find meaning in the many details of school life.

[3] Simon, 2001, pp. 78, 87. Simon explores these challenges throughout chapter 4 of her book. The chapter is entitled, "We could argue about that all day: missed opportunities for exploring moral questions" (Simon, 2001, pp. 53–98).

Judd Kruger Levingston is head of upper school at Chestnut Hill Academy, Philadelphia, PA. He was ordained as a rabbi and he received his doctorate at the Jewish Theological Seminary in New York.

TECHNOLOGY

Coherent Curriculum and Technology

By Bernadine Sommer, Jill Gerber, & Suzanne Gill

A comprehensive tool that links standards and instruction, assessment and evaluation, the IMSeries™ is a relational database, accessible by teachers at school or at home, that connects the innumerable pieces of the curriculum, and continues a child's record across grade levels. The software helps ensure that the designed curriculum is implemented—that units teach to Forsyth's standards and assessments tell how the students are "doing" in the standards. When the system is fully implemented, teachers, administrators, and parents will be able to view a student's progress and achievement in real time and over the continuum of years.

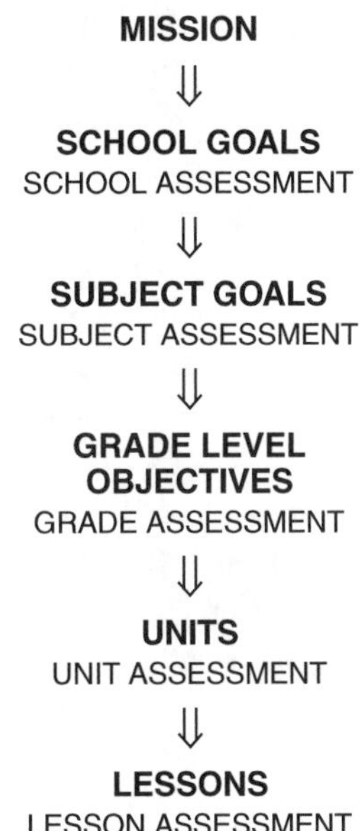

Figure 1 Mission-Driven Curriculum

In 1995, in response to an ISACS evaluation, Forsyth School began its design of a coherent curriculum tied to the mission of the school. Dr. Findlay McQuade was the consultant who taught the faculty "the architecture of curriculum" (fig. 1.) Over the course of four years, the faculty revised the curriculum under his guidance, so that the lofty ideals of the mission were reflected in every aspect of the day-to-day life of the school.

MISSION

The mission of Forsyth School is to provide children with a supportive atmosphere and opportunities for success in order that they may develop self-confidence and a love of learning.

SCHOOL GOALS

Forsyth students will learn to:

- cultivate curiosity and ask questions
- enjoy challenge, take risks, and solve problems
- be honest, fair, compassionate, and kind
- develop leadership and cooperative skills
- read well, write well, and compute well
- be as interested in process as in outcome
- gather, organize, and construct the meaning of a large body of knowledge
- connect their studies to the world outside school and use their knowledge as responsible members of a democratic society
- respect, understand, and appreciate differences between people and use their knowledge as responsible members of a pluralistic world
- express themselves joyfully and creatively in the visual and performing arts
- use computer technology as a means of expression and investigation
- participate regularly in physical activity and value the role of physical activity in maintaining a healthy lifestyle
- recognize and appreciate their own individual strengths, take responsibility for their own learning, and develop self-discipline.

Figure 2 Mission-driven School Goals

As a first step toward having the mission drive the curriculum, the trustees and faculty translated the mission into School Goals (fig. 2), which provided the foundation for all the layers that followed. The second step was the design of the subject area standards, derived from the school goals, national standards, school traditions, and best practice. Next, the subject area standards were broken down by grade level and each grade's contribution to the child's achievement of the goals, over time, was articulated. After that, the units that would 'teach' the grade level objectives were determined, and so on into unit design, activities and lessons. The documents all began with the stem, "The students will be able to . . ."

Another design element of the structure is that each subject area is sub-divided into strands. There are several reasons. The strands facilitate documentation and discourse, assessment of student achievement, and evaluation of program design. For example, the strands in language arts are process, listening, reading, speaking, writing, and language.

In social studies, the strands are process, history, geography, culture, current events, and citizenship.

An essential characteristic of the curriculum design is that it is built for change, not stasis (fig. 3.). The interplay between the standards, instruction, and assessment and the evaluation of assessment data provides us with information about individual students. Over time, the assessment data can also provide feedback on program, by grade level and by subject, and teachers, administrators, and curriculum committees can base their decisions on school-generated research.

Dynamic Curriculum

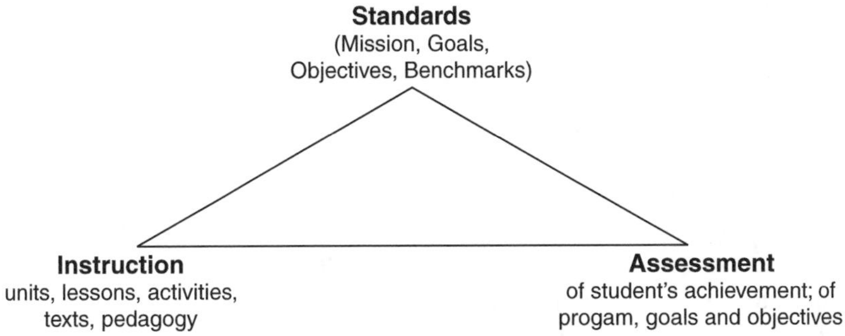

Figure 3

With the standards in place, the next stage of the curriculum overhaul involved unit design, and an integral part of unit design was assessment. Aligning mission to classroom content was a logical step, almost self-evident once started. However, other changes were not quite so self-evident. Schoolwide, shifts in thinking occurred in two major areas. One was focus. Since the school's business is students and their learning, the design decision to begin each curriculum document with the stem, "The students will be able to . . ." put the students, and the content of their learning, overtly at the center of the endeavor. The importance of the teacher did not change. However, switching to a particular emphasis on the student has been powerful. The second shift in thinking was about assessment. As a community of teachers, we are relearning assessment, and coming to understand and apply three main categories: skills assessment, performance-type assessments, and authentic assessment.

Throughout the various stages of this curriculum alignment, one-day meetings for groups of faculty were scheduled. Although such all-day meetings were demanding, the groups developed understanding of curricular relationships in the constructivist mode, and in a collegial and convivial atmosphere. Typically the day began with talk about challenges and hopes; what was going on in schools locally, nationally, internationally; and the state of the standards, if any. Following that, the conversation moved on to the current situation at the school in broad outline. Mapping was a useful tool. Analysis of overlaps, holes, and inconsistencies led to evaluation and examination of possible courses of action. Faculty discussed, negotiated, and reached consensus on what to move, adapt, add, and subtract. When finally the negotiations were complete, the result was a designed, coherent experience for the student.

At the completion of every stage throughout the four-year process, faculty thought, "Now, we're done!" Invariably, there was yet another layer of program to be articulated, yet another more detailed version of the same material to be written. One document after another, teachers developed the various layers—subject goals, grade level objectives, performance assessments, course descriptions, the scope and sequence of units, skills checklists in mathematics and language arts, and finally units, units, units. Well into the process, as each document begat its several sub-documents, and drafts succeeded drafts, and the proliferation seemed to be a curricular form of the "Sorcerer's Apprentice," we heard of a promising software package. We researched several systems. However, only the IMSeries™ (Learning Technology Systems) linked standards to instruction to assessment. Only IMSeries continued student records across grade levels.

Forsyth teachers began pioneering the software in 1998. IMSeries is a powerful system that enables the faculty to link every part of the instructional process together: horizontally, at grade level, and vertically, by subject. It is a comprehensive tool that has the potential to allow us to align—at every level—all our standards and benchmarks, units, instruction, assessment, and evaluation, as we strive to make sure all our students fulfill the school's mission. It helps us ensure we teach the designed curriculum, assess what we teach, and teach what we assess.

Figure 4 Standards-Based Instructional Framework

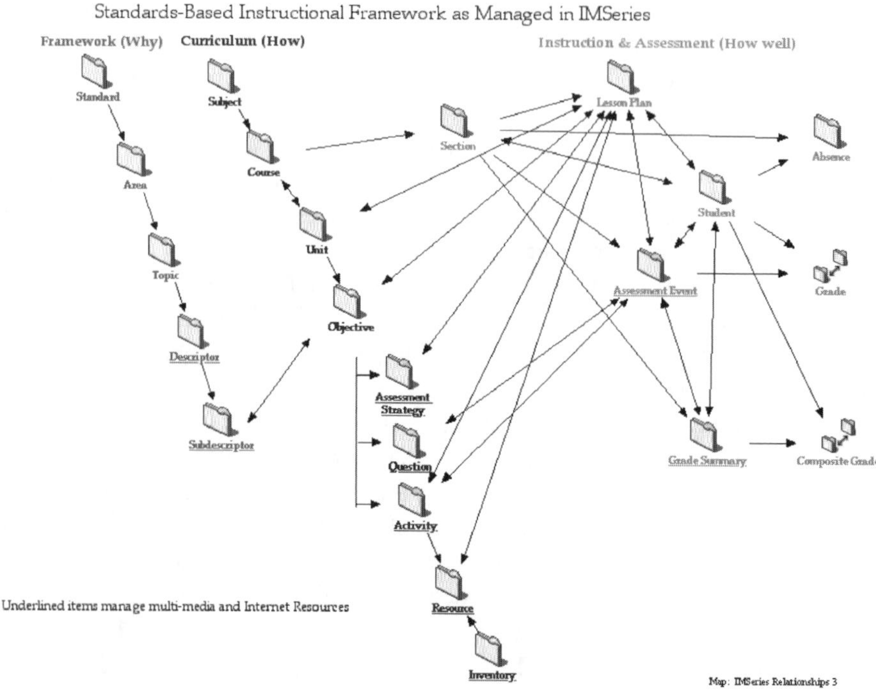

The process is slow because the strength of IMSeries is its complexity and flexibility. Its structure is designed to incorporate our originally designed curriculum. Therefore, the care with which the curriculum elements go in, and the quality of what goes in, determines what eventually comes out. The IMSeries program has enormous potential to track the effectiveness of our curriculum, child by child, throughout his or her education here, but not until all the pieces have been entered all the way down to the assessment level.

The process of entering data is an ongoing challenge. In order to be able to analyze what is taught, assessed, and mastered, instructional units are broken down into a unit objective, activities, resources, and assessment structure. Each of these variables is linked to subject goals and grade level objectives. While the prospect of real-time access to a student's performance over time is exciting, the task of entering data with such detail can overwhelm teachers who are not particularly technologically savvy. In an attempt to address this issue while also maintaining momentum, the faculty designs units following a template that makes entering the data into the database easier. A person specifically trained and charged with entering teacher-generated units helped the school gather the instructional information without having a negative impact on morale.

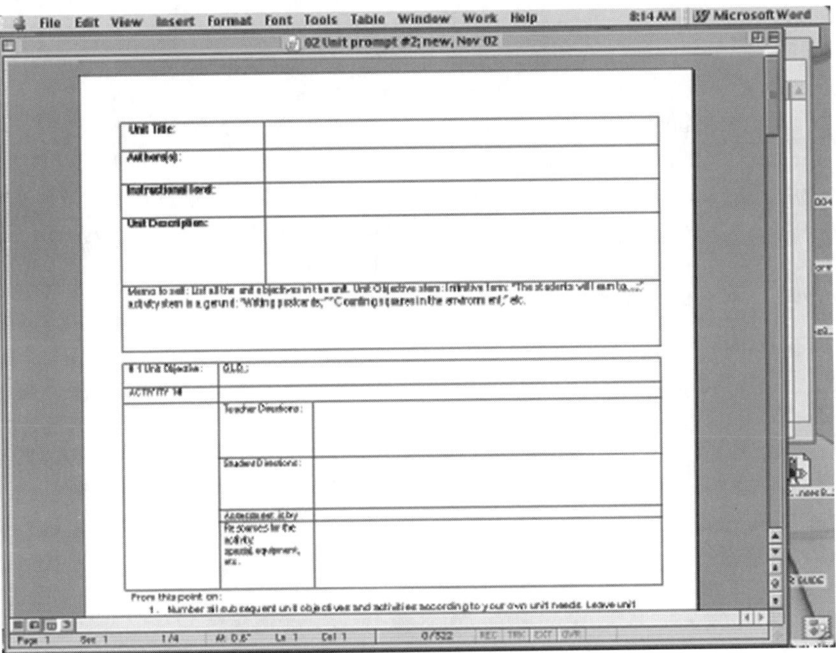

Figure 5 IM Series (Unit Prompt)

Well-designed assessments are the key for the schoolwide analysis and communication we strive to achieve. IMSeries allows users to graph student progress over time on particular objectives, analyze class performance, compare performance based on gender or section, and articulate achievement of a subject goal over years. In order for this analysis to be useful, assessments must be well designed and accurately reflect the objectives being assessed. This takes time and professional development. In spite of the challenges it brought, IMSeries aided our community in articulating clearly our curriculum, our instruction, and how students demonstrate what they have learned. Could we have evolved to our current state in our quest for a clearly articulated, coherent curriculum without IMSeries? Probably, in time. However, IMSeries's linking structure illuminated the holes in our curriculum and guided our discussions in a more purposeful direction, saving us time and frustration.

At every stage, the software has served us well. In the early stages, determining which pieces connected to which other pieces engendered much discussion and deepened people's understanding. Unit writing is well under way, and again, the non-negotiability of the format "forced" understanding of the components of a unit, of assessment in general and rubrics in particular. Many teachers record attendance in IM, and we hope to have a new progress report, aligned to standards and unit achievement, ready and in use by winter 2003.

Bernadine Sommer is director of studies and division head at Forsyth School, St. Louis. Originally from Ireland, she trained as a teacher at Carysfort and her B.A. and M.A. are from Trinity College, Dublin. **Jill Gerber,** now at Crossroads School, taught at Forsyth at several grade levels and guided the process of adapting the instructional management software to Forsyth's requirements. She received the Independent Schools of St. Louis award and the Edison award for Teacher of the Year, 2002. She is a 2004 Emerson Electric Excellence in Education Award winner and 2003 ISSL Teacher of Distinction. **Suzanne Gill,** (A.M.L.S., University of Michigan; B.A., Fontbonne University) is director of curriculum resources, She is the author of *File Management and Information Retrieval Systems* (1st, 2nd, 3rd eds) (Libraries Unlimited) and is listed in *Who's Who in Information Science* (American Library Association).

Technology and "All Kinds of Minds"

By Jim Heynderickx

Mel Levine's books and theories can stimulate interesting conversations and re-evaluations of long-held beliefs, and sending teachers to his "Schools Attuned" training programs has become a tradition at some independent schools.[1] To many educators, his work represents a unified theory of child development and learning, designed to be understood by teachers, parents, and the students themselves. Through research and brief case studies, Levine argues for child-centered attitudes toward assessment and new opportunities for student growth.

References to student technology use appear throughout Levine's *A Mind at a Time*. He doesn't hesitate to criticize certain types of technology use as unproductive, repetitive activities that can delay student growth. Levine believes that many television shows, for example, "offer stimulation in small chunks without much call for sustained attention or deep concentration."[2] He also notes that Internet access and research, if misused, may be "a new mode of passive learning."[3]

More frequently, however, Levine offers examples of how technology can be used to help students cope with developmental weaknesses or excel in an area of personal affinity. He is critical of technology, yet he recognizes that it is a permanent and often important part of students' lives. If a school adopted the core tenants of Levine's work, how would student technology use change?

Defining Misuses of Technology

To begin, a school should define and acknowledge Levine's criticisms and warnings about misuses of technology. A clear set of recommendations and guidelines for television viewing, video and computer gaming, Internet research, and related issues should be shared with students, parents, and faculty. More than a few parents may be modeling unproductive technology use at home, and the recommendations may take some time to take hold. In my experience, however, a large percentage of parents are interested in qualified recommendations on these issues.

Assistive Technology Use

Levine's approach uses surveys and assessments to create a profile of each student according to seven neurodevelopmental areas (genetics, temperament and emotions, influence of peers, physical health, educational experience, cultural values, family factors, and environmental influences).[4] He notes that all of us are weak in one or more of the seven areas, and most of us will remain functionally limited in those areas for all of our lives.[5] In most cases, these weaknesses do not stop adults from leading productive lives or having highly successful careers. Technology use can help students improve or cope in areas where they are weak, just as it helps adults in the working world.

Word processing is one of the most important ways technology can help students cope with "graphomotor function," the specific motor skills involved with handwriting.[6] Put simply, many students struggle with the basic motor control issues related to writing by hand, and this leads to frustration with the entire composition process. Levine argues that early implementation of word processing (third or fourth grade) can help these students sidestep disabling composition issues. For most students (and adults), composing or note-taking at a keyboard can be a much more fluid, complete, and rewarding process.

The issue of keyboarding raises another avenue for investigation—the intersection of automatic language and writing as seen in student instant messaging use. As Levine notes, many students can have brilliant expressive language (oral, automatic), but then seem incapable of writing a paper using literate language. Without question, instant messaging is the "invisible elephant" in the room during student technology discussions. While the Pew Research Center reports that 74% of online teens use instant messaging, only a small percentage of teachers have ever tried it, and most schools go to significant lengths to ban it from their networks.[7] Currently, only a handful of teachers communicate with students through instant messaging, but they report that students can use their comfort and skills in this mode of writing to improve and grow in the literate language modes expected and required by school. A writing conference held through instant messaging, for example, creates a written transcript that can be used by both student and teacher when discussing the next draft of the paper.

Levine also emphasizes the importance of "mapping out" clear definitions of problems and processes for students. Graphical mapping software can help students develop confidence and clarity in a number of neurodevelopmental areas. Inspiration® software, for example, is an easy-to-use two-dimensional mapping tool for organizing and revising ideas and terms.[8] Many students like its format and colorful yet clear charts, graphs, and outlines. Inspiration® can help students diagram sentences and verb tenses, create graphical outlines for writing projects, and visualize major concepts in all disciplines. The drawing functions in most word processors can create similar visual maps, and encouraging this type of approach could help students in a range of areas.

Students with organizational, scheduling, and sequencing weaknesses may benefit from using personal digital assistants, tape recorders, digital cameras, or similar tools. The evaluation of personal performance (during an oral book report, presentation, dance, athletics, or even just classroom behavior) can benefit greatly from video taping and guided analysis. Using video tape as a way to share student work with parents or peers can also radically improve students' approach, appreciation, and motivation.[9]

Creative Technology Use in Student Affinity Areas

Many students find ownership and excitement as they explore and attempt to master different types of technology use (graphic design, statistics, digital images and video, simulations, web page creation, online publication and communication, and other areas). In some cases (online "blogs" or journals, for example), students may invest large amounts of effort that are valued by audiences other than teachers and parents. In effect, they gain respect and a sense of achievement in unrecognized areas of affinity.

Alan November notes that students can often be "fearless learners" in areas of their own choosing, to the extent that their level of achievement is far beyond any homework or class project.[10] Levine recognizes the importance of allowing "students to strengthen strengths" by doing in-depth work in areas of personal affinity, and in many cases this involves student technology use.

In *A Mind at a Time,* Levine tells the story of a boy who had motor development issues that made him fearful of all types of athletic performance.[11] Along with other issues, his social standing, confidence, and self-esteem were dangerously low. When a school coach invited him to become a team statistician, the boy used his innate love of numbers, statistics, and technology to immerse himself in the work. The student gathered performance data and processed it through spreadsheets and other software to create professional reports for a wide range of athletes at his school. His social standing and self-confidence made a remarkable turnaround as he became the essential "mathlete" of the sports program.

Structurally, the recognition and support of in-depth student work in affinity areas can have a major impact on the curriculum, schedule, and learning environment. High Tech High in San Diego has extended this concept to the point of creating individual and small-group student work spaces so that up to half of the school day is spent in an office setting instead of in classrooms.[12] At other schools, many students already have all the basic equipment of a home office (mid-level computer, Internet access, printer, and other peripherals) that could be utilized in a similar way.

The Broader Communicative Mission

Traditionally, the analysis of an educational therapist or counselor may be phrased in terms that are not understood, used, or even shared with individual students. Levine advocates a more inclusive approach, in that students themselves learn language and concepts that clearly define their strengths, weaknesses, and the specific steps needed to improve their situations. In his view, no student chooses to fail, and the painful issues that students face are more than enough motivation to learn new terms and approaches that will help them improve.

Teachers who attend the Schools Attuned program receive access to increasing amounts of online information. The "Views Attuned" information is designed to help teachers become careful observers of students and make informed decisions about how to help. Information is also gathered from parents and students, so that multiple perspectives are part of the profile creation process. The Schools Attuned week-long sessions are not simple and brief: Many teachers respond that the overarching construct is best understood through the graphics and charts that show the interconnectedness of the concepts. The main criticism of Levine's approach is that it is "too time consuming" for typical teachers, but the online database helps with the time-effective processing of information. In the future, the online materials could also be used by parents and students, since one of the core tenants of Levine's mission is a shared understanding of concepts and recommendations.

Many schools and teachers still teach technology as a separate subject or an "added-on" project requirement. Levine's approach is more varied and integrated. An advanced program based on his ideas would create and support technology opportunities according to individual student profiles. This child-centered approach may be more complicated than uniform expectations, but the benefits for students could be much greater. Working toward this goal also returns educational technology to its original mission: to increase independence, individualization, and self-direction in the learning process. These objectives fit well with Levine's philosophy, and the structural change that allows and values these changes has just begun.

Notes

[1] For more information about Schools Attuned, see www.allkindsofminds.org.

[2] Mel Levine, *A Mind at a Time* (New York: Simon & Schuster, 2002) 43.

[3] Levine 43.

[4] Levine 42.

[5] Levine 15.

[6] Levine 173.

[7] Pew Research Center, (June 20, 2001), "Teenage Life Online: The Rise of the Instant-Message Generation and the Internet's Impact on Friendships and Family Relationships." *Pew Internet and Family Life Project* [Online]. http://www.pewinternet.org/reports/toc.asp?Report=36.

[8] For more information about Inspiration® software, see www.inspiration.com.

[9] Alan November, "Creating A New Culture of Teaching and Learning." *Alan November Presents . . .* [Online]. http://www.anovember.com/articles/asilomar.html.

[10] Alan November, "A Morning with Alan November." Technology in Education Conference, (June 26, 2003). For more information, see www.tie-online.org.

[11] Levine 323.

[12] For more information about High Tech High, see www.hightechhigh.org.

Jim HeyndErickx has worked with educational technology since 1989 at American University, George Washington University, Trinity College, and the Lowell School in Washington, D.C. He is currently the director of technology at Oregon Episcopal School in Portland, OR.

From Blackboards to SMART Boards

By Elizabeth Hofreuter-Landoni

> "There have been only two major technological impacts on mainstream U.S. K–12 education in our country's history . . . the use of blackboards and mass-produced textbooks."
>
> —Randy Pausch, "A Curmudgeon's Vision for Technology in Education"

Depending on whose article you are reading or in whose office you are sitting, computer technology is either the bane of our existence or the greatest hope for educational reform. Both are wrong. Stop for a minute and consider that a blackboard or a pencil were once new technologies in the classroom. Both were met with caution and engendered extreme reactions. Consider their impact now. Both enhanced teaching and learning because they were tools used to accomplish things in the classroom that were not possible without them. These "new" technologies also required a shift in the thinking of the time. As Randy Pausch describes, "Blackboards took the 'personal slate' and made a large communal display." The teacher was no longer a personal mentor for a roomful a students; he was a sage on the stage. Oddly enough, here we are so many years later trying to get off the stage to return to our role as the guide on the side.

Why were these technologies successful? By looking at the answer, we can learn from two lessons. First of all, they allowed teachers to accomplish something that they could not have done otherwise. Until the installation of the blackboard, there was no communal display, no way for all students to see the same drawing, or word, or sentence at the same time. In her research of current educational technology, Stone Wiske (2002) puts it this way: "To enable technology to have important educational effect, technology must afford significant educational advantage." So technology is powerful in education if it accomplishes something in the classroom that we could not do, or could not do well, without it. The pencil allowed students to erase and learn from mistakes. The second lesson is that these technologies were tools that supported the goals for learning. The curriculum was forefront. The pencil, or the blackboard, was simply a tool. As James Marshall warns us today, "Poorly designed programs that lack an instructional foundation; casual, purposeless use of technology in the classroom; and lack of alignment between desired learning outcomes and the application of educational technology all threaten the success of any learning-by-technology endeavor. Successful technology-based learning relies heavily on a context for use" (2002). Granted, there has to be a supportive administration, a willing and trained teacher, and appropriate funding. With those things in place, the technology will be successful only when it is used to achieve educational goals and affords the teacher and students an opportunity to accomplish something they had not done without it.

Technology Must Afford Significant Educational Advantage

What does it mean practically for technology to provide significant educational advantage? Let's begin with a classroom example. In the English department at The Linsly School, of which I have been a member for 12 years, all students are required to write in a journal every day. Teachers accommodate that requirement in different ways. For me, students wrote in a literary notebook. There were approximately 75 thin spiral notebooks to contend with each time I graded journals. I snagged more sweaters on loose spirals than I care to remember. Grading them was always put off until it was a monstrous task, and no entry received the attention it deserved. Then we became a "wired" school. Based on work I was required to do in a graduate class (a.k.a. training and support), I created an asynchronous list serv for my students—an electronic journal. Now in lieu of assigning journal writing in class, I post a question or an opinion each night and ask the students in my humanities class to respond to it. Sometimes it serves to continue our discussion after the bell has rung. Other times it serves as a precursor for the next class topic. Regardless, it allows us to communicate outside of our prescribed class time—something I could not do before the advent of the technology.

The electronic journal has several additional benefits. First, it allows students the time and privacy to organize their thoughts before they respond, as they might not be able to do orally in class. In some cases, it lets them get their heads around a difficult concept before having to face the class discussion the next day. Secondly, each post is read not just by me, but by others in class and possibly by parents, peers, and strangers. There is pride taken in these nightly responses. At times, I have invited authors to log on and post their ideas. Given the ambiguous audience, students' responses are solid, and often thought provoking. Some exhibit humor that I never witness in class. Others are verbose when they tend to be reticent face to face.

This is a prime example of the changing role of the teacher. As Patrick Bassett predicted for us in the spring of 2002, "We are in a revolution where the idea of the academy is shifting to the notion of a learning organization; that it's really not about the teacher or the scholar. It's about the learner." I set the discussion in motion and then I read. Sometimes I respond—jump into the fray—but mostly I just read. It is in this arena of my class that I feel most like a coach. I throw the ball out there and then I watch while they practice the very skills they need to compete. I blow the whistle every once in a while, but mostly I let them scrimmage. What they do well or poorly dictates my focus for class the next day. This is a significant educational advantage to me. It solved a problem I knew I had. My students weren't taking daily writing exercises seriously because no one cared. They knew there was a good chance most entries would not be read or that they would get to choose their best ones (portfolio fashion), and as a result they wrote very little of significance. Now thanks to the electronic journal, I not only have a handle on grading journals, but my students have benefited tenfold. The technology gave them a new canvas to express themselves. It gave me a chance to shift focus to student inquiry.[1]

It is important to note that the U.S. Department of Education sees a future in online learning. The technology briefs for *No Child Left Behind* state, "Online courses are coming into widespread use at the high school level. These online courses extend options available to students; for example, advanced placement courses can be provided online when they could not be provided otherwise due to geographical distances or insufficient resources. Online courses can enable sharing resources . . . so that a specialized topic taught by a teacher in one school can be made available to students in other schools. Online courses can also better serve students who cannot attend school due to health or other reasons, and provide alternative approaches to learning for students who don't do well with traditional classroom approaches."[2]

Clearly, not everyone who wants to test the waters online will have the necessary training and support available to them. However, online class elements are available through many portals online, one of which is Blackboard.com. Serving over one thousand schools and colleges, the company has one goal: to transform the Internet into a powerful environment for teaching and learning. Some of its Learning System services include a course management system, electronic class discussion boards, and online assessments. With Blackboard, faculty can post syllabi, multimedia files, course documents and other materials available to students anytime, anywhere.[3]

In my humanities example, the technology solved a problem for me. This is a good starting point for a teacher to make a connection between the curriculum and technology. Educators may see a fit within a classroom activity that they currently find incomplete, inefficient or frustrating. Consider a Linsly School colleague of mine, Dennis Hon, who uses the white board, the colorful descendent of the blackboard, to passionately introduce a new calculus concept to the class. Regularly, he demonstrates an example and solves the first problem with a flair that keeps students motivated and interested. Subsequent problems are discussed and students offer input toward solutions. Inevitably, though, there are one, two, or more students who are absent. Be it cold and flu season, the day of the Math League test, or a college visit, there comes a time each year when absences are the rule of thumb in the classroom. Student absences mean they don't benefit from the classroom examples, group problems, or teacher's impact. For years I heard complaints from him that he simply couldn't teach all that he had to for the AP exam given the diminishing hours available for instruction. Enter *mimio,* and when funds allowed, a *SMART board*—the technology that makes a white board electronic.[4]

Already adept with graphing calculators in his classroom, Hon embarked on a new technology path by installing a SMART board at the front of the room. With this presentation technology, he sets up the problem on the white board, and the technology records what is written or drawn on the board as well as the voice of the teacher. When a student is available, he or she can play and repeat the lesson. There on the computer screen is the whiteboard information as she would have experienced in second period had she been there. Moreover, the student who struggles with the concept or loses focus during the teacher's explanation can play the lesson again and repeat it as necessary during study hall or flex period. In time, if the broadband allows, Hon's lessons can even be posted on a secure school website for students (and parents) to review at night during homework. As Jan Hawkins's research would confirm, the technology alone did not make a difference. The technology is effective because it is embedded in the classroom in a rational way (1997). In this upper level math class the technology makes a difference. Again there is an element of anytime, anywhere learning, but more important, there is a solution to a problem of class absences. There is significant educational advantage for students and the teacher alike.

Technology Must Achieve Clear Educational Goals

Let's revisit Hawkins's observation, "technology alone never makes a difference; it must be embedded in classrooms in rational ways" (1997). The idea is that technology cannot be an appendage to a lesson; it must be a means to achieving clear educational goals. Perhaps the NEA Foundation for the Improvement of Education (NFIE) puts it best. Based on research of pilot projects, NFIE recommends, "Start with what you want to achieve. Let desired student outcomes guide technology selection and use. Clear academic goals should govern, so that the focus is on outcomes rather than on dazzling technological tools" (Connecting). Indeed, the technology briefs of President Bush's *No Child Left Behind* policy gently urges us to begin with these questions, "What do students need to learn, and how can technology promote those learning goals?" (Technology).

How does technology promote learning goals? In 1975 I was in elementary school. I was asked to write a report on my hero. I copied facts verbatim from the World Book Encyclopedia on a person I can no longer remember. I recall the assignment so clearly because I put very little effort or time into it, but received glowing compliments on my work. Even as a young child I knew my teacher and I had misconnected. The good grade was a hollow achievement. I think of that experience often when I make assignments and write comments on student papers. I can't begin to tell you what the educational goal of that assignment was. Goals, or better yet essential questions, offer the students a problem to solve and a roadmap for a project. I did not have either. I had an assignment. When technology is imbedded in a rational way in that project, it deepens the student's educational experience. Janis Friesler at Frank Lloyd Wright Middle School has a similar project in which she asks eighth graders "How do events in history turn ordinary people into heroes?" Her students research the Holocaust and the Underground Railroad on the Internet and in the school library to investigate the events and the heroes who changed history.[5] In the end students create a PowerPoint slide show to visually depict key elements of an oral presentation to the class. Rubrics and guiding questions allow students to stay on track as they research the information that will give their oral presentation the sophistication and impact of which they can be proud.

Another classroom example comes from Cold Springs School in New Haven, CT. In this case, technology allows middle school children to become real-world field scientists. Recognized by NAIS as a 2003 Leading Edge honoree in technology, Cold Spring teacher Karen Zwick wants her students to practice problem-solving skills that apply to their study of science. The students use Palm handhelds to investigate the river that surrounds their school. Attaching probes to handhelds, they measure pH, water and air temperature, dissolved oxygen, and alkalinity. The students also study the plants along the river by taking pictures with the handhelds equipped with attachable cameras. "Initially, integrating the handhelds took effort—but that's part of my philosophy about how technology works," explains Zwick. "There's a process when you're first learning a new technology and it takes time. Then you get to a point where things run smoothly. In this case, the handheld technology makes investigations easier and learning richer. In the end, it's incredibly worthwhile."[6]

The Cold Spring project culminated in the students creating a virtual guide to the Mill River on the school website. As is often the case with technology, there were unexpected outcomes as well. The public access to the site allowed their work to catch the attention of state legislators. Ultimately, the middle school students were asked to display their site to Connecticut legislators at the Legislative Technology Conference. The students had become teachers. They realized that their ideas and their work were valuable not only in the context of the assignment, but in their community as well. Again, the role of teacher and students has shifted as adults learn from these adolescents.

Another Leading Edge honoree, the D.E.E.P. project at St. Matthew's School, experienced a similar shift in roles as their students became experts. In the D.E.E.P. project, students create a website to publish the results of science and math experiments, which they have designed, based on the principles of scuba diving. The teachers found that some of their students were being asked if their research could be used in college lecture notes. As described by one participating teacher, Christine Lorenz, "We often get e-mail from university professors asking if they can use a student's project as an example in their own classes. Sometimes we get requests from teachers at schools in which technology is just being introduced, and they want advice on how to implement something like this in their curriculum. The kids could not be more proud of their hard work on those occasions and neither can we. To have students *learn* difficult concepts is one thing; to have students learn and *teach* others is another."[7]

While there is much discussion about access to information as a key benefit to the incorporation of technology into the classroom, there is also something powerful in the access to a wider audience for student work. Lorenz comments, "It's very important to us that other educators understand how creative and innovative teaching in combination with technology can change the common classroom into a worldwide university of shared experiences." While this was not one of the initial goals of the project, this unexpected development has improved the quality of student work. Indeed, publication on the web improved the quality of the project. "When we added the web publishing component, it became eighth graders doing college level work."

Be it publication on the web, a presentation in PowerPoint, or even a class premier of a digital video, technology promotes learning goals as students construct knowledge and demonstrate their understanding with sophostication. Their work makes an impact. After all, they are an MTV generation. Computers are their medium for personal communication as instant messaging replaces the telephone. It is natural, then, that technology is also their medium for producing quality work in school.

Technology in the Classroom Gives Us Pause

I have shared with you a few class activities that "work"—that show a meaningful connection between technology and the curriculum. By no means is this an exhaustive list of best practices; they are simply examples of technology "affording a significant technological impact" while being imbedded in the educational objectives of each course. I include these examples to keep this discussion practical—theories do very little for us when the eyes of our students our upon us. Think of them as discussion points to which you will respond with other colleagues. Let them generate inquiry and, I hope, reflection.

This brings me to a line from Lewis Carroll's *Alice's Adventure in Wonderland.* "Would you tell me please, which way I ought to go from here?" To which the cat responds, "That depends a good deal on where you want to get to."

I don't pretend to know where we are headed with technology. Looking ahead to that future is uncertain. Are we on our way to virtual schools? Routine distance-learning programs? Shared virtual spaces? For that advice, I would suggest a collection of essays accumulated by the U.S. Department of Commerce, called *2020 Visions: Transforming Education and Training Through Advanced Technologies*. These authors take that leap of faith and make some predictions based on current research and development. As for me, I cannot tell you where technology will take us, for it depends on "where you want to get to." I am at peace simply returning to Pat Bassett's question, "How will technology make us better learners?" By deciding what technology we will choose to embrace in our classrooms and what we will ignore, the debate affords us the opportunity to reflect on our teaching and our academic goals.

Whatever its place in your classroom or school, technology can offer teachers a chance to give pause. In a daily schedule that barely leaves time to go to the bathroom or swallow a sandwich, there is too little time set aside to asking essential questions about improving teaching and learning. For me, and many others, the question of whether technology would improve my teaching or their learning gave me that much-needed pause. Even if the answer was no. No, there is no need for technology in this lesson. No, there is not enough money in the budget for that piece of hardware. No, we cannot support that type of software in our school. Still, it gave me a chance to consider the possibilities. The idea of integrating technology afforded me the opportunity to re-examine my goals for each classroom, for our school, for our students.

Regardless, the advent of technology in the classroom made me a better teacher. I was forced to ask myself, Could I do that unit better? Could that activity benefit from the access and communication available through the Internet? Could my students be more engaged in this lesson? It was always self-affirming to sincerely answer *no,* no technology needed. It was also professionally appealing to learn the technological skills to make my teaching better in some cases. Today, I offer my students a classroom that stretches beyond the concrete gray walls of our hallways and beyond the limitations of the daily schedule. But I also feel confident when I discuss a social issue as they see it without access to anything but their imaginations. I am proud when they learn about architecture through web resources, but ecstatic when they touch the walls at Fallingwater (one of Frank Lloyd Wright's most widely acclaimed works, Fallingwater is a house built over a waterfall), and later manipulate balsa wood to build cantilevers of their own.

Knowing when there will be a significant educational impact within the scope of the academic goals, and when there will not be, is the key to successful technology integration in any classroom. In the preceding classroom examples, technology is an item in the list of materials for each unit, and the impact on education takes place because students are motivated to learn and encouraged to be use their minds.

I look forward to the day when we discuss student learning and innovations in the curriculum without fanfare over the use of technology. How absurd it would seem today to remark on the inclusion of blackboards, or white boards, in every room as if their hanging on the wall alone said something about the learning experience taking place in that classroom.

Bibliography

Bassett, Patrick. "Bassett Unbound" [interviewed by W.E. DeLamater and S. A. Ward] *Independent School Technology Letter,* number 32, March 2002.

"Connecting the Bits," NEA Foundation for the Improvement of Education (NFIE). July 16 , 2003, http://nfie.org/publications/connecting.htm.

Dickard, Norris, Ed. *The Sustainability Challenge: Taking Edtech to the Next Level.* Benton Foundation, 2003.

Hawkins, Jan. " Dilemmas of Technology in Education." [Address to the Harvard Graduate School of Education.] Cambridge, MA, March 21, 1997.

Marshall, James. "Learning with Technology: Evidence that Technology Can and Does Support Learning," May, 2002. Cable in the Classroom. July 18, 2003, http://www.ciconline.org/enrichment/teaching/researchanalysis/learning_with_technology_white_paper.htm.

Pausch, Randy. "A Curmudgeon's Vision for Technology in Education," in *2020 Visions: Transforming Education and Training through Advanced Technologies,* Washington D.C.: U.S. Department of Commerce, 2002.

"Technology Briefs for NCLB Planners," May 23, 2003. The Northeast and the Islands Regional Technology Consortium (NEIR*TEC). July 8,2003, www.neirtec.org/products/techbriefs.

Wiske, Martha Stone. "A New Culture of Teaching for the 21st Century." July 6, 2003, http://learnweb.harvard.edu/ent/library/teaching_culture_article.pdf.

Notes

[1] Feel free to check out the electronic journal at any time. Indeed, all I ask is that you join in the discussion rather than lurk unannounced. You'll find us during the school year at www.linsly.org/humanities.

[2] You can access the NCLB technology briefs developed by the Northeast and the Islands Regional Technology Consortium (NEIR*TEC) at www.neirtec.org/products/techbriefs.

[3] Teachers who want to experiment with aspects of online learning can do so at www.blackboard.com.

[4] You can get access information about mimio technology at www.mimio.com. Information about SMART boards is available online www.smarttech.com.

[5] You can learn more about Friesler's project at www.knowledgeloom.org/gmott/resources/frieslerunit.pdf, where it was spotlighted by NEIR.TEC for making good use of technology. The entire hero unit is available as an Adobe Acrobat file.

[6] You can investigate the Cold Spring Mill River Project online when you access http://www.coldspringschool.org/csspages.html.

[7] Teachers and professors learn about the St Matthew's DEEP project online at http://www.stmatthewsschool.com/deep/intro.html.

After having taught English at both the middle and high school levels, **Elizabeth Hofreuter-Landini** turned her energies toward the meaningful incorporation of technology in schools. Currently, she serves as the director of curriculum and technology at The Linsly School in Wheeling, WV, teaching humanities, expository writing and web page design. She has an A.B. at Princeton University and an M.Ed. from Harvard University.

Weaving a Student-Written Textbook into the Web: The Story of *The Andover Reader*

By John A. Gould

It's a dangerous medium for us teachers, the Internet is. Lots of us don't much like it. Its tone is fast and jazzy, click you're here, click you're gone. I'm sure that this ephemerality is the source of much of our discontent. Scholars like stability, and we don't trust research that relies on fancy skywriting. Heaven knows, we're right a good deal of the time; there's enough junk out there in cyberspace. But when teachers start to take control of the Internet's content, when they start to publish their own materials on it, when they start to set up classes around it, that's when cybersurf starts to become home turf.

Remember, students in the twenty-first century are completely at ease with the Internet, a fact we older educators have to get used to. Even the youngest of them can navigate easily from site to site. They know how to extract information: text and images and sound-files. They can communicate: instant messaging and e-mail. They live with both the power and the weakness of the tool; like weather, it's everywhere all at once, good, bad, indifferent. They don't much care. Their problem isn't lack of skill; it's lack of discrimination.

Despite sharing these misgivings, during the last five years I've discovered some powerful ways to use the web in the classroom. Phillips Academy in Andover, like many independent schools nowadays, supports its own web presence; our domain is andover.edu. Half a dozen years ago, when andover.edu was a new, highly suspicious toy, a ninth-grader named Sam Antonaccio taught me how to create a website so I could publish some photographs I had taken of Thomas Hardy's settings in Dorset, England. It wasn't that hard, really; in a less than a month Sam taught me enough HTML to turn a Microsoft Word document into web text and tuck a picture underneath it. And this was before Word developed its capacity to save as HTML. Nowadays an alert monkey can make a web page.

English 200, the tenth-grade course at Andover, begins with a full term of expository writing, really creative nonfiction, taught primarily from prose models. I have often been impressed with essays the students wrote, and occasionally used to borrow a particularly successful one to show the next year's crop of beginning writers. For years I published the best papers in 5.5 × 8.5 magazines. I would gather copies of their best work, reduce the pages on the photocopier, arrange them in signatures, print a double-sided run large enough for all the members of the classes, collate and fold them in the middle, and somehow find a stapler that could reach into the center of the page to bind them. (Often this last task was the most difficult.) This labor of love took about a day and a half of sweat and groaning and (once in a while) cursing.

After Sam had taught me how to build a website, I saw immediately the advantages of using andover.edu as a classroom publishing tool. It was free, for one thing, and so easy. If the papers were submitted electronically, all I had to do was convert them to HTML—not hard—and arrange them with links to a table of contents. Four years ago, another teacher, Paul Kalkstein, who is more literate in web design than I am, and I created the *The English 200 Reader,* a "zine" or online journal, to which all our tenth-grade teachers invited their students to contribute particularly good work. Last year the *2002–03 Reader* published over 45 of these essays, all free, all accessible to students and to their parents, too, no matter where they lived. Proud parents and grandparents in Kansas or California or India or Asia or South America could see their [grand]children's work. The *Reader* generated excitement and pride for both student and family, and incidentally for the course itself.

The first edition of *The English 200 Reader* appeared on andover.edu in 1999, and it is still there, although I suspect only the proudest of grandparents refer to it now. By the end of our second year, Paul Kalkstein and I felt proud of what we were doing with *The Reader;* students, teachers, and those happy, hubristic grandparents all continued to take pride in seeing work published on the Internet. And then I remembered using those particularly fine student essays as models.

"Couldn't we," I asked Paul, "collect the best essays from the last couple of years, and make a *textbook?*"

Textbooks have always been one of our biggest stumbling blocks in English 200. Many teachers had been using large, bulky anthologies containing far more essays then they could use; students were paying big bucks for big texts that they used comparatively little. We felt guilty. Also quality was an issue, both for us and for the students. Teachers found many of the anthologized pieces substandard or inappropriate, and—for other reasons—so did the kids. But suppose we used *their* work? Some of our students had written truly wonderful pieces, pieces too that had been created in response to our own assignments. Thus they would serve as accurate models of what we were trying to get them to write. And best of all, if it was on the web, it would be free.

Incidentally, a few years earlier Paul and I had toyed with collecting professional essays for a web anthology for English 200—which would be free—but quickly gave up the project when we realized the horrors of getting copyright releases for all of them. The use of student papers would solve this problem, too; we would publish uncopyrighted essays, asserting copyright on behalf of the young authors. So,

"Sure," said Paul. "Let's call it *The Andover Reader.*"

We got to work. Paul designed the site: because English 200 is taught by "modes"—description, narration, comparison, cause/effect, and so on—he created a frame that contained links to each mode, then constructed a page to hold each collection of essays written in a particular one. I wrote a short introduction to each mode, illustrated by a photograph I had taken. For instance, on the "Definition" page I put up an image of Stonehenge. Then I wrote,

> To define something is to lasso it, to get control of it by putting a rope around it. It comes from the Latin: "de"—"about"; "fine"—"end" or "limit"; thus, "define"—"to put limits about something." We can define anything—a person, a place, a thing, an idea—by telling both what it is and what it is not. Look at this weird collection of granite slabs. Imagine the first Roman legionnaires ever to see it. How could they put limits about it, explain what it was and wasn't, so people back in Rome could understand?

After the illustrations were in place, we worked out backgrounds and font colors for each page. For the home page I chose one of my favorite photographs—a dark red *Masdevillia* orchid from Venezuela, which to me looks like a ballet dancer. Below it I placed Yeat's wonderful lines about the mystery of art: "O body swayed to music, O brightening glance, / How can we know the dancer from the dance?" When composing the "Analogy" page, I used the *Masdevillia* as well, since my feelings toward it seemed largely allegorical. Paul colored the title and navigation frames a dramatic mauve pink that picked up some highlights from the flower.

Finally we selected essays. We found wonders. Some pieces are hilarious. A parodic comparison of Mr. and Mrs. Potato Head notes that both Mr. and Mrs. P. H. boast "a convenient storage area located in the buttocks region of the potato figure," which "serves as a garage of sorts for appendages that are not being used on the spud." A process paper on how to "Procrastinate Like a Pro" remarks, "as a first time procrastinator, you'll have to start small. You have to walk before you can crawl." Other pieces are deeply moving: a reflection on a schoolmate's suicide, an instance of religious intolerance, a profound moment when a Korean girl sees Michelangelo's *Pieta* and starts to pray.

I was able to illustrate a number of these essays with photographs. Next to a process paper explaining brilliantly how Nomar Garciaparra of the Boston Red Sox fields a ground ball, I set a picture of the Man himself, poised exactly as the essay describes him. Mr. and Mrs. Potato Head appear, of course, and the *David,* mentioned in the essay about the *Pieta*. One essay writes about Louis Armstrong's "Wonderful World," and I was able to find a song clip, used as an advertisement, that plays the first line. (It would be nice to have the whole song, but once again, copyright issues are too complex.)

We obtained releases from the young writers for permission to use their essays as long as *The Andover Reader* exists, promising that we would assert copyright on their behalf. For each essay I wrote a one- or two-line introduction and three or four questions at the end. One young writer wrote back with his release, "I never imagined that anything I wrote would have *study questions* at the end!" These questions looked at stylistic issues the writers had dealt with—use of present tense, flashbacks, passive voice, second-person narrators, and so on—as well as questions of content. To facilitate the *Reader*'s use for teachers, I wrote a general introduction in which I indexed a number of these issues, linking the entries to the relevant essays.

And so we released *The Andover Reader* upon an unsuspecting public. It was a distinct success. Some two hundred teachers used it as their primary text, I being one of them. Others used it as a resource, sending students to it for inspiration and guidance.

The students' reactions were almost without exception positive. They may not have liked all the essays, but they liked most of them, and they read them all far more closely than they had the old anthologies. They understood the reasons for the "study questions," for they were going to be writing essays like these. In my classes I found the students were imitating the models far more consciously than they had done before, thus engaging more fully with the act of writing. And the whole process became a huge morale boost: the writers often told me that the new two hundred students were complimenting them on their pieces. They were celebrities, and I felt a bit like Oprah and her book club.

There are now 42 essays in the anthology. In the last couple of years, *The Andover Reader* has been gaining wider readership. Last year the Words Work Network—a website that "exists solely to reinvent and restore to prominence the art of writing in American high schools"—invited us to be hosted on the WoW server as well as that of andover.edu. An occasional e-mail informs us that another teacher has discovered the *Reader* and has used it in class. Paul and I are delighted by this acceptance. In the Introduction we wrote, "we mean the text to be used by anyone, without charge." (We do throw in a plug for a scholarship fund at Phillips Academy, however.) As the WoW network makes clear, other teachers are gaining similar results by web publication of student work like ours. We would urge any educator to use both our product and our process in any way that benefits her students.

Come visit the *Reader* at http://www.andover.edu/english/200/reader/. We welcome commentary and questions. We'll leave a light on for you, as you join those faithful grandparents who still visit all the way from Kansas and Seoul.

John Gould has been teaching English for more than thirty years, more than twenty of these at Phillips Academy. He is the author of a novel, a memoir, a grammar textbook, and a cookbook containing one hundred ways of preparing hot dogs.

Building Learning Communities with Online Learning

By ChristineBridge

Want the best of online learning in your school? To make the most of this powerful learning tool, leaders should ensure three things: (1) teachers have ongoing professional development in information literacy; (2) teachers know how to build learning communities; (3) teachers learn new ways of conducting authentic assessment.

Last year our administration tried a new initiative whereby senior students received eight hours of online instruction as part of their course work. This meant eight hours less instructional time in the classroom, and Fridays became a shortened day, with classes ending two hours earlier than usual. The trial year is now complete and overall, online learning has met with success. What follows is a brief explanation of the results of our school's initiative, followed by an explanation of the three recommendations listed above.

Our Online Program

I am a senior English teacher at a small college preparatory K–12 day school south of a major city in Canada. It has been a laptop school for three years now; students are introduced to the laptop program in grade seven. I was new to the school this year, and although I have ten years' teaching experience, in many ways, it was a year of firsts. It was the first time I had the opportunity to have three of my classes completely wired, and it was the first time I was expected to design online course materials. This was overwhelming, as I had little understanding of how to employ online learning tools. I also knew little about instructional design. I was not alone in my trepidation. Staff was also uneasy about how students would use the half-day academic time on Friday afternoons.

After a one-year trial, reaction from staff and students has been mixed. Both were surveyed in the spring months. Extra or free academic time on Fridays was seen as a success for most students and teachers. Who wouldn't relish the idea of finishing classes early Friday afternoons! Many students used provided time to work (particularly our IB students), to see teachers for extra help, or arrange meetings with groups of students for projects. As one senior English teacher commented after the first month of the initiative, "I have three students coming for help this Friday. The use of this time for meeting with teachers has quickly become the norm for many students." What didn't go so well was that few students used the time on Friday afternoons to complete online assignments, which was the main intent.

Online instruction employed WebCT course management application. WebCT (much like Blackboard) provides user-friendly components, such as electronic messaging systems, collaborative grouping, student grading assessment tools, and file transfer. Each senior course was required to have a classroom homepage that included a course calendar and syllabus. Staff was instructed to use discussion options and post assignments. The directive from our high school principal was straightforward: "Fundamentally, [online learning] should offer independence to students; it should pursue the objectives of your course, and it should employ technology in that pursuit. I can't help thinking that the best way to harness technology is to maximize its capacity in two ways: to communicate and to access information. Ideally, I'd love to see students offered the opportunity to pursue trans-disciplinary projects—true to life problems, which they attempt to solve, provoking them to learn along the way."

Reaction to WebCT was not clearly definable. The greatest difficulty in the school's one-year trial was consistency of use. Most of us were learning WebCT for the first time in September, a week before classes were to begin. Several teachers, particularly in English and social studies, went on to use the program with great success. It was, however, difficult for administration to get several staff members "on board." The reasons for this were due to time constraints, follow-up, and types of curriculum. Faculty believed some courses were more conducive to online learning than others.

Recommendations

Independent schools will adopt online learning programs for various reasons; however, the goals for each school will probably be quite similar. Online learning is a powerful tool. It is unique to classroom learning in that it empowers learners by expanding the boundaries of the classroom. Online learning means increased

1. ability to access information
   - for students
   - for teachers
   - for community and global projects
2. Ability to develop relationships with
   - other teachers
   - parents
   - community
   - students around the world
3. ability to conduct authentic assessment
   - with field experts and professionals
   - with other students around the world
   - with surveys and polls internally or externally

Schools able to employ all of these facets of online learning will achieve a rich learning environment for their students, teachers, and community. However, in order to get to that point, school leaders need to ensure that their faculty has the necessary tools. Teachers need to be given ample time for professional development prior to and during implementation of an online program. And there is no more important place to start than with workshops on information literacy.

Information Literacy

Teachers need to know how to validate information they find online. They should know the grammar and rules of the Internet: how to properly read web addresses, conduct meaningful searches, trace backward and forward links from any site, find out how much a search term is going for on the market. If we want to teach our students to think critically about information, we must know how to ourselves.

We have all grown up with print; in fact, we have been "paper trained"—we know how books work, how libraries work, how to access fiction from non-fiction and periodicals from reference sections. But the Internet is entirely different; categories of information are organized in entirely different ways. We need to ensure that our students are as comfortable surfing the Internet as they are looking for a book in the library. There are no ISBN numbers, references, or indices with Internet information; however, there are simple ways of validating information and categorizing it appropriately.

We want our students to be discerning about information they find. We also want them to develop critical thinking skills. It's naïve to believe that teachers will know how to foster these skills in their students if they are not completely comfortable and knowledgeable in the grammar rules of the Internet themselves. The goal is to access meaningful authentic information. It's there, but we just need to arm teachers and students with the necessary tools to find it.

Information literacy and critical thinking skills are important for more than just validating information. It's also about protecting our students from what's "out there." Many Internet sites provide potentially harmful information or are just plain inappropriate. Too often, educators rely entirely on school filters to block potentially harmful sites. This provides a sense of false security. Students are seven times more likely to use computers at home, where there may be no filters whatsoever, than at school. We need to teach them how do deal with the power of the Internet within safe environments. We need to prepare them for what is "out there."

Workshops or websites on information literacy are great places to start. There are many web sites that deal with literacy issues. Two of note are: www.anovember.com and http://school.discovery.com/schrockguide/. Most literacy workshops will start with the premise that teachers and students should regularly evaluate the websites they research or use in class. Web evaluations serve as a building block of validation and provoke students to think critically about information. Website evaluations are simple and easy to use. For a complete list of generic evaluation forms, try http://www.lib.vt.edu/research/evaluate/evalbiblio.html#forms.

Being versed in the grammar of the Internet also means teachers know how to efficiently access information meaningful for them and their students. It means access to thousands of lessons plans, global projects, educational databases. Knowing how to conduct proper searches with good search engines, using link commands, and advanced searches can only help improve the learning environment of any classroom. Just ask a class to search for projects or assignments within a certain discipline on the Internet. You will be amazed at what they discover, what interests them, and the quality of work upon which they are willing to embark.

Building Learning Communities

One of the most exciting features of technology is that it provides students with the tools to access and build relationships with other students all over the world. Students and teachers can build relationships with other students, other teachers, parent groups, or with members of the community. There are many ways to build learning communities. Teachers can start small with epals and discussions boards. Discussions boards can lead to all sorts of exciting opportunities for learning. I have had great success with using them as literature circles, peer editing, prewriting activities, and debriefing after classroom activities. Some teachers use them as an opportunity for students to submit stories based on characters or storylines from other works, similar to www.fanfiction.net. These stories are written by students using pen names and reviewed by other students in the school, or within the district. Discussion boards should extend outside the boundaries of the classroom to include parents and other members of the community. Having parents join in on literature circles with my classes last year proved a great success.

The power of online relationships means students can build projects with professionals, authentic materials, and data. For example, local government and politicians can be reached and asked about real problems in the community. Students can find out about issues in their community or pending laws that might serve as a springboard for further historical study or data recovery. Primary resources can be researched through the National Archives. There are many valuable lesson plans currently available at http://www.archives.gov/digital_classroom/index.html. Or www.firstgov.gov provides an extensive directory of government agencies that link to numerous scientific research sites and provide real data, which can be incorporated into science, math, history, and geography lessons.

Students should be encouraged to seek contact and build relationships with other students. Web Quests (www.webquest.org) are a great place to start. Web Quests are Internet lessons designed for online learners. They include standards, methods of assessment, and step-by-step lesson plans for all ages. They are collaboratively developed both by students and teachers around the world. Another site worth review is www.iearn.org. Here you will find lists of global projects that students may wish to join. In building a learning community, students learn how to communicate with people of different cultures, ages, races, and religions. We need to encourage our communities to grow and build stronger relationships with other cultures around the world. In researching various projects at www.iearn.org, one can quickly imagine the effects these meaningful global projects must have on the young people involved.

Authentic Assessment

It's also important for students to publish their work online and know that their audience reaches further than their teacher or members of their class. The website http://www.andover.edu/english/200/reader/ has brilliant student essays available, complete with questions that serve as discussion points for other essay writers around the country. What better way for a teacher to demonstrate quality work than showing her students essays from other students? What better motivator can there be than an authentic audience? Students want to rise to the level of their peers, if not surpass it. Why restrict them to publishing for one person when they can publish for the whole world?

The concept of authentic audience and assessment is integral to building a learning community. It makes learning real and meaningful. Consider the Slam poetry contest held in the South Bronx each school year. Middle school students, in one of the toughest school districts in the country, compete in a poetry contest whereby they workshop and are judged by local poets in New York City through video conferencing. The students write and perform their works to a live authentic audience and the results are amazing.

Authentic assessment could mean having work assessed by a group of poets, or a group of other students, or perhaps another teacher. Anonymity can be a tremendous bonus for assessment, as students are often more open and straightforward with people they do not know. Why not present a math problem to a bank manager or a physics lab to an engineer? The possibilities for independent schools to harness their communities to create vehicles of authentic assessment are unique and relatively untapped.

Authentic assessment can also come in the form of polls and surveys. Consider the power of polling your students during class to find out if they truly understand a concept you've just taught. Anonymous responses to your polls will be far more accurate than a show of individual responses. Also, surveys can be used throughout the school year among staff to provide feedback on school issues, goals, or initiatives. Not only are online polls a great indicator of current thoughts or feelings, they may re-energize discussion or prompt action.

Conclusion

Any school can have a good online learning program. But a program that bases itself on the importance of building relationships between individuals and the community will be the great one. In building a learning community, teachers need to be well versed in the grammar of the Internet: They need to know how to validate information. They also should understand the importance of authentic audience and its impact on student motivation and assessment.

My school fell short of its goals for online learning in its inaugural year. But we believe that we will improve and our learning community will grow. Every school has to start somewhere, and the goal for senior teachers to develop a class website with course outline and discussion board was certainly realistic and reasonable. Staff was given various workshops in September, told of the expectations, and given various avenues of support. But as any teacher will attest, throughout the course of the school year there are never enough hours in the day. For many, online course development fell by the wayside.

Our school will press on. Faculty agrees our initiatives need consistent revisiting, combined with continual professional development and the sharing of ideas. The more information literate we become and the more we harness the power of authentic assessment, the stronger the relationships in our learning community will be.

Christine Bridge has over ten years' teaching experience in independent schools in Western Canada. She now works with Alan November at Building Learning Communities in Marblehead, MA. She is a writer, researcher, and presenter of educational workshops on technology and writing.

Technology Usage and Administration at the Independent School: Balancing Control and Autonomy

By Stewart Crais & Lorrie Jackson

Almost overnight, the digital age has transformed the independent school. Computers have crept into the K–12 classroom, often in the hands of each student. Software or online primary resources have replaced the traditional textbook in many classes. Meanwhile, integrated programs handle all aspects of student and campus data: from admissions to development to grades to cafeteria supplies and more. On many campuses, the infusion of technology is so pervasive and integrated in daily operations that one would be hard-pressed to find any aspect of campus life operating without technology.

This transformation has allowed teachers, administrators, students and others to take ownership in the use of technology, yet such diffusion comes with a price. A secretary may buy a printer, not knowing if the school has the staff or the ink to support it. Administrators might purchase division-wide software programs, not knowing if similar programs already exist on campus or if the program even works with existing network or hardware specs. A teacher might load a school-owned word processing program onto a home computer, not knowing the legality of that action.

Without centralization of purchases, maintenance, and actual usage, school money is wasted, faculty members are frustrated, and legal issues arise. Yet, how does the independent school balance this need for control with the inherent autonomy given to many faculty and staff on how their classrooms or offices operate? Lausanne Collegiate School found that by introducing technology with appropriate staffing, communication, collaboration and empowerment, an effective and cost-saving compromise between control and autonomy could be achieved in the school's technology program.

Overview

Lausanne Collegiate School is a diverse, independent, coeducational, nonsectarian school serving a diverse student body in Memphis, TN. Approximately 750 students in grades pre-K–12 attend Lausanne. As part of its mission to prepare students for college and for life in a global environment, the school emphasizes technology in every grade and content area.

Lausanne's Laptop Program exemplifies this commitment, with all seventh through twelfth grade students purchasing IBM ThinkPads for use in their classrooms. Teachers with laptops, a wireless campus, a 5th/6th grade laptop cart, computer centers in grades pre-K–4 , and a schoolwide commitment to technology integration complete the picture. Lausanne's technology program—from laptops to online teacher training resources—has been recognized as a model for technology integration at public and independent schools.[1]

Infusion of Technology Through Appropriate Staffing

Infusing technology throughout all the departments and divisions helps to ensure the acceptance of technology in an independent school. The basis for this infusion, however, begins in the appropriate structuring of the Technology and Media Services department that provides, and should retain, the central locus of control.

In this example, the Technology and Media Services Department encompasses all computer hardware, software, media (e.g., TVs, VCRs, projectors) as well as the Library / Media Center. Personnel include a director, a systems administrator, a technology support specialist, an instructional technology coordinator, a technology education specialist, a library/media specialist, and an assistant library/media specialist (see figure below).

The director is a school administrator who reports to the headmaster and therefore serves on the administrative team along with the heads of the other divisions. Through weekly administrative team meetings and quarterly retreats, the director is able to offer input at the top decision-making level in the school, beginning the technology infusion process. The director is also the chair of the communications committee (a committee required by the school's accreditation body) and a member of the building and grounds committee (a board committee), ensuring that technology is a component of decision making school-wide. Through monthly meetings with both of these committees, technology is continually looked upon as an alternative for collaboration, communication, and problem-solving.

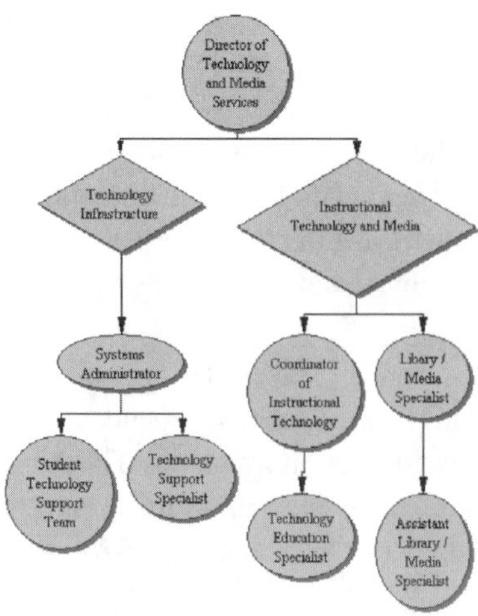

Lausanne chose to combine the library and the technology departments in order to foster more collaboration, a common trend in independent schools seeking to foster information literacy across campus. This combination allows for the coordinator of instructional technology to work closely with the library/media center personnel as students and teachers seek ways to use information, both electronic and otherwise. Technology and library classes can be combined so that students begin learning how to access information electronically at an early age.

The coordinator of instructional technology is responsible for helping the teachers use technology in their classrooms. This includes assisting in the classrooms during lessons, researching Internet sites for lessons, teacher training, and providing opportunities for technology leadership within the faculty. Types of leadership may include serving on their divisional technology committee, becoming one of six tech mentors, or presenting any classroom best practices at a faculty meeting or outside conference. This position allows for the infusion of technology throughout the faculty and staff by encouraging them to have ownership and decision-making opportunities.

The technology education specialist is responsible for teaching technology classes school-wide as well as heading the student technology clubs and other extracurricular activities. This position works closely with the coordinator of instructional technology in ensuring that appropriate skills are taught at the appropriate grade levels, following the school's technology scope and sequence and vertical teaming plans. Constant communication and collaboration with the students allows for the infusion of technology throughout the student body, preparing them for the ability to use technology to enhance their education.

The systems administrator works closely with the director of technology, ensuring that the appropriate hardware and software is deployed in the best possible way. Support of the workstations, servers, network, and overseeing of the school's laptop program are the responsibilities of this person, assisted by the technology support specialist and the student technology support team.

Having the appropriate personnel structure allows for ownership of technology decisions to become the responsibility of many players, including board members, administrators, staff, faculty, and students, while still allowing for a central locus of control. Participants learn to appreciate and understand the importance that technology can have in a school environment. More important, students enter college and the work force with the understanding of how to use technology to their benefit.

Communication

Communication is a two-way street: committees, tech mentors, and others allow faculty and staff to communicate their needs, while departmental reports to the faculty and board make clear the goals and steps to get there. Current projects, long-range plans, and appropriate feedback must all be communicated to the school community in order for a technology program to be successful and not perceived as a top-down approach. Lausanne uses several types of communication practices in order to encourage that both the ownership and growth of the technology program rely on the involvement of the entire school community.

The three divisional technology committees determine the issues and needs from their areas. Members of these committees are mostly faculty, but may also include administrative staff. These committees are headed by the coordinator of instructional technology and allow for the input of all parties involved. The members of these committees express their joys, concerns, and ideas related to technology in their classrooms. This information is then addressed by a member of the technology department, or communicated to and addressed by the administrative team via a monthly meeting, focusing primarily on technology.

Another component of communication is a quarterly newsletter published by the department. This newsletter spotlights various teachers and their use of technology in their classrooms. It also provides a space to announce new initiatives by the department, including new software, hardware, or other changes that are taking place at the time. The newsletter balances information from each division of the school, allowing for the audience (parents, teachers, and students) to read about technology schoolwide, thus contributing to the communication and understanding of technological endeavors.

Communication to the board of trustees concerning technology is an important piece as well. This helps the board recognize some of the needs of technology as well as the advances that have been made over the years. The department accomplishes this by conducting a "State of Technology" presentation to the board each year. This presentation includes information about what has happened in technology over the previous year, which projects are currently under way, and plans for the following year. This presentation gives the board the information they need in order to make the budget decisions that greatly shape the program's growth.

Ongoing communication in these areas shares the understanding and ownership of technology with the entire school community, not just one department.

Collaboration and Empowerment

Leadership style is an extremely important component of a successful technology program at any school. From the examples above, one can see that decisions should not be made without input and direction from the various constituencies. Teamwork is strongly encouraged among the technology and media services staff, allowing for understanding of each member's various duties and responsibilities. Large projects, such as the yearly laptop rollout, enjoy the support of the entire department, not just the systems administrator. These policies foster a "whatever it takes" attitude among all members.

In order to develop ownership in the department, the director holds weekly meetings in which the technology staff is asked for input about current projects and upcoming plans. Important decisions are not made without input from the entire department, which in turn has input from teachers, staff, and students. This shifts the locus of control away from the director and even the department and allows many players to participate in decision-making.

This sense of collaboration permeates the technology staff's interactions with the rest of the campus community as well. Rather than spending an unexpected money windfall on software of her choice, the coordinator of instructional technology delegates that decision to the middle school's technology committee members, faculty who use technology in their teaching and can best provide input on those decisions. The coordinator remains involved in the discussion, providing guidance as to compatibility with existing hardware/ software, but the teachers have the chance to offer their suggestions and voice their concerns.

Similarly, the systems administrator looks to his student tech support team for guidance on how best to resolve minor laptop usage issues or how to resolve tricky repair or maintenance issues. Team members know that their suggestions will be listened to and often acted upon by their supervisor.

Such mutual respect and collaborative style lets users feel that their input and ideas are valid while ensuring that tech staff are always aware of issues and concerns that impact the school. In fact, it is this department's belief that without empowerment and collaboration, true technology integration can never happen.

Recently, a kindergarten teacher observed a classroom at another school and was impressed at how projectors and interactive software were being used in early childhood. Despite her self-avowed beginner's skills, she shared her impressions with the technology staff and the headmaster, explaining in writing how she would utilize similar technology in her classroom if given the chance. Shortly, monies became available, and she was given the technology. She quickly learned how to use the equipment and began incorporating it in daily lessons, transforming her classroom overnight into a tech-infused learning space. Had the decision to purchase that equipment come top-down or had she not felt that her opinions would be valued and heard, such a transformation would never have happened.

Conclusion

The compromise between tightening the reins on technology and letting go a little is never easy, and even with the best of intentions, mistakes do happen. It is important that a school's technology department involve itself in all levels of school decision-making. This helps reduce buildings being built, purchases being made, or teachers being hired without the input of the tech staff. The system is not a perfect one, but with an ongoing commitment to collaborating, communicating, staffing, and centralizing technology administration, the independent school can continue to move toward a money-saving and sound curricular solution.

Note

[1] "School Site of the Month," *Teaching and Learning Magazine,* February, 2003, http://www.techlearning.com/db_area/archives/TL/2003/02/schoolsite.html "Best Bet." *USAТodayEducation,* March, 2003, http://www.usatoday.com/educate/home.htm "Lausanne Collegiate School Prepares Students for College Programs with IBM Tools," *IBM,* 2002, http://www-3. ibm.com/software/success/cssdb.nsf/CS/JMAY-5EVTAE?OpenDocument&Site=default

In his tenth year at Lausanne Collegiate School (Memphis, TN), **Stewart Crais,** director of technology, oversees the entire technology and media services department, handling purchasing, software licensing, and overall technology planning. In addition to these duties, Stewart also manages the servers, the website, and Lausanne's data and voice networks. Stewart is an MCSE (Microsoft Certified Systems Engineer) and earned his B.A. from Rhodes College.

As coordinator of instructional technology for Lausanne Collegiate School (Memphis, TN), **Lorrie Jackson** helps pre-K–12 teachers integrate technology into the regular classroom. She also writes *EducationWorld*'s weekly column "TechTorials," as well as its monthly series entitled *Teaching Teachers.* Lorrie has written several book chapters on technology in the classroom and is the moderator of [http://www.topica.com/lists/techtrainers] Techtrainers@topica.com, a mail list for teachers and teacher trainers. Lorrie earned her B.A. and M.A.T. from the University of Memphis.

The Small Market School and Technological Improvements

By Palmer Bell

The 2000–2001 NAIS Statistical Resources Report revealed that nationally the average member day school is able to designate an amount equal to 1.2% of budget per year for technological expenses. My personal experience suggests that there is a group of member schools that for a variety of reasons will never enjoy this luxury. Obviously, most independent schools utilize annual tuition revenue as their primary funding source. Collecting revenue that adequately funds the educational program offered is a fundamental issue within all tuition-driven schools. Schools that operate in geographic or economic "small markets" that necessitate establishing lower than average tuitions, schools that feel "mission pressure" to maintain lower tuitions, and/or schools that simply have short-term funding issues that require alternative spending priorities are under-funded, and therefore present unique educational and financial leadership challenges. The reality is that not only do such schools struggle to generate sufficient tuition revenue to meet current expenses, but they then are compelled to use fund-raising activities to cover annual expenses. Furthermore, schools within such a financial cycle compound their future financial pictures through an inability to set aside cash reserves and endowment funds, which other schools use to augment stronger tuition revenue receipts.

The temptation for those serving in schools that face financial issues is to resist proactively exploring and recommending new educational opportunities, such as those currently presented through technology. When I assumed the headship of just seven years ago, technology on our PK–8 campus of 350 students consisted of eleven Apple IIe computers, four VHS recorders, and four office computers. My vision for technological improvements faced initial costs that appeared prohibitive and ongoing costs that were a certainty. However, I believe that to resist the educational revitalization that technology is providing is potentially detrimental to the students and the institutions we serve. Perhaps the following suggestions will support leaders who face similar dilemmas to frame a vision that can stimulate the adoption of costly technological improvements.

What Is a Small School to Do?

Write a Specific Plan

For the small school, writing a detailed technology plan is essential. Such plans serve important functions both internally and externally for a school. As the plan guides internal acquisitions, it also signals to the external community your vision for the future.

A technology plan should document what technology objectives are to be addressed at each grade level or within each classroom and link those objectives to the school mission as appropriate. The rationale at the planning stage is that foreseeing that a class will be photo-editing or producing short movies distinguishes the technology needs for that class from a class requiring Internet access for a group writing exercise or from one needing simple word processing capabilities.

A specific, written technology plan should isolate the required types of technology desired while documenting the number and cost of each component needed and prioritizing the stages required to reach each specific goal. You will have to decide whether this is best tackled as a committee assignment or entrusted to a knowledgeable individual. Whichever methodology is best in your school, this process should include time to consider computer processors, memory requirements, and drive types so that these details can be added to the plan. If a computer network is necessary, how extensive must it be, and will the network also require Internet access? Ensure that your plan addresses the additional growth of the program, the ongoing training of staff, the timely replacement of outdated components, and the licensing of software. Carefully consider all forms of technology that the school requires. Many individuals use the terms *technology* and *computer* synonymously. Have you included television monitors, DVD/VHS players, PDAs, printers, scanners, digital cameras, video projectors, calculators and other technological hardware that your educational objectives suggest are needed? A site plan that maps the locations within each building that will house the newly acquired equipment may reveal additional hidden expenses that need to be addressed. The point here is what carpenters call "measure twice—cut once." Spending significant planning time will potentially save wasting thousands of precious dollars that could be better allocated.

The careful writing of a detailed technology plan is vital for more than merely the internal planning process. A further advantage to specifically planning for technological needs relates to potential gifts. School constituents with whom the plan is shared see both the vision and the opportunity to support it, confident that their gifts can be targeted to a specific area of need. When tight budgets restrict funds for acquiring new technological equipment, the small school may find it difficult to resist becoming a "dumping ground" for donated used equipment. A technology plan that designates the types, specifications, and numbers of desired equipment that fit the school's needs helps to guide decisions to accept gifts-in-kind. Obviously, a specific written plan is also instrumental in successfully applying for technology grants or matching funds when the time is right.

Affording Your Technology Plan

Once you contemplate technological improvements, you realize that available funding is a limiting factor in attaining stated objectives. Small schools that are funding their operations largely with annual tuition revenue must creatively approach any attempt at making major technological advancements. Include *budget* lines that support the annual stages you have established in the technology plan. Even if these budget entries must be reduced or eliminated during the school's annual budgeting process, this step forces all decision makers to become invested in the financial choices surrounding technology acquisitions. Choose to *re-direct* common budget items to support stated goals within the technology plan. For example, money from professional development workshops may be targeted for the technology training of faculty and staff. At different stages of your technology adoption all faculty may need similar training, while at other stages faculty should be allowed to choose their areas of personal need. Publish *wish-lists* of needed technological components that support your plan with the associated costs. Nothing encourages gifts faster than visible, tangible results that directly impact students. Contact local businesses and share your wish list. Businesses that routinely upgrade their equipment can be a valuable resource for used hardware that will still meet a school's specific needs. Leasing companies or computer stores that lease equipment may appreciate having a market for items being returned at lease-end.

Financing and/or leasing technological equipment should be explored creatively. Unfortunately, because the useful life of electronic equipment is relatively short, financing and leasing often require similar interest payments. Therefore, small schools may do better approaching board members when they need to finance periodic acquisitions. Board-designated *financial reserves* or restricted funds may be a source of funds for purchases if those designated funds can be tapped by board action. *Technology fees or tuition increases* when they support directly observable benefits can be justified to meet added technology costs. However, in many small markets any tuition or fee increase can be detrimental to student enrollment and therefore must be weighed carefully. *Vendor discounts and/or bid pricing* can significantly reduce the outlay for technology. Even small schools can qualify as volume buyers and should request the bid department price for technology components. Simply contact each company with the specific items you desire using detailed specifications or catalog ID numbers and allow the vendor to refuse to bid a lower price for that product. Annual fundraising banquets or auctions may target support for the technology plan. Once again, small schools that require such funds to "close the budget gap" need to tread carefully here, but even in such cases an appeal that promises that all funds above a threshold amount will be used to support technology can significantly increase the overall giving at such an event. Above all, remember to utilize creatively the hardware you do acquire. Resist throwing anything away, as older computers can become print servers, firewalls, web servers, classroom stations for younger students, or at the very least a source of parts to repair other similar hardware.

Examples of Technological Support to a Small School (last seven years)

- A local web design firm produces a school website and hosts the site (with e-mail server) at no charge
- CISCO Systems award grant for network equipment and training
- Local phone company wires a 20-computer lab for network as community service by employees
- School employee donates hours of free time to repair hardware and install equipment
- School benefactor uses past employer's donation program to double his gift to support technology, providing $20,000 for laptop computers
- Numerous donations of new hardware and software to fill important links in the technology plan (e.g., computers, printers, a digital movie camera, and library software)
- Company discounts support high-speed DSL, phone service, hardware and software acquisitions
- Hours of "teachers training teachers" in-house workshops cover a variety of software and hardware training issues
- Donations of used but appropriate hardware components including, 46 computers, video cameras, printers, a 10-bay CD tower, a network switch
- Partnership with the local state Educational Service Center to support a successful $585,000 T.A.R.G.E.T. grant that will provide off-site two-way video conferencing, teacher training and connect teachers/students to the Texas State Aquarium videoconferencing network

Conclusion

Small schools and/or schools in economically challenging markets have numerous hurdles to overcome. This is especially true when educational upheavals, such as we are currently experiencing in the technological revolution, threaten to leave such schools behind, outdated or financially strapped. The successful school must construct an attainable strategy guided by sound educational reasoning and one that recognizes it cannot match its wealthier cousins. Heads of small schools must distill the essence of educational trends and not chase the peaks and valleys showcased over the short term. However, as small schools strategize, and by necessity take baby steps, they have the advantage of recognizing and funding only the truly innovative, worthy advances. Small school leaders must be comfortable watching others explore the fad-induced expenses, trusting that many will be found undesirable and quickly abandoned. In all likelihood, small market schools will not have the latest, the fastest, or the trendiest technological advances. This is a vast improvement over having no advances. It has been my experience that aware, small schools, especially those in challenging economic regions, are excellent stewards of the revenue they receive, diligent in balancing innovation against educational mission and superior at delivering high value educational and yes, technological, experiences for their students at lower than average tuition cost. Therefore, the educational technological revolution need not be delayed.

Over the last 31 years **Palmer Bell** has served in six different NAIS schools across a broad geographic and educational spectrum. His training and degrees in the sciences have provided a unique basis for a career that has included positions as a teacher/coach, department head, dean, division head, assistant headmaster, and now for the last eight years a headmaster at St. James Episcopal School.

Dealing with Obsolescence: A Citrix Server Solution—St. Paul's School, A Case Study

By Mona Miller and Susan Kearney

Introduction

In 1999, during the planning phase for a new middle school building, the technology committee at St. Paul's School, a K–12 independent school in Brooklandville, MD, chose to implement a school-wide thin client network solution. In July 2003, six servers and 260 terminals compose the back end of this implementation. "Smart" terminals and PCs view a standard Windows desktop accessed on one of six servers in the "server farm." The ability to access a host of applications from a central server offers an ideal scenario for the recycling of outdated computers. St. Paul's School has realized significant financial savings by extending the life of aging computers and decreasing maintenance costs. This case study explains the philosophy and analysis behind the choice of a Citrix solution, the implementation, and the benefits to students.

The middle school at St. Paul's School is composed of fifth through eighth grades. The fifth grade is housed in a separate building. The old building, for sixth through eighth grades, was small and outdated, and contained only one computer lab for all middle school students. The lab was over-scheduled, making integration of technology into the curriculum difficult for most teachers and impossible for others. There was a definite and demonstrated need for more access to technology. Room organization was based on the departmental model. The new building was to be built with a wing for each grade (a cluster model) with a science lab, a modern language room, and three other classrooms.

Three options were considered before the plan to employ a Citrix based solution was chosen: the inclusion of a computer lab for each grade, small computer clusters in each classroom, and laptops for each student—traditional solutions in many schools. The first, a computer lab in each wing, was quickly discarded as requiring the building to be bigger and more costly than planned. Hardware would cost fifteen hundred for each station, and three more rooms would need to be added to the building. Scheduling of the lab would also still be an issue and spontaneous use impossible. The issue of obsolescence would need to be addressed every three to five years, and maintenance and setup would be required for each desktop.

The provision of four or five computers in each classroom would not allow for class-wide use at any time and, although the number of computers school-wide might be sufficient, they would not provide simultaneous use by an entire class. Issues of the initial price of hardware, subsequent replacement due to obsolescence, and increased desktop maintenance would exist as in the computer lab proposal.

Many schools have provided laptops for each student or require parents to purchase one for each of their children in the school. St. Paul's school chose not to burden families with this cost, families who for the most part already have computers in their homes. The care of a laptop by a middle school student is fraught with risks and presents greater physical burden. Laptops would not provide the same ease of switching gears that teachers want for their curriculum. Start-up requires time, and issues of worn batteries and failed systems present problems, interrupting the flow of teaching. Again, issues of initial price, maintenance, and obsolescence are inherent in this possible solution.

Citrix Solution

The Citrix Server solution selected by St. Paul's represents a return to a centralized, server-based computing environment. All the power and processing power resides on a collection of servers known as the server "farm." The servers must be equipped with multiple processors and enough RAM to accommodate simultaneous sessions of twenty to thirty users. While there is a significant up-front cost building the powerful infrastructure, these costs are offset by low terminal costs, extended life of aging, and often fully depreciated, PCs, decreased maintenance expense on workstations, and (although harder to quantify) efficiencies gained in network management.

The six servers in the SPnet farm use Citrix Metaframe 1.8 software. Tricerat Desktop software is used to manage and maintain standard desktops for students, faculty, and administrators. All servers are Compaq Proliant DL380s, with dual Pentium III 1.3 gHz processors, 2gb of RAM, two 35gb mirrored drives, and redundant power supplies. One server functions as the "load balancer," dividing up user sessions between the remaining five servers in the farm.

Software programs are installed on each server and monitored using a variety of methods. St. Paul's participates in a software licensing consortium agreement with Microsoft and area independent schools for access to Microsoft applications on PCs and terminals at schools. The school has also purchased a program (KeyServer) that meters licenses in a thin client environment. Every software package has run with no loss of functionality or performance penalty.

In the fall of 2000, a pilot program for the Citrix system was implemented in the fifth grade building that was not involved in construction. The four classrooms were each equipped with twenty "smart" terminals, named CompuDesks by St. Paul's. The instant access to the CompuDesks quickly changed how the integration of technology into every curricular area occurred. Technology is ubiquitous and can be used instantly for five minutes or for forty-five minutes. Students and teachers learned to make technology a dynamic part of each day.

The pilot program, in fact, proved so successful that two classrooms in every grade were similarly equipped in the new construction of the middle school. One more classroom was added in each grade the next year. The program has been expanded to the upper school, equipping one lab with thirty terminals. There are now a total of 260 terminals accessing Citrix at St. Paul's and hundreds accessing Citrix remotely in student, faculty, and administrator's homes.

Access to files and school resources from home was not an initial goal of the project. It has, however, become an indispensable feature provided in the Citrix environment deployed at St. Paul's. Students are able to continue schoolwork at home, accessing their personal files and library databases, such as SIRS Researcher and Electric Library. Faculty use the school's reporting systems, previously FileMaker Pro and now Senior Systems, the school software at home.

Conclusion

While the initial setting up of a Citrix solution requires powerful servers, the longer-term cost benefits from using older computers and from decreased network and computer maintenance and management have made the savings real. The CompuDesks have provided ubiquitous computing in a secure environment with no cost to families. The uninterrupted flow of teaching has changed teaching and learning at St. Paul's School, and off campus access to all school software, library databases, and files has bridged the divide between home and school.

Susan Kearney has been director of network services at St. Paul's School since 1995 and has 15 years experience in the technology industry.

Mona Miller has extensive experience in the use of technology in pre-collegiate education, having worked in this field for twenty years.

Thought, Technology, and the Stories of Our Lives: Reflecting on the Raw Material of Education

By Eric K. Neufer

You arrive at work and immediately encounter the billboards of our profession: books, newspapers, magazines, e-mails, websites, minutes from meetings, advertisements of many forms, sheets of paper that spew from the copy machine that is now digital and receiving data from every informational device around your campus. "Information superhighway," now a quaint term, doesn't capture the hustle and bustle of ideas that greet you every day. Everywhere behind the scenes, people's ideas are being actively marketed—with a variety of motives. Some are from companies that are working hard to survive and grow. Others wend their way from universities where the best of intentions are at work to transform everything within their reach. Many others linger in the hallways, born out of committee meetings and administrators' minds, generally with sincere intentions to make your school a place that serves everyone. By the time you walk into your classroom, you've taken a hearty dip in the pool of others' thoughts, not to mention your own. You've made a myriad of tiny decisions because each thought you experience prompts a response. Most, if not all, of those decisions are made with no awareness of what is happening. Your responses are carefully orchestrated, managed as they are by a crack team of internal administrative assistants whose job it is to keep "who you are" intact and consistent.

Contemplation of the educational landscape from a higher altitude than where we usually find ourselves on a day-to-day basis cannot help but make us uneasy about this flood of information and the tools for working and playing with it. Because one of our primary jobs is to help children make the best use of their minds, we must face the fact that it is the environment of the mind that is undergoing a profound transformation. We have never encountered anything like this deluge in known human history since Noah's flood. This ability we have, to think, has never had so much at its disposal and at its service as it does now. And it will have more tomorrow.

It is information technology, of course, that is giving the human mind, and its thoughts, unprecedented power. It is both the speed at which thoughts can travel and the speed at which thought leads to matter that are increasing. We see the former so vividly as a few stray words in an e-mail sent to the wrong person bring down an individual's career. A speech, every recorded word of which is run through the media mill until what appears to be every possible meaning is extracted, can bring about the same kind of devastation. The latter is obvious as computer programs play an increasing role in all aspects of our lives. The most vivid example is the machine that can take instructions in one end and give you the desired physical object out the other.

As we ponder our situation, we find ourselves face to face with the conundrum that we've never been able to adequately explain the nature of thought, the currency of our profession. We don't know what it is, yet we create the illusion that we do. We create pictures of reality that many students dutifully assume represent truth without questioning their integrity or their origins. But the emerging informational tools are serving to undermine this arrangement by opening wide channels of access to systems of thought much different from the "standard" ones, fostering the kind of questioning that we're seeing encouraged in constructivist environments. Technology, in short, is prompting us to think about the ways we teach and the ways students learn. As a result, discomfort with some of the deepest underlying assumptions about how we carry out the process of education is on the rise. We realize that it's time we do some basic things differently. We need to introduce students to many points of view and points of reference, thus challenging the idea of the teacher-centered class or the academic text as a sole source of information, static and unassailable. Furthermore, we need to do things that help us do basic things differently. Being creatures of habit, we are not chomping at the bit to reexamine our learning environments. Investment is high in the status quo. We just know, deep down, that something needs to happen to shake us loose from the comfortable.

In attempting to make some sense of it all, we soon realize that the very process we are trying to better understand is the process with which we are doing the understanding. We find ourselves thinking about thinking. This is, of course, metacognition, a branch of philosophy that generally doesn't attract large crowds. But, as we ponder the ever-shifting cognitive landscape, we come to see it as an increasingly practical skill. In fact, it can be a very effective tool for helping us be midwives to change. Jerome Bruner, in his book *The Culture of Education,* sees it as one of the "three classic antidotes" for the "unconsciousness of the automatic," that is, one of the ways we can better comprehend our own behavior.[1] And as our behavior continues to include increasingly powerful uses of technology, it becomes ever so vital that we redefine our educational strategies to address the way ideas are generated, communicated, and processed.

So then, how do we go about addressing the nature of thought, itself? Furthermore, how do we do it in a way that serves us, rather than merely adding to the number of scholarly books in the library? As we contemplate the nature of thought, we are faced with the problem that many of our contemplations are merely collections of the familiar. The task requires us to think outside the box, something for which there is generally little support. We come to realize that holding our ground at the frontier of understanding the mind is a difficult process, because each thought that arises can so easily be part of a conspiracy to push that frontier further away from us.

Before we get too timid, let's consider some language that might loosen up the habits that guide our thinking.

Sharing in the process of metacognition requires a vocabulary: words with agreed upon meanings to keep us from wandering off into our own solitary mental worlds. The words are not defined to argue for a particular interpretation of reality or to be some claim to ultimate truth. The goal, rather, is to fashion a set of tools that can help us maintain a conscious awareness of our thoughts as entities unto themselves, as opposed to mere labels for some so-called "reality." These tools also help to avoid the trap of mistaking our mental constructions of the world for the world, itself. What follows has arisen from my own intuitive and analytical experiences with metacognition. As Robert Kegan and Lisa Laskow Lahey advise in reference to their work with helping people change, "You are not required to buy any of these ideas; you're just renting them, for the time you spend with this book, to see if something new and useful appears to you as a result."[2]

Our definitions begin with the concept of *energy*. Take a moment to examine your own understanding of that term. Most of us have grown up under the boughs of Einstein's vision that tell us that everything is energy. And for our purposes, that will work just fine. It is, indeed, a word we'll use for *everything,* including every thought that arises in our minds.[3] The second concept is that energy is either in motion, which I'll call *flow,* or it is static, which I'll call *structure*. The next concept is *intention,* which I'll define as the decision to direct energy in a particular *direction*. In order to do so, some of the energy must be static, that is, its motion is somewhat or even completely curtailed with the interest of directing other energy that remains in motion, or flow. I'll make the claim that everything (energy) is naturally in a state of flow unless intention arises to keep it from being so.

In essence, intention produces structure; it creates what could be termed either *guidance* or *obstruction* for the flow, that is, the energy that is in motion. In our business, such guidance or obstruction takes the form of everything from rules to curricula to school buildings. (The picture that emerges is similar to a river, where intention is the formation of ice to channel the remaining liquid water. In fact, by defining these terms, I am creating structure to consciously guide the further flow of our discussion in a particular manner.) Structure created by human beings initially takes the form of *thought*. We'll use the word *concept* for those thoughts that maintain a perceivable existence over time. Thoughts and concepts are mental, or *inner* structures. *Matter,* is, of course, physical, or *outer* structure. In essence, *creativity* is the flow that leads to structure that in turn sets the parameters for subsequent flow. As such a process unfolds, we find ourselves amidst creations of greater and greater *complexity,* having increasingly intricate interactions of flow and structure. Finally, we need a term for what occurs in the world as a result of our intentions. (That is, we have a pile of nouns; we need a verb.) *Action* will do.

So far, the concepts I have defined are *objective,* that is, they have more of a feel of looking *at* reality rather than being *in* it. (As philosopher Ken Wilber insists, neither the objective nor the subjective can ultimately be reduced to the other with the process of thinking.[4] I'll come back to this important idea in a bit.) We need a corresponding set of concepts to use as labels for the *subjective* aspect of our lives. We'll use *meaning* for our experience of energy, *ideas* for our experience of mental structure, and *feeling* for our experience of flow. Our initial experience of an intention is the *desire* to have an influence on the next moment of life. Structure, beginning with thought (ideas), arises out of the intention (desire), followed by feeling and, generally, action. Complexity can bring the experience of *interest* or *confusion*. It becomes quickly obvious, given the general ongoing experience of thoughts, that intentions (desires) are constantly arising, often at cross purposes, much like what happens when many stones are dropped in a pond and ripples go out in all directions. Awareness of an individual intention appears almost impossible, much like the difficulty of determining which stone caused which ripple. As metacognition engages us in prolonged attention to our inner landscape, a desire inevitably arises for the ability to slow or even stop the seemingly never-ending stream of intentions and resulting thoughts so we can get a better look at them. We have a desire for greater clarity and seek respite from the increasingly annoying cacophony.

The observation of thoughts that leads to a slowing down of their appearance is one aspect of an ancient process known as *meditation*. If you are a meditator, then you already have some degree of understanding of this tool or art form. (If you are not, take the opportunity to observe what arises in response to the idea. Watch the power that some of your opinions have to distract you from the flow of this essay.) Developing a practice of meditation is a very helpful step for effective metacognition. A regular daily experience of going consciously "inside" does indeed slow the stream of thought.

*****

So far, our collection of tools for exploring the nature of thinking includes shared structure and a practice for clearer inner observation. Another essential class of resources includes insights from others who have traveled this road ahead of us: the philosophers and other thinkers who have specialized in this area. Since our purpose here is to put together a practical toolkit for employing metacognition in the service of education and our time and space are limited, we'll focus on three ideas with connections to important issues in our field.

The first idea relates to our growing understanding of constructivist learning, providing insight into why increasing numbers of teachers are working to integrate its practices into their classrooms. In the language of this essay, we would say that constructivist learning is the process by which students play a conscious role in the formation of their own inner structures, rather than merely incorporating those of their teachers and textbooks. Research reveals two types of structures in organizations: *designed* and *emergent*. *Designed* structures are created analytically with disciplined use of thought. *Emergent* structures come into being seemingly on their own, made possible by what could be termed the *fertility* of an organization, that is, the creative quality of the environment or the degree to which flow is both possible and encouraged. Physicist Fritjof Capra describes them:

> Emergent structures . . . provide novelty, creativity, and flexibility. They are adaptive, capable of changing and evolving. In today's complex . . . environment, purely designed structures do not have the necessary responsiveness and learning capability. They may be capable of magnificent feats, but since they are not adap-

tive, they are deficient when it comes to learning and changing, and thus liable to be left behind.[5]

The idea of emergent structures reminds one of what happens during improvisation, both in drama and in music. In fact, David Thornburg, a well-known educational futurist and amateur jazz musician, referring to it as *jamming,* sees it as a pedagogical model. He relates the following key elements of a jam session to educational practice:

- jamming requires more than one person
- jamming follows rules
- everyone helps everyone else
- everyone gets to solo
- jamming goes to new places
- jamming builds rapport[6]

In our model, what we see here is the spontaneous arising of intentions among different individuals that leads to shared structures of increasing interest-generating complexity. The rules Thornburg refers to are designed structures to create a fertile environment for the subsequent arising of the emergent ones. The rapport he speaks of is, of course, flow, or the movement of energy. It is a powerful environment for learning when the emergent structures are the understanding that is unfolding for the students. Furthermore, those who experience effective improvisation of any kind often identify it with high levels of meaning in their lives.[7]

Our second idea, an important one in metacognitive circles, is the relationship between the objective and the subjective viewpoints of reality. Our subjective experience, furthermore, expresses itself both at the individual and communal level. Ken Wilber calls it the "The Big Three": *I, we,* and *it,* and is emphatic on the point that one cannot be reduced to the other through any act of thought.[8] Such a claim prevents *it,* or the scientific viewpoint, from ever fully capturing the entire essence of reality. Our subjective experience provides something unique, without which our understanding of reality would be incomplete. While science currently has the upper hand for determining so much of our structure in the modern era, the deepening understanding of the process of storytelling is an indication that we are moving beyond the objective to a more comprehensive view of our experience.

Storytelling provides us with a powerful tool for restoring some stature to the subjective side of life: that of *story*. Objectively, a story is an energetic process. Subjectively, a story is a carrier of meaning through ideas that arise and the feeling they evoke. Objectively, like viewing a play, we see the props, the stage, even the script—static (structure) and moving (flow) energy. Subjectively, we step inside and become part of the story. From the subjective vantage point, life is experienced as stories within stories, where each story is a world unto itself, possessing all of the qualities of the world outside of it: a fractal and holographic arrangement (to represent this idea objectively). In essence, every thought possesses the potential for a story.[9]

The final idea we will consider is what we've all come to know as "school reform," our ongoing attempts to make meaningful and lasting changes in our educational institutions. As Kegan and Lahey observe:

> The word *reform* has become so attached to the words *school, health care,* and *court* that one has the impression the professions of education, medicine, and the judiciary are in continuous reconstruction.[10]

Anyone involved with trying to bring about such change knows how difficult it can be. The structures in need of attention feel like rock to our pickaxes, and there are additional forces, as well, that appear to work actively against our efforts. One of the problems we encounter is *attachment,* the tendency to be so caught up in our own stories that we fail to adequately understand or even notice the stories of others. Part of the rock we chip away at is the difficulty we all have at perceiving the cues that provide the clues as to the best ways to proceed.

Much of the work that needs to be done is on our inner structures, and we are seeing a growing variety of ideas and practices that is giving rise to a host of tools for helping us. Meditation, as we have seen, is one of these. Another is systems thinking and the work of Peter Senge, Margaret Wheatley, and others whose aim is to foster greater awareness of our thought processes.[11] Yet another approach is that of Kegan and Lahey, whose work with a wide variety of organizations addresses the role of language in maintaining and moving beyond the status quo.[12] The use of computer software can also help in that it enables us to manipulate our structures in more fluid ways than in days past. Disciplines such as the martial arts and hatha yoga, as well as massage therapy, chiropractics, and acupuncture work to loosen the structure and increase the flow of energy in the physical body, itself.

It is not which of these tools we use that is important, so much as the awareness with which we undertake their use—which, of course, is the same awareness we are trying to cultivate by using them! Unfortunately, as we seek to overcome attachment, it remains a problem when we attribute more meaning to the tool than is appropriate, giving it more importance than its due. The tool defines the underlying structure of the new story we find ourselves in and we become increasingly deaf and blind to other ways of viewing our situation. The awareness we're working on, however, can help us muster the discipline to move back into the objective realm so we can better comprehend the larger story. In Kegan and Lahey's words, "We tell our stories so we can stop *being* our stories and become persons who have these stories. We tell these stories so we can become more responsible for them."[13] In essence, this awareness manifests as our ability to maintain a dynamic balance between structure and flow, objective and subjective viewpoints, facts and stories. The creation and active support of this awareness at all levels of school operation can be a new experience for many of us. The title of a recent book by the systems thinking folks sums up the road ahead: *Schools That Learn.*[14]

*****

The applications of metacognition are indirect, having more to do with our assumptions about our actions than the actions themselves. The structures that emerge from our inner work and the expanding possibilities of information technology combine to bring many of these assumptions into question. An important one for us. as educators, to consider is the nature of *interpersonal communication*. We go about our day-to-day interactions with people based on many unexamined beliefs. At the same time, the quality of the human relationships in an educational community is of the utmost importance as the increasing complexity of our lives heightens the need to merge our creativity, which requires greater flow and less attachment between us. The alternative is to have too much of our energy tied up in maintaining the structures that determine our personal stories, keeping us apart.

We need to be teaching children how to manage this increasing flow at the same time we are learning to work with it ourselves. An excellent illustration of where this can happen is the growing use of digital video in the classroom. By putting filmmaking, a powerful form of storytelling, into the hands of the common man, students and teachers have tremendous opportunities for exploring the potential of collaborative work. Furthermore, filmmaking can provide direct contact with the flow of many aspects of life that, heretofore, could only be accessed at the level of structure. The editing made possible with this tool can also enable a depth of interaction with emergent structures that is rich with meaning.

There are many other assumptions that unconsciously guide the flow of our educational communities. As we work together to deepen our awareness of structure and flow in an attempt to unearth these assumptions, we find ourselves on many frontiers. As many of us are discovering, dialogue is just a beginning to our explorations. We need to prepare ourselves for the increasing flow of emergent structures that will suggest new ways of carrying out our business: new ways that may run counter to some very old, but potentially very out-of-date habits. We must work to create structures that will help each of us cope with the very unsettled future this portends. In essence, we must do what will be asked of us to apply our knowledge—of how our thoughts, with the help of a growing collection of technologies, become the stories of our lives—to the task of increasing the flow of meaning into the lives of our students. My goal has been to suggest some structure and to initiate some flow with this in mind. My wish is that the time we've spent together has been meaningful.

Bibliography

Bohm, David. *On Dialogue*. New York: Routledge, 1996.

Bruner, Jerome. *The Culture of Education*. Cambridge: Harvard University Press, 1996.

Capra, Fritjof. *Hidden Connections: Integrating the Biological, Cognitive, and Social Dimensions of Life into a Science of Sustainability*. New York: Random House, 2002.

Csikszentmihalyi, Mihaly. *Flow: The Psychology of Optimal Experience*. New York: Harper & Row, 1990.

Kegan, Robert and Lisa Laskow Lahey. *How the Way We Talk Can Change the Way We Work: Seven Languages for Transformation*. San Francisco: Jossey-Bass, 2001.

Thornburg, David. *The New Basics: Education and the Future of Work in the Telematic Age*. Alexandria: Association for Supervision and Curriculum Development, 2002.

Senge, Peter M. *The Fifth Discipline: The Art & Practice of the Learning Organization*. New York: Currency Doubleday, 1994.

Senge, Peter, Nelda Cambron-McCabe, Timothy Lucas, Bryan Smith, Janis Dutton, and Art Kleiner. *Schools That Learn*. New York: Doubleday, 2000.

Wheatley, Margaret. *Leadership and the New Science: Discovering Order in a Chaotic World*. San Francisco: Berrett-Koehler, 2001.

Wilber, Ken. *A Theory of Everything: An Integral Vision for Business, Politics, Science, and Spirituality*. Boston: Shambhala, 2001.

———. *Sex, Ecology, and Spirituality: The Spirit of Evolution*. Boston: Shambhala, 1995.

Notes

[1] Jerome Bruner, *The Culture of Education,* page 147. The other two antidotes are contrast and confrontation.

[2] Robert Kegan and Lisa Laskow Lahey, *How the Way We Talk Can Change the Way We Work: Seven Languages for Transformation,* page 49. This is a wonderful book for practicing metacognition.

[3] *Energy* has a long tradition of uses in science, philosophy, psychology, and religion. Physics has its notions of kinetic and potential energy. Mihaly Csikszentmihalyi, in his book *Flow,* refers to psychic energy as a way to talk about that which is flowing. Hinduism speaks of *prana* and *shakti,* Buddhism refers to *chi,* and Taoism is based on the Tao.

[4] Any serious student of philosophy needs to spend significant time with Wilber's work. His magnum opus is *Sex, Ecology, and Spirituality: The Spirit of Evolution*. A more accessible and better introductory book would be *A Theory of Everything*.

[5] Fritjof Capra, *Hidden Connections,* page 121.

[6] David Thornburg, *The New Basics: Education and the Future of Work in the Telematic Age,* page 95.

[7] A growing number of people are working with the tools of dialogue, which is the application of the principles of improvisation to oral communication. Physicist David Bohm's book *On Dialogue* is an excellent introduction.

[8] It is beyond thought, in realms of greater complexity, where the three viewpoints come together. One of the most important of Wilber's ideas is that there are levels of awareness, accessible to all of us, that transcend our thinking.

[9] Jerome Bruner's essay "The Narrative Construal of Reality" in *The Culture of Education* discusses the same ideas from a somewhat different perspective.

[10] Kegan and Lahey, pg. 61.

[11] Refer to Senge's Fifth Discipline work and Wheatley's *Leadership and the New Science* for more information.

[12] Kegan and Lahey.

[13] Kegan and Lahey, pg. 37, original italics.

[14] *Schools That Learn* by Peter Senge et al. is a rich collection of systems-thinking theory and experience as it applies to education.

Eric Neufer is the director of faculty technology development and the community website Manager at Phoenix Country Day School, a pre-K–12 day school in Paradise Valley, AZ. During his twenty years of work life, he has also been an educational software programmer; a teacher of programming, applications software, and mathematics; a director of information technology; and the author of a book entitled *Murder at Mythical Micro,* which used a murder mystery as a tool for mastering the original AppleWorks program.

Patrick F. Bassett
President
National Association of Independent Schools

Patrick F. Bassett became the president of the National Association of Independent Schools (NAIS) in August 2001. NAIS is a voluntary membership organization for more than 1,200 independent (private) schools and associations of schools in the U.S. and abroad.

Bassett began his career in independent schools in 1970 as an English teacher and lacrosse coach at Woodberry Forrest School (Virginia), an all-boys boarding school. In 1980, he became headmaster of an all-girls school, Stuart Hall (VA), where he remained until 1989. From 1981 to 1989, Bassett served on the Executive Committee of the Virginia Association of Independent Schools (VAIS), and he was president from 1988–1989. From 1985 to 1989, he served on the board of directors of the National Association of Independent Schools (NAIS). He was named a Kellogg National Leadership Fellow from 1986–1989. Bassett became the head of Pomfret School (CT), a coed, boarding day high school, in 1989.

From 1993 to 2001, Bassett was the president of the Independent Schools Association of the Central States (ISACS). ISACS provides accreditation, consultations, professional development events, and statistics gathering and reporting for more than 200 independent schools in the 15 states of the Midwest. He also served on the board of directors of The Multicultural Alliance (1994–2000), and he has served on the board of the Council for Spiritual and Ethical Education (CSEE) since 1996 and the board and Executive Committee of CAPE, the Council for American Private Education, since 2001. In March 2000, Bassett was honored by The Klingenstein Center of Teachers College (Columbia University) with the Educational Leadership Award. In 2001, he was invited by the president of Teachers College to join the Advisory Board of The Klingenstein Center, Teachers College, Columbia University.

Bassett is the author of numerous book chapters and articles, including several commentary pieces in *Education Week:* "The End of Independent Schools" (March 13, 1996); "Why Good Schools Are Countercultural" (February 6, 2002), and "Testing, Accountability, and Independence" (August 19, 2002); "Searching for Great Teachers" (February 26, 2003). He has also contributed chapters and served as co-editor for *Looking Ahead: Independent School Issues and Answers,* Avocus Books 1994 (1st ed.) and 2004 (2nd ed.).

Patrick Bassett is a Phi Beta Kappa, magna cum laude graduate of Williams College (MA). He also holds a master's degree from Northwestern University (IL). He and his wife, Barbara, have two grown daughters and two grandchildren.

NAIS is the national institutional advocate for independent pre-collegiate education. NAIS provides independent school leaders with products, services, and professional development opportunities.

July 2003